Computer Graphics

AN INTRODUCTION TO THE MATHEMATICS AND GEOMETRY

Computer Graphics

AN INTRODUCTION TO THE MATHEMATICS AND GEOMETRY

M. E. Mortenson

Industrial Press Inc.
200 Madison Avenue, New York, New York 10016-4078

LIBRARY OF CONGRESS
Library of Congress Cataloging-in-Publication Data

Mortenson, Michael E., 1939–
Computer graphics: an introduction to the mathematics and geometry/M.E. Mortenson.
p. cm.
Includes index.
ISBN 0-8311-1182-8
1. Computer graphics. I. Title.
T385.M668 1988
006.6—dc19

88-21518
CIP

INDUSTRIAL PRESS INC
200 Madison Avenue
New York, NY 10016-4078
First Printing

Computer Graphics: An Introduction to the Mathematics and Geometry

Composition, printing and binding by Edwards Brothers, Incorporated, Ann Arbor, Michigan

2 4 6 8 7 5 3

Preface

COMPUTER GRAPHICS: AN INTRODUCTION TO THE MATHEMATICS AND GEOMETRY introduces the mathematical and geometric principles supporting computer graphics and a large class of applications referred to as geometric modeling. This textbook is intended for the lower-division college student majoring in computer science, engineering, or applied mathematics whose special interests are in computer graphics, CAD/CAM systems, geometric modeling, or related subjects. *Computer Graphics* can also serve as a supplement to upper-division and graduate-level courses or as a useful addition to the reference libraries of professionals.

Prerequisites include college-preparatory mathematics through trigonometry; an introduction to solid geometry would be useful. At least one course in computer programming would be helpful, since programming *per se* is not a subject of this textbook. Calculus is not required, although a prior or concurrent course in elementary calculus would be of benefit to understanding certain topics here. Some elementary calculus is introduced where tangents and normals to curves and surfaces are discussed.

A set of integrated concepts is presented whose mastery is necessary for a thorough understanding of the mathematics and geometry underlying computer graphics. Several important concepts are emphasized throughout this text. These concepts include parametric geometry; transformations; vectors; matrix methods; and, to a lesser extent (although nonetheless important), data structures, algorithm development, and computational efficiency.

The text is interspersed with "boxes"—one page or two facing pages—presenting tightly focused information on a specific problem elaborating on a concept in the text proper. Of course, there are many exercises, and the answers to some are provided. A suggestion: Read all the exercises (even those not assigned); they are a good sampling of problems that may be faced in a professional capacity.

Much of the work in Section 1.4, Display Coordinate Systems, and Chapter

16, Display and Scene Transformations, was inspired by the work of Bill Miller, whose IMAGINATOR three-dimensional graphics program effectively demonstrates the application of these concepts.

Thanks to James Geronimo and Woodrow Chapman of Industrial Press for their thoughtful and professional guidance throughout the preparation of this textbook.

Finally, thanks to my wife, Janet. This is the second time in five years that she has devoted much time and talent to the production of a very difficult manuscript. *Mahalo nui loa.*

Contents

Computer Graphics

AN INTRODUCTION TO THE MATHEMATICS AND GEOMETRY

1. Coordinate Systems

GEOMETRIC OBJECTS have many important characteristics, such as size and shape, location and orientation, and certain spatial relationships to each other. To describe, measure, and analyze these characteristics consistently and quantitatively requires a frame of reference called a **coordinate system.** There are many kinds of coordinate systems, each offering special advantages depending on the problem to be solved. In fact, a coordinate system is, in and of itself, a kind of geometric object.

When you complete your studies in this chapter, you will be acquainted with a variety of coordinate systems and will begin to understand something of their application and versatility. You will learn that one kind of system can be transformed (changed) into another kind, and you will be prepared to work with the combinations of coordinate systems needed to generate computer graphic displays.

So now let us look at the coordinate systems used in computer graphics.

1.1. One-Dimensional Coordinate Systems

Perhaps the most important feature of a coordinate system is its number of dimensions. The simplest system is one dimensional and consists of an unbounded straight line (Fig. 1.1). A reference point, O, the **origin,** allows you to locate, construct, and measure geometric objects; in this system, objects are limited to points and lines. Locate a point, $\mathbf{p}$, by giving its distance, x, from the origin. This single number, or **coordinate,** is sufficient to describe $\mathbf{p}$. A plus or minus sign indicates the direction of the point relative to the origin. Mathematicians call this system the **real line,** because there is a one-to-one correspondence between the points on the line and the set of real numbers. (Note that a boldface, lowercase $\mathbf{p}$ denotes a geometric point. You will find this notation used throughout the

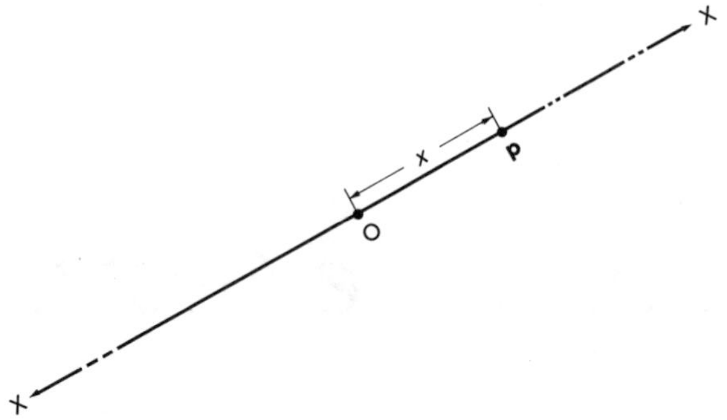

Fig. 1.1. One-dimensional coordinate system. (Note that coordinate systems need not be horizontal.)

text, with some minor exceptions usually related to algebraic considerations.)

The location of the origin is arbitrary. Choosing a new origin, O^*, does not change the geometric characteristics of objects defined in the system (Fig. 1.2). For example, the distance between points $\mathbf{p}_1$ and $\mathbf{p}_2$ is the same for either the O or O^* system. Let O and O^* be separated by a distance d. The coordinate of O^* in terms of the initial coordinate system, O, is $x_T = -d$. Then, in the O^* system, the coordinate of $\mathbf{p}_1$ is $x_1 + d$, and that of $\mathbf{p}_2$ is $x_2 + d$. This process of changing the origin is known as a **transformation.** Of course, O^* could just as easily be to the right of O. If that were the case, the two preceding expressions would not give correct results. To account for this, use the algebraic value of the coordinate of O^* in the O system, x_T. This produces the following correct expression relating the coordinate x of any point $\mathbf{p}$ in the O system to its coordinate x^* in the O^* system:

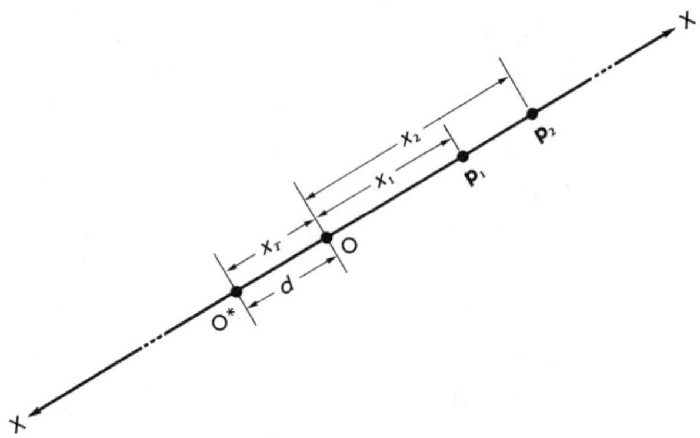

Fig. 1.2. Changing the origin.

$$x^* = x - x_T \tag{1.1}$$

The asterisk denotes the coordinate of **p** in the new or transformed system. Equation (1.1) is called a transformation equation. The concept of a transformation is an important one in geometric modeling and computer graphics. In your studies you will encounter many other coordinate system transformations as well as many other kinds of transformations.

One-dimensional coordinate systems are not the most exciting topics you will study, but they are not without some interesting properties, and they give rise to a rich assortment of concepts. For example, consider an interval on the real line, bounded by the points x_a and x_b (Fig. 1.3), where $x_a < x_b$. (It is easy to think of this interval as merely a line segment, but you should also try to keep in mind the concept of the interval as a set of continuous points.)

An arbitrary point, x, is either in this interval (a member of the set of points) or outside of it. If the bounding points x_a and x_b are declared to be in the interval (or set) and if $x_a \leq x \leq x_b$, then x is in the interval (or set). This is a **closed interval** because the boundary or limit points are included. An **open interval** looks like $x_a < x < x_b$; here the boundary points are not included. If you want to use more concise notation, then write

$$x \in [a, b] \qquad \text{for a closed interval} \tag{1.2}$$

$$x \in (a, b) \qquad \text{for an open interval} \tag{1.3}$$

Read the symbol $\in$ as "is an element (or member) of." This notation from set theory applies to many algebraic and geometric situations you will encounter. A small refinement of interpretation with considerable geometric significance is: If $x = a$ or $x = b$, then x is on the boundary.

Other examples of "geometry" on this line include relationships among points, points and lines, and lines. Does one point fall between two other points? Do two line segments overlap? What is the length of a line segment? You can discover many other properties and rules. Try some.

One-dimensional coordinate systems need not be limited to unbounded straight lines. Consider a semiinfinite line (or half line) or finite line segment. And then there are coordinate systems and geometries you could construct on closed curves. These more exotic systems are not just mental exercises; their usefulness is apparent in other branches of math-

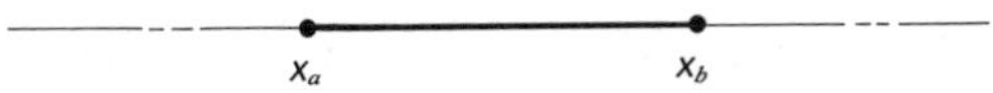

Fig. 1.3. An interval on the real line.

ematics and in the physical sciences. Think of coordinate systems as geometric tools available to you to help you understand and solve many kinds of problems. But first, it is important that you understand them and their versatility, and how to use them to advantage.

EXERCISES

1. Given the interval defined by a set of points x such that $x \in [-3.5, 8]$, state whether the following points are inside or outside the interval:

a. (2)
b. (0)
c. (−4)
d. (7)
e. (9.5)
f. (3.5)
g. (−8)
h. (8.1)
i. (−1.5)
j. (4)

2. If line segments in a one-dimensional coordinate system are given by the interval notation, then describe the relationship of each of the following six lines to the other five:

a. $x_A \in [-3, -1]$
b. $x_B \in [4, 10]$
c. $x_C \in [12, 16]$
d. $x_D \in [-4, 1]$
e. $x_E \in [2, 5]$
f. $x_F \in [5, 7]$

3. Given the 10 points a–j of Exercise 1, state whether they are inside or outside each of the following four intervals:

a. $x_A \in [3, 9.5]$
b. $x_B \in (-4, 4)$
c. $x_C \in [0, 10.1]$
d. $x_D \in (-1, 3.5)$

4. Show that the distance between $\mathbf{p}_1$ and $\mathbf{p}_2$ in Fig. 1.2 is the same in both coordinate systems.

5. Describe some of the features of a closed, circular one-dimensional coordinate system. *Hint:* How would you locate points and intervals? What about segments longer than the circumference?

1.2. Two-Dimensional Coordinate Systems

Early in the 17th century, the French mathematician and philosopher René Descartes revolutionized the study of geometry. Descartes recognized that algebraic functions could be interpreted geometrically by graphing them onto a two-dimensional coordinate system. This idea supported earlier notions of a one-to-one correspondence between algebra and geometry. Not only could algebraic equations be interpreted as graphed curves, but, also, many geometric figures were found to have simple algebraic equivalents. In fact, we now know, thanks to Descartes and others, that all geometric objects—curves, surfaces, and more exotic types—can be described algebraically. And all algebraic functions have a geometric interpretation. This large and important branch of mathematics is called **analytic geometry,** and Descartes is its founder. The rectangular, two-dimensional system of coordinates he used to graph the algebraic functions (although not invented by him) is called a **Cartesian coordinate system.**

Two unbounded straight lines intersecting at right angles form the **principal axes,** x and y, of the coordinate system. Their point of intersection, O, is the origin. A grid of equally spaced lines may be laid out parallel to the principal axes, although this is not strictly necessary. Now every point in the plane is located and defined by a pair of numbers (x, y), the coordinates of the point. In Fig. 1.4 the coordinates of the point $\mathbf{p}_1$ are (x_1, y_1). At x_1 on the x axis, construct a line parallel to the y axis. Similarly, at y_1 on the y axis, construct a line parallel to the x axis. These two lines intersect at $\mathbf{p}_1$.

Note that the principal axes do not necessarily have to be at right angles to each other; but if they are not, it is no longer a *Cartesian* system. Computations in a skewed-axis system are somewhat more complex, and trigonometric relationships are more cumbersome to express. The coor-

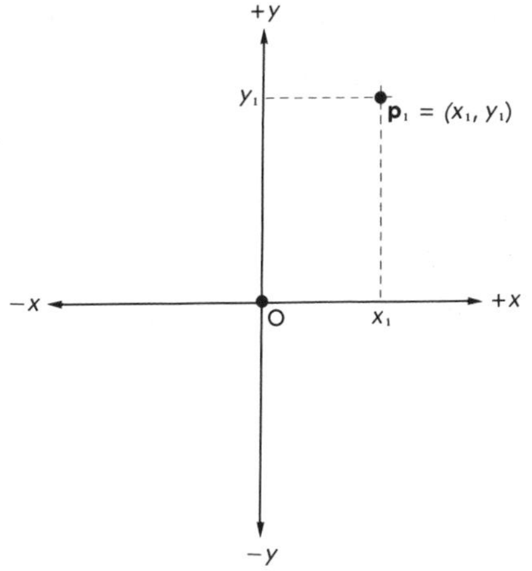

Fig. 1.4. Two-dimensional Cartesian coordinate system.

dinate system establishes a frame of reference for making quantitative measurements: position, angle, distance, area, length, and so forth. These measurements are easier to make and interpret if the axes are at right angles and if the scales on them are linear and equal.

Again, the location of the origin is arbitrary. Let us see what happens to the coordinates of a point when you change the location of the origin. Study the change shown in Fig. 1.5. The new system is translated x_T and y_T relative to the initial system. The coordinate transformation is given by

$$x^* = x - x_T, \qquad y^* = y - y_T \tag{1.4}$$

Do you see another way to establish a new coordinate system? It is also possible to rotate O^*. The rotational transformations are developed later.

There are many other two-dimensional coordinate systems, none of which are Cartesian. There is one in particular with which you are surely familiar: It is the system of coordinates on the surface of a sphere, called longitude and latitude, and used, of course, to map the geography of our planet. Later you will encounter other two-dimensional coordinate systems on more general surfaces.

Computer graphic displays are almost invariably constructed in a two-dimensional Cartesian coordinate system. Even three-dimensional objects must be projected and displayed in two dimensions (with the exception of holographic displays). Later on you will study screen coordinate systems and understand them as special adaptations of the Cartesian coordinates.

POLAR COORDINATE SYSTEM

There is one other two-dimensional coordinate system we will briefly consider now, the **polar coordinate system,** although its use is very lim-

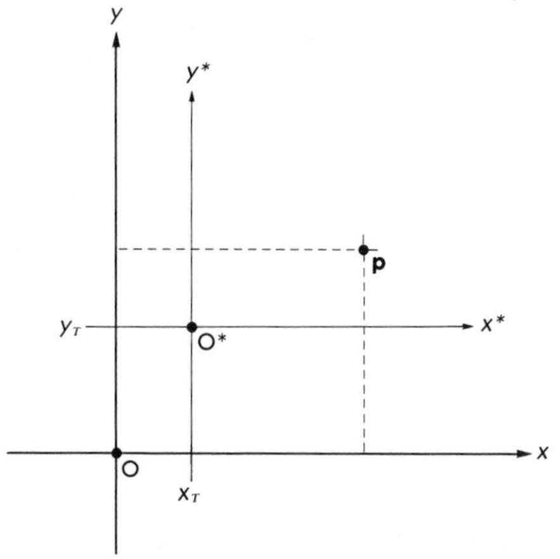

Fig. 1.5. Changing the origin in a two-dimensional system.

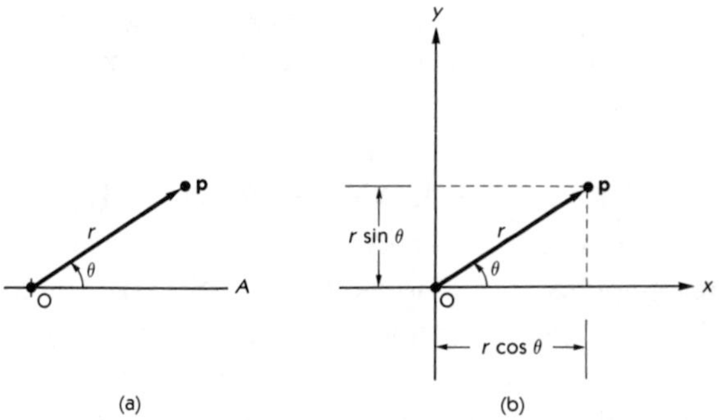

Fig. 1.6. Polar coordinates.

ited in geometric modeling and computer graphics. (It is used principally in navigation and air-traffic-control systems.) Figure 1.6a shows the elements of a polar coordinate system, and Fig. 1.6b shows this polar coordinate system with a Cartesian coordinate system superimposed on it. The polar coordinates of a point are given by a radial distance, r, from an origin and an angle, θ, between the line of r and some reference line, say OA. The relationship between the Cartesian and polar coordinates of a point are readily apparent in Fig. 1.6b. The transformation from polar to Cartesian coordinates is given by

$$x = r\cos\theta \qquad \text{and} \qquad y = r\sin\theta \tag{1.5}$$

The inverse of this transformation is

$$r = |(x^2 + y^2)^{1/2}| \qquad \text{and} \qquad \theta = \tan^{-1}(y/x) \tag{1.6}$$

Note that the origins of the polar and Cartesian systems coincide, as do the angle reference line, OA, and the x axis.

EXERCISES

1. The coordinates of each of the following 10 points are with respect to an initial Cartesian coordinate system, O. Find the coordinates of these points in the O^* system, where O^* is at $(-4, 3)$ in the O system.

a. $\mathbf{p}_1 = (2, -1)$
b. $\mathbf{p}_2 = (-3, 1)$
c. $\mathbf{p}_3 = (2, 0)$
d. $\mathbf{p}_4 = (0, 0)$
e. $\mathbf{p}_5 = (0, 3)$
f. $\mathbf{p}_6 = (3, 5)$
g. $\mathbf{p}_7 = (-2, 5)$
h. $\mathbf{p}_8 = (-6, 2)$
i. $\mathbf{p}_9 = (-3, -4)$
j. $\mathbf{p}_{10} = (-4, 3)$

2. Show that the distance between two arbitrary points is independent of coordinate system transformations. (*Note:* You do not have to consider rotational transformations for this exercise.)

3. Derive the transformation equations (translation only) between two similarly oriented polar coordinate systems whose origins do not coincide.

1.3. Three-Dimensional Coordinate Systems

The coordinate system most frequently used in geometric modeling and computer graphics is the three-dimensional Cartesian coordinate system (Fig. 1.7). A simple extension of the two-dimensional Cartesian coordinate system, the three-dimensional system consists of three mutually perpendicular reference axes labeled x, y, and z, called the **principal coordinate axes.**

As a matter of convention, the positive x axis is drawn to the right, the positive y axis is up, and the positive z axis extends out from the origin toward the reader at right angles to the x and y axes. This is called a **right-hand coordinate system** and is the coordinate system most often used for referencing all geometric data.

It is called a right-hand system because if the fingers of your right hand are curled so that they attempt to rotate the $+x$ axis into the $+y$ axis, your thumb will point in the direction of the $+z$ axis. This defines a positive rotation about the z axis. Let us extend this idea a little. Rotating the $+y$ axis about the x axis and toward the $+z$ axis is a positive rotation. Finally, rotating the $+z$ axis into the $+x$ axis, about the y axis, is also defined as a positive rotation. Do you see the cyclic nature of this convention? ... x,

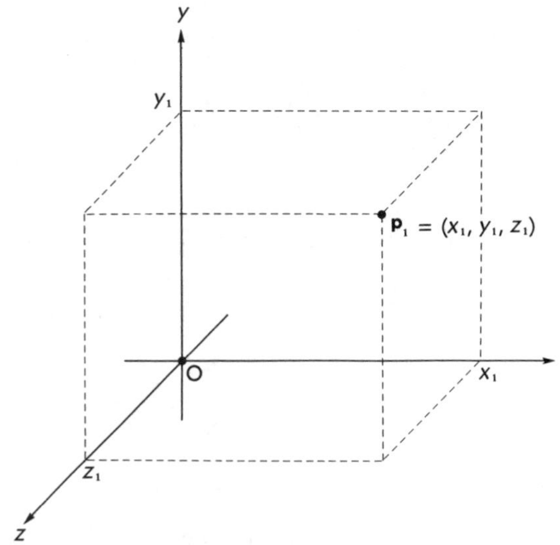

Fig. 1.7. Three-dimensional Cartesian coordinate system.

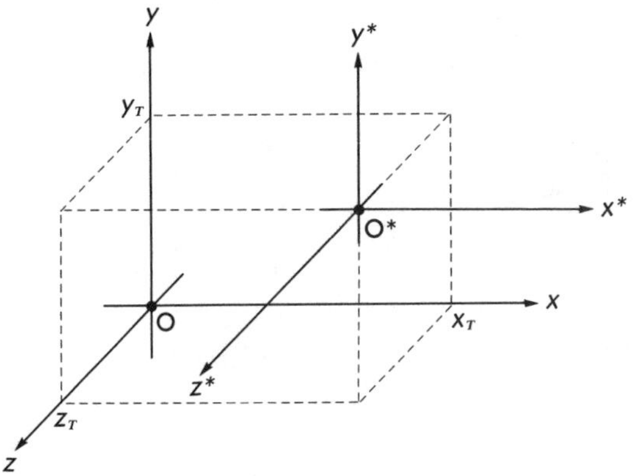

Fig. 1.8. Changing the origin in a three-dimensional system.

y, z, x, y .... The reverse cycle, x, z, y, x, z ..., establishes a left-hand system.

Imagine a three-dimensional grid constructed of three mutually perpendicular sets of lines parallel to each of the principal coordinate axes. These form a framework in which you can locate geometric objects and make measurements. Now, every point in space is located and defined by a set of three real numbers, a triplet, the coordinates (x,y,z). In Fig. 1.7 the coordinates of the point $\mathbf{p}_1$ are (x_1, y_1, z_1).

Remember, the location and orientation of the origin are arbitrary (Fig. 1.8). Consider transformations between two Cartesian coordinate systems whose corresponding principal axes are parallel. (Later you will study more general transformations, including rotations.) You can specify the coordinates of any point $\mathbf{p}$ in terms of either system. The coordinates are related by the following equations [analogous to Eq. (1.5)]:

$$\begin{aligned} x^* &= x - x_T \\ y^* &= y - y_T \\ z^* &= z - z_T \end{aligned} \tag{1.7}$$

Now let us consider two other, more specialized, three-dimensional coordinate systems: cylindrical and spherical. Various forms of both of these systems find applications in physics and engineering.

CYLINDRICAL COORDINATE SYSTEM

Figure 1.9 shows a cylindrical coordinate system with a Cartesian coordinate system superimposed on it. The cylindrical coordinates of a point, $\mathbf{p}$, are (r, θ, z): a radial distance, r, from the origin; an angle θ between

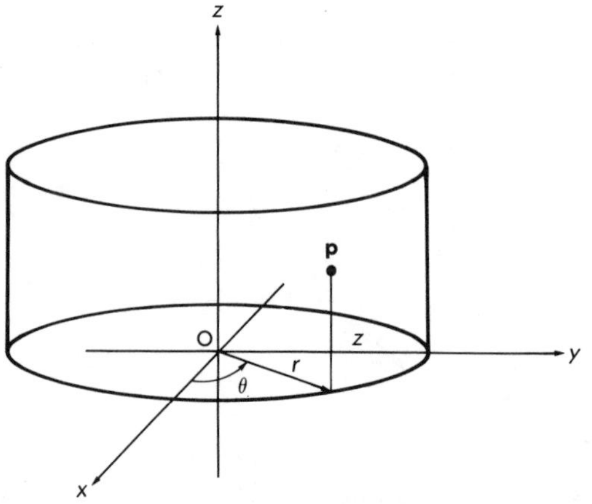

Fig. 1.9. Cylindrical coordinate system.

the line of r and some reference line, say the $+x$ axis; and a distance, z, from the plane containing the line of r and the reference line.

You can easily derive the transformation relationships between the Cartesian and cylindrical coordinates of a point. From the figure, find

$$\begin{aligned} x &= r\cos\theta \\ y &= r\sin\theta \\ z &= z \end{aligned} \tag{1.8}$$

Note that you generate a cylindrical surface if you hold r constant while varying θ and z. What geometric objects result if θ or z are held constant while the other two coordinates vary?

SPHERICAL COORDINATE SYSTEM

Figure 1.10 shows a spherical coordinate system with a Cartesian coordinate system superimposed on it. The spherical coordinates of a point, **p**, are (r, θ, ϕ): a radial distance from the origin, r, and two angles, θ and ϕ.

The transformation relationships between the Cartesian and spherical coordinates of a point are

$$\begin{aligned} x &= r\sin\phi\cos\theta \\ y &= r\sin\phi\sin\theta \\ z &= r\cos\phi \end{aligned} \tag{1.9}$$

Note that if you hold ϕ constant while allowing r and θ to vary, you

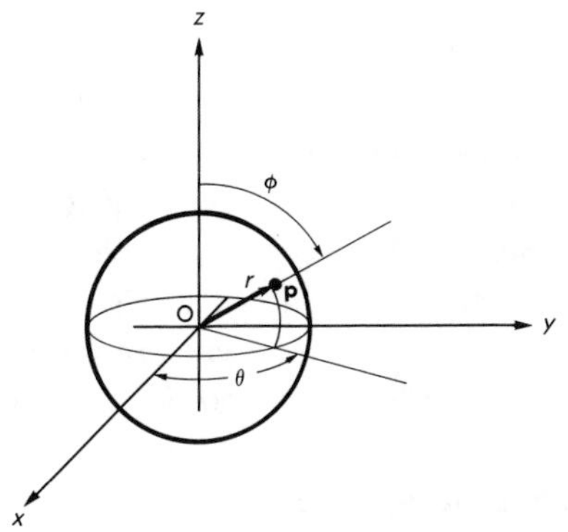

Fig. 1.10. Spherical coordinate system.

generate a conical surface. What is the result of fixing r while θ and ϕ vary? Or, fixing θ and allowing r and ϕ to vary?

EXERCISES

1. The coordinates of each of the following 10 points are with respect to an initial Cartesian coordinate system, *O*. Find the coordinates of these points in O^*, where O^* is at (6, 4, −2) in the *O* system.

a. $\mathbf{p}_1 = (0, 0, 0)$
b. $\mathbf{p}_2 = (6, 1, 1)$
c. $\mathbf{p}_3 = (-4, 2, -3)$
d. $\mathbf{p}_4 = (6, 4, -2)$
e. $\mathbf{p}_5 = (-3, -9, 0)$
f. $\mathbf{p}_6 = (5, -7, -1)$
g. $\mathbf{p}_7 = (-9, -1, -3)$
h. $\mathbf{p}_8 = (2, -3, -2)$
i. $\mathbf{p}_9 = (8, 5, 8)$
j. $\mathbf{p}_{10} = (1, 0, 0)$

2. Derive the inverse of the transformation given by Eq. (1.9). That is, given the Cartesian coordinates of a point, find the equivalent polar coordinates.

3. Use the results of Exercise 2 to compute the polar coordinates of the points given in Exercise 1.

4. Derive the inverse of the transformation given by Eq. (1.8). That is, given the Cartesian coordinates of a point, find the equivalent cylindrical coordinates.

5. Use the results of Exercise 4 to compute the cylindrical coordinates of the points given in Exercise 1.

6. Derive the transformation equations (translation only) between two similarly oriented cylindrical coordinate systems.

7. Derive the transformation equations (translation only) between two similarly oriented spherical coordinate systems.

1.4. Display Coordinate Systems

Most three-dimensional computer graphics systems use a variety of both two- and three-dimensional coordinate systems. A name and unique set of axes identifies each coordinate system and indicates how each is used.

A typical three-dimensional computer graphics system uses five different coordinate systems. These are shown in Fig. 1.11. What follows is an initial, nonmathematical introduction to each of these systems to help you develop an intuitive notion of their use, properties, and relationship to one another.

The **global coordinate system,** also called the **world coordinate system,** is the principal frame of reference. This three-dimensional system is the basis for defining and locating in space all objects in a computer graphics scene, including the observer's position and line of sight. The global coordinate system serves as the master reference system in which all other coordinate systems are defined.

A **local coordinate system** is used to define the geometry of an object independently of the global system. Do this when you want to define an object without giving it a specific location in the global system. Once you define the object "locally," you can place it in the global system simply by specifying the location and orientation of the origin of the local system within the global system, then mathematically transforming the point coordinates defining the object from the local to the global system.

The **view coordinate system** locates objects in three-dimensional space relative to the location of the observer. Use it, if necessary, to simplify the mathematics for projecting an image of the object onto the picture plane.

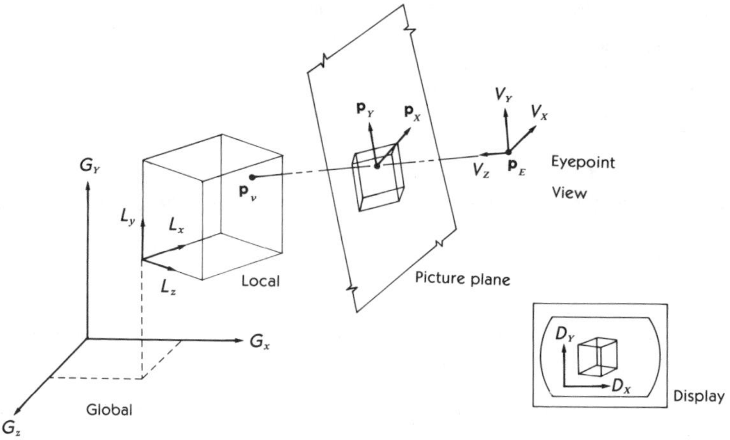

Fig. 1.11. Coordinate systems used to construct a computer graphics display.

As you might presume, the location and orientation of the view coordinate system change each time the view changes.

The **picture-plane coordinate system** is two dimensional and locates points on the picture plane, sometimes called the **projection plane.**

The **screen coordinate system** locates points on the surface of a particular computer graphic display device, such as a graphics monitor or plotter. *Note:* There will most likely be a separate coordinate system for each display device.

Let us now examine how these coordinate systems relate to each other and how they are used to form the basis for a three-dimensional computer graphics system.

OBJECTS IN THREE-DIMENSIONAL SPACE

The first step in this process is to represent objects in three-dimensional space. To do this, you must create geometric models of the objects. Many objects are adequately represented as a set of points and lines. For example, see the object in Fig. 1.12.

Define points by their three-dimensional coordinates in the global coordinate system by using a local system linked by a set of transformation equations to the global system. Define lines by their end points. Chapters 2 and 3 develop the concepts of points and lines more fully.

Now, return to the object in Fig. 1.12. Note that it is defined by a set of four points whose coordinates are

$$\mathbf{p}_1 = (1, 0, 1) \qquad \mathbf{p}_3 = (6, 0, 1)$$
$$\mathbf{p}_2 = (4, 0, 4) \qquad \mathbf{p}_4 = (3, 4, 2)$$

and a set of six lines whose end points are

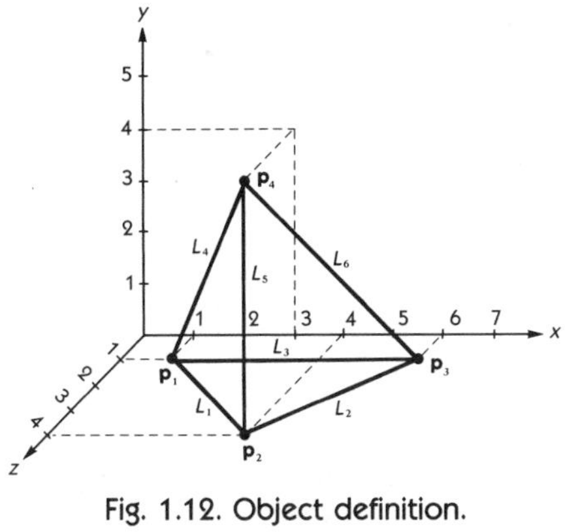

Fig. 1.12. Object definition.

$$L_1 = (\mathbf{p}_1, \mathbf{p}_2) \qquad L_4 = (\mathbf{p}_1, \mathbf{p}_4)$$
$$L_2 = (\mathbf{p}_2, \mathbf{p}_3) \qquad L_5 = (\mathbf{p}_2, \mathbf{p}_4)$$
$$L_3 = (\mathbf{p}_3, \mathbf{p}_1) \qquad L_6 = (\mathbf{p}_3, \mathbf{p}_4)$$

This type of specification produces a **wireframe** model of the object, whose display makes the object's surfaces appear transparent. Most objects, however, are solid and opaque, so this type of model, although popular, is somewhat limited.

To represent an object as a solid, we must provide additional information. This usually requires some data format to identify the planes defining the surface of the object. It also requires considerably more computations to determine which planes are visible in a particular view and which planes are not visible. Most microcomputers do not have the memory or processing speed to meet these additional modeling demands in a satisfactory way; therefore, to conserve memory and to reduce computation time, many microcomputer graphics systems display objects as wireframe models.

THE OBSERVER

Once an object is defined in the global system, you can compute a view of it from any direction. To do this, you must first have a way to represent the location of the observer (or more precisely, the eye of the observer) and the direction of the observer's line of sight.

Define an eyepoint, $\mathbf{p}_E$, located by specifying its coordinates in the global system (Fig. 1.13). Next, specify the observer's line of sight in either of

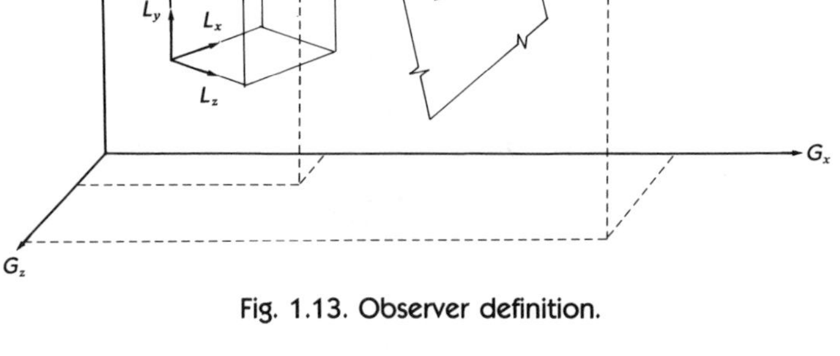

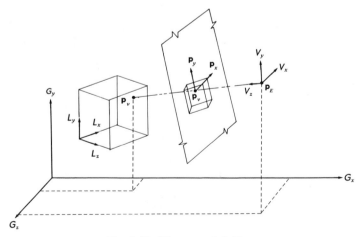

Fig. 1.13. Observer definition.

two ways: as a set of direction angles (or direction cosines) defining the direction of the line of sight in the global system, or by specifying the location of a viewpoint, $\mathbf{p}_v$, that lies somewhere along the line of sight. Once this is done, rotate the observer's eye about the line of sight to produce the final view. Specify this rotation by simply giving the angle of rotation about the line of sight.

CHANGING VIEWS

Any subsequent view of the object assumes that either the object itself moves or the eye of the observer moves. To move the object requires transforming all object-defining points to new positions corresponding to the new position of the object. To move the observer only requires specifying a new eyepoint location and, if necessary, a new orientation for the line of sight. Most computer graphics systems assume the eye of the observer moves to create a new view of the object.

Relocate the eyepoint, $\mathbf{p}_E$, by specifying its new coordinates. There are three ways to do this: by specifying absolute values relative to the global system, by specifying incremental moves relative to the current position in the global system, and by specifying incremental moves relative to the view coordinate system.

Define a new orientation for the line of sight by specifying a new location for the viewpoint, $\mathbf{p}_v$, or by specifying new direction angles for the line of sight. As with the eyepoint, relocate the viewpoint by specifying its new coordinates relative to the global system, by specifying incremental moves relative to its current position in the global system, or as incremental moves relative to the view system. Specify new direction angles relative to either the global or view systems.

As you can see, changing views could be complicated and confusing. This is further compounded because each new view requires a new set of numbers (angles or coordinates) that are often difficult to determine. Most computer graphics systems attempt to simplify this process by limiting the options available to you or by making some general assumptions about the type of moves you will most likely make. The challenge is to develop a strategy for quickly and easily moving about the object or scene without sacrificing versatility of control over the movement.

Consider the following four modes for moving the eye of the observer. The first mode allows you to specify directly through numerical input the parameters affecting a particular view, such as the location of the eyepoint, the location of the viewpoint, the distance of the picture plane from eyepoint, and the type of view desired. There are also three somewhat more geometric and interactive modes, known as **Aim, Orbit,** and **Pan,** that let you quickly move the eyepoint in and around the object or scene using simple commands, such as "up," "down," "left," "right," "forward," and "back." The mathematical basis for these view-changing movements appears in later chapters of this text.

TWO-DIMENSIONAL PICTURES

Assume that you have selected a particular view of a three-dimensional object. What happens next? Project the three-dimensional geometry of the object onto a two-dimensional view surface, called a **picture plane.** You must do this each time the view changes. In fact, for perspective projections, the picture of the object changes if the location of the picture plane changes (that is, the distance of the eyepoint, $\mathbf{p}_E$, from the picture plane) even though $\mathbf{p}_E$ and the line of sight are unchanged. This means that the location of the picture plane is an integral, important part of the view process.

The picture plane usually is located between the object and the observer and is perpendicular (normal) to the line of sight. This condition is shown in Fig. 1.14, where the picture plane is clearly outside of the object.

Let us assume that the distance between the eyepoint and the picture plane is fixed. Now imagine the eyepoint and picture plane moving together toward the object until the picture plane lies inside the object (in this case the object might be a building). This condition is shown in Fig. 1.15, and you will encounter it when the observer wishes to move into an object and look around. Note how the picture has been truncated or "clipped" at the picture plane. This prevents distortion and eliminates lines that would tend to confuse the image on the picture plane.

Lines located wholly or partially between the eyepoint and the picture plane become distorted when their end points are projected onto the pic-

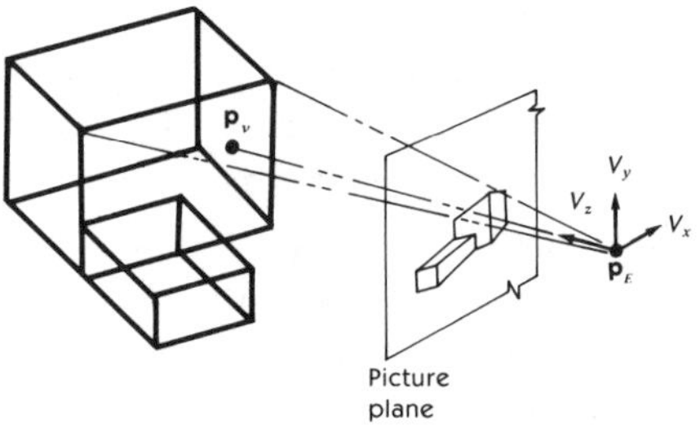

Fig. 1.14. Picture plane: outside location.

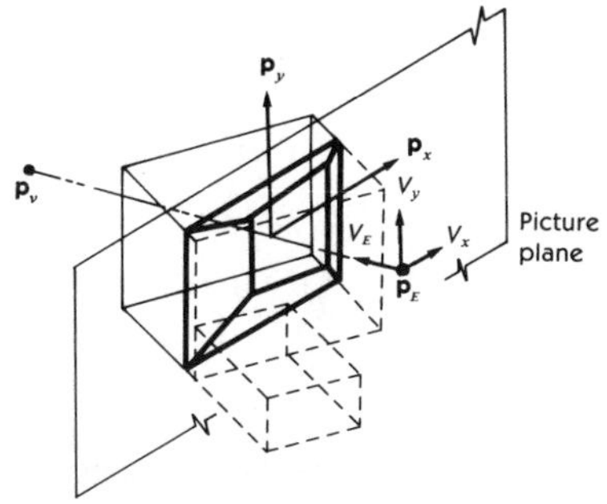

Fig. 1.15. Picture plane: inside location.

ture plane. Furthermore, lines located wholly or partially behind the eyepoint become inverted when they are projected onto the picture plane. Both of these conditions can create visual confusion and should be avoided.

One way to avoid this condition is to keep the eye of the observer and its corresponding picture plane outside of the object or objects in the scene. This approach, however, does not allow the observer to move around inside an object or scene. The preferred procedure, shown in Fig. 1.15, clips or truncates all lines at the picture plane that are partially on the observer's side of the picture plane and eliminates all lines that are wholly on the observer's side of the picture plane. This approach eliminates distortion and allows the observer to look around inside an object. A similar set of conditions arises if the eyepoint is inside the object and the picture plane is beyond it.

Note that both Fig. 1.14 and Fig. 1.15 show the lines of projection converging on the eyepoint. This type of projection produces a **perspective** image of the object on the picture plane. (See also Fig. 1.16.) The main advantage of a perspective picture is that it looks more realistic. It accurately represents what the eye sees from the specified eyepoint. You will

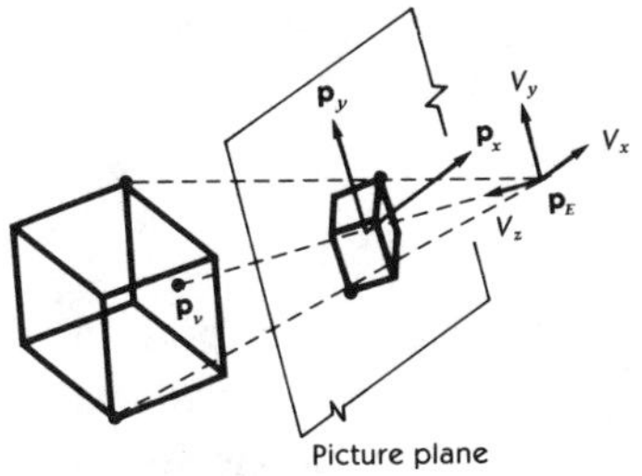

Fig. 1.16. Perspective projection.

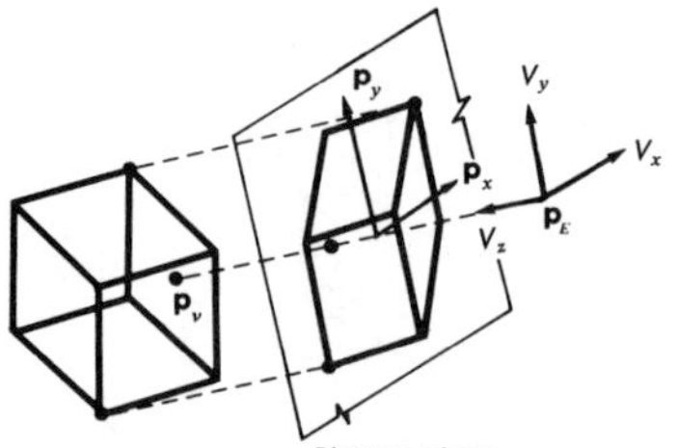

Fig. 1.17. Orthographic projection.

encounter the mathematics of **perspective projections** and their transformation equations in later chapters.

Another type of projection is created by constructing the lines of projection so that they are parallel to the line of sight. This type of projection is called a **parallel projection** or an **orthographic projection** (if perpendicular to the picture plane) (Fig. 1.17).

The main advantage of an orthographic projection is that the unit of distance measured along all lines parallel to the picture plane remains uniform and constant. This makes it easier to measure distances in an orthographic projection, a convenience more valuable when the "picture" is in the hardcopy form of a plot or drawing.

GRAPHIC DISPLAYS

You should note that all "pictures" projected onto the picture plane are "mathematical pictures" only; they are data sets in the computer's memory computed from the underlying data set representing the geometric model. As such, you do not see them directly.

To create the picture of an object that you actually see on the computer graphic display screen, first mathematically transfer or map the picture-plane data set of the object from the picture plane to the surface of the display device. Do this by transforming the coordinates of the point on the picture plane to appropriate coordinates in the display-screen coordinate system. This introduces the idea of the window and viewport.

1.5. Window and Viewport

Often you will want to map only a portion of the "picture" on the picture plane onto the display-screen coordinate system. Do this by specifying a rectangular boundary, called a **window**, around that portion of the object or scene on the picture plane that you want to display. Then map the image within this window to yet another bounded area, called a **viewport,** on the screen coordinate system. The image in the viewport is the one that you actually see.

The coordinate system of the display screen has, of course, horizontal and vertical limits, established by the number of horizontal and vertical locations accessible to the screen electron beam generating the display. Two integers specify the beam location. Usually the first number indicates the beam's horizontal displacement from some reference or "zero" location (ordinarily in the lower left corner of the screen), and the second number indicates the vertical displacement. The beam, if in the "on" mode, creates a small but finite spot of light at the location to which it is directed. This spot defines a discrete, uniquely addressable picture element, a **pixel** (Fig. 1.18). The rectangular array or assemblage of these discrete pixels forms the screen coordinate system. Again, note that points on it are always integers, always positive. Furthermore, the horizontal (H) and vertical (V) dimensions of a screen are not necessarily equal (in Fig. 1.18 they are). An important sequence of transformations, then, is from the infinite, continuous three-dimensional space of points in a world coordinate system to the finite and discrete two-dimensional screen system. (Box 1.1 elaborates on this point.)

Let us now derive the transformation from the picture plane to the screen coordinate system. A simple case is shown in Fig. 1.19. Here you see the arbitrary point, $\mathbf{p}$, at x, y in the picture plane (which in this case corresponds to the x, y plane in the world system). The problem is to assign appropriate display-screen coordinates to it, thus defining $\mathbf{p}_s$. So, given $\mathbf{p}$, find $\mathbf{p}_s$. You need some supporting geometric information. To do this, you must make some assumptions: First, assume that the display is on an $H \times V$ pixel screen. Next, assume that you want to display everything in an area of the world coordinate system defined by the boundaries Wx_L, Wx_R, Wy_T, Wy_B (the window) within the area in the screen defined by

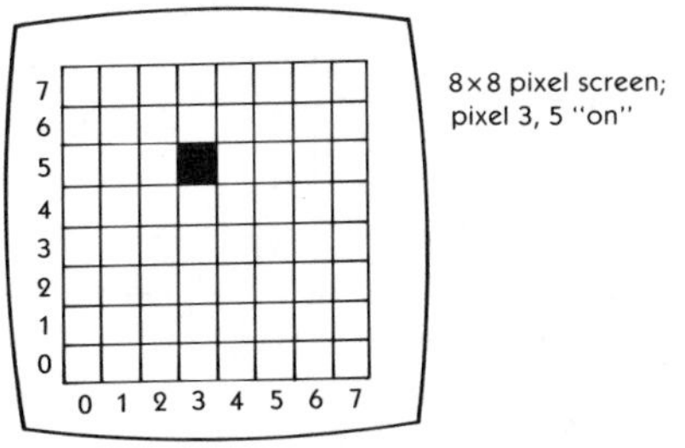

Fig. 1.18. Display-screen coordinate system.

Box 1.1. Object Space to Image Space: Units of Measure

You will frequently see the terms **object space** and **image space.** Object space corresponds to the world coordinate system, image space to the display-screen coordinate system. Object space is an unbounded, infinite collection of continuous points. It may have any number of dimensions, but you will usually develop models in a three-dimensional object space.

Compare this three-dimensional object space to the bounded and discrete image space of two dimensions. How do you reconcile these two spaces? Through the special transformations developed in Section 1.5, Eqs. (1.11). Note a subtle problem, however. Computing x_s and y_s results in real, noninteger numbers for screen coordinates. Ordinarily, you can merely truncate them if the decimal portion is less than 0.5, or round up if it is 0.5 or greater, and thus convert x_s and y_s to integers.

A word of caution: It is not a good practice to try to recover x and y from image space (screen coordinates), since in initially computing integer x_s and integer y_s you irretrievably lose information. Nor is it a good practice to compute global scene or geometric analysis using the screen coordinates. Always save object space coordinates, both for subsequent view changes and for possible future scene analysis. Usually you will save the object space definition of a model for other reasons, so this is not a problem.

Vx_L, Vx_R, Vy_T, Vy_B (the viewport). In doing this, you are establishing a one-to-one correspondence between points in the picture-plane window and points in the screen viewport. You are "mapping" points in the world system onto the screen. It sounds rather ominous and rigorous, but you can do it rather easily by using simple ratios of the geometric relationships of

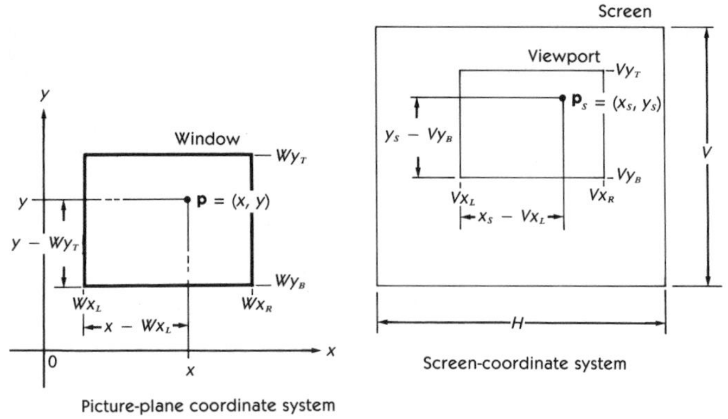

Fig. 1.19. Transformation from picture plane to screen coordinates.

the points $\mathbf{p}$ and $\mathbf{p}_S$ to their locations within their respective regions. The ratios are

$$\frac{x_S - Vx_L}{Vx_R - Vx_L} = \frac{x - Wx_L}{Wx_R - Wx_L}$$
$$\frac{y_S - Vy_B}{Vy_T - Vy_B} = \frac{y - Wy_B}{Wy_T - Wy_B} \tag{1.10}$$

Solve these equations for x_S and y_S to obtain

$$x_S = \frac{x - Wx_L}{Wx_R - Wx_L}(Vx_R - Vx_L) + Vx_L$$
$$y_S = \frac{y - Wy_B}{Wy_T - Wy_B}(Vy_T - Vy_B) + Vy_B \tag{1.11}$$

Here is an important feature about these equations:

$$x_{\text{scale factor}} = \frac{Vx_R - Vx_L}{Wx_R - Wx_L}$$
$$y_{\text{scale factor}} = \frac{Vy_T - Vy_B}{Wy_T - Wy_B} \tag{1.12}$$

There is no distortion in the horizontal and vertical interrelationships between points mapped onto the screen relative to their original interrelationships in the world system if, and only if, $x_{\text{scale factor}} = y_{\text{scale factor}}$. For example, with equality of the scale factors, four points in the world system defining the vertices of a square when mapped onto the screen will continue to define the vertices of a square-appearing figure. (Box 1.2 suggests a mathematical way to accommodate a variety of screen sizes.)

SUMMARY

To model and display an object in three-dimensional space, first establish the global coordinate system. This is the frame of reference for defining and locating all objects and observers. Next, locate the observer's eyepoint and line of sight. Specify the location of the picture plane, assumed to be perpendicular to the line of sight, by giving its distance from the eyepoint.

To create an image of the object on the picture plane, you can make one of two types of projection. Make a perspective projection by projecting lines from each point on the object to the eyepoint. Then create the perspective image on the picture plane by connecting the points of inter-

Box 1.2. Normalized Graphics Device Coordinates

To accommodate a variety of graphics devices (a variety of screen sizes) on an extensive graphics network, you have a mathematical technique called **normalization.** Compute the coordinates for an imaginary screen whose horizontal and vertical dimensions are $H = 1.0$, $V = 1.0$, respectively. This is a unit or normalized screen (see the figure).

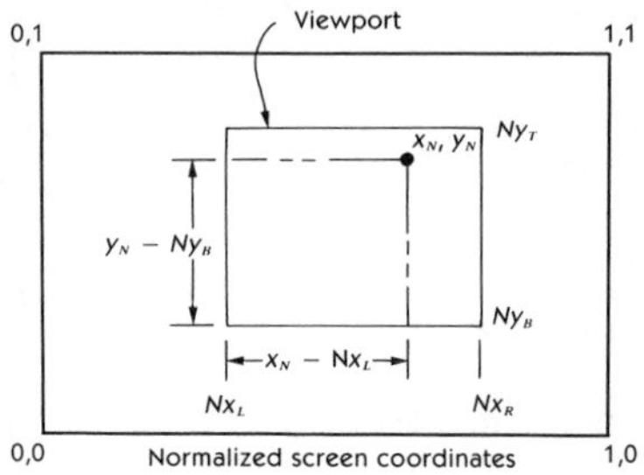

Modify Eq. (1.11) appropriately to obtain

$$x_N = \frac{x - x_L}{x_R - x_L}(Nx_R - Nx_L) + Nx_L$$

$$y_N = \frac{y - y_B}{y_T - y_B}(Ny_T - Ny_B) + Ny_B$$

where, clearly, $0 \le Nx_L, Nx_R, Ny_T, Ny_B \le 1.0$, meaning that $0 \le x_N, y_N \le 1.0$. Finally, transmit x_N and y_N, then transform them locally by multiplying each normalized coordinate by the appropriate horizontal and vertical scales, so that

$$x_s = Hx_N$$
$$y_s = Vy_N$$

If a particular screen size is 1024×768, then

$$x_s = 1024x_N$$
$$y_s = 768y_N$$

section of these lines with the picture plane in the same way they are connected to form the original object. Make an orthographic projection by projecting lines from each of the points on the object to the picture plane so that the projection lines are parallel to the line of sight. The line of sight itself must be perpendicular to the picture plane. Then create the orthographic image on the picture plane by appropriately connecting the points of intersection of these lines with the picture plane.

Map the mathematical picture-plane image of the object stored in the computer's memory to the screen coordinates. The display device (graphics monitor, plotter, and so on) then produces the actual image of the object seen by the observer.

This chapter has sketched in only the broadest outlines the various coordinate systems used in computer graphics. Each system and the transformations required to move data from one system to another are further developed in later chapters.

EXERCISES

1. If the point $\mathbf{p} = (x_L, y_B)$ in the picture-plane coordinate system is made to correspond with the origin of the screen coordinate system, then show how this affects Eq. (1.11).

2. Given points $\mathbf{p}_1 = (4.5, 6.8)$, $\mathbf{p}_2 = (-1.2, 1.0)$, and $\mathbf{p}_3 = (8.4, -2.5)$, find their respective screen coordinates. Use the following assumptions: The screen is 512 × 512 pixels and the window is the minimum square that encloses the points and fills the upper left quadrant of the screen.

2. Points

You saw in Chapter 1 that it was quite impossible to talk about coordinate systems without also talking about points. We did not exhaust the subject. There is much more to be said about points and their importance to geometric modeling and computer graphics.

The **point** is the simplest geometric object. It cannot be defined in terms of anything simpler. In fact, as you will see in later chapters, the point is the basic building block for all the other geometric objects you will study. Recall from elementary geometry how many simple figures were defined as a locus of points with certain constraining properties. For example, a circle is the locus of points equidistant from a given point and all lying in a common plane. This principle is easily extended to more complex curves and also to surfaces and solids. To do this, merely use sets of equations to define the locus of points. This is a much more powerful way of describing geometric objects; it allows you to analyze and quantify their properties and relationships. And most important, points and analytical techniques for controlling their generation, location, and transformation are central to developing computer graphic displays.

2.1. Definition and Properties

A point has two important aspects. First, a point suggests the notion of place or location. This is its fundamental geometric aspect. Second, a point has latent quantitative properties; it is specified by a set of one or more real numbers: its coordinates. This is its analytic aspect. These two aspects coalesce when you apply the principles of analytic geometry. The set of real numbers—the coordinates of the point—not only locate the point in a hypothetical coordinate system, but also locate it with respect to other points in the system.

Define a point in n-dimensional space by a set of real numbers:

$$\mathbf{p} = (x_1, x_2, \ldots, x_n) \tag{2.1}$$

where x_1, x_2, ..., x_n are the real-number coordinates of $\mathbf{p}$ and n is the number of dimensions of the coordinate system. Remember, we will use a boldface, lowercase letter $\mathbf{p}$ to denote a point.

Almost all of the points used in modeling and computer graphics are defined in two- or three-dimensional space, so you will not again encounter Eq. (2.1) in this form. Note here, though, that each coordinate has an identifying number (subscript). This is usually not necessary if the geometry is in two or three dimensions; then you have plenty of letters with which to name the coordinates, such as x, y, and, if necessary, z. In fact, the global or world coordinate system will be exclusively a three-dimensional coordinate system, so that the points in it are given by

$$\mathbf{p} = (x, y, z) \tag{2.2}$$

A subscript is used to identify a specific point. For example,

$$\mathbf{p}_1 = (x_1, y_1, z_1) \tag{2.3}$$

If you review Chapter 1, you will see that points are an integral part of the definition of a coordinate system. Now you can use an extension of the definition of a point to define a Cartesian coordinate system in another way. Let us do this for three dimensions: Define the three-dimensional space with a Cartesian coordinate system as the set of all points defined by the triplet of real numbers (x, y, z), where $x, y, z \in (-\infty, +\infty)$. From this definition you can derive all the other characteristics of the coordinate system. For example, the origin is the point with $x = 0$, $y = 0$, and $z = 0$, or $\mathbf{p} = (0, 0, 0)$. The x axis is the set of points $\mathbf{p} = (x, 0, 0)$, where $x \in (-\infty, +\infty)$. How would you define the y and z axes?

By itself, a point has no geometric or analytic properties other than place. It has no size, orientation, length, area, or volume. It has no inside or outside, nor any other common geometric characteristics. But when you have defined two or more points, you can compute and test many interesting properties.

Given two points in space, $\mathbf{p}_1$ and $\mathbf{p}_2$, compute the distance, d, between them by using the Pythagorean theorem. (see Fig. 2.1):

$$d = \sqrt{(x_2 - x_1)^2 + (y_2 - y_1)^2 + (z_2 - z_1)^2} \tag{2.4}$$

The distance d is itself a real number; it is always positive. You may assign a specific unit of measurement to the coordinate system: centimeters, meters, light-years, and so on. The distance is then given in terms of this unit

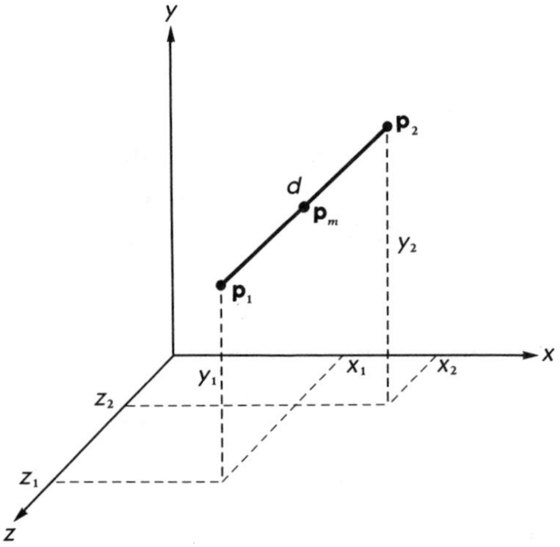

Fig. 2.1. Distance between two points.

of measurement. Although the choice you make is arbitrary, you must be consistent throughout the model.

The coordinates of the midpoint, call it $\mathbf{p}_m$, between these two points are

$$\mathbf{p}_m = [(x_1 + x_2)/2, (y_1 + y_2)/2, (z_1 + z_2)/2] \tag{2.5}$$

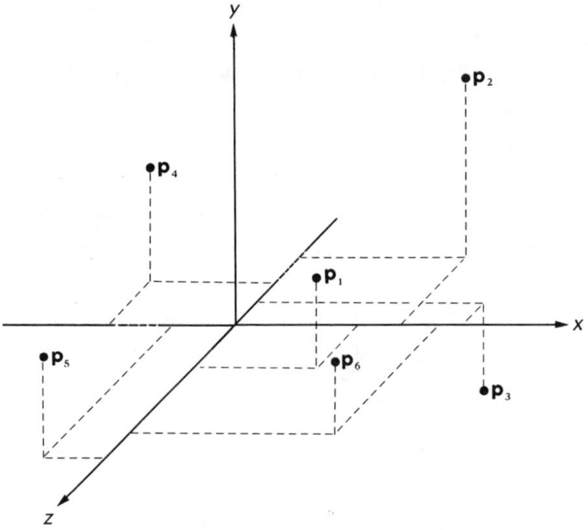

Fig. 2.2. A set of points.

Now let us add more points to the system (Fig. 2.2). Given the coordinates of each point, then for any point in the set compute which other point is closest and which is farthest. You could compute d for each pair of points. But wait; d^2 will do just as well! You will save an "expensive" computation. Can you think of any other computational shortcuts?

Finding the vertices of a rectangular solid, or box, which just contains all the points of a given set, is often useful in geometric modeling and computer graphics if you must detect relationships between two or more sets of points or the containment of a point in a given volume of space. Can you devise a way to compute the coordinates of the eight vertices of the box? *Hint*: Find the maximum and minimum x, y, and z coordinates of the point set. Assume the "edges" of the box are parallel to the coordinate axes. (You are asked to complete this solution in Exercise 10.)

An interesting problem may arise when you display three or more points. See Box 2.1.

Box 2.1. Pixels and Point Resolution

You may not always be able to resolve every point in a set of points that you want to display. Consider, for example, the three points, $\mathbf{p}_1$, $\mathbf{p}_2$, $\mathbf{p}_3$, in the figure below. For simplicity, arrange them on a common horizontal line so that $y_1 = y_2 = y_3$. Now only the x values determine their separation. If the number of pixels, H, between $\mathbf{p}_1$ and $\mathbf{p}_3$ is less than the ratio of the separations of $\mathbf{p}_1$ and $\mathbf{p}_3$ to $\mathbf{p}_1$ and $\mathbf{p}_2$, then $\mathbf{p}_1$ and $\mathbf{p}_2$ cannot be resolved. That is, $\mathbf{p}_1$ and $\mathbf{p}_2$ will not be displayed as two separate and distinct points. This relationship is expressed by the inequality

$$\frac{x_3 - x_1}{x_2 - x_1} > H_{\text{pixels}}$$

If the inequality is true, then $\mathbf{p}_1$ and $\mathbf{p}_2$ cannot be resolved.

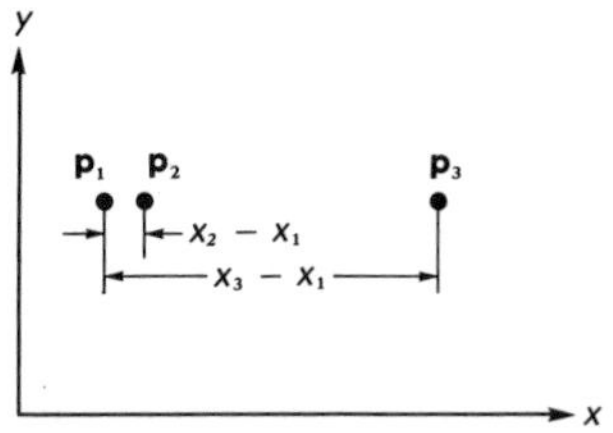

EXERCISES

1. Define a polar coordinate system and its principal characteristics as a set of points.

2. Define a spherical coordinate system and its principal characteristics as a set of points.

3. Define a cylindrical coordinate system and its principal characteristics as a set of points.

4. Find the distances between the following pairs of points:

a. (−2, 8, 0), (7, 5, 11)
b. (3, 3, −4), (1, 0, 9)
c. (1.1, 7.3, −2), (6.7, 8, 0)
d. (−5, −1, 0), (4, 9, 1)
e. (0, 0, 1), (0, 0, 1)
f. (−3, 0, 0), (7, 0, 0)
g. (1, 1, 0), (4, 6, −3)
h. (−2.7, 6.5, 0.8), (5.1, −5.7, 1.9)
i. (7, −4, 2), (0, 2.7, −0.3)
j. (10, 9, −1), (3, 8, 3)

5. Generalize Eq. (2.4) so that it is applicable to points in a Cartesian space of n dimensions.

6. Compute the coordinates of points in Exercise 4 relative to a coordinate system located at (−2, 8, 0) in the original system and parallel to it.

7. Compute the distance between each pair of transformed points in Exercise 6.

8. Show that the distance between any pair of points is independent (invariant) of the coordinate system.

9. Find the midpoint between each pair of points in Exercise 4.

10. Find the coordinates of the eight vertices of a rectangular box that just encloses an arbitrary set of points.

11. Find the coordinates of the eight vertices of a rectangular box that just encloses the set of 20 points given in Exercise 4.

12. Write a procedure to compute the eight vertices of a rectangular box that just contains a set of points. Denote this as **BOX** (N, P, BOX), where

N is the input number of points.
P (N,3) is the input array of point coordinates (x, y, z), and
BOX (8,3) is the output array of the box vertex point coordinates.

2.2. Displaying Points

A computer graphics display allows you to inspect visually a geometric model. Assume that you must construct and display a geometric model consisting of a set of points whose coordinates are known, and the points are more or less randomly distributed throughout a limited region of three-dimensional space. Furthermore, assume that you want to view these points by looking toward the origin from some point on the $+z$ axis and outside the set. You are suddenly faced with several important questions:

1. How are the points entered into the computer graphics display program?

2. How are they identified and stored?

3. How is a set of data describing three-dimensional objects (points, in this case) transformed into a two-dimensional display?

Each of these rather general questions quickly blossoms into many detailed questions. For example, as to the first question, you can directly enter the coordinates of points by typing them in on the keyboard of the computer graphics terminal, by using logical inferences based on geometric relationships or constructions (that is, the midpoint between two existing points or the point of intersection of two straight lines), or by indicating physically with a light pen or similar device. The graphics program interprets the message and displays the points accordingly; or another computer program may generate output data in the form of point coordinates and transmit these data to the graphics program for subsequent display.

The first example—entering the points directly—requires the careful design of interactive procedures: how to communicate information to the computer graphics program via the display terminal or work station. The second example, using another computer program, requires an equally well-designed data interface between the two programs. You will briefly explore some of the principles underlying the design and implementation of these aspects of computer graphics program design.

When a point is entered into the program, its coordinates are stored in an **array**; an array is an ordered arrangement of numbers or other mathematical elements. This array may include a unique identifying number for each point, or the position of the coordinates of a point within the array may be all the "identification" required. Figure 2.3 shows the coordinates of six points arranged as a rectangular array of 18 numbers. This is a convenient mathematical technique for representing and manipulating related groups of numbers, although, strictly speaking, the numbers are not stored in the computer in "rectangular" configurations (to be discussed subsequently).

Give an array an identifying symbol, say A, and use double subscripts on this symbol to identify particular numbers in the array; for example, A_{ij}.

	Column 1	Column 2	Column 3	
	x	y	z	
Row 1	−2.5	3.2	1.7	← Point 1
Row 2	2.0	6.0	6.0	← Point 2
Row 3	9.5	−0.2	−4.3	← Point 3
Row 4	0.1	6.3	−5.2	← Point 4
Row 5	8.8	6.9	3.7	← Point 5
Row 6	−0.7	0.0	−3.9	← Point 6

Fig. 2.3. Coordinates of six points arranged as a rectangular array of numbers.

The subscript i denotes the particular row and j denotes the particular column in which the number A_{ij} appears. For example, the value of $A_{5,2}$ of the array in Fig. 2.3 is 6.9.

The stored coordinates are usually accessible to the graphics display program as a linear (one-at-a-time) sequence of numbers. An exception to this is in a parallel processing environment where each of the three coordinates of a point is simultaneously accessible to three separate processors and program segments. (This type of system is not considered here.) There are two ways to form a linear sequence of coordinate values for n points; both are illustrated in Fig. 2.4. Sometimes point identifying information is included in these data arrays. In Fig. 2.4a, the coordinates of each point are grouped together in sequence. In Fig. 2.4b, all the x coordinate values are grouped together, followed by the y and z coordinate values.

Part of the answer to the third question, how to transform three-dimensional data into a two-dimensional format, is given in Sections 1.4 and 1.5. There you saw how points are transformed from a two-dimensional world coordinate system onto the bounded screen coordinate system [Eq. (1.11)]. Most of the models you deal with, however, are defined by three-dimensional points. How to transform these points onto the two-dimensional picture plane is the subject of Chapter 5. Meanwhile, you still have several other problems to consider.

You can define **absolute points** or **relative points**. This distinction arises because of the way point coordinates are computed and the way points are plotted or displayed. Absolute points are given directly by their coordinates, in whatever system they are in: world, screen, and so on. Thus, a set of absolute points is

$$\text{Absolute point } \mathbf{p}_i = (x_i, y_i) \qquad i = 1, \ldots, n \tag{2.6}$$

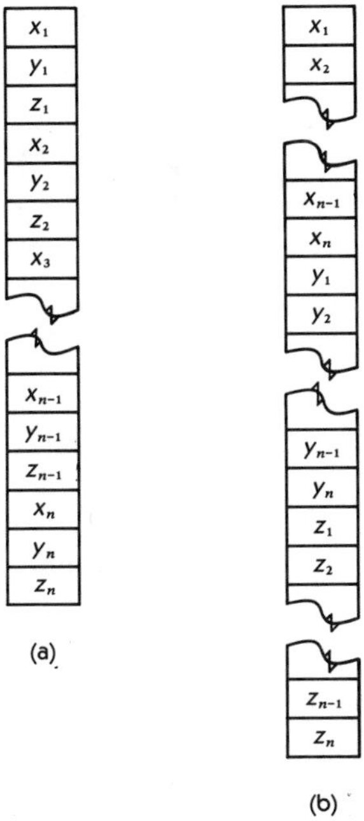

Fig. 2.4. Two kinds of linear sequences of point coordinates.

The coordinates of each relative point are defined relative to the coordinates of the point preceding it. This is best demonstrated by the following expression:

$$\text{Relative point } \mathbf{p}_i = \mathbf{p}_{i-1} + \Delta_i \qquad i = 1, \ldots, n \tag{2.7}$$

where $\mathbf{p}_0$ is some initial point (it could, of course, be the origin), and where $\Delta_i = (\Delta x_i, \Delta y_i)$. This is illustrated in Fig. 2.5. Such a sequence may be generated in the course of some numerical analysis or when computing points on lines, curves, or surfaces, for example.

Now let us turn to another point display problem. You will often find it necessary to define a window that just encloses a specific set of points. How do you do this? Investigate each point, $\mathbf{p}_i$, searching for the maximum and minimum x and y values. Then,

$$\begin{aligned} Wx_R &= \max x \\ Wx_L &= \min x \\ Wy_T &= \max y \\ Wy_B &= \min y \end{aligned} \tag{2.8}$$

Study the example in Fig. 2.6. Here are seven points with coordinates: $\mathbf{p}_1$

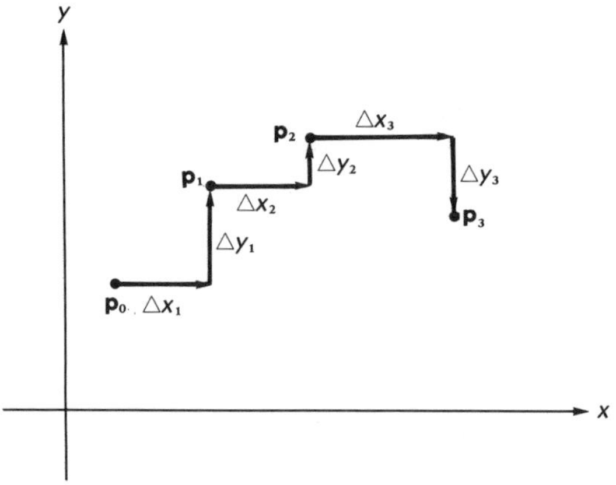

Fig. 2.5. Relative points.

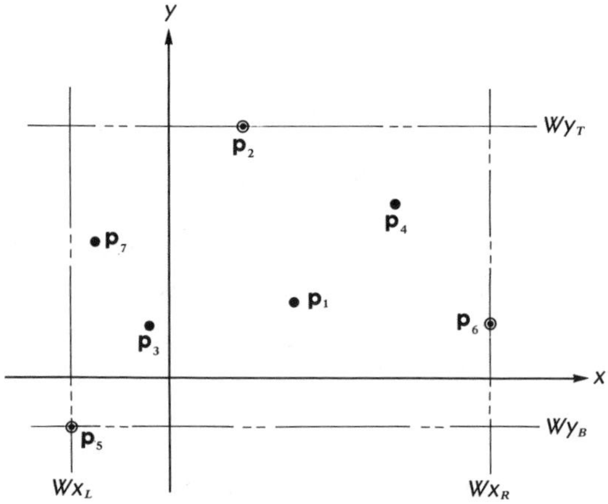

Fig. 2.6. Defining a window for a set of points.

$= (3.0, 1.5)$, $\mathbf{p}_2 = (2.0, 4.0)$, $\mathbf{p}_3 = (-0.5, 0.7)$, $\mathbf{p}_4 = (5.0, 3.0)$, $\mathbf{p}_5 = (-2.5, -1.0)$, $\mathbf{p}_6 = (7.0, 0.6)$, and $\mathbf{p}_7 = (-2.0, 2.0)$. It is easy to find that max $x = x_6$, min $x = x_5$, max $y = y_2$, and min $y = y_5$, so that $Wx_R = 7.0$, $Wx_L = -2.5$, $Wy_T = 4.0$, and $Wy_B = -1.0$. Confirm this visually by inspecting the figure.

EXERCISES

1. Given Δ_i = constant for all $\mathbf{p}_i$, find $\mathbf{p}_4$.

2. Find the set of Δ_i's for the vertex points of a square whose lower left corner

coincides with the origin and whose sides are four units long. Assume that the square is oriented parallel to the x, y coordinate axes. Let $\mathbf{p}_0 = (0, 0)$, and proceed counterclockwise.

3. Same as Exercise 2, except let $\mathbf{p}_0 = (0, 4)$ and proceed clockwise.

4. Write a procedure to compute the window boundaries that just enclose a set of points. Denote this as **BOX2D** (N, P, WXR, WXL, WYT, WYB), where

N is the input number of points
P (3, N) is the input array of point coordinates
WXR, WXL, WYT, WYB are the output window boundaries

2.3. Point Containment

It is very useful to know if a given point in the picture plane is inside or outside the window region. Let the coordinates of the test point be x, y. The point is inside the window if and only if both of the following inequalities are true:

$$Wx_L \leq x \leq Wx_R \quad \text{and} \quad Wy_B \leq y \leq Wy_T \tag{2.9}$$

EXERCISES

1. If $Wx_R = 14$, $Wx_L = -2$, $Wy_T = 8$, and $Wy_B = -4$, then determine which of the following points are in the window:

a. $\mathbf{p}_1 = (0, 0)$
b. $\mathbf{p}_2 = (0, 10)$
c. $\mathbf{p}_3 = (8, -6)$
d. $\mathbf{p}_4 = (16, -6)$
e. $\mathbf{p}_5 = (-1, 10)$
f. $\mathbf{p}_6 = (15, 4)$
g. $\mathbf{p}_7 = (3, 10)$
h. $\mathbf{p}_8 = (14, 2)$
i. $\mathbf{p}_9 = (-2, 8)$
j. $\mathbf{p}_{10} = (10, 10)$

2. What are the coordinates of the four window corner points in Exercise 1?

3. Derive a test to determine if a point is contained in a rectangular volume (a box) in three-dimensional space. Define all the parameters.

4. What are the coordinates of the eight vertices of the box defined in Exercise 3?

2.4. Translation and Rotation of Points

You can move a point from one location to another in two ways: You can **translate** it from its current position to a new one, or you can **rotate** it about some axis to a new position. Describe a translation by giving rel-

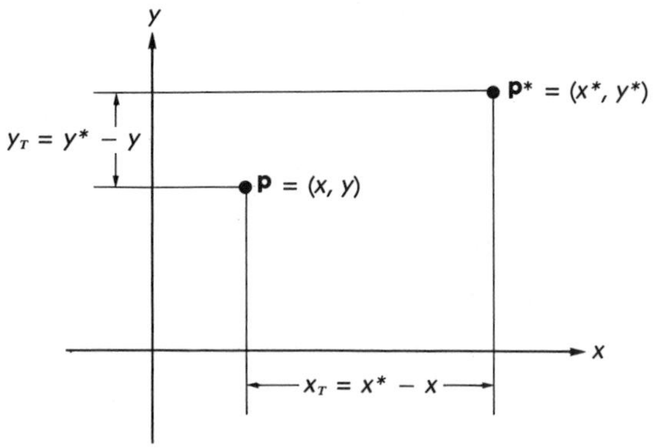

Fig. 2.7. Translating a point.

ative changes to a point's coordinates (Fig. 2.7). Denote these changes as x_T and y_T. Then,

$$\begin{aligned} x^* &= x + x_T \\ y^* &= y + y_T \end{aligned} \tag{2.10}$$

where x^* and y^* are the coordinates of the new location. Generalizing to three dimensions, or more, is obvious. Compare this equation to the one describing a coordinate-system transformation [Eqs. (1.5) and (1.7)].

The simplest rotation of a point you can describe in two dimensions is a rotation about the origin (Fig. 2.8). If you rotate a point **p** about the origin and through an angle θ, then you derive the coordinates of the transformed point **p*** as follows: Express x^* and y^* in terms of $\alpha + \theta$ and r^*; thus,

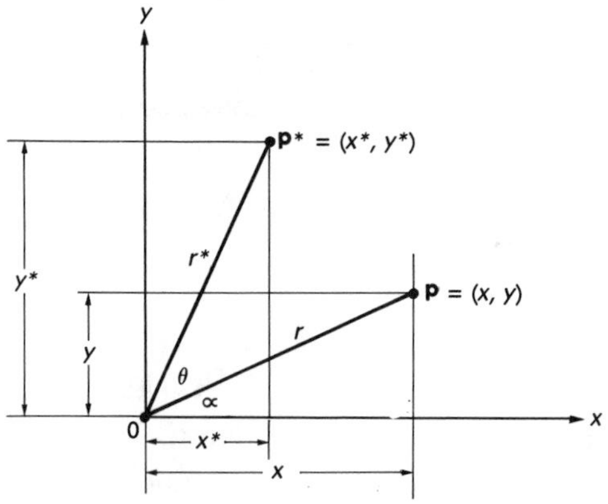

Fig. 2.8. Rotating a point about the origin.

$$x^* = r^* \cos(\alpha + \theta)$$
$$y^* = r^* \sin(\alpha + \theta) \quad (2.11)$$

Recall from elementary trigonometry that

$$\cos(\alpha + \theta) = \cos\alpha\cos\theta - \sin\alpha\sin\theta$$
$$\sin(\alpha + \theta) = \sin\alpha\cos\theta - \cos\alpha\sin\theta \quad (2.12)$$

Also,

$$\cos\alpha = \frac{x}{r}$$
$$\sin\alpha = \frac{y}{r} \quad (2.13)$$

Since $r = r^*$, with appropriate substitutions of the preceding expressions into Eq. (2.11), find

$$x^* = x\cos\theta - y\sin\theta$$
$$y^* = x\sin\theta + y\cos\theta \quad (2.14)$$

This is the set of rotation transformations you are after. To generalize this to three dimensions requires that you change from rotation about the origin—a point—to rotation about a straight line—an axis of rotation. In three dimensions, Eq. (2.14) describes the rotation of a point about the z axis. A positive rotation in two dimensions is counterclockwise about the origin.

You can produce a rotation transformation of the two-dimensional co-

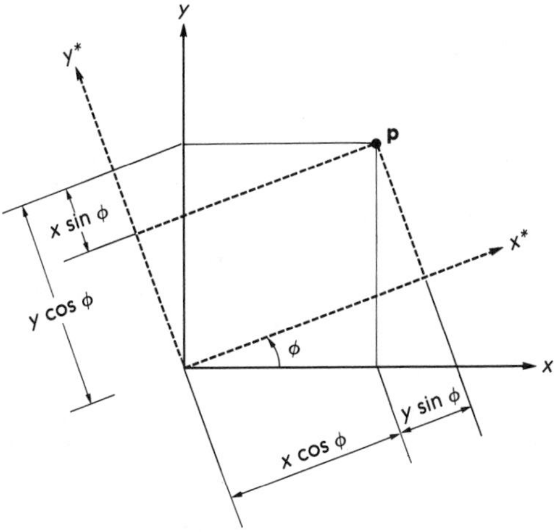

Fig. 2.9. Coordinate system rotation.

ordinate system by rotating the axes about the origin through an angle, ϕ (Fig. 2.9). The coordinates of a point are given by the following transformation equations:

$$\begin{aligned} x^* &= x \cos \phi + y \sin \phi \\ y^* &= -x \sin \phi + y \cos \phi \end{aligned} \tag{2.15}$$

EXERCISES

1. Derive the net transformation equations for a point that is first translated by x_T, y_T and then rotated by θ.

2. Derive the net transformation equations for a point that is first rotated by θ and then translated by x_T, y_T.

3. Compare the results of Exercises 1 and 2. What conclusion do you make?

4. How are Eqs. (2.14) and 2.15) related?

3. Lines

AFTER THE POINT, the straight line is the next simplest geometric object. Long before we abstract it from the context of the everyday physical world, and long before we even name it, we acquire an empirical, intuitive knowledge of the straight line. We observe that all physical manifestations of a straight line are finite **line segments** with definite end points and length. When we come to grips with the mathematical or geometric line, we must also consider the unbounded or infinite line and the semi-infinite or half-line.

In this chapter you will learn to represent these lines as the locus of points satisfying certain well-defined equations, called **linear parametric equations.** These equations allow you to define lines in spaces of two or more dimensions. They also allow you to analyze the geometric or spatial relationships between points and lines, another subject for your attention in this chapter.

You will revisit lines in Chapter 12, where you will see how to use vectors to define straight lines, and again in Chapter 13, where you will see that a straight line is a special form of curve.

3.1. Definition and Properties

Define a straight line in three-dimensional space as the locus of points satisfying a set of three linear equations,

$$\begin{aligned} x &= a_x u + b_x \\ y &= a_y u + b_y \\ z &= a_z u + b_z \end{aligned} \tag{3.1}$$

The dependent variables x, y, and z are the coordinates of a point. Note that Eqs. (3.1) generate a set of coordinates each time you specify a value for u, the parametric variable. The coefficients a_x, a_y, a_z, b_x, b_y, and b_z are constant for any given line.

Think of these three equations, taken together, as a point-generating machine. The fuel, or input, is values of u. The machine then produces coordinates of points on a line as output (Fig. 3.1). It produces a bounded line segment if you limit the range of values assigned to the parametric variable u. Usually you let u take values in the interval from 0 to 1, inclusive. (This is called the **unit interval.**) Express this as

$$u \in [0, 1] \tag{3.2}$$

By controlling the interval limits, you control the nature of the line, making it a line segment, a semi-infinite line, or an infinite line. The concept of the interval is developed more fully in Box 3.1.

You can see that if you insert values of $u = 0$ and $u = 1$ into the point-generating machine of Fig. 3.1, then you obtain the end-point coordinates $\mathbf{p}_0 = (4, 2, -2)$ and $\mathbf{p}_1 = (1, 6, 4)$. If you choose to characterize a line segment by the coordinates of its end points, then you must modify Eq. (3.1) accordingly. Identify the end points of the line segment, as above, by $\mathbf{p}_0$ and $\mathbf{p}_1$ (Fig. 3.2). Substitute $u = 0$ into Eq. (3.1) to obtain

$$\begin{aligned} b_x &= x_0 \\ b_y &= y_0 \\ b_z &= z_0 \end{aligned} \tag{3.3}$$

where x_0, y_0, z_0 are the coordinates at the $u = 0$ end point of the line. For $u = 1$,

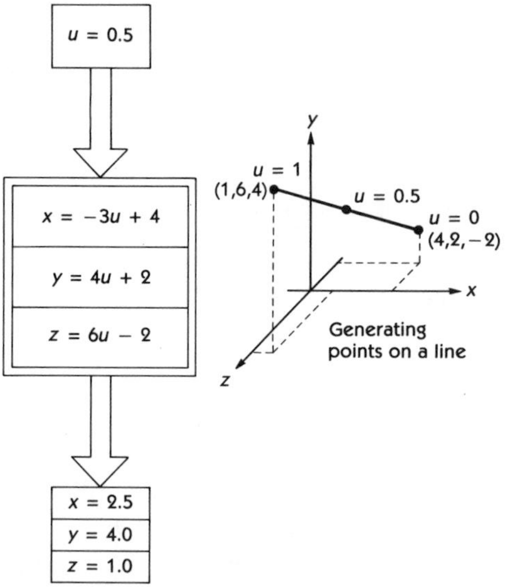

Fig. 3.1. A point-generating machine.

Box 3.1. Intervals

Consider the continuous set of points defining the real line x. Let an interval on x be defined by $a < x < b$, where a and b are limiting points of the interval. This is an **open interval** because it does *not* contain its limit points. Conversely, if $a \le x \le b$, then it is a **closed interval** because it *does* contain its limit points.

A closed interval is denoted [a,b], using brackets, with the interval limits separated by a comma. An open interval is denoted (a,b), using parentheses, with the interval limits again separated by a comma. Write (for a closed interval, for example)

$$x \in [a, b]$$

Read this as: x is an element (or member) of the interval $[a, b]$. These intervals briefly appeared in your study of one-dimensional coordinate systems (Section 1.1). The unit interval is a special case [Eq. (3.2)] and is often used in geometric modeling and computer graphics.

All the intervals mentioned so far are one dimensional, but, of course, there are two-, three-, or even n-dimensional analogs. For example, $u,v \in [0,1]$ and $u, v, w \in [0,1]$ are unit regions in two and three dimensions, respectively.

These concepts are borrowed from set theory. You can interpret the interval as a subset (open or closed) and x as a member of this subset if it falls appropriately in the specified interval:

$$a < x < b \text{ or } x \in (a, b)$$

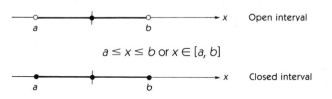

Open interval

$$a \le x \le b \text{ or } x \in [a, b]$$

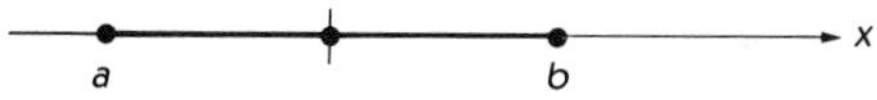

Closed interval

There are also discrete intervals. Consider, for example, the set of positive integers 1, 2, 3, ..., N. Denote a closed interval in this set as $[a : b]$, where a and b are integers and are separated by a colon.

$$\begin{aligned} x_1 &= a_x + x_0 \\ y_1 &= a_y + y_0 \\ z_1 &= a_z + z_0 \end{aligned} \tag{3.4}$$

or

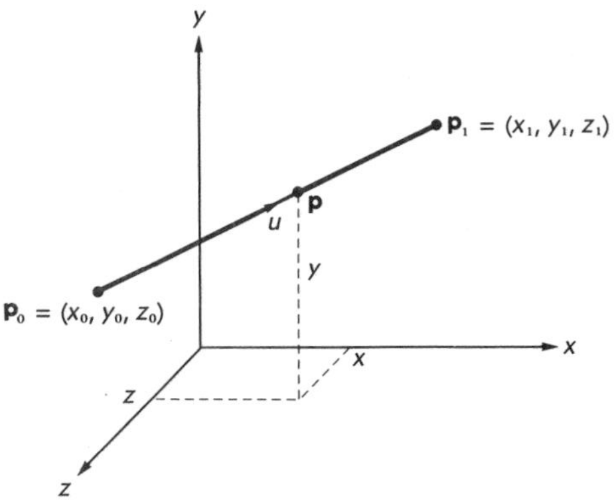

Fig. 3.2. Characteristics of a line segment.

$$
\begin{aligned}
a_x &= x_1 - x_0 \\
a_y &= y_1 - y_0 \\
a_z &= z_1 - z_0
\end{aligned}
\tag{3.5}
$$

Now substitute the results of Eq. (3.3) and Eq. (3.5) into Eq. (3.1) to obtain

$$
\begin{aligned}
x &= (x_1 - x_0)\,u + x_0 \\
y &= (y_1 - y_0)\,u + y_0 \qquad u \in [0, 1] \\
z &= (z_1 - z_0)\,u + z_0
\end{aligned}
\tag{3.6}
$$

This is a very useful set of equations. It means that if you know the end-point coordinates of a line segment, then you can immediately write a parametric equation for it and find any intermediate points on it. And the parametric variable u quite conveniently ranges through the closed interval from zero to one.

The length of a line segment is found simply by applying the Pythagorean theorem to the end-point coordinate differences:

$$L = \sqrt{(x_1 - x_0)^2 + (y_1 - y_0)^2 + (z_1 - z_0)^2} \tag{3.7}$$

Every line has three numbers associated with it that uniquely describe its angular orientation in space. These numbers are called direction cosines (or direction numbers). Denote them as σ_x, σ_y, and σ_z. The computations are simple:

$$\sigma_x = \frac{x_1 - x_0}{L}$$

$$\sigma_y = \frac{y_1 - y_0}{L} \tag{3.8}$$

$$\sigma_z = \frac{z_1 - z_0}{L}$$

Figure 3.3 is a geometric interpretation of the direction cosine σ_x. A similar interpretation applies to σ_y and σ_z. Here the edges of the auxiliary rectangular solid are parallel to the coordinate axes, and $\mathbf{p}_0$, A, and $\mathbf{p}_1$ define a right triangle at A. You can clearly see that

$$\sigma_x = \cos\theta \tag{3.9}$$

The sum of the squares of the direction cosines is one; therefore, any two of them suffice to determine the third:

$$\sigma_x^2 + \sigma_y^2 + \sigma_z^2 = 1 \tag{3.10}$$

A final observation: Direction cosines do not completely specify a line. They tell nothing about the location of the line. For example, any two parallel lines in space have the same direction cosines. In fact, this is a good way to test for parallelism.

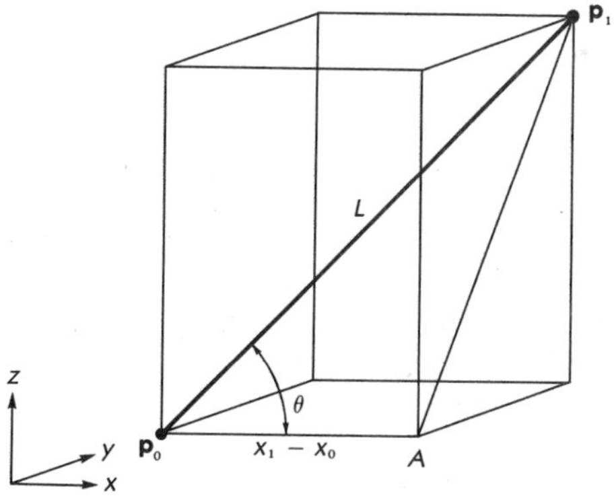

$$\sigma_x = \frac{x_1 - x_0}{L} = \cos\theta$$

Fig. 3.3. Direction cosines of a line segment.

EXERCISES

1. Show that the sum of the squares of the direction cosines of a line is equal to one.

2. Compute the length and direction cosines for each of the following lines, which are defined by their end points:

a. $\mathbf{p}_0 = (4, 3, 6)$, $\mathbf{p}_1 = (4, 3, 10)$
b. $\mathbf{p}_0 = (-1, 0, 7)$, $\mathbf{p}_1 = (5, -4, 0)$
c. $\mathbf{p}_0 = (0, 0, 0)$, $\mathbf{p}_1 = (1, 0, 0)$
d. $\mathbf{p}_0 = (0, 0, 0)$, $\mathbf{p}_1 = (0, 1, 0)$
e. $\mathbf{p}_0 = (0, 0, 0)$, $\mathbf{p}_1 = (0, 0, 1)$

3. Compute the length and direction cosines for each of the following lines, which are defined by their end points:

a. $\mathbf{p}_0 = (3.7, 9.1, 0.2)$, $\mathbf{p}_1 = (0.9, -2.6, 2.6)$
b. $\mathbf{p}_0 = (2.1, -6.4, 0)$, $\mathbf{p}_1 = (3.3, 0.7, -5.1)$
c. $\mathbf{p}_0 = (10.3, 4.2, 3.7)$, $\mathbf{p}_1 = (6.0, 10.3, 9.2)$
d. $\mathbf{p}_0 = (5.3, -7.9, 1.4)$, $\mathbf{p}_1 = (0, 4.1, 0.7)$

4. Check the direction cosines computed in Exercise 2 and Exercise 3 by showing that $\sigma_x^2 + \sigma_y^2 + \sigma_z^2 = 1$. (More realistically, $\sigma_x^2 + \sigma_y^2 + \sigma_z^2 = 1 \pm \epsilon$, where $\epsilon << 1$.)

5. Write the parametric equations for each line in Exercise 2.

6. Write the parametric equations for each line in Exercise 3.

7. Reverse the end-point order of the lines in Exercise 2 and Exercise 3. Does this affect their length or direction cosines? (Prove it.) What inference do you draw about the algebraic signs of the respective direction cosines?

8. Show algebraically that the direction cosines of a line segment are dependent on the order of the end points (that is, the direction of parametrization).

9. Reverse the end-point order of the lines in Exercise 2, and then write their parametric equations. Compare your results to the equations you derived from Exercise 5.

10. Given a line defined by the end points (5, 3, 9) and (2, 7, 1), find the two sets of parametric equations corresponding to each of the two possible directions of parametrization, for $u \in [0, 1]$.

11. Given a line defined by the end points $\mathbf{p}_0 = (0, 8, 3)$ and $\mathbf{p}_1 = (4, -2, 9)$, write the parametric equations for segments of this line in the following intervals:

a. $u \in [0, 0.5]$
b. $u \in [0.5, 0]$

c. $u \in [0.1, 0.3]$
d. $u \in [0.4, 0.9]$
e. $u \in [0.2, 0.6]$

12. Given a line whose initial point is (3, 4, 8) and whose final point is (7, −6, 9), derive its parametric equations corresponding to each of the following intervals of parametrization:

a. $u \in [0, 1]$
b. $u \in [1, 2]$
c. $u \in [-1, 1]$
d. $u \in [1, 3]$
e. $u \in [0, 2]$

3.2. Computing Points on a Line

The parametric representation of a line developed in Section 3.1 is particularly useful for computing points on a line. An important class of points on a line frequently used in geometric modeling and computer graphics consists of the points that occur at equal intervals along the line. There are two ways to compute the coordinates for these points, one considerably faster and more efficient than the other. We will look at both.

Given a line, find the coordinates of points on it at n equal intervals. Since you already know $\mathbf{p}_0$ and $\mathbf{p}_1$, there remain $n - 1$ intermediate points to compute. Figure 3.4 shows a line with six equal intervals.

One option is to use Eq. (3.6), $x = (x_1 - x_0)u + x_0, \ldots$, for each $n - 1$ points. There are $n - 1$ values of the parametric variable, given by

$$u = \frac{1}{n}, \frac{2}{n}, \frac{3}{n}, \ldots, \frac{n-1}{n} \tag{3.11}$$

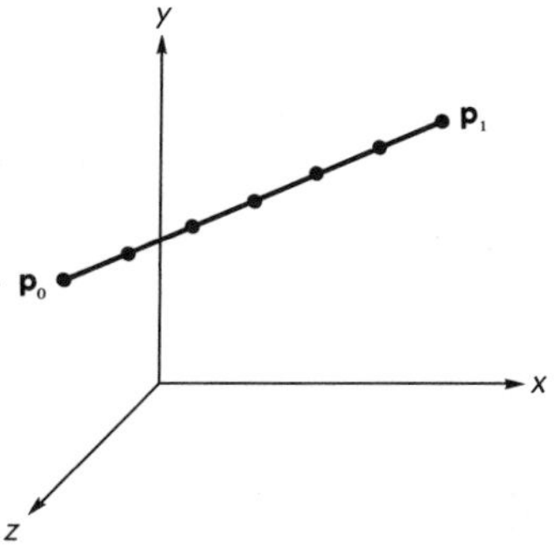

Fig. 3.4. Computing points at equal intervals along a line.

requiring $n - 1$ divisions to compute. For the x coordinates there are $n - 1$ multiplications and n additions (including finding $x_1 - x_0$). The totals for all coordinates are $3n$ additions, $3(n - 1)$ multiplications, and $n - 1$ divisions.

You can do much better than this. First, note that u always changes by a constant amount, Δu, where

$$\Delta u = \frac{1}{n} \tag{3.12}$$

Next, observe that for any x_i

$$x_i = (x_1 - x_0)\, u_i + x_0 \tag{3.13}$$

and for x_{i+1}

$$x_{i+1} = (x_1 - x_0)\, u_{i+1} + x_0 \tag{3.14}$$

But since $u_{i+1} = u_i + \Delta u$, we rewrite Eq. (3.14) as

$$x_{i+1} = (x_1 - x_0)(u_i + \Delta u) + x_0 \tag{3.15}$$

or

$$x_{i+1} = (x_1 - x_0)\, u_i + (x_1 - x_0)\Delta u + x_0 \tag{3.16}$$

But $(x_1 - x_0)\, u_i + x_0 = x_i$, so

$$x_{i+1} = x_i + (x_1 - x_0)\Delta u \tag{3.17}$$

and $(x_1 - x_0)\Delta u$ is a constant, so let $\Delta x = (x_1 - x_0)\Delta u$. Therefore,

$$x_{i+1} = x_i + \Delta x \tag{3.18}$$

This tells you that you find each successive x coordinate by adding a constant to the previous value. Very neat! Now let us count the computations: To compute Δu requires one division. To compute Δx requires one addition and one multiplication. For the x coordinates there are $n - 1$ additions. So the totals for all coordinates are $3n$ additions, 3 multiplications, and 1 division. Quite a savings. You will encounter extensions of this technique, called the **forward difference method,** in Chapter 13.

EXERCISES

1. Compute the $n - 1$ intermediate points for each of the following lines, which are defined by their end points:

   a. $\mathbf{p}_0 = (0, 0, 0)$, $\mathbf{p}_1 = (10, 0, 0)$, for $n = 10$.
   b. $\mathbf{p}_0 = (-1, 0, 0)$, $\mathbf{p}_1 = (0, 1, 0)$, for $n = 2$.

c. $\mathbf{p}_0 = (7, 3, 9)$, $\mathbf{p}_1 = (7, 3, 0)$, for $n = 3$.
d. $\mathbf{p}_0 = (-4, 6, 0)$, $\mathbf{p}_1 = (2, 11, -7)$, for $n = 4$.
e. $\mathbf{p}_0 = (0, 0, 6)$, $\mathbf{p}_1 = (6, 1, -5)$, for $n = 4$.

2. Write a procedure to compute points along a line at equal intervals of the parametric variable. Denote this as **LINEPT**(P0, P1, N, POUT), where

P0(3) are the input coordinates of $\mathbf{p}_0$,
P1(3) are the input coordinates of $\mathbf{p}_1$,
N is the input number of intervals on the line, and
POUT(N + 1,3) is the output array of point coordinates, including $\mathbf{p}_0$ and $\mathbf{p}_1$.

3. Show that equal intervals in u correspond to equal lengths on a straight line.

3.3. Point and Line Relationships

A test point, $\mathbf{q}$, is either on or off a given line (Fig. 3.5). If it is on the line, it is either between the end points, $\mathbf{q}_1$, on the backward extension of the line, $\mathbf{q}_2$, or on the forward extension, $\mathbf{q}_3$.

Write Eq. (3.6) in terms of u to obtain

$$u_x = \frac{x - x_0}{x_1 - x_0}$$
$$u_y = \frac{y - y_0}{y_1 - y_0} \tag{3.19}$$
$$u_z = \frac{z - z_0}{z_1 - z_0}$$

The subscript on u identifies the source of its computed value. Now, given the coordinates of any point $\mathbf{q} = (x, y, z)$, compute u_x, u_y, u_z. If, and only if, $u_x = u_y = u_z$, then point $\mathbf{q}$ is on the line; otherwise it is off the line. (*Note:* The test for equality should allow some small but finite deviation; for example, $|u_x - u_y| = \epsilon$, where $\epsilon << 1$.) If $\mathbf{q}$ is on the line, then the

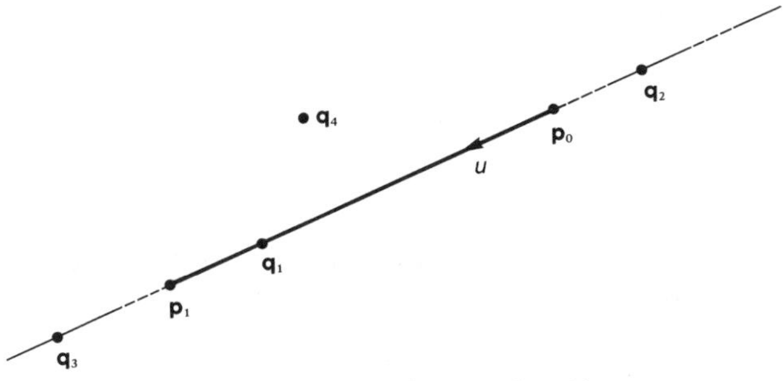

Fig. 3.5. Point and line relationships.

Box 3.2. Position of a Point Relative to a Line

In a plane, to determine the position of a point relative to a line, solve the parametric equations to obtain the implicit equation

$$f(x,y) = (x - x_0)(y_1 - y_0) - (y - y_0)(x_1 - x_0)$$

For a reference point $\mathbf{p}_R$ not on the line, compute $f(x_R, y_R)$. For any arbitrary test point, $\mathbf{p}_T$, compute $f(x_T, y_T)$. If $f(x_T, y_T) = 0$, then $\mathbf{p}_T$ is on the line. If $f(x_T, y_T)$ and $f(x_R, y_R)$ have the same sign [that is, $f(x_T, y_T) > 0$ and $f(x_R, y_R) > 0$, or $f(x_T, y_T) < 0$ and $f(x_R, y_R) < 0$], then $\mathbf{p}_T$ and $\mathbf{p}_R$ are on the same side of the line; otherwise they are on opposite sides.

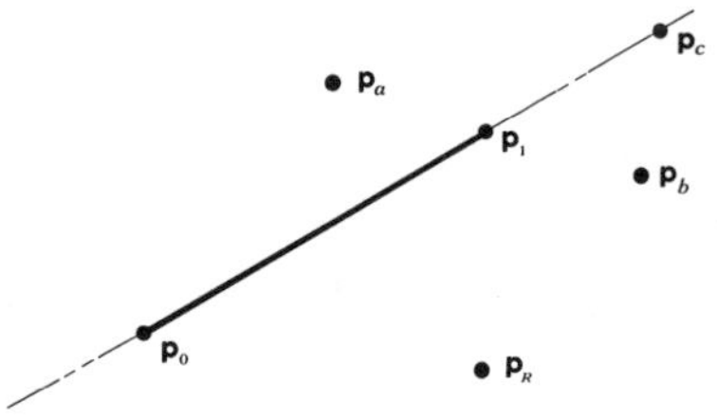

Here is one way to choose a reference point: Let $\mathbf{p}_R = (x_0 + 1, y_0)$. Then $\mathbf{p}_R$ is to the right of the line. If $y_0 = y_1$ (the line is horizontal), then let $\mathbf{p}_R = (x_0, y_0 + 1)$, placing $\mathbf{p}_R$ above the line.

value of u indicates its precise position. Box 3.2 shows how to determine another important relationship between a point and a line.

EXERCISES

1. Compute the relationships of the following points to the line given by the points $\mathbf{p}_0 = (6, 4, 8)$ and $\mathbf{p}_1 = (8, 8, 12)$:

a. $\mathbf{q}_1 = (6, 4, 12)$
b. $\mathbf{q}_2 = (8, 8, 16)$
c. $\mathbf{q}_3 = (4, 0, 4)$
d. $\mathbf{q}_4 = (12, -8, 20)$
e. $\mathbf{q}_5 = (7, 6, 10)$
f. $\mathbf{q}_6 = (10, 4, 12)$
g. $\mathbf{q}_7 = (10, 12, 16)$
h. $\mathbf{q}_8 = (6.5, 5, 9)$
i. $\mathbf{q}_9 = (6.5, 6, 8)$
j. $\mathbf{q}_{10} = (6, 8, 8)$

2. Write a procedure to test the relationship between a point and a line. Denote this as **PTLNRL**(PT, P0, P1, IT, U), where

PT(3) are the input coordinates of the test point,

P0(3), P1(3) are the input coordinates of the end points defining a line,
IT is the output test result. If
- IT = 0, the point is off the line,
- IT = 1, the point is on the line between $\mathbf{p}_0$ and $\mathbf{p}_1$, inclusive,
- IT = 2, the point is on the back extension of the line, and
- IT = 3, the point is on the forward extension of the line; and

U is the output value of u if the point is on the line.

3.4. Intersection of Lines

If two lines intersect, then they have a common point—the point of intersection. We now discuss the problem of determining if two lines defined in three-dimensional space intersect, and then the special case of the intersection of a line in two dimensions intersecting with a second line that is either horizontal or vertical (Fig. 3.6).

Suppose you have two lines, a and b. If they intersect, then there is a point (the point of intersection) such that

$$\begin{aligned} x_a &= x_b \\ y_a &= y_b \\ z_a &= z_b \end{aligned} \tag{3.20}$$

It follows that from Eq. (3.6),

$$\begin{aligned} (x_{1,a} - x_{0,a})\,u_a + x_{0,a} &= (x_{1,b} - x_{0,b})\,u_b + x_{0,b} \\ (y_{1,a} - y_{0,a})\,u_a + y_{0,a} &= (y_{1,b} - y_{0,b})\,u_b + y_{0,b} \\ (z_{1,a} - z_{0,a})\,u_a + z_{0,a} &= (z_{1,b} - z_{0,b})\,u_b + z_{0,b} \end{aligned} \tag{3.21}$$

You obtain three equations in two unknowns, u_a and u_b. Use any two of the three equations to solve for u_a and u_b. Substitute u_a and u_b into the third, or remaining, equation to verify the solution. If the solution cannot be verified, then the lines do not intersect. Finally, if both u_a and u_b are in the interval 0 to 1, inclusive, then the intersection is valid.

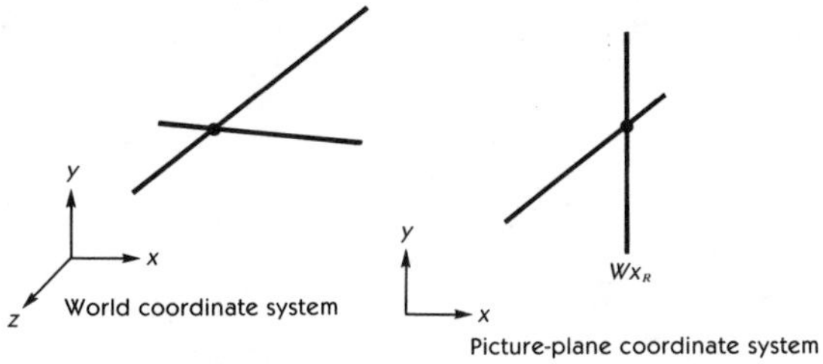

Fig. 3.6. Intersection of lines.

Next, suppose you have an arbitrary line in a two-dimensional space, say the picture plane. (For now assume it to be the x,y plane.) You must determine if this line intersects with Wx (right or left) or Wy (top or bottom). Wx is a vertical line whose equation is $x = Wx$, where Wx is a constant, of course. Wy is a horizontal line, where $y = Wy$. If $x = Wx$ intersects our arbitrary line, then

$$u = \frac{Wx - x_0}{x_1 - x_0} \tag{3.22}$$

If you find a value of u in the unit interval, then use it to compute the y coordinate of the point of intersection. If the arbitrary line itself is vertical, then it does not intersect Wx, since for a vertical line $x_0 = x_1$, and, therefore, $x_1 - x_0 = 0$. Apply a similar procedure when computing line intersections with Wy.

EXERCISES

1. Find the point of intersection (if any) between the following pairs of lines. Describe the characteristics of the intersections you find.

a. $\mathbf{p}_{0,a} = (2, 4, 6)$, $\mathbf{p}_{1,a} = (4, 6, -4)$;
$\mathbf{p}_{0,b} = (0, 0, 1)$, $\mathbf{p}_{1,b} = (6, 8, -6)$

b. $\mathbf{p}_{0,a} = (2, 4, 6)$, $\mathbf{p}_{1,a} = (4, 6, -4)$;
$\mathbf{p}_{0,b} = (4, 3, 5)$, $\mathbf{p}_{1,b} = (2.5, 4.5, 3.5)$

c. $\mathbf{p}_{0,a} = (2, 4, 6)$, $\mathbf{p}_{1,a} = (4, 6, -4)$;
$\mathbf{p}_{0,b} = (3, 5, 1)$, $\mathbf{p}_{1,b} = (0, 2, 16)$

d. $\mathbf{p}_{0,a} = (10, 8, 0)$, $\mathbf{p}_{1,a} = (-1, -1, 0)$;
$\mathbf{p}_{0,b} = (13, 2, 0)$, $\mathbf{p}_{1,b} = (4, 7, 0)$

e. $\mathbf{p}_{0,a} = (5, 0, 0)$, $\mathbf{p}_{1,a} = (2, 0, 0)$;
$\mathbf{p}_{0,b} = (8, 0, 0)$, $\mathbf{p}_{1,b} = (10, 0, 0)$

2. Find the point of intersection (if any) between the following lines and the picture-plane boundaries (assumed to be the x,y plane). The boundaries are $Wx_R = 8$, $Wx_L = -3$, $Wy_T = 6$, $Wy_B = -2$. Describe the characteristics of the intersections you find; the lines are defined by their end points. *Note:* Solutions must be analytical, not graphical.

a. $\mathbf{p}_0 = (-1, 0)$, $\mathbf{p}_1 = (-4, -3)$

b. $\mathbf{p}_0 = (-1, 2)$, $\mathbf{p}_1 = (3, 0)$

c. $\mathbf{p}_0 = (6, 2)$, $\mathbf{p}_1 = (2, 8)$

d. $\mathbf{p}_0 = (9, 4)$, $\mathbf{p}_1 = (9, 8)$

e. $\mathbf{p}_0 = (9, 0)$, $\mathbf{p}_1 = (13, 4)$

3.5. Line Containment and Clipping

Only line segments within a window are displayed. This means that you need a test to decide if a line segment is wholly inside, partially inside, or entirely outside the window area (Fig. 3.7). A line is completely within the window area if, and only if, all the following inequalities are true:

$$Wx_L \leq x_0, \quad x_1 \leq Wx_R, \quad \text{and} \quad Wy_B \leq y_0, y_1 \leq Wy_T \tag{3.23}$$

otherwise the line is only partially inside the window or entirely outside it. Clearly, Line 1 in the figure passes the test of Eq. (3.23). This simply means that both end points are in the window area.

If only one end point is contained by the window, as in the case of Line 2, then compute the point of intersection between the line and the appropriate window boundary (Fig. 3.8). Since, in our example, $x_0 > Wx_R$ and $y_0 > Wy_B$, it is not necessary to calculate intersections with Wx_L and Wy_B. Knowing that $y_0 > Wy_T$ does not add anything to your knowledge of the situation, since either one of two distinct line orientations is possible. This means that you must compute intersections with Wx_R and Wy_T. The u-value closest to that of the contained point corresponds to the appropriate point of intersection. This point of intersection becomes the new end point of the line. This segment of the line is saved and displayed. This process is called **clipping,** because that part of a line not within the window boundaries is "clipped" off. A line is completely outside the window if any one of the following sets of inequalities is true:

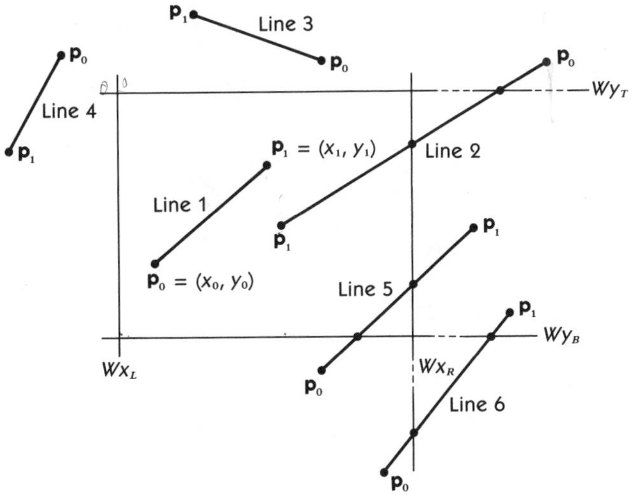

Fig. 3.7. Line containment.

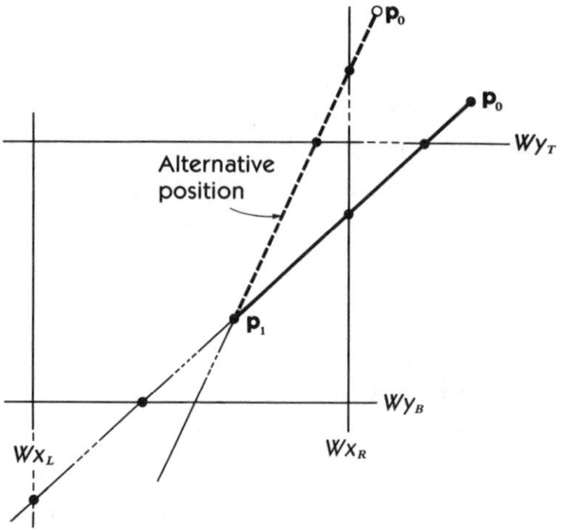

Fig. 3.8. Line–window intersection.

$$x_0, x_1 < Wx_L, \qquad x_0, x_1 > Wx_R \tag{3.24}$$
$$y_0, y_1 < Wy_B, \qquad y_0, y_1 > Wy_T$$

You can easily verify why this must be true by studying carefully Fig. 3.7 again.

There are other possible line–window arrangements. It may be that none of the preceding conditions obtains. In that case, you are faced with a condition analogous to one of the alternatives in Fig. 3.9. One approach is to compute all possible intersection points, $\mathbf{p}_i$, then use the u_i, x_i, y_i

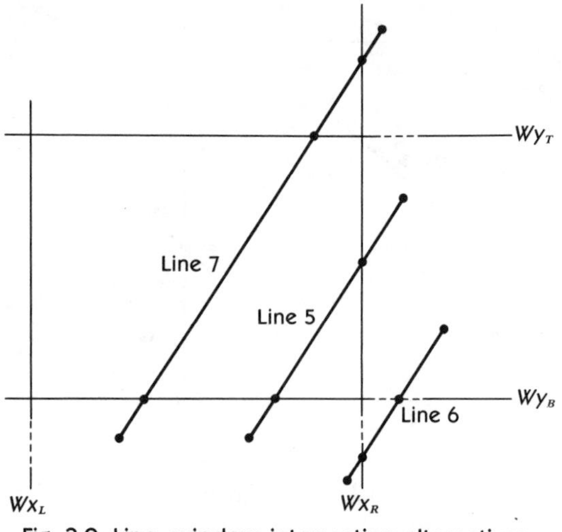

Fig. 3.9. Line–window intersection alternatives.

values of each of these points to determine the two points that appropriately bound that portion of the line contained within the window.

If you convert the window boundaries into parametric line segments (Fig. 3.10), then the clipping procedure is somewhat simplified, because all valid points of intersection on the window boundary lines must be within the unit interval on these lines. For example, the parametric equations for Line B are

$$x = (Wx_R - Wx_L)u + Wx_L \qquad (3.25)$$
$$y = Wy_B$$

The intersection of Line B with some arbitrary Line A is given by solving the two simultaneous equations

$$(x_1 - x_0)\,u_A + x_0 = (Wx_R - Wx_L)\,u_B + Wx_L$$
$$(y_1 - y_0)\,u_A + y_0 = Wy_B \qquad (3.26)$$

for u_A and u_B. Do this and obtain

$$u_A = \frac{Wy_B - y_0}{y_1 - y_0}$$
$$u_B = \left(\frac{x_1 - x_0}{y_1 - y_0}\right)\left(\frac{Wy_B - y_0}{Wx_R - Wx_L}\right) + \left(\frac{x_0 - Wx_1}{Wx_R - Wx_L}\right) \qquad (3.27)$$

Let us review and summarize the line containment and clipping process. First, perform two sets of tests on the end points of a line. The first test says that if both $Wx_L \le x_0, x_1 \le Wx_R$ and $Wy_B \le y_0, y_1 \le Wy_T$ are true, then the line is contained in the window, so no intersection computations are required. If the first test is not true, then perform a second set of tests: If any of the following four inequalities is true, namely, $x_0, x_1 < Wx_L$; $x_0, x_1 > Wx_R$; $y_0, y_1 < Wy_B$; or $y_0, y_1 > Wy_T$, then the line lies entirely outside the window. In the event that neither of these two sets

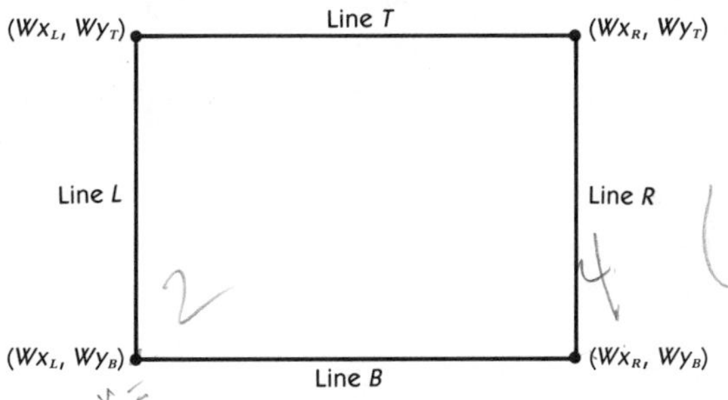

Fig. 3.10. The window defined by four parametric lines.

Box 3.3. Algorithm: Clip Lines

Here is an algorithm to clip a set of lines against the boundaries of a given window. The algorithm assumes that the lines are defined by parametric equations whose coefficients are determined by the line end points. Parametrization is over the unit interval. Window boundaries are also represented parametrically.

CLIPLINES(NLINES,LINETYPE,LINES,WINDOW,LINESOUT)

NLINES: The number of lines to be clipped.
LINETYPE: Absolute or relative.
LINES(4,NLINES): The input array of line end-point coordinates.
WINDOW4: The input window boundaries: Wx_L, Wx_R, Wy_T, Wy_B.
LINESOUT(4,M): The output array of coordinates defining the end points of lines in the window.

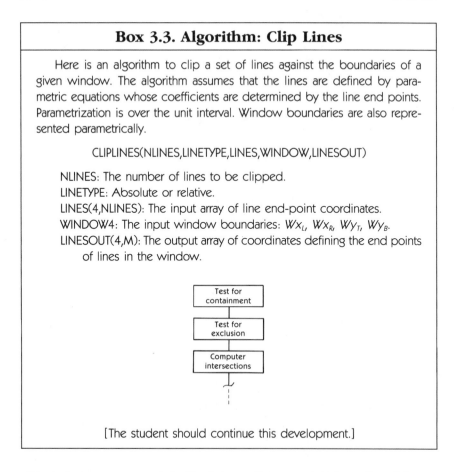

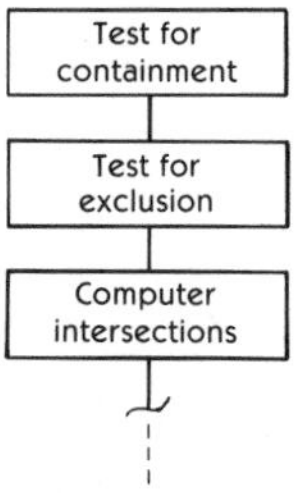

[The student should continue this development.]

of tests is true, you must do the intersection computations. Box 3.3 suggests the outline of an algorithm to clip lines.

EXERCISES

1. Clip and redefine (as necessary) the end points of the following lines with respect to a window whose boundaries are $Wx_L = 2$, $Wx_R = 14$, $Wy_B = -2$, and $Wy_T = 10$. Describe each line's relationship to the window (inside, outside, intersecting):

a. Line 1: $\mathbf{p}_0 = (-5, 4)$, $\mathbf{p}_1 = (1, 13)$
b. Line 2: $\mathbf{p}_0 = (7, 4)$, $\mathbf{p}_1 = (5, 9)$
c. Line 3: $\mathbf{p}_0 = (12, 6)$, $\mathbf{p}_1 = (12, 0)$
d. Line 4: $\mathbf{p}_0 = (5, 12)$, $\mathbf{p}_1 = (-3, -4)$
e. Line 5: $\mathbf{p}_0 = (2, -2)$, $\mathbf{p}_1 = (6, 2)$
f. Line 6: $\mathbf{p}_0 = (4, 3)$, $\mathbf{p}_1 = (8, -4)$

g. Line 7: $\mathbf{p}_0 = (2, 1)$, $\mathbf{p}_1 = (2, 12)$
h. Line 8: $\mathbf{p}_0 = (12, -6)$, $\mathbf{p}_1 = (6, 13)$
i. Line 9: $\mathbf{p}_0 = (11, 7)$, $\mathbf{p}_1 = (15, 7)$
j. Line 10: $\mathbf{p}_0 = (13, -5)$, $\mathbf{p}_1 = (18, 4)$

3.6. Displaying Lines

Strings of connected line segments, relative and absolute lines, line data formats, and the window–viewport transformation for lines are subjects you must become familiar with in order to understand just how a mathematically defined line or set of lines is appropriately displayed on a computer graphics screen. We explore these subjects in this section. Do not let the dearth of quantitative data here mislead you. The logical concepts, although relatively simple, are nonetheless important in both geometric modeling and computer graphics.

You can arrange and sequentially connect a set of points with straight lines to form both open and closed figures (Fig. 3.11). There is what you might call the "brute-force" approach: Define each line separately. In other words, for n lines,

$$\begin{aligned} \text{Line } 1 &= \mathbf{p}_0, \mathbf{p}_1 \\ \text{Line } 2 &= \mathbf{p}_1, \mathbf{p}_2 \\ \text{Line } 3 &= \mathbf{p}_2, \mathbf{p}_3 \\ &\vdots \\ \text{Line } n &= \mathbf{p}_{n-1}, \mathbf{p}_n \end{aligned} \tag{3.28}$$

Interpret the equal sign to read "is defined by." Using this approach you must store the coordinates of $2n$ points in the geometric data base.

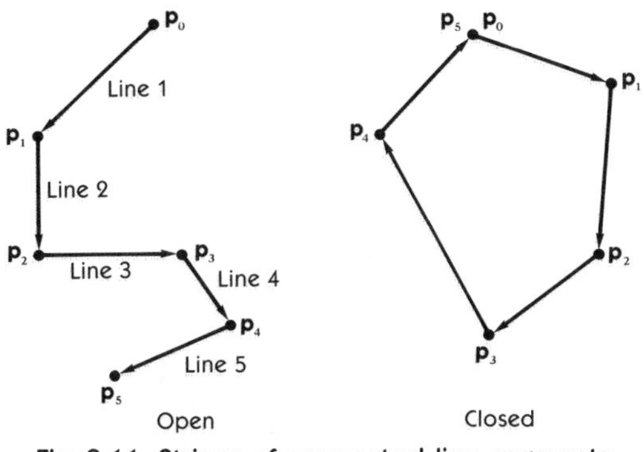

Fig. 3.11. Strings of connected line segments.

There is a subtler approach. Identify a single series of points as a line string and arrange the line algorithms to interpret them as follows:

$$
\begin{aligned}
\text{Line } 1 &= \begin{cases} \mathbf{p}_0 \\ \mathbf{p}_1 \end{cases} \\
\text{Line } 2 &= \begin{cases} \mathbf{p}_1 \\ \mathbf{p}_2 \end{cases} \\
\text{Line } 3 &= \begin{cases} \mathbf{p}_2 \\ \mathbf{p}_3 \end{cases} \\
&\vdots \\
\text{Line } n &= \begin{cases} \mathbf{p}_{n-1} \\ \mathbf{p}_n \end{cases}
\end{aligned}
\tag{3.29}
$$

Coordinates are not duplicated in the data base as they are in Eq. (3.28), and you store the coordinates of only $n + 1$ points.

Both of the preceding methods use the absolute line definition or representation, so called because the point coordinates are given directly. Now consider a slight variation: the relative line definition. Here, define relative offsets or displacements, with each point in a sequence derived relative to the previous point (Fig. 3.12). This looks like:

$$
\begin{aligned}
\text{Line } 1 &= \begin{cases} \mathbf{p}_0 = \text{initial point} \\ \mathbf{p}_1 = \mathbf{p}_0 + \Delta_1 \end{cases} \\
\text{Line } 2 &= \begin{cases} \mathbf{p}_1 = \mathbf{p}_0 + \Delta_1 \\ \mathbf{p}_2 = \mathbf{p}_1 + \Delta_2 \end{cases} \\
\text{Line } 3 &= \begin{cases} \mathbf{p}_2 = \mathbf{p}_1 + \Delta_2 \\ \mathbf{p}_3 = \mathbf{p}_2 + \Delta_3 \end{cases} \\
&\vdots \\
\text{Line } n &= \begin{cases} \mathbf{p}_{n-1} = \mathbf{p}_{n-2} + \Delta_{n-1} \\ \mathbf{p}_n = \mathbf{p}_{n-1} + \Delta_n \end{cases}
\end{aligned}
\tag{3.30}
$$

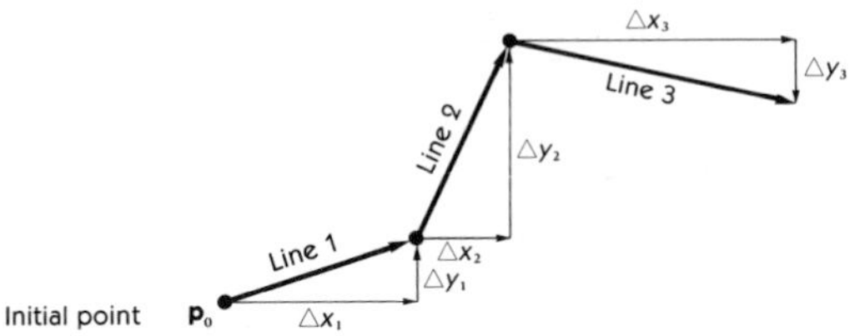

Fig. 3.12. Relative lines.

where $\Delta_i = (\Delta x_i, \Delta y_i)$. Your data base now contains the initial point, $\mathbf{p}_0$, and the Δ's; all the $\mathbf{p}_i$'s are computed sequentially from these data. The data base is no more or less crowded than for the previous method. It is easy to convert from relative lines to absolute lines and vice versa. Either format is useful in both world and screen coordinates. In fact, both the electron beam and the pen plotter are driven by incremental movement commands based on differential or relative line definitions. (Note the increasing use of subscripts. You will quickly grow accustomed to them and use them to great advantage as you progress.)

The transformation of lines (previously clipped) from the picture plane to a screen viewport proceeds simply by applying Eq. (1.11) to each line end point, while preserving the data defining their connectivity (Fig. 3.13).

EXERCISES

1. The six points whose coordinates are listed below define a sequence of connected lines, in the order shown. Use this information to construct each of the three line data formats we have just discussed. Label the formats appropriately.

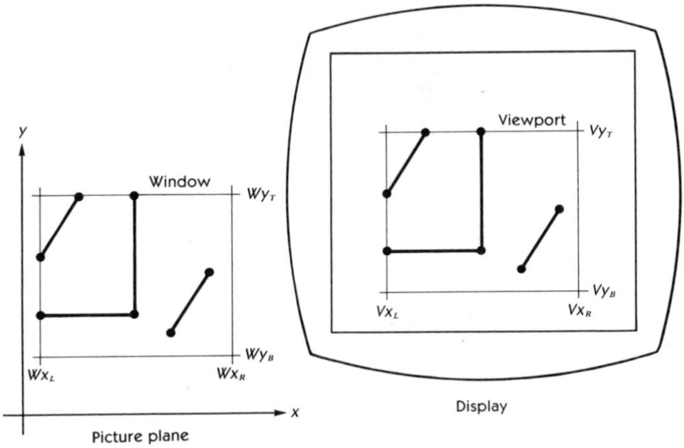

Fig. 3.13. Window–viewport transformation of lines.

The point coordinates are: $\mathbf{p}_0 = (1, 3)$, $\mathbf{p}_1 = (4, 5)$, $\mathbf{p}_2 = (4, 8)$, $\mathbf{p}_3 = (9, 5)$, $\mathbf{p}_4 = (5, 1)$, $\mathbf{p}_5 = (7, -3)$.

3.7. Translation and Rotation of Lines

Translate a line by translating its end-point coordinates (Fig. 3.14). The end-point translations must be identical or the transformed line will have a different length or angular orientation, or both. In two dimensions, we have

$$x_0^* = x_0 + x_T, \qquad x_1^* = x_1 + x_T$$
$$y_0^* = y_0 + y_T, \qquad y_1^* = y_1 + x_T \tag{3.31}$$

In doing this kind of translation, the line always moves parallel to its original position and its length does not change. Do you see that all points on the line are translated equally? This is sometimes called a **rigid body translation.** Here, again, the generalization to three or more dimensions is obvious and simple.

The simplest rotation of a line that you can describe in two dimensions is about the origin (Fig. 3.15). Rotate both end points, $\mathbf{p}_0$ and $\mathbf{p}_1$, through an angle, θ, about the origin. Then the coordinates of the transformed end points, $\mathbf{p}_0^*$ and $\mathbf{p}_1^*$, are given by applying Eq. (2.14):

$$x_0^* = x_0 \cos\theta - y_0 \sin\theta, \qquad x_1^* = x_1 \cos\theta - y_1 \sin\theta$$
$$y_0^* = x_0 \sin\theta + y_0 \cos\theta, \qquad y_1^* = x_1 \sin\theta + y_1 \cos\theta \tag{3.32}$$

This produces a rigid body rotation of the line. To generalize this to three dimensions, proceed as you would for points.

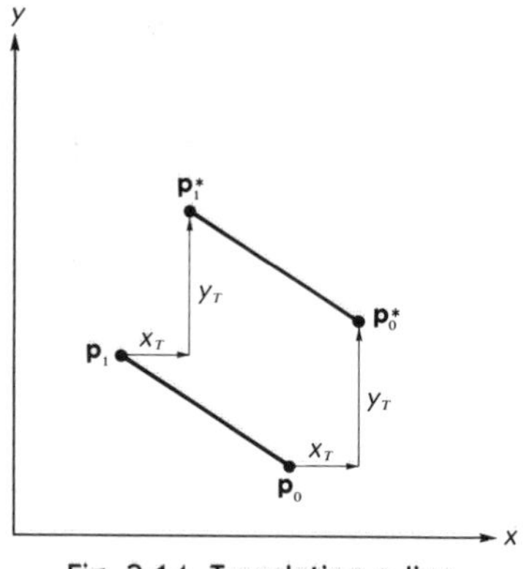

Fig. 3.14. Translating a line.

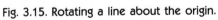

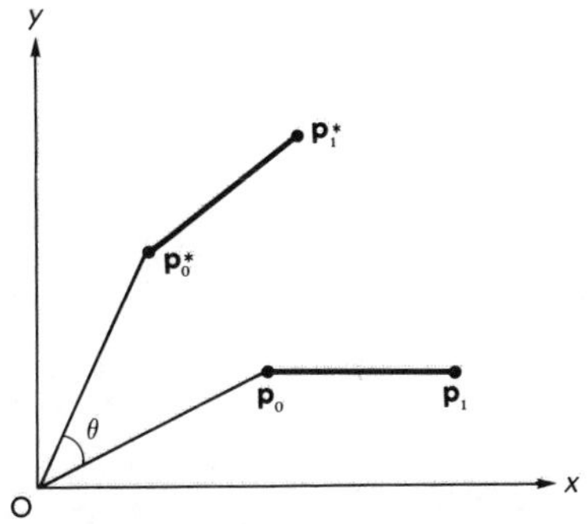

Fig. 3.15. Rotating a line about the origin.

4. Planes

PLANES ARE UBIQUITOUS in computer graphics. You have already crossed paths with a variety of uses for them: picture planes, screen planes, principal planes, clipping planes, and intersection planes, to name a few. Thus far, however, there has been only an unspoken appeal to intuition regarding the properties of planes. Now you will investigate their more quantitative, analytical aspects.

Do you recall from Euclidean geometry the definition of a plane as the locus of points equidistant from two fixed points? This plane is the perpendicular bisector of the line joining the two points. This is a demonstrative or constructive definition. However, from now on you will attach and associate appropriate algebraic equations to the planes you work with.

4.1. Definition and Properties

For the moment let us depart from the parametric format and discuss an implicit equation defining a plane. You will discover a more powerful and more intuitively geometric definition after studying vectors in Chapter 12. For now and for many applications, the following equation of a plane is appropriate; this equation defines the locus of points that lie in a plane:

$$Ax + By + Cz + D = 0 \tag{4.1}$$

This is a linear equation in x, y, and z. Select values for the constant coefficients A, B, C, and D and you define a specific plane in space. It is an arbitrary plane in that, depending on the values of the coefficients, it can assume any orientation (Fig. 4.1).

If the coordinates of a point satisfy Eq. (4.1), then the point lies on the plane. Arbitrarily specify any two coordinates, say x and y, and determine the third coordinate, z (in this case), by solving Eq. (4.1).

You obtain a more restricted version of the general equation by dropping one of the terms containing a coordinate variable, z, for example, as in

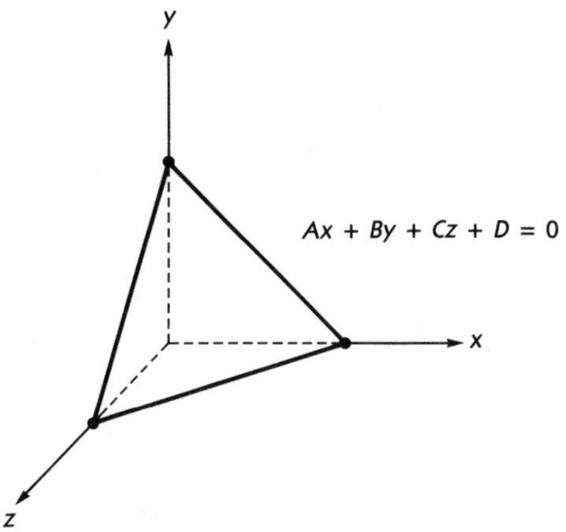

Fig. 4.1. General plane. (Only that part of the plane in the positive octant is shown.)

$$Ax + By + D = 0 \tag{4.2}$$

This means that the z coordinate of an arbitrary point can take on any value whatever. The remaining coordinates are constrained by the relationship imposed by the equation. All planes defined with this restriction are perpendicular to the principal plane identified by the two remaining coordinate values. In the case of Eq. (4.2), then, the plane is always perpendicular to the x,y plane. Note that the equation defines the line of intersection between the plane and the principal x,y plane. Look at the illustration of these concepts in Fig. 4.2.

You can probably surmise what the final possible restriction on Eq.

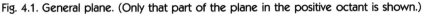

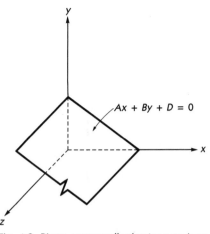

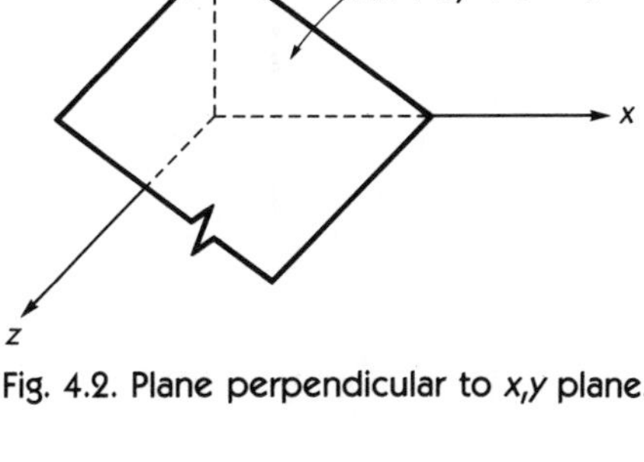

Fig. 4.2. Plane perpendicular to x,y plane.

(4.1) is. Drop any two of the coordinate-variable-containing terms, x and y, for example, as in

$$Cz + D = 0 \qquad \text{or} \qquad z = k \tag{4.3}$$

where k is a constant. Now look at the interpretation of this in Fig. 4.3. In this example ($z = k$), the plane is perpendicular to the z axis and intersects it at k.

These planes are unbounded. They extend (mathematically) indefinitely. The figures show them somewhat bounded, but of course this is only to highlight graphically the position and orientation of the planes. There are such things as bounded planes, and you will examine them in the chapter on polygons.

See Boxes 4.1 and 4.2 for other ways of defining a plane.

EXERCISES

1. Given three points on a plane, $\mathbf{p}_1 = (a, 0, 0)$, $\mathbf{p}_2 = (0, b, 0)$, and $\mathbf{p}_3 = (0, 0, c)$, show that

$$\frac{x}{a} + \frac{y}{b} + \frac{z}{c} = 1$$

2. Derive the relationships among d, σ_x, σ_y, σ_z, and A, B, C, D expressed in Box 4.1.

4.2. Point and Plane Relationships

To determine the position of a test point, $\mathbf{p}_T$, relative to a plane, first define some convenient reference point, $\mathbf{p}_R$ (Fig. 4.4). Then, using the im-

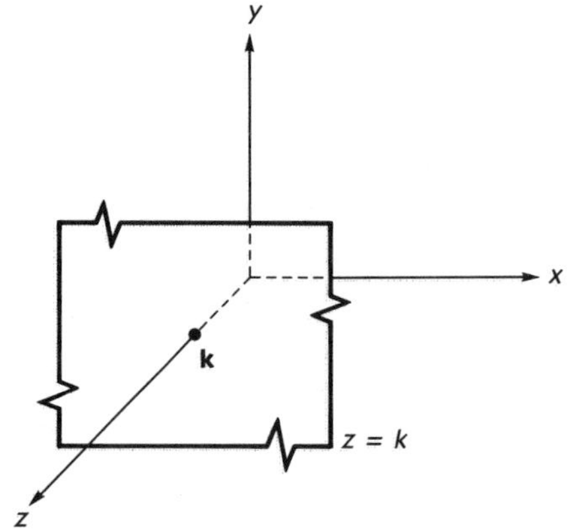

Fig. 4.3. Plane perpendicular to the z axis.

Box 4.1. Normal Form of Plane Equation

An interesting way to define a plane is by giving its perpendicular distance, d, from the origin and the direction cosines of the line defined by d: σ_x, σ_y, and σ_z (also known as the direction cosines of the plane). This is all the data we need to define the intersection of the plane with each of the coordinate axes. To derive a, b, and c, below, observe that $O\mathbf{p}_d\mathbf{p}_a$ is a right triangle; if d is perpendicular to the plane, then any line in the plane through $\mathbf{p}_d$ is necessarily perpendicular to d. Thus,

$$a = \frac{d}{\sigma_x}$$

$$b = \frac{d}{\sigma_y}$$

$$c = \frac{d}{\sigma_z}$$

This yields the three points $\mathbf{p}_a = (a, 0, 0)$, $\mathbf{p}_b = (0, b, 0)$, and $\mathbf{p}_c = (0, 0, c)$. Write the implicit form of the plane equation in terms of the distance, d, and its direction cosines as

$$\sigma_x x + \sigma_y y + \sigma_z z - d = 0$$

Do not be mistaken in thinking that, in general, $\sigma_x = A$, $\sigma_y = B$, $\sigma_z = C$, and $d = D$. These relationships are true only if $A^2 + B^2 + C^2 = 1$. However, given $Ax + By + Cz + D = 0$, then

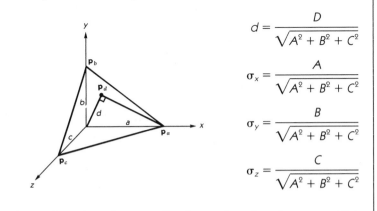

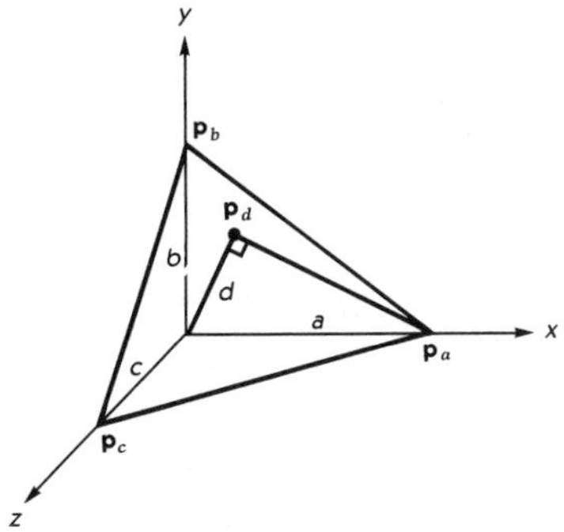

$$d = \frac{D}{\sqrt{A^2 + B^2 + C^2}}$$

$$\sigma_x = \frac{A}{\sqrt{A^2 + B^2 + C^2}}$$

$$\sigma_y = \frac{B}{\sqrt{A^2 + B^2 + C^2}}$$

$$\sigma_z = \frac{C}{\sqrt{A^2 + B^2 + C^2}}$$

Clearly, if two planes have the same direction cosines, then they are parallel.

Box 4.2. A Plane Defined by Three Noncollinear Points

Three noncollinear points in space are necessary and sufficient to define a plane. Demonstrate the proof of this assertion as follows: Let the coordinates of the three points be $\mathbf{p}_1 = (x_1, y_1, z_1)$, $\mathbf{p}_2 = (x_2, y_2, z_2)$, and $\mathbf{p}_3 = (x_3, y_3, z_3)$; furthermore, let $A' = A/D$, $B' = B/D$, and $C' = C/D$. The latter assumption yields, for the implicit equation of a plane,

$$A'x + B'y + C'z + 1 = 0$$

Using this equation and the coordinates of the three points, write

$$\begin{aligned} A'x_1 + B'y_1 + C'z_1 + 1 &= 0 \\ A'x_2 + B'y_2 + C'z_2 + 1 &= 0 \\ A'x_3 + B'y_3 + C'z_3 + 1 &= 0 \end{aligned}$$

Here are three equations in three unknowns: A', B', and C'. Note that two points are not sufficient to determine A', B', and C', and a fourth point would not necessarily fall on the plane.

plicit form of the plane equation, $f(x, y, z) = Ax + By + Cz + D$, compute $f(x_R, y_R, z_R)$ and $f(x_T, y_T, z_T)$. Decide which relationship is present according to the following conditions:

a. If $f(x_T, y_T, z_T) = 0$, then $\mathbf{p}_T$ is on the plane.

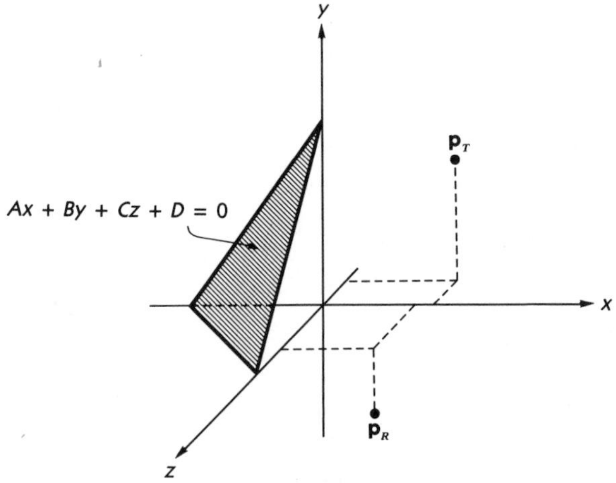

Fig. 4.4. Point and plane relationship.

b. If $f(x_T, y_T, z_T) > 0$ and $f(x_R, y_R, z_R) > 0$, then $\mathbf{p}_T$ is on the same side of the plane as $\mathbf{p}_R$.

c. If $f(x_T, y_T, z_T) < 0$ and $f(x_R, y_R, z_R) < 0$, then $\mathbf{p}_T$ is on the same side of the plane as $\mathbf{p}_R$.

d. If none of the conditions *a*, *b*, or *c* obtain, then $\mathbf{p}_T$ is on the opposite side of the plane relative to $\mathbf{p}_R$.

The origin often conveniently serves as $\mathbf{p}_R$.

You will see that these relationships are useful in determining if a point is inside or outside a given solid. You will find such tests useful in model synthesis and analysis, as well as display construction.

EXERCISES

1. Find the relationships between the following points and the plane $y = -3$, where $\mathbf{p}_R$ is the origin:

a. $\mathbf{p}_1 = (4, 2, 5)$
b. $\mathbf{p}_2 = (3, -3, 0)$
c. $\mathbf{p}_3 = (-2, 4, 6)$
d. $\mathbf{p}_4 = (5, -4, 3)$
e. $\mathbf{p}_5 = (-3, -7, 8)$

2. Find the relationships between the following points and the plane $3x - 2y - 3z + 12 = 0$, where $\mathbf{p}_R$ is the origin:

a. $\mathbf{p}_1 = (1, 2, 3)$
b. $\mathbf{p}_2 = (-2, 5, 4)$
c. $\mathbf{p}_3 = (-1, 8, 2)$
d. $\mathbf{p}_4 = (0, 0, 4)$
e. $\mathbf{p}_5 = (2, 0, 0)$

3. Find the relationships between the following points and the plane $4y - 3z - 24 = 0$, where $\mathbf{p}_R$ is the origin:

a. $\mathbf{p}_1 = (6, 2, 4)$
b. $\mathbf{p}_2 = (-3, 6, 0)$
c. $\mathbf{p}_3 = (8, 0, -8)$
d. $\mathbf{p}_4 = (2, 2, -9)$
e. $\mathbf{p}_5 = (-1, 7, -1)$

4.3. Intersections

If a line and plane intersect, then they have a point in common, $\mathbf{p}_i$ (Fig. 4.5). To find the coordinates of $\mathbf{p}_i$, you must solve the following four equations in four unknowns:

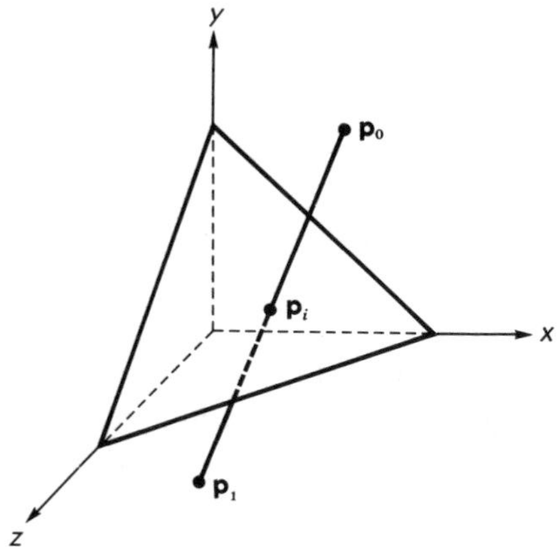

Fig. 4.5. Line and plane intersection.

$$
\begin{aligned}
Ax_i + By_i + Cz_i + D &= 0 \\
x_i &= (x_1 - x_0)u_i + x_0 \\
y_i &= (y_1 - y_0)u_i + y_0 \\
z_i &= (z_1 - z_0)u_i + z_0
\end{aligned}
\tag{4.4}
$$

Solve these equations for u_i:

$$u_i = \frac{Ax_0 + By_0 + Cz_0 + D}{A(x_1 - x_0) + B(y_1 - y_0) + C(z_1 - z_0)} \tag{4.5}$$

If $u_i \in [0, 1]$, then solve for x_i, y_i, z_i. If $Ax_0 + By_0 + Cz_0 + D = 0$ and $Ax_1 + By_1 + Cz_1 + D = 0$, then the line lies in the plane. If $u_i = \infty$; that is, if $A(x_1 - x_0) + B(y_1 - y_0) + C(z_1 - z_0) = 0$, then the line is parallel to the plane and does not intersect it. (Is it not amazing how much information is contained in a few simple equations? Learn the meanings of the symbols and the rules for manipulating them, and you soon understand and control a powerful array of geometric concepts.)

Now consider the somewhat more difficult problem: Find the intersection between two unbounded planes. Your geometric intuition should tell you that two unbounded nonparallel planes intersect in a straight line. You will find some of the key ingredients for this problem illustrated in Fig. 4.6. Begin with the two equations in three unknowns:

$$
\begin{aligned}
A_1x + B_1y + C_1z + D_1 &= 0 \\
A_2x + B_2y + C_2z + D_2 &= 0
\end{aligned}
\tag{4.6}
$$

Here the extra unknown (call it an extra **degree of freedom**) implies that the solution is a line, not a point (which requires a third equation).

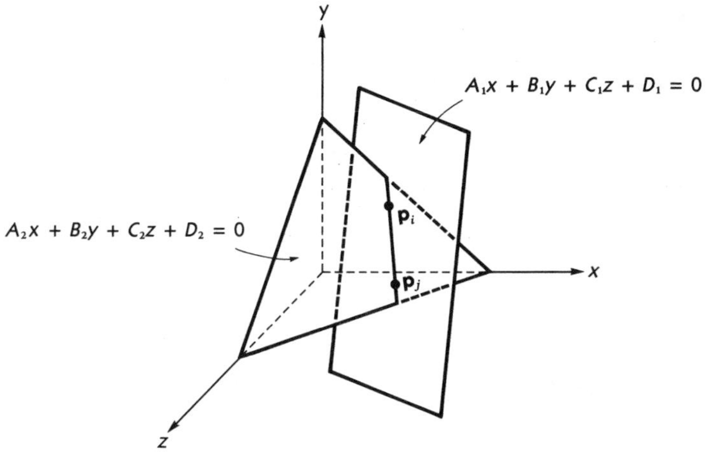

Fig. 4.6. The intersection of two planes.

Now assign a value to one of the unknown variables, say $z = z_i$, so that you have two equations in two unknowns:

$$\begin{aligned} A_1x + B_1y &= -(C_1z_i + D_1) \\ A_2x + B_2y &= -(C_2z_i + D_2) \end{aligned} \tag{4.7}$$

Solve these for x and y and label the solutions x_i, y_i. You now have one point on the line of intersection: $\mathbf{p}_i = (x_i, y_i, z_i)$.

Next, assign a new value to z, say $z = z_j$, to obtain

$$\begin{aligned} A_1x + B_1y &= -(C_1z_j + D_1) \\ A_2x + B_2y &= -(C_2z_j + D_2) \end{aligned} \tag{4.8}$$

Solve again for x and y and label the solutions x_j, y_j. You now have another point on the line of intersection: $\mathbf{p}_j = (x_j, y_j, z_j)$.

Two points are all you need to completely define the line of intersection in parametric form:

$$\begin{aligned} x &= (x_i - x_j)u + x_j \\ y &= (y_i - y_j)u + y_j \\ z &= (z_i - z_j)u + z_j \end{aligned} \tag{4.9}$$

If you want different end points, then simply reparametrize as necessary, computing new points using these equations. Since the planes are unbounded, you can also treat the line of intersection as unbounded. Bounded elements are shown in Fig. 4.6, for clarity.

EXERCISES

1. Find the intersections, if any, between the plane $3x + 4y + z = 24$ and the following lines whose end points are given. Comment on the nature of the intersection.

a. Line 1: $\mathbf{p}_0 = (4, 0, 4)$, $\mathbf{p}_1 = (4, 6, 4)$
b. Line 2: $\mathbf{p}_0 = (10, 0, 2)$, $\mathbf{p}_1 = (10, 2, 2)$
c. Line 3: $\mathbf{p}_0 = (10, -10, 2)$, $\mathbf{p}_1 = (10, 2, 2)$
d. Line 4: $\mathbf{p}_0 = (0, 0, 24)$, $\mathbf{p}_1 = (8, 0, 0)$
e. Line 5: $\mathbf{p}_0 = (0, 9, 0)$, $\mathbf{p}_1 = (0, 0, 25)$

2. Find the intersections, if any, between the following planes:

a. $3x + 4y + z = 24$ and $-2x + 4y + z = 24$
b. $3x + 4y + z = 24$ and $y = 2$
c. $3x + 4y + z = 24$ and $2x - 3y = 0$
d. $3x + 4y + z = 24$ and $5x - 3y + 5z = 15$
e. $x = 7$ and $z = -5$.

5. Projections

Model or object space is not only three dimensional, but it is also unlimited, embedded as it is in the world coordinate system. Image or display space is the two-dimensional space of the display screen, limited by definite boundaries, with discrete, discontinuously accessible points called pixels.

These facts suggest that you must resolve two separate problems when constructing the display of a geometric model: How much of the model do you actually see in the display, and how do you convert three-dimensional model data into its correct two-dimensional representation. The window–viewport transformation handles the first problem. This means that the second problem is one of transforming the three-dimensional data onto the two-dimensional picture plane. This kind of transformation is called a **projection transformation.**

5.1. Orthographic Projection

There are many kinds of projections; two are of particular interest to us in computer graphics: **orthographic projection** and **perspective projection.** First to consider is the simpler orthographic projection. You will study perspective projections in the next section. Now you will focus mainly on projecting points in the world coordinate system onto the **picture plane,** also called the **projection plane.**

Two geometric constructs are required: a projection plane and projection lines. Define a projection plane by its equation and specify a rule or procedure for constructing projection lines. A projection line originates at the point to be projected and ends at the point where it intersects the projection plane. The rule is this: **In an orthographic projection, the lines of projection are perpendicular to the plane of projection.** Consequently, the projection lines are all parallel. Look at the general case illustrating these concepts in Fig. 5.1. The projected image of a point is at the intersection of its line of projection and the projection plane.

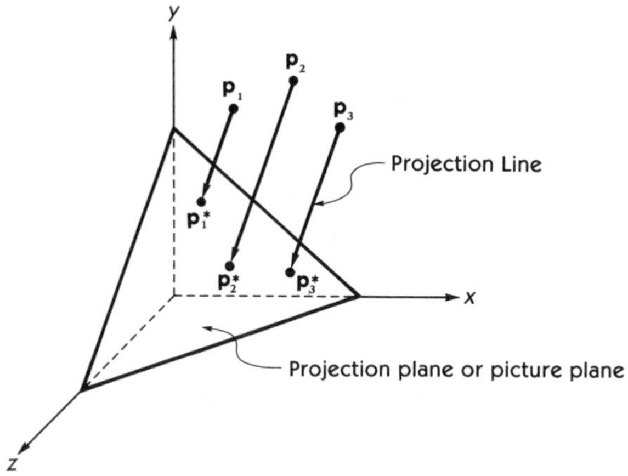

Fig. 5.1. Projection lines and plane.

In Fig. 5.1, points $\mathbf{p}_1$, $\mathbf{p}_2$, and $\mathbf{p}_3$ are projected onto the indicated plane. Their images are $\mathbf{p}_1^*$, $\mathbf{p}_2^*$, and $\mathbf{p}_3^*$. The lines $\mathbf{p}_1\mathbf{p}_1^*$, $\mathbf{p}_2\mathbf{p}_2^*$, and $\mathbf{p}_3\mathbf{p}_3^*$ are all mutually parallel, and all are perpendicular to the plane.

A much simpler case is shown in Fig. 5.2. Suppose you want to project the image of $\mathbf{p}_1$ and other points onto a picture plane. Select the x,y plane as the picture plane, or plane of projection. This means that the projection lines are all perpendicular to the x,y plane and parallel to the z axis. If the coordinates of $\mathbf{p}_1$ are (x_1, y_1, z_1), then the coordinates of its projected image, $\mathbf{p}_1^*$, are $(x_1^*, y_1^*, 0)$, where $x_1^* = x_1$, $y_1^* = y_1$, and $z_1^* = 0$.

The case you have just seen is special because the orientation of the projection plane simplifies the mathematics. Remember, however, that you

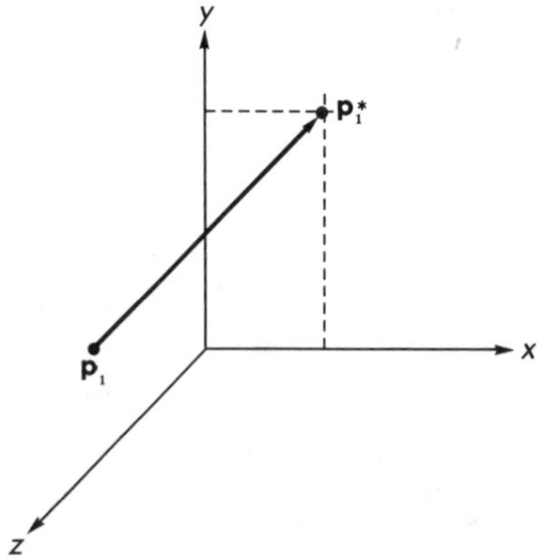

Fig. 5.2. Projection onto $z = 0$ plane.

can select any arbitrarily positioned and oriented projection plane. The mathematics of the general case is more complex, and you will consider it after you have acquired more powerful mathematical tools. For now, consider only projections onto planes parallel to the principal planes.

How do you decide which plane to use? Are the $z = 0$, $z = 2$, or $z = a$ planes not all equivalent, for example, as far as constructing an orthographic projection? The answer is: Yes and no, of course! Yes, because the projected image of any set of points exhibits an identical configuration on each of these planes. No, because so far you have not accounted for the observer. To do this, specify the position of the observer's eye and the direction in which he or she is looking. There are some nifty mathematical devices for doing this, as you will discover in later chapters.

Orthographic projections have several advantages. They are computationally simple, particularly if you select one of the principal planes. The projections are a reasonably good approximation of the visual image if the field of view is not too deep (that is, if the distance between the closest and farthest points is small with respect to the distance from the observer). Orthographic projections are compatible with the requirements of mechanical drawing in that measurements of lines parallel to the plane are in uniform and constant units.

EXERCISES

1. Demonstrate that to produce the orthographic projection of a line, it is sufficient to project its end points.

2. Compute the orthographic projection of each of the points *a* through *e* onto each of the planes *f* through *j*, independent of the position of an observer:

Point a. $\mathbf{p}_1 = (7, 9, -10)$
b. $\mathbf{p}_2 = (10, 8, 8)$
c. $\mathbf{p}_3 = (-10, 6, 2)$
d. $\mathbf{p}_4 = (-4, -5, -4)$
e. $\mathbf{p}_5 = (-10, 6, -1)$
Plane f. $z = 0$
g. $y = 0$
h. $x = 0$
i. $z = -2$
j. $x = 1$

3. Repeat Exercise 2 for the picture plane $x = 1$ with an observer at the origin looking in the $+x$ direction.

4. Repeat Exercise 2 for the picture plane $z = 0$ with an observer at $z = 4$ looking toward the origin.

5. Show that the orthogonal projection of the midpoint of a line is the midpoint of the similarly projected line.

6. What are some invariant properties of arrangements of points and lines subjected to orthographic projection?

5.2. Perspective Projection

A perspective projection produces a realistic image, lacking only the stereo effect of binocular vision. The key components are an eyepoint, $\mathbf{p}_E$, and a projection plane (Fig. 5.3). All lines of projection converge on the eyepoint; consequently, they are neither perpendicular to the projection plane nor are they mutually parallel. One way to find the perspective transformation of any point is to compute the intersection of its projection line with the projection plane. Another solution, usually more effective and computationally efficient, involves nothing more complicated than solving similar triangles (Fig. 5.4). Note that $\lambda = z_E - z_c$, where λ is the distance from the eyepoint to the plane. If the eyepoint is on the $+z$ axis, then from similar triangles,

$$
\begin{aligned}
x^* &= \frac{\lambda x}{z_E - z} \\
y^* &= \frac{\lambda y}{z_E - z} \qquad (5.1) \\
z^* &= z_c
\end{aligned}
$$

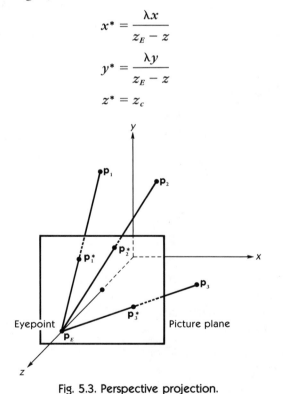

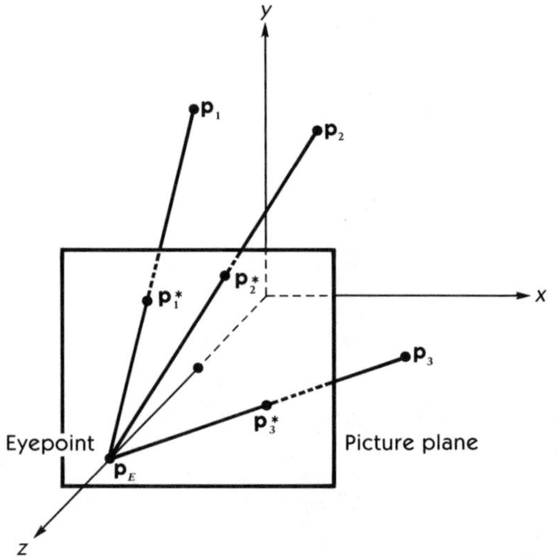

Fig. 5.3. Perspective projection.

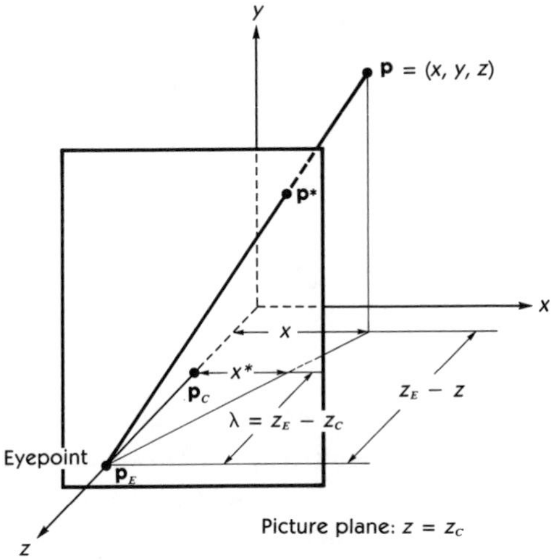

Fig. 5.4. Perspective projection: a geometric solution.

If the projection plane coincides with the x,y plane ($z = 0$), then, since $z_c = 0$ and $z_E = \lambda$, Eqs. (5.1) become

$$
\begin{aligned}
x^* &= \frac{\lambda x}{\lambda - z} \\
y^* &= \frac{\lambda y}{\lambda - z} \\
z^* &= 0
\end{aligned}
\tag{5.2}
$$

EXERCISES

1. Derive Eq. (5.2) for a left-hand coordinate system with the eyepoint on the $-z$ axis.

2. Compute the perspective projection of the following onto the $z = 0$ plane where the eyepoint is at $z = 20$.

a. $\mathbf{p}_1 = (-6, 4, -2)$
b. $\mathbf{p}_2 = (3, 10, 0)$
c. $\mathbf{p}_3 = (7, 5, 6)$
d. $\mathbf{p}_4 = (4, -9, 16)$
e. $\mathbf{p}_5 = (-1, 0, 12)$

6. Polygons

A **POLYGON** IS A MANY-SIDED two-dimensional figure bounded by a circuit of straight-line segments joining successive pairs of points. The line segments are **edges** and the points are **vertices.** It is important to note that an edge is a bounded straight-line segment, a finite length of an otherwise unbounded straight line. A polygon, then, is a finite, closed, two-dimensional area bounded by edges and vertices. If the vertices, or vertex points, are coplanar (that is, if they all lie in the same plane), then the polygon is a **plane polygon;** otherwise it is a **skew polygon.** We will be concerned only with plane polygons here, so the qualifying term "plane" will be omitted.

Polygons in computer graphics are as ubiquitous as planes. It is easy to subdivide and approximate the surfaces of many solids with planes bounded by polygons. You can then project, fill, and shade them to create a very realistic display of the image of the solid. You will encounter many applications of these useful geometric forms.

6.1. Definition and Properties

Study the examples of polygons in Fig. 6.1. There are three-, four-, five-, and six-sided polygons in this figure; of course, there is no limit to the number of sides or edges a polygon can have. Also, there is an infinite number of each type; that is, there is an infinite number of three-sided or triangular polygons. The same is true of four-sided, five-sided, or n-sided polygons.

Note that in all cases the number of vertices equals the number of edges; thus,

$$V - E = 0 \tag{6.1}$$

where V denotes the number of vertices and E denotes the number of edges. Also notice that a plane polygon must have at least three sides in

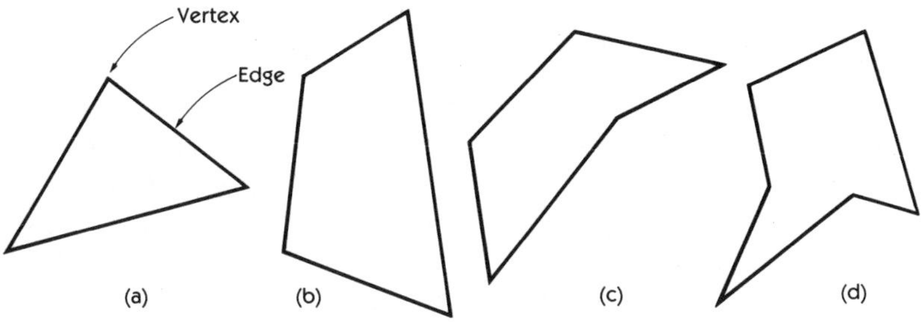

Fig. 6.1. Polygons.

order to enclose a finite area. Curiously, you can create nonplanar polygons that have only two sides. Consider the two noncoincident great-circle arcs connecting antipodal points on a sphere in Fig. 6.2. Such a polygon is called a **digon.**

Polygons can be convex, concave, or stellar. If no straight lines that are prolongations of the bounding edges penetrate the interior, then the polygon is **convex.** To be convex also requires that the edges intersect the polygon only at vertices; otherwise the polygon is **concave.** Any concave polygon can be minimally contained by a convex one (see Box 6.1). The polygons in Fig. 6.1a and Fig. 6.1b are convex; those in Fig. 6.1c and Fig. 6.1d are concave. If the edges of the polygon intersect at points in addition to the vertex points, then it is called a **stellar polygon** (Fig. 6.3). Remember, edges are line segments and not unbounded straight lines.

A **regular polygon** lies in a plane, has straight line edges all of equal length, and all vertex angles are equal. It can be inscribed in a circle with which it shares a common geometric center. Figure 6.4 shows several regular polygons.

A polygon is equilateral if all of its sides are equal and equiangular if all of its angles are equal. If the number of sides (edges) is greater than three, then it can be equilateral without being equiangular (and vice versa). A rhombus is equilateral (Fig. 6.5a); a rectangle is equiangular (Fig. 6.5b).

The sum of the exterior angles of a plane polygon (not a stellar poly-

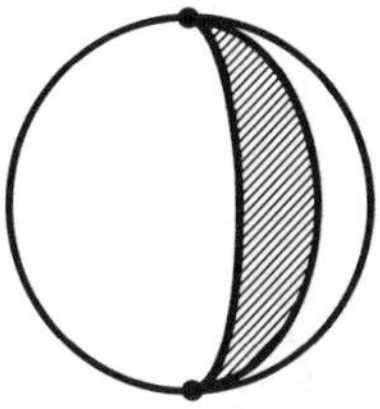

Fig. 6.2. A digon.

Box 6.1. Convex Hull of a Polygon

The **convex hull** of any polygon is the convex polygon that would be formed if a rubber band were stretched over the vertex points. The convex hull of a convex polygon has sides corresponding identically to those of the polygon, while the convex hull of a concave polygon always has fewer sides than the polygon, some sides of which are not collinear. Observe the convex hull of the concave polygon in the figure. It has only four sides; the concave polygon has five.

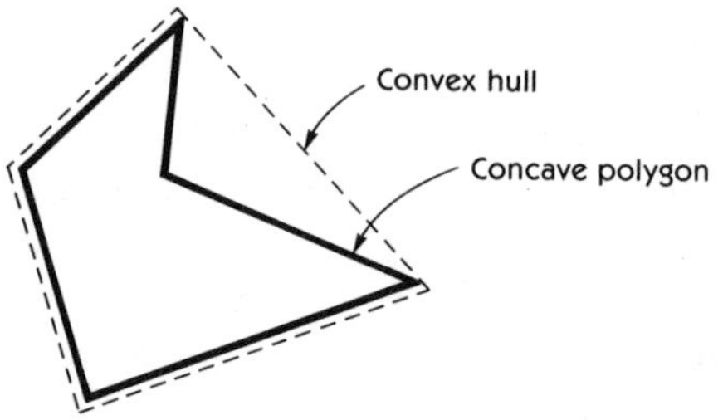

gon) is 2π; therefore, each exterior angle of a regular polygon is $2\pi/E$ and its interior angle (the supplement) is $(1 - 2/E)\pi$ (Fig. 6.6).

The perimeter of a regular polygon is

$$\text{Perimeter} = EL \tag{6.2}$$

where E denotes the number of edges and L is the length of an edge.

The area of a regular polygon is

$$A = \frac{EL^2}{4} \cot\left(\frac{\pi}{E}\right) \tag{6.3}$$

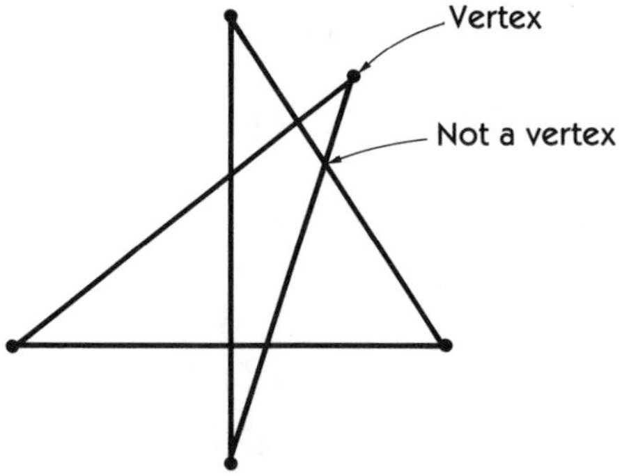

Fig. 6.3. Stellar polygon.

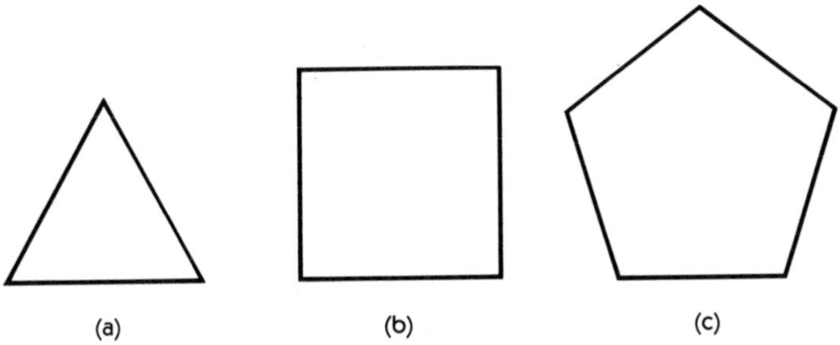

Fig. 6.4. Regular polygons.

Denote a polygon lying in the x,y plane by the boldface capital letters **PG**, and define it as follows:

$$\mathbf{PG} = \mathbf{PG}\,(n, x_1, y_1, x_2, y_2, \ldots, x_n, y_n) \tag{6.4}$$

where n denotes the number of vertices (or sides) of the polygon and x_1, y_1, x_2, $y_2, \ldots$, x_n, y_n are the coordinates of the vertices. Define the edges by successive vertex points, producing the last edge by constructing a line between (x_n, y_n) and (x_1, y_1).

Given a polygon of the form defined by Eq. (6.4), how are its geometric center, perimeter, and area computed? The polygon is the form (or one very much like it) you will most likely use in geometric modeling, so it is important to discover a computational procedure to determine its properties. Stellar polygons are seldom used in computer graphics modeling situations, and you can usually safely assume that any given polygon is not a stellar polygon. Later you will see how to build a stellar polygon detector. The following procedures apply to convex polygons only.

Compute the geometric center $\mathbf{p}_{CG}$ of a convex polygon by simply computing the average x and y value of the coordinates of its vertices; thus,

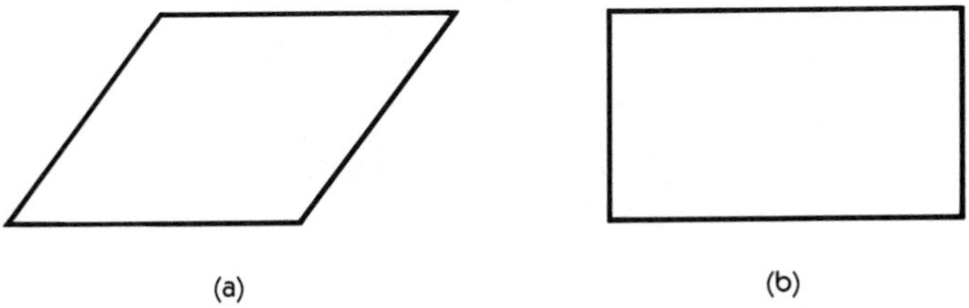

Fig. 6.5. (a) Rhombus and (b) rectangle.

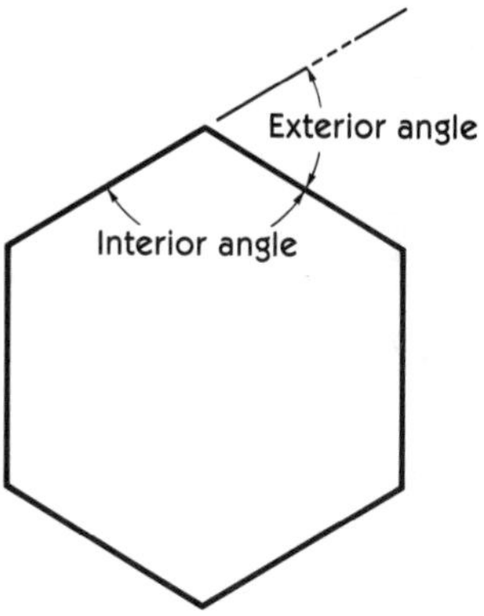

Fig. 6.6. Interior and exterior angles.

$$x_{CG} = \frac{x_1 + x_2 + \cdots + x_n}{n}$$
$$y_{CG} = \frac{y_1 + y_2 + \cdots + y_n}{n} \tag{6.5}$$

Given a convex polygon and its $\mathbf{p}_{CG}$, compute its area as follows: First, divide the n-sided polygon into n triangles using the point $\mathbf{p}_{CG}$ as a common vertex point for all the triangles and each edge of the polygon as part of a separate triangle, as shown in Fig. 6.7. Next, compute the length of each edge and radiant from $\mathbf{p}_{CG}$ to each vertex—with elementary geometry, calculate the area of a triangle given the length of its three sides.

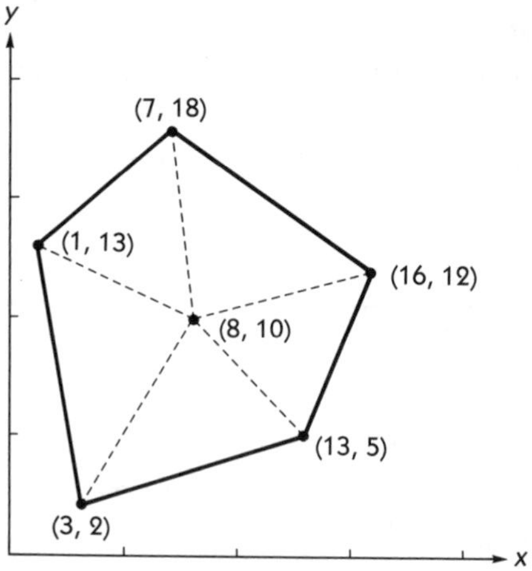

Fig. 6.7. Computing the area of a convex polygon.

Finally, sum the areas of all the triangles to find the area of the convex polygon.

The perimeter of a convex or concave polygon is the sum of the length of each edge; thus,

$$L = \sqrt{(x_1 - x_2)^2 + (y_1 - y_2)^2} + \sqrt{(x_2 - x_3)^2 + (y_2 - y_3)^2} + \cdots + \sqrt{(x_n - x_1)^2 + (y_n - y_1)^2} \tag{6.6}$$

A stellar polygon is a likely result of connecting vertices with edges out of order. Check a polygon to make sure you have not accidentally created an unwanted stellar polygon. To detect a stellar polygon, use the fact that their edges intersect at points in addition to their vertices.

Study the polygon in Fig. 6.8. Check each edge for the possibility of its intersection with other edges. Note that edges meeting at a vertex do not intersect each other elsewhere. Checking for intersections with a given edge can be more efficient by not considering the edges immediately preceding and succeeding it. Edge 2,3 of the polygon shown in the figure, for example, can intersect edges 1,2 and 3,4 only at vertices 2 and 3, respectively. That means that only edges 4,5 and 5,1 remain as candidates for intersection with edge 2,3.

In the figure, points of intersection are produced at a and b. In a stellar polygon these points must be between the vertex points of the edge in question. It is easy to test to determine if this is true; in the example,

$$\begin{aligned} x_2 < x_a, \quad x_b < x_3 \\ y_2 < y_a, \quad y_b < y_3 \end{aligned} \tag{6.7}$$

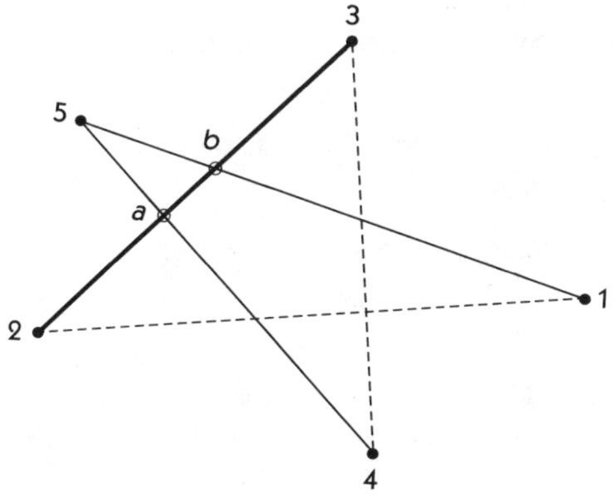

Fig. 6.8. Detecting a stellar polygon.

Compare the x,y coordinates of the point of intersection to the minimum and maximum x,y coordinates of the vertices bounding the edge.

EXERCISES

1. Classify the following polygons as concave, convex, or stellar:

a. $\mathbf{PG}_1 = \mathbf{PG}_1(5,-2,8,1,13,0,7,-2,13,2,10)$
b. $\mathbf{PG}_2 = \mathbf{PG}_2(4,4,12,7,13,9,11,7,15$
c. $\mathbf{PG}_3 = \mathbf{PG}_3(3,-1,2,2,3,2,-1)$
d. $\mathbf{PG}_4 = \mathbf{PG}_4(8,4,7,7,7,7,6,6,6,6,4,7,4,7,2,4,2)$
e. $\mathbf{PG}_5 = \mathbf{PG}_5(4,9,5,12,3,13,8,9,9)$

2. Specify the polygon defining the convex hull of each polygon given in Exercise 1.

3. Compute the exterior and interior angles for regular polygons with three, four, five, six, and eight sides, respectively.

4. Compute the perimeter and area of each of the polygons in Exercise 3; assume unit length edges.

5. Compute the perimeter and $\mathbf{p}_{CG}$ for $\mathbf{PG} = \mathbf{PG}(5,4,4,10,2,12,8,6,11,3,9)$.

6. Compute the area of each of the following convex polygons:

a. $\mathbf{PG}_1 = \mathbf{PG}_1(5,-3,5,1,5,3,7,3,11,-3,7)$
b. $\mathbf{PG}_2 = \mathbf{PG}_2(3,5,3,7,6,5,10)$
c. $\mathbf{PG}_3 = \mathbf{PG}_3(6,9,4,11,4,14,6,14,9,12,9,9,7)$
d. $\mathbf{PG}_4 = \mathbf{PG}_4(4,-3,0,0,-2,6,0,0,4)$
e. $\mathbf{PG}_5 = \mathbf{PG}_5(4,6,-3,13,-3,13,-2,9,1)$

7. Compute the perimeter and $\mathbf{p}_{CG}$ for each of the polygons defined in Exercise 6.

8. Show graphically that concave polygons can be divided into a set of convex polygons.

9. Write a procedure to compute the perimeter of a polygon. Denote this as **LPG**(N,P1,P2,...,PN,L) where

N is the input number of edges of the polygon,
P1(3), P2(3),...,PN(3) are the input coordinates of the vertices, and
L is the output perimeter

10. Write a procedure to compute the geometric center of a polygon. Denote this as **PCGPG**(N,P1,P2,...,PN,PCG) where PCG(3) are the output coordinates of the geometric center and the remaining arguments are defined as for **LPG** in Exercise 9.

6.2. Displaying Polygons

Here is an important problem in computer graphics: Given an arbitrary polygon, find the intersections between it and a series of horizontal lines. This is a big part of the so-called **polygon-filling** problem, where you want to turn on the pixels on those segments of the raster scan lines that are inside the polygon.

Refer to Fig. 6.9 while you discover a way to solve this problem: Assume that the polygon is defined in the display-screen coordinate system. Observe that a straight line intersects a polygon an even number of times. In general, if n_i is the number of intersections between a line and a polygon, then $n_i/2$ is the number of segments of the line inside the polygon. Now look at Line A in the figure. Define its end points and those of all other horizontal lines (for example, scanlines) as follows: The x coordinate ranges from $x = 0$ to $x = x_H$, where x_H is the display width and the y coordinate is constant for any specific line. Represent each polygon edge as a parametric line.

Search for and compute all intersections between Line A and lines a through h of the polygon. Expedite this search by considering only those edges whose end-point y-coordinate values are such that one is greater than and the other is less than y_A. This obviously eliminates lines b through g. The parametric equations for Line A are

$$x = x_H u \quad \text{and} \quad y = y_A \tag{6.8}$$

and for line a:

$$x = (x_{a,1} - x_{a,0})\,t + x_{a,0} \quad \text{and} \quad y = (y_{a,1} + y_{a,0})\,t + y_{a,0} \tag{6.9}$$

(The letter t denotes the parametric variable on line a to distinguish it

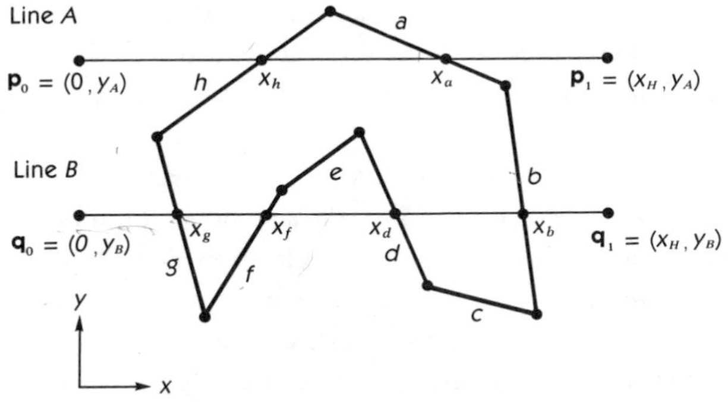

Fig. 6.9. Line and polygon intersection.

from u on Line A.) Equate the y coordinates at the point of intersection to obtain

$$(y_{a,1} - y_{a,0})\, t + y_{a,0} = y_A \tag{6.10}$$

Solve this equation for t:

$$t = \frac{y_A - y_{a,0}}{y_{a,1} - y_{a,0}} \tag{6.11}$$

Substitute this value of t into Eq. (6.9) to find the x coordinate of the point of intersection:

$$x_a = \frac{(x_{a,1} - x_{a,0})\,(y_A - y_{a,0})}{(y_{a,1} - y_{a,0}) + x_{a,0}} \tag{6.12}$$

Proceed similarly to find x_b. Since there are only two points of intersection, there is only one segment of line a in the on state, that segment between x_b and x_a.

What about Line B? There are four intersections whose x coordinates are x_b, x_d, x_f, and x_g. Pair these off in ascending order: (x_g, x_f) and (x_d, x_b). These segments are in the "on" state. These concepts and processes also apply to point containment tests. See Box 6.2.

Certainly, polygon filling is an important problem, and you have just explored one of many ways to solve it. Now let us turn to another similar problem. What happens, for example, when a polygon in the picture plane does not lie entirely in the window area (Fig. 6.10)?

Begin the solution by testing in sequence each vertex point for containment in the window. If all vertex points fall inside the window, then the entire polygon falls inside the window. Compute window boundary intersections for every edge with one or both vertices outside the window. (Note that having both vertices outside the window does not necessarily mean that the edge lies entirely outside the window.) When all the intersection points have been found, order them so as to define the clipped polygon.

Ordering and tracing schemes are relatively easy to invent. For example, start with intersection points on a window boundary. These are easy to find because you know one of their coordinate values must equal the window-boundary coordinate. Sort them in ascending or descending order. Do this for all window boundaries. Now, using the list of sorted window intersection points and the sequential list of coordinates of the original unclipped polygon, construct a new vertex list for the clipped polygon in proper sequential order.

Box 6.2.
Point Containment Test

Given a test point, $\mathbf{p}_T$, determine if it is inside, outside, or on the boundary of a polygon. In the set of vertex points find x_{min}, x_{max}, y_{min}, and y_{max}. If $\mathbf{p}_T$ is not inside the min–max box, it is not inside the polygon. If it is inside the min–max box, then it may or may not be inside the polygon. Compute the intersections of $y = y_T$ with the edges of the polygon. Consider only edges whose end points straddle $y = y_T$. There is always an even number of intersections (count intersection with a vertex as two). Pair the x coordinates of the intersections in ascending order; for example, (x_1, x_2), (x_3, x_4), and so on. If x_T falls inside an interval, for example, $x_1 < x_T < x_2$, then it is inside the polygon. If x_T is identically equal to one of the interval limits, then it is on the boundary. Otherwise it is outside the polygon. This procedure works for both convex and concave polygons.

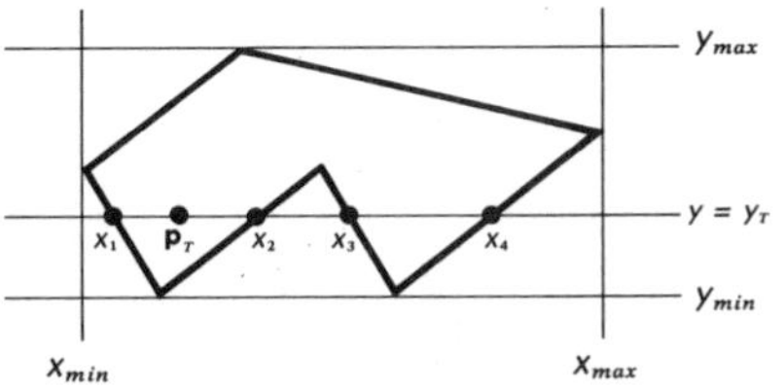

The following test applies only to convex polygons. Establish a reference point, $\mathbf{p}_R$, known to be inside the polygon; for example, $[(x_1 + x_3)/2, (y_1 + y_3)/2]$. Write the implicit equation of each edge, $f_{1,2}(x,y)$, $f_{2,3}(x,y)$, $f_{3,4}(x,y)$, and so on. For each and every edge compute and compare $f_{i,j}(x_T,y_T)$ and $f_{i,j}(x_R,y_R)$. If the evaluated functions, in pairs, have the same sign, then $\mathbf{p}_T$ is inside the polygon. If any one $f_{i,j}(x_T,y_T) = 0$ and if otherwise the preceding conditions obtain, then the point is on the boundary (an edge) of the polygon; otherwise it is outside the polygon. Demonstrate why this procedure will not work for concave polygons.

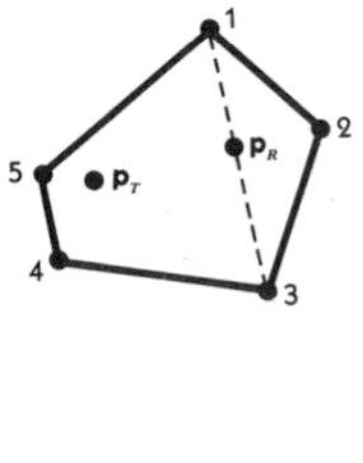

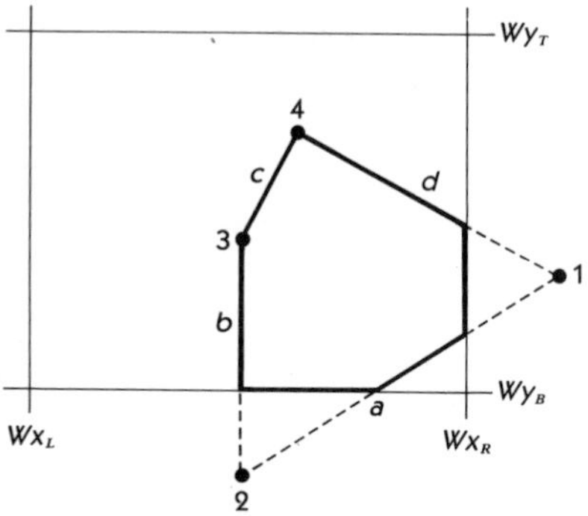

Fig. 6.10. Polygon clipping.

Box 6.3. Polygon–Polygon Containment and Clipping

Given two convex polygons, if all the vertices of one are contained in the other, then the first polygon is inside the second. This test alone does not work for all cases with concave polygons, where intersection computations are required to eliminate ambiguities.

Polygon–polygon clipping proceeds by computing intersections between likely pairs of edges (some combinations are easily discarded). Then use a sorting and tracing scheme to construct the clipped polygon. Note that internal or external clipping is possible. You can interpret the results of the clipping in several ways, each resulting in new polygons.

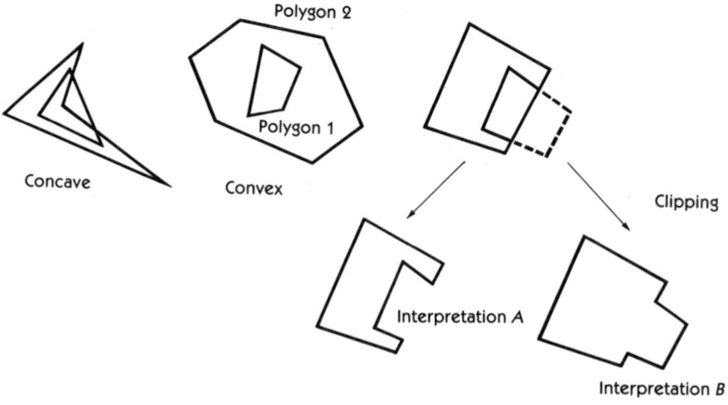

Since the window is itself nothing more or less than a polygon, it seems reasonable to extend these ideas—to generalize them—to apply to any two polygons. This is done in Box 6.3.

EXERCISES

1. Develop in greater detail than presented above an algorithm for clipping a polygon.

7. Polyhedra

THREE-DIMENSIONAL SOLID SHAPES with plane faces in their infinite variety have been the fount of mystery and the object of study for at least 2500 years, and probably for much longer. The Platonic solids and a few semi-regular derivative shapes were early stimulants of humankind's powers of abstraction. Yet polyhedral forms were also expressed concretely in civil structures and monumental architecture. Their usefulness to us is undiminished. Today we use polyhedra in the abstract in mathematics and modeling, to represent other, more complex, shapes. We use them in the aggregate, assemblies of them, like building blocks, in our computer graphics displays. One at a time and in combination, their properties are relatively easy to compute, since all possible polyhedra are defined by only the three simplest of geometric elements: points, lines, and planes—vertices, edges, and faces.

7.1. Definition and Classification

A **polyhedron** is a multifaceted three-dimensional solid bounded by a finite, connected set of plane polygons such that every edge of each polygon belongs also to just one other polygon. The polygonal faces taken together form a closed surface, dividing space into two regions, interior and exterior. A cube is an example of a polyhedron.

Study the examples of polyhedra in Fig. 7.1. All the faces are plane polygons, and all the edges are straight line segments. The simplest possible polyhedron, one with four faces, is shown in Fig. 7.1b. The polyhedra in Figs. 7.1a, 7.1b, and 7.1d are convex, and the one in Fig. 7.1c is concave. Note that in every case each polyhedral edge is shared by exactly two polygonal faces.

Three geometric elements characterize all polyhedra: vertices (V), edges (E), and faces (F). Each vertex subtends an equal number of edges and

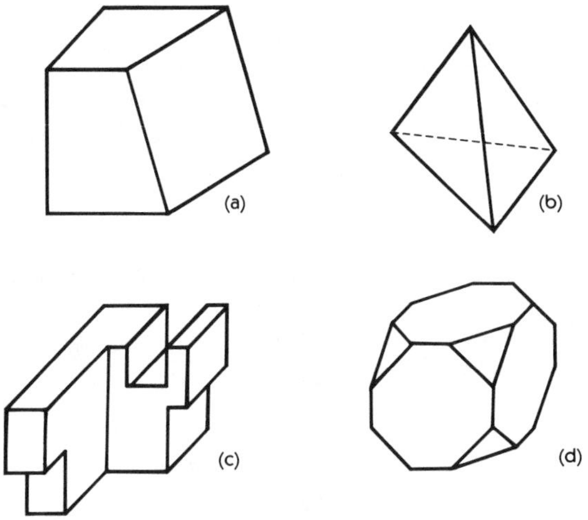

Fig. 7.1. Polyhedra.

faces, each edge is bounded by two vertices and two faces, and each face is bounded by a closed loop of coplanar edges forming a polygon. Finally, the angle between faces that intersect at a common edge is called the **dihedral angle.** The cube in Fig. 7.2 illustrates these elements of a polyhedron. Box 7.1 offers an analytical definition of a convex polyhedron.

A polyhedral convex hull is analogous to the convex hull for a polygon (see Box 6.1), but in three dimensions, of course. The convex hull of a convex polyhedron is identical to the polyhedron itself. The convex hull of a concave polyhedron is formed by "wrapping" the concave polyhedron in a rubber sheet, producing an enveloping convex polyhedron. The concave polyhedron shown in Fig. 7.3a, for example, has the convex hull in Fig. 7.3b. In essence, a convex hull is the minimum convex polyhedron that will enclose the concave polyhedron.

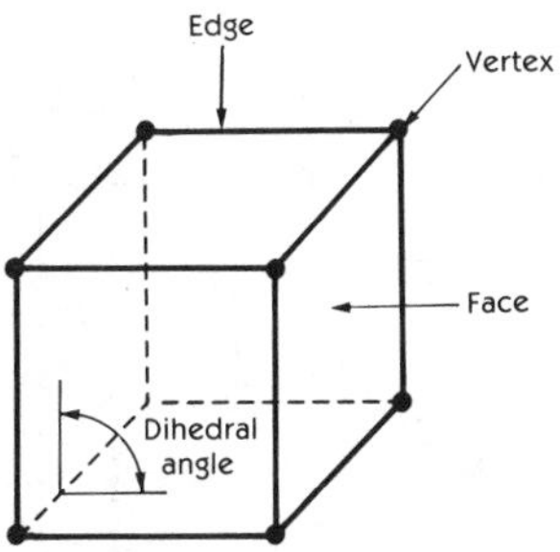

Fig. 7.2. Polyhedron elements.

Box 7.1. Cartesian Definition

A convex polyhedron with n faces can be defined by a consistent system of n inequalities constructed as follows: The plane equation of each face is expressed as an inequality. For the ith face, write

$$A_i x + B_i y + C_i z + D_i > 0$$

Adjust the sign of the expression on the left so that arbitrary points on the same side of this plane as the polyhedron vertices satisfy the inequality. Any point that satisfies all n inequalities lies inside the polyhedron. Here is an example:

$$\begin{aligned} x &> 0 \\ -x + 4 &> 0 \\ y &> 0 \\ -y + 4 &> 0 \\ z &> 0 \\ -z + 4 &> 0 \end{aligned}$$

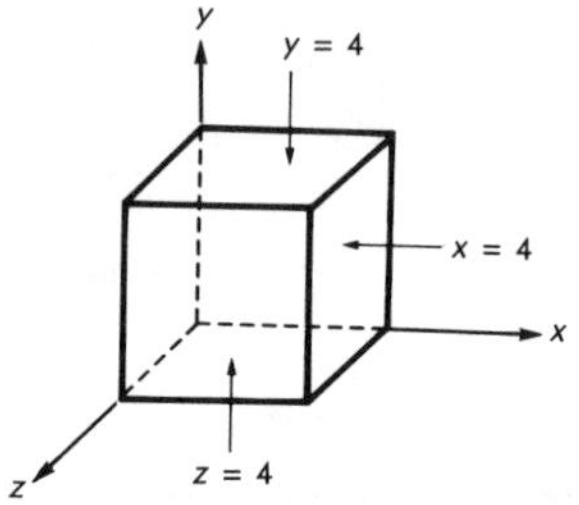

This system of six inequalities defines a cube aligned with the coordinate axes, with edges of length 4. Test a variety of points against these inequalities.

A convex polyhedron is a **regular polyhedron** if its faces are regular polygons and equal, and if its vertices are surrounded alike. As in the example of a cube, then, all faces are identical and all edges are of equal length. It turns out that in three-dimensional space there are only five regular polyhedra: the tetrahedron, hexahedron (cube), octahedron, dodecahedron, and icosahedron. These are also called **the five Platonic solids.** Box 7.2 presents their properties, and Fig. 7.4 illustrates them.

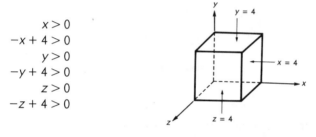

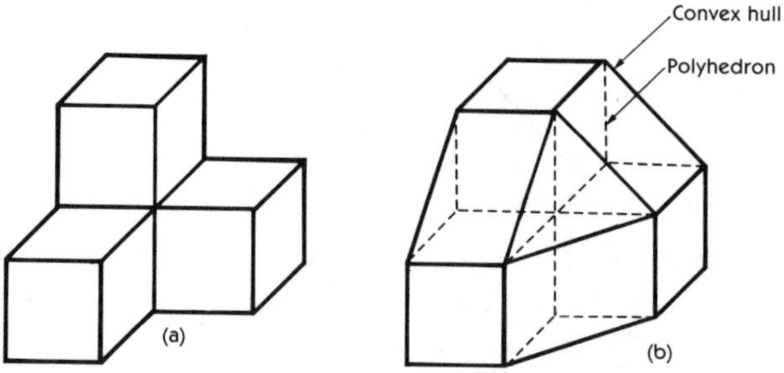

Fig. 7.3. The convex hull revisited.

Box 7.2. Properties of Regular Polyhedra

Polyhedron Name	Face Polygons	Vertices	Edges	Faces	Faces at a Vertex
Tetrahedron	Triangles	4	6	4	3
Octahedron	Triangles	6	12	8	4
Icosahedron	Triangles	12	30	20	5
Hexahedron (cube)	Squares	8	12	6	3
Dodecahedron	Pentagons	20	30	12	3

Note that the sum of all face angles at a vertex of a convex polygon is always less than 2π. Otherwise, one of two conditions will prevail: The edges meeting at the vertex are coplanar (sum of the angles $= 2\pi$) or some of the edges at the vertex must be reentrant and the polyhedron is concave (sum of the angles $> 2\pi$).

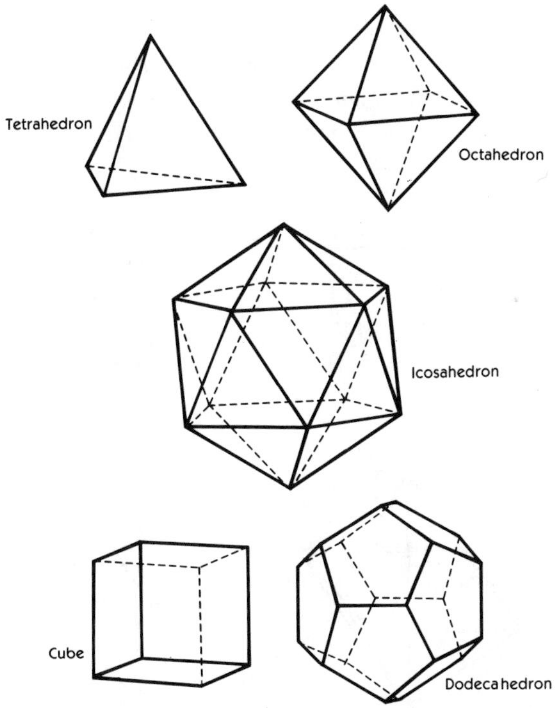

Fig. 7.4. The five regular polyhedra.

7.2. Euler's Formula

A mathematical relationship exists among the number of vertices (V), edges (E), and faces (F) of a **simple polyhedron;** this relationship is called **Euler's** (pronounced "oiler") **formula** for polyhedra. It is stated as

$$V - E + F = 2 \tag{7.1}$$

Applying this to a cube, for example, yields $8 - 12 + 6 = 2$. The term **simple polyhedron** refers to any polyhedron that can be continuously deformed into a sphere, assuming that its faces are treated like rubber sheets.

To apply Euler's formula, other conditions must be met:

1. All faces are bounded by a single ring of edges, and there are no holes in the faces.

2. The polyhedron has no holes through it.

3. Each edge adjoins exactly two faces and is terminated by a vertex at each end.

4. At least three edges meet at each vertex.

Study the examples in Fig. 7.5. Note that the polyhedra satisfy the four conditions and, therefore, satisfy Euler's formula.

Vertices, edges, and faces added to a polyhedron must produce a result that satisfies Euler's formula and the four conditions. In Fig. 7.6a, an edge is added joining Vertex 1 to 3 and dividing Face 1,2,3,4 into two separate

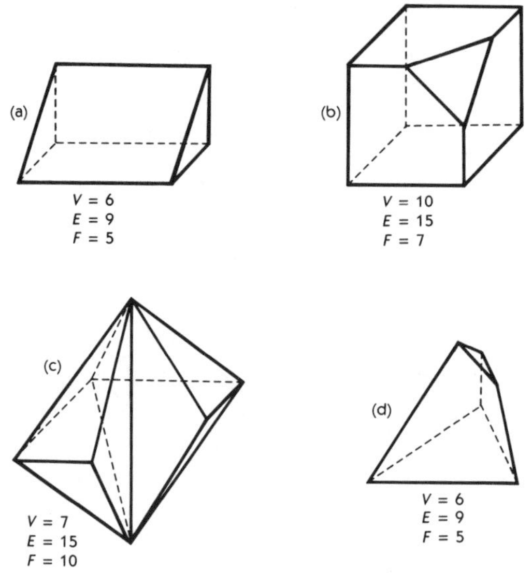

Fig. 7.5. Polyhedra elements for Euler's formula.

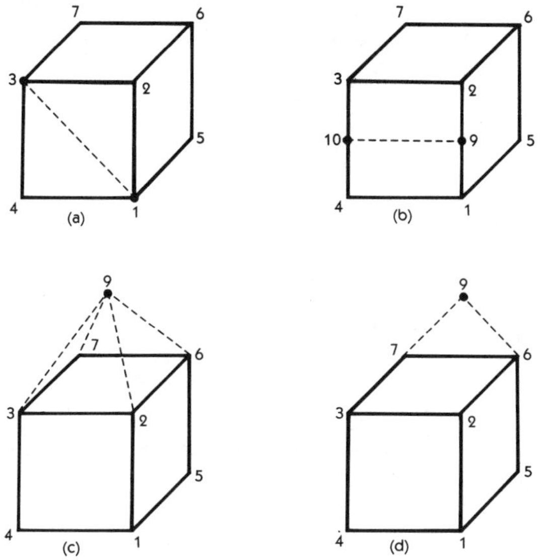

Fig. 7.6. Modifying a polyhedron.

faces; thus, we have added one face and one edge. These additions produce no net change to Euler's formula, and the change to the network of vertices, edges, and faces is legitimate. In Fig. 7.6b, Vertices 9 and 10 are added and joined with an edge. The new vertices divide Edges 1,2 and 3,4, and the new Edge 9,10 divides Face 1,2,3,4. These changes, too, produce no net change to Euler's formula (since $2 - 3 + 1 = 0$). In Fig. 7.6c one vertex, four edges, and four faces are added; the existing Face 2,6,7,3, however, is deleted. Again, no net change is made to Euler's formula (since $1 - 4 + 3 = 0$). In Fig. 7.6d the change is not acceptable—one vertex, two edges, and one face are added. Although this change preserves Euler's formula (since $1 - 2 + 1 = 0$), it does not satisfy the conditions requiring each edge to adjoin exactly two faces and at least three edges to meet at each vertex.

There are two kinds of changes illustrated in the figure. In Fig. 7.6a and Fig. 7.6b the solid shape of the polyhedron (in this case, a cube) is preserved, and only the network of vertices, edges, and faces is modified. In Fig. 7.6c the solid shape itself is modified by a change in the network defining it.

Euler's formula provides direct and simple proof that there are only five regular polyhedra. Let us now determine all possible regular polyhedra. Remember that a regular polyhedron is one with every face having the same number of edges, say h, every vertex having the same number of edges radiating from it, say k, and every edge having the same length.

Since every edge has two vertices and belongs to exactly two faces, it follows that $hF = 2E = kV$. Substitute this into Euler's formula:

$$\frac{2E}{k} - E + \frac{2E}{h} = 2 \tag{7.2}$$

or

$$\frac{1}{E} = \frac{1}{h} + \frac{1}{k} - \frac{1}{2} \tag{7.3}$$

For a polyhedron, assume that $h, k \geq 3$. If both h and k are larger than 3, then Eq. (7.3) implies that

$$0 < \frac{1}{E} = \frac{1}{h} + \frac{1}{k} - \frac{1}{2} \leq \frac{1}{4} + \frac{1}{4} - \frac{1}{2} = 0 \tag{7.4}$$

which is impossible; therefore, either h or k equals 3. If $h = 3$, then

$$0 < \frac{1}{E} = \frac{1}{3} + \frac{1}{k} - \frac{1}{2} \tag{7.5}$$

implies that $3 \leq k \leq 5$. Similarly, if $k = 3$, then $3 \leq h \leq 5$. Therefore, $(h,k,E) = (3,3,6)$, $(4,3,12)$, $(3,4,12)$, $(5,3,30)$, and $(3,5,30)$ are the only possibilities. These are realized by the tetrahedron, cube, octahedron, dodecahedron, and icosahedron. Note that we did not have to use the fact that the edges of the polyhedron all have the same length.

EXERCISES

1. Verify Euler's formula applied to the five regular polyhedra.

2. Study Figs. 7.7a and 7.7b. Describe what is wrong with each in terms of Euler's formula and the four conditions.

7.3. Connectivity Matrix

How are the data describing a polyhedron organized? Here is one way: List the vertices and their coordinates, then find a simple way to connect

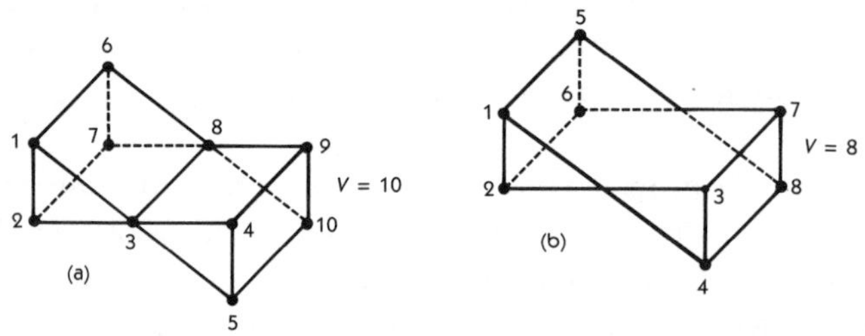

Fig. 7.7. Exercise 2.

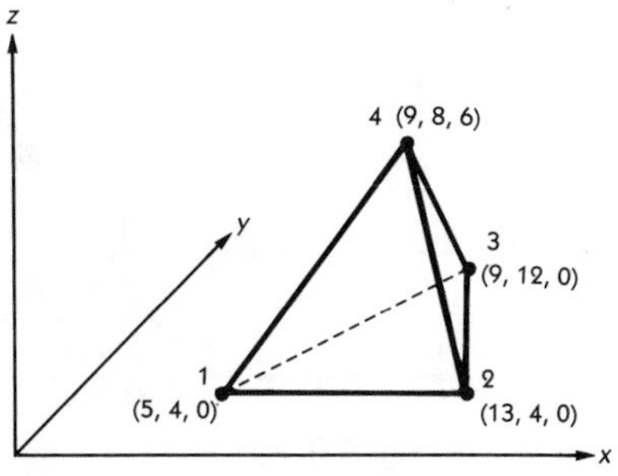

Fig. 7.8. Tetrahedron.

the vertices: use a **connectivity matrix**—a two-dimensional list or table.

Try this on a general tetrahedron (Fig. 7.8). First, number each vertex, then list the coordinates as follows:

Vertex	Coordinates
1	(5,4,0)
2	(13,4,0)
3	(9,12,0)
4	(9,8,6)

Next, construct a table (the connectivity matrix) showing how to connect the vertices to form the edges:

Vertex	1	2	3	4
1	0	1	1	1
2	1	0	1	1
3	1	1	0	1
4	1	1	1	0

The table has 16 entries; its dimensions are four rows by four columns. An entry of 0 means that the vertex heading the row in which the entry appears is not connected to the vertex heading the column in which the entry appears. An entry of 1 means that the vertices are connected. For simplicity, omit the row and column headings identifying the vertices, and the matrix becomes

$$\text{Tetrahedron connectivity matrix} = \begin{bmatrix} 0 & 1 & 1 & 1 \\ 1 & 0 & 1 & 1 \\ 1 & 1 & 0 & 1 \\ 1 & 1 & 1 & 0 \end{bmatrix} \tag{7.6}$$

Number the columns of the matrix consecutively from left to right and the rows from top to bottom; enclose the matrix in brackets.

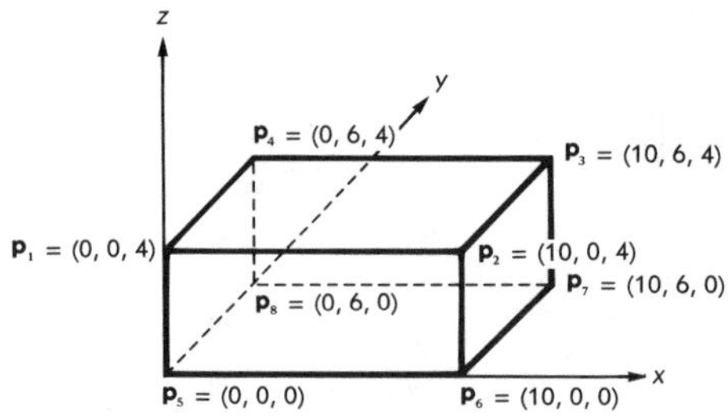

Fig. 7.9. Block.

The connectivity matrix for the tetrahedron is not very exciting, so try one for the block shown in Fig. 7.9. Define the list of its vertex coordinates by a matrix. Let each row, in order, be a specific vertex, then the entry in Column 1 is the x coordinate, in Column 2 the y coordinate, and in Column 3 the z coordinate. Write the vertex coordinates matrix as follows:

$$\mathbf{V} = \begin{bmatrix} 0 & 0 & 4 \\ 10 & 0 & 4 \\ 10 & 6 & 4 \\ 0 & 6 & 4 \\ 0 & 0 & 0 \\ 10 & 0 & 0 \\ 10 & 6 & 0 \\ 0 & 6 & 0 \end{bmatrix} \tag{7.7}$$

From the matrix **V**, for example, the coordinates of Vertex 3 from the third row are $\mathbf{p}_3 = (10,6,4)$. The connectivity matrix for this block is

$$\mathbf{C} = \begin{bmatrix} 0 & 1 & 0 & 1 & 1 & 0 & 0 & 0 \\ 1 & 0 & 1 & 0 & 0 & 1 & 0 & 0 \\ 0 & 1 & 0 & 1 & 0 & 0 & 1 & 0 \\ 1 & 0 & 1 & 0 & 0 & 0 & 0 & 1 \\ 1 & 0 & 0 & 0 & 0 & 1 & 0 & 1 \\ 0 & 1 & 0 & 0 & 1 & 0 & 1 & 0 \\ 0 & 0 & 1 & 0 & 0 & 1 & 0 & 1 \\ 0 & 0 & 0 & 1 & 1 & 0 & 1 & 0 \end{bmatrix} \tag{7.8}$$

Note that **C** is doubly redundant. Imagine a line drawn diagonally from the zero in Row 1 and Column 1 to the zero in Row 8 and Column 8. The triangular array of elements on one side of this diagonal is the mirror image of the array on the other side. It is easy to see why; for example, the 1 in Row 7 and Column 3 says that Vertex 7 is joined to Vertex 3 by an edge; the 1 in Row 3 and Column 7 says that Vertex 3 is joined to Vertex 7 with an edge—two identical pieces of information. The redundancy is not only tolerable but useful, because any search of these data for connectivity is more direct.

The information in the **V** and **C** matrices defines a **wireframe** model of the block. But what about the faces? Imagine devising a procedure to analyze **V** and **C** to flesh out the wireframe with planar polygonal faces by searching for planar loops or circuits of edges. There is also a more direct way. Simply include in the data a list of sequences of vertices defining closed loops of edges bounding the faces. Using the block previously defined as an example, form a matrix with each row containing the vertex sequence bounding a face; thus,

$$\mathbf{F} = \begin{bmatrix} 1 & 2 & 3 & 4 \\ 8 & 7 & 6 & 5 \\ 5 & 6 & 2 & 1 \\ 6 & 7 & 3 & 2 \\ 7 & 8 & 4 & 3 \\ 8 & 5 & 1 & 4 \end{bmatrix} \tag{7.9}$$

Row 3 gives the vertices surrounding Face 3. This means that the vertices are connected by edges in the order given, including an implied closing or loop-completing edge: 5-to-6-to-2-to-1-to-5, producing the correct four edges. Note that the vertex sequences are consistently given in *counterclockwise* order when viewing the face from outside the solid. This convention helps you determine which side of a face is inside and which is outside. If you curl the fingers of your right hand in the counterclockwise direction around the edges of a face (that is, in the order in which the vertices surrounding that face are listed), then your thumb points outward from the interior of the polyhedron.

Box 7.3 offers a slight digression, suggesting that, on occasion, data should be tested and verified.

EXERCISES

1. Compute the sum of the angles between adjacent edges at a vertex of each of the regular polyhedra.

2. Compute the sum of the angles between adjacent edges at each of the following vertices:

a. Vertex 4, Fig. 7.10a
b. Vertex 14, Fig. 7.10b
c. Vertex 8, Fig. 7.10c
d. Vertex 3, Fig. 7.10d
e. Vertex 7, Fig. 7.10d

3. Give the connectivity matrix for the polyhedron shown in Fig. 7.10a.

Box 7.3. Face Planarity Test

How valid are the data defining a polyhedron? One of the first questions you might ask yourself is: Do the specified vertices surrounding each face lie in a plane? This is easy to test. First, using any three vertex points surrounding a face, define the plane containing the face. Then all other vertex points surrounding the face must satisfy this equation.

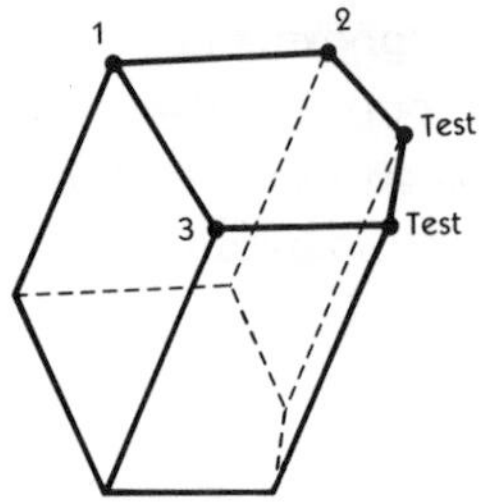

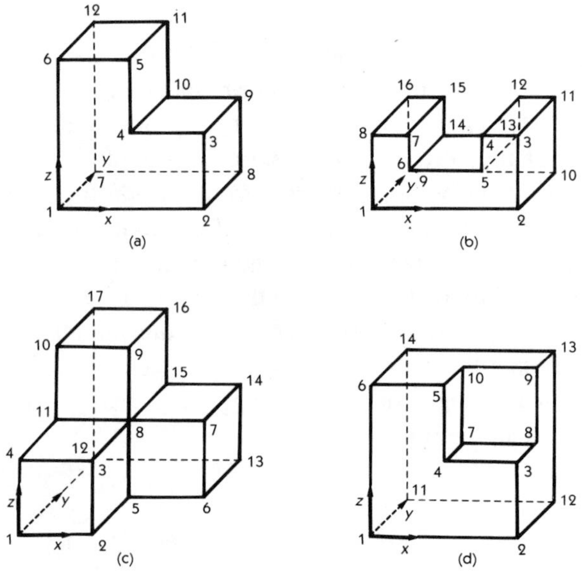

Fig. 7.10. Polyhedra.

4. Give the connectivity matrix for the polyhedron shown in Fig. 7.10b.

5. Give the connectivity matrix for the polyhedron shown in Fig. 7.10c.

6. Give the connectivity matrix for the polyhedron shown in Fig. 7.10d.

7. Give the vertex sequence matrix defining the faces of the polyhedron shown in Fig. 7.10a.

8. Give the vertex sequence matrix defining the faces of the polyhedron shown in Fig. 7.10b.

9. Give the vertex sequence matrix defining the faces of the polyhedron shown in Fig. 7.10c.

10. Give the vertex sequence matrix defining the faces of the polyhedron shown in Fig. 7.10d.

7.4. Displaying Polyhedra

In this section you will explore a few of the problems encountered in creating a realistic display of a polyhedron. Since you have not yet studied vectors (Chapter 12) or surfaces (Chapter 14), you will study only edge visibility here.

Each face of a polyhedron is a polygon. So to project a polyhedron, simply project each face polygon onto the picture plane and then onto the display screen (with clipping, as necessary). By doing this and nothing more, you produce something analogous to Fig. 7.11a. Each edge is visible, as if the faces were transparent, or as if the polyhedron were merely a wire-framework construction—a so-called **wireframe** model. The all-edges-visible wireframe model does give a pretty good idea of the polyhedron's shape, but a more realistic image discriminates between visible and hidden edges. Look at two different ways to achieve this in Figs. 7.11b and 7.11c.

Determining the edge visibility of a convex polyhedron is much simpler than for a concave polyhedron. Given a convex polyhedron (Fig. 7.12), compute vertex visibility as follows:

1. Project the face polygons onto the picture plane (preferably the x,y plane).

2. Write the plane equation for each face, using the world-system coordinates of any three vertex points of the face polygon.

3. Write the parametric equation (in the world system) of the line between each vertex, point $\mathbf{p}_V$, and the eyepoint, $\mathbf{p}_E$. For each line, assume $u = 0$ at $\mathbf{p}_E$ and $u = 1$ at $\mathbf{p}_V$. These are called **vertex projection lines.**

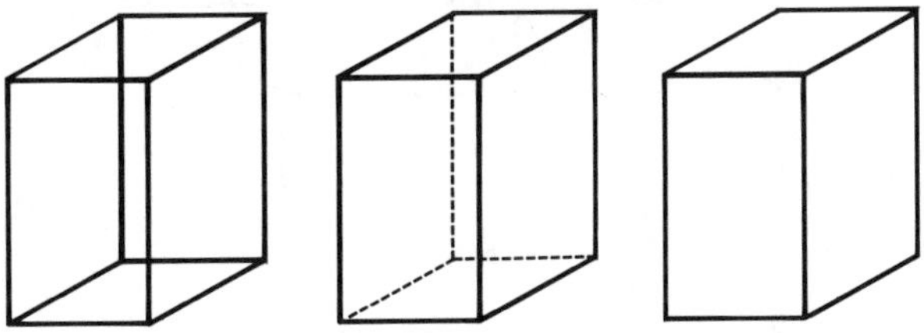

(a) (b) (c)

Fig. 7.11. Edge visibility.

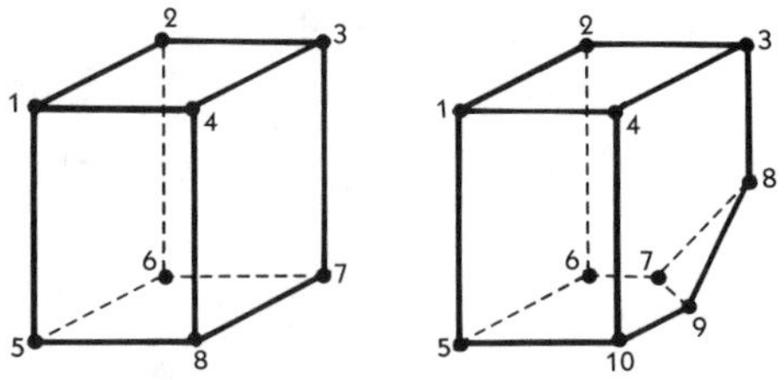

Fig. 7.12. Edge visibility: convex polyhedra.

4. Compute the intersection between the vertex projection line and each face plane (exclude the faces bounding the vertex). Do this for each vertex projection line. If a vertex projection line intersects any face such that the point of intersection, $\mathbf{p}_I$, lies between $\mathbf{p}_E$ and $\mathbf{p}_V$, that is, $0 < u_I < 1$, then $\mathbf{p}_V$ is hidden. Otherwise $\mathbf{p}_V$ is visible. (Some elaboration is necessary here. Not only must the line intersect the plane of the face in the world system, but the point of intersection must be inside the projected polygon defining the boundary of the face in the picture plane. This requires a containment test in the picture-plane system.)

If the vertex of a convex polyhedron is hidden, then all edges radiating from it are also hidden. Two examples in Fig. 7.12 support this assertion. In Fig. 7.12a, vertex 6 is hidden; therefore, edges 6–2, 6–5, and 6–7 are hidden. The edge visibility procedure for convex polyhedrons is relatively easy to state, but many computations are required to make the final determination.

The relationship between vertex and edge visibility asserted above for convex polyhedra does not apply to concave polyhedra. Look at the polyhedron of Fig. 7.13. Although vertex 8 is hidden, edge 3–9 is not (completely) hidden. Here is an interesting feature about concave polyhedra: An edge can be partly hidden (or visible). Compare this to convex polyhedra, where an edge is either entirely visible or entirely hidden. All is

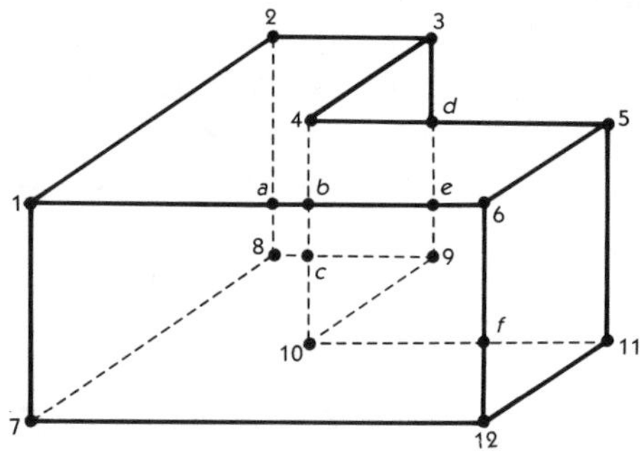

Fig. 7.13. Edge visibility: concave polyhedra.

not lost, however. You can solve edge visibility for concave polyhedra, but, of course, you will need more computations. Use the polyhedron in Fig. 7.13 as an example. This is how to proceed:

1. Test vertex visibility (as above for convex polyhedra). If a vertex is hidden, then at least some portion of each edge radiating from it is hidden. Denote them as *H*? edges. All other edges are entirely visible. (Column 1 of Table 7.1 summarizes the results of this step for the polyhedron of Fig. 7.13.)

2. Compute intersections (in the picture plane) of each *H*? with all other edges (including other *H*? edges). Preserve those intersections within the *H*? edge unit interval. Those *H*? edges with no intersections are completely hidden (*H*). See column 2 of Table 7.1.

3. Segment each remaining *H*? edge at the intersection points on it, and test the visibility of each segment. (For example, test the visibility of the midpoint of each segment.)

Observe that the visibility of an edge changes only at its intersection with another edge. Confirm this via the polyhedron in the figure, or any arbitrary concave polyhedron you might construct.

Note that in both of these procedures, you are determining only edge visibility. Although you use some of the geometric properties of the faces, you have not considered filling them, shading them, or otherwise using

Table 7.1

Vertex	Results of Step 1	Edge	Results of Step 1	Results of Step 2	Results of Step 3
1	*V*	1–2	*V*		
2	*V*	2–3	*V*		
3	*V*	3–4	*V*		
4	*V*	4–5	*V*		
5	*V*	5–6	*V*		
6	*V*	6–1	*V*		
7	*V*	7–8	*H*?	*H*	
8	*H*?	8–9	*H*?		8–*c* *H*; *c*–9 *H*
9	*H*?	9–10	*H*?	*H*	
10	*H*?	10–11	*H*?		10–*f* *H*; *f*–11 *H*
11	*V*	11–12	*V*		
12	*V*	12–7	*V*		
		1–7	*V*		
		2–8	*H*?		2–*a* *H*; *a*–8 *H*
		3–9	*H*?		3–*d* *V*; *d*–*e* *H*; *e*–9 *H*
		4–10	*H*?		4–*b* *H*; *b*–*c* *H*; *c*–10 *H*
		5–11	*V*		
		6–12	*V*		

them more directly as, for example, in the **painter's algorithm.** The painter's algorithm is derived from the artist's technique of painting the background first, then painting each succeeding layer of subject up to the topmost, foreground detail. Each layer appropriately obscures that which is immediately behind it, or hidden from the observer. An analog of this technique applied to raster graphics images allows sorting, filling, and displaying surfaces in levels from far to near (relative to the observer) and thereby building up an appropriate set of hidden and visible regions into a realistic display.

Vectors (Chapter 12) allow you to assign a direction to each face, enabling you to determine if the outside of the face is pointed toward or away from you. You can visualize this as an outward-pointing arrow on each face (Fig. 7.14). Then, for a convex polyhedron, observe that an edge is hidden if both its bounding faces point away from you. Otherwise it is visible.

Here is a slightly different problem, but nonetheless with an applicability to the visible-edge problem: Given a convex polyhedron, find the set of edges defining its silhouette. The sequence of edges defining the silhouette of the polyhedron in Fig. 7.15 is: (1,2), (2,3), (3,4), (4,5), (5,11), (11,12), (12,7), (7,1). Here is the procedure:

1. Project the polyhedron onto the picture plane (say the *x,y* plane).

2. Compute the implicit equation of each edge, *f*(*x,y*).

3. Test each edge *f*(*x,y*) for all vertices (except the two end points of the edge in question). If *f*(*x,y*) is the same sign or zero for all vertices, then the edge is on the silhouette.

Intuitively you can visualize this with the following example: Extend edge 1–2 indefinitely. Note that all vertices are on the same side of this edge. That tells you it is a silhouette edge. Do the same for edge 5–6. Do you see the difference?

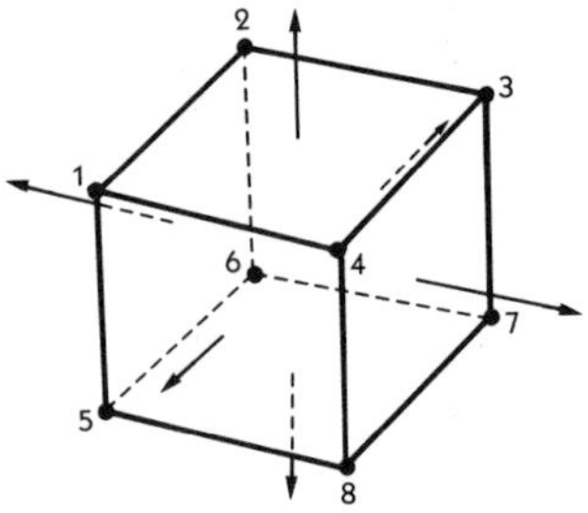

Fig. 7.14. Directed polyhedron faces.

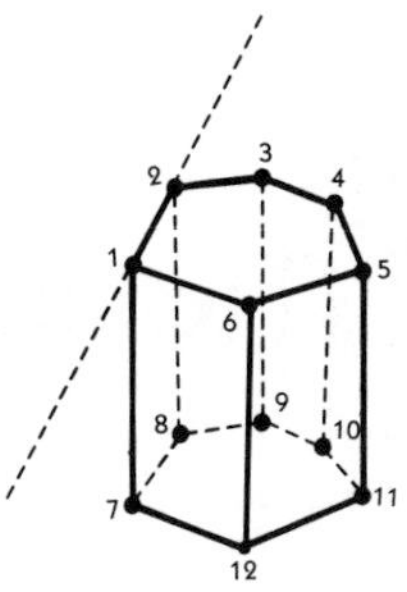

Fig. 7.15. Silhouette of a convex polyhedron.

Now, once you know the silhouette edges, you also know that they are visible, and so are the silhouette vertices. Test all other vertices for visibility, as above, and apply the results to determine the visibility of the remaining edges.

EXERCISES

1. Several assertions are made in this section. See if you can find any examples to contradict any of them.

2. Using the Cartesian definition of a polyhedron presented in Box 7.2, describe how to recognize a point on the face, edge, or vertex, or outside the polyhedron.

8. Two-Dimensional Constructions

MANY COMPLEX TWO-DIMENSIONAL shapes are combinations of squares, rectangles, and circles. Modeling these shapes correctly and unambiguously is necessary to produce accurate computer graphic displays and to compute their geometric properties and relationships. The mathematical representations of these simple two-dimensional shapes and the operations that combine them to form more complex shapes have three-dimensional analogs, which you will study in Chapter 9.

In this chapter, you will study models of squares, rectangles, and circles in the two-dimensional Cartesian coordinate plane. You will consider only squares and rectangles whose sides are parallel to the coordinate system axes. Circles, of course, have no such orientation constraints. Your intuitive notion of these simple shapes is sufficient, so we will dispense with their formal definitions.

The square, rectangle, and circle are so widely used in computer graphics and geometric modeling that it is very useful, if not necessary, to describe them concisely. It is also useful to know which points are inside, outside, or on the boundary of these figures and how to combine them to produce more complex figures. You will find out how to do these things in the following sections.

8.1. Squares

Describe a square by giving the coordinates of one of its vertices and the length of a side. Remember, for the moment consider only squares whose sides are parallel to the coordinate axes; for convenience and consistency, always specify the coordinates of a square's lower left vertex. This will always be the vertex with the minimum coordinate values relative to the other three vertices, $\mathbf{p} = (x_{\min}, y_{\min})$.

Denote a square symbolically with the capital letters **SQ** (shown boldface throughout the text). You can indicate a specific square by adding an alphabetic or numeric subscript, $\mathbf{SQ}_i$ for example. Thus, to specify a square, write:

$$\mathbf{SQ} = \mathbf{SQ}\,(x_0, y_0, a) \tag{8.1}$$

where x_0, y_0 are the coordinates of the lower left, or minimum, vertex and a is the length of the side. Read this expression as: A square is a function of the coordinates of its minimum vertex and the length of its side. The quantities inside parentheses are the **arguments** of the function; see several examples in Fig. 8.1. These three numbers, plus some code identifying what it is they describe, are all you need to describe a square in two dimensions with sides parallel to the principal axes.

Note that x_0 and y_0 can have positive or negative values, but values of a must always be positive, since a square whose side has a negative length is geometrically undefined or meaningless.

A great deal of information is contained in the three arguments. The location of a square is, of course, given by x_0, y_0; its perimeter is $4a$ and its area is a^2. The coordinates of its maximum vertex are simply $x_0 + a$, $y_0 + a$. In fact, to display a square, you must first compute the coordinates of all four vertex points and then progress as for polygons. In counterclockwise order from the minimum vertex, they are

$$\begin{aligned} \mathbf{p}_0 &= (x_0, y_0) \\ \mathbf{p}_1 &= (x_0 + a, y_0) \\ \mathbf{p}_2 &= (x_0 + a, y_0 + a) \\ \mathbf{p}_3 &= (x_0, y_0 + a) \end{aligned} \tag{8.2}$$

Again use a lowercase boldface **p** to denote a point and a subscript to indicate a specific point, as in Fig. 8.2. Note that $\mathbf{p}_{min} = \mathbf{p}_0$ and $\mathbf{p}_{max} = \mathbf{p}_2$.

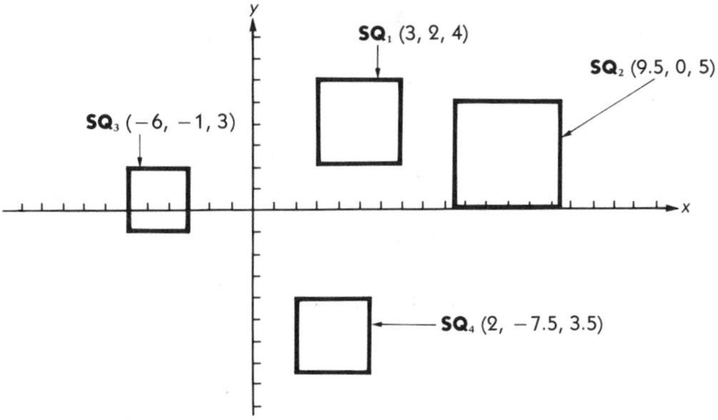

Fig. 8.1. Squares defined on the x, y plane.

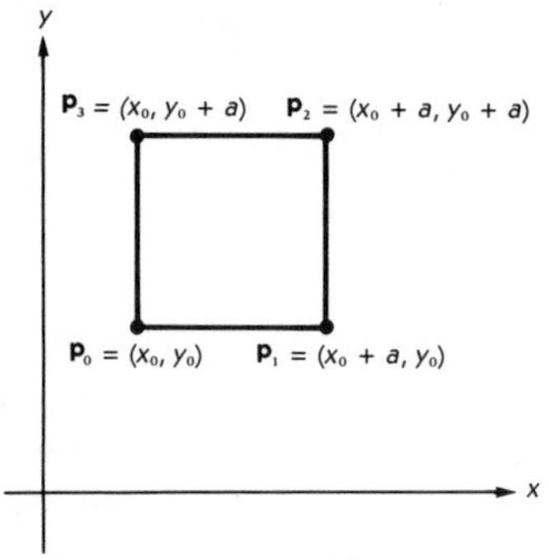

Fig. 8.2. Coordinates of the vertex points of a square.

Here, min and max refer to relative values of the coordinates and not to the points as such.

The geometric center of a square is at the point

$$\mathbf{P}_{CG} = \left(x_0 + \frac{a}{2}, y_0 + \frac{a}{2} \right) \tag{8.3}$$

Now look at the example of $\mathbf{SQ}_1 = \mathbf{SQ}_1(-4,-3,10)$ in Fig. 8.3. Compute the following properties:

Perimeter:	$4a$	$= 40$
Area:	a^2	$= 100$
Centroid:	$\mathbf{P}_{CG}$	$= (1,2)$
Minimum Vertex:	$\mathbf{p}_{min}$	$= (-4,-3)$
Maximum Vertex:	$\mathbf{p}_{max}$	$= (6,7)$

Many computer graphics problems require that you determine if a given

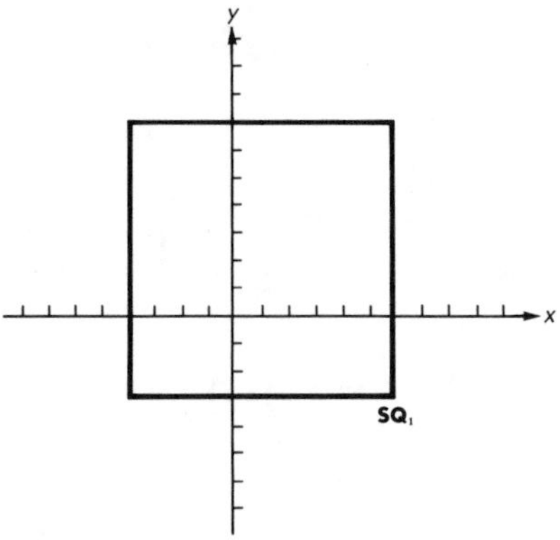

Fig. 8.3. $\mathbf{SQ}_1 = \mathbf{SQ}_1(-4,-3,10)$.

point is inside, outside, or on the boundary of a closed shape. Given a point $\mathbf{p} = (x,y)$, test its coordinates against those of $\mathbf{p}_{min}$ and $\mathbf{p}_{max}$. If the point is *inside* the square, then *both* of the following conditions must be satisfied.

$$x_{min} < x < x_{max} \quad \text{and} \quad y_{min} < y < y_{max} \tag{8.4}$$

If the point is *outside* the square, then *at least one* of the following conditions is true:

$$x < x_{min}, \quad x > x_{max}, \quad y < y_{min}, \quad \text{or} \quad y > y_{max} \tag{8.5}$$

If the point is on the boundary of the square, then

$$\left.\begin{array}{c} x = x_{min} \\ \text{or} \\ x = x_{max} \end{array}\right\} \text{ and } y_{min} \le y \le y_{max} \tag{8.6}$$

or

$$\left.\begin{array}{c} y = y_{min} \\ \text{or} \\ y = y_{max} \end{array}\right\} \text{ and } x_{min} \le x \le x_{max} \tag{8.7}$$

This procedure is called **point classification.** Given $\mathbf{SQ}_1 = \mathbf{SQ}_1(4,-2,8)$, for example, classify the three points $\mathbf{p}_1 = (2,-5)$, $\mathbf{p}_2 = (12,3)$, and $\mathbf{p}_3 = (6,3)$. See Fig. 8.4.

First compute $\mathbf{p}_{min} = (4,-2)$ and $\mathbf{p}_{max} = (12,6)$ for $\mathbf{SQ}_1$; thus, $x_{min} = 4$, $x_{max} = 12$, $y_{min} = -2$, and $y_{max} = 6$. Now test each point. Point $\mathbf{p}_1$ must

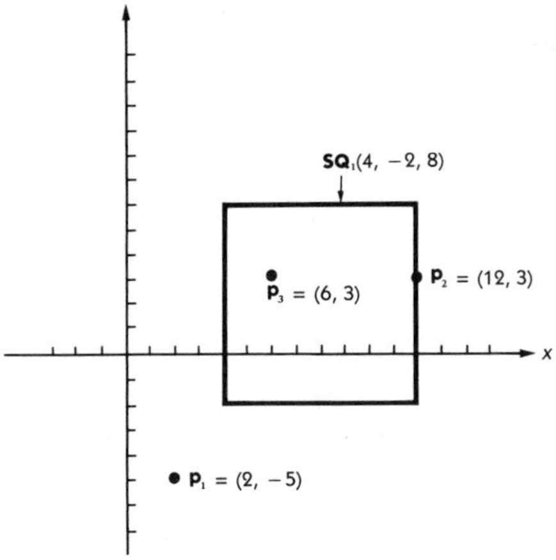

Fig. 8.4. Point classification with respect to a square.

be outside the square since it satisfies only the conditions defined in Eq. (8.5), so that $2 < 4$ and $-5 < -2$.

Point $\mathbf{p}_2$ must be on the boundary of the square since it satisfies only the conditions defined in Eq. (8.6), so that $12 = 12$ and $-2 \le 3 \le 6$.

Point $\mathbf{p}_3$ must be inside the square since it satisfies only the conditions defined in Eq. (8.4), so that $4 < 6 < 12$ and $-2 < 3 < 6$.

You can easily extend containment and classification testing to determine the relationships possible between two squares. One square may lie entirely within the other, the two squares may be entirely disjoint (one is entirely outside the other), or the two squares may intersect.

$\mathbf{SQ}_1$ is inside $\mathbf{SQ}_2$ if and only if $\mathbf{p}_{\text{min},1} \ge \mathbf{p}_{\text{min},2}$ and $\mathbf{p}_{\text{max},1} \le \mathbf{p}_{\text{max},2}$. Here the test for inequality applies to the coordinates. Note that both inequalities must be true; see Fig. 8.5a. Another way to express this is: $\mathbf{SQ}_1$ $\langle$inside$\rangle$ $\mathbf{SQ}_2$ if and only if

$$\begin{matrix} x_{\text{min},1} \ge x_{\text{min},2} \\ y_{\text{min},1} \ge y_{\text{min},2} \end{matrix} \quad \text{and} \quad \begin{matrix} x_{\text{max},1} \le x_{\text{max},2} \\ y_{\text{max},1} \le y_{\text{max},2} \end{matrix} \tag{8.8}$$

where the symbols $\langle\ \rangle$ denote a relationship. Note that if Eq. (8.8) is true, then it is also true that $a_1 < a_2$.

Furthermore, $\mathbf{SQ}_1$ $\langle$outside$\rangle$ $\mathbf{SQ}_2$ if and only if

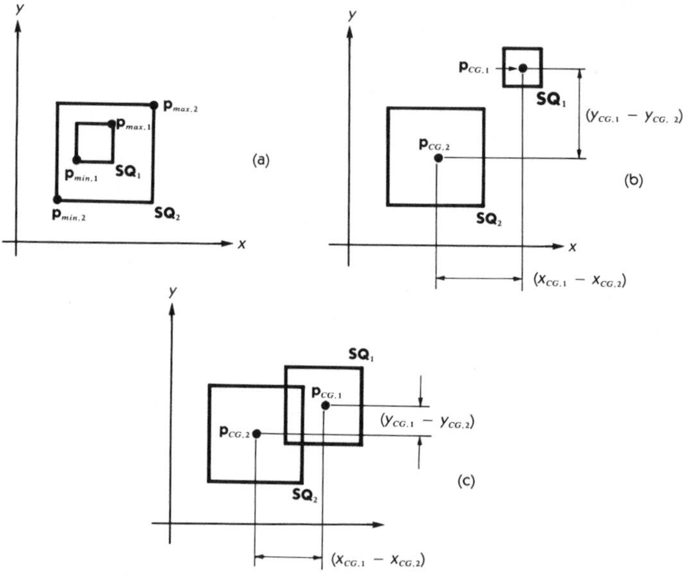

Fig. 8.5. Relationships between two squares.

$$|x_{CG,1} - x_{CG,2}| \geq \frac{a_1 + a_2}{2}$$

or (8.9)

$$|y_{CG,1} - y_{CG,2}| \geq \frac{a_1 + a_2}{2}$$

This relationship between two squares and the conditions giving rise to it are shown in Fig. 8.5b. Note that this relationship is symmetrical: if $\mathbf{SQ}_1$ is outside $\mathbf{SQ}_2$, then $\mathbf{SQ}_2$ is outside $\mathbf{SQ}_1$. Verify that the inside relationship is not symmetrical.

Finally $\mathbf{SQ}_1$ ⟨intersect⟩ $\mathbf{SQ}_2$ if and only if

$$\frac{|a_1 - a_2|}{2} < |x_{CG,1} - x_{CG,2}| < \frac{a_1 + a_2}{2}$$

and (8.10)

$$\frac{|a_1 - a_2|}{2} < |y_{CG,1} - y_{CG,2}| < \frac{a_1 + a_2}{2}$$

See Fig. 8.5c.

Now consider the conditions describing two squares that share a boundary. How many ways can you imagine this condition occurring? Figure 8.6a shows four ways that two squares can share a y = const boundary. Express these as

$$\left\{\begin{matrix} y_{\max,1} = y_{\min,2} \text{ or} \\ y_{\max,1} = y_{\max,2} \text{ or} \\ y_{\min,1} = y_{\min,2} \text{ or} \\ y_{\min,1} = y_{\max,2} \end{matrix}\right\} \text{ and } |x_{CG,1} - x_{CG,2}| < \frac{a_1 + a_2}{2} \tag{8.11}$$

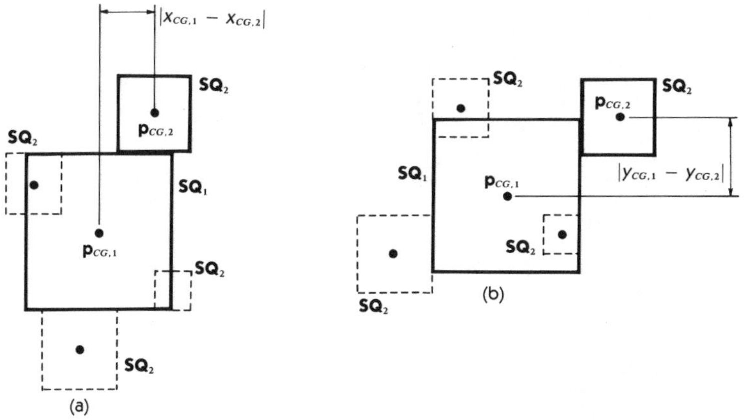

Fig. 8.6. Squares with a common boundary.

Figure 8.6b shows four ways that two squares can share an x = const boundary. Express these as

$$\left\{\begin{matrix} x_{\min,1} = x_{\max,2} \text{ or} \\ x_{\min,1} = x_{\min,2} \text{ or} \\ x_{\max,1} = x_{\max,2} \text{ or} \\ x_{\max,1} = x_{\min,2} \end{matrix}\right\} \text{ and } |y_{CG,1} - y_{CG,2}| < \frac{a_1 + a_2}{2} \qquad (8.12)$$

EXERCISES

1. Which of the following expressions improperly specify a square, and why?
   a. $\mathbf{SQ}_1(-2,0,3)$
   b. $\mathbf{SQ}_2(7,1,-2)$
   c. $\mathbf{SQ}_3(-0.5,0.5,0.01)$
   d. $\mathbf{SQ}_4(0,0,1)$
   e. $\mathbf{SQ}_5(-1,-2.5)$
   f. $\mathbf{SQ}_6(8,10,0.5)$
   g. $\mathbf{SQ}_7(0,-6.5,2,3.5)$
   h. $\mathbf{SQ}_8(0.002,-0.002,3.000)$
2. Draw the following squares on graph paper:
   a. $\mathbf{SQ}_1(-2,-2,4)$
   b. $\mathbf{SQ}_2(4,-1,5)$
   c. $\mathbf{SQ}_3(5,4,2)$
   d. $\mathbf{SQ}_4(-6,-6,6)$
   e. $\mathbf{SQ}_5(-4,1,3)$
3. Compute the coordinates of the vertices of each of the squares given in Exercise 2.
4. Write the arguments for the squares shown in Fig. 8.7.

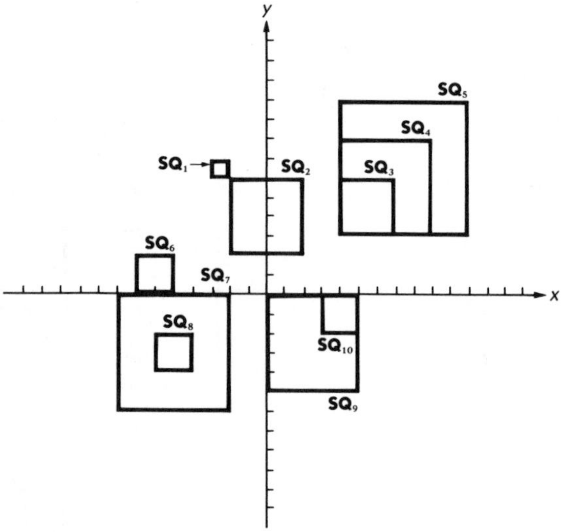

Fig. 8.7. Ten squares.

5. Compute $\mathbf{p}_{max}$ and $\mathbf{p}_{CG}$ for the squares shown in Fig. 8.7.

6. Given $\mathbf{SQ}_1 = \mathbf{SQ}_1(-2,-2,8)$, classify the following points. Solve this problem analytically, not graphically.

a. $\mathbf{p}_1 = (8,6)$
b. $\mathbf{p}_2 = (-2,6)$
c. $\mathbf{p}_3 = (-1,3)$
d. $\mathbf{p}_4 = (2,-2)$.
e. $\mathbf{p}_5 = (-1,-4)$

7. Given $\mathbf{SQ}_1 = \mathbf{SQ}_1(-4,-4,8)$ and $\mathbf{SQ}_2 = \mathbf{SQ}_2(-2,-2,4)$, where $\mathbf{SQ}_2$ defines a hole in $\mathbf{SQ}_1$, classify the following points as being inside, outside, or on the boundary of the resulting shape:

a. $\mathbf{p}_1 = (-2,4)$
b. $\mathbf{p}_2 = (6,3)$
c. $\mathbf{p}_3 = (-2,1)$
d. $\mathbf{p}_4 = (1,1)$
e. $\mathbf{p}_5 = (4,1)$
f. $\mathbf{p}_6 = (-6,-2)$
g. $\mathbf{p}_7 = (3,-3)$

8. Given $\mathbf{SQ}_1 = \mathbf{SQ}_1(-2,2,5)$, classify the following squares with respect to $\mathbf{SQ}_1$:

a. $\mathbf{SQ}_2 = \mathbf{SQ}_2(-4,6,3)$
b. $\mathbf{SQ}_3 = \mathbf{SQ}_3(3,6,2)$
c. $\mathbf{SQ}_4 = \mathbf{SQ}_4(0,4,2)$
d. $\mathbf{SQ}_5 = \mathbf{SQ}_5(-2,2,3)$
e. $\mathbf{SQ}_6 = \mathbf{SQ}_6(-3,2,2)$
f. $\mathbf{SQ}_7 = \mathbf{SQ}_7(-5,-3,4)$

9. Show that $\mathbf{p}_{CG} = (\mathbf{p}_{min} + \mathbf{p}_{max})/2$.

10. Write a procedure to compute the coordinates of four vertex points of a square. Denote this as **SQVP**(SQ,VP0,VP1,VP2,VP3) where (using array notation)

SQ(3) are the input values of x_0, y_0, and a; and
VP0(2), VP1(2), VP2(2), VP3(2) are the output coordinates of the vertex points.

11. Write a procedure to compute $\mathbf{p}_{min}$ and $\mathbf{p}_{max}$ of a square. Denote this as **SQMM**(SQ,PMIN,PMAX), where

SQ(3) are the input values of x_0, y_0, and a,
PMIN(2) are the output coordinates of $\mathbf{p}_{min}$, and
PMAX(2) are the output coordinates of $\mathbf{p}_{max}$.

12. Write a procedure to compute the perimeter, area, and $\mathbf{p}_{CG}$ of a square. Denote this as **SQPROP**(SQ,P,A,PCG) where

SQ(3) are the input values of x_0, y_0, and a,
P is the output perimeter,
A is the output area, and
PCG(2) are the output coordinates of $\mathbf{p}_{CG}$.

13. Write a procedure to classify a point with respect to a square. Denote this as **SQPT**(SQ,PT,ICLS), where

SQ(3) are the input values of x_0, y_0, and a,
PT(2) are the input coordinates of a point, and
ICLS is the output classification of the point:
ICLS = 1 if the point is outside,
ICLS = 2 if the point is inside, and
ICLS = 3 if the point is on the boundary.

14. Write a procedure to classify the relationship between two squares. Denote this as **SQSQ**(SQ1,SQ2,ICLS) where

SQ1(3), SQ2(3) are the input values of x_0, y_0, and a for each of the two squares and
ICLS is the output classification of SQ1 with respect to SQ2:
ICLS = 1 if SQ1 is outside SQ2 with no common boundary,
ICLS = 2 if SQ1 is inside SQ2 with no common boundary,
ICLS = 3 if SQ1 intersects SQ2 with no common boundary,
ICLS = 4 if SQ1 is outside SQ2 with a common boundary,
ICLS = 5 if SQ1 is inside SQ2 with a common boundary,
ICLS = 6 if SQ1 intersects SQ2 with a common boundary,
ICLS = 7 if SQ1 contains SQ2 with no common boundary, and
ICLS = 8 if SQ1 contains SQ2 with a common boundary.

8.2. Rectangles

Describe a rectangle by giving the coordinates of one of its vertices and the lengths of its two principal dimensions. Consider, for the moment, only rectangles whose sides are parallel to the coordinate axes. As with squares, specify the coordinates of the rectangle's lower left vertex.

Denote a rectangle symbolically with the boldface capital letters **RN**. Again, indicate a specific rectangle by adding an alphabetic or numeric subscript: $\mathbf{RN}_1$, for example. Thus, to specify a rectangle, write:

$$\mathbf{RN} = \mathbf{RN}(x_0, y_0, a_x, a_y) \tag{8.13}$$

where x_0 and y_0 are the coordinates of the lower left or minimum vertex and a_x and a_y are the principal dimensions parallel to the x and y axes, respectively. Read this expression as: A rectangle is a function of the coordinates of a vertex and the lengths of its principal dimensions; see several examples in Fig. 8.8.

Note that x_0 and y_0 can take on positive or negative values; however,

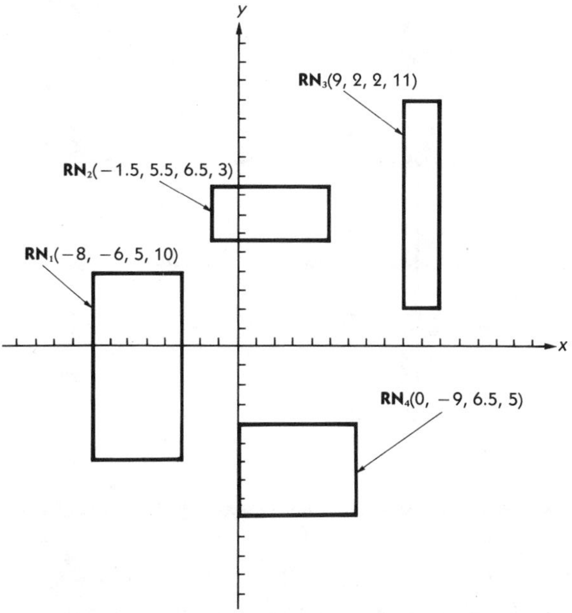

Fig. 8.8. Rectangles defined on the *x*, *y* plane.

a_x and a_y must always be positive, since rectangles with negative dimensions are undefined.

A rectangle has the following properties:

$$\text{perimeter} = 2\,(a_x + a_y)$$
$$\text{area} = a_x a_y$$
$$\mathbf{p}_{CG} = \left(x_0 + \frac{a_x}{2}, y_0 + \frac{a_y}{2}\right)$$
$$\mathbf{p}_{\min} = (x_0, y_0)$$
$$\mathbf{p}_{\max} = (x_0 + a_x, y_0 + a_y)$$

To display a rectangle, you must first compute the coordinates of the four vertex points. In counterclockwise order from the minimum vertex, they are (Fig. 8.9)

$$\begin{aligned}\mathbf{p}_0 &= (x_0, y_0)\\ \mathbf{p}_1 &= (x_0 + a_x, y_0)\\ \mathbf{p}_2 &= (x_0 + a_x, y_0 + a_y)\\ \mathbf{p}_3 &= (x_0, y_0 + a_y)\end{aligned} \tag{8.14}$$

Classifying a point with respect to a rectangle is the same as for a square. In fact, since classification depends only on $\mathbf{p}_{\min}$ and $\mathbf{p}_{\max}$, Eqs. (8.4)–(8.7)

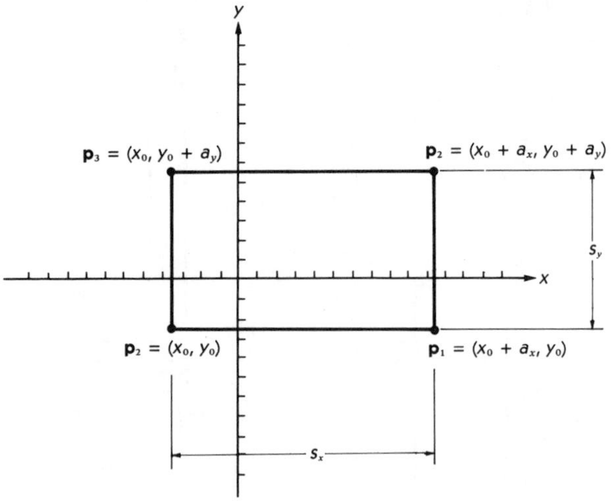

Fig. 8.9. Coordinates of the vertex points of a rectangle.

for squares also apply to rectangles. The same classification applies to two rectangles that share a boundary (or a rectangle and square, for that matter), and Eqs. (8.11) and (8.12) also apply to rectangles.

Classifying the spatial relationship between two rectangles requires that we modify slightly some of the equations describing the relationships between squares. Equation (8.8) still applies. The rest are changed as you can see in the following equations; thus $\mathbf{RN}_1$ ⟨outside⟩ $\mathbf{RN}_2$ if and only if

$$|x_{CG,1} - x_{CG,2}| \geq \frac{a_{x,1} + a_{x,2}}{2}$$

or (8.15)

$$|y_{CG,1} - y_{CG,2}| \geq \frac{a_{y,1} + a_{y,2}}{2}$$

$\mathbf{RN}_1$ ⟨intersects⟩ $\mathbf{RN}_2$ if and only if

$$\frac{|a_{x,1} - a_{x,2}|}{2} < |x_{CG,1} - x_{CG,2}| < \frac{a_{x,1} + a_{x,2}}{2}$$

and/or (8.16)

$$\frac{|a_{y,1} - a_{y,2}|}{2} < |y_{CG,1} - y_{CG,2}| < \frac{a_{y,1} + a_{y,2}}{2}$$

Note that the rectangle is more general and, therefore, is a more powerful form of representation than the square. The rectangle represents a square if $a_x = a_y$. Although the rectangle requires four numbers to specify

it completely, it can represent a greater variety of shapes, and so it is more useful.

EXERCISES

1. Which of the following expressions improperly specify a rectangle, and why?

   a. $\mathbf{RN}_1(0.012,-3.065,7.5,0.21)$
   b. $\mathbf{RN}_2(-3,-3,3,3)$
   c. $\mathbf{RN}_3(2.75,3.50,6.0,-6.0)$
   d. $\mathbf{RN}_4(3760,0,253,11)$
   e. $\mathbf{RN}_5(6.0,-9.5,1.0,0)$
   f. $\mathbf{RN}_6(0,0,1,2)$
   g. $\mathbf{RN}_7(0,0,-1,-1)$
   h. $\mathbf{RN}_8(-3.9,-1.7,6.5,7.2,1.3)$
   i. $\mathbf{RN}_9(8,3,3,9)$
   j. $\mathbf{RN}_{10}(612,108,43,37)$

2. Draw the following rectangles on graph paper:

   a. $\mathbf{RN}_1(-6,1,2,5)$
   b. $\mathbf{RN}_2(-2,2,5,4)$
   c. $\mathbf{RN}_3(0,0,7,1)$
   d. $\mathbf{RN}_4(-5,-3,5,3)$
   e. $\mathbf{RN}_5(-1,-4,3,3)$

3. Represent the following squares as rectangles:

   a. $\mathbf{SQ}_1(-2,-2,4)$
   b. $\mathbf{SQ}_2(4,-1,5)$
   c. $\mathbf{SQ}_3(5,4,2)$

4. Compute the coordinates of the vertices of each of the rectangles defined in Exercise 2.

5. Write the defining arguments for the rectangles in Fig. 8.10.

6. Compute $\mathbf{p}_{max}$ and $\mathbf{p}_{CG}$ for the rectangles in Fig. 8.10.

7. Given $\mathbf{RN}_1 = \mathbf{RN}_1(-3,2,9,3)$, classify the following points. Solve this problem analytically, not graphically.

   a. $\mathbf{p}_1 = (1,4)$
   b. $\mathbf{p}_2 = (-3,3)$
   c. $\mathbf{p}_3 = (-5,2)$
   d. $\mathbf{p}_4 = (6,5)$
   e. $\mathbf{p}_5 = (6,1)$

8. Given $\mathbf{RN}_1 = \mathbf{RN}_1(-4,-1,8,5)$ and $\mathbf{SQ}_1 = \mathbf{SQ}_1(0,0,3)$, where $\mathbf{SQ}_1$ defines a hole in the shape defined by $\mathbf{RN}_1$, classify the following points as being inside, outside, or on the boundary of the net shape:

   a. $\mathbf{p}_1 = (-1,6)$
   b. $\mathbf{p}_2 = (0,4)$
   c. $\mathbf{p}_3 = (-5,3)$
   d. $\mathbf{p}_4 = (-3,3)$
   e. $\mathbf{p}_5 = (4,3)$
   f. $\mathbf{p}_6 = (6,3)$

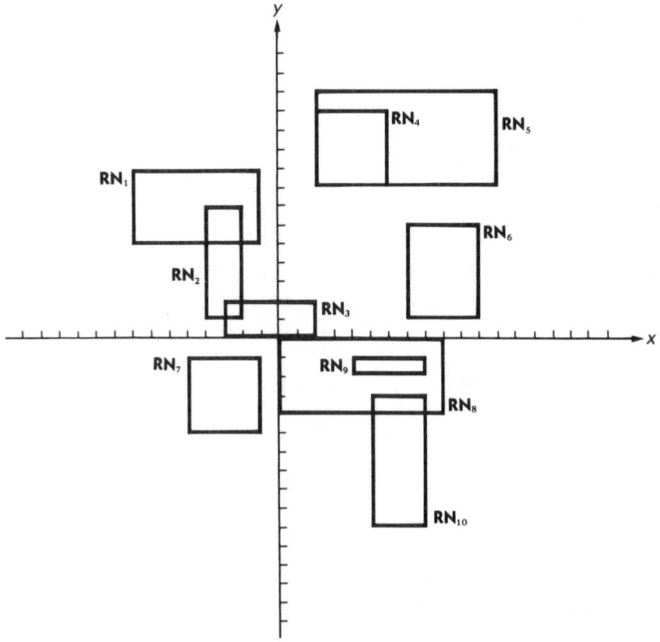

Fig. 8.10. Ten rectangles.

g. $\mathbf{p}_7 = (1,1)$
h. $\mathbf{p}_8 = (-3,0)$
i. $\mathbf{p}_9 = (3,0)$
j. $\mathbf{p}_{10} = (3,-3)$

9. Given $\mathbf{RN}_1 = \mathbf{RN}_1(2,2,8,5)$, classify the following squares and rectangles with respect to $\mathbf{RN}_1$:

a. $\mathbf{RN}_2(-4,2,2,5)$
b. $\mathbf{RN}_3(-1,6,6,3)$
c. $\mathbf{RN}_4(7,7,4,2)$
d. $\mathbf{SQ}_1(-1,-1,4)$
e. $\mathbf{SQ}_2(4,2,3)$
f. $\mathbf{RN}_5(8,3,1,3)$
g. $\mathbf{SQ}_3(11,4,2)$
h. $\mathbf{RN}_6(10,1,3,1)$
i. $\mathbf{SQ}_4(2,-4,3)$
j. $\mathbf{RN}_7(6,-2,3,4)$

10. Write a procedure to compute the coordinates of the four vertex points of a rectangle. Denote this as **RNVP**(RN,VP0,VP1,VP2,VP3), where

RN(4) are the input values of x_0, y_0, a_x, and a_y and
VP0(2), VP1(2), VP2(2), VP3(2) are the output coordinates of the vertex points.

11. Write a procedure to compute $\mathbf{p}_{min}$ and $\mathbf{p}_{max}$ of a rectangle. Denote this as **RNMM**(RN,PMIN,PMAX), where

RN(4) are the input values of x_0, y_0, a_x, and a_y,
PMIN(2) are the output coordinates of $\mathbf{p}_{min}$, and
PMAX(2) are the output coordinates of $\mathbf{p}_{max}$.

12. Write a procedure to compute the perimeter, area, and $\mathbf{p}_{CG}$ of a rectangle. Denote this as **RNPROP**(RN,P,A,PCG), where

RN(4) are the input values of x_0, y_0, a_x, and a_y,
P is the output perimeter,
A is the output area, and
PCG(2) are the output coordinates of $\mathbf{p}_{CG}$.

13. Write a procedure to classify a point with respect to a rectangle. Denote this as **RNPT**(RN,PT,ICLS), where

RN(4) are the input values of x_0, y_0, a_x, and a_y,
PT(2) are the input coordinates of a point, and
ICLS is the output classification of the point:
ICLS = 1 if the point is outside,
ICLS = 2 if the point is inside, and
ICLS = 3 if the point is on the boundary.

14. Write a procedure to classify the relationship between two rectangles. Denote this as **RNRN**(RN1,RN2,ICLS), where

RN1(4), RN2(4) are the input values of x_0, y_0, a_x, and a_y and
ICLS is the output classification of RN2 with respect to RN1:
ICLS = 1 if RN1 is outside RN2 with no common boundary,
ICLS = 2 if RN1 is inside RN2 with no common boundary,
ICLS = 3 if RN1 intersects RN2 with no common boundary,
ICLS = 4 if RN1 is outside RN2 with a common boundary,
ICLS = 5 if RN1 is inside RN2 with a common boundary,
ICLS = 6 if RN1 intersects RN2 with a common boundary,
ICLS = 7 if RN1 contains RN2 with no common boundary, and
ICLS = 8 if RN1 contains RN2 with a common boundary.

8.3. Circles

To describe a circle, give the coordinates of its center point and its radius. Since a circle is radially symmetrical, it has no preferred orientation in the x, y coordinate plane. All orientations are geometrically equal.

Denote a circle symbolically with the boldface capital letters **CR**. You can add a subscript to indicate a specific circle, $\mathbf{CR}_i$ for example. Thus, to specify a circle, write:

$$\mathbf{CR} = \mathbf{CR}(x_c, y_c, r) \tag{8.17}$$

where x_c, y_c are the coordinates of the center point and r is the radius (Fig. 8.11). Read this expression as: A circle is a function of the coordinates

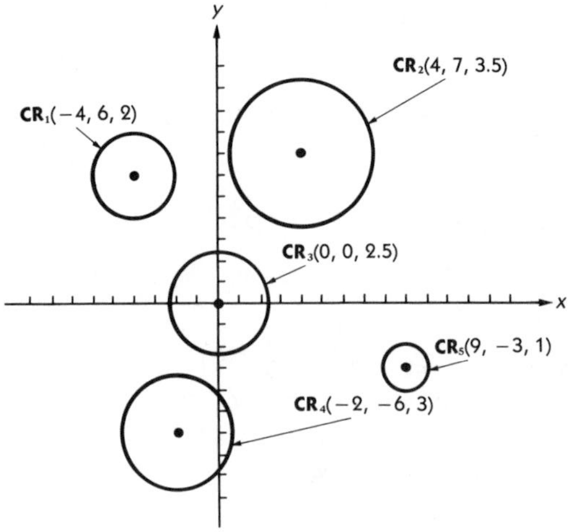

Fig. 8.11. Circles defined on the *x*, *y* plane.

of its center point and its radius. Note that x_c and y_c can take on positive or negative values, but r must always be positive, since circles with negative radii are undefined.

To display a circle, compute points on its circumference. Interpret these as the vertices of a polygon approximating the circle (Box 8.1).

A circle has the following properties:

$$\text{perimeter} = 2\pi r$$
$$\text{area} = \pi r^2$$
$$\mathbf{p}_{CG} = (x_c, y_c)$$

The $\mathbf{p}_{min}$ and $\mathbf{p}_{max}$ vertices of squares and rectangles that were so valuable in computing relationships are not characteristics of a circle.

You can classify points with respect to a circle simply by computing a distance (Fig. 8.12). Given a point, $\mathbf{p}_i = (x_i, y_i)$, compute its distance from the center of a given circle. Denote the distance as d_i; thus

$$d_i = \sqrt{(x_i - x_c)^2 + (y_i - y_c)^2} \tag{8.18}$$

Then

$$\mathbf{p}_i \langle\text{inside}\rangle\ \mathbf{CR} \text{ if and only if } d_i < r \tag{8.19}$$

$$\mathbf{p}_i \langle\text{outside}\rangle\ \mathbf{CR} \text{ if and only if } d_i > r \tag{8.20}$$

$$\mathbf{p}_i \langle\text{boundary}\rangle\ \mathbf{CR} \text{ if and only if } d_i = r \tag{8.21}$$

Given two circles, the following spatial relationships are possible between them: One circle may lie entirely within the other, the two circles

Box 8.1. Displaying a Circle

A simple and direct way to display a circle begins with the unit circle, with its center at the origin. Define and compute the coordinates of a set of points equally spaced around its circumference. These coordinates are given by $\mathbf{p}(\theta) = (\cos\theta, \sin\theta)$.

For an arbitrary circle in the x, y plane, of radius r and located at x_c, y_c, first multiply the coordinates of each point on the unit circle by r (this is a scaling transformation). This produces a new set of points; these fall on the circumference of a circle of radius r, centered at the origin. Next, add x_c and y_c to the x and y coordinates, respectively, of these points (this is a translation transformation). This produces the final set of points; they are on the circumference of the circle of radius r, centered at x_c, y_c. Connect these (vertex) points to define a polygon approximating the circle. The more points, the better the approximation, and the smoother the curve.

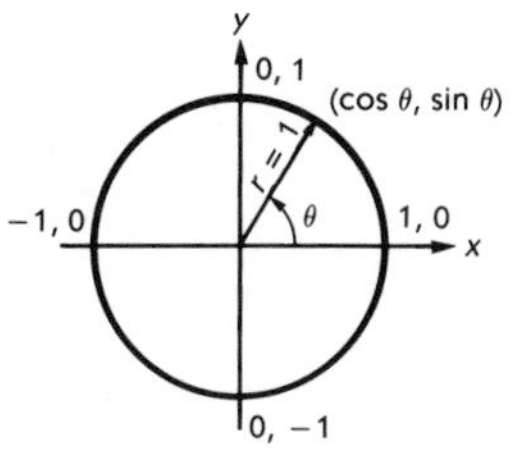

Do this for **CR** = (3, 2, 1.5). If the unit circle is approximated by a 16-sided polygon, then its vertex coordinates are:

$\mathbf{p}_1 = (1, 0)$
$\mathbf{p}_2 = (0.924, 0.383)$
$\mathbf{p}_3 = (0.707, 0.707)$
$\mathbf{p}_4 = (0.383, 0.924)$
$\mathbf{p}_5 = (0, 1)$
$\mathbf{p}_6 = (-0.383, 0.924)$
$\mathbf{p}_7 = (-0.707, 0.707)$
$\mathbf{p}_8 = (-0.924, 0.383)$
$\mathbf{p}_9 = (-1, 9)$
$\mathbf{p}_{10} = (-0.924, -0.384)$
$\mathbf{p}_{11} = (-0.707, -0.707)$
$\mathbf{p}_{12} = (-0.383, -0.924)$
$\mathbf{p}_{13} = (0, -1)$
$\mathbf{p}_{14} = (0.383, -0.924)$
$\mathbf{p}_{15} = (0.707, -0.707)$
$\mathbf{p}_{16} = (0.924, -0.383)$

(continued)

Box 8.1. (Continued)

The scaling transformation produces:

$\mathbf{p}_1 = (1.5, 0)$
$\mathbf{p}_2 = (1.386, 0.574)$
$\mathbf{p}_3 = (1.061, 1.061)$
$\mathbf{p}_4 = (0.574, 1.386)$
$\mathbf{p}_5 = (0, 1.5)$
$\mathbf{p}_6 = (-.574, 1.386)$
$\mathbf{p}_7 = (-1.061, 1.061)$
$\mathbf{p}_8 = (-1.386, 0.574)$
$\mathbf{p}_9 = (-1.5, 0)$
$\mathbf{p}_{10} = (-1.386, -0.574)$
$\mathbf{p}_{11} = (-1.061, -1.061)$
$\mathbf{p}_{12} = (-0.574, -1.386)$
$\mathbf{p}_{13} = (0, -1.5)$
$\mathbf{p}_{14} = (0.574, -1.386)$
$\mathbf{p}_{15} = (1.061, -1.061)$
$\mathbf{p}_{16} = (1.386, -0.574)$

And finally, the translation transformation produces:

$\mathbf{p}_1 = (4.5, 2.0)$
$\mathbf{p}_2 = (4.386, 2.574)$
$\mathbf{p}_3 = (4.061, 3.061)$
$\mathbf{p}_4 = (3.574, 3.386)$
$\mathbf{p}_5 = (3.0, 3.5)$
$\mathbf{p}_6 = (2.426, 3.386$
$\mathbf{p}_7 = (1.939, 3.061)$
$\mathbf{p}_8 = (1.614, 2.574)$
$\mathbf{p}_9 = (1.5, 2.0)$
$\mathbf{p}_{10} = (1.614, 1.426)$
$\mathbf{p}_{11} = (1.939, 0.939)$
$\mathbf{p}_{12} = (2.426, 0.614)$
$\mathbf{p}_{13} = (3.0, 0.5)$
$\mathbf{p}_{14} = (3.574, 0.614)$
$\mathbf{p}_{15} = (4.061, 0.939)$
$\mathbf{p}_{16} = (4.386, 1.426)$

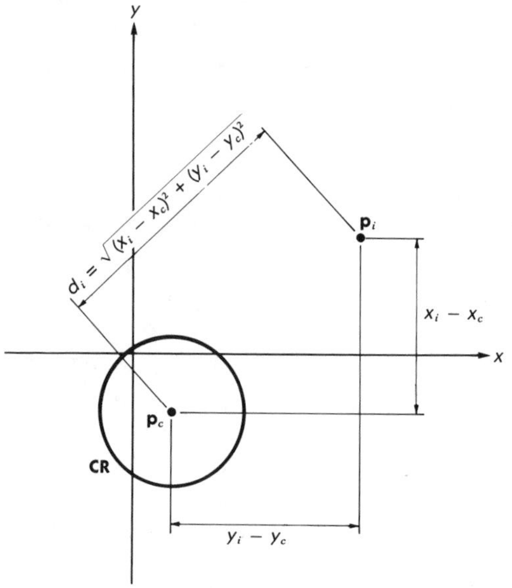

Fig. 8.12. Point classification with respect to a circle.

may be entirely disjoint, they may intersect, or they may be tangent. Determine these relationships by computing the distance, d, between the centers of the two circles; thus

$$\mathbf{CR}_1 \ \langle\text{inside}\rangle\ \mathbf{CR}_2 \text{ if and only if } d < r_2 - r_1 \tag{8.22}$$

where $r_2 > r_1$; see Fig. 8.13a.

$$\mathbf{CR}_1 \ \langle\text{outside}\rangle\ \mathbf{CR}_2 \text{ if and only if } d > r_1 + r_2 \tag{8.23}$$

See Fig. 8.13b.

$$\mathbf{CR}_1 \ \langle\text{intersect}\rangle\ \mathbf{CR}_2 \text{ if and only if } r_2 - r_1 < d < r_1 + r_2 \tag{8.24}$$

See Fig. 8.13c.

$$\mathbf{CR}_1 \ \langle\text{internally tangent}\rangle\ \mathbf{CR}_2 \text{ if and only if } d = r_2 - r_1 \tag{8.25}$$

See Fig. 8.13d.

$$\mathbf{CR}_1 \ \langle\text{externally tangent}\rangle\ \mathbf{CR}_2 \text{ if and only if } d = r_1 + r_2 \tag{8.26}$$

See Fig. 8.13e.

Now consider the classification of a circle and a rectangle. This is a much more complex problem and requires several steps to solve it. First rewrite Eq. (8.18), expressing the geometric condition that it implies as a function of an arbitrary point $\mathbf{p}_i$; see Fig. 8.14. Thus,

$$f(\mathbf{p}_i) = (x_i - x_c)^2 + (y_i - y_c)^2 - r^2 \tag{8.27}$$

where $\mathbf{p}_i = (x_i, y_i)$. It is easy to see that

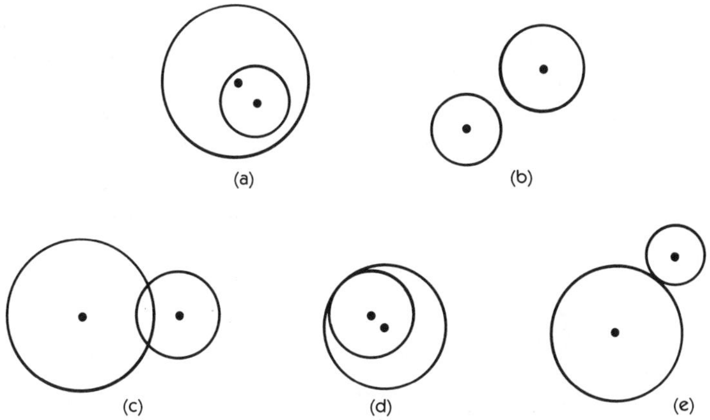

Fig. 8.13. Relationships between two circles.

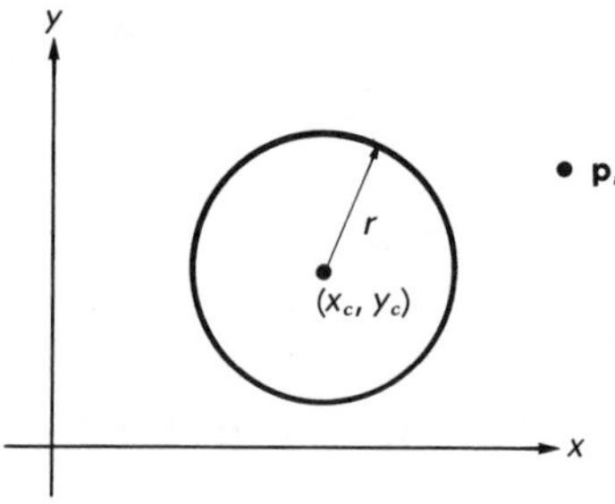

Fig. 8.14. A circle and an arbitrary point.

$$
\begin{aligned}
&\text{If } f(\mathbf{p}_i) > 0, \text{ then } \mathbf{p}_i \ \langle\text{outside}\rangle\ \mathbf{CR}\\
&\text{If } f(\mathbf{p}_i) < 0, \text{ then } \mathbf{p}_i \ \langle\text{inside}\rangle\ \mathbf{CR}\\
&\text{If } f(\mathbf{p}_i) = 0, \text{ then } \mathbf{p}_i \ \langle\text{boundary}\rangle\ \mathbf{CR}
\end{aligned}
\tag{8.28}
$$

Next, given a specific rectangle and circle, classify each vertex point of the rectangle with respect to the circle using Eq. (8.28). Table 8.1 lists all the possible distributions of vertex points, with the resulting rectangle and circle classification. See illustrations of each distribution in Fig. 8.15.

Conditions 14 and 15 are indeterminate solely on the basis of the distribution of the rectangle's vertex point; we need to analyze this further. Figures 8.15l and 8.15m show that we can further subdivide these con-

Table 8.1. Rectangle and Circle Classification

Condition	Rectangle Vertex Point Distribution: Inside Circle	Boundary of Circle	Outside Circle	Classification
1	4	0	0	**RN** ⟨inside⟩ **CR**
2	3	1	0	**RN** ⟨inside⟩ **CR**
3	3	0	1	**RN** ⟨intersect⟩ **CR**
4	2	2	0	**RN** ⟨inside⟩ **CR**
5	2	1	1	**RN** ⟨intersect⟩ **CR**
6	2	0	2	**RN** ⟨intersect⟩ **CR**
7	1	3	0	[a]
8	1	2	1	**RN** ⟨intersect⟩ **CR**
9	1	1	2	**RN** ⟨intersect⟩ **CR**
10	1	0	3	**RN** ⟨intersect⟩ **CR**
11	0	4	0	**RN** ⟨inside⟩ **CR**
12	0	3	1	[a]
13	0	2	2	**RN** ⟨intersect⟩ **CR**
14	0	1	3	Indeterminate
15	0	0	4	Indeterminate

[a] Conditions 7 and 12 are the same as Condition 11. In fact, if three rectangle vertex points are on the boundary of the circle, then the fourth point must also be on the boundary.

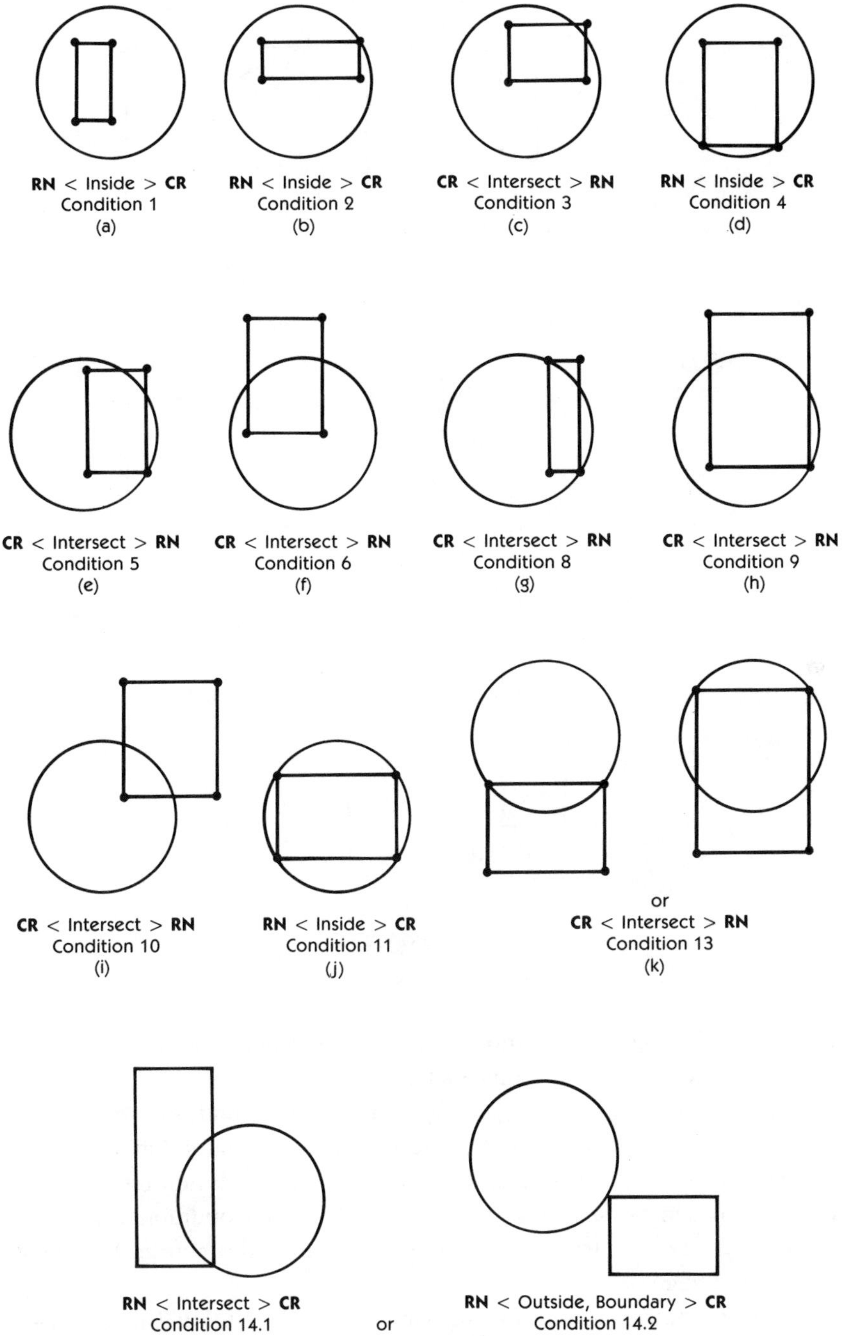

Fig. 8.15. Rectangle vertex point distribution with respect to a circle.

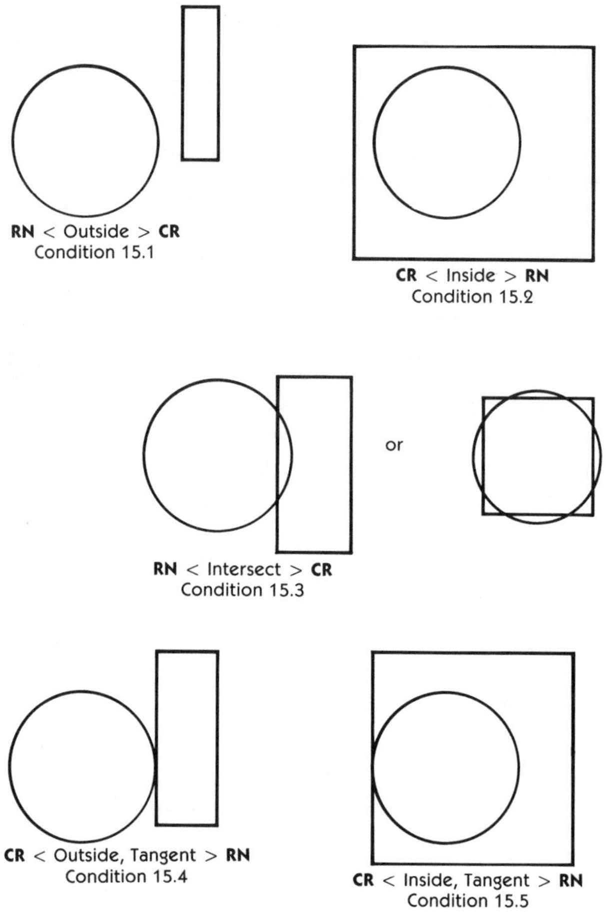

Fig. 8.15 (continued)

ditions. If the point distribution indicates that Condition 14 exists, then distinguish between Conditions 14.1 and 14.2 as follows.

If $x_{min} < x_c < x_{max}$ or $y_{min} < y_c < y_{max}$, then Condition 14.1 exists; otherwise Condition 14.2 exists. The coordinate conjunction "or" is inclusive, meaning either "one or the other" or "both." When the center of the circle lies in the shaded region in Fig. 8.16, then Condition 14.1 exists. Both inequalities are true if the center of the circle lies within the boundary of the rectangle.

There is another way to distinguish between Condition 14.1 and 14.2; use the following set of inequalities, so that if

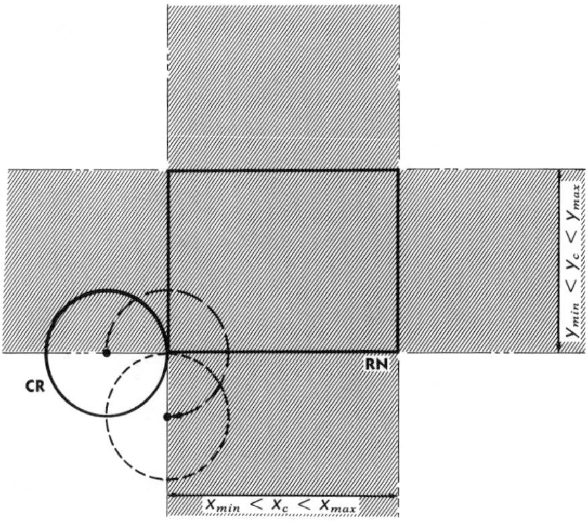

Fig. 8.16. Condition 14 requirements.

$$\begin{aligned} &x_c \leq x_{\min} \text{ and } y_c \leq y_{\min} \text{ or} \\ &x_c \geq x_{\max} \text{ and } y_c \leq y_{\min} \text{ or} \\ &x_c \geq x_{\max} \text{ and } y_c \geq y_{\max} \text{ or} \\ &x_c \leq x_{\min} \text{ and } y_c \geq y_{\max} \end{aligned} \tag{8.29}$$

then Condition 14.2 exists; otherwise Condition 14.1 exists. This time the "or" is exclusive, meaning "one or the other, but not both." These inequalities define the shaded regions in Fig. 8.17. The center of the circle

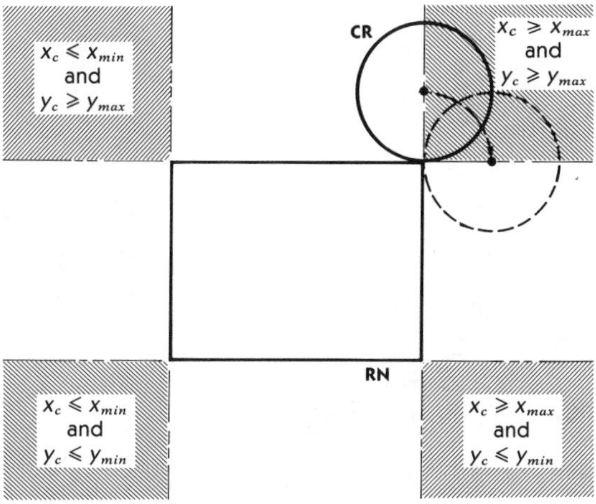

Fig. 8.17. Alternative condition 14 requirements.

lies in one of them if exactly one of the four sets of inequalities in Eq. (8.29) is true.

If the point distribution indicates that Condition 15 exists, then distinguish between the five possible subdivisions as follows:

1. **RN** ⟨outside⟩ **CR** if one of the following inequalities is true:

$$\begin{aligned} &x_{\min} - x_c > r \text{ or (exclusive)} \\ &x_c - x_{\max} > r \text{ or (inclusive)} \\ &y_{\min} - y_c > r \text{ or (exclusive)} \\ &y_c - y_{\max} > r \end{aligned} \tag{8.30a}$$

Then Condition 15.1 exists. See the example of Fig. 8.18a; here the first and third instance of the coordinate conjunction "or" is exclusive, because the two inequalities with $x_{\min}$ and $x_{\max}$ terms cannot be simultaneously true, and similarly for the two inequalities with $y_{\min}$ and $y_{\max}$ terms.

The rectangle may be outside the circle even though none of the inequalities of Eq. (8.30a) are true. Thus, **RN** ⟨outside⟩ **CR** if one of the following conditions are true; see Fig. 8.18b.

$$\begin{aligned} &x_c < x_{\min} \text{ and } y_c < y_{\min} \text{ and } \sqrt{(x_{\min} - x_c)^2 + (y_{\min} - y_c)^2} \geq r \text{ or} \\ &x_c < x_{\min} \text{ and } y_c > y_{\max} \text{ and } \sqrt{(x_{\min} - x_c)^2 + (y_{\max} - y_c)^2} \geq r \text{ or} \\ &x_c > x_{\max} \text{ and } y_c < y_{\min} \text{ and } \sqrt{(x_{\max} - x_c)^2 + (y_{\min} - y_c)^2} \geq r \text{ or} \\ &x_c > x_{\max} \text{ and } y_c > y_{\max} \text{ and } \sqrt{(x_{\max} - x_c)^2 + (y_{\max} - y_c)^2} \geq r \end{aligned} \tag{8.30b}$$

2. **CR** ⟨inside⟩ **RN** if and only if all of the following inequalities are true:

$$\begin{aligned} &x_c - x_{\min} > r \text{ and} \\ &x_{\max} - x_c > r \text{ and} \\ &y_c - y_{\min} > r \text{ and} \\ &y_{\max} - y_c > r \end{aligned} \tag{8.31}$$

Then Condition 15.2 exists; see Fig. 8.19.

3. **RN** ⟨intersect⟩ **CR** if and only if

$$\begin{aligned} &|x_{\min} - x_c| < r \text{ or} \\ &|x_c - x_{\max}| < r \text{ or} \\ &|y_{\min} - y_c| < r \text{ or} \\ &|y_c - y_{\max}| < r \end{aligned} \tag{8.32}$$

Then Condition 15.3 exists. Here "or" is inclusive; see Fig. 8.20.

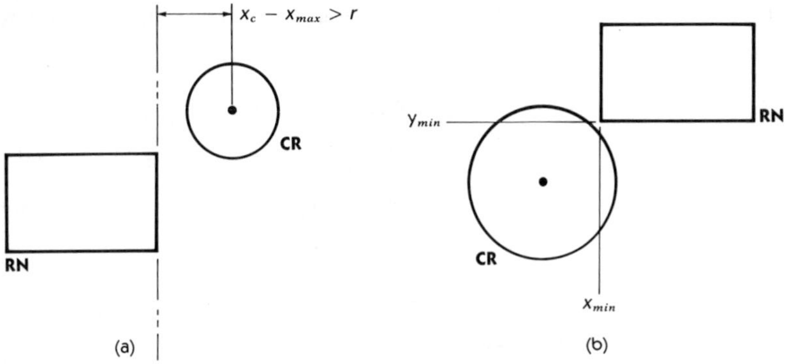

Fig. 8.18. Condition 15.1.

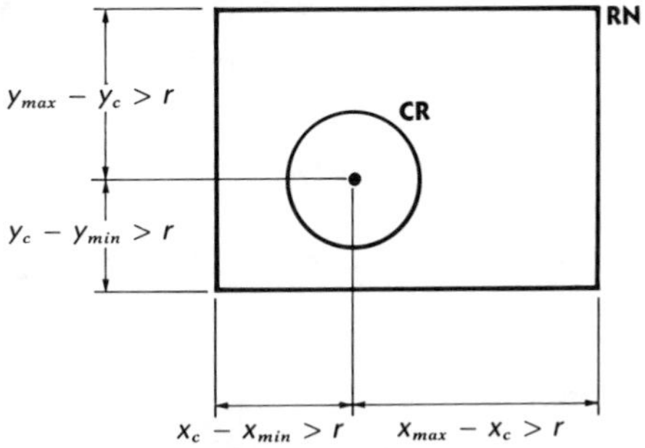

Fig. 8.19. Condition 15.2.

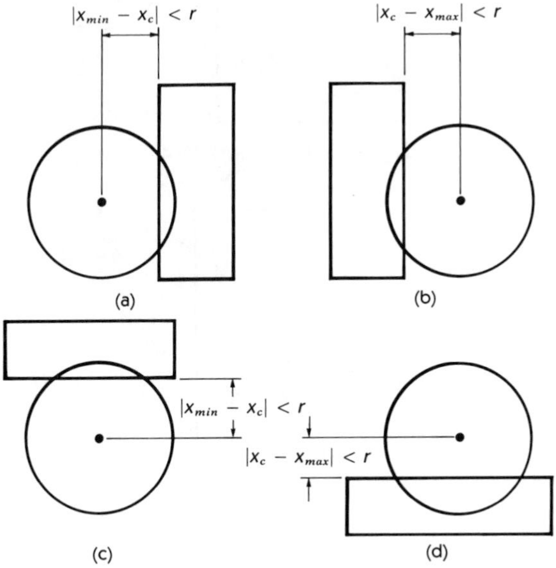

Fig. 8.20. Condition 15.3.

4. **CR** ⟨outside, tangent⟩ **RN** if and only if one of the following four sets of equations and inequalities is true:

$$x_{\min} - x_c = r \text{ and } y_{\min} < y_c < y_{\max} \text{ or} \tag{8.33}$$

$$x_c - x_{\max} = r \text{ and } y_{\min} < y_c < y_{\max} \text{ or} \tag{8.34}$$

$$y_{\min} - y_c = r \text{ and } x_{\min} < x_c < x_{\max} \text{ or} \tag{8.35}$$

$$y_c - y_{\max} = r \text{ and } x_{\min} < x_c < x_{\max} \tag{8.36}$$

Then Condition 15.4 exists. Here "or" is exclusive. See the example illustrating Eq. (8.36) in Fig. 8.21.

5. **CR** ⟨inside, tangent⟩ **RN** if and only if

$$\begin{aligned} x_c - x_{\min} &\geq r \text{ and} \\ x_{\max} - x_c &\geq r \text{ and} \\ y_c - y_{\min} &\geq r \text{ and} \\ y_{\max} - y_c &\geq r \end{aligned} \tag{8.37}$$

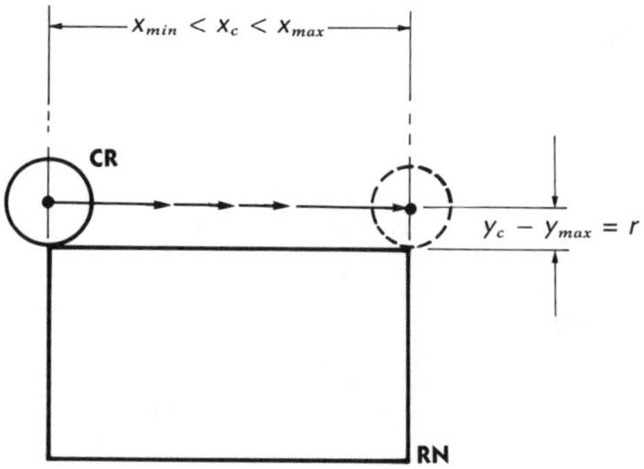

Fig. 8.21. Condition 15.4.

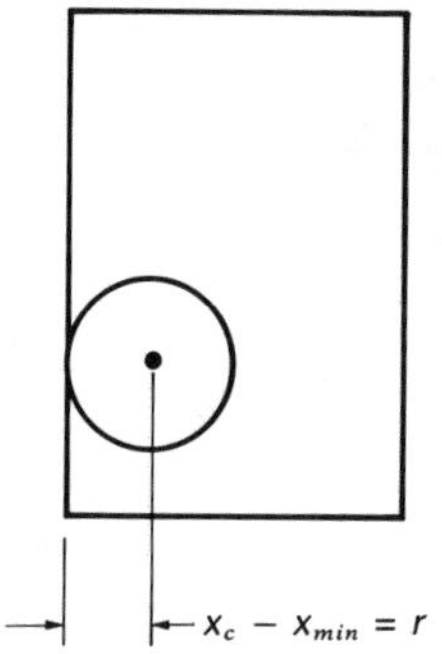

Fig. 8.22. Condition 15.5.

where at least one of the four expressions is an equality; then Condition 15.5 exists. See Fig. 8.22, which illustrates that the first expression is satisfied as an equality and that the remaining expressions are true inequalities.

EXERCISES

1. Which of the following expressions improperly specify circles, and why?

a. $\mathbf{CR}_1(0,0,0)$	f. $\mathbf{CR}_6(7,10,3)$
b. $\mathbf{CR}_2(0,0,-1)$	g. $\mathbf{CR}_7(3.5,2.5,50.5)$
c. $\mathbf{CR}_3(0,0,1)$	h. $\mathbf{CR}_8(7.5,-0.5)$
d. $\mathbf{CR}_4(-3,2,6)$	i. $\mathbf{CR}_9(0,0,49.50)$
e. $\mathbf{CR}_5(7,10,2,1)$	j. $\mathbf{CR}_{10}(1,1,1)$

2. Draw the following circles on graph paper:

   a. $\mathbf{CR}_1(-1.5,0,1.5)$
   b. $\mathbf{CR}_2(0,0,1)$
   c. $\mathbf{CR}_3(0.75,2.50,0.75)$
   d. $\mathbf{CR}_4(3,2,1.5)$
   e. $\mathbf{CR}_5(4,-0.5,0.75)$

3. Write the defining arguments for the circles shown in Fig. 8.23.

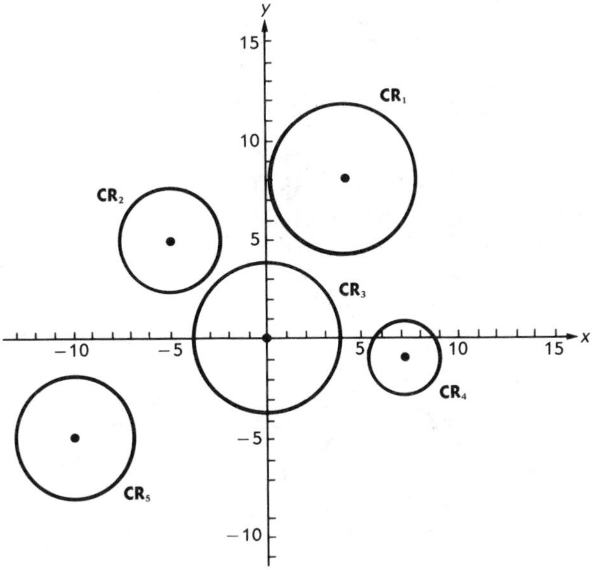

Fig. 8.23. Five circles.

4. Given $\mathbf{CR}_1 = \mathbf{CR}_1(4,1,3)$, classify the following points. Solve this problem analytically, not graphically.

a. $\mathbf{p}_1 = (1,1)$
b. $\mathbf{p}_2 = (4,3)$
c. $\mathbf{p}_3 = (6,4)$
d. $\mathbf{p}_4 = (5, 1 - \sqrt{8})$
e. $\mathbf{p}_5 = (5, \sqrt{10})$

5. Given $\mathbf{CR}_0 = \mathbf{CR}_0(-1,-1,3)$, classify the following circles with respect to $\mathbf{CR}_0$:

a. $\mathbf{CR}_1(-3,5,1.4)$
b. $\mathbf{CR}_2(5,5,0.75)$
c. $\mathbf{CR}_3(-1,0,3)$
d. $\mathbf{CR}_4(0,2,0.75)$
e. $\mathbf{CR}_5(-2,1,0.5)$
f. $\mathbf{CR}_6(-1,-1,1.5)$
g. $\mathbf{CR}_7(-5,-1,1)$
h. $\mathbf{CR}_8(0.5,1,1.5)$
i. $\mathbf{CR}_9(-1,-5,1)$
j. $\mathbf{CR}_{10}(4,-3,2)$

6. Given $\mathbf{RN}_1 = \mathbf{RN}_1(0,0,12,6)$, $\mathbf{CR}_1 = \mathbf{CR}_1(3,3,1.5)$, and $\mathbf{CR}_2 = \mathbf{CR}_2(9,3,1.5)$, assume that the two circles define holes in a solid rectangular shape. Classify the following points with respect to this shape. Note that you should classify points in the holes as outside the shape. (*Hint*: Use a systematic approach, and classify each point with respect to the rectangle first; then only those that fall inside the rectangle require further testing and classifying with respect to the circles.)

a. $\mathbf{p}_1 = (0,4)$
b. $\mathbf{p}_2 = (2,5)$
c. $\mathbf{p}_3 = (8,6)$
d. $\mathbf{p}_4 = (9,9)$
e. $\mathbf{p}_5 = (15,6)$
f. $\mathbf{p}_6 = (3,4)$
g. $\mathbf{p}_7 = (6,3)$
h. $\mathbf{p}_8 = (9,3)$
i. $\mathbf{p}_9 = (9,1.5)$
j. $\mathbf{p}_{10} = (3,-1)$

7. Classify the relationship of the following sets of circles and squares:

a. $\mathbf{CR} = \mathbf{CR}(1,-1,3)$, $\mathbf{RN} = \mathbf{RN}(-2,-4,8,7)$
b. $\mathbf{CR} = \mathbf{CR}(-2,3,1.5)$, $\mathbf{RN} = \mathbf{RN}(-2,-3,5,5)$
c. $\mathbf{CR} = \mathbf{CR}(0,0,2)$, $\mathbf{RN} = \mathbf{RN}(-3,-1,6,2)$
d. $\mathbf{CR} = \mathbf{CR}(4,5,3)$, $\mathbf{RN} = \mathbf{RN}(2,3,1,4)$
e. $\mathbf{CR} = \mathbf{CR}(3,4,2)$, $\mathbf{RN} = \mathbf{RN}(-1,1,2,5)$

8. Write a procedure to compute the perimeter and area of a circle. Denote this as **CRPROP**(CR,P,A), where

CR(3) are the input values of x_c, y_c, and r,
P is the output perimeter, and
A is the output area.

9. Write a procedure to classify a point with respect to a circle. Denote this as **CRPT**(CR,PT,ICLS), where

CR(3) are the input values of x_c, y_c, and r,
PT(2) are the input coordinates of the point, and
ICLS is the output classification of the point:
ICLS = 1 if the point is outside,
ICLS = 2 if the point is inside, and
ICLS = 3 if the point is on the boundary.

10. Write a procedure to classify the relationship between two circles. Denote this as **CRCR**(CR1,CR2,ICLS) where

CR1(3), CR2(3) are the input values of x_c, y_c, and r, and
ICLS is the output classification of CR1 with respect to CR2:
ICLS = 1 if $\mathbf{CR}_1$ ⟨outside⟩ $\mathbf{CR}_2$,
ICLS = 2 if $\mathbf{CR}_1$ ⟨outside, tangent⟩ $\mathbf{CR}_2$,
ICLS = 3 if $\mathbf{CR}_1$ ⟨intersect⟩ $\mathbf{CR}_2$,
ICLS = 4 if $\mathbf{CR}_1$ ⟨inside⟩ $\mathbf{CR}_2$,
ICLS = 5 if $\mathbf{CR}_2$ ⟨inside⟩ $\mathbf{CR}_1$,
ICLS = 6 if $\mathbf{CR}_1$ ⟨inside, tangent⟩ $\mathbf{CR}_2$,
ICLS = 7 if $\mathbf{CR}_2$ ⟨inside, tangent⟩ $\mathbf{CR}_1$,
ICLS = 8 if $\mathbf{CR}_1$ ⟨inside, concentric⟩ $\mathbf{CR}_2$,
ICLS = 9 if $\mathbf{CR}_2$ ⟨inside, concentric⟩ $\mathbf{CR}_1$, and
ICLS = 10 if $\mathbf{CR}_1$ ⟨concentric, equal⟩ $\mathbf{CR}_2$.

11. Write a procedure to classify the relationship between a circle and a rectangle. Denote this as **CRRN** (CR, RN, ICLS), where

CR(3) are the input values of x_c, y_c, and r,
RN(4) are the input values of x_0, y_0, a_x, and a_y, and
ICLS is the output classification:
ICLS = 1 if **CR** ⟨outside⟩ **RN**,
ICLS = 2 if **CR** ⟨outside, tangent⟩ **RN**,
ICLS = 3 if **CR** ⟨intersect⟩ **RN**,
ICLS = 4 if **CR** ⟨inside⟩ **RN**,
ICLS = 5 if **RN** ⟨inside⟩ **CR**, and
ICLS = 6 if **CR** ⟨inside, tangent⟩ **RN**.

8.4. Combining Elements

Combining elementary shapes to form more complex shapes is an important part of computer graphics and geometric modeling. You will study three kinds of combining operations: **union, difference,** and **intersect**. Box 8.2 and Box 8.3 elaborate on these and other concepts of set theory.

Box 8.2. Set Theory: Basic Concepts

The term **set** means any well-defined collection of objects. Objects belonging to a set are its elements, or members. In the geometry of computer graphics, the basic element is the point.

A set containing all the elements of all the sets under consideration is the **universal set,** symbolized by *E*. In geometry, for example, *E* is often taken as all the points in two- (or three-) dimensional space. The **complement** of a set, *A*, with respect to a universal set, *E*, is the set of all elements in *E* that are not elements in *A*, written cA.

A **null set** is a set having no elements at all, symbolized by $\emptyset$. It is sometimes called the empty set or the void set.

Any set *A* is a subset of *B* only if every element in *A* is also an element in *B*. The symbol $\subset$ indicates the subset relationship. Thus, $A \subset B$ means that *A* is a subset of *B*. If *B* consists of the points on the unit interval, then the interval from 0.1 to 0.3 is a subset of *B*.

New sets are formed by combining the elements in two or more sets. For example, given sets *A* and *B*, construct a third set, *C*, whose elements are all the elements in *A* plus all the elements in *B*. Write this as

$$C = A \cup B$$

This is the **union** of two sets. For example, if $A = \{a, b, c\}$ and $B = \{c, d, e, f\}$, then $C = A \cup B = \{a, b, c, d, e, f\}$

You can form a set, *D*, containing only elements common to both *A* and *B*. Set *D* is called the **intersection** of *A* and *B* and is written as

$$D = A \cap B$$

So, if $A = \{a, b, c, d\}$, and $B = \{c, d, e, f, g\}$, then $D = \{c, d\}$.

Finally, $A - B$ denotes the set of elements in *A* that are not also elements in *B*. This is the difference of two sets.

(See Box 8.3 for a more graphic view of set theory.)

UNION

The union operator unites, or adds, two shapes to form a third shape. It is denoted by the symbol $\cup$. If *A* and *B* are two shapes, then $A \cup B = C$, where the shape *C* consists of all points that are in *A*, in *B*, or in both *A* and *B*. Use ordinary capital letters to denote arbitrary, general shapes, and **SQ**, **RN**, and **CR** to denote the three special elementary shapes.

Let $\mathbf{RN}_1 = \mathbf{RN}_1(4,4,8,5)$ and $\mathbf{RN}_2 = \mathbf{RN}_2(9,6,7,5)$, and then represent the union of these two rectangles as $A = \mathbf{RN}_1 \cup \mathbf{RN}_2$; see the result in Fig. 8.24. A bold line defines the boundary of the new shape, and a shaded area

Box 8.3. Venn Diagrams

A convenient way to study sets and subsets is by using Venn diagrams. Venn diagrams graphically interpret the properties of, and operations on, sets. In computer graphics and geometric modeling, sets consist of points, and the universal set E is the set of points defining a Euclidean space with a dimension of your choice. Set theory, through Venn Diagrams, suggests ways to operate on these points and classify them according to such properties as inside, outside, or on the boundary of some geometric object.

Study the four Venn diagrams below. Each circular region represents something, perhaps geometric points (or a surface or solid, for example), perhaps types of demographic data. The shaded region in each diagram is the outcome of the indicated operations.

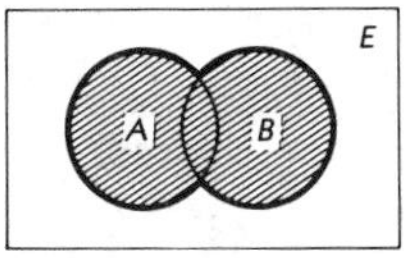

$A \cup B$

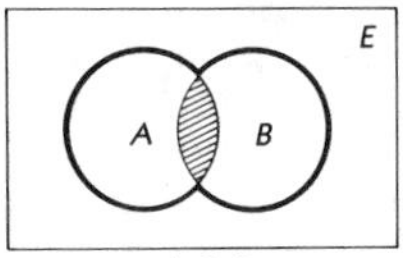

$A \cap B$

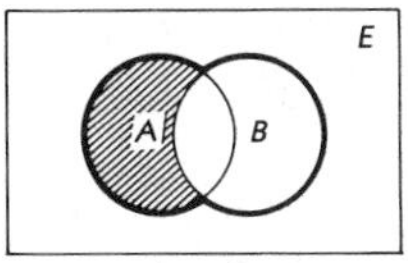

$A - B$

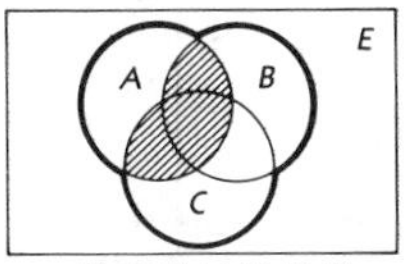

$(A \cap B) \cup (A \cap C)$

defines the interior of it. Note that there are two kinds of points in A: those inside it and those on its boundary; express this as

$$A = bA \cup iA \tag{8.38}$$

where b indicates boundary and i indicates interior. This equation means that a shape A consists of the union of its boundary points, bA, and interior points, iA. Similar expressions for $\mathbf{RN}_1$ and $\mathbf{RN}_2$ are

$$\mathbf{RN}_1 = b\mathbf{RN}_1 \cup i\mathbf{RN}_1 \quad \text{and} \quad \mathbf{RN}_2 = b\mathbf{RN}_2 \cup i\mathbf{RN}_2 \tag{8.39}$$

Note in Fig. 8.24 that the boundary of A consists of part of the boundary of $\mathbf{RN}_1$ and part of the boundary of $\mathbf{RN}_2$. No interior points of $\mathbf{RN}_1$ and $\mathbf{RN}_2$ contribute to the boundary of $\mathbf{RN}_1 \cup \mathbf{RN}_2$, but iA consists of points from both the boundary and interior of $\mathbf{RN}_1$ and $\mathbf{RN}_2$.

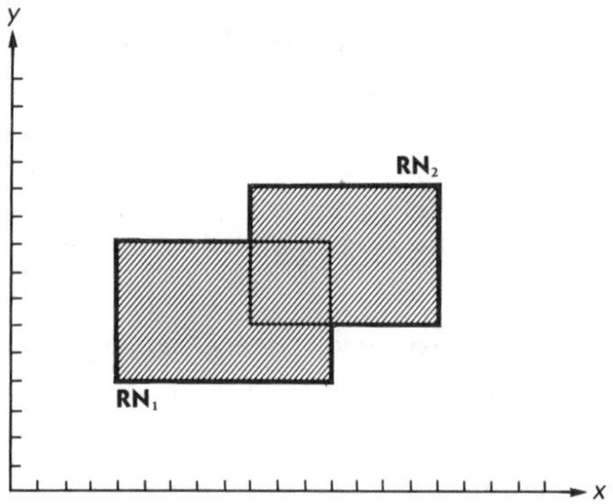

Fig. 8.24. Union of two rectangles.

How are points classified with respect to the result of the union of two shapes? More specifically, how are points on the elementary shapes classified with respect to the result of their union? Figure 8.25 shows four important spatial arrangements to distinguish among when analyzing the union of two rectangles. Table 8.2 presents the eight possible combinations of point classification for two rectangles joined by the union operator. Points falling outside both $\mathbf{RN}_1$ and $\mathbf{RN}_2$ are not included.

Note that only Condition 2 is indeterminate. Here a point lies on the boundary of both $\mathbf{RN}_1$ and $\mathbf{RN}_2$, and we need to analyze it further. Figures

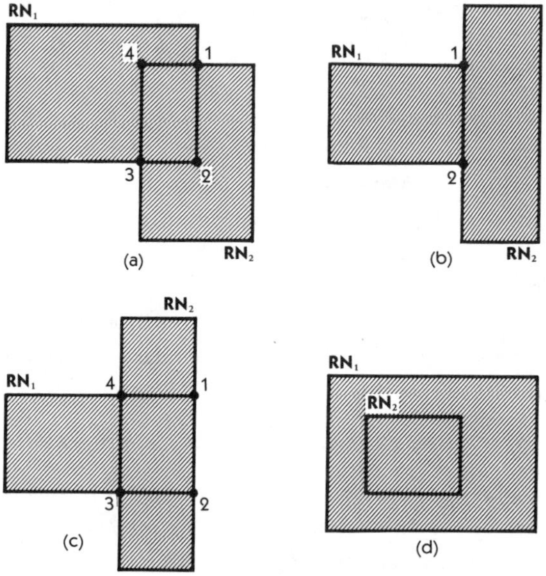

Fig. 8.25. $\mathbf{RN}_1 \cup \mathbf{RN}_2$: four important spatial arrangements.

Table 8.2. $RN_1 \cup RN_2$: Point Classification

	If				Then	
Condition	$b\mathbf{RN}_1$	$i\mathbf{RN}_1$	$b\mathbf{RN}_2$	$i\mathbf{RN}_2$	$b(\mathbf{RN}_1 \cup \mathbf{RN}_2)$	$i(\mathbf{RN}_1 \cup \mathbf{RN}_2)$
1	X				X	
2	X		X		Indeterminate	
3	X			X		X
4		X				X
5		X	X			X
6		X		X		X
7			X		X	
8				X		X

8.25b and 8.25c show two ways rectangle boundaries may coincide. In Fig. 8.25b the coincident segments of the boundaries are part of $i(\mathbf{RN}_1 \cup \mathbf{RN}_2)$; in Fig. 8.25c they are part of $b(\mathbf{RN}_1 \cup \mathbf{RN}_2)$. Distinguish between them as follows:

For two rectangles, only four spatial arrangements produce coincident boundary segments interior to their union; see Fig. 8.26. These arrangements satisfy one and only one of the following four conditions

$$\begin{aligned} x_{\max,1} &= x_{\min,2} \text{ or} \\ x_{\min,1} &= x_{\max,2} \text{ or} \\ y_{\max,1} &= y_{\min,2} \text{ or} \\ y_{\min,1} &= y_{\max,2} \end{aligned} \tag{8.40}$$

where "or" is exclusive.

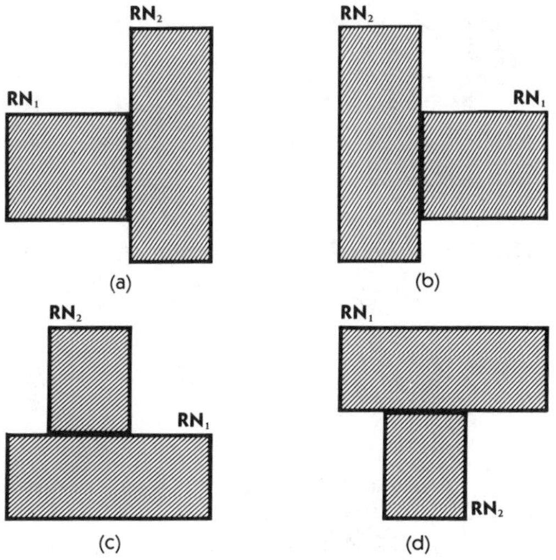

Fig. 8.26. $\mathbf{RN}_1 \cup \mathbf{RN}_2$: coincident interior boundaries.

For two rectangles, only four spatial arrangements will produce coincident boundary segments on the boundary of their union; see Fig. 8.27. These arrangements satisfy one or more of the following four conditions:

$$
\begin{aligned}
x_{\max,1} &= x_{\max,2} \text{ or} \\
x_{\min,1} &= x_{\min,2} \text{ or} \\
y_{\max,1} &= y_{\max,2} \text{ or} \\
y_{\min,1} &= y_{\min,2}
\end{aligned}
\tag{8.41}
$$

where "or" is inclusive.

The union of two circles produces classification results nearly identical to the results for two rectangles; see Fig. 8.28. Table 8.3 presents the eight possible combinations of point classification for two circles joined by the

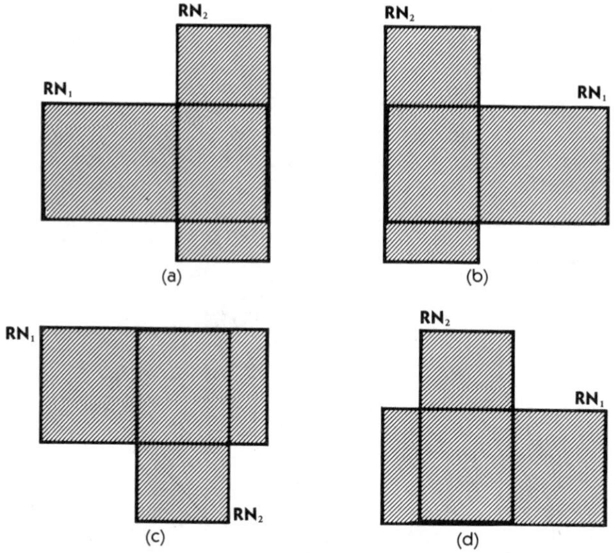

Fig. 8.27. **RN_1** ∪ **RN_2**: Coincident exterior boundaries.

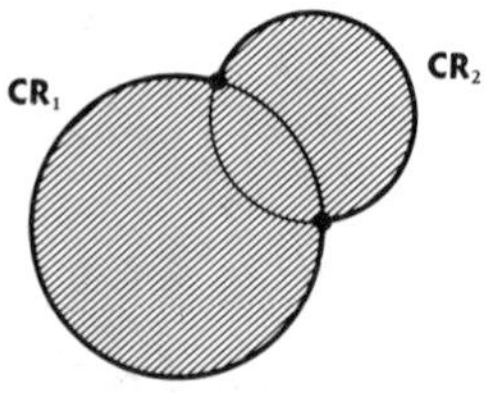

Fig. 8.28. Union of two circles.

Table 8.3. $\mathbf{CR}_1 \cup \mathbf{CR}_2$: Point Classification

	If				Then	
Condition	$b\mathbf{CR}_1$	$i\mathbf{CR}_1$	$b\mathbf{CR}_2$	$i\mathbf{CR}_2$	$b(\mathbf{CR}_1 \cup \mathbf{CR}_2)$	$i(\mathbf{CR}_1 \cup \mathbf{CR}_2)$
1	X				X	
2	X		X		X	
3	X			X		X
4		X				X
5		X	X			X
6		X		X		X
7			X		X	
8				X		X

union operator. Again, points falling outside both of these elements are not included.

Note that for two circles Condition 2 is not indeterminate. Only the two points of intersection satisfy this condition, and they are clearly on $b(\mathbf{CR}_1 \cup \mathbf{CR}_2)$.

The union of a rectangle and a circle produces classification results identical to results for two circles; see Fig. 8.29 and Table 8.4. In fact, this same approach to classifying points applies to the union of any two arbitrary shapes, and you can construct a similar table of classification combinations; see Table 8.5.

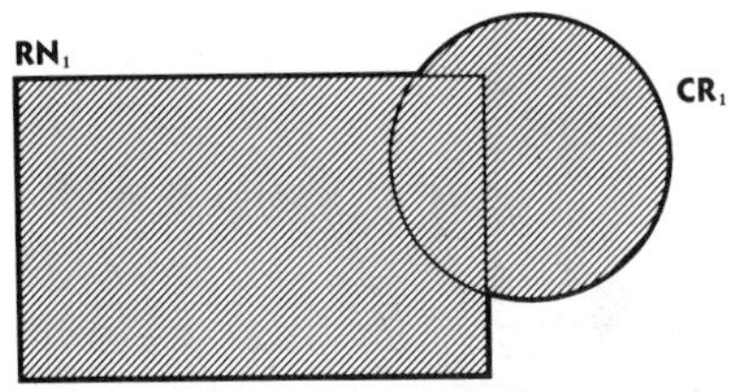

Fig. 8.29. Union of a rectangle and a circle.

Table 8.4. $\mathbf{RN}_1 \cup \mathbf{CR}_1$: Point Classification

	If				Then	
Condition	$b\mathbf{RN}_1$	$i\mathbf{RN}_1$	$b\mathbf{CR}_2$	$i\mathbf{CR}_2$	$b(\mathbf{RN}_1 \cup \mathbf{CR}_1)$	$i(\mathbf{RN}_1 \cup \mathbf{CR}_1)$
1	X				X	
2	X		X		X	
3	X			X		X
4		X				X
5		X	X			X
6		X		X		X
7			X		X	
8				X		X

Table 8.5. $A \cup B$: Point Classification

	If				Then	
Condition	*bA*	*iA*	*bB*	*iB*	$b(A \cup B)$	$i(A \cup B)$
1	X				X	
2	X		X		Indeterminate (?)	
3	X			X		X
4		X				X
5		X	X			X
6		X		X		X
7			X		X	
8				X		X

Applying the union operator sequentially to a series of shapes produces a new shape; thus,

$$A_0 = A_1 \cup A_2 \cup A_3 \cup \cdots \cup A_n \tag{8.42a}$$

The order of a sequence of union operations is not important; thus

$$A = B \cup C \cup D = C \cup B \cup D \tag{8.42b}$$

See the example in Fig. 8.30. The more complex shape A can itself be combined with another shape or shapes to produce new, even more complex shapes. The geometric model of shape A_0, given by Eq. (8.42a), consists of a set of other shapes A_i and the operators that combine them.

For a complex model defined by the union of many simpler shapes (such as rectangles and circles), classify the points as follows: First classify the given point with respect to each of the simple shapes, then evaluate the results.

1. If the point lies in the interior of any one of the simple shapes, then classify it as being inside the combined shape, regardless of its classification with respect to the remaining simple shapes.

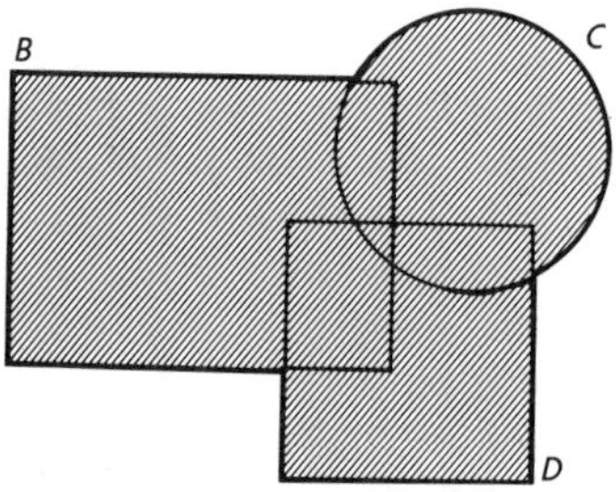

Fig. 8.30. Union of three shapes.

2. If the point lies on the boundary of one and only one of the simple shapes, then classify it as being on the boundary of the combined shape.

3. If the point lies on the boundary of more than one simple shape and is inside none of them, then analyze it further.

The ability to classify a point with respect to a geometric model is central to analyzing it quantitatively and understanding it. Our experience so far with a model tells us that we must be able to determine which points are inside the model, which are on its boundary, and which are outside of the model. We will continue to use point classification when we analyze the difference and intersect operators.

DIFFERENCE

The difference operator subtracts one shape from another to form a third shape; it is denoted by the minus sign. If A and B are two shapes, then $C = A - B$, where the shape C consists of all points in A that are not also in B. Figure 8.31 shows the difference between two rectangles; note that

$$\mathbf{RN}_1 - \mathbf{RN}_2 \neq \mathbf{RN}_2 - \mathbf{RN}_1 \tag{8.43}$$

and in general,

$$C - D \neq D - C \tag{8.44}$$

Thus, the order of the operands is important.

Using the difference operator, you can easily create holes in shapes; see Fig. 8.32. In fact, you can entirely negate a shape; for example, if A ⟨inside⟩ B, then $A - B = \emptyset$, where the symbol $\emptyset$ denotes a **null** object or the

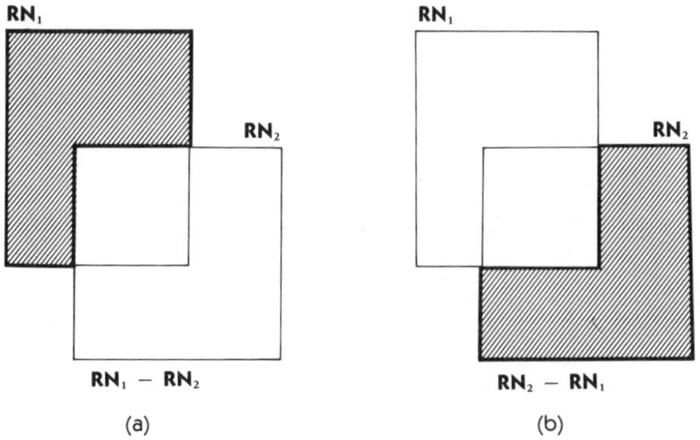

Fig. 8.31. Difference between two rectangles.

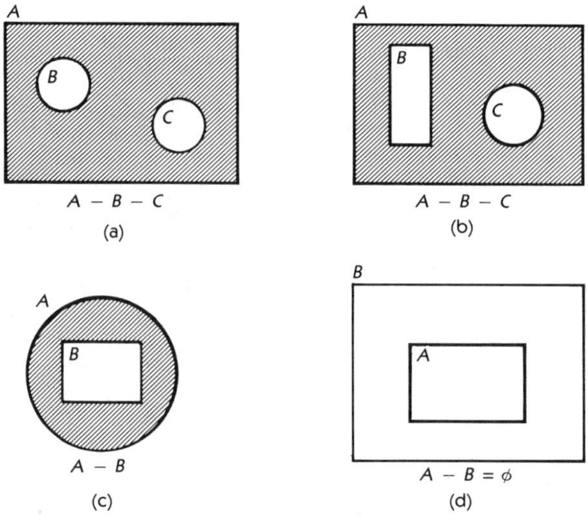

Fig. 8.32. Creating holes with the difference operator.

nonexistence of any object. This is equivalent to the arithmetic zero; see Fig. 8.32d. As you might suspect, you can use the difference operator to create two or more disjoint (unconnected) shapes from one initial shape; Fig. 8.33 shows several examples.

How are points classified with respect to the result of the difference between two shapes? Figure 8.34 shows four spatial arrangements to distinguish between. We use rectangles because they are likely to have coincident boundaries. Table 8.6 presents the eight possible combinations of point classification for two rectangles joined by the difference operator. Again, points falling outside both $\mathbf{RN}_1$ and $\mathbf{RN}_2$ are not included.

The last column of the table is labeled $o(\mathbf{RN}_1 - \mathbf{RN}_2)$, and it denotes points on $\mathbf{RN}_1$ or $\mathbf{RN}_2$ but outside the result of their difference.

Condition 2 is indeterminant. For the particular case of rectangles whose sides are parallel to the coordinate axes, distinguish the arrangements shown

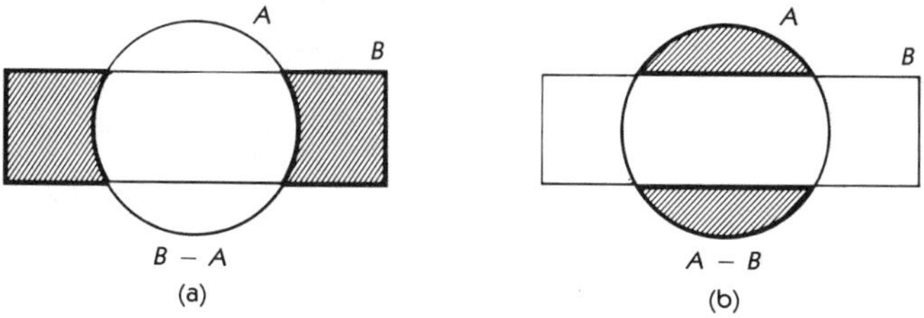

Fig. 8.33. Creating two shapes with the difference operator.

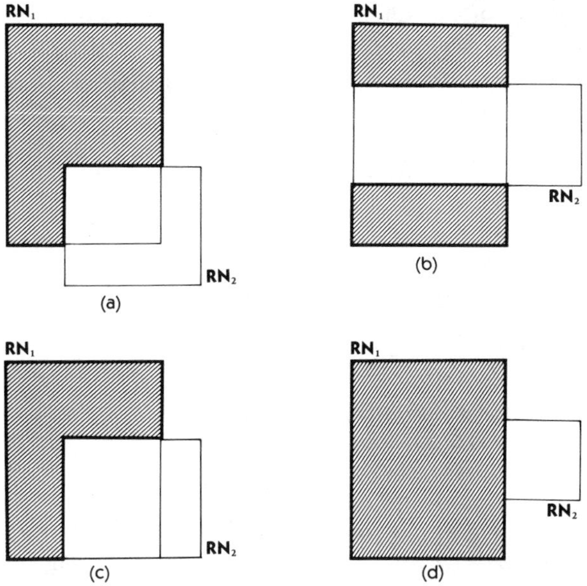

Fig. 8.34. $\mathbf{RN}_1 - \mathbf{RN}_2$: point classification and the difference operator.

in Fig. 8.34b and Fig. 8.34c from that shown in Fig. 8.34d as follows:

1. If $x_{min,1} = x_{min,2}$ or $x_{max,1} = x_{max,2}$ or $y_{min,1} = y_{min,2}$ or $y_{max,1} = y_{max,2}$ then $\mathbf{p} \in o(\mathbf{RN}_1 - \mathbf{RN}_2)$.

2. If $x_{min,1} = x_{max,2}$ or $x_{max,1} = x_{min,2}$ or $y_{min,1} = y_{max,2}$ or $y_{max,1} = y_{min,2}$, then $\mathbf{p} \in b(\mathbf{RN}_1 - \mathbf{RN}_2)$.

Remember, the symbol $\in$ means "is a member or element of"; for example, $\mathbf{p} \in o(\mathbf{RN}_1 - \mathbf{RN}_2)$ reads as follows: "Point $\mathbf{p}$ is a member of those points lying outside the shape produced by $\mathbf{RN}_1 - \mathbf{RN}_2$." There are, of course, more sophisticated techniques for doing point classification that

Table 8.6. $\mathbf{RN}_1 - \mathbf{RN}_2$: Point Classification

	If				Then		
Condition	$b\mathbf{RN}_1$	$i\mathbf{RN}_1$	$b\mathbf{RN}_2$	$i\mathbf{RN}_2$	$b(\mathbf{RN}_1 - \mathbf{RN}_2)$	$i(\mathbf{RN}_1 - \mathbf{RN}_2)$	$o(\mathbf{RN}_1 - \mathbf{RN}_2)$
1	X				X		
2	X		X		Indeterminate		
3	X			X			X
4		X				X	
5		X	X		X		
6		X		X			X
7			X				X
8				X			X

do not depend on the parallel orientation condition, and you will examine them later.

If a new shape is defined by a sequence of difference operations as follows

$$A = B - C_1 - C_2 - C_3 - \cdots - C_n \tag{8.45}$$

then rewrite this as

$$A = B - (C_1 \cup C_2 \cup C_3 \cup \cdots \cup C_n) \tag{8.46}$$

Let $D = C_1 \cup C_2 \cup C_3 \cup \cdots \cup C_n$, then Eq. (8.46) becomes

$$A = B - D \tag{8.47}$$

Apply the point classification scheme as shown in Table 8.6.

INTERSECT

The intersect operator is the converse of the difference operator and limits two shapes to form a third; it is denoted by $\cap$, similar to an inverted symbol for the union operator. If A and B are two shapes, then $C = A \cap B$, where the shape C consists of all points in A that are also in B. Figure 8.35 shows the intersection of a rectangle and circle; note that

$$\mathbf{RN}_1 \cap \mathbf{CR}_1 = \mathbf{CR}_1 \cap \mathbf{RN}_1 \tag{8.48}$$

and in general,

$$A \cap B \cap C = A \cap C \cap B \tag{8.49}$$

Figure 8.36 demonstrates this for the case of three intersecting rectangles. The order of the operands is not important in a sequence of intersection operations.

If two shapes are disjoint, then their intersection is null; this is expressed as

$$A \cap B = \emptyset, \text{ if } A \ \langle\text{outside}\rangle\ B \tag{8.50}$$

How are points classified with respect to the result of the intersection

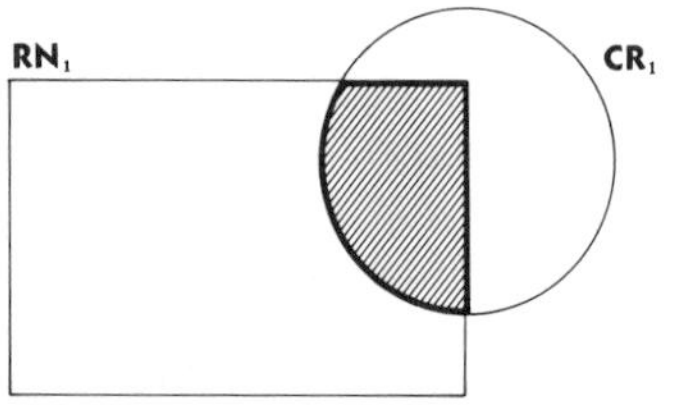

Fig. 8.35. Intersection of a rectangle and circle.

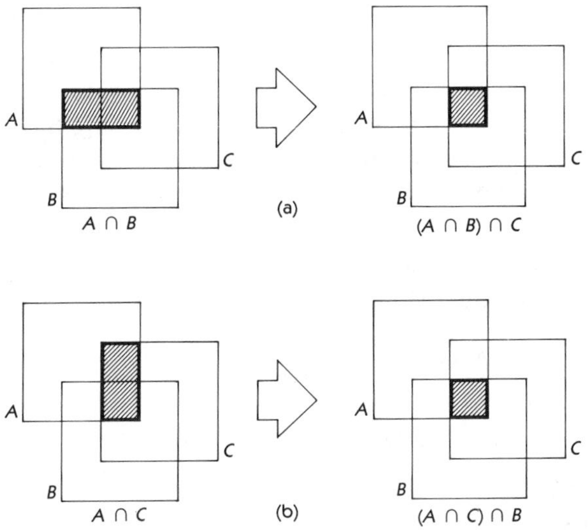

Fig. 8.36. Order independence of a sequence of intersection operations.

of two shapes? Figure 8.37 shows five spatial arrangements to distinguish between. In Fig. 8.37b the rectangle and circle do not intersect, so $A \cap B = \emptyset$. In Fig. 8.37c only a segment of *bA* intersects with a segment of *bB*, and this condition too produces a null result. This is because $bA \cap bB$ stands alone and is not dimensionally similar to *A* or *B*. *A* and *B* are two-dimensional objects. The result of the intersection for the arrangement in

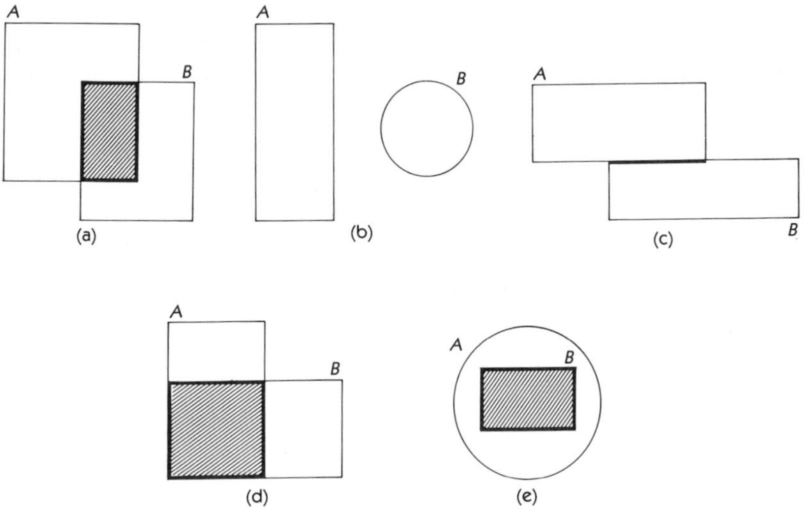

Fig. 8.37. $A \cap B$: five important spatial arrangements.

Fig. 8.37c is a line—a one-dimensional object. Sometimes this is called a **dangling edge.**

Table 8.7 presents the eight possible combinations of point classification for two shapes used to create a third shape using the intersect operator. Again, points falling outside both A and B are not included.

Condition 2 is indeterminate because both arrangements c and d in Fig. 8.37 yield the same tabulated point classification with respect to *A* and *B*. This is possible only when both shapes are rectangles. Analyze this further by performing the following additional tests for two rectangles.

1. If $x_{min,1} = x_{max,2}$ or $x_{max,1} = x_{min,2}$ or $y_{min,1} = y_{max,2}$ or $y_{max,1} = y_{min,2}$, then $A \cap B \neq 0$.

2. If $x_{min,1} = x_{min,2}$ or $x_{max,1} = x_{max,2}$ or $y_{min,1} = y_{min,2}$ or $y_{max,1} = y_{max,2}$, then $\mathbf{p} \in b(A \cap B)$.

You can easily use combinations of these three operators to create complex shapes. Study the example in Fig. 8.38. Here the elementary shapes are defined as follows:

a. $A = \mathbf{CR}_1(0,0,4)$

b. $B = \mathbf{RN}_1(-5,-2,10,4)$

c. $C = \mathbf{RN}_2(-2,-1,4,2)$

d. $D = \mathbf{CR}_2(-2,0,1)$

e. $E = \mathbf{CR}_3(2,0,1)$

The points of intersection between the boundaries of combined two-dimensional shapes are often useful when computing analytical properties of these complex shapes or when creating a computer graphic display of them. This is an important part of the general problem of computing the

Table 8.7. $A \cap B$: Point Classification

	If				Then		
Condition	*bA*	*iA*	*bB*	*iB*	$b(A \cap B)$	$i(A \cap B)$	$o(A \cap B)$
1	X						X
2	X		X		Indeterminate		
3	X			X	X		
4		X					X
5		X	X		X		
6		X		X		X	
7			X				X
8				X			X

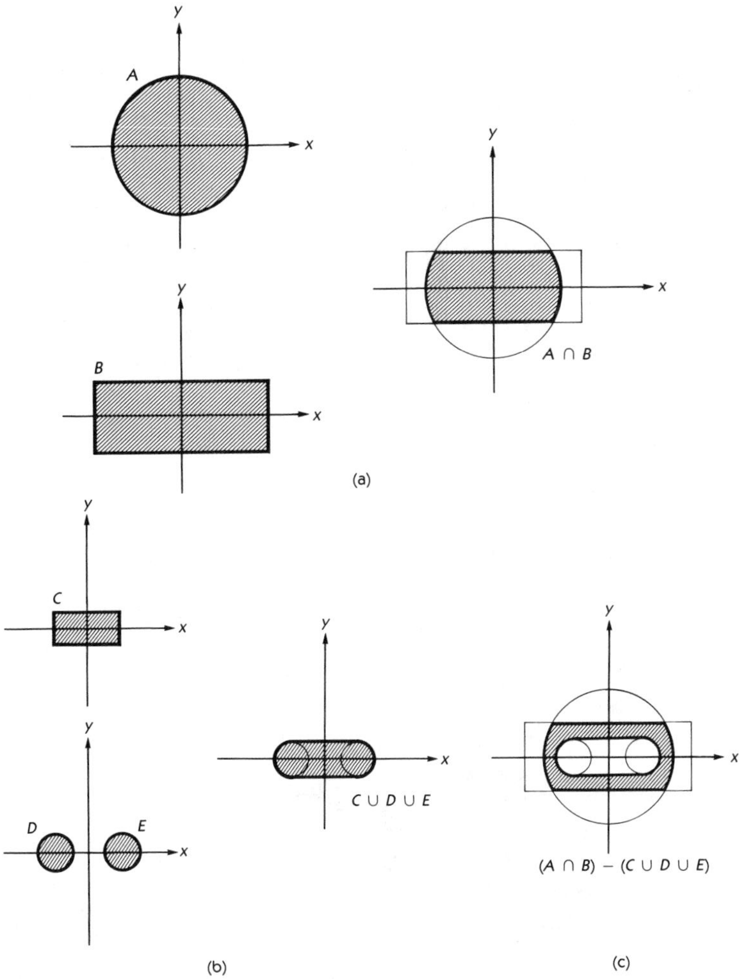

Fig. 8.38. Combining simple shapes to create a complex shape.

geometric intersection between more complex three-dimensional shapes. The intersection of two surfaces is usually a curve, for example; how we find such a curve and describe it analytically is a complex and sophisticated computation problem. Although the solution to this particular problem is beyond the scope of this textbook, the intersection problems we do consider are necessary conceptual and computational prerequisites to the more complex problems.

Now consider the points of intersection produced by the following combinations: two rectangles, a rectangle and circle, and two circles. Figure 8.39 shows three possible intersections of two rectangles and the re-

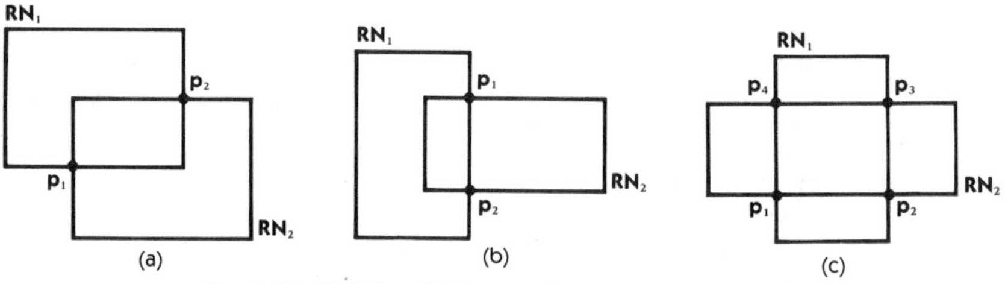

Fig. 8.39. Points of intersection: two rectangles.

sulting points of intersection. It is not difficult to find the coordinates of these points.

In Fig. 8.39a,

$$b\mathbf{RN}_1 \cap b\mathbf{RN}_2 = \{\mathbf{p}_1, \mathbf{p}_2\} \tag{8.51}$$

where the elements within the curly brackets are the set of points of intersection. The coordinates are

$$\mathbf{p}_1 = (x_{\min,2}, y_{\min,1}), \quad \mathbf{p}_2 = (x_{\max,1}, y_{\max,2}) \tag{8.52}$$

In Fig. 8.39b the coordinates are

$$\mathbf{p}_1 = (x_{\max,1}, y_{\min,2}), \quad \mathbf{p}_2 = (x_{\max,1}, y_{\max,2}) \tag{8.53}$$

In Fig. 8.39c,

$$b\mathbf{RN}_1 \cap b\mathbf{RN}_2 = \{\mathbf{p}_1, \mathbf{p}_2, \mathbf{p}_3, \mathbf{p}_4\} \tag{8.54}$$

where the coordinates are

$$\begin{aligned} \mathbf{p}_1 &= (x_{\min,1}, y_{\min,2}), & \mathbf{p}_2 &= (x_{\max,1}, y_{\min,2}) \\ \mathbf{p}_3 &= (x_{\max,1}, y_{\max,2}), & \mathbf{p}_4 &= (x_{\min,1}, y_{\max,2}) \end{aligned} \tag{8.55}$$

Consider the intersection of the rectangle and circle shown in Fig. 8.40. Point $\mathbf{p}_1$ is at the intersection of the circle and $x_{\min}$; thus, the x coordinate

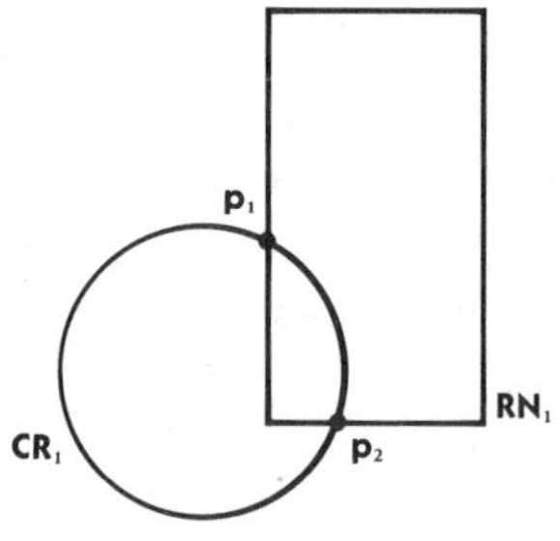

Fig. 8.40. Points of intersection: a rectangle and circle.

of $\mathbf{p}_1$ is denoted as x_1, where $x_1 = x_{min}$. The algebraic equation of the circle is

$$(x - x_c)^2 + (y - y_c)^2 = r^2 \tag{8.56}$$

Let $x = x_1$, then solve for $y = y_1$. The equation has two roots. Only those solutions in the interval $y_{min} \leq y_1 \leq y_{max}$ are acceptable (other solutions do not lie on the rectangle boundary).

Point $\mathbf{p}_2$ is at the intersection of the circle and y_{min}; thus, the y coordinate of $\mathbf{p}_2$ is $y_1 = y_{min}$. Substitute $y = y_1$ into Eq. (8.56) and solve for $x = x_1$. Only those solutions in the interval $x_{min} \leq x_1 \leq x_{max}$ are acceptable.

A general approach is to compute the intersections of the circle with each of the four lines: $x = x_{min}$, $x = x_{max}$, $y = y_{min}$, and $y = y_{max}$. Use only those solutions producing intersection point coordinates in the intervals $x \in [x_{min}, x_{max}]$ and $y \in [y_{min}, y_{max}]$.

Finally, consider the intersection of the two circles shown in Fig. 8.41. Let (x_i, y_i) denote the coordinates of the point of intersection $\mathbf{p}_i$, where $i = 1, 2$. Then x_i and y_i must satisfy Eq. (8.56). Two quadratic equations in two unknowns result:

$$\begin{aligned}(x_i - x_{c,1})^2 + (y_i - y_{c,1})^2 &= r_1^2 \\ (x_i - x_{c,2})^2 + (y_i - y_{c,2})^2 &= r_2^2\end{aligned} \tag{8.57}$$

The trigonometry of the problem provides a direct solution; refer to Fig. 8.42 for this development. Given three sides of a triangle a, b, and c

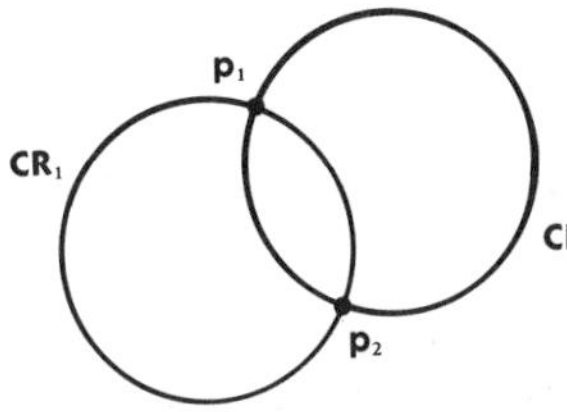

Fig. 8.41. Points of intersection: two circles.

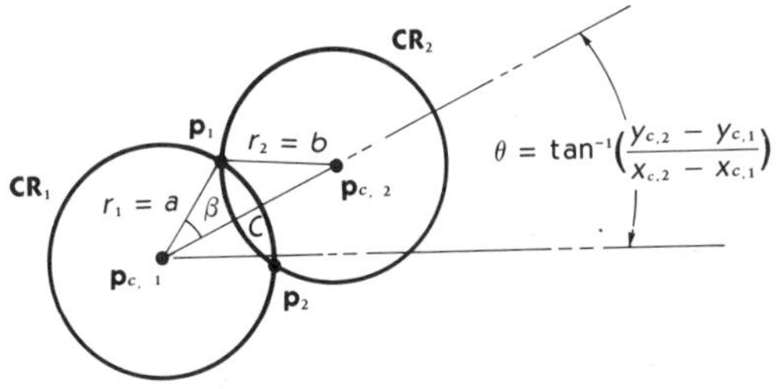

Fig. 8.42. Intersection of two circles: elements of a solution.

where

$$\begin{aligned} a &= r_1 \\ b &= r_2 \\ c &= \sqrt{(x_{c,2} - x_{c,1})^2 + (y_{c,2} - y_{c,1})^2} \end{aligned} \tag{8.58}$$

so that if

$$s = \tfrac{1}{2}(a + b + c) \tag{8.59}$$

$$d = \sqrt{\frac{(s - a)(s - b)(s - c)}{s}} \tag{8.60}$$

then determine β from

$$\tan\left(\frac{\beta}{2}\right) = \frac{d}{s - b} \tag{8.61}$$

Now compute the coordinates of $\mathbf{p}_1$ as

$$\begin{aligned} x_1 &= x_{c,1} + r_1 \cos(\theta + \beta) \\ y_1 &= y_{c,1} + r_1 \sin(\theta + \beta) \end{aligned} \tag{8.62a}$$

and compute the coordinates of $\mathbf{p}_2$ as

$$\begin{aligned} x_2 &= x_{c,1} + r_2 \cos(\theta - \beta) \\ y_2 &= y_{c,1} + r_2 \sin(\theta - \beta) \end{aligned} \tag{8.62b}$$

where

$$\theta = \tan^{-1}\left(\frac{y_{c,2} - y_{c,1}}{x_{c,2} - x_{c,1}}\right) \tag{8.63}$$

The square has not been mentioned in this section because the rectangle is a more general, inclusive element, but these procedures apply equally to squares.

The properties of the union and intersect operators are summarized in Box 8.4.

EXERCISES

1. Accurately sketch on graph paper the union of the following pairs of elements:

   a. $\mathbf{RN}_1(-3,-2,5,4)$, $\mathbf{RN}_2(-1,-1,5,4)$
   b. $\mathbf{RN}_3(-4,4,3,5)$, $\mathbf{RN}_4(-3,6,2,3)$

Box 8.4. Properties of Boolean Operators

Union Properties

1. $A \cup B$ is a set	Closure
2. $A \cup B = B \cup A$	Commutative
3. $(A \cup B) \cup C = A \cup (B \cup C)$	Associative
4. $A \cup 0 = A$	Identity
5. $A \cup A = A$	Idempotent
6. $A \cup cA = E$	Complement

Intersection Properties

1. $A \cap B$ is a set	Closure
2. $A \cap B = B \cap A$	Commutative
3. $(A \cap B) \cap C = A \cap (B \cap C)$	Associative
4. $A \cap E = A$	Identity
5. $A \cap A = A$	Complement

Distributive Properties

1. $A \cup (B \cap C) = (A \cup B) \cap (A \cup C)$	Union is distributive over intersection.
2. $A \cap (B \cup C) = (A \cap B) \cup (A \cap C)$	Intersection is distributive over union.

Complementation Properties

1. $cE = \emptyset$	
2. $c\emptyset = E$	
3. $c(cA) = A$	
4. $c(A \cup B) = cA \cap cB$	de Morgan's Law
5. $c(A \cap B) = cA \cup cB$	

c. $\mathbf{CR}_1(4,7,1.5)$, $\mathbf{RN}_5(3,7,4,2)$
d. $\mathbf{CR}_2(10,-2,3)$, $\mathbf{RN}_6(9,-7,2,9)$
e. $\mathbf{CR}_3(9,11,2)$, $\mathbf{CR}_4(12,9, 3)$

2. Accurately sketch on graph paper the difference of the following pairs of elements:

a. $\mathbf{CR}_1 - \mathbf{RN}_1$, where $\mathbf{CR}_1 = \mathbf{CR}_1(0,0,3)$ and $\mathbf{RN}_1 = \mathbf{RN}_1(-1,-1,5,5)$
b. $\mathbf{RN}_2 - \mathbf{RN}_3$, where $\mathbf{RN}_2 = \mathbf{RN}_2(-5,5,3,3)$ and $\mathbf{RN}_3 = \mathbf{RN}_3(-4,4,1,5)$
c. $\mathbf{RN}_4$, $-$ $\mathbf{RN}_5$, where $\mathbf{RN}_4 = \mathbf{RN}_4(0,0,5,5)$ and $\mathbf{RN}_5 = \mathbf{RN}_5(0,0,4,4)$
d. $\mathbf{RN}_6 - \mathbf{RN}_7$, where $\mathbf{RN}_6 = \mathbf{RN}_6(7,-2,4,4)$ and $\mathbf{RN}_7 = \mathbf{RN}_7(8,-1,2,2)$
e. $\mathbf{RN}_8 - \mathbf{CR}_2$, where $\mathbf{RN}_8 = \mathbf{RN}_8(6,5,3,4)$ and $\mathbf{CR}_2 = \mathbf{CR}_2(8,7,1.5)$

3. Accurately sketch on graph paper the intersection of the following pairs of elements:

a. $\mathbf{RN}_1(0,0,2,7)$, $\mathbf{RN}_2(-2,2,6,3)$
b. $\mathbf{RN}_3(0,0,3,4)$, $\mathbf{RN}_4(4,4,1,3)$
c. $\mathbf{RN}_5(0,-5,5,5)$, $\mathbf{CR}_1(0,0,3)$
d. $\mathbf{CR}_2(-3,5,2)$, $\mathbf{RN}_6(-6,2,6,8)$
e. $\mathbf{CR}_3(7,4,3)$, $\mathbf{RN}_7(5,0,4,8)$

4. Write expressions describing each of the five shapes shown in Fig. 8.43.

5. Classify the following points with respect to $\mathbf{RN}_1 \cup \mathbf{RN}_2$, where $\mathbf{RN}_1 = \mathbf{RN}_1(2,2,6,3)$ and $\mathbf{RN}_2 = \mathbf{RN}_2(2,5,3,3)$:

a. $\mathbf{p}_1 = (8,8)$
b. $\mathbf{p}_2 = (3,6)$
c. $\mathbf{p}_3 = (4,5)$
d. $\mathbf{p}_4 = (7,4)$
e. $\mathbf{p}_5 = (6,2)$

(Do this problem analytically, not graphically, and show your work.)

6. Classify the following points with respect to $\mathbf{CR}_1 \cup \mathbf{RN}_1$, where $\mathbf{CR}_1 = \mathbf{CR}_1(4,3,2)$ and $\mathbf{RN}_1 = \mathbf{RN}_1(4,3,3,5)$:

a. $\mathbf{p}_1 = (4,5)$
b. $\mathbf{p}_2 = (6,5)$

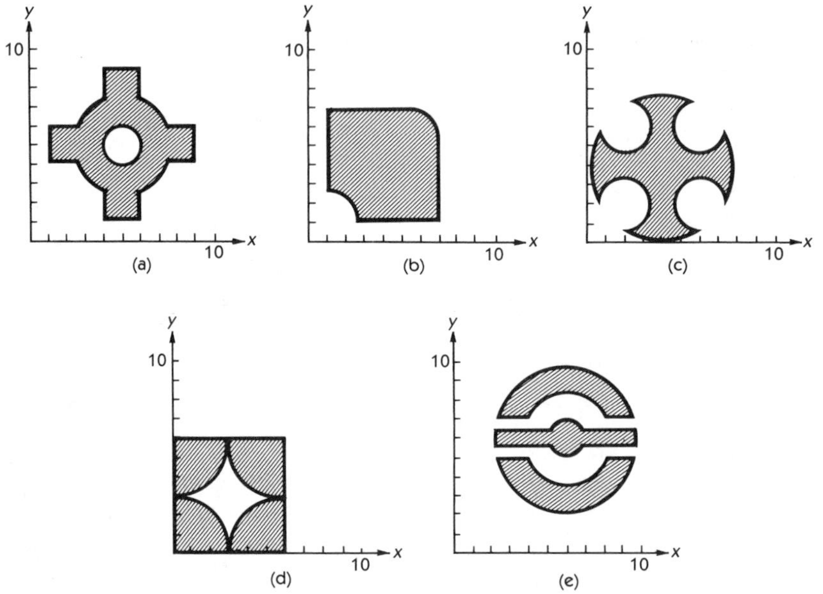

Fig. 8.43. Exercise 4.

c. $\mathbf{p}_3 = (9,3)$
d. $\mathbf{p}_4 = (5,2)$
e. $\mathbf{p}_5 = (2,1)$

(Do this problem analytically, not graphically, and show your work.)

7. Classify the following points with respect to $\mathbf{CR}_1 \cup \mathbf{CR}_2$, where $\mathbf{CR}_1 = \mathbf{CR}_1(3,3,2)$ and $\mathbf{CR}_2 = \mathbf{CR}_2(6,3,3)$:

a. $\mathbf{p}_1 = (2,4)$
b. $\mathbf{p}_2 = (7,5.828)$
c. $\mathbf{p}_3 = (4,2)$
d. $\mathbf{p}_4 = (6,1)$
e. $\mathbf{p}_5 = (10,3)$

(Do this problem analytically, not graphically, and show your work).

8. Classify the following points with respect to $\mathbf{CR}_1 - \mathbf{RN}_1$, where $\mathbf{CR}_1 = \mathbf{CR}_1(4,4,3)$ and $\mathbf{RN}_1 = \mathbf{RN}_1(3,0,2,8)$:

a. $\mathbf{p}_1 = (4.5,7.5)$
b. $\mathbf{p}_2 = (2,5)$
c. $\mathbf{p}_3 = (3.5,3.5)$
d. $\mathbf{p}_4 = (6.828,5)$
e. $\mathbf{p}_5 = (4,1)$

(Do this problem analytically, not graphically, and show your work.)

9. Classify the following points with respect to $\mathbf{CR}_1 - \mathbf{CR}_2$, where $\mathbf{CR}_1 = \mathbf{CR}_1(6,4,3)$ and $\mathbf{CR}_2 = \mathbf{CR}_2(6.5,4.5,1.5)$:

a. $\mathbf{p}_1 = (3,6)$
b. $\mathbf{p}_2 = (6.5,5)$
c. $\mathbf{p}_3 = (5,4.5)$
d. $\mathbf{p}_4 = (8.5,3)$
e. $\mathbf{p}_5 = (5,2)$

(Do this problem analytically, not graphically, and show your work.)

10. Classify the following points with respect to $\mathbf{CR}_1 \cap \mathbf{RN}_1$, where $\mathbf{CR}_1 = \mathbf{CR}_1(3.5,3.5,2.5)$ and $\mathbf{RN}_1 = \mathbf{RN}_1(3.5,0,4.5,3.5)$:

a. $\mathbf{p}_1 = (0.5,5.5)$
b. $\mathbf{p}_2 = (3,5)$
c. $\mathbf{p}_3 = (5,5.5)$
d. $\mathbf{p}_4 = (2,3)$
e. $\mathbf{p}_5 = (5,3)$
f. $\mathbf{p}_6 = (8,3.5)$
g. $\mathbf{p}_7 = (3.5,2)$
h. $\mathbf{p}_8 = (5,1.5)$
i. $\mathbf{p}_9 = (3.5,1)$
j. $\mathbf{p}_{10} = (6.5,0.5)$

(Do this problem analytically, not graphically, and show your work.)

11. Find the coordinates of the points of intersection between the boundaries of the following pairs of shape elements:

a. $\mathbf{RN}_1(3,1,3,7)$, $\mathbf{RN}_2(2,4,3,3)$
b. $\mathbf{CR}_1(4,5,3)$, $\mathbf{RN}_2(3,4,6,2)$
c. $\mathbf{CR}_1(3,4,2)$, $\mathbf{CR}_2(7,5,3)$
d. $\mathbf{CR}_1(5,4,2.5)$, $\mathbf{RN}_1(3,3,4,1)$
e. $\mathbf{CR}_1(3.5,5.5,1)$, $\mathbf{SQ}(4,1,3)$

(Do this problem analytically, not graphically, and show your work.)

12. Write a procedure to classify a point with respect to the union of two rectangles. Denote this as **RURPT**(RN1,RN2,PT,ICLS), where

RN1(4),RN2(4) are the input values of x_0, y_0, a_x, and a_y,
PT(2) are the input coordinates of the point, and
ICLS is the output classification of the point:
ICLS = 1 if the point is outside,
ICLS = 2 if the point is inside, and
ICLS = 3 if the point is on the boundary.

13. Write a procedure to classify a point with respect to the difference of two rectangles $\mathbf{RN}_1 - \mathbf{RN}_2$. Denote this as **RDRPT**(RN1,RN2,PT,ICLS), where the arguments are defined as for **RURPT**.

14. Write a procedure to classify a point with respect to the intersection of two rectangles $\mathbf{RN}_1 \cap \mathbf{RN}_2$. Denote this as **RIRPT**(RN1,RN2,PT,ICLS) where the arguments are defined as for **RURPT**.

15. Write a procedure to compute the points of intersection between two rectangles. Denote this as **RNRN**(RN1,RN2,INTNO,POI), where

RN1(4),RN2(4) are the input values of x_0, y_0, a_x, and a_y,
INTNO is the output number of intersections found, and
POI(2,INTNO) is the output array of coordinates of the points of intersection.

9. Three-Dimensional Constructions

WE CAN DESCRIBE many complex three-dimensional objects as combinations of cubes, blocks, cylinders, and spheres. These simple shapes and the operations that combine them into more complex shapes are the basis of elementary solid modeling, which is key to many computer graphics applications.

Solid objects are usually defined in the three-dimensional world coordinate system. In this chapter you will study cubes, blocks, and cylinders whose plane faces are parallel to the principal coordinate planes. The edges of cubes and blocks are parallel to the coordinate axes, and the axis of symmetry of a cylinder is parallel to one of the three coordinate axes. Again, your intuitive notion of these simple shapes is sufficient here.

Although not quite as commonplace as the square, rectangle, and circle, the cube block, cylinder, and sphere are used often enough in modeling and computer graphics to warrant developing efficient, concise data formats for describing them. And, as with their two-dimensional relatives, you must often determine if a point is inside, outside, or on a boundary of one of these three-dimensional objects.

9.1. Cubes

Describe a cube by giving the coordinates of one of its vertices and the length of its side. Note that for now you will consider only cubes whose edges are parallel to the three coordinate axes. Always specify the vertex that has the minimum coordinates relative to the other vertices.

Denote a cube symbolically with the boldface capital letters **CB**. Again, indicate a specific cube by adding an alphabetic or numeric subscript, for example $\mathbf{CB}_i$. Thus, to specify a cube, write:

$$\mathbf{CB} = \mathbf{CB}\,(x_0, y_0, z_0, a) \tag{9.1}$$

where x_0, y_0, and z_0 are the coordinates of the minimum vertex and a is the length of the side. Read this expression as: A cube is a function of the coordinates of its minimum vertex and the length of its side. Note that x_0, y_0, and z_0 can be positive or negative and a must always be positive. See Fig. 9.1 and Box 9.1.

As with the square, a great deal of information is contained in the cube's four arguments. The location is given, of course, by x_0, y_0, z_0. The cube's surface area is $6a^2$, and its volume is a^3. The coordinates of its maximum vertex are simply $\mathbf{p}_{max} = (x_0 + a, y_0 + a, z_0 + a)$. The coordinates of the eight vertices are (Fig. 9.2):

$$\begin{aligned} &\mathbf{p}_0 = (x_0, y_0, z_0), && \mathbf{p}_4 = (x_0, y_0, z_0 + a) \\ &\mathbf{p}_1 = (x_0 + a, y_0, z_0), && \mathbf{p}_5 = (x_0 + a, y_0, z_0 + a) \\ &\mathbf{p}_2 = (x_0 + a, y_0 + a, z_0), && \mathbf{p}_6 = (x_0 + a, y_0 + a, z_0 + a) \\ &\mathbf{p}_3 = (x_0, y_0, + a, z_0), && \mathbf{p}_7 = (x_0, y_0 + a, z_0 + a) \end{aligned} \tag{9.2}$$

The **centroid**, or geometric center, of a cube is at point

$$\mathbf{p}_{CG} = x_0 + \frac{a}{2}, y_0 + \frac{a}{2}, z_0 + \frac{a}{2} \tag{9.3}$$

For a specific example, say $\mathbf{CB}_1 = \mathbf{CB}_1\ (2,1,2,3)$ in Fig. 9.3, compute the following properties:

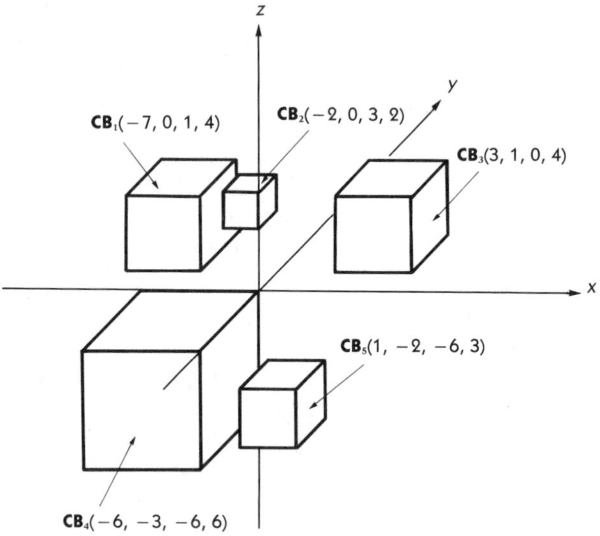

Fig. 9.1. Cubes.

Box 9.1. Displaying a Cube or Block

A cube is obviously nothing more than a very special polyhedron. In fact, it is a regular polyhedron, one of the five Platonic solids. The notational format suggested by Eq. (9.1) is a convenient way for a graphics user to define a cube, using a minimal amount of data. These data can be subsequently expanded by appropriate algorithms: computing all the vertex points, the connectivity matrix defining edges, and the array organizing the edges into the polygonal faces. Beyond this, the mathematics and geometry of displaying a cube are precisely those of displaying a polyhedron. Refer to Section 7.4. A similar approach applies to blocks.

Surface area:	$6_a^2 = 54$
Volume:	$a^3 = 27$
Centroid:	$\mathbf{p}_{CG} = (3.5, 2.5, 3.5)$
Minimum vertex:	$\mathbf{p}_{\min} = (2,1,2)$
Maximum vertex:	$\mathbf{p}_{\max} = (5,4,5)$

Classify an arbitrary point $\mathbf{p} = (x, y, z)$ with respect to a cube as follows:

p ⟨inside⟩ **CB** if and only if all of the following conditions are true:

$$x_{\min} < x < x_{\max}, \quad y_{\min} < y < y_{\max}, \quad \text{and} \quad z_{\min} < z < z_{\max} \tag{9.4}$$

p ⟨outside⟩ **CB** if and only if one or more of the following six conditions is true:

$$\begin{aligned} x &< x_{\min}, & x &> x_{\max} \\ y &< y_{\min}, & y &> y_{\max} \\ z &< z_{\min}, & z &> z_{\max} \end{aligned} \tag{9.5}$$

p ⟨boundary⟩ **CB** if

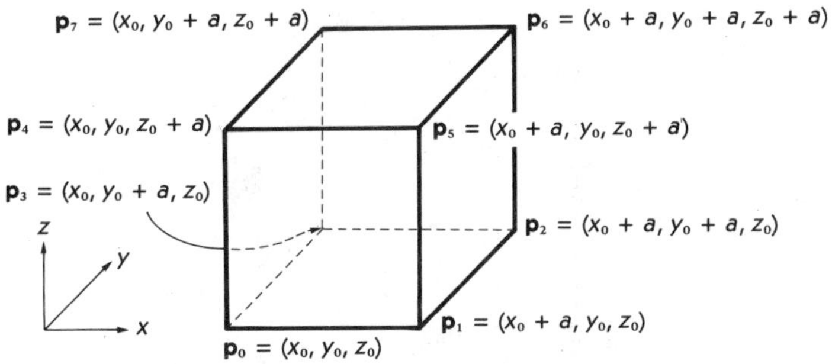

Fig. 9.2. Coordinates of the vertex points of a cube.

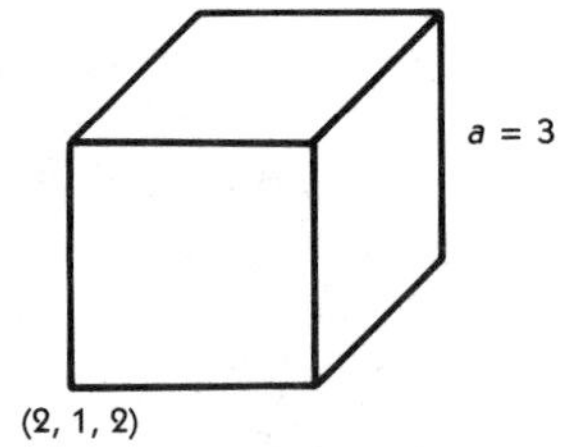

Fig. 9.3. $\mathbf{CB}_1 = \mathbf{CB}_1(2, 1, 2, 3)$.

$$\left\{\begin{matrix} x = x_{min} \\ \text{or} \\ x = x_{max} \end{matrix}\right\} \quad \text{and} \quad y_{min} < y < y_{max} \quad \text{and} \quad z_{min} < z < z_{max} \qquad (9.6)$$

or

$$\left\{\begin{matrix} y = y_{min} \\ \text{or} \\ y = y_{max} \end{matrix}\right\} \quad \text{and} \quad x_{min} < x < x_{max} \quad \text{and} \quad z_{min} < z < z_{max} \qquad (9.7)$$

or

$$\left\{\begin{matrix} z = z_{min} \\ \text{or} \\ z = z_{max} \end{matrix}\right\} \quad \text{and} \quad x_{min} < x < x_{max} \quad \text{and} \quad y_{min} < y < y_{max} \qquad (9.8)$$

Given $\mathbf{CB}_1 = \mathbf{CB}_1(0,0,0,4)$ in Fig. 9.4, for another example, classify the following points with respect to it: $\mathbf{p}_1 = (2,2,4)$, $\mathbf{p}_2 = (-2,2,2)$, and $\mathbf{p}_3 = (3,3,1)$. Compute $\mathbf{p}_{min} = (0,0,0)$ and $\mathbf{p}_{max} = (4,4,4)$ for $\mathbf{CB}_1$. For $\mathbf{p}_1$, $z_1 = 4 = z_{max}$ and $x_{min} < x_1 < x_{max}$, y_{min}, $< y < y_{max}$; therefore, $\mathbf{p}_1$ ⟨boundary⟩ $\mathbf{CB}_1$. For $\mathbf{p}_2$, $x_2 < x_{min}$, and, therefore, $\mathbf{p}_2$ ⟨outside⟩ $\mathbf{CB}_1$. Finally, for $\mathbf{p}_3$, $0 < x_3 < 4$, $0 < y_3 < 4$, and $0 < z_3 < 4$, and, therefore, $\mathbf{p}_3$ ⟨inside⟩ $\mathbf{CB}_1$.

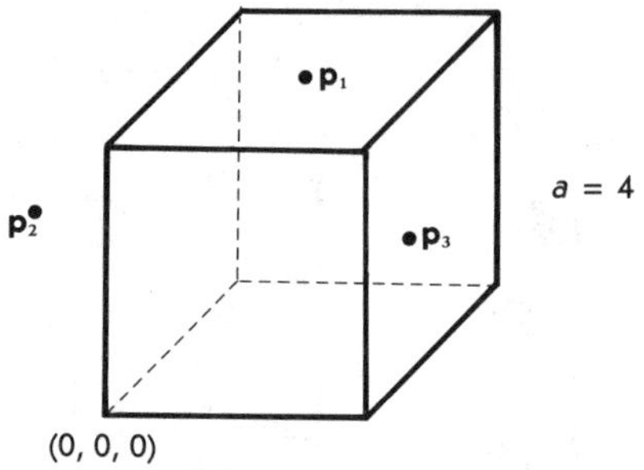

Fig. 9.4. Point classification with respect to a cube.

Given two cubes, the following spatial relationships can occur between them: One cube may lie entirely within the other, the two cubes may be disjoint, or the two cubes may intersect; see Fig. 9.5. Express these relationships as follows:

CB$_1$ ⟨inside⟩ **CB**$_2$ if and only if

$$\begin{Bmatrix} x_{\min,1} \geq x_{\min,2} \\ y_{\min,1} \geq y_{\min,2} \\ z_{\min,1} \geq z_{\min,2} \end{Bmatrix} \quad \text{and} \quad \begin{Bmatrix} x_{\max,1} \leq x_{\max,2} \\ y_{\max,1} \leq y_{\max,2} \\ z_{\max,1} \leq z_{\max,2} \end{Bmatrix} \tag{9.9}$$

Also, if Eq. (9.9) is true, then it is also true that $a_1 < a_2$; see Fig. 9.5a.

CB$_1$ ⟨outside⟩ **CB**$_2$ if and only if one or more of the following six conditions is true:

$$\begin{aligned} x_{\max,1} &\leq x_{\min,2} \quad \text{or} \quad x_{\min,1} \geq x_{\max,2} \\ y_{\max,1} &\leq y_{\min,2} \quad \text{or} \quad y_{\min,1} \geq y_{\max,2} \\ z_{\max,1} &\leq z_{\min,2} \quad \text{or} \quad z_{\min,1} \geq z_{\max,2} \end{aligned} \tag{9.10}$$

Again, note that if **CB**$_1$ ⟨outside⟩ **CB**$_2$, then it is also true that **CB**$_2$ ⟨outside⟩ **CB**$_1$; see Fig. 9.5b.

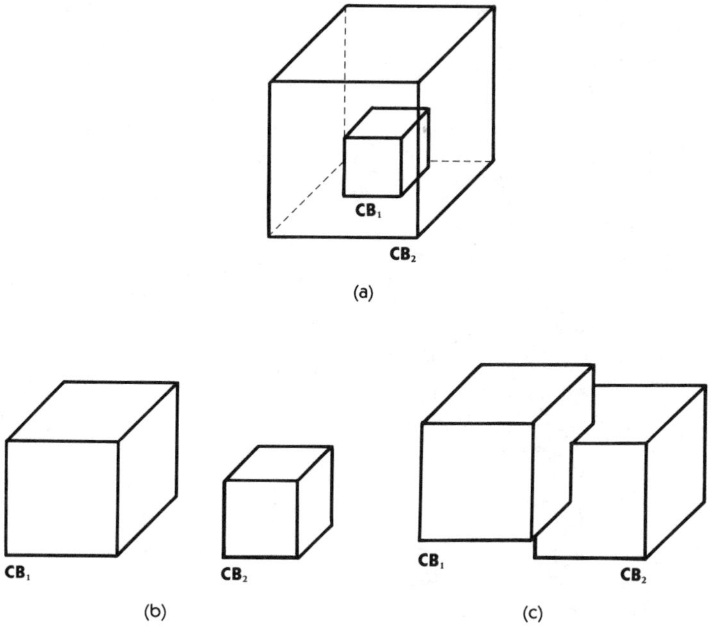

Fig. 9.5. Relationships between two cubes.

$\mathbf{CB}_1$ ⟨intersect⟩ $\mathbf{CB}_2$ if all of the following conditions are true:

$$\frac{|a_1 - a_2|}{2} < |x_{CG,1} - x_{CG,2}| < \frac{a_1 + a_2}{2}$$

and

$$\frac{|a_1 - a_2|}{2} < |y_{CG,1} - y_{CG,2}| < \frac{a_1 + a_2}{2} \tag{9.11}$$

and

$$\frac{|a_1 - a_2|}{2} < |z_{CG,1} - z_{CG,2}| < \frac{a_1 + a_2}{2}$$

The intersection of two cubes is shown in Fig. 9.5c.

Now consider the conditions describing two cubes that share a boundary face. Figure 9.6 shows two cubes externally tangent; that is, in all three cases $\mathbf{CB}_1$ ⟨outside⟩ $\mathbf{CB}_2$, but they are in face-to-face contact. Denote these conditions as $\mathbf{CB}_1$ ⟨outside, tangent⟩ $\mathbf{CB}_2$. Express these conditions algebraically as follows:

$\mathbf{CB}_1$ ⟨outside, tangent⟩ $\mathbf{CB}_2$ if and only if one of the following three sets of conditions is true:

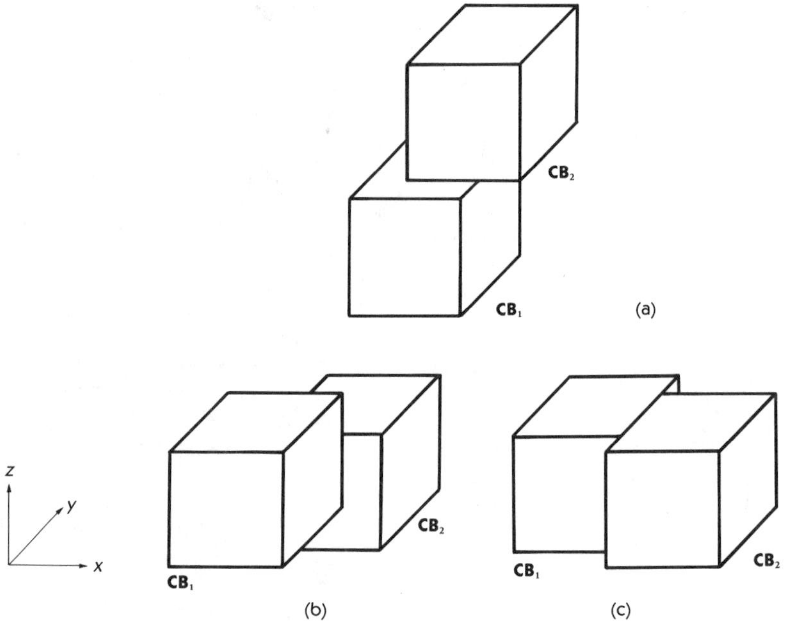

Fig. 9.6. Cubes with a common boundary.

$$\left\{\begin{matrix} z_{max,1} = z_{min,2} \\ \text{or} \\ z_{min,1} = z_{max,2} \end{matrix}\right\} \text{ and } \left\{\begin{matrix} |x_{CG,1} - x_{CG,2}| < (a_1 + a_2)/2 \\ \text{and} \\ |y_{CG,1} - y_{CG,2}| < (a_1 + a_2)/2 \end{matrix}\right\}$$

or

$$\left\{\begin{matrix} y_{max,1} = y_{min,2} \\ \text{or} \\ y_{min,1} = y_{max,2} \end{matrix}\right\} \text{ and } \left\{\begin{matrix} |x_{CG,1} - x_{CG,2}| < (a_1 + a_2)/2 \\ \text{and} \\ |z_{CG,1} - z_{CG,2}| < (a_1 + a_2)/2 \end{matrix}\right\} \quad (9.12)$$

or

$$\left\{\begin{matrix} x_{max,1} = x_{min,2} \\ \text{or} \\ x_{min,1} = x_{max,2} \end{matrix}\right\} \text{ and } \left\{\begin{matrix} |y_{CG,1} - y_{CG,2}| < (a_1 + a_2)/2 \\ \text{and} \\ |z_{CG,1} - z_{CG,2}| < (a_1 + a_2)/2 \end{matrix}\right\}$$

$\mathbf{CB}_1$ ⟨inside, tangent⟩ $\mathbf{CB}_2$ if and only if Eqs. (9.9) are true, with the exception that one or more of the six expressions must produce a condition of equality, for example, $x_{max,1} = x_{max,2}$.

$\mathbf{CB}_1$ ⟨intersect, tangent⟩ $\mathbf{CB}_2$ if and only if one or two of the following three sets of conditions is true:

$$\left\{\begin{matrix} z_{max,1} = z_{max,2} \\ \text{or} \\ z_{min,1} = z_{min,2} \end{matrix}\right\} \text{ and } \left\{\begin{matrix} |x_{CG,1} - x_{CG,2}| < (a_1 + a_2)/2 \\ \text{and} \\ |y_{CG,1} - y_{CG,2}| < (a_1 + a_2)/2 \end{matrix}\right\}$$

or

$$\left\{\begin{matrix} y_{max,1} = y_{max,2} \\ \text{or} \\ y_{min,1} = y_{min,2} \end{matrix}\right\} \text{ and } \left\{\begin{matrix} |x_{CG,1} - x_{CG,2}| < (a_1 + a_2)/2 \\ \text{and} \\ |z_{CG,1} - z_{CG,2}| < (a_1 + a_2)/2 \end{matrix}\right\} \quad (9.13)$$

or

$$\left\{\begin{matrix} x_{max,1} = x_{max,2} \\ \text{or} \\ x_{min,1} = x_{min,2} \end{matrix}\right\} \text{ and } \left\{\begin{matrix} |y_{CG,1} - y_{CG,2}| < (a_1 + a_2)/2 \\ \text{and} \\ |z_{CG,1} - z_{CG,2}| < (a_1 + a_2)/2 \end{matrix}\right\}$$

EXERCISES

1. Which of the following expressions improperly specify a cube, and why?
   a. $\mathbf{CB}_1(-3,6,0,1)$
   b. $\mathbf{CB}_2(0,0,0,-1)$
   c. $\mathbf{CB}_3(2.5,0.5,1.0,21.5)$
   d. $\mathbf{CB}_4(-0.5,-2.4,-0.5,1,1)$
   e. $\mathbf{CB}_5(7.5,-1.0,2.0)$
   f. $\mathbf{CB}_6(0,0,0,0)$
   g. $\mathbf{CB}_7(0,1,2,3)$
   h. $\mathbf{CB}_8(5,0,7,-6)$
2. Compute the coordinates of the vertices for each of the following cubes:
   a. $\mathbf{CB}_1(0,0,0,1)$
   b. $\mathbf{CB}_2(-2,3,0,2)$
   c. $\mathbf{CB}_3(6.1,2.7,3.5,0.5)$
   d. $\mathbf{CB}_4(-10,-10,-10,10)$
   e. $\mathbf{CB}_5(21.5,17.3,0,7.2)$

3. Compute $\mathbf{p}_{CG}$ for each of the cubes defined in Exercise 2.

4. Compute the surface area and volume of each of the cubes defined in Exercise 2.

5. Given $\mathbf{CB}_1 = \mathbf{CB}_1(0,0,0,3)$, classify the following points:

a. $\mathbf{p}_1 = (2,2,3)$
b. $\mathbf{p}_2 = (0.01,2.99,2.99)$
c. $\mathbf{p}_3 = (1,1,-2)$
d. $\mathbf{p}_4 = (1.5,1.5,3)$
e. $\mathbf{p}_5 = (2,4,2)$

6. Given $\mathbf{CB}_1 = \mathbf{CB}_1(0,2,2,4)$, classify $\mathbf{CB}_1$ with respect to the following cubes:

a. $\mathbf{CB}_2(0,2,2,5)$
b. $\mathbf{CB}_3(4,3,3,4)$
c. $\mathbf{CB}_4(0,0,0,1)$
d. $\mathbf{CB}_5(0,5,1,8)$
e. $\mathbf{CB}_6(0.5,2.5,2.5,3)$

7. Write a procedure to compute the coordinates of the eight vertex points of a cube. Denote this as **CBVP**(CB,VP), where

CB(4) are the input values x_0, y_0, z_0, and a and
VP(3,8) are the input coordinates of the vertex points.

8. Write a procedure to compute the surface area, volume, and $\mathbf{p}_{CG}$ of a cube. Denote this as **CBPROP**(CB,A,V,PCG), where

CB(4) are the input values x_0, y_0, z_0, and a,
A is the output area,
V is the output volume, and
PCG(3) are the output coordinates of $\mathbf{p}_{CG}$.

9. Write a procedure to classify a point with respect to a cube. Denote this as **CBPT**(CB,PT,ICLS), where

CG(4) are the input values x_0, y_0, z_0, and a,
PT(3) are the input coordinates of a point, and
ICLS is the output classification of this point:
ICLS = 1 if the point is outside,
ICLS = 2 if the point is inside, and
ICLS = 3 if the point is on the boundary.

10. Write a procedure to classify the relationship between two cubes. Denote this as **CBCB**(CB1,CB2,ICLS), where

CB1(4), CB2(4) are the input values x_0, y_0, z_0, and a for each of the two cubes and

ICLS = 1 if $\mathbf{CB}_1$ ⟨outside⟩ $\mathbf{CB}_2$,
ICLS = 2 if $\mathbf{CB}_1$ ⟨outside, tangent⟩ $\mathbf{CB}_2$,
ICLS = 3 if $\mathbf{CB}_1$ ⟨intersect⟩ $\mathbf{CB}_2$,
ICLS = 4 if $\mathbf{CB}_1$ ⟨intersect, tangent⟩ $\mathbf{CB}_2$,
ICLS = 5 if $\mathbf{CB}_1$ ⟨inside⟩ $\mathbf{CB}_2$,
ICLS = 6 if $\mathbf{CB}_1$ ⟨inside, tangent⟩ $\mathbf{CB}_2$,
ICLS = 7 if $\mathbf{CB}_2$ ⟨inside⟩ $\mathbf{CB}_1$, and
ICLS = 8 if $\mathbf{CB}_2$ ⟨inside, tangent⟩ $\mathbf{CB}_1$.

11. Derive the expression(s) describing cubes that are joined only along an edge.

12. Derive the expression(s) describing cubes that are joined only at a vertex.

9.2. Blocks

To describe a block, give the coordinates of one of its vertices and the lengths of its three principal dimensions. You will consider here only blocks whose edges are parallel to the coordinate axes. As with cubes, always specify the vertex that has the minimum coordinates relative to the other vertices.

Denote a block symbolically with the boldface capital letters **BK**, and specify it as follows:

$$\mathbf{BK} = \mathbf{BK}(x_0, y_0, z_0, a_x, a_y, a_z) \tag{9.14}$$

where x_0, y_0, and z_0 are the coordinates of the minimum vertex and a_x, a_y, and a_z are the principal dimensions parallel to the x, y, and z axes, respectively. Read this expression as: A block is a function of the coordinates of its minimum vertex and the lengths of its sides. See several samples in Fig. 9.7. (Refer again to Box 9.1.)

A block has the following properties: Its surface area is $2(a_x a_y + a_x a_z + a_y a_z)$, and its volume is $a_x a_y a_z$. The coordinates of its maximum vertex are simply $\mathbf{p}_{max} = (x_0 + a_x, y_0 + a_y, z_0 + a_z)$. The coordinates of its eight vertices are (see Fig. 9.8)

$$\begin{aligned}
\mathbf{p}_0 &= (x_0, y_0, z_0)\\
\mathbf{p}_1 &= (x_0 + a_x, y_0, z_0)\\
\mathbf{p}_2 &= (x_0 + a_x, y_0 + a_y, z_0)\\
\mathbf{p}_3 &= (x_0, y_0 + a_y, z_0)\\
\mathbf{p}_4 &= (x_0, y_0, z_0 + a_z)\\
\mathbf{p}_5 &= (x_0 + a_x, y_0, z_0 + a_z)\\
\mathbf{p}_6 &= (x_0 + a_x, y_0 + a_y, z_0 + a_z)\\
\mathbf{p}_7 &= (x_0, y_0 + a_y, z_0 + a_z)
\end{aligned} \tag{9.15}$$

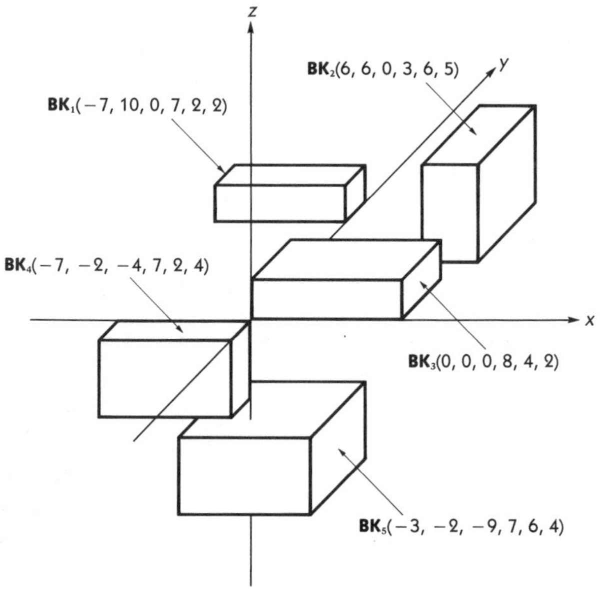

Fig. 9.7. Blocks.

The centroid, or geometric center, of a block is located at the point

$$\mathbf{p}_{CG} = \left(x_0 + \frac{a_x}{2}, y_0 + \frac{a_y}{2}, z_0 + \frac{a_z}{2} \right) \tag{9.16}$$

Study the block shown in Fig. 9.9, and compute the following properties:

Surface area:	$2\,(a_x a_y + a_x a_z + a_y a_z) = 368$
Volume:	$a_x a_y a_z = 384$
Centroid:	$\mathbf{P}_{CG} = (7,2,9)$
Minimum vertex:	$\mathbf{p}_{\min} = (4,0,1)$
Maximum vertex:	$\mathbf{p}_{\max} = (10,4,17)$

Classify an arbitrary point $\mathbf{p} = (x, y, z)$ with respect to a block as follows:

1. $\mathbf{p}$ ⟨inside⟩ **BK** if and only if all of the following conditions are true:

$$x_{\min} < x < x_{\max}, \quad y_{\min} < y < y_{\max}, \quad \text{and} \quad z_{\min} < z < z_{\max} \tag{9.17}$$

2. $\mathbf{p}$ ⟨outside⟩ **BK** if and only if at least one of the following sets of conditions is true:

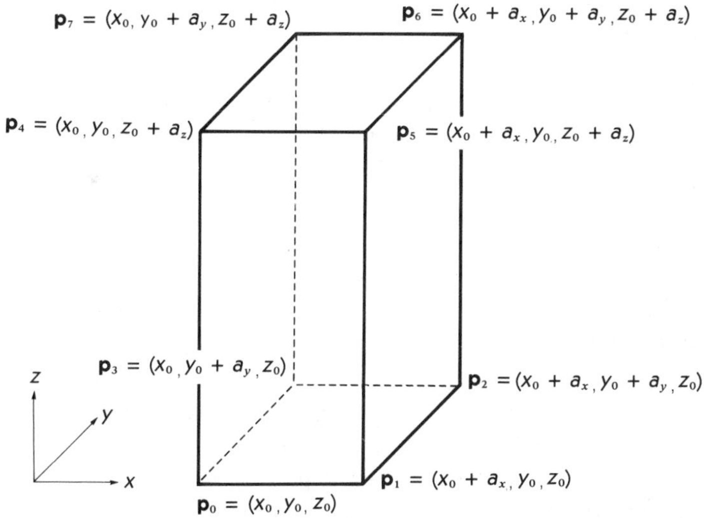

Fig. 9.8. Coordinates of the vertex points of a block.

$$\begin{aligned} x &< x_{\min} \quad \text{or} \quad x > x_{\max} \\ y &< y_{\min} \quad \text{or} \quad y > y_{\max} \\ z &< z_{\min} \quad \text{or} \quad z > z_{\max} \end{aligned} \tag{9.18}$$

3. **p** ⟨boundary⟩ > **BK** if

$$\left\{ \begin{matrix} x = x_{\min} \\ \text{or} \\ x = x_{\max} \end{matrix} \right\} \quad \text{and} \quad y_{\min} < y < y_{\max} \quad \text{and} \quad z_{\min} < z < z_{\max} \tag{9.19}$$

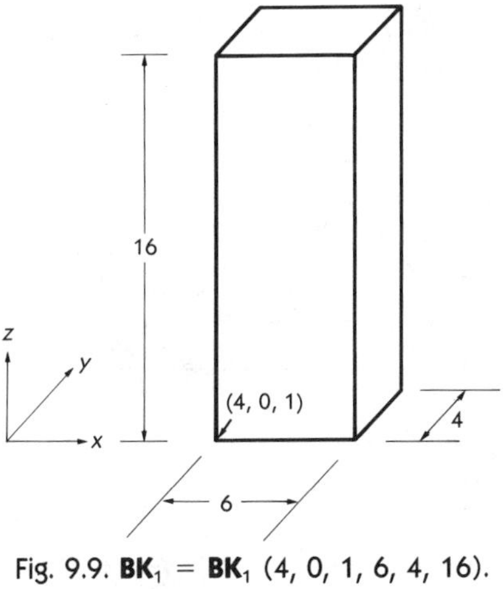

Fig. 9.9. $\mathbf{BK}_1 = \mathbf{BK}_1\ (4, 0, 1, 6, 4, 16)$.

or

$$\begin{Bmatrix} y = y_{\min} \\ \text{or} \\ y = y_{\max} \end{Bmatrix} \quad \text{and} \quad x_{\min} < x < x_{\max} \quad \text{and} \quad z_{\min} < z < z_{\max} \tag{9.20}$$

or

$$\begin{Bmatrix} z = z_{\min} \\ \text{or} \\ z = z_{\max} \end{Bmatrix} \quad \text{and} \quad x_{\min} < x < x_{\max} \quad \text{and} \quad y_{\min} < y < y_{\max} \tag{9.21}$$

Note that Eqs. (9.17)–(9.21) are identical in form to Eqs. (9.4)–(9.8); the difference, of course, lies in the computation of $\mathbf{p}_{\min}$ and $\mathbf{p}_{\max}$.

Given $\mathbf{BK}_1 = \mathbf{BK}_1(-7,-4,-1,14,8,2)$, classify the following points with respect to it: $\mathbf{p}_1 = (-7,2,0)$, $\mathbf{p}_2 = (4,4,6)$, and $\mathbf{p}_3 = (4,0,0)$; see Fig. 9.10. For $\mathbf{p}_1$, $x_1 = -7 = x_{\min}$ and $y_{\min} < y_1 < y_{\max}$, $z_{\min}$, $< z_1 < z_{\max}$; therefore, $\mathbf{p}_1$ ⟨boundary⟩ $\mathbf{BK}_1$. For $\mathbf{p}_2$, $z_2 = 6 > z_{\max}$ and, therefore, $\mathbf{p}_2$ ⟨outside⟩ $\mathbf{BK}_1$. Finally, for $\mathbf{p}_3$, $-7 < x_3 < 7$, $-4 < y_3 < 4$, and $-1 < z_3 < 1$, and, therefore, $\mathbf{p}_3$ ⟨inside⟩ $\mathbf{BK}_1$.

Given two blocks, the following spatial relationships can occur between them: One block may lie entirely within the other, the two blocks may be disjoint, or the two blocks may intersect; see Fig. 9.11. Express these relationships as follows:

$\mathbf{BK}_1$ ⟨inside⟩ $\mathbf{BK}_2$ if and only if

$$\begin{Bmatrix} x_{\min,1} \geq x_{\min,2} \\ y_{\min,1} \geq y_{\min,2} \\ z_{\min,1} \geq z_{\min,2} \end{Bmatrix} \quad \text{and} \quad \begin{Bmatrix} x_{\max,1} \leq x_{\max,2} \\ y_{\max,1} \leq y_{\max,2} \\ z_{\max,1} \leq z_{\max,2} \end{Bmatrix} \tag{9.22}$$

Furthermore, if Eq. (9.22) is true, then it is also true that $a_{x,1} < a_{x,2}$, $a_{y,1} < a_{y,2}$, and $a_{z,1} < a_{z,2}$; see Fig. 9.11a.

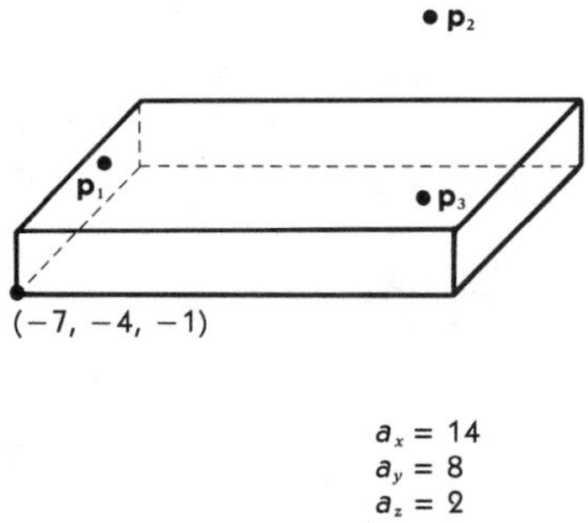

Fig. 9.10. Point classification with respect to a block.

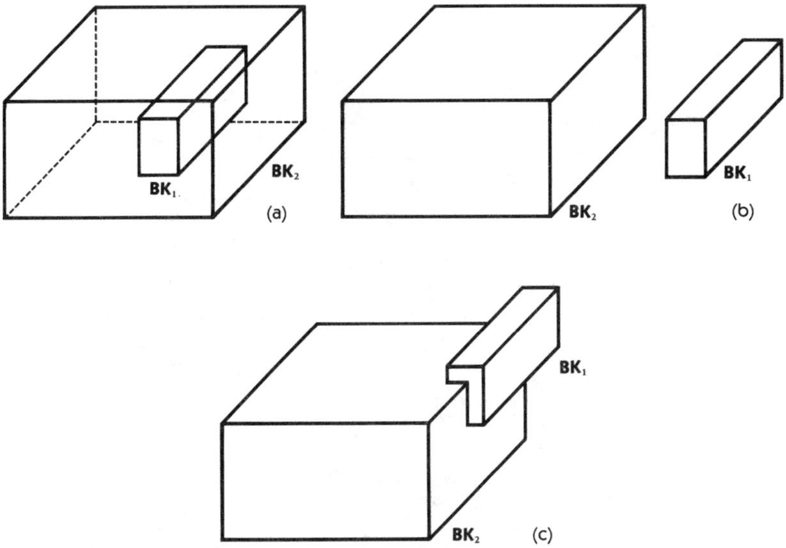

Fig. 9.11. Relationships between two blocks.

$\mathbf{BK}_1$ ⟨outside⟩ $\mathbf{BK}_2$ if and only if one or more of the following six conditions is true:

$$\begin{aligned} x_{\max,1} &\le x_{\min,2} \quad \text{or} \quad x_{\min,1} \ge x_{\max,2} \\ y_{\max,1} &\le y_{\min,2} \quad \text{or} \quad y_{\min,1} \ge y_{\max,2} \\ z_{\max,1} &\le z_{\min,2} \quad \text{or} \quad z_{\min,1} \ge z_{\max,2} \end{aligned} \tag{9.23}$$

If $\mathbf{BK}_1$ ⟨outside⟩ $\mathbf{BK}_2$, then $\mathbf{BK}_2$ ⟨outside⟩ $\mathbf{BK}_1$; see Fig. 9.11b.

$\mathbf{BK}_1$ ⟨intersect⟩ $\mathbf{BK}_2$ if all of the following conditions are true (see Fig. 9.11c):

$$\frac{|a_{x,1} - a_{x,2}|}{2} < |x_{CG,1} - x_{CG,2}| < \frac{a_{x,1} + a_{x,2}}{2}$$

and

$$\frac{|a_{y,1} - a_{y,2}|}{2} < |y_{CG,1} - y_{CG,2}| < \frac{a_{y,1} + a_{y,2}}{2} \tag{9.24}$$

and

$$\frac{|a_{z,1} - a_{z,2}|}{2} < |z_{CG,1} - z_{CG,2}| < \frac{a_{z,1} + a_{z,2}}{2}$$

Finally, consider two blocks that share a boundary face. Figure 9.12 shows two blocks externally tangent; that is, in all three cases $\mathbf{BK}_1$ ⟨out-

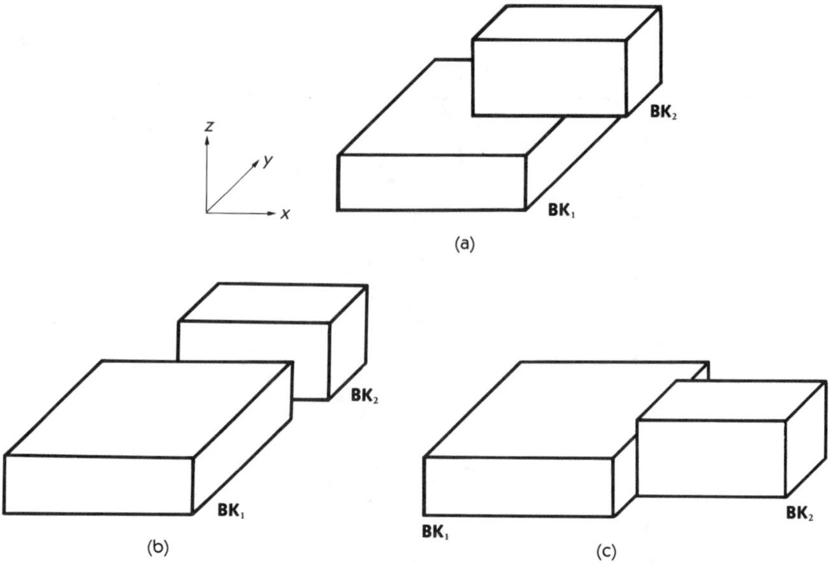

Fig. 9.12. Blocks with a common boundary.

side⟩ $\mathbf{BK}_2$, but they are in face-to-face contact. Denote these conditions as $\mathbf{BK}_1$ ⟨outside, tangent⟩ $\mathbf{BK}_2$. Express this algebraically as follows:

$\mathbf{BK}_1$ ⟨outside, tangent⟩ $\mathbf{BK}_2$ if and only if one of the following three sets of conditions is true:

$$\left\{\begin{matrix} z_{\max,1} = z_{\min,2} \\ \text{or} \\ z_{\min,1} = z_{\max,2} \end{matrix}\right\} \text{ and } \left\{\begin{matrix} |x_{CG,1} - x_{CG,2}| < (a_{x,1} + a_{x,2})/2 \\ \text{and} \\ |y_{CG,1} - y_{CG,2}| < (a_{y,1} + a_{y,2})/2 \end{matrix}\right\}$$

or

$$\left\{\begin{matrix} y_{\max,1} = y_{\min,2} \\ \text{or} \\ y_{\min,1} = y_{\max,2} \end{matrix}\right\} \text{ and } \left\{\begin{matrix} |x_{CG,1} - x_{CG,2}| < (a_{x,1} + a_{x,2})/2 \\ \text{and} \\ |z_{CG,1} - z_{CG,2}| < (a_{z,1} + a_{z,2})/2 \end{matrix}\right\} \quad (9.25)$$

or

$$\left\{\begin{matrix} x_{\max,1} = x_{\min,2} \\ \text{or} \\ x_{\min,1} = x_{\max,2} \end{matrix}\right\} \text{ and } \left\{\begin{matrix} |y_{CG,1} - y_{CG,2}| < (a_{y,1} + a_{y,2})/2 \\ \text{and} \\ |z_{CG,1} - z_{CG,2}| < (a_{z,1} + a_{z,2})/2 \end{matrix}\right\}$$

$\mathbf{BK}_1$ ⟨inside, tangent⟩ $\mathbf{BK}_2$ if and only if Eqs. (9.22) are true, with the exception that one or more of the six expressions must produce a condition of equality, for example, $x_{\max,1} = x_{\max,2}$.

$\mathbf{BK}_1$ ⟨intersect, tangent⟩ $\mathbf{BK}_2$ if and only if one or two of the following three sets of conditions is true:

$$\left\{\begin{array}{c} z_{\max,1} = z_{\max,2} \\ \text{or} \\ z_{\min,1} = z_{\min,2} \end{array}\right\} \quad \text{and} \quad \left\{\begin{array}{c} |x_{CG,1} - x_{CG,2}| < (a_{x,1} + a_{x,2})/2 \\ \text{and} \\ |y_{CG,1} - y_{CG,2}| < (a_{y,1} + a_{y,2})/2 \end{array}\right\}$$

or

$$\left\{\begin{array}{c} y_{\max,1} = y_{\max,2} \\ \text{or} \\ y_{\min,1} = y_{\min,2} \end{array}\right\} \quad \text{and} \quad \left\{\begin{array}{c} |x_{CG,1} - x_{CG,2}| < (a_{x,1} + a_{x,2})/2 \\ \text{and} \\ |z_{CG,1} - z_{CG,2}| < (a_{z,1} + a_{z,2})/2 \end{array}\right\} \qquad (9.26)$$

or

$$\left\{\begin{array}{c} x_{\max,1} = x_{\max,2} \\ \text{or} \\ x_{\min,1} = x_{\min,2} \end{array}\right\} \quad \text{and} \quad \left\{\begin{array}{c} |y_{CG,1} - y_{CG,2}| < (a_{y,1} + (a_{y,2})/2 \\ \text{and} \\ |z_{CG,1} - z_{CG,2}| < (a_{z,1} + a_{z,2})/2 \end{array}\right\}$$

EXERCISES

1. Which of the following expressions improperly specify a block, and why?

a. $\mathbf{BK}_1(0,0,0,1,-1,4)$
b. $\mathbf{BK}_2(-2.5,7.2,1.3,17.6,4.3,8.1)$
c. $\mathbf{BK}_3(0.017,0.714,-1.003,2.001,0.001,0.509)$
d. $\mathbf{BK}_4(12.1,7.8,-0.9,2.5,2.5)$
e. $\mathbf{BK}_5(3,3,1,1,1,1,3)$
f. $\mathbf{BK}_6(-6.5,-6.5,-6.5,13,13,13)$
g. $\mathbf{BK}_7(0,0,0,1,1,1)$
h. $\mathbf{BK}_8(2.1,0.8,-0.5,2.1,0.8,0.5)$
i. $\mathbf{BK}_9(-8,-5,2,0,4,4)$
j. $\mathbf{Bk}_{10}(A,B,C,D,E,F)$

2. Compute the coordinates of the vertices for each of the following blocks

a. $\mathbf{BK}_1(0,0,0,3,8,1)$
b. $\mathbf{BK}_2(-4,-2,-6,8,4,12)$
c. $\mathbf{BK}_3(3,1,1,5,2,8)$
d. $\mathbf{BK}_4(7,-6,2,5,5,1)$
e. $\mathbf{BK}_5(0,-0.5,2.5,1.3,7.0,7.2)$

3. Compute $\mathbf{p}_{CG}$ for each of the blocks defined in Exercise 2.

4. Compute the surface area and volume of each of the blocks defined in Exercise 2.

5. Given $\mathbf{BK}_1 = \mathbf{BK}_1(0,0,2,1,8,4)$, classify the following points:

a. $\mathbf{p}_1 = (0,0,0)$
b. $\mathbf{p}_2 = (0,5,3)$

c. $\mathbf{p}_3 = (0,0,4)$
d. $\mathbf{p}_4 = (-1,0,4)$
e. $\mathbf{p}_5 = (0.8,7.1,2.1)$

6. Given $\mathbf{BK}_1 = \mathbf{BK}_1(0,0,2,1,8,4)$, classify $\mathbf{BK}_1$ with respect to the following blocks:

a. $\mathbf{BK}_2(0,6,2,1,8,4)$
b. $\mathbf{BK}_3(0,8,2,1,8,4)$
c. $\mathbf{BK}_4(0,0,2,8,4,1)$
d. $\mathbf{BK}_5(0,0,0,1,8,1.99)$
e. $\mathbf{BK}_6(0,0,2,1,8,5)$

7. Write a procedure to compute the coordinates of the eight vertex points of a block. Denote this as **BKVP**(BK,VP), where

BK(6) are the input values x_0, y_0, z_0, a_x, a_y, and a_z and
VP(3,8) are the output coordinates of the vertex points.

8. Write a procedure to compute the surface area, volume, and $\mathbf{p}_{CG}$ of a block. Denote this as **BKPROP**(BK,A,V,PCG), where

BK(6) are the input values x_0, y_0, z_0, a_x, a_y, and a_z
A is the output area
V is the output volume, and
PCG(3) are the output coordinates of $\mathbf{p}_{CG}$.

9. Write a procedure to classify a point with respect to a block. Denote this as **BKPT**(BK,PT,ICLS), where

BK(6) are the input values x_0, y_0, z_0, a_x, a_y, and a_z
PT(3) are the input coordinates of a point, and
ICLS is the output classification of the point:
ICLS = 1 if the point is outside,
ICLS = 2 if the point is inside, and
ICLS = 3 if the point is on the boundary.

10. Write a procedure to classify the relationship between two blocks. Denote this as **BKBK**(BK1,BK2,ICLS), where

BK1(6), BK2(6) are the input values x_0, y_0, z_0, a_x, a_y, and a_z for each of the two blocks and
ICLS is the output classification:
ICLS = 1 if $\mathbf{BK}_1$ ⟨outside⟩ $\mathbf{BK}_2$,
ICLS = 2 if $\mathbf{BK}_1$ ⟨outside, tangent⟩ $\mathbf{BK}_2$,
ICLS = 3 if $\mathbf{BK}_1$ ⟨intersect⟩ $\mathbf{BK}_2$
ICLS = 4 if $\mathbf{BK}_1$ ⟨intersect, tangent⟩ $\mathbf{BK}_2$
ICLS = 5 if $\mathbf{BK}_1$ ⟨inside⟩ $\mathbf{BK}_2$,
ICLS = 6 if $\mathbf{BK}_1$ ⟨inside, tangent⟩ $\mathbf{BK}_2$,

ICLS = 7 if $\mathbf{BK}_2$ ⟨inside⟩ $\mathbf{BK}_1$, and
ICLS = 8 if $\mathbf{BK}_2$ ⟨inside, tangent⟩ $\mathbf{BK}_1$.

11. Derive expression(s) describing blocks that share only a common edge.

12. Derive expression(s) describing blocks that share only a common vertex.

9.3. Cylinders

To describe a cylinder, give the coordinates of the center point of one of its circular faces, a number indicating the orientation of the cylinder's axis, its radius, and its length. You will consider only right circular cylinders whose axes are parallel to one of the three coordinate axes. There are two circular face center points; use the minimum point in the definition.

Denote a cylinder symbolically with the boldface capital letters **CL**, and specify it as follows:

$$\mathbf{CL} = \mathbf{CL}\,(x_c, y_c, z_c, k, r, L) \tag{9.27}$$

where x_c, y_c, and z_c are the coordinates of the minimum center point, k is a number indicating the orientation of the axis, r is the radius, and L is the length. If $k = 1$, then the cylinder's axis is parallel to the x axis; if $k = 2$, then it is parallel to the y axis; if $k = 3$, then it is parallel to the z axis (Fig. 9.13). See Box 9.2.

A cylinder has the following properties: Its surface area is $2\pi r(r + L)$, and its volume is $\pi r^2 L$. The coordinates of its centroid, or geometric center, depend on the orientation of its axis. Thus, if $k = 1$, then

$$\mathbf{p}_{CG} = \left(x_c + \frac{L}{2}, y_c, z_c\right) \tag{9.28}$$

If $k = 2$, then

$$\mathbf{p}_{CG} = \left(x_c, y_c + \frac{L}{2}, z_c\right) \tag{9.29}$$

If $k = 3$, then

$$\mathbf{p}_{CG} = \left(x_c, y_c, z_c + \frac{L}{2}\right) \tag{9.30}$$

Study the cylinder shown in Fig. 9.14, and compute the following properties:

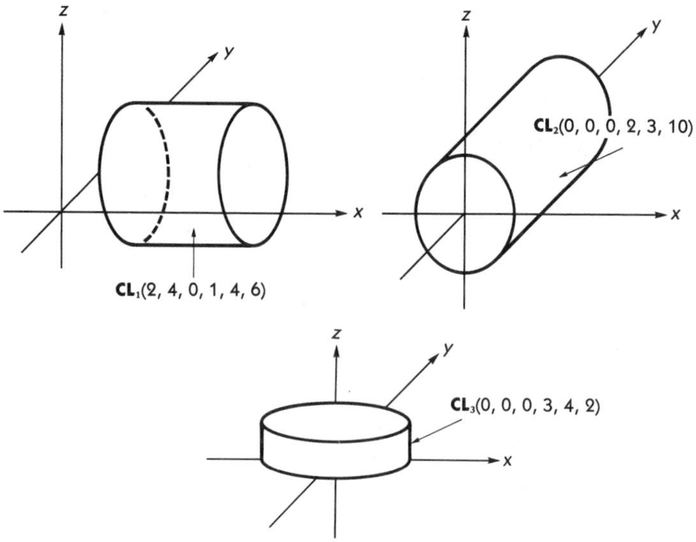

Fig. 9.13. Cylinders defined in *x, y, z* coordinate space.

$$\begin{aligned} &\text{Surface area:} & 2\pi r(r + L) &= 326.73 \\ &\text{Volume:} & \pi r^2 L &= 452.39 \\ &\text{Centroid:} & \mathbf{p}_{CG} &= (0,0,4.5) \end{aligned}$$

Classify an arbitrary point $\mathbf{p} = (x,y,z)$ with respect to a cylinder as follows:

1. When $k = 1$, **p** ⟨inside⟩ **CL** if and only if all of the following conditions are true:

$$x_c < x < x_c + L, \qquad \sqrt{(y - y_c)^2 + (z - z_c)^2} < r \tag{9.31}$$

2. When $k = 1$, **p** ⟨outside⟩ **CL** if and only if at least one of the following sets of conditions is true:

$$\begin{aligned} &x < x_c \quad \text{or} \quad x > x_c + L \\ &\sqrt{(y - y_c)^2 + (z - z_c)^2} > r \end{aligned} \tag{9.32}$$

3. When $k = 1$, **p** ⟨boundary⟩ **CL** if

$$\begin{Bmatrix} x = x_c \\ \text{or} \\ x = x_c + L \end{Bmatrix} \quad \text{and} \quad \sqrt{(y - y_c)^2 + (z - z_c)^2} \le r \tag{9.33}$$

or

Box 9.2. Displaying a Cylinder

The approach here is to approximate the cylinder with an appropriate polyhedron. The two circular faces become n-sided polygons, whose corresponding vertices are connected by straight lines, forming rectangular facets defining the cylindrical surface. Special algorithms interpret the concise data of Eq. (9.27) by computing all the polyhedron vertex points, point-connectivity-defining edges, and edge connectivity defining the polygonal faces. Now you may proceed as with the display of any polyhedron (Section 7.4).

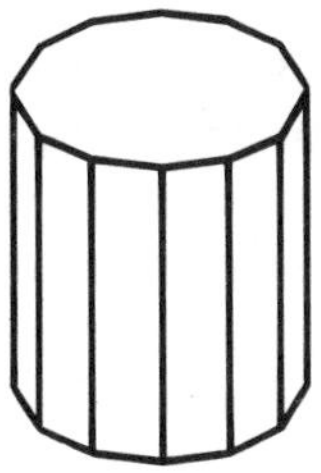

$$x_c < x < x_c + L \quad \text{and} \quad \sqrt{(y - y_c)^2 + (z - z_c)^2} = r \qquad (9.34)$$

There are similar expressions for $k = 2$ and $k = 3$. Try to derive them. Note that the expression $\sqrt{(y - y_c)^2 + (z - z_c)^2}$ gives the distance of the point from the axis of the cylinder. If $k = 1$, then the y, z coordinates of any point on the cylinder's axis are y_c, z_c, respectively.

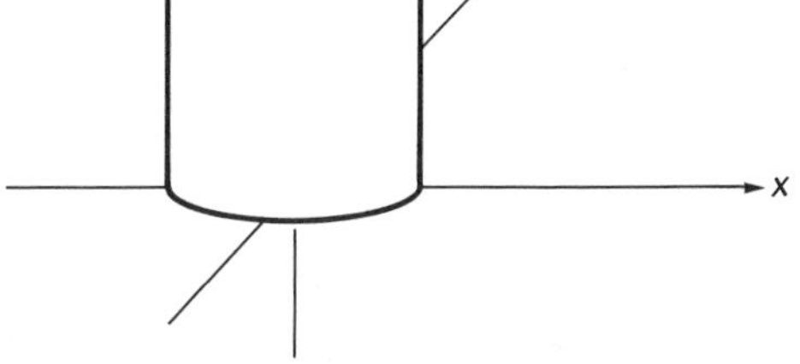

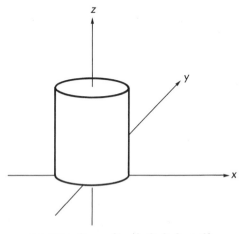

Fig. 9.14. $\mathbf{CL}_1 = \mathbf{CL}_1$ (0, 0, 0, 3, 4, 9).

Given $\mathbf{CL}_1 = \mathbf{CL}_1(0,0,0,3,4,9)$, the cylinder shown in Fig. 9.14, classify the following points with respect to it: $\mathbf{p}_1 = (1,1,6)$, $\mathbf{p}_2 = (0,-4,1)$, and $\mathbf{p}_3 = (-1,-1,-1)$. $\mathbf{p}_1$ ⟨inside⟩ $\mathbf{CL}_1$ because $z_c < z_1 < z_c + L$ and $\sqrt{(x_1 - x_c)^2 + (y_1 - y_c)^2} < r$. $\mathbf{p}_2$ ⟨boundary⟩ $\mathbf{CL}_1$, because $z_c < z_2 < z_c + L$ and $\sqrt{(x_2 - x_c)^2 + (y_2 - y_c)^2} = r$. Finally $\mathbf{p}_3$ ⟨outside⟩ $\mathbf{CL}_1$, because $z_3 < z_c$.

Given two cylinders $\mathbf{CL}_1$ and $\mathbf{CL}_2$, the following spatial relationships can occur between them, depending on the orientation of their axes: One cylinder may lie entirely within the other, the two cylinders may be disjoint, or the two cylinders may intersect.

First consider the relationships between two cylinders whose axes are parallel, that is, $k_1 = k_2$. In the expressions that follow, $k_1 = k_2 = 3$. Here the axes of the cylinders are parallel to the z axis. Again, there are similar expressions for $k_1 = k_2 = 1$ or 2. Figure 9.15 shows the three principal relationships for this case. These relationships are expressed as follows:

When $k_1 = k_2$, $\mathbf{CL}_1$ ⟨inside⟩ $\mathbf{CL}_2$ if and only if all of the following conditions are true:

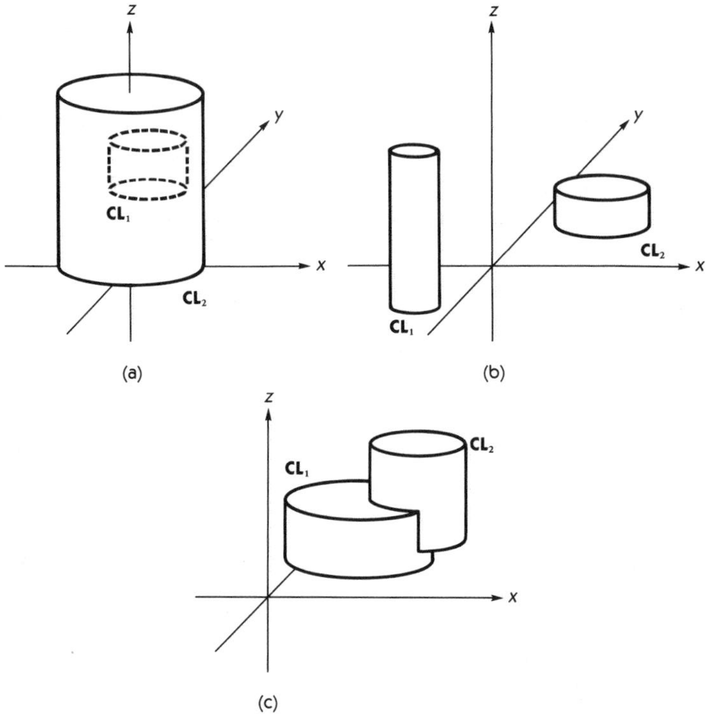

Fig. 9.15. Relationships between two cylinders for $a_1 = a_2$.

$$r_1 \leq r_2$$

$$\sqrt{(x_{c,1} - x_{c,2})^2 + (y_{c,1} - y_{c,2})^2} \leq r_2 - r_1 \tag{9.35}$$

$$z_{c,1} > z_{c,2} \quad \text{and} \quad z_{c,1} + L_1 < z_{c,2} + L_2$$

Figure 9.16a shows two views of this relationship. The geometry exhibited in these views clearly illustrates the conditions in Eqs. (9.35).

When $\boldsymbol{k}_1 = \boldsymbol{k}_2$, $\mathbf{CL}_1$ ⟨outside⟩ $\mathbf{CL}_2$ if and only if at least one of the following conditions is true (see Fig. 9.16b):

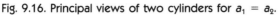

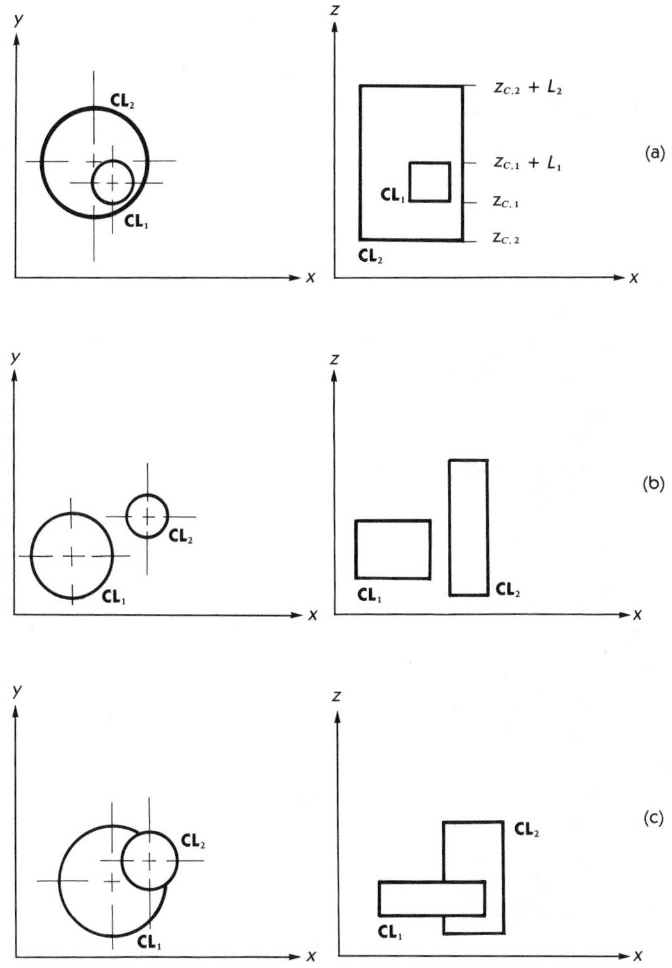

Fig. 9.16. Principal views of two cylinders for $a_1 = a_2$.

$$\sqrt{(x_{c,1} - x_{c,2})^2 + (y_{c,1} - y_{c,2})^2} \geq r_1 + r_2$$
$$\begin{Bmatrix} z_{c,1} \geq z_{c,2} + L \\ \text{or} \\ z_{c,1} + L \leq z_{c,2} \end{Bmatrix} \tag{9.36}$$

When $k_1 = k_2$, $\mathbf{CL}_1$ ⟨intersect⟩ $\mathbf{CL}_2$ if one of the following two sets of conditions is true:

$$\begin{gathered} |r_1 - r_2| < \sqrt{(x_{c,1} - x_{c,2})^2 + (y_{c,1} - y_{c,2})^2} < r_1 + r_2 \\ \text{and} \\ z_{c,2} < z_{c,1} < z_{c,2} + L_2 \quad \text{and, or} \quad z_{c,2} < z_{c,2} + L_2 \end{gathered} \tag{9.37}$$

or (exclusive)

$$\begin{gathered} \sqrt{(x_{c,1} - x_{c,2})^2 + (y_{c,1} - y_{c,2})^2} < r_1 + r_2 \\ \text{and} \\ z_{c,2} < z_{c,1} < z_{c,2} + L_2 \quad \text{or} \quad z_{c,2} < z_{c,1} < z_{c,2} + L_2 \end{gathered} \tag{9.38}$$

See Fig. 9.16c.

Next consider the relationships between two cylinders whose axes are not parallel, that is, $k_1 \neq k_2$. There are six possible combinations; they are: $k_1 = i$, $k_2 = j$ where $i, j = 1,2,3$ and $i \neq j$. Figure 9.17 shows the three principal relationships when $k_1 = 3$ and $k_2 = 1$. Similar results obtain for the other five combinations. The conditions that define these relationships are as follows:

When $k_1 = 3$ and $k_2 = 1$, $\mathbf{CL}_1$ ⟨inside⟩ $\mathbf{CL}_2$ if and only if all of the following conditions are true:

$$\begin{gathered} \sqrt{(x_{c,1} - x_{c,2})^2 + (y_{c,1} - r_1 - y_{c,2})^2} < r_2 \\ \sqrt{(x_{c,1} - x_{c,2})^2 + (y_{c,1} + r_1 - y_{c,2})^2} < r_2 \\ \sqrt{(x_{c,1} + L_1 - x_{c,2})^2 + (y_{c,1} + r_1 - y_{c,2})^2} < r_2 \\ \sqrt{(x_{c,1} + L_1 - x_{c,2})^2 + (y_{c,1} - r_1 - y_{c,2})^2} < r_2 \\ \begin{cases} z_{c,1} + r_1 < z_{c,2} + L_2 \\ z_{c,1} - r_1 > z_{c,2} \end{cases} \end{gathered} \tag{9.39}$$

Figure 9.18a shows two views of this relationship. Study the geometry of these views to discover how the conditions expressed in Eqs. (9.39) are derived. Similar expressions apply to $\mathbf{CL}_2$ ⟨inside⟩ $\mathbf{CL}_1$.

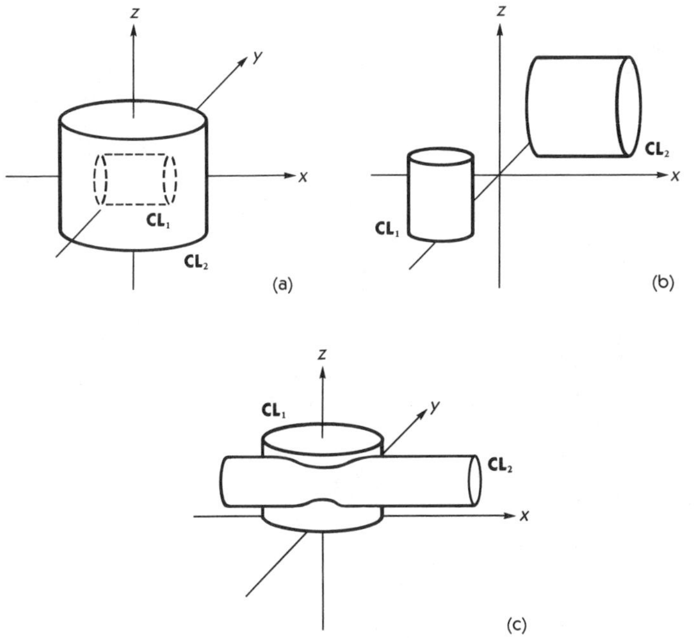

Fig. 9.17. Relationships between two cylinders for $a_1 = 3$ and $a_2 = 1$.

When $k_1 = 3$ and $k_2 = 1$, $\mathbf{CL}_1$ ⟨outside⟩ $\mathbf{CL}_2$ if and only if one or more of the following conditions is true (see Fig. 9.18b):

$$\begin{aligned} &x_{c,1} - x_{c,2} \geq r_2 &&\text{or}\quad x_{c,2} - x_{c,1} \geq L_1 + r_2 \\ &y_{c,1} - y_{c,2} \geq r_1 + r_2 &&\text{or}\quad y_{c,2} - y_{c,1} \geq r_1 + r_2 \\ &z_{c,1} - z_{c,2} \geq r_1 + L_2 &&\text{or}\quad z_{c,2} - z_{c,1} \geq r_1 \end{aligned} \tag{9.40}$$

When $k_1 = 3$ and $k_2 = 1$, $\mathbf{CL}_1$ ⟨intersect⟩ $\mathbf{CL}_2$ if $\mathbf{CL}_1$ ⟨not inside⟩ $\mathbf{CL}_2$, $\mathbf{CL}_2$ ⟨not inside⟩ $\mathbf{CL}_1$, and $\mathbf{CL}_1$ ⟨not outside⟩ $\mathbf{CL}_2$.

This is a somewhat different approach from previous ones, but equally valid. Note that if two objects intersect, they must be seen to intersect from any point of view; see Fig. 9.18c.

You will not study here the conditions that indicate internal or external tangency between two cylinders. They are easy to develop, both for cylinders whose axes are parallel and for those whose axes are not. For cylinders whose axes are parallel, for example, a necessary though not sufficient condition for tangency is that the distance between their axes must equal $r_1 + r_2$, unless the cylinders are tangent at their circular, plane faces. Figure 9.19 shows several examples of cylinder–cylinder tangency.

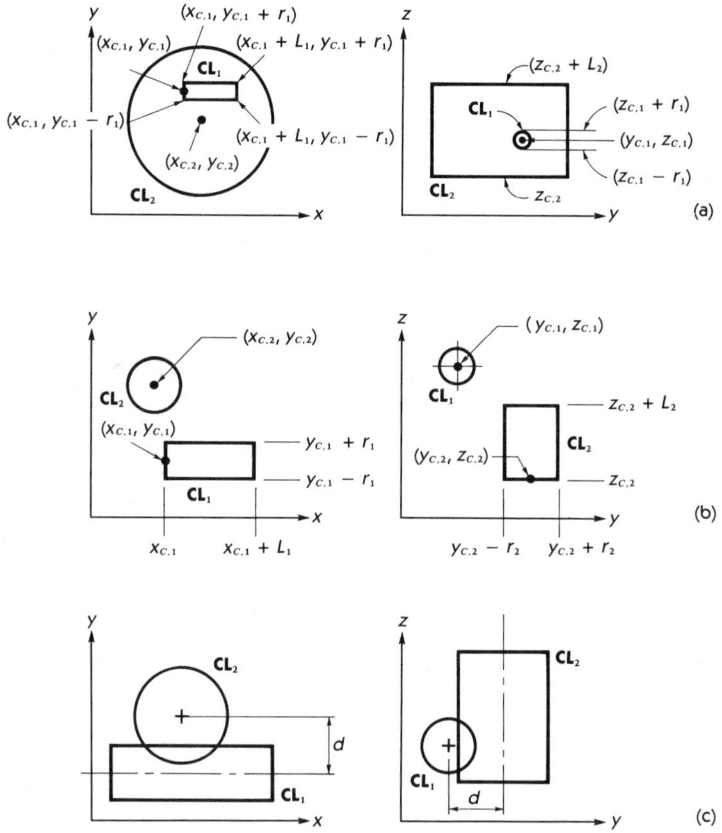

Fig. 9.18. Principal views of two cylinders for $a_1 = 3$ and $a_2 = 1$.

EXERCISES

1. Which of the following expressions improperly specify a cylinder, and why?

a. $\mathbf{CL}_1(0,0,0,1,2,6)$
b. $\mathbf{CL}_2(-1,7,0,4,2,10)$
c. $\mathbf{CL}_3(6.2,-1.3,5.0,2,2.5,2.5)$
d. $\mathbf{CL}_4(1,1,1,3,2.4,3.2,1.6)$
e. $\mathbf{CL}_5(8.3,9.7,3.6,1.2,3.1,1.1)$
f. $\mathbf{CL}_6(16,16,0,1,16,0.5)$
g. $\mathbf{CL}_7(3.5,8.2,-1.5,2,21.5,59.6)$
h. $\mathbf{CL}_8(-1.5,-1.5,0,3,1.5,-2.0)$
i. $\mathbf{CL}_9(4,8,8,1,8,1)$
j. $\mathbf{CL}_{10}(7.5,7.5,0,3,7.5)$

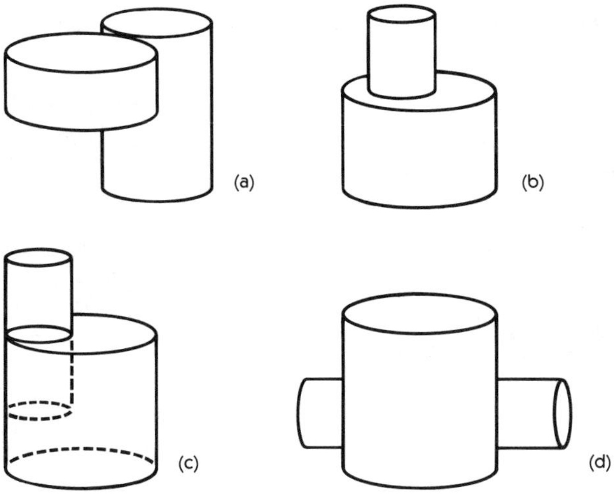

Fig. 9.19. Tangent cylinders.

2. Compute the coordinates of the maximum center point for each of the following cylinders:

a. $\mathbf{CL}_1(0,0,-6,3,1,4)$
b. $\mathbf{CL}_2(4,1,-1,3,1.5,3)$
c. $\mathbf{CL}_3(0,1,0,2,0.5,10)$
d. $\mathbf{CL}_4(-2,-2,1,1,3,16)$
e. $\mathbf{CL}_5(8,0,-6,2,2,9)$

3. Compute $\mathbf{p}_{CG}$ for each of the cylinders defined in Exercise 2.

4. Compute the surface area and volume for each of the cylinders defined in Exercise 2.

5. Given $\mathbf{CL}_1 = \mathbf{CL}_1(2,2,0,3,1,7)$, classify the following points with respect to it:

a. $\mathbf{p}_1 = (2,2,-1)$
b. $\mathbf{p}_2 = (2,3,7)$
c. $\mathbf{p}_3 - (2.5,2,1)$
d. $\mathbf{p}_4 = (1,2,0)$
e. $\mathbf{p}_5 = (3,3,6)$

6. Given $\mathbf{CL}_1 = \mathbf{CL}_1(2,2,0,3,1,7)$, classify $\mathbf{CL}_1$ with respect to the following cylinders:

a. $\mathbf{CL}_2(2,2,0,3,2,1)$
b. $\mathbf{CL}_3(0,2,2,1,1,5)$
c. $\mathbf{CL}_4(1.5,2,3,3,0.5,2.5)$
d. $\mathbf{CL}_5(0,0,1,3,3,1)$
e. $\mathbf{CL}_6(0,-2,2,2,0.25,16)$

7. Write a procedure to compute the surface area, volume, and $\mathbf{p}_{CG}$ of a cylinder. Denote this as **CLPROP**(CL,A,V,PCG), where

CL(6) are the input values x_c, y_c, z_c, k, r, L,
A is the output area,
V is the output volume, and
PCG(3) are the output coordinates of $\mathbf{p}_{CG}$.

8. Write a procedure to classify a point with respect to a cylinder. Denote this as **CLPT**(CL,PT,ICLS) where

CL(6) are the input values x_c, y_c, z_c, k, r, L,
PT(3) are the input coordinates of a point, and
ICLS is the output classification of this point:
ICLS = 1 if the point is outside,
ICLS = 2 if the point is inside, and
ICLS = 3 if the point is on the boundary.

9. Write a procedure to classify the relationship between two cylinders $\mathbf{CL}_1$ and $\mathbf{CL}_2$. Denote this as **CLCL**(CL1,CL2,ICLS), where

CL1(6), CL2(6) are the input values x_c, y_c, z_c, k, r, L for each of the two cylinders and
ICLS is the output classification:
ICLS = 1 if $\mathbf{CL}_1$ ⟨outside⟩ $\mathbf{CL}_2$,
ICLS = 2 if $\mathbf{CL}_1$ ⟨outside, tangent⟩ $\mathbf{CL}_2$,
ICLS = 3 if $\mathbf{CL}_1$ ⟨intersect⟩ $\mathbf{CL}_2$,
ICLS = 4 if $\mathbf{CL}_1$ ⟨intersect, tangent⟩ $\mathbf{CL}_2$,
ICLS = 5 if $\mathbf{CL}_1$ ⟨inside⟩ $\mathbf{CL}_2$,
ICLS = 6 if $\mathbf{CL}_1$ ⟨inside, tangent⟩ $\mathbf{CL}_2$,
ICLS = 7 if $\mathbf{CL}_2$ ⟨inside⟩ $\mathbf{CL}_1$, and
ICLS = 8 if $\mathbf{CL}_2$ ⟨inside, tangent⟩ $\mathbf{CL}_1$.

9.4. Spheres

To describe a sphere, give the coordinates of its center point and its radius. Since a sphere is radially symmetrical, it has no preferred or distinguishing orientation in space. All orientations are geometrically equal.

Denote a sphere symbolically with the boldface capital letters **SP**. Use a subscript to indicate a specific sphere, $\mathbf{SP}_i$ for example. Thus, to specify a sphere, write

$$\mathbf{SP} = \mathbf{SP}(x_c, y_c, z_c, r) \tag{9.41}$$

where x_c, y_c, and z_c are the coordinates of the center point and r is the radius. Read this expression as: A sphere is a function of the coordinates of its center point and its radius. See Fig. 9.20 and discussion in Box. 9.3.

A sphere has the following properties:

Circumference:	$C = 2\pi r$
Surface area:	$A = 4\pi r^2$
Volume:	$V = \frac{4}{3}\pi r^3$
$\mathbf{p}_{CG}$:	(x_c, y_c, z_c)

Continue to classify the points by computing distance. Given a point $\mathbf{p} = (x,y,z)$, compute its distance from the center of a given sphere. Denote this distance as d. Thus,

$$d = \sqrt{(x - x_c)^2 + (y - y_c)^2 + (z - z_c)^2} \tag{9.42}$$

Then

$$\mathbf{p}\ \langle\text{inside}\rangle\ \mathbf{SP} \text{ if and only if } d < r \tag{9.43}$$

$$\mathbf{p}\ \langle\text{outside}\rangle\ \mathbf{SP} \text{ if and only if } d > r \tag{9.44}$$

and

$$\mathbf{p}\ \langle\text{boundary}\rangle\ \mathbf{SP} \text{ if and only if } d = r \tag{9.45}$$

Figure 9.21 illustrates the point classification geometry.

Given two spheres $\mathbf{SP}_1$ and $\mathbf{SP}_2$, the spatial relationships that can occur between them are: One sphere may lie entirely within the other, the two spheres may be disjoint, or they may intersect. Decide which relationship

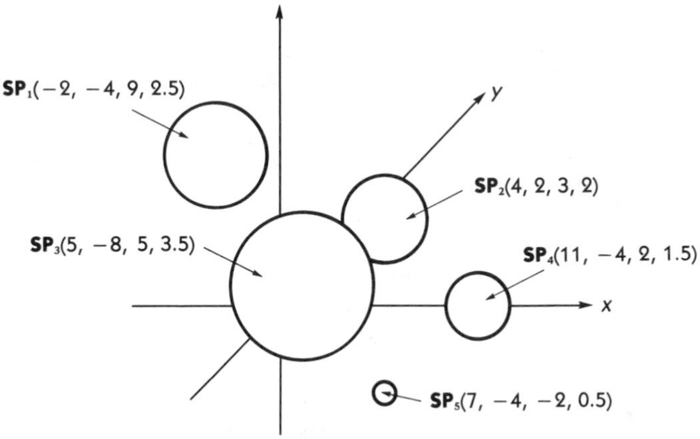

Fig. 9.20. Spheres.

Box 9.3. Displaying a Sphere

Use the concise data defining a sphere [Eq. (9.41)] to construct a polyhedron that approximates it. Then proceed as with the display of any polyhedron (Section 7.4).

exists by computing the distance between the centers of the two spheres, denoted d_c, where

$$d_c = \sqrt{(x_{c,2} - x_{c,1})^2 + (y_{c,2} - y_{c,1})^2 + (z_{c,2} - z_{c,1})^2} \qquad (9.46)$$

Thus,

$$\mathbf{SP}_1 \langle \text{inside} \rangle \mathbf{SP}_2 \text{ if and only if } d_c \leq r_2 - r_1 \qquad (9.47)$$

$$\mathbf{SP}_2 \langle \text{inside} \rangle \mathbf{SP}_1 \text{ if and only if } d_c \leq r_1 - r_2 \qquad (9.48)$$

$$\mathbf{SP}_1 \langle \text{outside} \rangle \mathbf{SP}_2 \text{ if and only if } d_c \geq r_1 + r_2 \qquad (9.49)$$

$$\mathbf{SP}_1 \langle \text{intersect} \rangle \mathbf{SP}_2 \text{ if and only if } r_2 - r_1 < d_c < r_1 + r_2 \qquad (9.50)$$

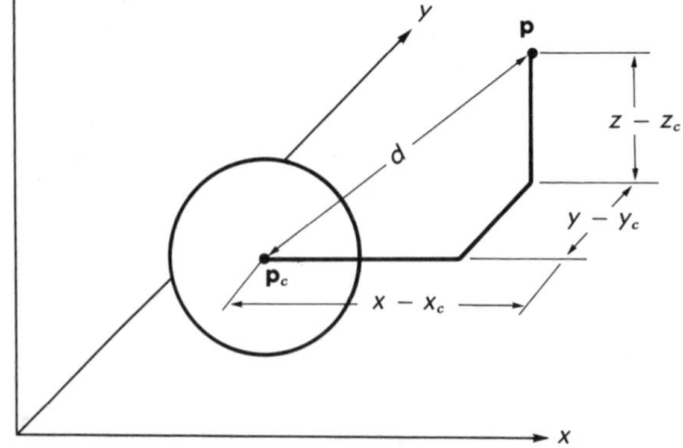

Fig. 9.21. Point classification with respect to a sphere.

See Fig. 9.22 for examples of these relationships.

There are three possible tangency conditions:

$$\mathbf{SP}_1 \ \langle \text{outside, tangent} \rangle \ \mathbf{SP}_2 \text{ if and only if } d_c = r_1 + r_2 \tag{9.51}$$

or

$$\mathbf{SP}_1 \ \langle \text{inside, tangent} \rangle \ \mathbf{SP}_2 \text{ if and only if } d_c = r_2 - r_1 \tag{9.52}$$

or

$$\mathbf{SP}_2 \ \langle \text{inside, tangent} \rangle \ \mathbf{SP}_1 \text{ if and only if } d_c = r_1 - r_2 \tag{9.53}$$

See Figs. 9.22e and 9.22f.

Classifying the possible spatial relationships between a sphere and a block is a more complex problem and is similar to the problem of the circle and rectangle. Several steps are required to solve it: First, classify the vertex points of the block with respect to the sphere. A block vertex point is either inside the sphere, outside it, or on its boundary. There are 45 combinations of vertex point distributions. You will examine some of them now.

Table 9.1 lists some of the distribution combinations; several are shown in Fig. 9.23. (Are all 45 combinations geometrically possible or unique?) Note that for Condition 2 the sphere is circumscribed about the block, and the geometric center of the sphere and block coincide.

Conditions 6, 7, 13, 14, and 15 are geometrically impossible. There can

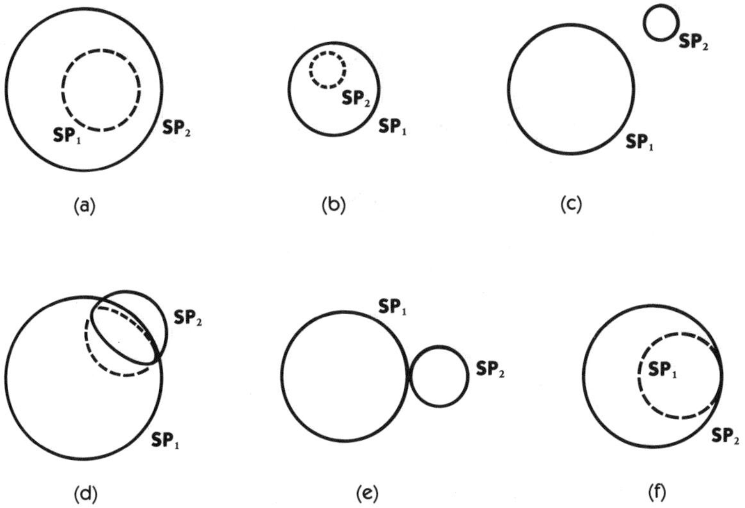

Fig. 9.22. Relationships between two spheres.

Table 9.1. Block and Sphere Classification

Condition	Block Vertex Point Distribution: Inside Sphere	Boundary of Sphere	Outside Sphere	Classification
1	8	0	0	**BK** ⟨inside⟩ **SP**
2	0	8	0	**BK** ⟨inside⟩ **SP**
3	0	0	8	Indeterminate
4	7	1	0	**BK** ⟨inside⟩ **SP**
5	7	0	1	**BK** ⟨intersect⟩ **SP**
6	1	7	0	Geometrically impossible
7	0	7	1	Geometrically impossible
8	1	0	7	**BK** ⟨intersect⟩ **SP**
9	0	1	7	Indeterminate
10	6	2	0	**BK** ⟨inside⟩ **SP**
11	6	1	1	**BK** ⟨intersect⟩ **SP**
12	6	0	2	**BK** ⟨intersect⟩ **SP**
13	2	6	0	Geometrically impossible
14	1	6	1	Geometrically impossible
15	0	6	2	Geometrically impossible
16	2	0	6	**BK** ⟨intersect⟩ **SP**
17	1	1	6	**BK** ⟨intersect⟩ **SP**
18	0	2	6	**BK** ⟨intersect⟩ **SP**

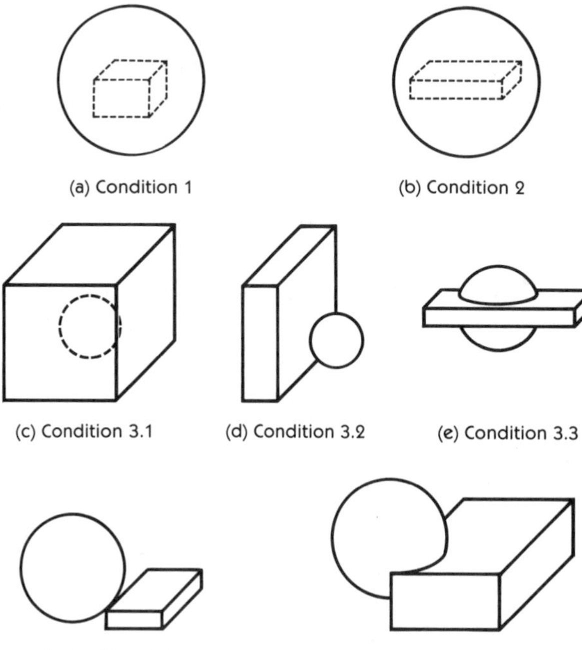

(a) Condition 1 (b) Condition 2 (c) Condition 3.1 (d) Condition 3.2 (e) Condition 3.3 (f) Condition 9.1 (g) Condition 9.2

Fig. 9.23. Block vertex point distribution with respect to a sphere.

be one, two, three, four or eight block vertex points on the boundary (or surface) of a sphere.

Conditions 3 and 9 are indeterminate solely on the basis of the distribution of block vertex points. See Figs. 9.23c–9.23g. There are three possible classifications for Condition 3 (inside, intersect, and outside) and two for Condition 9 (intersect and outside).

If the distribution of points indicates that Condition 3 exists, then distinguish between the three possibilities as follows:

SP ⟨inside⟩ **BK** if and only if all of the following six conditions are true:

$$\begin{aligned} &x_c - x_{\min} \geq r \quad \text{and} \quad x_{\max} - x_c \geq r, \quad \text{and} \\ &y_c - y_{\min} \geq r \quad \text{and} \quad y_{\max} - y_c \geq r, \quad \text{and} \\ &z_c - z_{\min} \geq r \quad \text{and} \quad z_{\max} - z_c \geq r \end{aligned} \tag{9.54}$$

SP ⟨outside⟩ **BK** if at least one of the following six conditions is true:

$$\begin{aligned} &x_{\min} - x_c \geq r \quad \text{or} \quad x_c - x_{\max} \geq r, \quad \text{or} \\ &y_{\min} - y_c \geq r \quad \text{or} \quad y_c - y_{\max} \geq r, \quad \text{or} \\ &z_{\min} - z_c \geq r \quad \text{or} \quad z_c - z_{\max} \geq r \end{aligned} \tag{9.55}$$

SP ⟨intersect⟩ **BK** if at least one of the following conditions is true:

$$\begin{aligned} &x_c - r \leq x_{\min} \leq x_c + r \quad \text{or} \quad x_c - r \leq x_{\max} \leq x_c + r, \quad \text{or} \\ &y_c - r \leq y_{\min} \leq y_c + r \quad \text{or} \quad y_c - r \leq y_{\max} \leq y_c + r, \quad \text{or} \\ &z_c - r \leq z_{\min} \leq z_c + r \quad \text{or} \quad z_c - r \leq z_{\max} \leq z_c + r \end{aligned} \tag{9.56}$$

Condition 9 is also indeterminate. Try to develop the criteria for resolving this.

The spatial relationships possible between a sphere and a cylinder are only slightly more difficult to classify. The following are the conditions required for a sphere and a cylinder to be disjoint, where the axis of the cylinder is parallel to the z axis. The other two axis orientations produce similar results.

SP ⟨outside⟩ **CL** if one of the following conditions is true (see Fig. 9.24a):

$$\begin{aligned} z_{CL} - z_c &\geq r_s \\ z_c - (z_{CL} + L) &\geq r_s \\ \sqrt{(x_c - x_{CL})^2 + (y_c - y_{CL})^2} &\geq r_s + r_c \end{aligned} \tag{9.57}$$

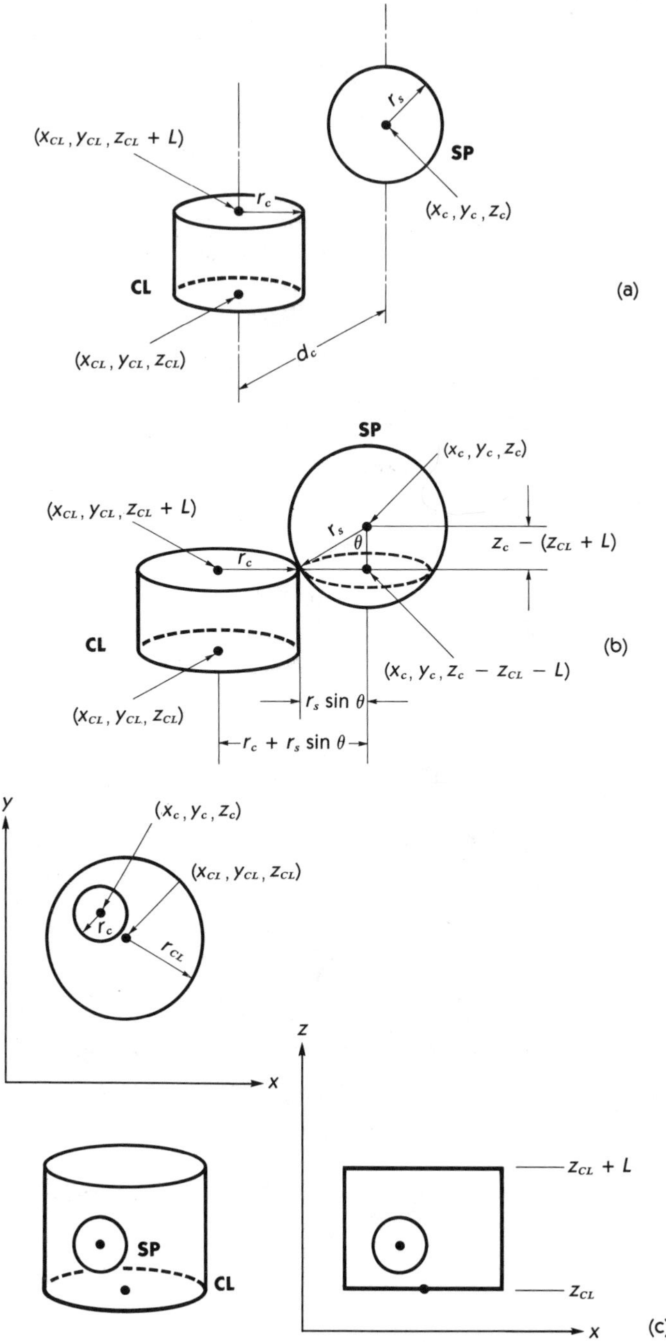

Fig. 9.24. (a) and (b) Sphere ⟨outside⟩ cylinder; (c) sphere ⟨inside⟩ cylinder.

SP ⟨outside⟩ **CL** if one of the following two sets of conditions is true:

$$0 \leq z_c - (z_{CL} + L) \leq r_s \quad \text{and} \\ \sqrt{(x_c - x_{CL})^2 + (y_c - y_{CL})^2} \geq r_c + r_s \sin\theta \tag{9.58}$$

where

$$\theta = \cos^{-1}\left(\frac{z_c - z_{CL} - L}{r_s}\right) \tag{9.59}$$

or

$$0 \leq z_{CL} - z_c \leq r_s \quad \text{and} \\ \sqrt{(x_c - x_{CL})^2 + (y_c - y_{CL})^2} \geq r_c + r_s \sin\theta \tag{9.60}$$

See Fig. 9.24b.

Next, consider the inside relationship between sphere and cylinder. Again, the axis of the cylinder is parallel to the z axis. Figure 9.24c shows the pertinent geometry.

SP ⟨inside⟩ **CL** if and only if all of the following conditions are true:

$$z_c - z_{CL} \geq r_c \\ z_{CL} + L - z_c \geq r_c \\ \sqrt{(x_c - x_{CL})^2 + (y_c - y_{CL})^2} \leq r_{CL} - r_c \tag{9.61}$$

CL ⟨inside⟩ **SP** if and only if any two of the following three conditions are true. (Note: If any two are true, then the third follows directly.) Figure 9.25 shows the geometry defining each condition.

$$\sqrt{(x_c - x_{CL})^2 + (y_c - y_{CL})^2} \leq r_c - r_{CL} \tag{9.62}$$

$$\left.\begin{array}{l} \sqrt{(x_c - x_{CL} + r_{CL})^2 + (z_c - z_{CL} - L)^2} \leq r_c \\ \sqrt{(x_c - x_{CL} - r_{CL})^2 + (z_c - z_{CL} - L)^2} \leq r_c \\ \sqrt{(x_c - x_{CL} + r_{CL})^2 + (z_c - z_{CL})^2} \leq r_c \\ \sqrt{(x_c - x_{CL} - r_{CL})^2 + (z_c - z_{CL})^2} \leq r_c \end{array}\right\} \tag{9.63}$$

$$\left.\begin{array}{l} \sqrt{(y_c - y_{CL} + r_{CL})^2 + (z_c - z_{CL} - L)^2} \leq r_c \\ \sqrt{(y_c - y_{CL} - r_{CL})^2 + (z_c - z_{CL} - L)^2} \leq r_c \\ \sqrt{(y_c - y_{CL} + r_{CL})^2 + (z_c - z_{CL})^2} \leq r_c \\ \sqrt{(y_c - y_{CL} - r_{CL})^2 + (z_c - z_{CL})^2} \leq r_c \end{array}\right\} \tag{9.64}$$

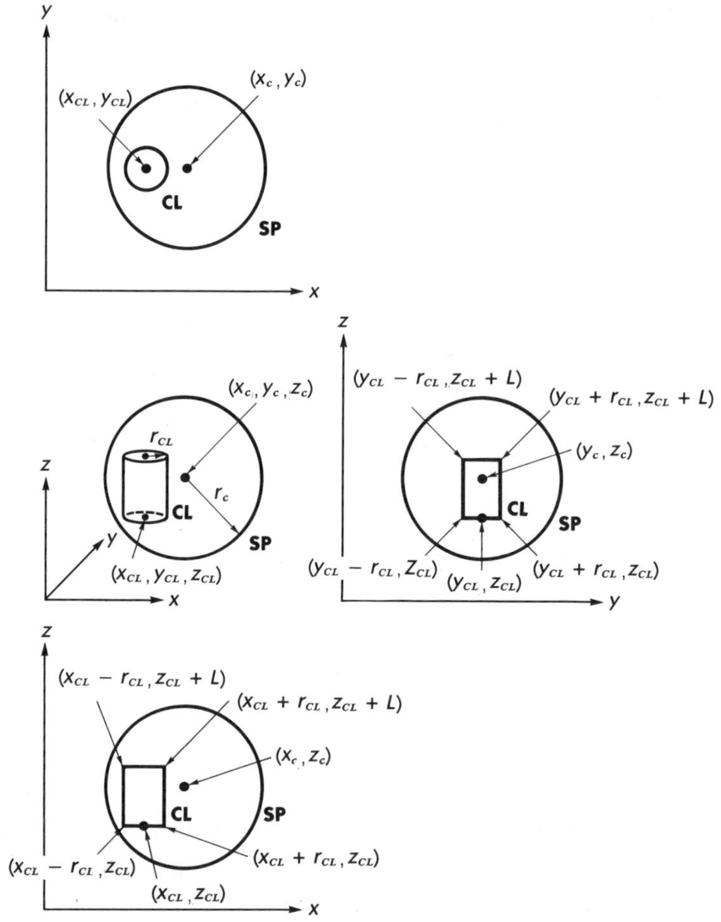

Fig. 9.25. Cylinder ⟨inside⟩ sphere.

Finally, **SP** ⟨intersect⟩ **CL** if and only if **SP** ⟨not inside⟩ **CL**, **CL** ⟨not inside⟩ **SP**, and **SP** ⟨not outside⟩ **CL**.

Can you think of a more direct test for **SP** ⟨intersect⟩ **CL**? Hint: Imagine the sphere and cylinder projected onto a plane perpendicular to the axis of the cylinder.

EXERCISES

1. Which of the following expressions improperly specify a sphere, and why?

   a. $\mathbf{SP}_1$ (0, 0, 0, 1)
   b. $\mathbf{SP}_2$ (−1, −1, 0, 0)

c. $\mathbf{SP}_3$ (7.2, 6.1, −2.5, 2.5)
d. $\mathbf{SP}_4$ (4, 2, 9, −2)
e. $\mathbf{SP}_5$ (−8.3, 0, −8.3, 4.5)

2. Compute the points of minimum and maximum x, y, and z for each of the following spheres:

a. $\mathbf{SP}_1$ (0, 0, 0, 1)
b. $\mathbf{SP}_2$ (3, 3, 0, 1)
c. $\mathbf{SP}_3$ (−2, 4, 6, 2)
d. $\mathbf{SP}_4$ (7.5, 5, 2, 2.5)
e. $\mathbf{SP}_5$ (0, 0, 10, 5)

3. Compute the circumference, surface area, volume, and $\mathbf{p}_{CG}$ for each of the spheres defined in Exercise 2.

4. Given $\mathbf{SP}_1 = \mathbf{SP}_1$ (0, 4, 0, 2), classify the following points with respect to it:

a. $\mathbf{p}_1 = (0, 4, 1)$
b. $\mathbf{p}_2 = (0, 4, 2)$
c. $\mathbf{p}_3 = (0, 0, 0)$
d. $\mathbf{p}_4 = (0, 4, 3)$
e. $\mathbf{p}_5 = (-1, -1, -1)$

5. Given $\mathbf{SP}_1 = \mathbf{SP}_1$ (0, 4, 0, 2), classify $\mathbf{SP}_1$ with respect to the following spheres:

a. $\mathbf{SP}_2$ (−1, 5, 1, 2)
b. $\mathbf{SP}_3$ (0, 3, 0, 1)
c. $\mathbf{SP}_4$ (4, 4, 0, 1)
d. $\mathbf{SP}_5$ (0, 4, −6, 4)
e. $\mathbf{SP}_6$ (0, 4, 0, 2)

6. Given $\mathbf{SP}_1 = \mathbf{SP}_1$ (0, 0, 0, 1), classify $\mathbf{SP}_1$ with respect to the following blocks:

a. $\mathbf{BK}_1$ (4, 0, 0, 1, 4, 1)
b. $\mathbf{BK}_2$ (−1, −1, −10, 2, 2, 9)
c. $\mathbf{BK}_3$ (−1, −1, 0, 2, 2, 9)
d. $\mathbf{BK}_4$ (−2, −3, −4, 6, 6, 12)
e. $\mathbf{BK}_5$ (−1, −1, −1, 2, 2, 2)

7. Given $\mathbf{SP}_1 = \mathbf{SP}_1$ (2, 4, 1, 2), classify $\mathbf{SP}_1$ with respect to the following cylinders:

a. $\mathbf{CL}_1$ (0, 0, 0, 2, 2, 6)
b. $\mathbf{CL}_2$ (0, 0, 0, 3, 2, 6)
c. $\mathbf{CL}_3$ (0, 4, 1, 1, 2, 6)
d. $\mathbf{CL}_4$ (2, 4, 0, 3, 1, 1)
e. $\mathbf{CL}_5$ (2, 4, −2, 3, 4, 1)

8. Write a procedure to compute the circumference, surface area, volume, and geometric center of a sphere. Denote this as **SPROP** (SP, C, A, V, PCG), where

SP(4) are the input values x_c, y_c, z_c, and r,
A is the output area,
V is the output volume, and
PCG(3) are the output coordinates of $\mathbf{p}_{CG}$.

9. Write a procedure to classify a point with respect to a sphere. Denote this as **SPT** (SP, PT, ICLS), where

SP(4) are the input values x_c, y_c, z_c, and r,
PT(3) are the input coordinates of the point, and
ICLS is the output classification of this point:
ICLS = 1 if the point is outside,
ICLS = 2 if the point is inside, and
ICLS = 3 if the point is on the boundary.

10. Write a procedure to classify the relationship between two spheres, $\mathbf{SP}_1$ and $\mathbf{SP}_2$. Denote this as **SPSP** (SP1, SP2, ICLS) where

SP1(4), SP2(4) are the input values x_c, y_c, z_c, and r for each of the two spheres and
ICLS is the output classification:
ICLS = 1 if $\mathbf{SP}_1$ ⟨outside⟩ $\mathbf{SP}_2$,
ICLS = 2 if $\mathbf{SP}_1$ ⟨outside, tangent⟩ $\mathbf{SP}_2$,
ICLS = 3 if $\mathbf{SP}_1$ ⟨intersect⟩ $\mathbf{SP}_2$,
ICLS = 4 if $\mathbf{SP}_1$ ⟨inside⟩ $\mathbf{SP}_2$,
ICLS = 5 if $\mathbf{SP}_1$ ⟨inside, tangent⟩ $\mathbf{SP}_2$,
ICLS = 6 if $\mathbf{SP}_2$ ⟨inside⟩ $\mathbf{SP}_1$, and
ICLS = 7 if $\mathbf{SP}_2$ ⟨inside, tangent⟩ $\mathbf{SP}_1$.

11. Write a procedure to classify the relationship between a sphere and a cylinder, $\mathbf{SP}_1$ and $\mathbf{CL}_1$. Denote this as **SPCL** (SP, CL, ICLS), where

SP(4) are the input values x_c, y_c, z_c, and r,
CL(6) are the input values x_c, y_c, z_c, k, r, and L, and
ICLS is the output classification:
ICLS = 1 if $\mathbf{SP}_1$ ⟨outside⟩ $\mathbf{CL}_1$,
ICLS = 2 if $\mathbf{SP}_1$ ⟨outside, tangent⟩ $\mathbf{CL}_1$,
ICLS = 3 if $\mathbf{SP}_1$ ⟨intersect⟩ $\mathbf{CL}_1$,
ICLS = 4 if $\mathbf{SP}_1$ ⟨intersect, tangent⟩ $\mathbf{CL}_1$,
ICLS = 5 if $\mathbf{SP}_1$ ⟨inside⟩ $\mathbf{CL}_1$,
ICLS = 6 if $\mathbf{SP}_1$ ⟨inside, tangent⟩ $\mathbf{CL}_1$,
ICLS = 7 if $\mathbf{CL}_1$ ⟨inside⟩ $\mathbf{SP}_1$, and
ICLS = 8 if $\mathbf{CL}_1$ ⟨inside, tangent⟩ $\mathbf{SP}_1$.

9.5. Combining Elements

Combining simple three-dimensional shapes to form complex solid geometric models proceeds in much the same way as when combining two-dimensional shapes. Again, you will use three kinds of combining operators: union, difference, and intersect; these have the same function and meaning, of course, that they had in Section 8.4.

UNION

First study the union of two blocks in Fig. 9.26. Table 9.2 presents the eight possible combinations of point classification for two blocks $\mathbf{BK}_1$ and $\mathbf{BK}_2$ joined by the union operator. Points falling outside both blocks are not included.

Only Condition 2 is indeterminate. This occurs when a point lies on the boundary of both $\mathbf{BK}_1$ and $\mathbf{BK}_2$. Further analysis is required to resolve the ambiguity. There are several ways the bounding surfaces of rectangles may coincide: some consist of points interior to the union; others consist of points on its boundary. Figure 9.27 shows examples of both. Any point $\mathbf{p}$ on the shaded areas of the solids in Figs. 9.27a and 9.27b is classified as follows:

$$\text{If } \mathbf{p} \in b\mathbf{BK}_1 \quad \text{and} \quad \mathbf{p} \in b\mathbf{BK}_2, \quad \text{then} \quad \mathbf{p} \in b(\mathbf{BK}_1 \cup \mathbf{BK}_2) \tag{9.65}$$

is true if and only if at least one of the following six conditions is true:

$$\begin{aligned} x_{\min,1} &= x_{\min,2}, & x_{\max,1} &= x_{\max,2} \\ y_{\min,1} &= y_{\min,2}, & y_{\max,1} &= y_{\max,2} \\ z_{\min,1} &= z_{\min,2}, & z_{\max,1} &= z_{\max,2} \end{aligned} \tag{9.66}$$

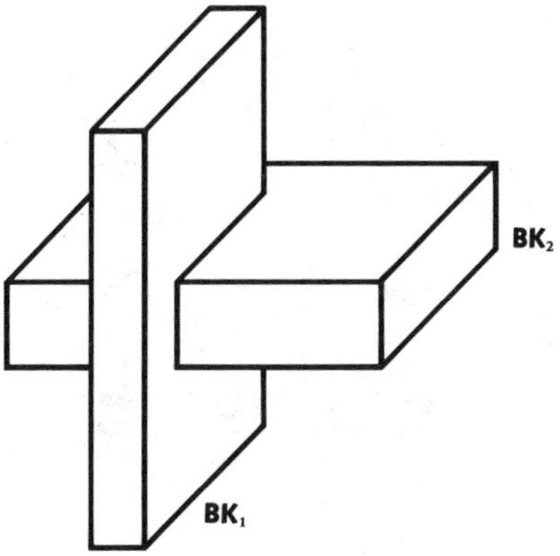

Fig. 9.26. Union of two blocks.

Table 9.2. $\mathbf{BK}_1 \cup \mathbf{BK}_2$: Point Classification

	If				Then	
Condition	$b\mathbf{BK}_1$	$i\mathbf{BK}_1$	$b\mathbf{BK}_2$	$i\mathbf{BK}_2$	$b(\mathbf{BK}_1 \cup \mathbf{BK}_2)$	$i(\mathbf{BK}_1 \cup \mathbf{BK}_2)$
1	X				X	
2	X		X		Indeterminate	
3	X			X		X
4		X				X
5		X	X			X
6		X		X		X
7			X		X	
8				X		X

Any point $\mathbf{p}$ on the shaded areas of the solids in Fig. 9.27c and Fig. 9.27d is classified as follows:

$$\text{If } \mathbf{p} \in b\mathbf{BK}_1 \quad \text{and} \quad \mathbf{p} \in b\mathbf{BK}_2, \quad \text{then} \quad \mathbf{p} \in i(\mathbf{BK}_1 \cup \mathbf{BK}_2) \qquad (9.67)$$

is true if and only if one of the following six conditions is true:

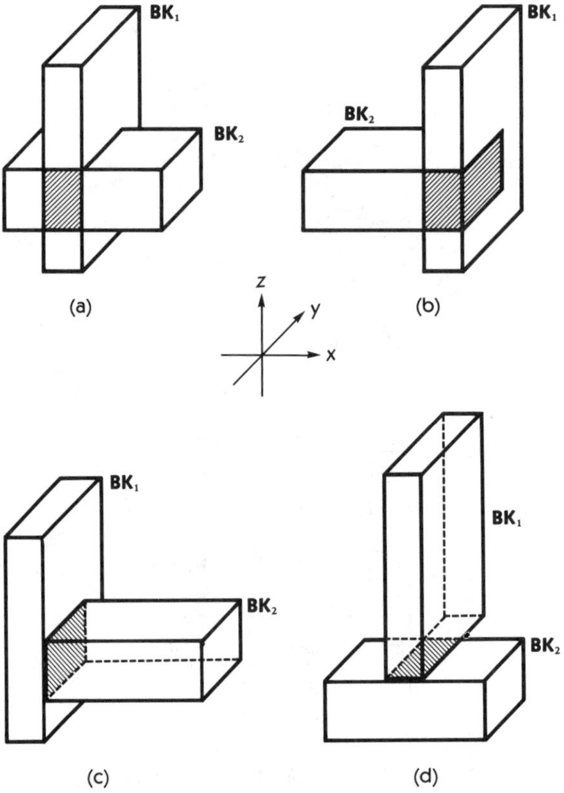

Fig. 9.27. $\mathbf{BK}_1 \cup \mathbf{BK}_2$: coincident boundaries.

$$\begin{aligned} x_{\min,1} &= x_{\max,2}, & x_{\max,1} &= x_{\min,2} \\ y_{\min,1} &= y_{\max,2}, & y_{\max,1} &= y_{\min,2} \\ z_{\min,1} &= z_{\max,2}, & z_{\max,1} &= z_{\min,2} \end{aligned} \tag{9.68}$$

Note that each of these conditions is mutually exclusive.

DIFFERENCE

Compare the possible results of the union operator to those of the difference operator acting on two blocks $\mathbf{BK}_1$ and $\mathbf{BK}_2$; see the example in Fig. 9.28. Table 9.3 presents the eight possible combinations of point classification for the difference of two blocks. Again, points falling outside both blocks are not included. Remember, the order of the operands is important.

Condition 2 is indeterminate. The ambiguity is resolved as follows, depending on which boundary surfaces of the blocks coincide. Figure 9.29 shows examples of two kinds of surface coincidence.

$$\text{If } \mathbf{p} \in b\mathbf{BK}_1 \quad \text{and} \quad \mathbf{p} \in b\mathbf{BK}_2, \quad \text{then} \quad \mathbf{p} \in o(\mathbf{BK}_1 - \mathbf{BK}_2) \tag{9.69}$$

is true if and only if at least one of the following six conditions is true (see Fig. 9.29a):

$$\begin{aligned} x_{\min,1} &= x_{\min,2}, & x_{\max,1} &= x_{\max,2} \\ y_{\min,1} &= y_{\min,2}, & y_{\max,1} &= y_{\max,2} \\ z_{\min,1} &= z_{\min,2}, & z_{\max,1} &= z_{\max,2} \end{aligned} \tag{9.70}$$

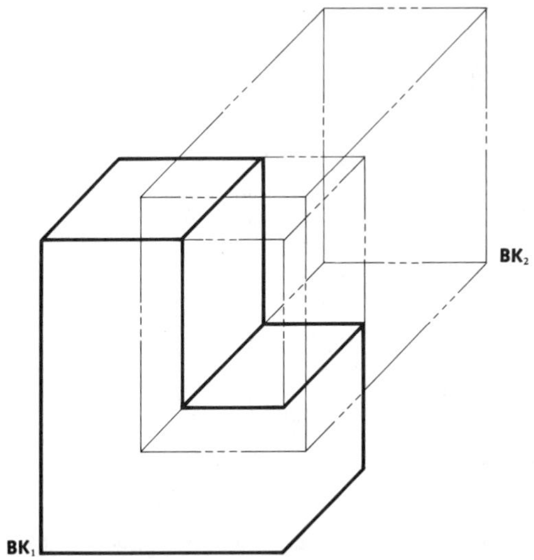

Fig. 9.28. Difference of two blocks.

Table 9.3. $\mathbf{BK}_1 - \mathbf{BK}_2$: Point Classification

	If				Then		
Condition	$b\mathbf{BK}_1$	$i\mathbf{BK}_1$	$b\mathbf{BK}_2$	$i\mathbf{BK}_2$	$b(\mathbf{BK}_1 - \mathbf{BK}_2)$	$i(\mathbf{BK}_1 - \mathbf{BK}_2)$	$o(\mathbf{BK}_1 - \mathbf{BK}_2)$
1	X				X		
2	X		X			Indeterminate	
3	X			X			X
4		X				X	
5		X	X		X		
6		X		X			X
7			X				X
8				X			X

The alternative condition is defined as follows:

$$\text{If } \mathbf{p} \in b\mathbf{BK}_1 \quad \text{and} \quad \mathbf{p} \in b\mathbf{BK}_2, \quad \text{then} \quad \mathbf{p} \in b(\mathbf{BK}_1 - \mathbf{BK}_2) \tag{9.71}$$

is true if and only if one of the following six conditions is true (see Fig. 9.29b):

$$\begin{aligned} x_{\min,1} &= x_{\max,2}, & x_{\max,1} &= x_{\min,2} \\ y_{\min,1} &= y_{\max,2}, & y_{\max,1} &= y_{\min,2} \\ z_{\min,1} &= z_{\max,2}, & z_{\max,1} &= z_{\min,2} \end{aligned} \tag{9.72}$$

Using the difference operator, it is easy to create geometric models of objects with cavities and passages; Fig. 9.30 shows several examples. In Fig. 9.30a a hemispherical depression is created in a block $\mathbf{BK}_1 - \mathbf{SP}_1$; in Fig. 9.30b a rectangular passage results from the difference of two blocks $\mathbf{BK}_1 - \mathbf{BK}_2$; in Fig. 9.30c a sphere with three mutually perpendicular circular passages results from the difference of a sphere and three cylinders $\mathbf{SP}_1 - \mathbf{CL}_1 - \mathbf{CL}_2 - \mathbf{CL}_3$.

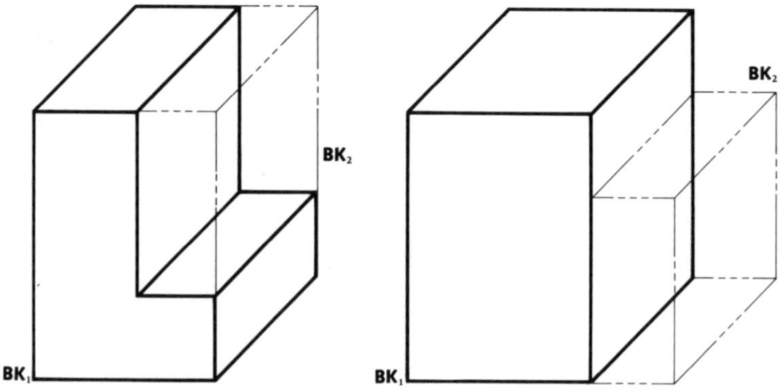

(a) (b)

Fig. 9.29. $\mathbf{BK}_1 - \mathbf{BK}_2$: coincident boundaries.

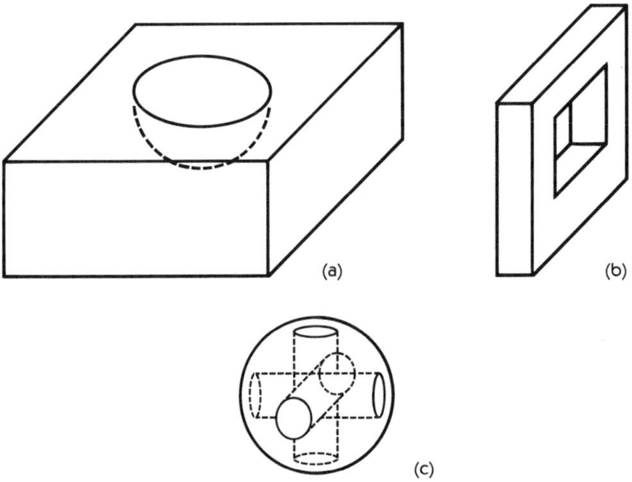

Fig. 9.30. Modeling with the difference operator.

INTERSECTION

The intersection of three-dimensional shapes is analogous to the intersection of two-dimensional shapes. Review Section 8.4.3. The intersection of two blocks $\mathbf{BK}_1$ and $\mathbf{BK}_2$ in Fig. 9.31 illustrates some of the properties of this combining operation. In Fig. 9.31a $\mathbf{BK}_3 = \mathbf{BK}_1 \cap \mathbf{BK}_2$. The arrangement in Fig. 9.31b produces a null result $\mathbf{BK}_1 \cap \mathbf{BK}_2 = \emptyset$. In Figs. 9.31c and 9.31d the operands are in a position such that some boundary faces are mutually coincident, producing an ambiguity when classifying points lying on these coincident faces. Table 9.4 presents the eight possible point classifications with respect to the intersection of two blocks. Points outside either block or both blocks are not considered, since they are clearly outside any shape resulting from the intersection operation.

The indeterminancy of Condition 2 is resolved as follows:

$$\text{If } \mathbf{p} \in b\mathbf{BK}_1 \quad \text{and} \quad \mathbf{p} \in b\mathbf{BK}_2, \quad \text{then} \quad \mathbf{p} \in b(\mathbf{BK}_1 \cap \mathbf{BK}_2) \tag{9.73}$$

is true if and only if at least one of the following six conditions is true (see Fig. 9.31c):

$$\begin{aligned} x_{\min,1} &= x_{\min,2}, & x_{\max,1} &= x_{\max,2} \\ y_{\min,1} &= y_{\min,2}, & y_{\max,1} &= y_{\max,2} \\ z_{\min,1} &= z_{\min,2}, & z_{\max,1} &= z_{\max,2} \end{aligned} \tag{9.74}$$

Alternatively,

$$\text{If } \mathbf{p} \in b\mathbf{BK}_1 \quad \text{and} \quad \mathbf{p} \in b\mathbf{BK}_2, \quad \text{then} \quad \mathbf{p} \in d(\mathbf{BK}_1 \cap \mathbf{BK}_2) \tag{9.75}$$

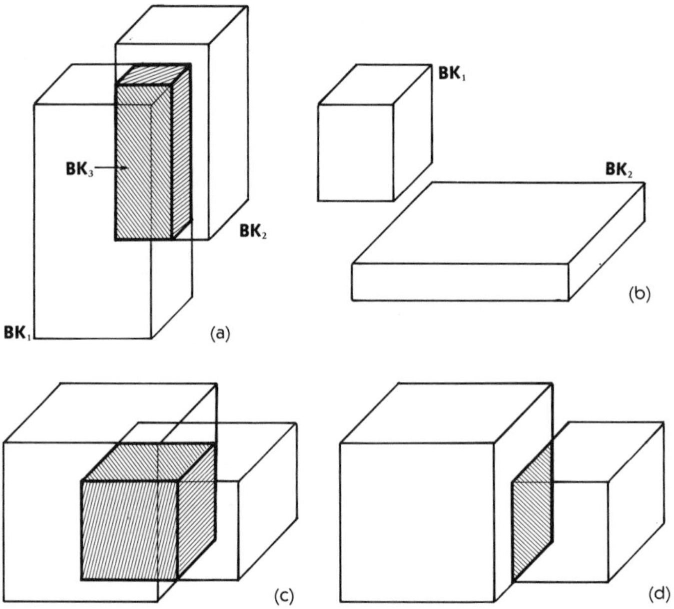

Fig. 9.31. Intersection of two blocks.

(the d notation is explained below) is true if and only if one of the following conditions is true (see Fig. 9.31d):

$$
\begin{aligned}
x_{\min,1} &= x_{\max,2}, \qquad & x_{\max,1} &= x_{\min,2} \\
y_{\min,1} &= y_{\max,2}, \qquad & y_{\max,1} &= y_{\min,2} \\
z_{\min,1} &= z_{\max,2}, \qquad & z_{\max,1} &= z_{\min,2}
\end{aligned}
\tag{9.76}
$$

Note that in this case the intersection produces an object that is not three dimensional. The object's dimensionality is different from the dimensionality of the blocks whose combination produced it, denoted by

Table 9.4. $BK_1 \cap BK_2$: Point Classification

	If				Then		
Condition	$b\mathbf{BK}_1$	$i\mathbf{BK}_1$	$b\mathbf{BK}_2$	$i\mathbf{BK}_2$	$b(\mathbf{BK}_1 \cap \mathbf{BK}_2)$	$i(\mathbf{BK}_1 \cap \mathbf{BK}_2)$	$o(\mathbf{BK}_1 \cap \mathbf{BK}_2)$
1	X						X
2	X		X			Indeterminate	
3	X			X	X		
4		X					X
5		X	X		X		
6		X		X		X	
7			X				X
8				X			X

the letter *d*, as in Eq. (9.75). Solid geometric modeling is usually used to produce only three-dimensional objects. Any other result is a null object and is ignored or discarded.

Most geometric modeling systems are designed to produce dimensionally homogeneous objects. Figure 9.32 shows examples of objects produced by the intersect operation that are dimensionally inhomogeneous or dimensionally dissimilar to the original combining objects. In Fig. 9.32a the two three-dimensional blocks are in a position such that their intersection produces a two-dimensional region; in Fig. 9.32b a one-dimensional object is produced; in Fig. 9.32c a point is produced. The intersection of the "L"-shaped object produced by $\mathbf{BK}_1 \cup \mathbf{BK}_2$ intersected with $\mathbf{BK}_3$ produces a dimensionally inhomogeneous object—it contains both a three-dimensional region and a two-dimensional region—while in Fig. 9.32e the operations produce a combination of three- and one-dimensional regions. In both Figs. 9.32d and 9.32e the three-dimensional regions are said to have a "dangling surface" or "dangling edge."

More advanced modeling techniques offer mathematical tests to detect these conditions. For now, only those products of any intersection operation that are three dimensional are valid.

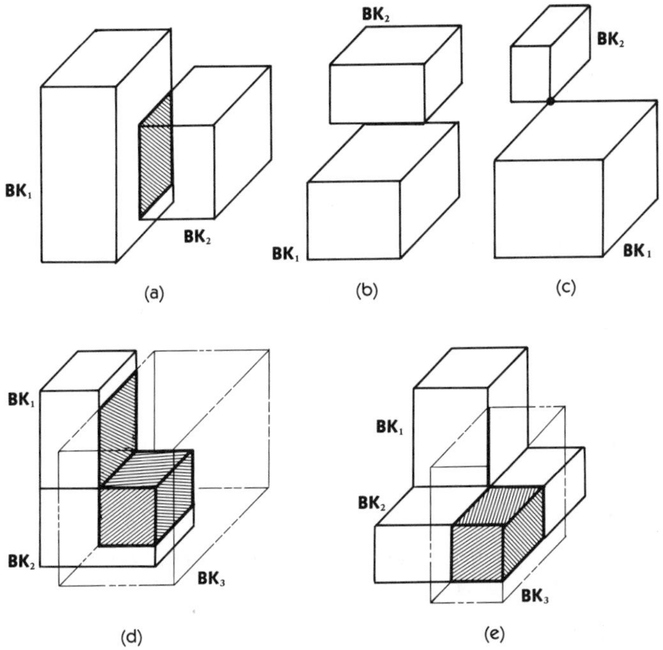

Fig. 9.32. Dimensionally inhomogeneous objects.

Although you have focused on blocks in your study of combining three-dimensional elements, the procedures apply equally to the other shapes.

EXERCISES

1. Accurately sketch on graph paper the union of the following pairs of elements:

a. $\mathbf{CB}_1$ (0, 0, 0, 6), $\mathbf{CB}_2$ (−1, −2, 3, 4)
b. $\mathbf{BK}_1$ (0, 0, 0, 3, 2, 9), $\mathbf{BK}_2$ (−1, −2, 3, 6, 6, 2)
c. $\mathbf{CL}_1$ (0, 0, 0, 3, 3, 4), $\mathbf{CL}_2$ (3, 0, 2, 3, 2, 1)
d. $\mathbf{SP}_1$ (0, 0, 0, 3), $\mathbf{SP}_2$ (0, 0, −4, 3)
e. $\mathbf{CL}_1$ (0, 0, 0, 3, 3, 6), $\mathbf{BK}_1$ (0, −3, 3, 5, 6, 2)

2. Accurately sketch on graph paper the difference between each element of the pairs of elements defined in Exercise 1.

a. $\mathbf{CB}_1 - \mathbf{CB}_2$
b. $\mathbf{BK}_1 - \mathbf{BK}_2$
c. $\mathbf{CL}_1 - \mathbf{CL}_2$
d. $\mathbf{SP}_2 - \mathbf{SP}_1$
e. $\mathbf{BK}_1 - \mathbf{CL}_1$

3. Accurately sketch on graph paper the intersection between each element of the pairs of elements defined in Exercise 1.

a. $\mathbf{CB}_1 \cap \mathbf{CB}_2$
b. $\mathbf{BK}_1 \cap \mathbf{BK}_2$
c. $\mathbf{CL}_1 \cap \mathbf{CL}_2$
d. $\mathbf{SP}_2 \cap \mathbf{SP}_1$
e. $\mathbf{BK}_1 \cap \mathbf{CL}_1$

4. Write expressions describing each of the five shapes shown in Fig. 9.33.

5. Write expressions describing each of the shapes shown in Fig. 9.34.

6. Classify the following points with respect to $\mathbf{BK}_1 - \mathbf{BK}_2$, where $\mathbf{BK}_1 = \mathbf{BK}_1$ (0, 0, 0, 6, 4, 4) and $\mathbf{BK}_2 = \mathbf{BK}_2$ (4, 0, 0, 2, 2, 4):

a. $\mathbf{p}_1 = (2, 4, 4)$
b. $\mathbf{p}_2 = (6, 0, 4)$
c. $\mathbf{p}_3 = (1, 3, 1)$
d. $\mathbf{p}_4 = (5, 1, 2)$
e. $\mathbf{p}_5 = (3, 0, 1)$

7. Classify the following points with respect to $\mathbf{BK}_1 \cup \mathbf{BK}_2$, where $\mathbf{BK}_1 = \mathbf{BK}_1$ (0, 0, 0, 4, 4, 4) and $\mathbf{BK}_2 = \mathbf{BK}_2$ (4, 2, 0, 2, 2, 4):

a. $\mathbf{p}_1 = (2, 4, 4)$
b. $\mathbf{p}_2 = (6, 0, 4)$

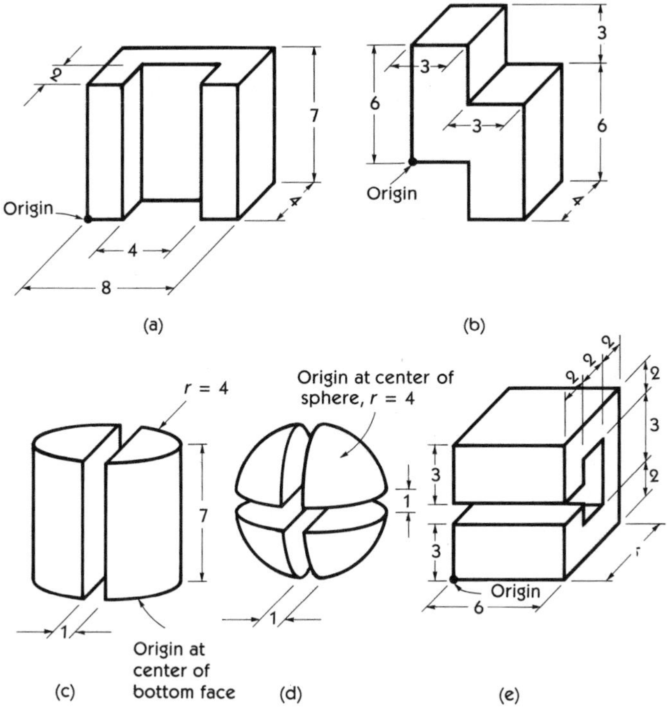

Fig. 9.33. Exercise 4.

c. $\mathbf{p}_3 = (1, 3, 1)$
d. $\mathbf{p}_4 = (5, 1, 2)$
e. $\mathbf{p}_5 = (3, 0, 1)$

8. Classify the following points with respect to $\mathbf{BK}_1 - \mathbf{CL}_1$, where $\mathbf{BK}_1 = \mathbf{BK}_1\,(3, 2, 0, 6, 4, 4)$ and $\mathbf{CL}_1 = \mathbf{CL}_1\,(8, 0, 3, 2, 2, 8)$:

a. $\mathbf{p}_1 = (4, 4, 4)$
b. $\mathbf{p}_2 = (9, 6, 4)$
c. $\mathbf{p}_3 = (5, 3, 2.5)$

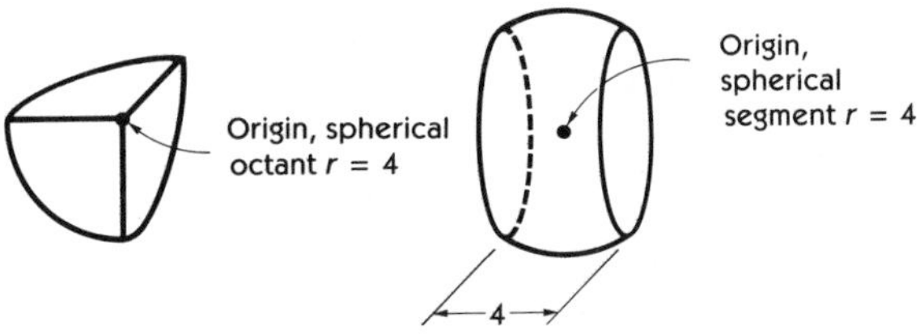

Fig. 9.34. Exercise 5.

d. $\mathbf{p}_4 = (6, 4, 3)$
e. $\mathbf{p}_5 = (8, 4, 3)$

9. Classify the following points with respect to $\mathbf{CL}_1 - \mathbf{BK}_1$, where $\mathbf{CL}_1 = \mathbf{CL}_1\,(0, 0, 0, 2, 3, 8)$ and $\mathbf{BK}_1 = \mathbf{BK}_1\,(0, 0, -4, 6, 4, 8)$:

a. $\mathbf{p}_1 = (0, 6, 0)$
b. $\mathbf{p}_2 = (3, 6, 0)$
c. $\mathbf{p}_3 = (-2, 2, 0)$
d. $\mathbf{p}_4 = (2, 2, 0)$
e. $\mathbf{p}_5 = (-2, 0, 0)$

10. Classify the following points with respect to $\mathbf{SP}_1 - \mathbf{BK}_1$, where $\mathbf{SP}_1 = \mathbf{SP}_1\,(0, 0, 0, 3)$ and $\mathbf{BK}_1 = \mathbf{BK}_1\,(-4, -4, -1, 8, 8, 2)$:

a. $\mathbf{p}_1 = (0, 0, 2)$
b. $\mathbf{p}_2 = (0, 0, 0)$
c. $\mathbf{p}_3 = (1, 1, -1)$
d. $\mathbf{p}_4 = (5, 0, -1)$
e. $\mathbf{p}_5 = (0, 0, -3)$

11. Classify the following points with respect to $\mathbf{BK}_1 \cap \mathbf{SP}_1$, where $\mathbf{BK}_1 = \mathbf{BK}_1\,(-2, -4, -4, 4, 8, 8)$ and $\mathbf{SP}_1 = \mathbf{SP}_1\,(0, 0, 0, 3)$:

a. $\mathbf{p}_1 = (3, 4, 1)$
b. $\mathbf{p}_2 = (0, 0, 3)$
c. $\mathbf{p}_3 = (0.5, 1, 1)$
d. $\mathbf{p}_4 = (-3, 0, 0)$
e. $\mathbf{p}_5 = (2, 0, -1)$

12. Classify the following points with respect to $[(\mathbf{BK}_1 \cup \mathbf{BK}_2) \cap \mathbf{BK}_3]$, where $\mathbf{BK}_1 = \mathbf{BK}_1\,(0, 0, 0, 4, 4, 3)$, $\mathbf{BK}_2 = \mathbf{BK}_2\,(0, 0, 3, 2, 4, 4)$, and $\mathbf{BK}_3 = \mathbf{BK}_3\,(2, 2, 0, 4, 6, 6)$:

a. $\mathbf{p}_1 = (1, 1, 7)$
b. $\mathbf{p}_2 = (2, 3, 4)$
c. $\mathbf{p}_3 = (5, 3, 4)$
d. $\mathbf{p}_4 = (3, 3, 3)$
e. $\mathbf{p}_5 = (3, 3, 1)$

13. Write a procedure to classify a point with respect to the union of two blocks. Denote this as **BUBPT** (BK1, BK2, PT, ICLS), where

BK1 (6), BK2 (6) are the input values of x_0, y_0, z_0, a_x, a_y, and a_z,
PT(3) are the input coordinates of the point, and
ICLS is the output classification of the point:
ICLS = 1 if the point is outside,

ICLS = 2 if the point is inside, and
ICLS = 3 if the point is on the boundary.

14. Write a procedure to classify a point with respect to the difference of two blocks $\mathbf{BK}_1 - \mathbf{BK}_2$; denote this as **BDBPT** (BK1, BK2, PT, ICLS), where the arguments are defined as for **BUBPT** in Exercise 13.

15. Write a procedure to classify a point with respect to the intersection of two blocks; denote this as **BIBPT** (BK1, BK2, PT, ICLS), where the arguments are defined as for **BUBPT** in Exercise 13.

16. Write a procedudre to determine the arguments of a block produced by the intersection of two other blocks.

17. Consider Eq. (9.68). Sketch and discuss the condition: $x_{max,1} = x_{min,2}$ and $y_{min,1} = y_{max,2}$. Find other similar conditions. What about sharing only a vertex?

10. Elementary Transformations

A TRANSFORMATION PRODUCES a change in a geometric object. Now consider two kinds of transformations: those that change the position and orientation of an object, and those that change its shape. **Translation** and **rotation** transformations alter position and orientation, while **scaling** transformations alter size and shape. You will see how these transformations apply to the special two- and three-dimensional objects you have studied in Chapters 8 and 9. You have already studied the translation of points and lines. Later, in Chapter 15, you will study more sophisticated and powerful transformations.

10.1. Translation

Translation produces change of position without change of shape or orientation (rotational position). Let us first investigate how to translate a rectangle. Then you can apply what you learn here to other shapes you have studied. Remember, a rectangle is specified by $\mathbf{RN} = \mathbf{RN}(x_0, y_0, a_x, a_y)$, where x_0 and y_0 are the coordinates of the minimum vertex and a_x and a_y are the lengths of the sides parallel to the x and y axes, respectively. Since translation does not change the size or shape of a rectangle, the arguments a_x and a_y are unchanged by this transformation.

If you move a rectangle, **RN**, in the x direction by an amount x_t and in the y direction by y_t, then x_0 and y_0 must change by precisely these amounts. Denote the components of translation by $\mathbf{T} = (x_t, y_t)$. Study the example in Fig. 10.1. The arguments of the transformed rectangle, **RN***, in terms of the initial rectangle are:

$$\begin{aligned} x_0^* &= x_0 + x_t \\ y_0^* &= y_0 + y_t \\ a_x^* &= a_x \\ a_y^* &= a_y \end{aligned} \tag{10.1}$$

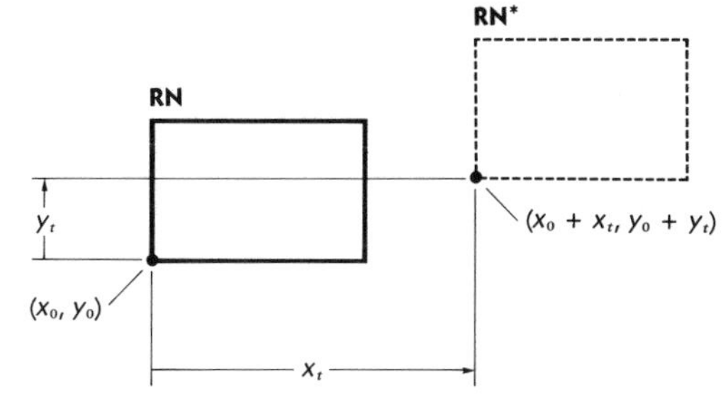

Fig. 10.1. Translating a rectangle.

Given x_0^* and y_0^*, you can easily compute x_t, y_t from

$$\begin{aligned} x_t &= x_0^* - x_0 \\ y_t &= y_0^* - y_0 \end{aligned} \tag{10.2}$$

Note that x_t and y_t can have positive or negative values.

Translate squares and circles in a similar way. For example, compare the translation of a circle to that of a rectangle in Figs. 10.1 and 10.2. Translate a circle, **CR**, by an (x_t, y_t) to obtain **CR***. Thus,

$$\begin{aligned} x_c^* &= x_c + x_t \\ y_c^* &= y_c + y_t \\ r_c^* &= r \end{aligned} \tag{10.3}$$

Transform all of the three-dimensional elements—the cube, block, disk, and sphere—in a similar way. Translate either the coordinates of the min-

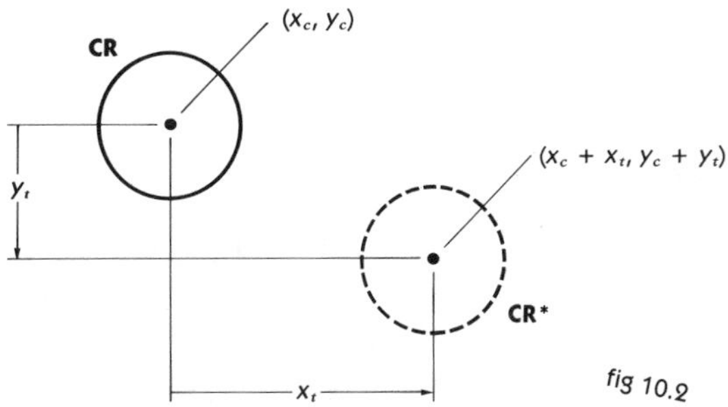

Fig. 10.2. Translating a circle.

imum vertex or center point. Note that in this case the components of translation are (x_t, y_t, z_t).

EXERCISES

1. Find the translation components (x_t, y_t) for each of the following pairs of objects:

a. **SQ**(3,0,8), **SQ***(6,−4,8)
b. **RN**(11,6,9,5), **RN***(10,6,9,5)
c. **RN**(5,1,1,1), **RN***(10,3,1,1)
d. **CR**(0,0,1), **CR***(−8,−6,1)
e. **CB**(−2,−2,0,1), **CB***(−1,5,−1,1)
f. **BK**(4,12,−6,8,8,2), **BK***(4,12,4,8,8,2)
g. **BK**(2,10,9,6,6,2), **BK***(8,16,15,6,6,2)
h. **CL**(7,4,14,2,1,10), **CL***(5,0,14,2,1,10)
i. **CL**(−8,3,−12,1,2,5), **CL***(−8,14,−4,1,2,5)
j. **SP**(1,−6,−7,4), **SP***(4,−6,−4,4)

2. Translate each of the following elements to the origin. Find the translation components (y_t, y_t) required and the arguments of the transformed elements.

a. **SQ**(3,0,8)
b. **RN**(11,6,9,5)
c. **RN**(5,1,1,1)
d. **CR**(0,0,1)
e. **CB**(−2,−2,0,1)
f. **BK**(4,12,−6,8,8,2)
g. **BK**(2,10,9,6,6,2)
h. **CL**(7,4,14,2,1,10)
i. **CL**(−8,3,12,1,2,5)
j. **SP**(1,−6,−7,4)

3. Translate a copy of the sphere **SP**(0,0,0,1) to each of the vertices of **BK**(0,0,0,2,5,5). Give the translation components required and the arguments of the transformed elements.

4. Write a procedure to translate a block. Denote this as **TRBK**(BKI,T,BLO), where

BKI(6) are the input values x_0, y_0, z_0, s_x, s_y, and s_z of the initial block,
T(3) are the input components x_t, y_t, and z_t of the translation, and
BKO(6) are the output values x_0^*, y_0^*, z_0^*, s_x^*, s_y^*, and s_z^* of the transformed block.

10.2. Rotation

Rotating an object changes its position and orientation. In this section you will consider only simple 90° rotations, or integer multiples of 90°. Let us begin with the rectangle. Deriving the expressions that describe the 90° rotations is simpler if the rectangle is initially in the positive x, y quadrant (the first quadrant).

Figure 10.3 shows both a 90° counterclockwise and a 90° clockwise rotation about the origin (or z axis) of a rectangle in the first quadrant. Denote a rotation by $\mathbf{R} = (a,b)$, where a is the axis of rotation (x axis = 1, y axis = 2, z axis = 3) and b is the angle (counterclockwise rotations are positive).

Study the example of the +90° rotation in Fig. 10.3. Note that the rotation changes the rectangle's orientation so that a new minimum vertex must be computed. The arguments of the transformed rectangle in terms of the initial rectangle for $\mathbf{R} = (3,90)$ are

$$\begin{aligned} x_0^* &= -(y_0 + a_y) \\ y_0^* &= x_0 \\ a_x^* &= a_y \\ a_y^* &= a_x \end{aligned} \tag{10.4}$$

For $\mathbf{R} = (3,-90)$,

$$\begin{aligned} x_0^* &= y_0 \\ y_0^* &= -(x_0 + a_x) \\ a_x^* &= a_y \\ a_y^* &= a_x \end{aligned} \tag{10.5}$$

See Fig. 10.4. If $\mathbf{R} = (3,\pm 180)$,

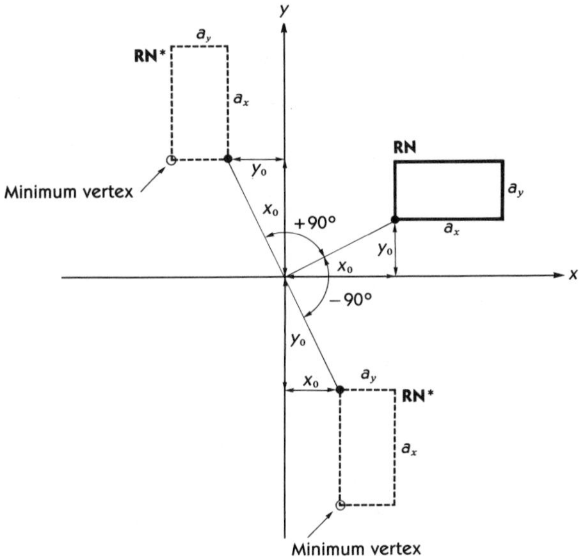

Fig. 10.3. Rotation of a rectangle ±90°.

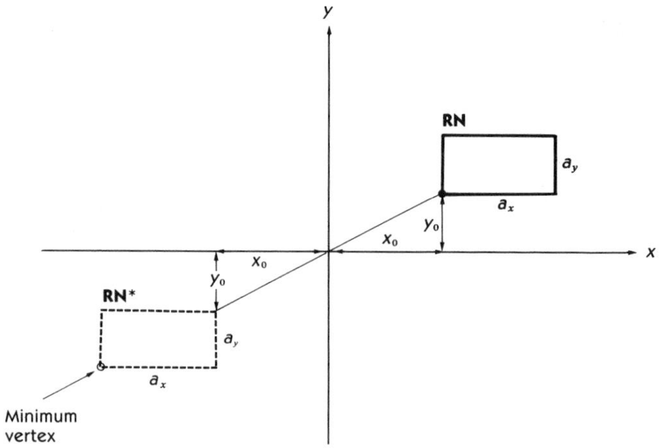

Fig. 10.4. Rotation of a rectangle ±180°.

$$
\begin{aligned}
x_0^* &= -(x_0 + a_x) \\
y_0^* &= -(y_0 + a_y) \\
a_x^* &= a_x \\
a_y^* &= a_y
\end{aligned}
\tag{10.6}
$$

Rotating a circle is simpler, since its radius is independent of its orientation. By studying Fig. 10.5 you can readily determine the transformation equations: for **R** = (3,90), the arguments of **CR*** are

$$
\begin{aligned}
x_c^* &= -y_c \\
y_c^* &= x_c \\
r^* &= r
\end{aligned}
\tag{10.7}
$$

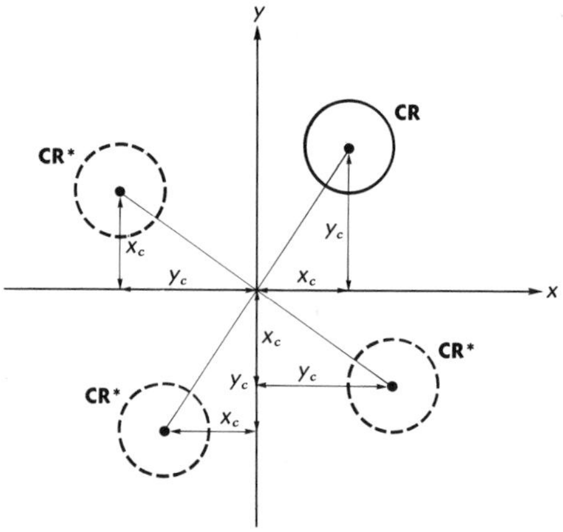

Fig. 10.5. Rotation of a circle.

for **R** = (3,−90), the arguments of **CR*** are

$$\begin{aligned} x_c^* &= y_c \\ y_c^* &= -x_c \\ r^* &= r \end{aligned} \tag{10.8}$$

and for **R** = (3,±180), the arguments of **CR*** are

$$\begin{aligned} x_c^* &= -x_c \\ y_c^* &= -y_c \\ r^* &= r \end{aligned} \tag{10.9}$$

These transformation equations are independent of the element's initial position and depend only on the angle of rotation.

Now consider simple rotations of the three-dimensional elements. Begin with the block, and study its positions shown in Fig. 10.6. The block in the figure is rotated ±90° about the y axis; thus, **R** = (2,±90).

The sign convention for rotations about the coordinate axes are given in Fig. 10.7. Again, use the so-called **right-hand convention:** If the thumb of your right hand points in the positive x, y, or z direction, then the fingers of your right hand curl in the positive angular or rotational sense. Use this convention throughout the rest of the text. Note that rotating the positive x axis in the direction of the positive y axis is a positive rotation about the z axis.

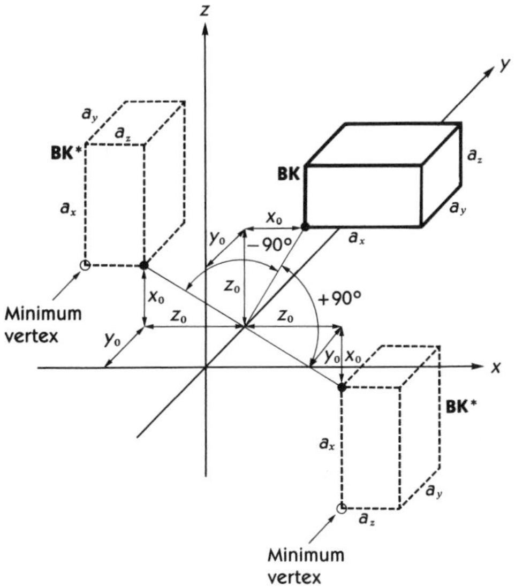

Fig. 10.6. Rotating a block ±90°.

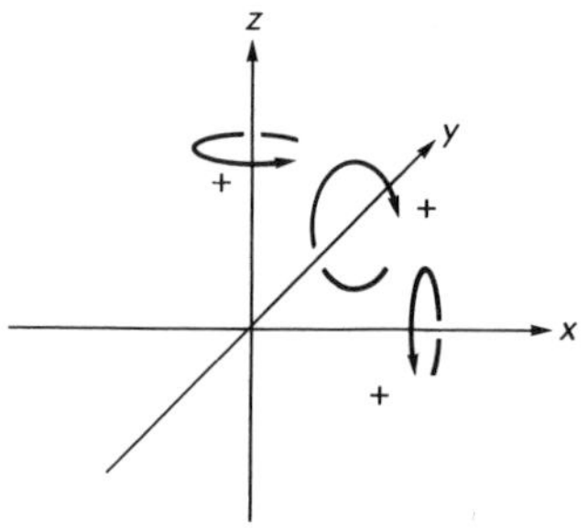

Fig. 10.7. Rotation sign convention.

Return now to the block rotation in Fig. 10.6. The transformation equations for **BK***, if **R** = (2,−90), are

$$\begin{aligned} x_0^* &= -(z_0 + a_z), & a_x^* &= a_z \\ y_0^* &= y_0, & a_y^* &= a_y \\ z_0^* &= x_0, & a_z^* &= a_x \end{aligned} \qquad (10.10)$$

for **R** = (2,90)

$$\begin{aligned} x_0^* &= z_0, & a_x^* &= a_z \\ y_0^* &= y_0, & a_y^* &= a_z \\ z_0^* &= -(x_0 + a_x), & a_z^* &= a_x \end{aligned} \qquad (10.11)$$

and for **R** = (2,±180)

$$\begin{aligned} x_0^* &= -(x_0 + a_x), & a_x^* &= a_x \\ y_0^* &= y_0, & a_y^* &= a_y \\ z_0^* &= -(z_0 + a_z), & a_z^* &= a_z \end{aligned} \qquad (10.12)$$

Note that the y components are unchanged by a rotation about the y axis. You will be asked to derive transformation equations for rotations about the x and z axes in Exercises 1 and 2 at the end of this section.

The rotation transformation equations of a cylinder are only slightly more difficult to determine; this is because the axis of the cylinder can be either parallel to the axis of rotation or perpendicular to it. The cylinder in Fig. 10.8 is **CL**($x_c, y_c, z_c, 3, r, L$). Note that $k = 3$ because the cylinder's axis is parallel to the z axis. If this cylinder is rotated about the z axis, as in Fig. 10.8a, then the transformation equations for **CL***, if **R** = (3,90), are

$$\begin{aligned} x_c^* &= -y_c, & k^* &= k \\ y_c^* &= x_c, & r^* &= r \\ z_c^* &= z_c, & L^* &= L \end{aligned} \qquad (10.13)$$

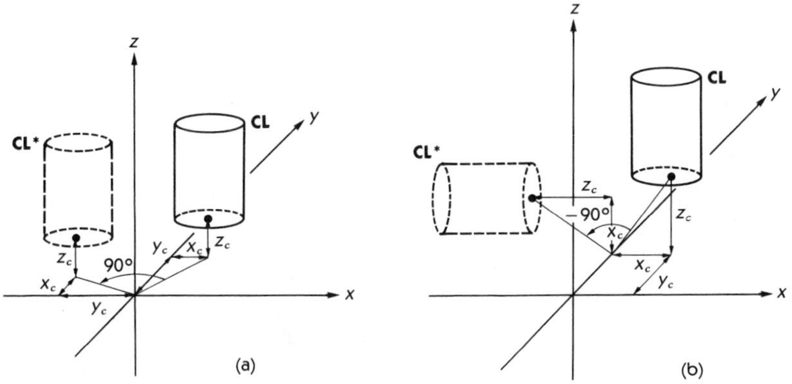

Fig. 10.8. Rotating a cylinder.

for **R** = (3,−90)

$$x_c^* = y_c, \qquad k^* = k$$
$$y_c^* = -x_c, \qquad r^* = r \tag{10.14}$$
$$z_c^* = z_c, \qquad L^* = L$$

for **R** = (3,±180)

$$x_c^* = -x_c, \qquad k^* = k$$
$$y_c^* = -y_c, \qquad r^* = r \tag{10.15}$$
$$z_c^* = z_c, \qquad L^* = L$$

Of course, the rotation does not change r and L, since they are properties of the cylinder itself and are independent of position or orientation. The cylinder's axis is parallel to the axis of rotation and also does not change. For a similar reason, z_c also does not change.

If this cylinder is rotated about the y axis, as in Fig. 10.8b, then the transformation equations for **CL***, if **R** = (2,90), are

$$x_c^* = z_c, \qquad k^* = 1$$
$$y_c^* = y_c, \qquad r^* = r \tag{10.16}$$
$$z_c^* = -x_c, \qquad L^* = L$$

for **R** = (2,−90)

$$x_c^* = -(z_c + L), \qquad k^* = 1$$
$$y_c^* = y_c, \qquad r^* = r \tag{10.17}$$
$$z_c^* = x_c, \qquad L^* = L$$

for **R** = (2,±180)

$$x_c^* = -x_c, \qquad k^* = 3$$
$$y_c^* = y_c, \qquad r^* = r \tag{10.18}$$
$$z_c^* = -(z_c + L), \qquad L^* = L$$

Note that the $\pm 90°$ rotation requires a change in k. Similar transformation equations apply to rotations of this cylinder about the x axis. In fact, all the other combinations of rotations and cylinder axis orientation are given by analogous equations.

Rotating a sphere is similar to rotating a point. Look at the possible rotations of the sphere in Fig. 10.9. The transformation equations for **SP***, if **R** = (2,90), are

$$x_c^* = z_c$$
$$y_c^* = y_c$$
$$z_c^* = -x_c \tag{10.19}$$
$$r^* = r$$

for **R** = (2,−90)

$$x_c^* = -z_c$$
$$y_c^* = y_c$$
$$z_c^* = x_c \tag{10.20}$$
$$r^* = r$$

and for **R** = (2,±180)

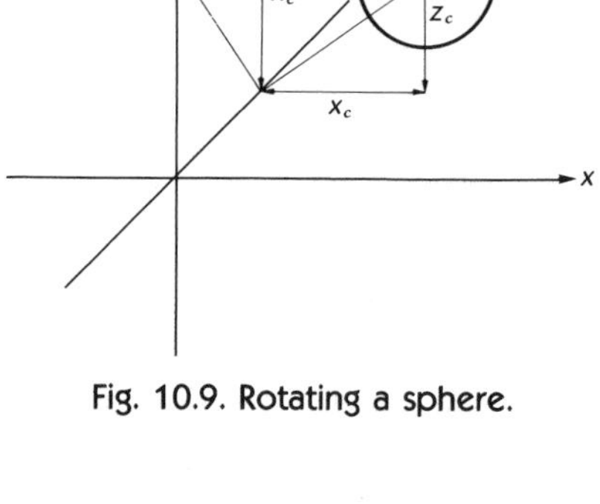

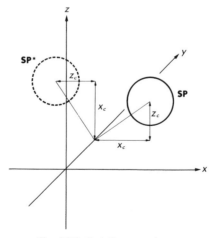

Fig. 10.9. Rotating a sphere.

$$
\begin{aligned}
x_c^* &= -x_c \\
y_c^* &= y_c \\
z_c^* &= -z_c \\
r^* &= r
\end{aligned}
\tag{10.21}
$$

Use similar transformations for rotations about the x and z axes.

Frequently you must both translate and rotate the geometric model of an object. The order in which you do this is important, for you can produce different results. Look at the rectangle in Fig. 10.10. Let **RN** = **RN**(5,3,3,6), **T** = (−4,−2), and **R** = (3,90), where **T** and **R** are the components of translation and rotation, respectively. Find **RN*** = (**RN**:**T**):**R** by first translating **RN** by **T**, then rotating the result by **R**, to give

$$\mathbf{RN}^* = \mathbf{RN}^*(-7,1,6,3) \tag{10.22}$$

Now find **RN*** = (**RN**:**R**):**T** by first rotating **RN** by **R**, then translating the result by **T**, to give

$$\mathbf{RN}^* = \mathbf{RN}^*(-13,3,6,3) \tag{10.23}$$

It is now obvious that (**RN**:**T**):**R** ≠ (**RN**:**R**):**T** and, indeed, order is important.

By using a combination of translation and rotation transformations, you can compute the rotation about any axis that is parallel to the principal axes. Study Fig. 10.11, for example. Assume that you must rotate the rectangle in Fig. 10.11a 90° counterclockwise about the vertex labeled "*a*." The problem is to find the arguments defining the rectangle in this new position. Let **RN** = **RN**(3,1,2,4); first, translate the rectangle so that its

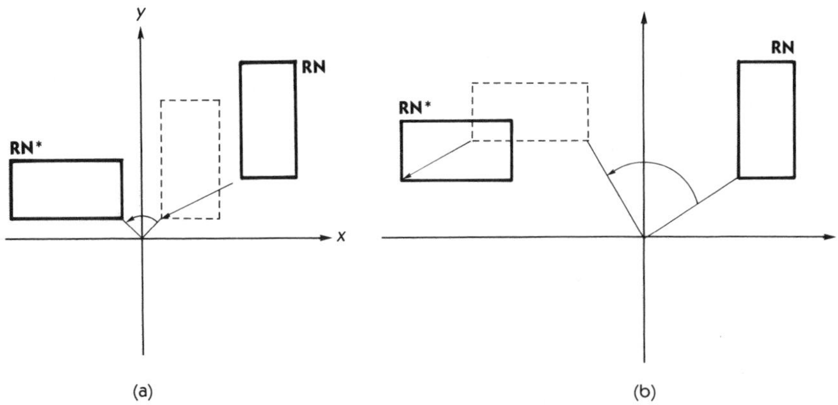

Fig. 10.10. Rotation and translation.

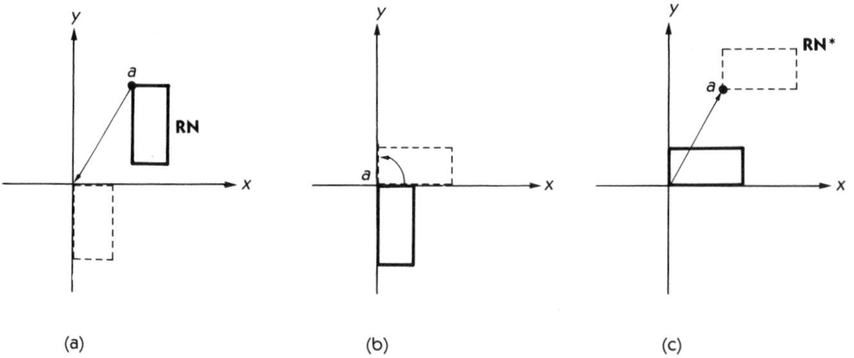

Fig. 10.11. General rotation.

vertex, a, is at the origin. For the example, this requires that $\mathbf{T} = (-3,-5)$. The translation is shown in Fig. 10.11a. Second, rotate this result by $\mathbf{R} = (3{,}90)$ about vertex a, which is now at the origin, as in Fig. 10.11b. Finally, reverse the initial translation to return vertex a to its original position, as in Fig. 10.11c. This requires $\mathbf{T} = (3{,}5)$. Express this maneuver symbolically as

$$\mathbf{RN}^* = ((\mathbf{RN}:\mathbf{T}_{a0}):\mathbf{R}):\mathbf{T}_{0a} \qquad (10.24)$$

where $\mathbf{T}_{a0}$ denotes a translation that moves point a to the origin and $\mathbf{T}_{0a}$ is the reverse translation. In fact, point a need not be a vertex; it can be any point. This procedure can easily apply to any two- or three-dimensional elements.

Throughout this section you have considered only 90° rotations or integer multiples of this angle. Later, in Chapter 15, you will investigate general rotations through any angle.

EXERCISES

1. Derive the transformation equations for a block rotated about the x axis: $\mathbf{R} = (1{,}90), (1,-90), (1,\pm180)$. Make a sketch similar to Fig. 10.6, showing the appropriate geometric components.

2. Derive the transformation equations for a block rotated about the z axis; $\mathbf{R} = (3{,}90), (3,-90), (3,\pm180)$. Make a sketch similar to Fig. 10.6, showing the appropriate geometric components.

3. Given $\mathbf{SQ}(-3,-4,2)$ and $\mathbf{R} = (3{,}90)$, compute $\mathbf{SQ}^* = \mathbf{SQ}:\mathbf{R}$.

4. Given $\mathbf{RN}(-4,1,1,4)$ and $\mathbf{R} = (3{,}180)$, compute $\mathbf{RN}^* = \mathbf{RN}:\mathbf{R}$.

5. Given $\mathbf{RN}(-2,1,5,2)$ and $\mathbf{R} = (3{,}90)$, compute $\mathbf{RN}^* = \mathbf{RN}:\mathbf{R}$.

6. Rotate **RN**(3,1,2,6) 90° clockwise about $\mathbf{p}_1 = (4,4,0)$. Compute $\mathbf{T}_{10}$, $\mathbf{T}_{01}$, **R**, and **RN***.

7. Rotate **BK**(−4,0,0,4,2,2) so that $\mathbf{p}_{min} = (-6,0,0)$ and $\mathbf{p}_{max} = (-4,2,4)$. Compute **T**, −**T**, **R**, and **BK***.

8. Rotate **CL**(0,0,3,3,2,3) by **R** = (2,90). Compute **CL*** = **CL**:**R**.

9. Write a procedure to rotate a rectangle about the origin. Denote this as **ROTREC**(RN1,R,RN2), where

RN1(4) are the input values x_0, y_0, a_x, and a_y,
R(2) are the input axis and angle, and
RN2(4) are the output values x_0^*, y_0^*, a_x^*, and a_y^*.

10. Write a procedure to rotate a rectangle about any point in its plane. Denote this as **RPTREC**(RN1,R,P,RN2), where

RN1(4) are the input values x_0, y_0, a_x, and a_y,
R(2) are the input axis parallel to the axis of rotation, and the angle,
P(2) are the input coordinates of the point, and
RN2(4) are the output values x_0^*, y_0^*, a_x^*, and a_y^*.

11. Write a procedure to rotate a block about any axis that is parallel to one of the three principal axes. Denote this as **ROTBK**(BK1,P,R,BK2), where

BK1(6) are the input values x_0, y_0, z_0, a_x, a_y, and a_z,
P(3) are the input coordinates of the point,
R(2) are the input values specifying the principal axis parallel to the rotation axis and the angle, and
BK2(6) are the output values x_0^*, y_0^*, z_0^*, a_x^*, a_y^* and a_z^*.

10.3. Scaling

Scaling is a transformation that changes the size or shape of an object. It is a very simple transformation to perform and to understand. The square, circle, cube, and sphere will change only in size. Let us see how this is done.

Recall that a square is given by $\mathbf{SQ}(x_0,y_0,a)$. You can change its size by multiplying the argument, a, by an appropriate factor while maintaining x_0 and y_0 unchanged. Denote the component(s) of the scaling transformation as $\mathbf{S}(s)$. Carry out the transformation operation so that arguments of $\mathbf{SQ}^*$ are

$$\begin{aligned} x_0^* &= x_0 \\ y_0^* &= y_0 \\ a^* &= sa \end{aligned} \tag{10.25}$$

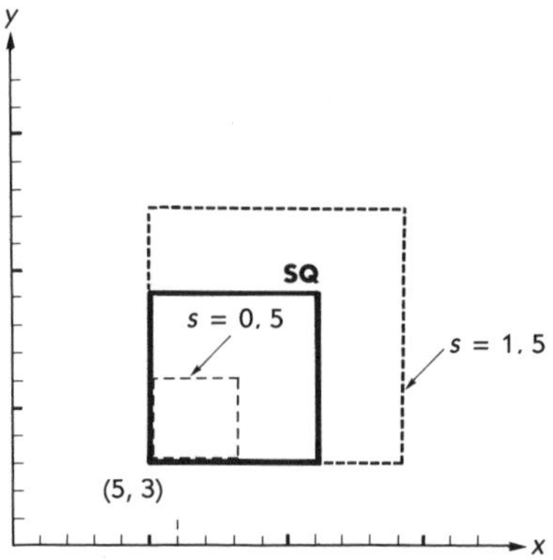

Fig. 10.12. Scaling a square.

where s must be positive. These are the scaling transformation equations for a square. Study the example in Fig. 10.12. It shows the result of two different scaling operations on **SQ**(5,3,6). In one case, $\mathbf{S}_1 = (0.5)$ and $\mathbf{SQ}_1^* = \mathbf{SQ}_1^*(5,3,3)$; in the other, $\mathbf{S}_2 = (1.5)$ and $\mathbf{SQ}_2^* = \mathbf{SQ}_2^*(5,3,9)$. Note that all the squares retain the same minimum or base vertex.

The circle, cube, and sphere are similarly scaled by multiplying r, a, and r, respectively, by appropriate scale factors. The circle and sphere expand or contract about their center points, while the cube, like the square, changes size while its minimum vertex remains in a fixed position. These differences are merely a result of the defining conventions.

The rectangle, block, and cylinder are susceptible to size and shape change. Recall that a rectangle is given by $\mathbf{RN}(x_0,y_0,a_x,a_y)$; its scaling transformation equations are

$$\begin{aligned} x_0^* &= x_0 \\ y_0^* &= y_0 \\ a_x^* &= s_x a_x \\ a_y^* &= s_y a_y \end{aligned} \tag{10.26}$$

where s_x and s_y are positive scale factors. If $s_x = s_y$, then only the size of the rectangle changes, and the sides maintain their original proportions. If $s_x \neq s_y$, then a shape change occurs. Look at an example. In Fig. 10.13a, **RN**(4,2,4,6) is scaled by $\mathbf{S} = (1.5,1.5)$, which simply changes its size, producing **RN***(4,2,6,9). In Fig. 10.13b the same initial rectangle is scaled by $\mathbf{S} = (2,0.5)$, which changes its shape, producing **RN***(4,2,8,3).

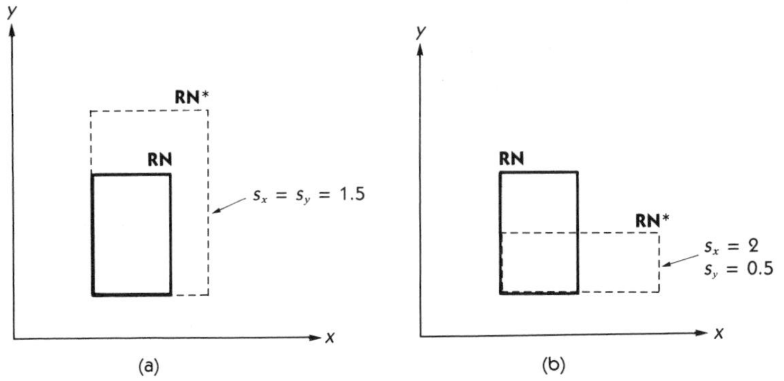

Fig. 10.13. Scaling a rectangle.

The scaling transformation equations for a block are

$$\begin{aligned} x_0^* &= x_0, & a_x^* &= s_x a_x \\ y_0^* &= y_0, & a_y^* &= s_y a_y \\ z_0^* &= z_0, & a_z^* &= s_z a_z \end{aligned} \tag{10.27}$$

For a cylinder they are

$$\begin{aligned} x_c^* &= x_c, & k^* &= k \\ y_c^* &= y_c, & r^* &= s_r r \\ z_c^* &= z_c, & L^* &= s_L L \end{aligned} \tag{10.28}$$

Note that any of the special shapes can be represented as a unit element transformed by appropriate scaling and translation operators. The unit elements are

Unit square: $\mathbf{SQ}_u = \mathbf{SQ}_u(0,0,1)$
Unit rectangle: $\mathbf{RN}_u = \mathbf{RN}_u(0,0,1,1)$
Unit circle: $\mathbf{CR}_u = \mathbf{CR}_u(0,0,1)$
Unit cube: $\mathbf{CB}_u = \mathbf{CB}_u(0,0,0,1)$
Unit block: $\mathbf{BK}_u = \mathbf{BK}_u(0,0,0,1,1,1)$
Unit cylinder: $\mathbf{CL}_{u,1} = \mathbf{CL}_{u,1}(0,0,0,1,1,1)$
Unit cylinder: $\mathbf{CL}_{u,2} = \mathbf{CL}_{u,2}(0,0,0,2,1,1)$
Unit cylinder: $\mathbf{CL}_{u,3} = \mathbf{CL}_{u,3}(0,0,0,3,1,1)$
Unit sphere: $\mathbf{SP}_u = \mathbf{SP}_u(0,0,0,1)$

A square is not a necessary element, since any square can be represented by a rectangle with $a_x = a_y$. Similarly, you can dispense with a cube, since you can represent any cube by a block with $a_x = a_y = a_z$. You can reduce the three unit cylinders to one, say $\mathbf{CL}_u(0,0,0,1,1,1)$, if you admit rotations into your unit element transformation scheme. Figure 10.14 shows the minimum set of unit elements.

Let us study an example. In Fig. 10.15 a unit block $\mathbf{BK}_u$ is transformed into a specific block $\mathbf{BK}_1$ as follows:

$$\mathbf{BK}_1 = (\mathbf{BK}_u : \mathbf{S}_1) : \mathbf{T}_1 \tag{10.29}$$

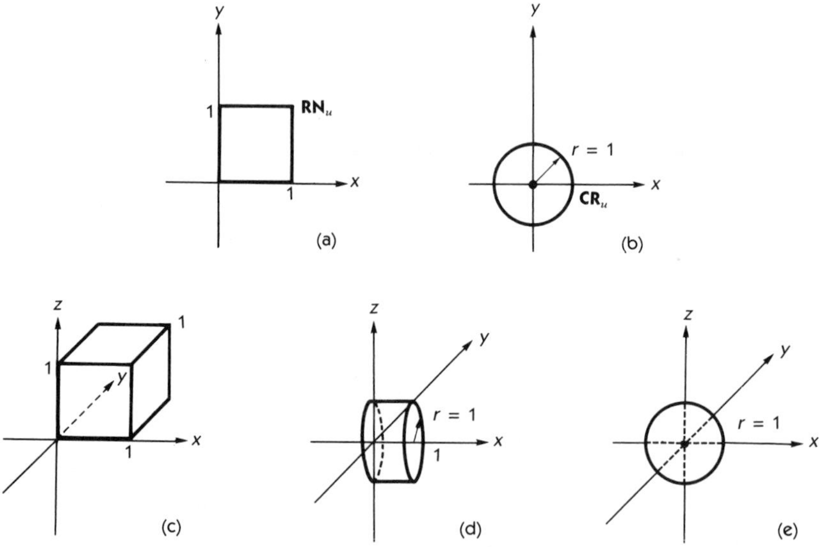

Fig. 10.14. Unit elements.

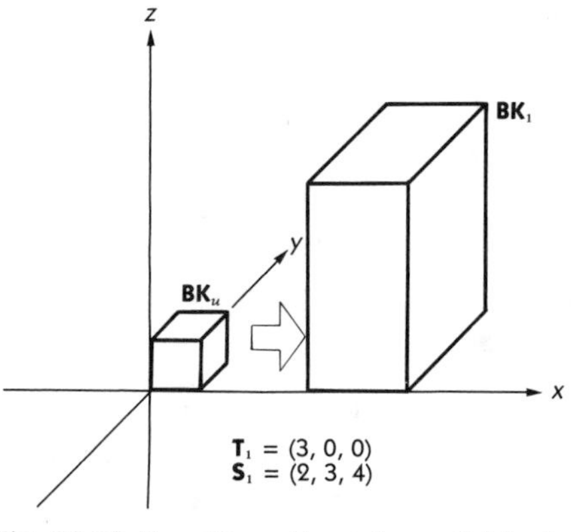

Fig. 10.15. Transformation of a unit block.

where $\mathbf{S}_1 = (2,3,4)$ and $\mathbf{T}_1 = (3,0,0)$; this produces $\mathbf{BK}_1 = (3,0,0,2,3,4)$. Thus, you can think of certain shape elements as transformations of unit elements. There are advantages to this in special circumstances beyond the scope of this discussion; for example, often you can reduce the number of basic shape elements in a geometric modeling system by using unit elements (sometimes called **primitives**).

EXERCISES

1. Double the size of the following geometric elements:

a. **CR**(−2,5,1.5)
b. **CR**(0,0,1)
c. **SP**(6.2,1.7,0,0.5)
d. **BK**(7.25,0,0,0.3,0.3,7.1)
e. **CL**(0,0,−2.5,3,0.5,1)
f. **CL**(8.1,9.7,0.25,2,0.25,2.5)
g. **RN**(−2.5,−2.5,2.5,6)
h. **SP**(1.5,0.75,0,3.25)
i. **BK**(8.25,3.15,6.5,7.25,4.5,6.25)
j. **CR**(3.1,2.7,0.75)

2. For each of the geometric elements in Exercise 1, give the appropriate unit element and the transformations necessary to define the element.

3. Give the transformations on a unit sphere necessary to create a sphere inscribed in a unit block.

4. Write a procedure to scale a block. Denote this as **SCALBK**(BK1,S,BK2), where

BK1(6) are the input values x_0, y_0, z_0, a_x, a_y, and a_z,
S(3) are the input scale factors s_x, s_y, and s_z, and
BK2(6) are the output values x_0^*, y_0^*, z_0^*, a_x^*, a_y^*, and a_z^*.

11. Matrix Methods

A MATRIX IS an array of numbers or other mathematical elements arranged in rows and columns. Not only is a matrix a convenient way to summarize and store mathematical data, but you can operate on a matrix mathematically. You can organize data defining geometric objects in the form of a matrix, including those you have already studied, as well as curves, surfaces, and other geometric forms. You will see that translation, rotation, and scaling can be best performed by matrices.

11.1. What is a Matrix?

A **matrix** is a rectangular array of numbers or other mathematical elements arranged in m rows and n columns. Denote a matrix with a boldface uppercase letter, such as **A**, **B**, or **C**, and use brackets to enclose the array. For example,

$$\mathbf{A} = \begin{bmatrix} a_{11} & a_{12} & a_{13} \\ a_{21} & a_{22} & a_{23} \\ a_{31} & a_{32} & a_{33} \\ a_{41} & a_{42} & a_{43} \end{bmatrix} \tag{11.1}$$

In this matrix the lowercase a denotes the elements. The double subscript indicates the position of the elements in the array by row and column number. Thus, a_{23} is in the second row and third column, and a_{ij} is the element in row i and column j.

An example of matrix representation are the coefficients in a set of simultaneous equations. In the set of equations

$$\begin{aligned} 2x - 3y + z &= 4 \\ -x + 2y + z &= 1 \\ 3x + y + 2z &= -3 \end{aligned} \tag{11.2}$$

the coefficients can be represented by a matrix, say **A**, so that

$$\mathbf{A} = \begin{bmatrix} 2 & -3 & 1 \\ -1 & 2 & 1 \\ 3 & 1 & 2 \end{bmatrix} \tag{11.3}$$

The right-hand side can also be represented by a matrix, say **B**, so that

$$\mathbf{B} = \begin{bmatrix} 4 \\ 1 \\ -3 \end{bmatrix} \tag{11.4}$$

Later you will see how to use matrix operations to solve such equations.

Determine the **order** of a matrix by the number of its rows and columns. State the order of a matrix by giving the number of rows first. The matrix in Eq. (11.1) has four rows and three columns and is of order 4 × 3, read "4 by 3." In general, a matrix with m rows and n columns is of order $m \times n$, read "m by n."

Two $m \times n$ matrices are equal if all corresponding elements are equal, but there can be no equality between matrices of different orders. Thus, given the three matrices **A**, **B**, and **C**,

$$\mathbf{A} = \begin{bmatrix} a_{11} & a_{12} \\ a_{21} & a_{22} \\ a_{31} & a_{32} \end{bmatrix}, \quad \mathbf{B} = \begin{bmatrix} b_{11} & b_{12} \\ b_{21} & b_{22} \\ b_{31} & b_{32} \end{bmatrix}, \quad \mathbf{C} = \begin{bmatrix} c_{11} & c_{12} & c_{13} \\ c_{21} & c_{22} & c_{23} \\ c_{31} & c_{32} & c_{33} \end{bmatrix} \tag{11.5}$$

then $\mathbf{A} = \mathbf{B}$ if and only if $a_{ij} = b_{ij}$ for $i = 1,2,3$ and $j = 1,2$. This statement means that $\mathbf{A} = \mathbf{B}$ if and only if $a_{11} = b_{11}$, $a_{12} = b_{12}$, $a_{21} = b_{21}$, $a_{22} = b_{22}$, $a_{31} = b_{31}$, and $a_{32} = b_{32}$. However, $\mathbf{A} \neq \mathbf{C}$ and $\mathbf{B} \neq \mathbf{C}$ because the elements cannot be equated one to one. Again, two matrices are equal if and only if they have the same order and if their corresponding elements are equal. Note that an $m \times n$ matrix cannot equal an $n \times m$ matrix.

If the number of rows equals the number of columns—if $m = n$—then the matrix is a **square matrix.** For example, matrix **C** in Eq. (11.5) is a square matrix.

A **row matrix** has a single row of elements, and a **column matrix** has a single column of elements. For example, in Eq. (11.6) **A** is a row matrix and **B** is a column matrix:

$$\mathbf{A} = [6 \quad 1 \quad 5], \qquad \mathbf{B} = \begin{bmatrix} 4 \\ 4 \\ -9 \end{bmatrix} \tag{11.6}$$

Column and row matrices are sometimes called **vectors.**

A **diagonal matrix** is a square matrix that has zero elements everywhere except on the main diagonal (from the upper-left-corner element to the lower-right-corner element). A diagonal matrix, **A**, requires that $a_{ij} = 0$ if $i \neq j$, and has the form

$$\mathbf{A} = \begin{bmatrix} a_{11} & 0 & 0 & \dots & 0 \\ 0 & a_{22} & 0 & \dots & 0 \\ 0 & 0 & a_{33} & \dots & 0 \\ \cdot & \cdot & \cdot & \dots & \cdot \\ 0 & 0 & 0 & \dots & a_{nn} \end{bmatrix} \tag{11.7}$$

A diagonal matrix that has unit-valued elements on the diagonal is called a **unit matrix** or **identity matrix.** The identity matrix is denoted by the symbol **I** and is defined as

$$\mathbf{I} = \delta_{ij} \tag{11.8}$$

where

$$\begin{aligned} \delta_{ij} &= 0 \text{ if } i \neq j \\ &= 1 \text{ if } i = j \end{aligned}$$

δ_{ij} is known as the **Kronecker delta.** An example of an identity matrix is

$$\mathbf{I} = \begin{bmatrix} 1 & 0 & 0 \\ 0 & 1 & 0 \\ 0 & 0 & 1 \end{bmatrix} \tag{11.9}$$

A **null matrix** is a matrix whose elements are all equal to zero. The usual notation for the null matrix is $\emptyset$.

A square matrix whose elements are symmetrical about the main diagonal is a **symmetric matrix.** If **B** is a symmetric matrix, then $b_{ij} = b_{ji}$. For example,

$$\mathbf{B} = \begin{bmatrix} 3 & 7 & -1 \\ 7 & -2 & 6 \\ -1 & 6 & 5 \end{bmatrix} \tag{11.10}$$

A matrix, **A**, is **antisymmetric** or **skew-symmetric** if $a_{ij} = -a_{ji}$, implying that $a_{ii} = 0$. For example,

$$\mathbf{A} = \begin{bmatrix} 0 & -8 & 3 \\ 8 & 0 & -4 \\ -3 & 4 & 0 \end{bmatrix} \tag{11.11}$$

EXERCISES

1. Let

$$A = \begin{bmatrix} 7 & 4 & 4 \\ 9 & 1 & 3 \\ 0 & 2 & 5 \end{bmatrix} \quad \text{and} \quad B = \begin{bmatrix} 6 & 5 \\ 8 & 1 \\ 3 & 9 \end{bmatrix}$$

a. Find a_{23}.
b. Find a_{12}.
c. Find a_{31}.
d. Find b_{11}
e. Find b_{32}.
f. What is the order of **A**?
g. What is the order of **B**?
h. Which matrix, if any, is a square matrix?
i. List the elements on the main diagonal of **A**.
j. Change a_{12}, a_{13}, and a_{23} so that **A** is a symmetric matrix.

2. Let

$$A = \begin{bmatrix} 1 & 0 & 0 \\ 0 & 1 & 0 \\ 0 & 0 & 1 \end{bmatrix}, \quad B = \begin{bmatrix} 7 \\ 4 \\ 9 \\ 5 \end{bmatrix} \quad \text{and} \quad C = [1 \quad -2 \quad 4 \quad 6]$$

a. Find a_{23}.
b. Find a_{32}.
c. Find b_{31}.
d. Find c_{14}.
e. What is the order of **A**?
f. What is the order of **B**?
g. What is the order of **C**?
h. Which is the column matrix?
i. Which is the row matrix?
j. Which is the identity matrix?

3. Let

$$A = [2 \quad -5 \quad 0] \quad \text{and} \quad B = \begin{bmatrix} 2 \\ -5 \\ 0 \end{bmatrix}$$

Are **A** and **B** equal?

4. Find the values of δ_{ij}.

a. $\delta_{3,2}$
b. $\delta_{1,4}$

c. $\delta_{3,3}$
d. $\delta_{7,10}$
e. $\delta_{1,1}$

5. Give the 2 × 2 null matrix.

6. Give the missing elements so that **A** = **B**:

$$\mathbf{A} = \begin{bmatrix} -0.5 & 0 & 6.25 & -4.75 \\ 1 & 7.25 & 5 & 0 \\ 2.5 & 3 & -1.25 & 9.25 \end{bmatrix}$$

$$\mathbf{B} = \begin{bmatrix} -0.5 & 0 & — & — \\ 1 & — & 5 & 0 \\ — & 3 & -1.25 & — \end{bmatrix}$$

7. Let

$$\mathbf{A} = \begin{bmatrix} 5 & 4 & 9 \\ 2 & 1 & 0 \\ 6 & 7 & 1 \end{bmatrix}$$

a. Change a_{12}, a_{13}, and a_{23} so that **A** becomes antisymmetric.
b. What other changes are necessary?

11.2. Matrix Operations

You can add or subtract two matrices if, and only if, they are of the same order. Adding **A** and **B** produces a third matrix, **C**, whose elements are equal to the sum of the corresponding elements of **A** and **B**. Write this as

$$\mathbf{A} + \mathbf{B} = \mathbf{C} \tag{11.12}$$

or

$$a_{ij} + b_{ij} = c_{ij} \qquad \text{for all } i,j \tag{11.13}$$

Similarly, the difference of two matrices, **A** and **B**, is another matrix, **D**, so that

$$\mathbf{A} - \mathbf{B} = \mathbf{D} \tag{11.14}$$

or

$$a_{ij} - b_{ij} = d_{ij} \qquad \text{for all } i,j \tag{11.15}$$

Clearly the matrix resulting from adding or subtracting two other matrices is of the same order as the original matrices. Furthermore, you can add and subtract more than two matrices. Thus,

$$\mathbf{A} + \mathbf{B} - \mathbf{C} = \mathbf{D} \tag{11.16}$$

or

$$a_{ij} + b_{ij} - c_{ij} = d_{ij} \qquad \text{for all } i,j \tag{11.17}$$

Look at an example: Given two 2 × 3 matrices, **A** and **B**,

$$\mathbf{A} = \begin{bmatrix} 6 & 5 & 9 \\ 3 & 7 & 1 \end{bmatrix} \quad \text{and} \quad \mathbf{B} = \begin{bmatrix} 4 & 0 & -3 \\ 1 & -4 & 1 \end{bmatrix} \tag{11.18}$$

then

$$\mathbf{C} = \mathbf{A} + \mathbf{B} = \begin{bmatrix} 6+4 & 5+0 & 9-3 \\ 3+1 & 7-4 & 1+1 \end{bmatrix} = \begin{bmatrix} 10 & 5 & 6 \\ 4 & 3 & 2 \end{bmatrix} \tag{11.19}$$

and

$$\mathbf{D} = \mathbf{A} - \mathbf{B} = \begin{bmatrix} 6-4 & 5-0 & 9+3 \\ 3-1 & 7+4 & 1-1 \end{bmatrix} = \begin{bmatrix} 2 & 5 & 12 \\ 2 & 11 & 0 \end{bmatrix} \tag{11.20}$$

Multiply a matrix, **A**, by some scalar constant, k, to produce a new matrix, **B**, of the same order as **A**. Produce each element of **B** by multiplying each element of **A** by k. Write this as

$$k\mathbf{A} = \mathbf{B} \tag{11.21}$$

or

$$ka_{ij} = b_{ij} \qquad \text{for all } i,j \tag{11.22}$$

For example, if $\mathbf{A} = [2 \quad 5 \quad 3]$ and $k = 3$, then

$$\mathbf{B} = k\mathbf{A} = [6 \quad 15 \quad 9] \tag{11.23}$$

You can multiply two matrices, **A** and **B**, to produce a third matrix, **C**, if and only if the number of columns of the first matrix is equal to the number of rows of the second matrix. The matrices **A** and **B** are **conformable** for multiplication when this condition is satisfied. Write the product of two matrices as

$$\mathbf{AB} = \mathbf{C} \tag{11.24}$$

where **A** is called the **premultiplier** and **B** is the **postmultiplier.** In general, $\mathbf{AB} \neq \mathbf{BA}$. If **A** is of order $m \times n$ and **B** of order $n \times p$, then **C** is of order $m \times p$. You will soon see how this comes about.

The product of two matrices, **A** and **B**, defined in terms of the elements of **A** and **B**, is:

$$c_{ij} = a_{i1}b_{1j} + a_{i2}b_{2j} + \dots + a_{in}b_{nj}.$$

Write this more compactly as

$$c_{ij} = \sum_{k=1}^{n} a_{ik}b_{kj} \tag{11.25}$$

Here is new notation that requires some explanation. The symbol Σ denotes summation (see Box 11.1). If **A** has three columns (and **B** has three rows), then $n = 3$, and Eq. (11.25) expands to

$$c_{ij} = a_{i1}b_{1j} + a_{i2}b_{2j} + a_{i3}b_{3j} \tag{11.26}$$

Thus, each element of **C** is the sum of the products of specific pairs of elements, one each from **A** and **B**. For example, for the element in row 2 and column 1 of **C**,

$$c_{21} = a_{21}b_{11} + a_{22}b_{21} + a_{23}b_{31} \tag{11.27}$$

There is structural meaning in this expression that reveals the need for conformable order. Take the example where **A** is of order 3 × 3 and **B** is 3 × 2. The structure of their product is revealed by arranging the matrix elements as shown in Eq. (11.28). The premultiplier **A** is to the left, and the postmultiplier **B** is above and to the right. The elements of **C** are produced at the intersection of the appropriate rows and columns of **A** and **B**, respectively:

$$\begin{array}{cc} & \begin{bmatrix} b_{11} & b_{12} \\ b_{21} & b_{22} \\ b_{31} & b_{32} \end{bmatrix} \\ \begin{bmatrix} a_{11} & a_{12} & a_{13} \\ a_{21} & a_{22} & a_{23} \\ a_{31} & a_{32} & a_{33} \end{bmatrix} & \begin{bmatrix} c_{11} & c_{12} \\ c_{21} & c_{22} \\ c_{31} & c_{32} \end{bmatrix} \end{array} \tag{11.28}$$

This structural relationship illustrates that c_{21}, for example, is determined by elements in row 2 of **A** and column 1 of **B**. Element c_{21} clearly lies at the intersection of this row-and-column pair. And, of course, summing the pairwise products of elements in this row and column produces a value for c_{21}. Also note how the orders of **A** and **B** determine the order of **C** and how this requirement for conformability arises.

Box 11.1. Summation Notation

Brevity and conciseness are achieved in mathematical expressions by using symbols. The Arabic numbers are more concise and also more powerful to work with than Roman numerals. The arithmetic symbols for addition, subtraction, multiplication, and division are certainly brief, yet they denote very powerful operators, otherwise very difficult to describe in ordinary language. The price you pay, of course, is the effort you must give to learning the meaning and proper use of symbols.

The uppercase Greek letter sigma, Σ, is the mathematical symbol for summation. Read the expression

$$\sum_{i=1}^{3} i$$

as "sigma i, i successively taking integer values from 1 to 3." It means: First insert the value 1 for i, then 2, and finally 3, and sum the results. Thus,

$$\sum_{i=1}^{3} i = 1 + 2 + 3 = 6$$

Other examples are:

$$\sum_{j=1}^{4} 2j = 2(1) + 2(2) + 2(3) + 2(4) = 20$$

$$\sum_{j=1}^{3} j^2 = (1)^2 + (2)^2 + (3)^2 = 14$$

$$\sum_{k=2}^{4} (5 - k) = (5 - 2) + (5 - 3) + (5 - 4) = 6$$

There are times when the upper limit for the summation is unknown or unspecified. Then you sum n terms and write

$$\sum_{i=1}^{n} i = 1 + 2 + 3 + \cdots + n$$

where the three dots are read "and so on."

The summation indices can be used as exponents or scalar multipliers, too, so that

$$\sum_{i=0}^{3} a_i x^i = a_0 + a_1 x + a_2 x^2 + a_3 x^3$$

(continued)

Box 11.1. (Continued)

Double summation provides compact notation for even more complex expressions. Interpret the equation

$$\sum_{i=1}^{2}\sum_{j=1}^{3} a_i x_j = b$$

in this way: Call the outer index i and the inner index j. Start by setting the outer index to 1, and then exhaust the inner index. This produces the following terms:

$$a_1x_1 + a_1x_2 + a_1x_3$$

Next, increment the outer index i by 1, and again exhaust the inner index j. This is the last step for this example and produces the final complete equation

$$a_1x_1 + a_1x_2 + a_1x_3 + a_2x_1 + a_2x_2 + a_2x_3 = b$$

Now work an example of matrix multiplication: If

$$\mathbf{A} = \begin{bmatrix} 4 & 2 & 1 \\ -3 & 6 & 0 \\ 7 & 8 & 5 \end{bmatrix} \quad \text{and} \quad \mathbf{B} = \begin{bmatrix} 1 & 0 \\ -4 & 2 \\ 3 & 5 \end{bmatrix}$$

then $\mathbf{C} = \mathbf{AB}$, with

$$\mathbf{C} = \begin{bmatrix} (4 \times 1) + (2 \times -4) + (1 \times 3) & (4 \times 0) + (2 \times 2) + (1 \times 5) \\ (-3 \times 1) + (6 \times -4) + (0 \times 3) & (-3 \times 0) + (6 \times 2) + (0 \times 5) \\ (7 \times 1) + (8 \times -4) + (5 \times 3) & (7 \times 0) + (8 \times 2) + (5 \times 5) \end{bmatrix} \tag{11.29}$$

or

$$\mathbf{C} = \begin{bmatrix} -1 & 9 \\ -27 & 12 \\ -10 & 41 \end{bmatrix} \tag{11.30}$$

Obtain the **transpose** of a matrix, **A**, denoted $\mathbf{A}^T$, by interchanging the rows and columns of **A**. For example, if

$$\mathbf{A} = \begin{bmatrix} 0.25 & 0.30 & 0.75 \\ 1.50 & -0.67 & 0.08 \\ 3 & -2.1 & 7.2 \end{bmatrix} \tag{11.31}$$

then

$$\mathbf{A}^T = \begin{bmatrix} 0.25 & 1.50 & 3 \\ 0.30 & -0.67 & -2.1 \\ 0.75 & 0.08 & 7.2 \end{bmatrix} \tag{11.32}$$

Note that for a square matrix, elements on the main diagonal do not change. However, all matrices have a transpose, not just square ones. Thus, if

$$\mathbf{B} = [x \quad y \quad z] \tag{11.33}$$

then

$$\mathbf{B}^T = \begin{bmatrix} x \\ y \\ z \end{bmatrix} \tag{11.34}$$

See a summary of matrix properties in Box 11.2.

Box 11.2. Matrix Properties

The properties of matrix addition and scalar multiplication are:

1. $A + B = B + A$
2. $A + (B + C) = (A + B) + C$
3. $b(A + B) = bA + bB$
4. $(b + d)A = bA + dA$
5. $b(dA) = (bd)A = d(bA)$

The properties of matrix multiplication are:

1. $(AB)C = A(BC)$
2. $A(B + C) = AB + AC$
3. $(A + B)C = AC + BC$
4. $A(kB) = k(AB) = (kA)B$

The properties of matrix transpose operations are

1. $(A + B)^T = A^T + B^T$
2. $(kA)^T = kA^T$
3. $(AB)^T = B^TA^T$

EXERCISES

1. Given $\mathbf{A} = [7 \quad 3 \quad 1]$, find $-\mathbf{A}$.

2. Given

$$\mathbf{A} = \begin{bmatrix} 3 & 2 & 0 \\ 4 & 5 & 1 \end{bmatrix}, \quad \mathbf{B} = \begin{bmatrix} 6 & 3 & 9 \\ 1 & 0 & 2 \end{bmatrix}, \quad \text{and} \quad \mathbf{C} = \begin{bmatrix} 4 & 8 & 1 \\ 3 & 1 & 5 \end{bmatrix}$$

find the following:

a. $\mathbf{A} + 2\mathbf{A}$
b. $\mathbf{B} + \mathbf{B}$
c. $2\mathbf{A} + \mathbf{B}$
d. $\mathbf{A} - \mathbf{B} - \mathbf{C}$
e. $\mathbf{A} + \mathbf{B} - 2\mathbf{C}$

3. Perform the indicated operation in each of the following expressions:

a. $\begin{bmatrix} 2 & 4 \\ 2 & 5 \end{bmatrix} + \begin{bmatrix} 0 & -4 \\ 3 & 8 \end{bmatrix}$

b. $\begin{bmatrix} 1 & 3 \\ 6 & 4 \\ 0 & 2 \end{bmatrix} - \begin{bmatrix} -4 & 7 \\ 1 & -2 \\ 5 & -1 \end{bmatrix}$

c. $\begin{bmatrix} 7 & 9 & 0 \\ 1 & 8 & -4 \\ 5 & 2 & -2 \end{bmatrix} - 2\begin{bmatrix} 3 & -1 & 4 \\ 5 & 0 & -3 \\ 6 & 6 & -2 \end{bmatrix}$

d. $[7 \quad 3 \quad 8 \quad 8] + [2 \quad -3 \quad -2 \quad 0]$

e. $\begin{bmatrix} 1 & 0 & 0 \\ 0 & 1 & 0 \\ 0 & 0 & 1 \end{bmatrix} + \begin{bmatrix} 1 & 0 & 0 \\ 0 & 1 & 0 \\ 0 & 0 & 1 \end{bmatrix}$

4. Let

$$\mathbf{A} = \begin{bmatrix} 6 & -2 \\ 1 & 0 \end{bmatrix}, \quad \mathbf{B} = \begin{bmatrix} 3 & 2 \\ 9 & -4 \end{bmatrix}, \quad \text{and} \quad \mathbf{C} = \begin{bmatrix} 5 & 3 \\ 2 & 1 \end{bmatrix}$$

a. Show that $\mathbf{A} + (-\mathbf{A}) = 0$
b. Show that $\mathbf{A} + \mathbf{B} = \mathbf{B} + \mathbf{A}$
c. Show that $\mathbf{A} + (\mathbf{B} + \mathbf{C}) = (\mathbf{A} + \mathbf{B}) + \mathbf{C}$

5. Find the values of the unknowns; show that the equations are true:

a. $[3x \quad -2y] = [12 \quad 4]$

b. $\begin{bmatrix} -2x \\ y \\ 0.5z \end{bmatrix} = \begin{bmatrix} -6 \\ 3 \\ 5 \end{bmatrix}$

c. $\begin{bmatrix} a & b \\ c & d \\ e & f \end{bmatrix} + \begin{bmatrix} 2 & 4 \\ 1 & 5 \\ 7 & 0 \end{bmatrix} = \begin{bmatrix} 0 & 0 \\ 0 & 0 \\ 0 & 0 \end{bmatrix}$

6. Find $\mathbf{I}^T$.

7. Given

$$\mathbf{A} = \begin{bmatrix} 4 & -2 \\ 1 & 0 \\ 6 & 7 \end{bmatrix} \quad \text{and} \quad \mathbf{B} = \begin{bmatrix} 1 & 1 \\ 5 & 2 \\ 2 & 4 \end{bmatrix}$$

a. Find $(\mathbf{A}^T)^T$
b. Find $(\mathbf{A} + \mathbf{B})^T$
c. Find $\mathbf{A}^T + \mathbf{B}^T$
d. Find $\mathbf{B}^T + \mathbf{A}^T$

8. If $\mathbf{A} = [3 \quad 5 \quad -7]$, compute $\mathbf{AI}$.

9. Show that $\mathbf{AI} = \mathbf{IA}$. (Hint: This assumes $\mathbf{A}$ and $\mathbf{I}$ are square.)

10. Find the product of the following matrices:

a. $[u^3 \quad u^2 \quad u \quad 1] \begin{bmatrix} a_x & a_y & a_z \\ b_x & b_y & b_z \\ c_x & c_y & c_z \\ d_x & d_y & d_z \end{bmatrix}$

b. $\begin{bmatrix} 2 & 1 \\ -4 & 0 \end{bmatrix} \begin{bmatrix} 6 & 3 \\ 1 & -5 \end{bmatrix}$

c. $\begin{bmatrix} 2 & 1 \\ -4 & 0 \end{bmatrix} \begin{bmatrix} 6 & 3 \\ 1 & -5 \end{bmatrix}^T$

d. $\begin{bmatrix} 2 & 1 \\ -4 & 0 \end{bmatrix}^T \begin{bmatrix} 6 & 3 \\ 1 & -5 \end{bmatrix}^T$

e. $\begin{bmatrix} 2 & 1 \\ -4 & 0 \end{bmatrix} \begin{bmatrix} 6 & 3 \\ 1 & -5 \end{bmatrix} \begin{bmatrix} -2 & 0 & 3 \\ 4 & -1 & 6 \end{bmatrix}$

11. If $\mathbf{P} = \mathbf{UMB}$ and the order of $\mathbf{U}$ is 1×4, the order of $\mathbf{M}$ is 4×4, and the order of $\mathbf{B}$ is 4×3, then what is the order of $\mathbf{P}$?

12. Write a procedure to compute the transpose of a 4×3 matrix.

13. Write a procedure to compute the product of a 4×4 matrix and a 4×3 matrix.

14. Write a procedure to compute the product of a 1×4 matrix and a 4×3 matrix.

11.3. Determinants

A **determinant** is a square array of elements that you can reduce to a single value by following a well-defined procedure. Write the 2×2 determinant of the square matrix

$$\mathbf{A} = \begin{bmatrix} a_{11} & a_{12} \\ a_{21} & a_{22} \end{bmatrix} \tag{11.35}$$

as

$$|\mathbf{A}| = \begin{vmatrix} a_{11} & a_{12} \\ a_{21} & a_{22} \end{vmatrix} \tag{11.36}$$

and evaluate it by

$$\begin{vmatrix} a_{11} & a_{12} \\ a_{21} & a_{22} \end{vmatrix} = a_{11}a_{22} - a_{12}a_{21} \tag{11.37}$$

A pair of vertical lines, not brackets, sets off and encloses a determinant.

A 3×3 determinant is defined by

$$\begin{vmatrix} a_{11} & a_{12} & a_{13} \\ a_{21} & a_{22} & a_{23} \\ a_{31} & a_{32} & a_{33} \end{vmatrix} = a_{11}\begin{vmatrix} a_{22} & a_{23} \\ a_{32} & a_{33} \end{vmatrix} - a_{12}\begin{vmatrix} a_{21} & a_{23} \\ a_{31} & a_{33} \end{vmatrix} + a_{13}\begin{vmatrix} a_{21} & a_{22} \\ a_{31} & a_{32} \end{vmatrix} \tag{11.38}$$

A matrix must be square to have a determinant. The determinant of a matrix, **A**, is denoted by $|\mathbf{A}|$. Note that there is a basic difference between a matrix and a determinant. A determinant, when expanded, has a numerical value, while matrices cannot be reduced to a single value. Matrices are, in fact, operators, and you should think of them as such.

Determinants often arise when performing matrix algebra, so you must know some of the fundamentals of determinants. Consider the simultaneous equations

$$\begin{aligned} a_{11}x + a_{12}y + a_{13}z &= b_1 \\ a_{21}x + a_{22}y + a_{23}z &= b_2 \\ a_{31}x + a_{32}y + a_{33}z &= b_3 \end{aligned} \tag{11.39}$$

The determinant of the coefficients a_{ij} is written

$$|\mathbf{A}| = \begin{vmatrix} a_{11} & a_{12} & a_{13} \\ a_{21} & a_{22} & a_{23} \\ a_{31} & a_{32} & a_{33} \end{vmatrix} \tag{11.40}$$

Recall Cramer's rule from elementary algebra. Use it to show that

$$x = \frac{\begin{vmatrix} b_1 & a_{12} & a_{13} \\ b_2 & a_{22} & a_{23} \\ b_3 & a_{32} & a_{33} \end{vmatrix}}{|\mathbf{A}|}$$

$$y = \frac{\begin{vmatrix} a_{11} & b_1 & a_{13} \\ a_{21} & b_2 & a_{23} \\ a_{31} & b_3 & a_{33} \end{vmatrix}}{|\mathbf{A}|} \tag{11.41}$$

$$z = \frac{\begin{vmatrix} a_{11} & a_{12} & b_1 \\ a_{21} & a_{22} & b_2 \\ a_{31} & a_{32} & b_3 \end{vmatrix}}{|\mathbf{A}|}$$

where $|\mathbf{A}|$ is given by Eq. (11.40). The solutions for x, y, and z require that $|\mathbf{A}| \neq 0$. If $b_1 = b_2 = b_3 = 0$, then Eqs. (11.41) are called **homogeneous equations.** For a set of homogeneous equations, where x, y, and z are not zero and, where a nontrivial solution is possible, the determinant of the coefficients, **A**, is equal to zero.

Note that you can write (Eq. 11.39) as a matrix equation:

$$\mathbf{AX} = \mathbf{B} \tag{11.42}$$

where

$$\mathbf{A} = \begin{bmatrix} a_{11} & a_{12} & a_{13} \\ a_{21} & a_{22} & a_{23} \\ a_{31} & a_{32} & a_{33} \end{bmatrix}, \quad \mathbf{X} = \begin{bmatrix} x \\ y \\ z \end{bmatrix}, \quad \text{and} \quad \mathbf{B} = \begin{bmatrix} b_1 \\ b_2 \\ b_3 \end{bmatrix}$$

In the next section you will see how a process called **matrix inversion** allows you to solve this matrix equation for **X**, that is, the elements of **X**. Before beginning this subject, you must first define the minor and cofactor of an element of a determinant.

The **minor** of the element a_{ij} of a determinant of size n is the determinant of size $n - 1$ obtained by deleting the ith row and jth column of the original determinant. In Eq. (11.40) the minor M_{ij} of element a_{23} is

$$M_{23} = \begin{vmatrix} a_{11} & a_{12} \\ a_{31} & a_{32} \end{vmatrix} \tag{11.43}$$

The **cofactor** of an element a_{ij} of a determinant is the minor of the element preceded by either a positive or a negative sign. The sign of the minor is determined by the expression

$$(-1)^{i+j} \tag{11.44}$$

Thus, the cofactor C_{ij} of element a_{23} in Eq. (11.40) is

$$\begin{aligned} C_{23} &= (-1)^{2+3} M_{23} \\ &= -M_{23} \end{aligned} \tag{11.45}$$

Evaluate a determinant, $|\mathbf{A}|$, of any order, $n \times n$, by summing the products of the elements of any single row or column with their cofactors. For example, given a 4×4 determinant, such as

$$|\mathbf{A}| = \begin{vmatrix} a_{11} & a_{12} & a_{13} & a_{14} \\ a_{21} & a_{22} & a_{23} & a_{24} \\ a_{31} & a_{32} & a_{33} & a_{34} \\ a_{41} & a_{42} & a_{43} & a_{44} \end{vmatrix} \tag{11.46}$$

compute its value. Use the elements in the first column to obtain

$$|\mathbf{A}| = a_{11}C_{11} + a_{21}C_{21} + a_{31}C_{31} + a_{41}C_{41} \tag{11.47}$$

The cofactors C_{11}, C_{21}, C_{31}, and C_{41} are themselves determinants. They are of order 3×3. Apply this same procedure to each of these cofactors, obtaining a set of 2×2 determinants. Then evaluate them using Eq. (11.37).

A summary of determinant properties appears in Box 11.3.

EXERCISES

1. Compute the value of each of the following determinants:

a. $\begin{vmatrix} -3 & 2 \\ 2 & 0 \end{vmatrix}$

b. $\begin{vmatrix} 1 & 4 \\ 2 & -5 \end{vmatrix}$

c. $\begin{vmatrix} 3 & 0 \\ 0 & 0 \end{vmatrix}$

Box 11.3. Determinant Properties
1. The determinant of a matrix is equal to the determinant of its transpose: $$\|\mathbf{A}\| = \|\mathbf{A}^T\|$$ 2. Interchanging any two rows (or columns) of **A** changes the sign of the determinant. Denote the changed matrix as **B**, then $$\|\mathbf{B}\| = -\|\mathbf{A}\|$$ 3. If you obtain matrix **B** by multiplying one row or column of **A** by a constant, c, then $$\|\mathbf{B}\| = c\|\mathbf{A}\|$$ 4. If two rows or columns of **A** are identical, then $$\|\mathbf{A}\| = 0$$ 5. If you derive **B** from **A** by adding a multiple of one row or column of **A** to another, then $$\|\mathbf{B}\| = \|\mathbf{A}\|$$ 6. If **A** and **B** are both $n \times n$ matrices, then the determinant of their product is $$\|\mathbf{AB}\| = \|\mathbf{A}\|\|\mathbf{B}\|$$

d. $\begin{vmatrix} 1 & 2 \\ 2 & 4 \end{vmatrix}$

e. $\begin{vmatrix} 2 & -3 \\ 5 & 1 \end{vmatrix}$

2. Let

$$|\mathbf{A}| = \begin{vmatrix} 3 & 0 & 1 \\ -2 & 4 & 2 \\ 5 & 1 & 3 \end{vmatrix}$$

Compute the following minors and cofactors:

a. M_{11}
b. M_{21}
c. M_{31}
d. M_{22}
e. M_{12}

f. C_{11}
g. C_{21}
h. C_{31}
i. C_{22}
j. C_{12}

3. Evaluate $|\mathbf{A}|$ in Exercise 2.

4. Interchange rows 1 and 2 of $|\mathbf{A}|$ (Exercise 2) to obtain $|\mathbf{B}|$. Thus,

$$|\mathbf{B}| = \begin{vmatrix} -2 & 4 & 2 \\ 3 & 0 & 1 \\ 5 & 1 & 3 \end{vmatrix}$$

Evaluate $|\mathbf{B}|$, and compare the result to $|\mathbf{A}|$.

5. Evaluate $|\mathbf{A}^T|$, and compare the result to $|\mathbf{A}|$.

6. Double the value of the elements in column 3 of $|\mathbf{A}|$ to obtain $|\mathbf{C}|$. Thus,

$$|\mathbf{C}| = \begin{vmatrix} 3 & 0 & 2 \\ -2 & 4 & 4 \\ 5 & 1 & 6 \end{vmatrix}$$

Evaluate $|\mathbf{C}|$, and compare the result to $|\mathbf{A}|$.

7. Write a procedure to evaluate a 4×4 determinant.

11.4. Matrix Inversion

To obtain the **inverse**, $\mathbf{A}^{-1}$, of an $n \times n$ matrix, **A**, replace each element in **A** by its cofactor and multiplying the transpose of the resulting matrix by $1/|\mathbf{A}|$. Let $\mathbf{C}_{ij}$ be the cofactor of a_{ij} of **A**, then

$$\mathbf{A}^{-1} = \frac{1}{|\mathbf{A}|} \begin{bmatrix} C_{11} & C_{21} & . & . & . & C_{n1} \\ C_{12} & . & . & . & . & . \\ \vdots & \vdots & \vdots & \vdots & \vdots & \vdots \\ C_{1n} & . & . & . & . & C_{nn} \end{bmatrix} \tag{11.48}$$

For example, find $\mathbf{A}^{-1}$ when

$$\mathbf{A} = \begin{bmatrix} 2 & 1 & 0 \\ -1 & -1 & 2 \\ 2 & 1 & 3 \end{bmatrix}$$

First compute $|\mathbf{A}| = -3$. Next replace each element of **A** by its cofactor, obtaining a new matrix, **B**:

$$\mathbf{B} = \begin{bmatrix} -5 & 7 & 1 \\ -3 & 6 & 0 \\ 2 & -4 & -1 \end{bmatrix} \tag{11.49}$$

Then find $\mathbf{B}^T$:

$$\mathbf{B}^T = \begin{bmatrix} -5 & -3 & 2 \\ 7 & 6 & -4 \\ 1 & 0 & -1 \end{bmatrix} \tag{11.50}$$

And $\mathbf{A}^{-1}$ follows directly:

$$\mathbf{A}^{-1} = -\frac{1}{3}\begin{bmatrix} -5 & -3 & 2 \\ 7 & 6 & -4 \\ 1 & 0 & -1 \end{bmatrix} \tag{11.51}$$

Note that for $\mathbf{A}^{-1}$ to exist, $|\mathbf{A}| \neq 0$. There is also a convenient test of the correctness of $\mathbf{A}^{-1}$, since $\mathbf{A}^{-1}\mathbf{A} = \mathbf{A}\mathbf{A}^{-1} = \mathbf{I}$. Do this for Eq. (11.51): Compute

$$\begin{aligned} -\frac{1}{3}\begin{bmatrix} -5 & -3 & 2 \\ 7 & 6 & -4 \\ 1 & 0 & -1 \end{bmatrix}\begin{bmatrix} 2 & 1 & 0 \\ -1 & -1 & 2 \\ 2 & 1 & 3 \end{bmatrix} \\ = -\frac{1}{3}\begin{bmatrix} -3 & 0 & 0 \\ 0 & -3 & 0 \\ 0 & 0 & -3 \end{bmatrix} = \begin{bmatrix} 1 & 0 & 0 \\ 0 & 1 & 0 \\ 0 & 0 & 1 \end{bmatrix} \end{aligned} \tag{11.52}$$

You can compare matrix inversion to taking the reciprocal of an expression in the course of an elementary algebraic analysis. Given the relationship

$$5x = 7 \tag{11.53}$$

compute the value of x by operating on 7 with the reciprocal of 5. Thus,

$$x = \frac{1}{5}7 \tag{11.54}$$

Similarly with matrix algebra, using matrix inversion, consider a set of n simultaneous linear equations with n unknown values of x. For example, given this set of equations as

$$\begin{aligned} a_{11}x_1 + a_{12}x_2 + \cdots + a_{1n}x_n &= b_1 \\ a_{21}x_1 + a_{22}x_2 + \cdots + a_{2n}x_n &= b_2 \\ \vdots \qquad\qquad\qquad & \quad \vdots \\ a_{n1}x_1 + a_{n2}x_2 + \cdots + a_{nn}x_n &= b_n \end{aligned} \tag{11.55}$$

you can readily rewrite this set as a matrix equation:

$$\mathbf{AX} = \mathbf{B} \tag{11.56}$$

Also, see Eq. (11.42). **A** is a $n \times n$ matrix, **X** is a $n \times 1$, and **B** is a $n \times 1$. Premultiply both sides of Eq. (11.56) to obtain

$$\mathbf{A}^{-1}\mathbf{A}\mathbf{X} = \mathbf{A}^{-1}\mathbf{B} \tag{11.57}$$

Since $\mathbf{A}^{-1}\mathbf{A} = \mathbf{I}$ and $\mathbf{I}\mathbf{X} = \mathbf{X}$, simplify Eq. (11.57) to obtain

$$\mathbf{X} = \mathbf{A}^{-1}\mathbf{B} \tag{11.58}$$

EXERCISES

Compute the inverse of the following matrices, if it exists.

1. $\begin{bmatrix} 1 & 0 & 0 \\ 0 & 1 & 0 \\ 0 & 0 & 1 \end{bmatrix}$ 2. $\begin{bmatrix} 3 & -1 & 2 \\ 1 & 2 & 1 \\ -2 & 1 & 3 \end{bmatrix}$ 3. $\begin{bmatrix} 1 & 0 & 0 \\ 2 & 1 & 3 \\ 1 & 1 & 2 \end{bmatrix}$

4. $\begin{bmatrix} 2 & 1 & 0 \\ 3 & 2 & 1 \\ -1 & 2 & 0 \end{bmatrix}$ 5. $\begin{bmatrix} 3 & -1 & 2 \\ 1 & 2 & 1 \\ 3 & -1 & 2 \end{bmatrix}$ 6. $\begin{bmatrix} 2 & 1 & 2 \\ 3 & 2 & 3 \\ -1 & 2 & -1 \end{bmatrix}$

Use matrix algebra to solve the following sets of simultaneous equations.

7. $4x + 3y + 2z = 5$
   $-3x + y - 2z = 1$
   $x + 2y + z = 1$

8. $-4x + 3y = -2$
   $-2x + y = 0$

9. $3x + 5y + z = 3$
   $2x + 2y + z = 5$
   $-x - y + 2z = 0$

10. Write a procedure to invert a 4×4 matrix, **A**. Denote this as **MATINV**(MI,MO), where

    MI(4,4) are the input elements of **A** and
    MO(4,4) are the output elements of $\mathbf{A}^{-1}$.

11.5. Transformations as Matrix Operations

You can represent both the data describing a geometric object and the data describing a transformation as matrices. Then apply matrix operations to compute the results of a transformation. Let the components of a point be given by a row matrix, $\mathbf{p} = [x \quad y \quad z]$, and translation components by another row matrix, $\mathbf{T} = [x \quad y \quad z]$. Then

$$\mathbf{p}^* = \mathbf{p} + \mathbf{T} \tag{11.59}$$

or

$$[x^* \quad y^* \quad z^*] = [x \quad y \quad z] + [x_T \quad y_T \quad z_T] \tag{11.60}$$

Express the arguments defining a rectangle as elements of a matrix:

$$\mathbf{RN} = [x_0 \quad y_0 \quad a_x \quad a_y] \tag{11.61}$$

Next, express the translation components of a rectangle as a matrix:

$$\mathbf{T}_{RN} = [x_T \quad y_T \quad 0 \quad 0] \tag{11.62}$$

Note that these two matrices are of the same order, 1 × 4. This means that you can add them together to form **RN***; thus,

$$\begin{aligned} \mathbf{RN}^* &= \mathbf{RN} + \mathbf{T}_{RN} \\ &= [x_0 + x_T \quad y_0 + y_T \quad a_x \quad a_y] \end{aligned} \tag{11.63}$$

This process applies to any of the geometric objects you have studied. For example, the cylinder translation, using matrix notation and operation, looks like this:

$$\mathbf{CL} = [x_c \quad y_c \quad z_c \quad k \quad r \quad L] \text{ and } \mathbf{T}_{CL} = [x_T \quad y_T \quad z_T \quad 0 \quad 0 \quad 0].$$

$$\begin{aligned} \mathbf{CL}^* &= \mathbf{CL} + \mathbf{T}_{CL} \\ &= [x_c + x_T \quad y_c + y_T \quad z_c + z_T \quad k \quad r \quad L] \end{aligned} \tag{11.64}$$

There are analogous matrix forms and translation operations for the other geometric objects. The inherent power and versatility of this technique is not so apparent here, but it will be by the time you complete Chapter 15.

But note that there are some shortcomings here. For one thing, the matrix order varies with object type. The matrix for a square is 1 × 3, for a rectangle 1 × 4, for a cylinder 1 × 6, and so on. Can you think of a way around this? Some of this awkwardness will be resolved when you use vectors to describe geometric objects.

These same principles apply to rotation transformations. To rotate a point, **p**, about the z axis, arrange the rotation components [from Eq. (2.14)] into the following matrix format:

$$\mathbf{R} = \begin{bmatrix} \cos\theta & \sin\theta & 0 \\ -\sin\theta & \cos\theta & 0 \\ 0 & 0 & 1 \end{bmatrix} \tag{11.65}$$

Then apply matrix multiplication to define **p**; thus,

$$[x^* \quad y^* \quad z^*] = [x \quad y \quad z]\begin{bmatrix} \cos\theta & \sin\theta & 0 \\ -\sin\theta & \cos\theta & 0 \\ 0 & 0 & 1 \end{bmatrix} \tag{11.66}$$

or, in shorter form,

$$\mathbf{p}^* = \mathbf{pR} \tag{11.67}$$

In fact, the same 3×3 rotation matrix, **R**, applies to a set of points. Arrange the coordinates in an $n \times 3$ matrix, **P**. Then $\mathbf{P}^* = \mathbf{PR}$, where $\mathbf{P}^*$ is also a $3 \times n$ matrix.

There is a rotation matrix, $\mathbf{R}_{RN}$, such that for a rectangle $\mathbf{RN}^* = \mathbf{RN} \times \mathbf{R}_{RN}$.

Since $\mathbf{RN} = [x_0 \quad y_0 \quad a_x \quad a_y]$, a 1×4 matrix, $\mathbf{R}_{RN}$ must be 4×4. You already know the form of $\mathbf{RN}^*$ for the various possible rotations. For example, if $\mathbf{R} = (3, 90)$, then $\mathbf{RN}^* = [-(y_0 + a_y) \quad x_0 \quad a_y \quad a_y \quad a_x]$. So it should be possible to construct a rotation matrix, $\mathbf{R}_{RN}$, for each of the possible rotations. And, indeed it is. For $\mathbf{R} = (3, 90)$, then

$$\mathbf{R}_{RN} = \begin{bmatrix} 0 & 1 & 0 & 0 \\ -1 & 0 & 0 & 0 \\ 0 & 0 & 0 & 1 \\ -1 & 0 & 1 & 0 \end{bmatrix} \tag{11.68}$$

For $\mathbf{R} = (3, 180)$, then

$$\mathbf{R}_{RN} = \begin{bmatrix} -1 & 0 & 0 & 0 \\ 0 & -1 & 0 & 0 \\ -1 & 0 & 1 & 0 \\ 0 & -1 & 0 & 1 \end{bmatrix} \tag{11.69}$$

You can easily determine the others. In fact, there are comparable matrices for the other geometric objects. Try to construct them.

Now you can express a sequence of translations and rotations as a series of matrix operations. For example, to translate, then rotate a rectangle:

$$\mathbf{RN}^* = (\mathbf{RN} + \mathbf{T}_{RN})\mathbf{R}_{RN} \tag{11.70}$$

Finally, there is a scaling matrix, $\mathbf{S}_{RN}$, such that

$$\mathbf{RN}^* = \mathbf{RN} \times \mathbf{S}_{RN} \tag{11.71}$$

Since $\mathbf{RN} = [x_0 \quad y_0 \quad a_x \quad a_y]$, a 1×4 matrix, $\mathbf{S}_{RN}$ must be 4×4. You already know the form of **RN***, so you can construct $\mathbf{S}_{RN}$:

$$\mathbf{S}_{RN} = \begin{bmatrix} 1 & 0 & 0 & 0 \\ 0 & 1 & 0 & 0 \\ 0 & 0 & s_x & 0 \\ 0 & 0 & 0 & S_y \end{bmatrix} \tag{11.72}$$

The scaling matrices for the others are easy to determine. Here they are for the three-dimensional objects you have studied:

$$\mathbf{S}_{CB} = \begin{bmatrix} 1 & 0 & 0 & 0 \\ 0 & 1 & 0 & 0 \\ 0 & 0 & 1 & 0 \\ 0 & 0 & 0 & s_a \end{bmatrix}, \quad \mathbf{S}_{BK} = \begin{bmatrix} 1 & 0 & 0 & 0 & 0 & 0 \\ 0 & 1 & 0 & 0 & 0 & 0 \\ 0 & 0 & 1 & 0 & 0 & 0 \\ 0 & 0 & 0 & s_x & 0 & 0 \\ 0 & 0 & 0 & 0 & s_y & 0 \\ 0 & 0 & 0 & 0 & 0 & s_z \end{bmatrix}$$
$$\mathbf{S}_{CL} = \begin{bmatrix} 1 & 0 & 0 & 0 & 0 & 0 \\ 0 & 1 & 0 & 0 & 0 & 0 \\ 0 & 0 & 1 & 0 & 0 & 0 \\ 0 & 0 & 0 & 1 & 0 & 0 \\ 0 & 0 & 0 & 0 & s_r & 0 \\ 0 & 0 & 0 & 0 & 0 & s_L \end{bmatrix}, \quad \mathbf{S}_{SP} = \begin{bmatrix} 1 & 0 & 0 & 0 \\ 0 & 1 & 0 & 0 \\ 0 & 0 & 1 & 0 \\ 0 & 0 & 0 & s_r \end{bmatrix} \tag{11.73}$$

It is appropriate to note here that applying these matrix methods uncritically or incautiously to solve geometric modeling problems of computer graphics is not always the most efficient course to follow. In many cases, the maximum value of matrix methods, both representational and operational, lies in applying them during intermediate phases, when a program's computation schemes are developing. Matrix methods often allow you to isolate quickly the computational key to a problem; at this point you can either carry through with these matrix methods or proceed in another direction. Many numerical methods have been developed to increase the speed and efficiency of matrix computations. These are more advanced subjects, and they are readily available in the literature.

12. Vectors

PERHAPS THE SINGLE most important mathematical device used in computer graphics and geometric modeling is the **vector**. Vectors are geometric objects of a sort, because, as you will soon see, they seem to fit one's notion of a displacement. (You can think of displacement as a change in position. If you move a book from a shelf to a table, you have displaced it a specific distance and direction.)

Vectors offer a distinct advantage over classical analytic geometry by minimizing your computational dependence on a specific coordinate system. At the very least, vectors allow you to postpone choosing a coordinate system until the later stages of solving a problem. It will be to your advantage to think geometrically and to compute with vectors.

12.1. What is a Vector?

A vector is a geometric object represented by an ordered set of numbers to which you assign certain properties. The properties are direction and magnitude. Vectors and vector algebra were invented to make it easier to analyze phenomena in physics and engineering that have these two properties. It turns out that vectors also prove to be invaluable to the study and application of geometry.

A vector is represented by a row or a column matrix; for example, $\mathbf{A} = [a, b]$, $\mathbf{B} = [a, b\ c]$, $\mathbf{C} = [a_1\ a_2\ \ldots\ a_n]$, $\mathbf{D} = [d\ e]^T$, $\mathbf{E} = [d\ e\ f]^T$, and $\mathbf{F} = [d_1\ d_2\ \ldots\ d_n]^T$ are all vectors. **A**, **B**, and **C** are row matrix vectors, and **D**, **E**, and **F** are column matrix vectors. **A** and **D** are two-dimensional vectors, **B** and **E** are three-dimensional vectors, and **C** and **F** are n-dimensional vectors.

Each element of a row or column matrix is called a **vector component**. Each vector component represents a **displacement**. Imagine receiving a note with instructions to walk 30 paces to the east, then 40 paces to the north. The instruction is a vector, with the first component a displacement 30 paces east, and the second component a displacement 40 paces north. Displacement, therefore, has both magnitude (length) and direction. The net result of these two component displacements is a total displacement of 50 paces in a generally northeast direction. Thus, the total vector has a length and direction, too, namely 50 paces northeast. Figure 12.1 illustrates this vector and its components. (Assume conventional map directions, with north upward and east to the right.) It is convenient to use arrows to graphically represent a vector. The length of the arrow represents the length or magnitude of the vector and vector components, and the orientation of the arrow represents their direction.

Let us encode these instructions, the "pacing" vector, into a more compact and convenient form. At the same time, let us also change the notation slightly so that the distinction between a vector and a general matrix is clear. Denote a vector with a boldface lowercase letter, such as **a**, **b**, **p**, **r**, or **u**. Represent the "pacing" vector by **d** and the previous instructions as

$$\mathbf{d} = [30 \;\; 40] \tag{12.1}$$

where the first component specifies the number of paces to be taken east (+) or west (−), and the second component specifies the number of paces north (+) or south (−).

Study the vectors in Fig. 12.2. The vectors are given by $\mathbf{a} = [8 \;\; 3]$, $\mathbf{b} = [-8 \;\; -3]$, $\mathbf{c} = [5 \;\; -5]$, and $\mathbf{d} = [-6 \;\; 8]$. Note how the components

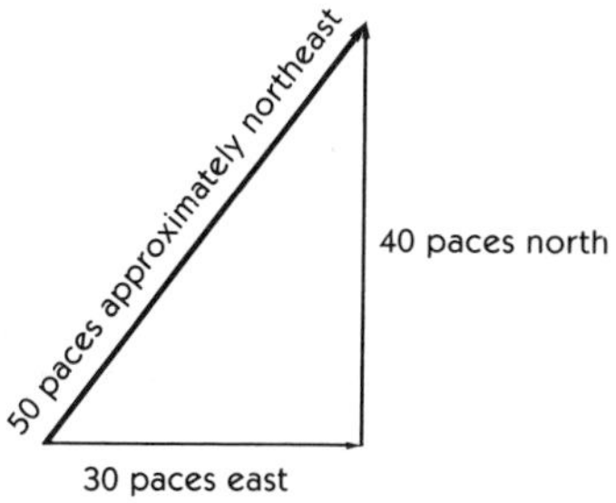

Fig. 12.1. Vectors and displacements.

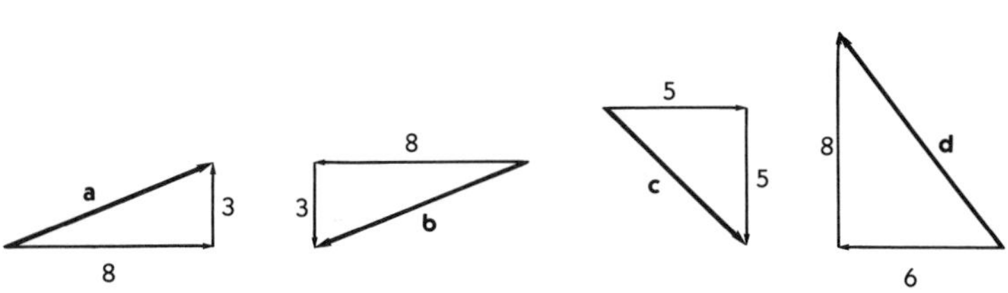

Fig. 12.2 Vectors.

control the direction of the vectors. For example, **a** and **b** are parallel and have the same length (magnitude), but they are in opposite directions. Use the Pythagorean theorem to determine the magnitudes of these vectors. Thus,

$$\begin{aligned} |\mathbf{a}| &= \sqrt{8^2 + 3^2} = 8.544 \\ |\mathbf{b}| &= \sqrt{(-8)^2 + (-3)^2} = 8.544 \\ |\mathbf{c}| &= \sqrt{5^2 + (-5)^2} = 7.071 \\ |\mathbf{d}| &= \sqrt{(-6)^2 + 8^2} = 10 \end{aligned} \tag{12.2}$$

where the vertical lines denote **absolute magnitude** and $|\mathbf{a}|$ is read "the absolute magnitude of **a**."

We will now explore other important characteristics of a vector besides direction and magnitude. Suppose you are given instructions to walk 60 paces east, then 20 paces north. The instructions in vector form are: $\mathbf{a} = [60 \;\; 20]$. When you do this, upon arriving at the specified destination, you receive further instructions: Walk 10 paces east, then 50 paces north. The instructions in the form of a vector are: $\mathbf{b} = [10 \;\; 50]$. When you do this you find yourself at yet another location. Could a single vector, say **c**, have brought you to this location from your initial position? Yes. You could have arrived at the same place by walking 70 paces east and 70 paces north: $\mathbf{c} = [70 \;\; 70]$. By adding the respective components of **a** and **b** we determine **c**. Thus,

$$\begin{aligned} \mathbf{c} = \mathbf{a} + \mathbf{b} &= [(60 + 10) \quad (20 + 50)] \\ &= [70 \;\; 70] \end{aligned} \tag{12.3}$$

Figure 12.3 shows graphically this process. This is **vector addition**. If you add two or more vectors, then you join the "tail" of each succeeding vector to the "head" of the preceding one. The resulting vector is represented

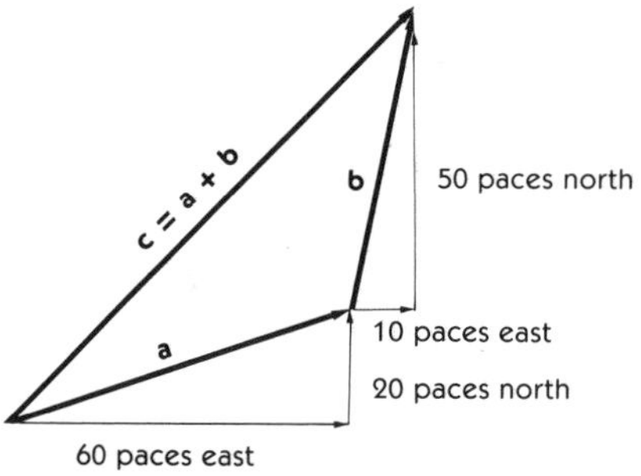

Fig. 12.3. Adding two vectors.

by an arrow from the tail of the first vector to the head of the last, as shown in Fig. 12.4.

Now add three vectors, **a**, **b**, and **c**, to obtain **d**. Denote the components of **a** by $[a_1 \;\; a_2]$, of **b** by $[b_1 \;\; b_2]$, and of **c** by $[c_1 \;\; c_2]$. If

$$\mathbf{d} = \mathbf{a} + \mathbf{b} + \mathbf{c} \tag{12.4}$$

then

$$\mathbf{d} = [d_1 \;\; d_2] \tag{12.5}$$

with

$$\begin{aligned} d_1 &= a_1 + b_1 + c_1 \\ d_2 &= a_2 + b_2 + c_2 \end{aligned} \tag{12.6}$$

Describing vectors with components given in terms of map directions certainly has intuitive appeal. It also has serious computational limitations. So, from now on, construct your vectors in two-dimensional and three-dimensional Cartesian coordinate systems. The first vector component will refer to displacement in the positive or negative x direction, the second to displacement in the positive or negative y direction, and the third component to displacement in the z direction. This means to write out the vector and its components as

$$\mathbf{a} = [a_x \;\; a_y \;\; a_z] \quad \text{or} \quad \mathbf{a} = \begin{bmatrix} a_x \\ a_y \\ a_z \end{bmatrix} \tag{12.7}$$

The geometric properties of a vector are independent of whether you express it as a row matrix vector or column matrix vector.

Note that so far you have not specified how to locate the vector on the "map," or coordinate system. That is because these are called **free vectors**. When you add them you simply add their components and produce another free vector. However, in geometric modeling, you will also

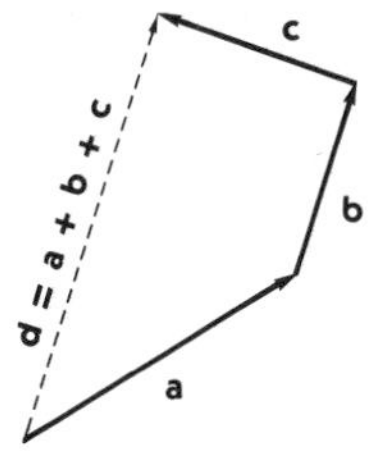

Fig. 12.4. Adding three vectors.

use a vector whose "tail" is assumed to be fixed at the origin of the coordinate system. Sometimes this ***fixed vector*** is denoted with the letter **p** for point vector or **r** for radius vector, both meaning essentially the same thing. Now the components of **p** are simply the coordinates of a point in space: $\mathbf{p} = [x \ y \ z]$; see Fig. 12.5.

If you add fixed vectors, you add their corresponding components and produce another fixed vector. Graphically you still construct the head-to-tail relationship described earlier. Thus, given $\mathbf{p}_1 = [x_1 \ y_1]$ and $\mathbf{p}_2 = [x_2 \ y_2]$, then $\mathbf{p}_3 = \mathbf{p}_1 + \mathbf{p}_2 = [(x_1 + x_2) \ (y_1 + y_2)]$; see Fig. 12.6.

Two vectors are equal when they have the same magnitude and direction. Represent them with parallel lines (arrows) of equal length when drawn to the same scale. Position is unimportant for equality. Algebraically, they have the same number of components, and corresponding components are equal.

To reverse the direction of a vector without changing its magnitude,

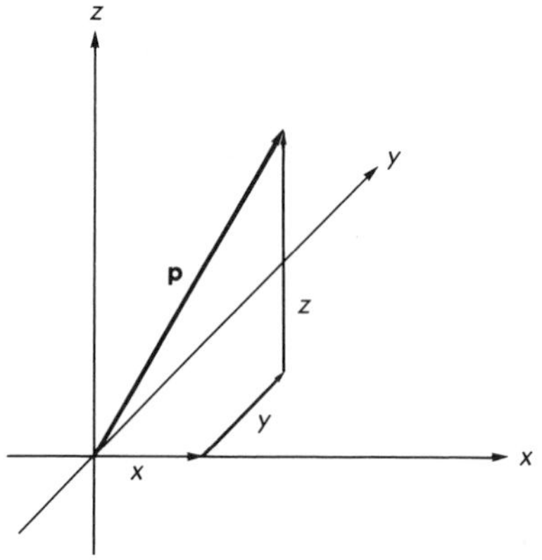

Fig. 12.5. Point vector.

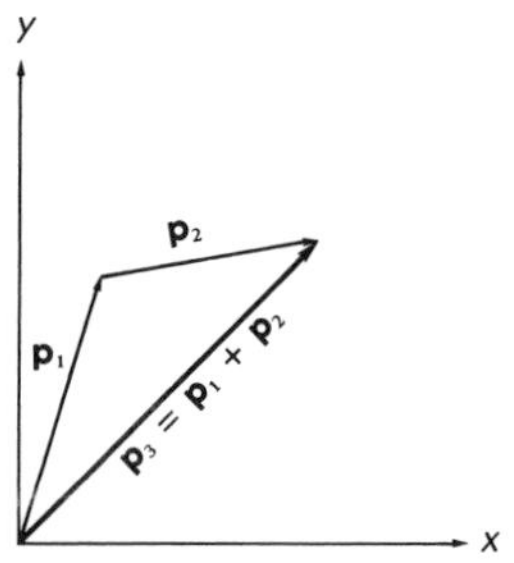

Fig. 12.6. Adding point vectors.

multiply each component by -1. So the reverse of $\mathbf{a}$ is $-\mathbf{a}$, and

$$-\mathbf{a} = -[a_x \; a_y \; a_z] = [-a_x \; -a_y \; -a_z] \tag{12.8}$$

For example, if $\mathbf{a} = [7 \;\; -2]$, then its reverse is
$\mathbf{b} = -\mathbf{a} = [-7 \;\; 2]$, illustrated in Fig. 12.7. Note that

$$\mathbf{a} + (-\mathbf{a}) = \emptyset \tag{12.9}$$

where $\emptyset$ is called the **null vector**. Now you have a way to subtract one vector from another, since

$$\mathbf{a} - \mathbf{b} = \mathbf{a} + (-\mathbf{b}) \tag{12.10}$$

and you merely subtract corresponding components of one vector from the other.

To increase or decrease the length (magnitude) of a vector, multiply it by a **scalar**. A scalar is a single number representing magnitude; it has no direction associated with it. Temperature and age are quantities measured by scalar numbers. Wind velocity and navigating instructions are quantities measured as vectors, because they have magnitude and direction. If $\mathbf{a} = 2\mathbf{b}$, then $\mathbf{a} = [2b_x \;\; 2b_y \;\; 2b_z]$ and $|\mathbf{a}| = 2|\mathbf{b}|$. Multiplying a vector by a scalar changes its magnitude but does not change its direction unless the scalar is negative, in which case the vector's direction is reversed. See Fig. 12.8. Thus, given a scalar, k, write

$$k\mathbf{a} = [ka_x \;\; ka_y \;\; ka_z] \tag{12.11}$$

Note that the components of a vector are themselves vectors, although

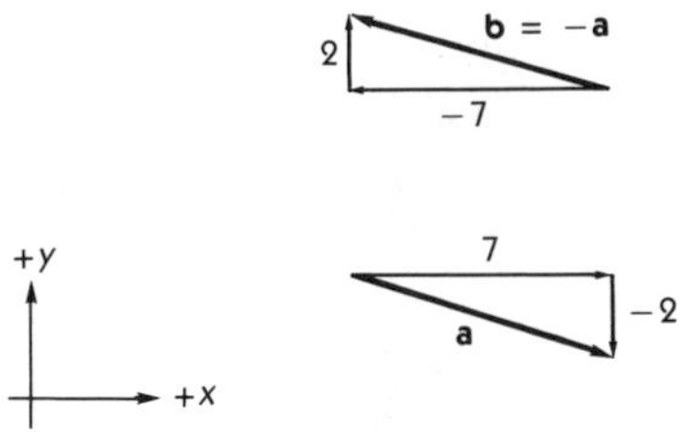

Fig. 12.7. Reversing the direction of a vector.

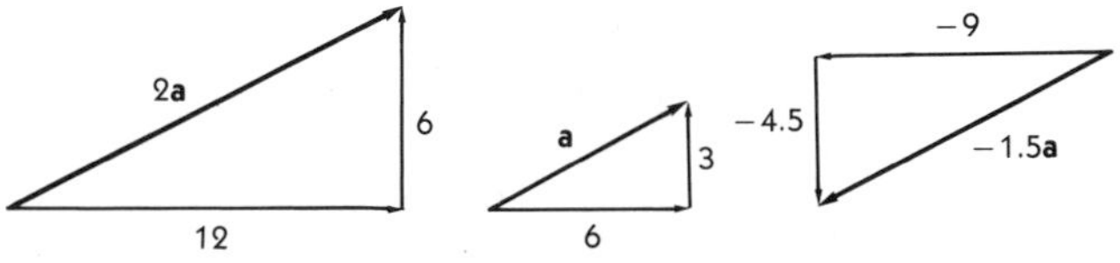

Fig. 12.8. Scalar multiplication.

you have not written them strictly as such. They certainly have both direction and magnitude. You could, of course, make the following definitions; let

$$\begin{aligned} \mathbf{a}_x &= [a_x \;\; 0 \;\; 0] \\ \mathbf{a}_y &= [0 \;\; a_y \;\; 0] \\ \mathbf{a}_z &= [0 \;\; 0 \;\; a_z] \end{aligned} \tag{12.12}$$

It is easy to see that

$$\mathbf{a} = \mathbf{a}_x + \mathbf{a}_y + \mathbf{a}_z = [a_x \;\; a_y \;\; a_z]$$

On this basis you define some special vectors, each of which have a unit length (magnitude = 1). Denote them as **i**, **j**, and **k**, where **i** is a unit vector in the x direction, **j** is in the y direction, and **k** is in the z direction. Now you can express a vector as

$$\mathbf{a} = a_x\mathbf{i} + a_y\mathbf{j} + a_z\mathbf{k} \tag{12.13}$$

where

$$\begin{aligned} \mathbf{i} &= [1 \;\; 0 \;\; 0] \\ \mathbf{j} &= [0 \;\; 1 \;\; 0] \\ \mathbf{k} &= [0 \;\; 0 \;\; 1] \end{aligned} \tag{12.14}$$

This formulation has some advantages in revealing geometric information inherent in more advanced vector operations, as you will see later.

The magnitude of any vector, **a**, is a scalar denoted as $|\mathbf{a}|$ and given by

$$|\mathbf{a}| = \sqrt{a_x^2 + a_y^2 + a_z^2} \tag{12.15}$$

A similar equation applies to two-dimensional vectors.

Define a **unit vector** as any vector whose magnitude is equal to one, no matter what its direction. (**i**, **j**, and **k** are special cases, with specific directions associated with them.) Denote a unit vector in the direction of **a** as $\mathbf{a}_u$. The components of $\mathbf{a}_u$ are

$$\mathbf{a}_u = \begin{bmatrix} \dfrac{a_x}{|\mathbf{a}|} & \dfrac{a_y}{|\mathbf{a}|} & \dfrac{a_z}{|\mathbf{a}|} \end{bmatrix} \tag{12.16}$$

Note that $\mathbf{a} = |\mathbf{a}|\mathbf{a}_u$. Let

$$\begin{aligned} x_u &= \frac{a_x}{|\mathbf{a}|} \\ y_u &= \frac{a_y}{|\mathbf{a}|} \\ z_u &= \frac{a_z}{|\mathbf{a}|} \end{aligned} \tag{12.17}$$

Then x_u, y_u, and z_u are the **direction cosines** of **a**, since $|\mathbf{a}_u| = 1$ and

$$x_u = \cos\alpha$$
$$y_u = \cos\beta \tag{12.18}$$
$$z_u = \cos\gamma$$

where α is the angle between **a** and the x axis, β is the angle between **a** and the y axis, and γ is the angle between **a** and the z axis. See Fig. 12.9. This is more clearly illustrated for two-dimensional vectors, as in Fig. 12.10.

Vectors offer a very compact form of representation and computation. You can carry out algebraic operations on the vectors themselves, rather than on each and every component. Look at how concise the representation is, for example:

$$\mathbf{x} = \mathbf{a} \tag{12.19}$$

If **x** and **a** are four component row vectors, then in expanded vector form Eq. (12.19) is

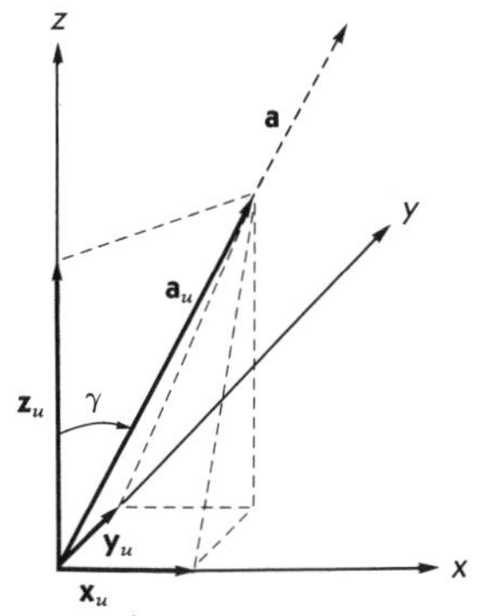

Fig. 12.9. Direction cosines of a three-dimensional vector.

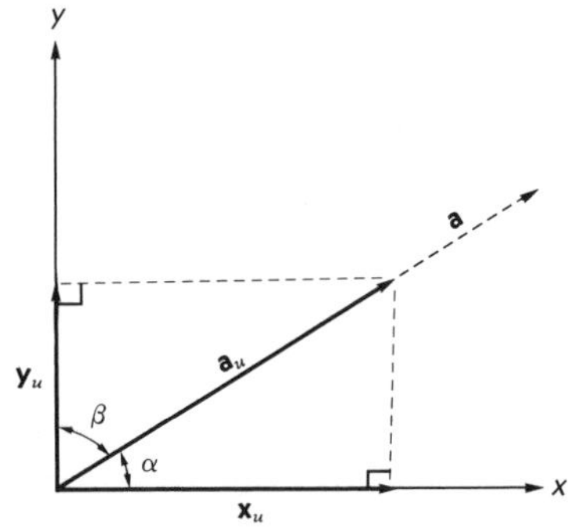

Figure 12.10. Direction cosines of a two-dimensional vector.

$$[x_1 \;\; x_2 \;\; x_3 \;\; x_4] = [a_1 \;\; a_2 \;\; a_3 \;\; a_4] \tag{12.20}$$

In ordinary algebraic form, Eq. (12.19) is a set of four separate equations:

$$\begin{aligned} x_1 &= a_1 \\ x_2 &= a_2 \\ x_3 &= a_3 \\ x_4 &= a_4 \end{aligned} \tag{12.21}$$

Scientists and engineers use vectors to compute the effects of physical forces. The complete vector algebra and calculus is complex and well developed. You will use only a small but important part of it in your studies of computer graphics and geometric modeling.

EXERCISES

1. Given the five vectors shown in Fig. 12.11, write them in component form.

2. Compute the magnitudes of the vectors given in Exercise 1.

3. Compute the direction cosines of the vectors given in Exercise 1.

4. If **x** and **r** are four-component row vectors, express the compact vector equation **x** = **r**

   a. in expanded vector form
   b. in ordinary algebraic form

5. If **a**, **b**, and **c** are three-component column vectors, express the compact vector equation **ax** + **by** = **c**

   a. in expanded vector form
   b. in ordinary algebraic form

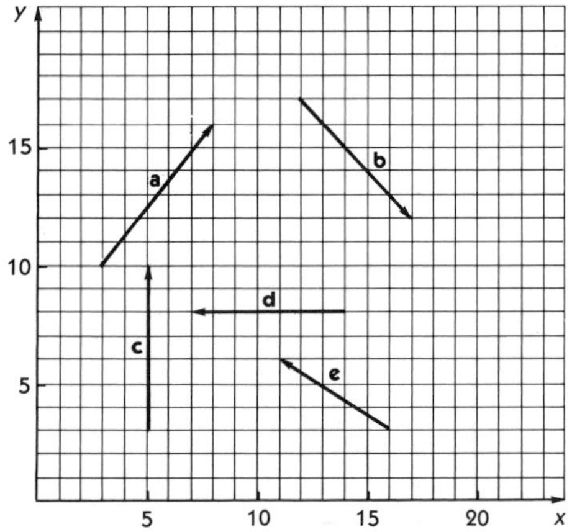

Fig. 12.11. Exercise 1.

6. If **r**, **s**, and **t** are two-component row vectors, express the compact vector equation **r** + **s** = **t**

   a. in expanded vector form
   b. in ordinary algebraic form

7. If **a** = [5 −1 7 4] and **x** is a four-component row vector, express $\mathbf{a}\mathbf{x}^T = 8$

   a. in expanded vector form
   b. in ordinary algebraic form

8. Given **a** = [2 3 5] and **b** = [6 −1 3], compute

   a. |**a**|
   b. |**b**|
   c. **c** = **a** + **b**
   d. **c** = **a** − **b**
   e. **c** = 2**a** + 3**b**

9. Given **a** = [−2 0 7] and **b** = [4 1 3], compute

   a. $\mathbf{a}_u$
   b. $\mathbf{b}_u$
   c. **c** = **a** − 2**b**
   d. **c** = 3**a**
   e. **c** = **a** + **b**

10. Show that the line joining the midpoints of two sides of a triangle is parallel to the third side and has one half its magnitude.

11. If **a** = [6 2 −5] and **b** = 2**a**, compare $\mathbf{a}_u$ and $\mathbf{b}_u$.

12.2. Scalar Product

The **scalar product** is the sum of the products of corresponding components of **a** and **b**. Write the scalar product of two three-dimensional vectors in expanded form as

$$\mathbf{a}\cdot\mathbf{b} = a_1b_1 + a_2b_2 + a_3b_3 \qquad (12.22)$$

The scalar product results in a single real number, a scalar. The scalar product of two vectors, **a** and **b**, is possible if, and only if, each has the same number of components. (Note that the scalar product is also called the **dot product**, since it is written as **a** · **b**.)

You can demonstrate that this product is the result of matrix multiplication by writing **a** as a row matrix and **b** as a column matrix.

$$\mathbf{a} \cdot \mathbf{b} = [a_1 \ \ a_2 \ \ a_3] \begin{bmatrix} b_1 \\ b_2 \\ b_3 \end{bmatrix} = a_1b_1 + a_2b_2 + a_3b_3 \tag{12.23}$$

For example, if $\mathbf{a} = [3 \ \ 1 \ \ 2]$ and $\mathbf{b} = [1 \ \ 4 \ \ -1]$, then $\mathbf{a} \cdot \mathbf{b} = 3 + 4 - 2 = 5$.

Note that if $\mathbf{a} = \mathbf{b}$ in Eq. (12.22), you obtain

$$\mathbf{a} \cdot \mathbf{a} = a_1^2 + a_2^2 + a_3^2 \tag{12.24}$$

or

$$\mathbf{a} \cdot \mathbf{a} = |\mathbf{a}|^2 \tag{12.25}$$

The angle, θ, between two vectors, **a** and **b**, satisfies the following equation:

$$\mathbf{a} \cdot \mathbf{b} = |\mathbf{a}||\mathbf{b}| \cos \theta \tag{12.26}$$

where $0 \leq \theta \leq \pi$. Solve Eq. (12.26) for θ to obtain

$$\theta = \cos^{-1} \frac{\mathbf{a} \cdot \mathbf{b}}{|\mathbf{a}||\mathbf{b}|} \tag{12.27}$$

See what a powerful geometric device this scalar product of two vectors is. If two vectors are perpendicular, then $\theta = 90°$ and $\cos \theta = 0$, and $\mathbf{a} \cdot \mathbf{b} = 0$. If $\theta = 0$, then they are parallel.

Join two arbitrary vectors, **a** and **b**, tail-to-tail as in Fig. 12.12. Draw a line from the head of **a** perpendicular to **b**. The line *ef* is called the **scalar projection** of **a** onto **b**, and its length is

$$L_P = \frac{\mathbf{a} \cdot \mathbf{b}}{|\mathbf{b}|} \tag{12.28}$$

where L_P denotes length of the projection. Note that since $\mathbf{b}/|\mathbf{b}| = \mathbf{b}_u$ you can also write Eq. (12.28) as

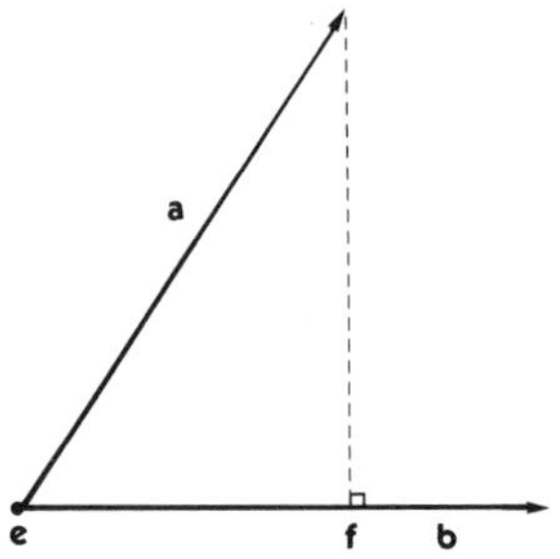

Fig. 12.12. Scalar and vector projection using the scalar product of two vectors.

$$L_P = \mathbf{a} \cdot \mathbf{b}_u \tag{12.29}$$

The vector drawn from e to f is the **vector projection** of **a** onto **b** and is given by

$$\mathbf{L}_P = (\mathbf{a} \cdot \mathbf{b}_u)\mathbf{b}_u \tag{12.30}$$

Exercises

1. Compute the following scalar products:

   a. $\mathbf{i} \cdot \mathbf{i}$
   b. $\mathbf{i} \cdot \mathbf{j}$
   c. $\mathbf{i} \cdot \mathbf{k}$
   d. $\mathbf{j} \cdot \mathbf{j}$
   e. $\mathbf{j} \cdot \mathbf{k}$
   f. $\mathbf{k} \cdot \mathbf{k}$

2. If $\mathbf{a} = [2 \; 0 \; 5]$, $\mathbf{b} = [-1 \; 3 \; 1]$, and $\mathbf{c} = [6 \; -2 \; -4]$, compute

   a. $\mathbf{a} \cdot \mathbf{a}$
   b. $\mathbf{a} \cdot \mathbf{b}$
   c. $\mathbf{a} \cdot \mathbf{c}$
   d. $\mathbf{b} \cdot \mathbf{b}$
   e. $\mathbf{b} \cdot \mathbf{c}$
   f. $\mathbf{c} \cdot \mathbf{c}$
   g. $\mathbf{b} \cdot \mathbf{a}$
   h. $\mathbf{c} \cdot \mathbf{b}$
   i. $\mathbf{a}_u \cdot \mathbf{a}_u$
   j. $\mathbf{a}_u \cdot \mathbf{b}_u$

3. If $\mathbf{a} = [4 \; -1]$, $\mathbf{b} = [2 \; 8]$, $\mathbf{c} = [-4 \; 1]$, and $\mathbf{d} = [3 \; 2]$, compute the angle between

   a. **a** and **b**
   b. **a** and **c**
   c. **c** and **b**
   d. **a** and **d**
   e. **c** and **d**

12.3. Vector Product

The **vector product** is written as $\mathbf{a} \times \mathbf{b}$ and is given by the expression

$$\mathbf{a} \times \mathbf{b} = \begin{vmatrix} \mathbf{i} & a_1 & b_1 \\ \mathbf{j} & a_2 & b_2 \\ \mathbf{k} & a_3 & b_3 \end{vmatrix} \tag{12.31}$$

where **i**, **j**, and **k** are the unit vectors in the **x**, **y**, and **z** directions. The vector product of two vectors, **a** and **b**, is possible if, and only if, they have the same number of components. The vector product is also called the **cross product**. Unlike the scalar product, which results in a scalar, the vector product, as you might guess, results in a vector. (In this section we will consider only the vector product of three-dimensional vectors.)

Compute the value of the determinant in Eq. (12.31) to obtain

$$\mathbf{a} \times \mathbf{b} = (a_2b_3 - a_3b_2)\mathbf{i} - (a_1b_3 - a_3b_1)\mathbf{j} + (a_1b_2 - a_2b_1)\mathbf{k} \quad (12.32)$$

In component form this is

$$\mathbf{a} \times \mathbf{b} = [(a_2b_3 - a_3b_2) \quad -(a_1b_3 - a_3b_1) \quad (a_1b_2 - a_2b_1)] \quad (12.33)$$

If $\mathbf{c} = \mathbf{a} \times \mathbf{b}$, then $\mathbf{c}$ is always perpendicular to both $\mathbf{a}$ and $\mathbf{b}$. You can best test this assertion by computing $\mathbf{a} \cdot \mathbf{c}$ and $\mathbf{b} \cdot \mathbf{c}$.

$$\begin{aligned} \mathbf{a} \cdot \mathbf{c} &= a_1(a_2b_3 - a_3b_2) - a_2(a_1b_3 - a_3b_1) + a_3(a_1b_2 - a_2b_1) \\ &= a_1a_2b_3 - a_1a_3b_2 - a_1a_2b_3 + a_2a_3b_1 + a_1a_3b_2 - a_2a_3b_1 \\ &= 0 \end{aligned} \quad (12.34)$$

If $\mathbf{a} \cdot \mathbf{c} = 0$, then $\mathbf{a}$ is perpendicular to $\mathbf{c}$. Similarly, it is easy to show that $\mathbf{b} \cdot \mathbf{c} = 0$. Thus, you successfully demonstrate the truth of the assertion.

If two vectors, $\mathbf{a}$ and $\mathbf{b}$, are parallel, then $\mathbf{a} \times \mathbf{b} = 0$. Let $\mathbf{b} = k\mathbf{a}$; this obviously makes $\mathbf{b}$ parallel to $\mathbf{a}$. Now compute $\mathbf{a} \times k\mathbf{a}$.

$$\begin{aligned} \mathbf{a} \times k\mathbf{a} = [&(ka_2a_3 - ka_3a_2) \\ &-(ka_1a_3 - ka_3a_1) \quad (ka_1a_2 - ka_2a_1)] \end{aligned} \quad (12.35)$$

This reduces to

$$\mathbf{a} \times k\mathbf{a} = [0 \ \ 0 \ \ 0] \quad (12.36)$$

the null vector. This also means that $\mathbf{a} \times \mathbf{a} = 0$.

Finally, observe that $\mathbf{b} \times \mathbf{a} = -(\mathbf{a} \times \mathbf{b})$. Reversing the order of the

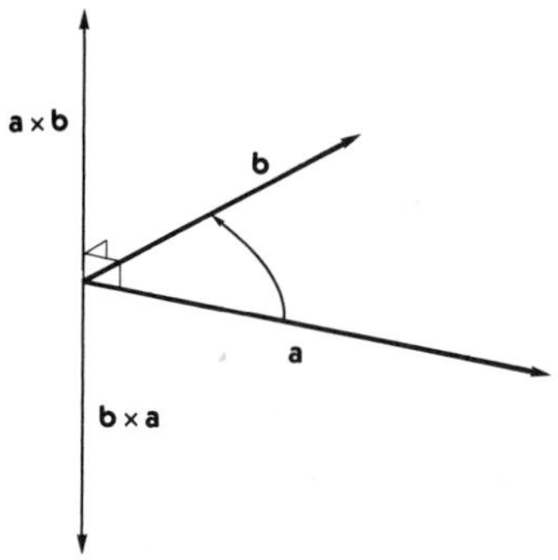

Fig. 12.13. Vector product.

vectors reverses the direction of their vector product. This is easy to verify algebraically. Try it.

The so-called ***right-hand rule*** gives an intuitive sense of the vector resulting from $\mathbf{a} \times \mathbf{b}$. Think of rotating **a** into **b** through the smallest angle, curling the fingers of your right hand in this angular direction. Then the extended thumb of your right hand will point in the direction of **c**, where $\mathbf{a} \times \mathbf{b} = \mathbf{c}$. Figure 12.13 shows some of these vector product characteristics. Note that division of vectors is not defined. (See the summary of vector properties in Box 12.1.)

Box 12.1. Vector Properties

Given vectors **p**, **q**, **r** and scalars k and l, then

1. $\mathbf{p} + \mathbf{q} = \mathbf{q} + \mathbf{p}$
2. $\mathbf{p} + (\mathbf{q} + \mathbf{r}) = (\mathbf{p} + \mathbf{q}) + \mathbf{r}$
3. $k(l\mathbf{p}) = kl\mathbf{p}$
4. $(k + l)\mathbf{p} = k\mathbf{p} + l\mathbf{p}$
5. $k(\mathbf{p} + \mathbf{q}) = k\mathbf{p} + k\mathbf{q}$

The scalar product has the following properties:

1. $\mathbf{p} \cdot \mathbf{r} = |\mathbf{p}||\mathbf{r}| \cos \theta$, where θ is the angle between **p** and **r**
2. $\mathbf{p} \cdot \mathbf{p} = |\mathbf{p}|^2$
3. $\mathbf{p} \cdot \mathbf{r} = \mathbf{r} \cdot \mathbf{p}$
4. $\mathbf{p} \cdot (\mathbf{r} + \mathbf{q}) = \mathbf{p} \cdot \mathbf{r} + \mathbf{p} \cdot \mathbf{q}$
5. $(k\mathbf{p}) \cdot \mathbf{r} = \mathbf{p} \cdot (k\mathbf{r}) = k(\mathbf{p} \cdot \mathbf{r})$
6. If **p** is perpendicular to **r**, then $\mathbf{p} \cdot \mathbf{r} = 0$

The vector product has the following properties:

1. $\mathbf{p} \times \mathbf{r} = \mathbf{s}$; **s** is perpendicular to both **p** and **r**
2. $\mathbf{p} \times \mathbf{r} = \begin{vmatrix} \mathbf{i} & \mathbf{j} & \mathbf{k} \\ p_x & p_y & p_z \\ r_x & r_y & r_z \end{vmatrix}$
3. $\mathbf{p} \times \mathbf{r} = |\mathbf{p}||\mathbf{r}|\mathbf{n} \sin \theta$; **n** is the unit vector perpendicular to the plane of **p** and **r**.
4. $\mathbf{p} \times \mathbf{r} = -\mathbf{r} \times \mathbf{p}$
5. $\mathbf{p} \times (\mathbf{r} + \mathbf{s}) = \mathbf{p} \times \mathbf{r} + \mathbf{p} \times \mathbf{s}$
6. $(k\mathbf{p}) \times \mathbf{r} = \mathbf{p} \times (k\mathbf{r}) = k(\mathbf{p} \times \mathbf{r})$
7. $\mathbf{i} \times \mathbf{j} = \mathbf{k}$, $\mathbf{j} \times \mathbf{k} = \mathbf{i}$, $\mathbf{k} \times \mathbf{i} = \mathbf{j}$
8. If **p** is parallel to **r**, then $\mathbf{p} \times \mathbf{r} = 0$
9. $\mathbf{p} \times \mathbf{p} = 0$

EXERCISES

1. Compute the following vector products:

a. $\mathbf{i} \times \mathbf{i}$
b. $\mathbf{j} \times \mathbf{j}$
c. $\mathbf{k} \times \mathbf{k}$
d. $\mathbf{i} \times \mathbf{j}$
e. $\mathbf{j} \times \mathbf{k}$
f. $\mathbf{k} \times \mathbf{i}$
g. $\mathbf{j} \times \mathbf{i}$
h. $\mathbf{k} \times \mathbf{j}$
i. $\mathbf{i} \times \mathbf{k}$

Remember: $\mathbf{i} = [1\ \ 0\ \ 0]$, $\mathbf{j} = [0\ \ 1\ \ 0]$, and $\mathbf{k} = [0\ \ 0\ \ 1]$.

2. Show that $\mathbf{b} \times \mathbf{a} = -(\mathbf{a} \times \mathbf{b})$.

3. Given $\mathbf{a} = [1\ \ 0\ \ -2]$, $\mathbf{b} = [3\ \ 1\ \ 4]$, and $\mathbf{c} = [-1\ \ 6\ \ 2]$, compute

a. $\mathbf{a} \times \mathbf{a}$
b. $\mathbf{a} \times \mathbf{b}$
c. $\mathbf{b} \times \mathbf{a}$
d. $\mathbf{b} \times \mathbf{c}$
e. $\mathbf{c} \times \mathbf{a}$

4. Given $\mathbf{a} = [5\ \ 2\ \ 0]$, $\mathbf{b} = [1\ \ 3\ \ 0]$, and $\mathbf{c} = [-10\ \ -4\ \ 0]$, compute

a. $\mathbf{a} \times \mathbf{b}$
b. $\mathbf{b} \times \mathbf{a}$
c. $\mathbf{c} \times \mathbf{b}$
d. $\mathbf{a} \times \mathbf{c}$
e. $\mathbf{a} \times (-\mathbf{c})$

12.4. Vector Equation of a Line

Now you will see how vectors represent geometric objects. Let us begin with straight lines. The vector equation of a line through the point, $\mathbf{p}_0$, and parallel to the vector, $\mathbf{t}$, is

$$\mathbf{p} = \mathbf{p}_0 + u\mathbf{t} \tag{12.37}$$

where u is a scalar variable multiplying $\mathbf{t}$. As u takes on successive numerical values, it generates a straight line whose corresponding successive coordinates are given by $\mathbf{p}$. To put it another way: Since $\mathbf{p}_0$ and $\mathbf{t}$ are constant, any real value of u generates a point on the same straight line. Figure 12.14 shows a geometric interpretation of this equation. As you increase the value of u, in this particular case, the vector $u\mathbf{t}$ increases in magnitude but does not change direction. So the point defined by $\mathbf{p} = \mathbf{p}_0 + u\mathbf{t}$ moves further up the line and to the right, always staying on the line. The reverse

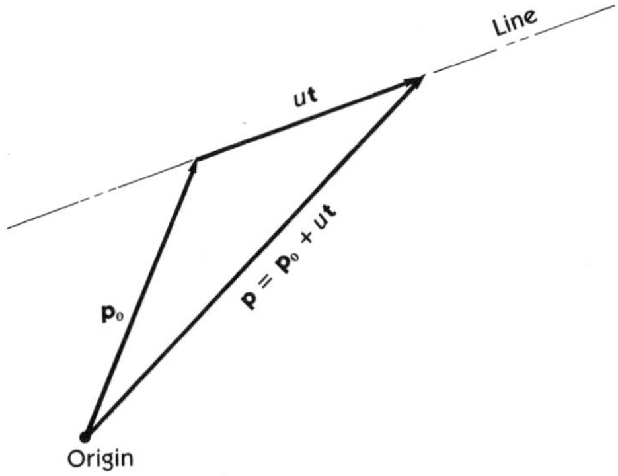

Fig. 12.14. Vector equation of a straight line.

occurs if you insert into the equation increasingly smaller or negative values of **u**.

If you write Eq. (12.37) in expanded vector form, you obtain (assuming column vectors)

$$\begin{bmatrix} x \\ y \\ z \end{bmatrix} = \begin{bmatrix} x_0 \\ y_0 \\ z_0 \end{bmatrix} + u \begin{bmatrix} t_x \\ t_y \\ t_z \end{bmatrix} \tag{12.38}$$

and in ordinary algebraic form

$$\begin{aligned} x &= x_0 + ut_x \\ y &= y_0 + ut_y \\ z &= z_0 + ut_z \end{aligned} \tag{12.39}$$

u is the independent variable; x, y, and z are dependent variables; and x_0, y_0, z_0, t_x, t_y, and t_z are constants. In fact, these are nothing more than the parametric equations of a straight line. You have met them before (Section 3.1).

Look at a two-dimensional example in Fig. 12.15. Since the line passes through (2,4) and parallel to the vector $\mathbf{t} = [2 \;\; 4]^T$, define $\mathbf{p}_0 = [2 \;\; 4]^T$, and write the equation as

$$\mathbf{p} = \mathbf{p}_0 + u\mathbf{t} \tag{12.40}$$

or

$$\begin{bmatrix} x \\ y \end{bmatrix} = \begin{bmatrix} 2 \\ 4 \end{bmatrix} + u \begin{bmatrix} 2 \\ 1 \end{bmatrix} \tag{12.41}$$

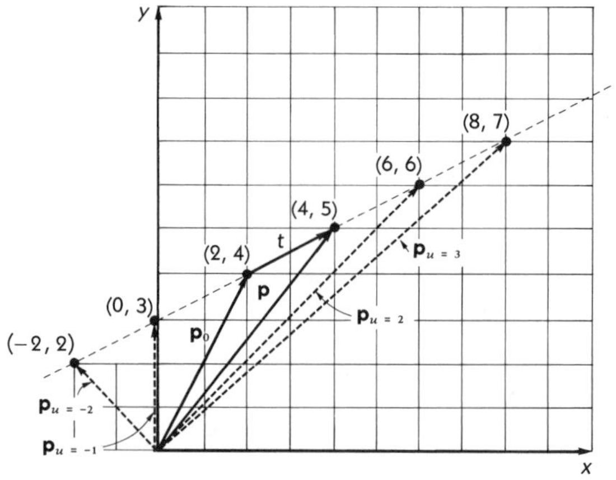

Fig. 12.15. Example of a vector equation of a straight line.

The ordinary algebraic equations are

$$x = 2 + 2u \qquad (12.42)$$
$$y = 4 + u$$

Compute pairs of x,y values for a variety of u values. For example:

u	x	y
−2	−2	2
−1	0	3
0	2	4
1	4	5
2	6	6
3	8	7

These points and their vector construction are plotted in Fig. 12.15.

Sometimes you must find the vector equation of a line through two points. To do this, first define the vectors to these two points: call them $\mathbf{p}_0$ and $\mathbf{p}_1$. $\mathbf{p}_0$ provides one of the two pieces of information required in Eq. (12.37). Now determine $\mathbf{t}$, and you have enough information in $\mathbf{p}_0$ and $\mathbf{p}_1$ to do this. From the vector constructions in Fig. 12.16 you will see that $\mathbf{t} = \mathbf{p}_1 - \mathbf{p}_0$, so substitute into Eq. (12.37) to obtain

$$\mathbf{p} = \mathbf{p}_0 + u(\mathbf{p}_1 - \mathbf{p}_0) \qquad (12.43)$$

If you limit the allowable values of u to those in the interval $0 \leq u \leq 1$, then this equation defines not an infinite or unlimited line, but instead a line segment extending from $\mathbf{p}_0$ to $\mathbf{p}_1$. You will usually need to specify this

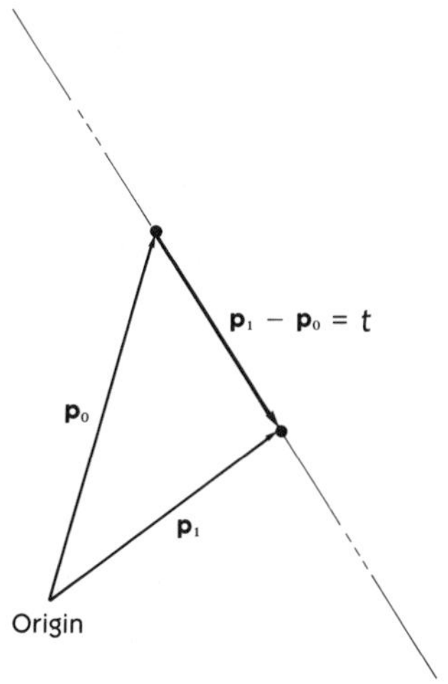

Fig. 12.16. Straight line between two points.

interval when defining a line segment, and, if you will recall, it is done this way:

$$u \in [0,1] \quad \text{also written as } 0 \leq u \leq 1 \tag{12.44}$$

Read the expression on the left as "u takes on values in the closed continuous interval extending from $u = 0$ to $u = 1$." Append this expression to the end of the equation, so that

$$\mathbf{p} = \mathbf{p}_0 + u(\mathbf{p}_1 - \mathbf{p}_0), \qquad u \in [0,1] \tag{12.45}$$

The limits on u of 0 and 1 will later prove to be useful for most applications, but of course you are free to choose any limits to specify a line segment. For example, $u \in [a,b]$, but in this case the line may extend beyond or terminate within the segment defined by $\mathbf{p}_0$ and $\mathbf{p}_1$.

So, Eq. (12.45) is a very convenient shorthand way to represent a straight line. But it is more than this, too, for you now have at your command all the power of vector geometry (see Box 12.2).

EXERCISES

1. If $\mathbf{a} = [6 \;\; -1 \;\; -2]$, $\mathbf{b} = [3 \;\; 2 \;\; 4]$, and $\mathbf{c} = [7 \;\; 0 \;\; 2]$, then write the vector equation of a line

   a. through $\mathbf{a}$ and parallel to $\mathbf{b}$,
   b. through $\mathbf{b}$ and parallel to $\mathbf{c}$,
   c. through $\mathbf{c}$ and parallel to $\mathbf{a}$,

Box 12.2. Solution of Vector Equations

Suppose you have the following vector equation:

$$\mathbf{a} + u\mathbf{b} + w\mathbf{c} = \mathbf{d} + t\mathbf{e}$$

This represents a system of three linear equations in three unknowns, u, w, and t. In nonvector form, it is expressed as

$$a_x + ub_x + wc_x = d_x + te_x$$
$$a_y + ub_y + wc_y = d_y + te_y$$
$$a_z + ub_z + wc_z = d_z + te_z$$

You can use the vector form to solve for u, w, and t by isolating each in turn. For example, for t apply $(\mathbf{b} \times \mathbf{c})$ as follows:

$$(\mathbf{b} \times \mathbf{c})\cdot(\mathbf{a} + u\mathbf{b} + w\mathbf{c}) = (\mathbf{b} \times \mathbf{c})\cdot(\mathbf{d} + t\mathbf{e})$$

Since $(\mathbf{b} \times \mathbf{c})$ is perpendicular to both $\mathbf{b}$ and $\mathbf{c}$, then

$$(\mathbf{b} \times \mathbf{c})\cdot\mathbf{a} = (\mathbf{b} \times \mathbf{c})\cdot\mathbf{d} + (t\mathbf{b} \times \mathbf{c})\cdot\mathbf{e}$$

Solve for t:

$$t = \frac{(\mathbf{b} \times \mathbf{c})\cdot\mathbf{a} - (\mathbf{b} \times \mathbf{c})\cdot\mathbf{d}}{(\mathbf{b} \times \mathbf{c})\cdot\mathbf{e}}$$

You can find similar expressions for u and w:

$$u = \frac{(\mathbf{c} \times \mathbf{e})\cdot\mathbf{d} - (\mathbf{c} \times \mathbf{e})\cdot\mathbf{a}}{(\mathbf{c} \times \mathbf{e})\cdot\mathbf{b}}$$

$$w = \frac{(\mathbf{b} \times \mathbf{e})\cdot\mathbf{d} - (\mathbf{b} \times \mathbf{e})\cdot\mathbf{a}}{(\mathbf{b} \times \mathbf{e})\cdot\mathbf{c}}$$

(*Note*: This happens to describe a very practical problem, that of the intersection between a plane and a straight line. You may want to refer to this box after studying the next section. Then try to reconstruct the first equation above using a more meaningful geometric notation for the vectors: that is, $\mathbf{p}_0$, $\mathbf{p}_1$, and so on.)

d. through $\mathbf{a}$ and parallel to $\mathbf{a}$, and
e. through $\mathbf{b}$ and parallel to the z axis.

2. Find the midpoint of the line segment between $\mathbf{p}_0 = [3\ \ 5\ \ 1]$ and $\mathbf{p}_1 = [-2\ \ 6\ \ 4]$.

3. Find the equations of the x, y, and z vector components, $x(u)$, $y(u)$, and $z(u)$, for each of the line segments given by the following pairs of end points:

a. $\mathbf{p}_0 = [0\ 0\ 0]$, $\mathbf{p}_1 = [1\ 1\ 1]$
b. $\mathbf{p}_0 = [-3\ 1\ 6]$, $\mathbf{p}_1 = [2\ 0\ 7]$
c. $\mathbf{p}_0 = [1\ 1\ -4]$, $\mathbf{p}_1 = [5\ -3\ 9]$
d. $\mathbf{p}_0 = [6\ 8\ 8]$, $\mathbf{p}_1 = [-10\ 0\ -3]$
e. $\mathbf{p}_0 = [0\ 0\ 1]$, $\mathbf{p}_1 = [0\ 0\ -1]$

4. Given $x = 3 + 2u$, $y = -6 + u$, $z = 4$, find $\mathbf{p}_0$ and $\mathbf{p}_1$.

5. What is the difference between the following two line segments: for line 1, $\mathbf{p}_0 = [2\ 1\ -2]$ and $\mathbf{p}_1 = [3\ -3\ 1]$; for line 2, $\mathbf{p}_0 = [3\ -3\ 1]$ and $\mathbf{p}_1 = [2\ 1\ -2]$?

6. Revise Eq. (12.45) so that $u \in [0,2]$.

7. Revise Eq. (12.45) so that $u \in [-1,1]$.

8. Find the midpoints of the lines given in Exercise 3.

9. Write a procedure to compute points on a straight line segment at intervals of 0.1 from $u = 0$ to $u = 1$. Denote this as **LNPTS**(P0, P1, PTS), where

P0(3) are the input coordinates of $\mathbf{p}_0$,
P1(3) are the input coordinates of $\mathbf{p}_1$, and
PTS(9) are the output coordinates of points at $u = 0.1, 0.2, 0.3, \ldots, 0.9$.

12.5. Vector Equation of a Plane

The vector equation of a plane through $\mathbf{p}_0$ and parallel to two independent vectors, $\mathbf{s}$ and $\mathbf{t}$ (where $\mathbf{s} \neq k\mathbf{t}$), is

$$\mathbf{p} = \mathbf{p}_0 + u\mathbf{s} + v\mathbf{t} \tag{12.46}$$

where u and v are scalar parametric variables. The vector $\mathbf{p}$ generates points on a plane as the parameters u and v vary independently. Figure 12.17 interprets this equation geometrically.

By writing Eq. (12.46) in expanded vector form, you obtain (using column vectors)

$$\begin{bmatrix} x \\ y \\ z \end{bmatrix} = \begin{bmatrix} x_0 \\ y_0 \\ z_0 \end{bmatrix} + u \begin{bmatrix} s_x \\ s_y \\ s_z \end{bmatrix} + v \begin{bmatrix} t_x \\ t_y \\ t_z \end{bmatrix} \tag{12.47}$$

and in ordinary algebraic form

$$\begin{aligned} x &= x_0 + us_x + vt_x \\ y &= y_0 + us_y + vt_y \\ z &= z_0 + us_z + vt_z \end{aligned} \tag{12.48}$$

Three points are also sufficient to define a plane in space. So refor-

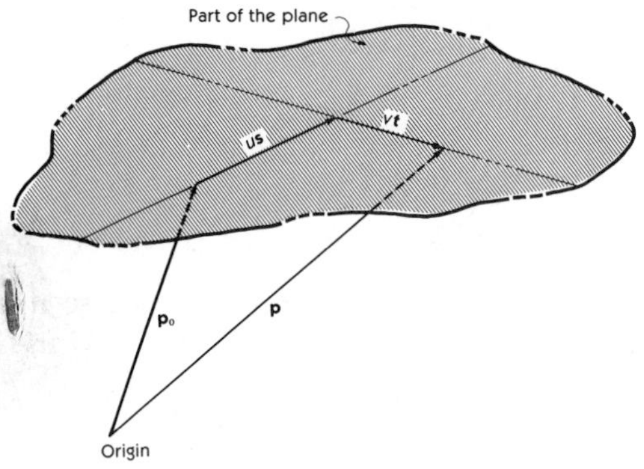

Fig. 12.17. Vector equation of a plane.

mulate Eq. (12.46) to reflect this. Figure 12.18 illustrates the vector geometry. Let the vectors $\mathbf{p}_0$, $\mathbf{p}_1$, and $\mathbf{p}_2$ represent the three points. Then the vector $\mathbf{p}_1 - \mathbf{p}_0$ defines one of the vectors to which the plane is parallel, and $\mathbf{p}_2 - \mathbf{p}_1$ defines the other. Thus, $\mathbf{p}_1 - \mathbf{p}_0 = \mathbf{s}$ and $\mathbf{p}_2 - \mathbf{p}_1 = \mathbf{t}$; substitute these values into Eq. (12.46) to obtain

$$\mathbf{p} = \mathbf{p}_0 + u(\mathbf{p}_1 - \mathbf{p}_0) + v(\mathbf{p}_2 - \mathbf{p}_1) \tag{12.49}$$

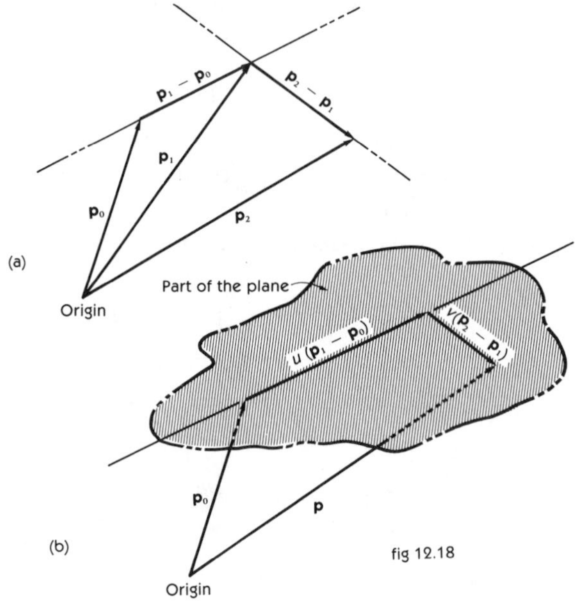

Fig. 12.18. Three points define a plane.

the vector equation of a plane guaranteed to pass through the points $\mathbf{p}_0$, $\mathbf{p}_1$, and $\mathbf{p}_2$. Again, as u and v vary independently, that is, when you substitute various numerical values for them, then $\mathbf{p}$ generates points on the plane, as in Fig. 12.18b.

A vector perpendicular to a plane (or any other geometric element, for that matter) is called the **normal vector**. It is usually denoted as $\mathbf{n}$. You now have two ways to compute it:

$$\mathbf{n} = \mathbf{s} \times \mathbf{t} \tag{12.50}$$

or

$$\mathbf{n} = (\mathbf{p}_1 - \mathbf{p}_0) \times (\mathbf{p}_2 - \mathbf{p}_1) \tag{12.51}$$

The magnitude of $\mathbf{n}$ is rarely of interest, so you may choose to work with the unit normal, $\mathbf{n}_u$, where

$$\mathbf{n}_u = \frac{\mathbf{n}}{|\mathbf{n}|} \tag{12.52}$$

In fact, it is common practice to drop the subscript u when it is clear that $\mathbf{n}$ must necessarily represent the unit normal.

Another way to define a plane is by a point through which it must pass, $\mathbf{p}_0$, and its unit normal, $\mathbf{n}$. Note that the normal to a plane is equal for all points on the plane. See the vector construction in Fig. 12.19. Then a point, $\mathbf{p}$, lies on the plane if, and only if, $\mathbf{p} - \mathbf{p}_0$ is perpendicular to $\mathbf{n}$, or

$$(\mathbf{p} - \mathbf{p}_0) \cdot \mathbf{n} = 0 \tag{12.53}$$

In vector component form this becomes

$$(x - x_0)n_x + (y - y_0)n_y + (z - z_0)n_z = 0 \tag{12.54}$$

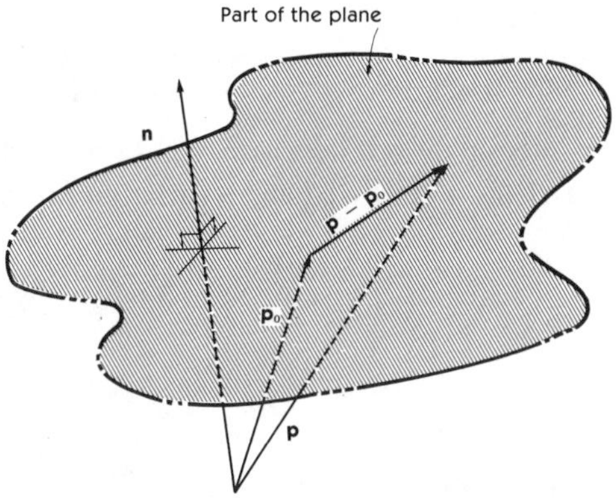

Fig. 12.19. Normal to a plane.

Box 12.3. Vector Equation of a Plane: Normal Form

Now you can apply vector geometry to reinterpret Box 4.1. Define a plane by giving the vector **d** from the origin and perpendicular to the plane. Then any point, **p**, on the plane must satisfy

$$(\mathbf{p} - \mathbf{d}) \cdot \mathbf{d} = 0$$

If you expand this equation in terms of its components, you obtain

$$(x - d_x)d_x + (y - d_y)d_y + (z - d_z)d_z = 0$$

or

$$d_x x + d_y y + d_z z - (d_x^2 + d_y^2 + d_z^2) = 0$$

This, of course, reduces to

$$\sigma_x x + \sigma_y y + \sigma_z z - d = 0$$

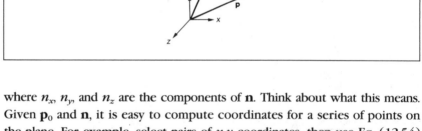

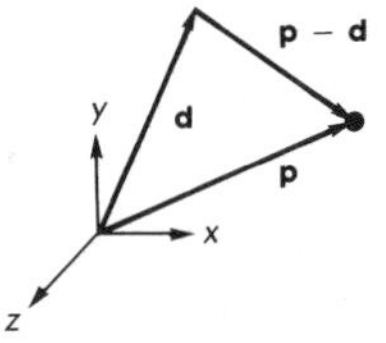

where n_x, n_y, and n_z are the components of **n**. Think about what this means. Given $\mathbf{p}_0$ and **n**, it is easy to compute coordinates for a series of points on the plane. For example, select pairs of x,y coordinates, then use Eq. (12.54) to compute the required corresponding z coordinate.

To define a rectangular bounded plane, simply specify limits on the parametric variables. Do this as follows:

$$\mathbf{p} = \mathbf{p}_0 + u\mathbf{s} + v\mathbf{t}, \qquad u,v \in [0,1] \tag{12.55}$$

Again, the limits or interval do not necessarily have to be the interval from 0 to 1; thus, $u \in [a,b]$ and $v \in [c,d]$. (For a variation on this problem, see Box 12.3.)

EXERCISES

1. Write the vector equation of the plane passing through **a** and parallel to **b** and **c**.

2. Write the vector equation of a plane that passes through the origin and is perpendicular to the y axis.

13. Curves

NO DOUBT YOU have a strong intuitive sense of what a curve is. It is unlikely that you have ever seen a curve floating around free of any object, but you can readily identify the curved edges and silhouettes of objects or the curve that describes the path of a moving object. Now you will explore some mathematical definitions of curves in a form that is very useful to geometric modeling and computer graphics: the **parametric curve.**

A parametric curve is one whose defining equations are given in terms of a single, common, independent variable called the **parametric variable.** You have already briefly encountered the parametric variable in Lines (Chap. 3) and Vectors (Chap. 12). Now its use and power will become even clearer.

Imagine a curve in three-dimensional space. Each point on the curve has a unique set of coordinates: a specific x value, y value, and z value. Next, assume that each coordinate is defined and controlled by a separate mathematical expression, so that

$$x = x(u), \qquad y = y(u), \qquad z = z(u) \tag{13.1}$$

where $x(u)$ stands for some as yet unspecified expression in which u is an independent variables; for example, $x(u) = au^2 + bu + c$, similarly for $y(u)$ and $z(u)$ (but remember that these are each independent expressions). You will see specific examples in a moment. First, a word about the symbols in Eq. (13.1): Each expression is a **parametric equation.** x, y, and z are dependent variables because their values depend on the value you assign to u, the **parametric variable.** People who do geometric modeling prefer these kinds of expressions because the coordinates x, y, and z are independent of each other; each is defined by its own parametric equation.

Now, back to curves: Think of each and every point on the curve as being defined by a vector, $\mathbf{p}$ (Fig. 13.1). The components of these vectors are $x(u)$, $y(u)$, and $z(u)$. Write this mathematically as

$$\mathbf{p} = \mathbf{p}(u) \tag{13.2}$$

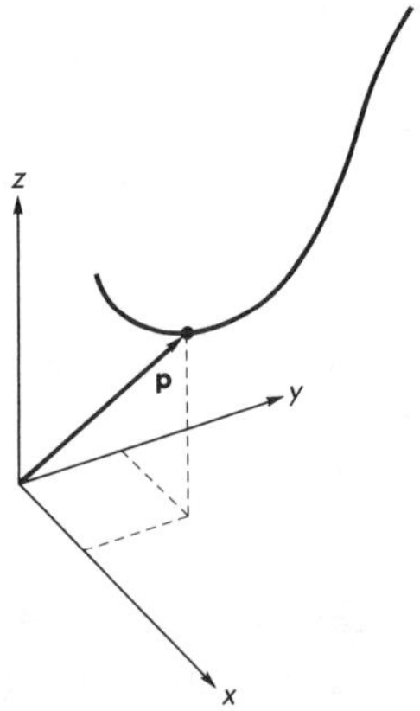

Fig. 13.1. Point on a curve defined by a vector.

This says that the vector **p** is a function of some variable, u. Here, again, the variable is the parametric variable.

There is a lot of information in Eq. (13.2). In component form, it becomes

$$\mathbf{p}(u) = [x(u) \ y(u) \ z(u)] \tag{13.3}$$

The specific functions that define the vector components of **p** determine the shape of the curve. In fact, this is the way to define a curve—by simply choosing or designing these mathematical functions. There are only a few simple rules you must follow: Define each component by a **single, common** parametric variable, and make sure that each point on the curve corresponds to a unique value of the parametric variable. The last rule can be put the other way around: Each value of the parametric variable must correspond to a unique point on the curve.

In the sections that follow, you will study expressions that define both plane curves and space curves. You will also find out what a tangent and tangent vector are and how to join many simple curve segments to form a more complicated curve.

13.1. Plane Curves

To define plane curves, use parametric functions that are second-degree polynomials. So, for $x(u)$,

$$x(u) = a_x u^2 + b_x u + c_x \tag{13.4}$$

with similar expressions for $y(u)$ and $z(u)$. The a, b, and c terms are constant coefficients. You can combine $x(u)$, $y(u)$, $z(u)$, and their respective coefficients into an equivalent, more concise, vector equation, thusly:

$$\mathbf{p}(u) = \mathbf{a}u^2 + \mathbf{b}u + \mathbf{c}, \qquad u \in [0,1] \tag{13.5}$$

The constant coefficients are in vector form: **a**, **b**, and **c**. Note: Do not interpret these coefficients as geometric points. Nonetheless, each has three components, for example, $\mathbf{a} = [a_x \; a_y \; a_z]$.

This is not the most versatile of plane curves, to be sure. For example, you cannot "design" one that has an inflection point, no matter what values you select for the constants **a**, **b**, and **c**. (Later you will see how to achieve this with cubic polynomials.)

How do you define a specific plane curve, one that you can plot, with definite end points and orientation in space? First, note in Eq. (13.5) that there are nine coefficients to specify: a_x, b_x, c_x, a_y, b_y, c_y, a_z, b_z, and c_z. If you know the two end points and an intermediate point on the curve, then you know nine quantities that you can express in terms of **a**, **b**, and **c** (3 points × 3 coordinates/point = 9 known quantities). By applying some simple algebra to these relationships, you can rewrite Eq. (13.5) in terms of the three known points: To one of the end points, assign $u = 0$, and to the other $u = 1$. To the intermediate point, arbitrarily assign $u = 0.5$. Write these points symbolically as

$$\begin{aligned} \mathbf{p}_0 &= [x_0 \; y_0 \; z_0] \\ \mathbf{p}_{0.5} &= [x_{0.5} \; y_{0.5} \; z_{0.5}] \\ \mathbf{p}_1 &= [x_1 \; y_1 \; z_1] \end{aligned} \tag{13.6}$$

Remember, assume that you know these nine coordinates that define these three points. You are interested in finding **a**, **b**, and **c** so that the curve $\mathbf{p}(u)$ passes through these points (Fig. 13.2). So, use Eq. (13.4) and find a_x, b_x, and c_x in terms of these point coordinates. At $u = 0$, $u = 0.5$, and $u = 1$,

$$\begin{aligned} x_0 &= c_x \\ x_{0.5} &= 0.25a_x + 0.5b_x + c_x \\ x_1 &= a_x + b_x + c_x \end{aligned} \tag{13.7}$$

Now solve these three equations in three unknowns for a_x, b_x, and c_x:

$$\begin{aligned} a_x &= 2x_0 - 4x_{0.5} + 2x_1 \\ b_x &= -3x_0 + 4x_{0.5} - x_1 \\ c_x &= x_0 \end{aligned} \tag{13.8}$$

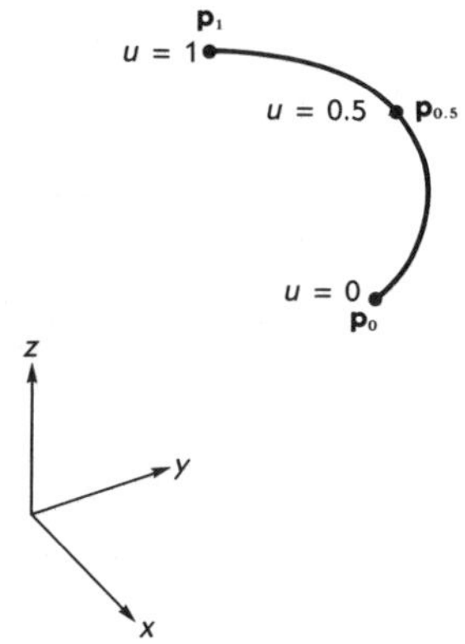

Fig. 13.2. Plane curve through three points.

Substitute these results into Eq. (13.4) to find

$$x(u) = (2x_0 - 4x_{0.5} + 2x_1)u^2 + (-3x_0 + 4x_{0.5} - x_1)u + x_0 \quad (13.9)$$

Of course, there are equivalent expressions for $y(u)$ and $z(u)$. But you are not through yet. One more step remains. Rewrite Eq. (13.9) as follows:

$$x(u) = (2u^2 - 3u + 1)x_0 + (-4u^2 + 4u)x_{0.5} + (2u^2 - u)x_1 \quad (13.10)$$

Again, since there are equivalent expressions for $y(u)$ and $z(u)$, summarize these relationships in one vector equation:

$$\begin{aligned}\mathbf{p}(u) = {} & (2u^2 - 3u + 1)\mathbf{p}_0 + (-4u^2 + 4u)\mathbf{p}_{0.5} \\ & + (2u^2 - u)\mathbf{p}_1 \quad u \in [0,1]\end{aligned} \quad (13.11)$$

Equation 13.5 produces the same plane curve in space as Eq. (13.11) when the relationships in Eq. (13.8) hold true. The curve will always lie in a plane no matter what three points you chose. If you are really curious, you may want to prove that this is so. (*Hint:* Any three points, not on a straight line, define a unique plane.) Another interesting observation is that the point on the curve at $u = 0.5$ (that is, $\mathbf{p}_{0.5}$) is not necessarily half way along the length of the curve between $\mathbf{p}_0$ and $\mathbf{p}_1$. You can show this quite convincingly by choosing three points to define a curve such that two of them are relatively close together. See an example of this in Fig. 13.3.

It is useful to call Eq. (13.5) the **algebraic form** and Eq. (13.11) the **geometric form.** Each of these equations can be written more compactly if you use matrices. Compactness is not the only advantage to matrix notation. Once in matrix form, you can use the full power of matrix algebra to solve modeling problems. Try it with Eq. (13.5) first. Study this equation with an eye to writing the right-hand side as the product of two matrices.

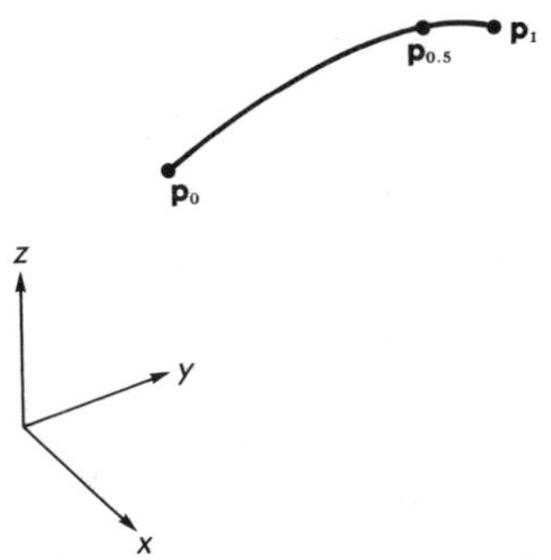

Fig. 13.3. Curve defined by three nonuniformly spaced points.

Try $[u^2 \ u \ 1]$ and $[\mathbf{a} \ \mathbf{b} \ \mathbf{c}]^T$. The first is a 1×3 row matrix, the second a 3×1 column matrix. If you multiply them in this order you get

$$[u^2 \ u \ 1]\begin{bmatrix}\mathbf{a}\\ \mathbf{b}\\ \mathbf{c}\end{bmatrix} = \mathbf{a}u^2 + \mathbf{b}u + c \tag{13.12}$$

This is the result you are looking for! Now let

$$\mathbf{U} = [u^2 \ u \ 1] \tag{13.13}$$

and

$$\mathbf{A} = [\mathbf{a} \ \mathbf{b} \ \mathbf{c}]^T \tag{13.14}$$

Then you can see that

$$\mathbf{p}(u) = \mathbf{UA}, \qquad u \in [0,1] \tag{13.15}$$

Remember that **A** is a matrix of three vectors, so that

$$\mathbf{A} = \begin{bmatrix}\mathbf{a}\\ \mathbf{b}\\ \mathbf{c}\end{bmatrix} = \begin{bmatrix} a_x & a_y & a_z \\ b_x & b_y & b_z \\ c_x & c_y & c_z \end{bmatrix} \tag{13.16}$$

The nine terms on the right are called the **algebraic coefficients.**

Now convert Eq. (13.11) into matrix form. The right-hand side looks like the product of

$$[(2u^2 - 3u + 1) \ \ (-4u^2 + 4u) \ \ (2u^2 - u)]$$

and

$$[\mathbf{p}_0 \ \mathbf{p}_{0.5} \ \mathbf{p}_1]^T$$

This means that

$$\mathbf{p}(u) = [(2u^2 - 3u + 1) \quad (-4u^2 + 4u) \quad (2u^2 - u)] \times [\mathbf{p}_0 \;\; \mathbf{p}_{0.5} \;\; \mathbf{p}_1]^T \tag{13.17}$$

Make the following substitutions; let

$$\mathbf{F} = [(2u^2 - 3u + 1) \quad (-4u^2 + 4u) \quad (2u^2 - u)] \tag{13.18}$$

and

$$\mathbf{B} = \begin{bmatrix} \mathbf{p}_0 \\ \mathbf{p}_{0.5} \\ \mathbf{p}_1 \end{bmatrix} = \begin{bmatrix} x_0 & y_0 & z_0 \\ x_{0.5} & y_{0.5} & z_{0.5} \\ x_1 & y_1 & z_1 \end{bmatrix} \tag{13.19}$$

The nine terms on the right are called the **geometric coefficients.**

Now you can see that

$$\mathbf{p}(u) = \mathbf{FB} \tag{13.20}$$

Write these curves in algebraic form, $\mathbf{p}(u) = \mathbf{UA}$, or geometric form, $\mathbf{p}(u) = \mathbf{FB}$. Since this is obviously true,

$$\mathbf{FB} = \mathbf{UA} \tag{13.21}$$

The **F** matrix is itself the product of two other matrices:

$$\mathbf{F} = [u^2 \;\; u \;\; 1] \begin{bmatrix} 2 & -4 & 2 \\ -3 & 4 & -1 \\ 1 & 0 & 0 \end{bmatrix} \tag{13.22}$$

The first matrix on the right you will recognize as **U**. Denote the rightmost matrix as

$$\mathbf{M} = \begin{bmatrix} 2 & -4 & 2 \\ -3 & 4 & -1 \\ 1 & 0 & 0 \end{bmatrix} \tag{13.23}$$

This means that

$$\mathbf{F} = \mathbf{UM} \tag{13.24}$$

and that you can rewrite Eq. (13.21) as

$$\mathbf{UMB} = \mathbf{UA} \tag{13.25}$$

or, more simply, as

$$\mathbf{MB} = \mathbf{A} \tag{13.26}$$

This expresses a simple relationship between the algebraic and geometric coefficients; so you have

$$\mathbf{A} = \mathbf{MB} \tag{13.27}$$

or

$$\mathbf{B} = \mathbf{M}^{-1}\mathbf{A} \tag{13.28}$$

The matrix **M** is called the **universal transformation matrix,** and **F** is called the **blending function matrix.** You will learn much more about these matrices and their uses in following sections.

EXERCISES

1. Find **a**, **b**, and **c** for each of the curves defined by the following sets of points:

a. $\mathbf{p}_0 = [0\ 2\ 2]$, $\mathbf{p}_{0.5} = [1\ 4\ 0]$, $\mathbf{p}_1 = [3\ 1\ 6]$
b. $\mathbf{p}_0 = [-1\ 0\ 4]$, $\mathbf{p}_{0.5} = [0\ 0\ 0]$, $\mathbf{p}_1 = [0\ -2\ -2]$
c. $\mathbf{p}_0 = [-3\ 7\ 1]$, $\mathbf{p}_{0.5} = [5\ 1\ 4]$, $\mathbf{p}_1 = [6\ 0\ 0]$
d. $\mathbf{p}_0 = [7\ 7\ 8]$, $\mathbf{p}_{0.5} = [2\ 0\ 3]$, $\mathbf{p}_1 = [2\ -4\ 1]$
e. $\mathbf{p}_0 = [0\ -1\ 2]$, $\mathbf{p}_{0.5} = [-1\ -3\ 7]$, $\mathbf{p}_1 = [0\ 5\ 2]$

2. Find $\mathbf{p}_0$, $\mathbf{p}_{0.5}$, and $\mathbf{p}_1$ for each of the curves defined by the following sets of algebraic vectors:

a. $\mathbf{a} = [1\ 0\ 0]$, $\mathbf{b} = [-3\ -3\ 0]$, $\mathbf{c} = [3\ 0\ 0]$
b. $\mathbf{a} = [6\ 9\ 8]$, $\mathbf{b} = [-8\ -2\ 4]$, $\mathbf{c} = [-4\ 6\ 1]$
c. $\mathbf{a} = [8\ 1\ -1]$, $\mathbf{b} = [5\ 4\ -5]$, $\mathbf{c} - [-10\ 4\ -3]$
d. $\mathbf{a} = [10\ 6\ 6]$, $\mathbf{b} = [-15\ -17\ -13]$, $\mathbf{c} = [7\ 7\ 8]$
e. $\mathbf{a} = [-2\ -4\ 4]$, $\mathbf{b} = [3\ 2\ -10]$, $\mathbf{c} = [-1\ 0\ 4]$

3. What are the dimensions of the matrices in Eq. (13.25)? Verify the dimensions of the product.

4. Find **A** when

$$\mathbf{B} = \begin{bmatrix} 0 & 1 & 1 \\ 3 & -2 & 0 \\ 2 & 5 & -4 \end{bmatrix}$$

5. Find $\mathbf{M}^{-1}$

6. Verify your answer to Exercise 5.

7. Describe the curve that results if $\mathbf{p}_0$, $\mathbf{p}_{0.5}$, and $\mathbf{p}_1$ are collinear.

8. Describe the curve that results if two of the points coincide. Note that there are two distinctly different combinations. What are they?

9. Give the general geometric coefficients of a curve that lies in the x, y plane.

10. Give the general geometric coefficients of a curve that lies in the $y = -3$ plane.

11. Give the geometric coefficients of a curve that approximates a 90° circular arc in the first quadrant of the x, y plane, centered at the origin and with a unit radius.

12. For the curve found for Exercise 11, compute the point at $u = 0.25$. How far does this deviate from a true circle? (Compute "radius" to point at $u = 0.25$.)

13. Consider Eq. (13.4). Show that if the right-hand side of the equation is linear in u, then a straight line results.

14. Consider Eq. (13.5). Show that this indeed generates only plane curves.

15. Show that Eq. (13.5) cannot produce a curve with an inflection point.

13.2. Space Curves

A space curve is not confined to a plane. It is free to twist through space like the path of a bumblebee through the blossoms of a cherry tree. For a space curve, you must use parametric functions that are cubic polynomials (or higher-degree polynomials). For $x(u)$, write

$$x(u) = a_x u^3 + b_x u^2 + c_x u + d_x \tag{13.29}$$

with similar expressions for $y(u)$ and $z(u)$. The a, b, c, and d terms are constant coefficients. As with plane curves, you can combine the $x(u)$, $y(u)$, and $z(u)$ expressions into a single vector equation:

$$\mathbf{p}(u) = \mathbf{a}u^3 + \mathbf{b}u^2 + \mathbf{c}u + \mathbf{d}, \qquad u \in [0,1] \tag{13.30}$$

This equation is analogous to Eq. (13.5). In fact, if $\mathbf{a} = 0$, then it is identical to the equation for plane curves.

You are again faced with the problem of how to use this equation to define a specific curve. Use the same approach as for plane curves. This time, though, there are 12 coefficients to determine. If you specify four points through which the curve must pass, you can easily determine $\mathbf{a}$, $\mathbf{b}$, $\mathbf{c}$, and $\mathbf{d}$. But which four points? Two are obvious: $\mathbf{p}_0$ and $\mathbf{p}_1$, the end points at $u = 0$ and $u = 1$. It turns out to be convenient to use two intermediate points and assign parametric values of $u = \frac{1}{3}$ and $u = \frac{2}{3}$ to them. (It is convenient when computing points at equal parametric intervals for computer graphic display and also for computing various geometric properties.)

So now you have the four points: $\mathbf{p}(0)$, $\mathbf{p}(\frac{1}{3})$, $\mathbf{p}(\frac{2}{3})$, and $\mathbf{p}(1)$. The notation is simpler if you make the following substitutions: $\mathbf{p}(0) = \mathbf{p}_1$, $\mathbf{p}(\frac{1}{3}) = \mathbf{p}_2$, $\mathbf{p}(\frac{2}{3}) = \mathbf{p}_3$, and $\mathbf{p}(1) = \mathbf{p}_4$; see Fig. 13.4. Next, use Eq. (13.29) to form the following four equations in four unknowns:

$$\begin{aligned} x_1 &= d_x \\ x_2 &= \tfrac{1}{27} a_x + \tfrac{1}{9} b_x + \tfrac{1}{3} c_x + d_x \\ x_3 &= \tfrac{8}{27} a_x + \tfrac{4}{9} b_x + \tfrac{2}{3} c_x + d_x \\ x_4 &= a_x + b_x + c_x + d_x \end{aligned} \tag{13.31}$$

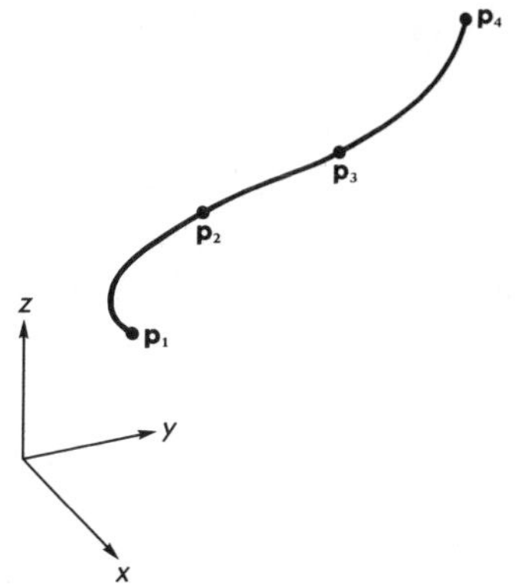

Fig. 13.4. Four points define a space curve.

Now find expressions for a_x, b_x, c_x, and d_x in terms of x_1, z_2, x_3, and x_4. After working out the algebra, you should get

$$\begin{aligned} a_x &= -\tfrac{9}{2}x_1 + \tfrac{27}{2}x_2 - \tfrac{27}{2}x_3 + \tfrac{9}{2}x_4 \\ b_x &= 9x_1 - \tfrac{45}{2}x_2 + 18x_3 - \tfrac{9}{2}x_4 \\ c_x &= -\tfrac{11}{2}x_1 + 9x_2 - \tfrac{9}{2}x_3 + x_4 \\ d_x &= x_1 \end{aligned} \tag{13.32}$$

Substitute these results into Eq. (13.29):

$$\begin{aligned} x(u) = &[-\tfrac{9}{2}x_1 + \tfrac{27}{2}x_2 - \tfrac{27}{2}x_3 + \tfrac{9}{2}x_4]u^3 \\ &+ [9x_1 - \tfrac{45}{2}x_2 + 18x_3 - \tfrac{9}{2}x_4]u^2 \\ &+ [-\tfrac{11}{2}x_1 + 9x_2 - \tfrac{9}{2}x_3 + x_4]u \\ &+ x_1 \end{aligned} \tag{13.33}$$

It all looks a bit messy now, but you will soon put it into a neater, more compact form. Next, rewrite Eq. (13.33) as follows:

$$\begin{aligned} x(u) = &(-4u^3 + 9u^2 - 5.5u + 1)x_1 \\ &+ (13.5u^3 - 22.5u^2 + 9u)x_2 \\ &+ (-13.5u^3 + 18u^2 - 4.5u)x_3 \\ &+ (4.5u^3 - 4.5u^2 + u)x_4 \end{aligned} \tag{13.34}$$

Since there are equivalent expressions for $y(u)$ and $z(u)$, summarize them with a vector equation:

$$\begin{aligned} \mathbf{p}(u) = &(-4u^3 + 9u^2 - 5.5u + 1)\mathbf{p}_1 \\ &+ (13.5u^3 - 22.5u^2 + 9u)\mathbf{p}_2 \\ &+ (-13.5u^3 + 18u^2 - 4.5u)\mathbf{p}_3 \\ &+ (4.5u^3 - 4.5u^2 + u)\mathbf{p}_4, \qquad u \in [0,1] \end{aligned} \tag{13.35}$$

This means that, given four points and successive values of u such that $u \in [0,1]$, Eq. (13.35) produces a curve that starts at $\mathbf{p}_1$, passes through $\mathbf{p}_2$ and $\mathbf{p}_3$, and ends at $\mathbf{p}_4$. Actually, nothing mysterious happens if you use values of u less than 0 or greater than 1. This just extends the curve beyond the range we are interested in (or else you would have chosen a different $\mathbf{p}_1$ or $\mathbf{p}_4$ or both).

Take one more step toward a more compact notation. Let the matrix $\mathbf{G} = [G_1 \; G_2 \; G_3 \; G_4]$, with

$$\begin{aligned} G_1 &= (-4u^3 + 9u^2 - 5.5u + 1) \\ G_2 &= (13.5u^3 - 22.5u^2 + 9u) \\ G_3 &= (-13.5u^3 + 18u^2 - 4.5u) \\ G_4 &= (4.5u^3 - 4.5u^2 + u) \end{aligned} \tag{13.36}$$

Then define a matrix $\mathbf{P} = [\mathbf{p}_1 \; \mathbf{p}_2 \; \mathbf{p}_3 \; \mathbf{p}_4]^T$, so that

$$\mathbf{p}(u) = \mathbf{GP}, \qquad u \in [0,1] \tag{13.37}$$

The matrix **G** is the product of two other matrices, **U** and **N**:

$$\mathbf{G} = \mathbf{UN} \tag{13.38}$$

where $\mathbf{U} = [u^3 \; u^2 \; u \; 1]$ and

$$\mathbf{N} = \begin{bmatrix} -4.5 & 13.5 & -13.5 & 4.5 \\ 9.0 & -22.5 & 18.0 & -4.5 \\ -5.5 & 9.0 & -4.5 & 1.0 \\ 1.0 & 0 & 0 & 0 \end{bmatrix} \tag{13.39}$$

Now, let

$$\mathbf{a} = \begin{bmatrix} \mathbf{a} \\ \mathbf{b} \\ \mathbf{c} \\ \mathbf{d} \end{bmatrix} = \begin{bmatrix} a_x & a_y & a_z \\ b_x & b_y & b_z \\ c_x & c_y & c_z \\ d_x & d_y & d_z \end{bmatrix} \tag{13.40}$$

Then write Eq. (13.30) with matrix notation as

$$\mathbf{p}(u) = \mathbf{UA}, \qquad u \in [0,1] \tag{13.41}$$

This looks a lot like Eq. (13.15) for plane curves, except that you have defined new **U** and **A** matrices. In fact, you can just forget about Eq. (13.15) because it is only a special case of the formulation for a space curve.

It is useful to be able to convert from the **A** matrix to the **P** matrix. This is easy if you do some simple matrix algebra using Eqs. (13.37), (13.38), and (13.41). You first get

$$\mathbf{GP} = \mathbf{UNP} \tag{13.42}$$

and then

$$\mathbf{UA} = \mathbf{UNP} \tag{13.43}$$

or more simply

$$\mathbf{A} = \mathbf{NP} \tag{13.44}$$

Another very clever way to define this space curve does not use intermediate points. You will study this next.

EXERCISES

1. Compute G_1, G_2, G_3, and G_4 at $u = 0$.

2. Compute G_1, G_2, G_3, and G_4 at $u = 1$.

3. Compute G_1, G_2, G_3, and G_4 at $u = \frac{1}{3}$.

4. Compute G_1, G_2, G_3, and G_4 at $u = \frac{2}{3}$.

5. What general condition must be imposed on the four points $\mathbf{p}_1$, $\mathbf{p}_2$, $\mathbf{p}_3$, and $\mathbf{p}_4$ to produce a curve that lies in the y, z plane?

6. Give four points that produce an approximation of a 90° circular arc lying in the first quadrant of the x, y plane, centered at the origin and with a unit radius.

7. For the curve found in Exercise 6, compute the point at $u = 0.5$. How far does this deviate from a true circle?

8. Show that Eq. (13.30) can produce a plane curve with an inflection point. Compare this to Eq. (13.5).

9. Describe various conditions on Eq. (13.30) that produce a straight line.

13.3. Tangents to Curves and Tangent Vectors

Every point on a curve has a straight line associated with it called the tangent line, or just **tangent.** It is very easy to construct the tangent line graphically. Figure 13.5 shows some of the key steps.

Suppose you want to find the tangent at point **p** on a curve. First find a neighboring point on this curve, say **1**, and draw a straight line through it and **p**. This is not the tangent. Try again. Choose another point closer to **p**, say **2**, and draw a straight line through it and **p**. This is not the tangent either, but it is closer to it than the first attempt. Now try the same thing with point **3**. Again, the line through it and **p** is not the tangent, but it is much better than the two earlier tries.

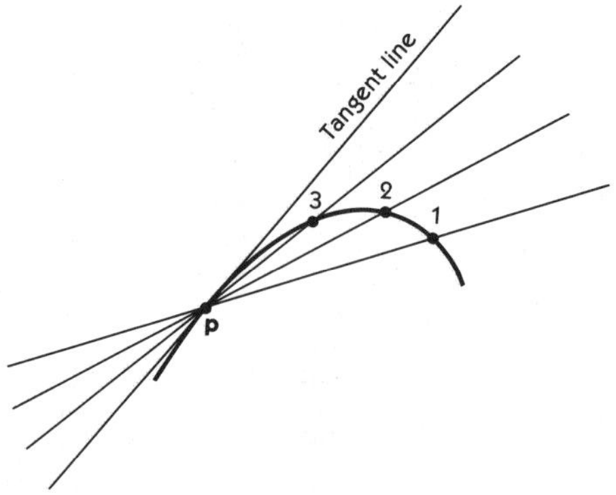

Fig. 13.5. Constructing a tangent line to a curve.

Now you know how to construct closer and closer approximations to the tangent line: by choosing closer and closer points to **p** through which to construct the lines. When the distance between **p** and the chosen point becomes vanishingly small, then the line through them is the tangent.

There is also a mathematical way to compute the tangent at any point on a curve, if the curve is defined by some sort of analytical function (such as a well-behaved equation). It is particularly easy if the function is a simple polynomial, such as those you have been using to produce plane and space curves. The only catch is that you will have to use some calculus to do it.

For the moment, at least, characterize the tangent line by its slope. Slope is nothing more than the ratio of the rise to the run of the tangent: the change in y per change in x for any interval on a line in the x, y plane. Study Fig. 13.6. For any interval on the line shown in this figure, say "a," compute Δx_a, "delta" x_a (where $\Delta x_a = x_2 - x_1$), and Δy_a (where $\Delta y_a = y_2 - y_1$). Then the slope is simply

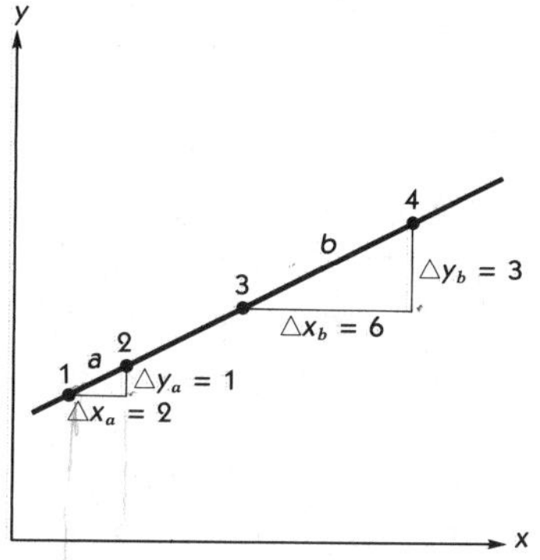

Fig. 13.6. The slope of a line.

$$\text{slope}_a = \frac{\Delta y_a}{\Delta x_a} = \frac{1}{2} \tag{13.45}$$

Do the same for interval "*b*" and find

$$\text{slope}_b = \frac{\Delta y_b}{\Delta x_b} = \frac{3}{6} = \frac{1}{2} \tag{13.46}$$

Clearly, $\text{slope}_a = \text{slope}_b$, since

$$\frac{\Delta y_a}{\Delta x_a} = \frac{\Delta y_b}{\Delta x_b} = \frac{1}{2} \tag{13.47}$$

So, no matter how small or how large the interval, the slope is constant and equal at all points on a given straight line.

What about the slope at any point on a curve? Let us use the example of the parabola: $y = x^2$. See Fig. 13.7. Start at some point on the curve whose coordinates are (x_1, y_1). To construct (mathematically and graphically) a tangent and compute its slope through this point, you need another point close to it. Since x is the independent variable, add a small increment to it, say Δx. You now have the x coordinate of the second point. The y coordinate is simply $(x_1 + \Delta x)^2$, because the point coordinates must, of course, satisfy the curve function, $y = x^2$. Now compute the slope from

$$x = (x_1 + \Delta x) - x_1 \tag{13.48}$$

and

$$y = (x_1 + \Delta x)^2 - y_1 \tag{13.49}$$

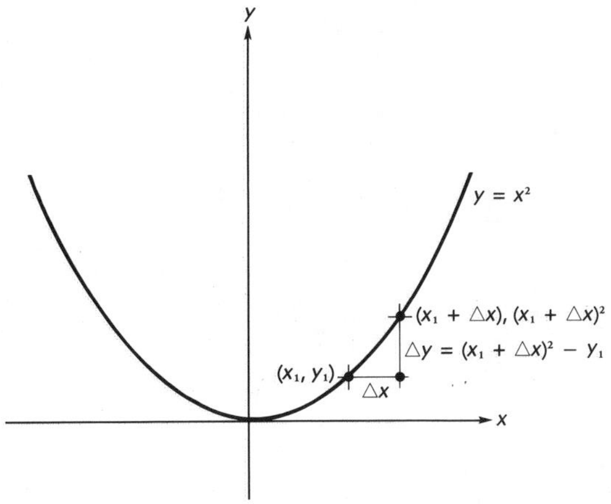

Fig. 13.7. The slope at a point on the curve $y = x^2$.

so that

$$\frac{\Delta y}{\Delta x} = \frac{(x_1 + \Delta x)^2 - y_1}{(x_1 + \Delta x) - x_1} = \frac{x_1^2 + 2x_1\Delta x + (\Delta x)^2 - y_1}{\Delta x} \qquad (13.50)$$

Note that $y_1 = x_1^2$ and that if Δx is small, then $(\Delta x)^2$ is so small you can ignore it. Let Δx approach arbitrarily close to zero, but not be set equal to zero. Write this as $\Delta x \to 0$. (You will see this in the introductory sections of elementary calculus textbooks.) Then,

$$\frac{\Delta y}{\Delta x} = 2x_1 \qquad (13.51)$$

or more generally,

$$\frac{\Delta y}{\Delta x} = 2x \qquad (13.52)$$

This is the slope at any point on the curve. Plot the curve and try Eq. (13.52) for various points. Just substitute their x values into this equation.

Try one more example before you make any assertions based on what you have found so far. Try the curve $y = x^3$; see Fig. 13.8. Again, start at some point on this curve. Say its coordinates are (x_1,y_1). Increment x_1 by Δx to find a nearby point, and proceed as before. First find Δx and Δy:

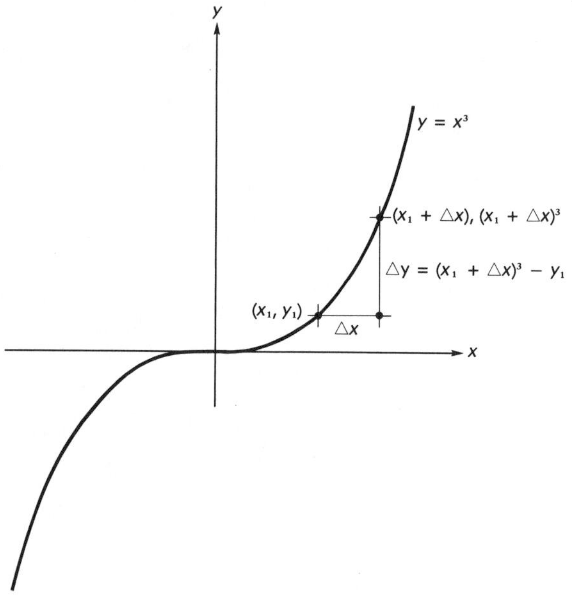

Fig. 13.8. The slope at a point on the curve $y = x^3$.

$$\Delta x = (x_1 + \Delta x) - x_1 \tag{13.53}$$

and

$$\Delta y = (x_1 + \Delta x)^3 - y_1 \tag{13.54}$$

so that

$$\frac{\Delta y}{\Delta x} = \frac{(x_1 + \Delta x)^3 - y_1}{(x_1 + \Delta x) - x_1} = \frac{x_1^3 + 3x_1^2\Delta x + 3x_1(\Delta x)^2 + (\Delta x)^3 - y_1}{\Delta x} \tag{13.55}$$

Since the terms containing $(\Delta x)^2$ and $(\Delta x)^3$ are negligibly small and since $y_1 = x_1^3$, Eq. (13.55) reduces to

$$\frac{\Delta y}{\Delta x} = 3x_1^2 \tag{13.56}$$

or, more generally,

$$\frac{\Delta y}{\Delta x} = 3x^2 \tag{13.57}$$

Note the interesting trend, that in general

$$\text{if } y = ax^n, \quad \text{then } \frac{\Delta y}{\Delta x} = nax^{n-1} \tag{13.58}$$

where "a" is any constant coefficient.

If you let Δx approach arbitrarily close to zero (Δy also proportionately approaches zero), then you must use a different set of symbols: In place of $\Delta y/\Delta x$ use dy/dx, a "d" instead of a "delta." This is certainly a confusing convention, because the natural tendency is to want to cancel the "d's," as in an ordinary algebraic quotient, so that $dy/dx = y/x$; but this is wrong because the d and y and the d and x are tied together to represent the concept in calculus called **differentiation,** which is what you just did. Sorry, but you are stuck with this convention. Now you can rewrite Eq. (13.58) as

$$\text{If } y = ax^n, \quad \text{then } \frac{dy}{dx} = nax^{n-1} \tag{13.59}$$

From all of this, you can correctly surmise that the slope at any point of a curve defined analytically by $y = f(x)$ is given by the first derivative of y with respect to x.

Given the polynomial,

$$y = x^3 + 2x^2 + 1 \tag{13.60}$$

then

$$\frac{dy}{dx} = 3x^2 + 4x \tag{13.61}$$

Each term in Eq. (13.60) is differentiated separately according to Eq. (13.59). Note that differentiating a constant results in zero. You can continue to perform a succession of these differentiating operations on a function. If you compute the derivative of a derivative, the result is called the **second derivative,** denoted as d^2y/dx^2—in other words, the second derivative of y with respect to x. Of course, you can continue indefinitely this process of differentiating as long as the prior result is a differentiable function.

Now you have the tools you need to compute the slope at any point on a curve given by a simple polynomial function. Simply take the derivative of the function and substitute the value of the independent variable (x in the example you have studied) into the result.

Several questions now arise: What about curves in three dimensions, and what about curves defined by parametric functions? Let us tackle the parametric functions first. Take the following example: If

$$x(u) = 2u \qquad \text{and} \qquad y(u) = 3u^2 \tag{13.62}$$

then

$$\frac{dx}{du} = 2 \qquad \text{and} \qquad \frac{dy}{du} = 6u \tag{13.63}$$

Now you can assert without rigorous proof that

$$\frac{dy}{dx} = \frac{dy/du}{dx/du} \tag{13.64}$$

Therefore, for this example,

$$\frac{dy}{dx} = \frac{6u}{2} = 3u \tag{13.65}$$

For curves in three dimensions given by parametric functions, like the space curves of the last section, you can compute several different slope combinations: dy/dx, dy/dz, and dz/dx, for example. Usually, though, it is easier to work with the direction cosines of the tangent line at a point on a curve; study Fig. 13.9.

Imagine a unit vector, **t**, that is collinear with the tangent to the curve

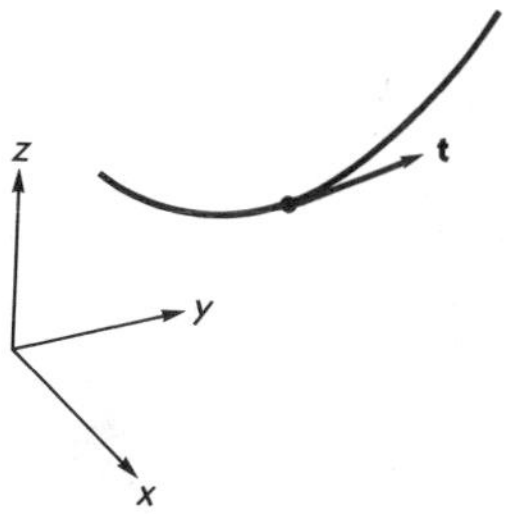

Fig. 13.9. Unit vector tangent to a curve.

at some arbitrary point on the curve. Its components t_x, t_y, and t_z are the direction cosines of the tangent line, and it is very easy to show that

$$\frac{dy}{dx} = \frac{t_y}{t_x}, \quad \frac{dy}{dz} = \frac{t_y}{t_z}, \quad \text{and} \quad \frac{dz}{dx} = \frac{t_z}{t_x} \tag{13.66}$$

and so on. Also, we know that

$$t_x^2 + t_y^2 + t_z^2 = 1 \tag{13.67}$$

So, given any two direction cosines, you can easily compute the third.

In what direction does **t** point along the tangent line? That is easy, too. The math works out so that it is always pointing in the direction along the curve in which the parametric variable is increasing.

If you compute the parametric derivative of each of the parametric functions $x(u)$, $y(u)$, and $z(u)$, such as those given by Eq. (13.29) or (13.30), then you get

$$\frac{dx(u)}{du}, \quad \frac{dy(u)}{du}, \quad \text{and} \quad \frac{dz(u)}{du} \tag{13.68}$$

Using Eq. (13.64), you can then compute, for example,

$$\frac{dy}{dx} = \frac{dy(u)/du}{dx(u)/du} \tag{13.69}$$

and so on. This means that you can treat $dx(u)/du$, $dy(u)/du$, and $dz(u)/du$ as components of a vector along the tangent to the curve. This vector is not necessarily the unit vector, because the same direction cosine ratios apply for any vector along a common tangent line. This is the **parametric tangent vector.** It is a very powerful idea, and you will now see how to use it.

Remember that in the last section you learned how to define a space curve by specifying four points and that by properly computing some coefficients the curve does pass through the four points. Now we have another way to define a space curve. You will still use the two end points, but instead of the two intermediate points, let us use the tangent vectors at each end. This will let you control the slope at each end. (This is called cubic **Hermite interpolation.**)

Study Fig. 13.10. It shows one way to represent graphically and symbolically the elements that describe the parametric cubic space curve. Note that a superscript u denotes differentiation with respect to u (and, of course, indicates the tangent vector) and that the subscript 0 or 1 denotes the local value of u with which these vectors are evaluated. Finally, note the arrowhead and associated letter u in the middle of the curve. They merely emphasize the direction along the curve in which u is increasing. (There is a way to change the parametrization without changing the shape or position of a curve. You will find this discussed in Box 13.1.) The vectors $\mathbf{p}_0$, $\mathbf{p}_1$, $\mathbf{p}_0^u$, and $\mathbf{p}_1^u$ are called the boundary conditions. They are all you need to define a parametric cubic space curve. Of course, you have already learned how to do this with four points, but two of the points were not on a boundary.

Now let us do some mathematics and see how to use these tangent vectors. First work out the x components. You know that for a parametric cubic space curve [from Eq. (13.29)]

$$x(u) = a_x u^3 + b_x u^2 + c_x u + d_x \tag{13.70}$$

Differentiate this to obtain a component of the tangent vector:

$$\frac{dx(u)}{du} = x^u = 3a_x u^2 + 2b_x u + c_x \tag{13.71}$$

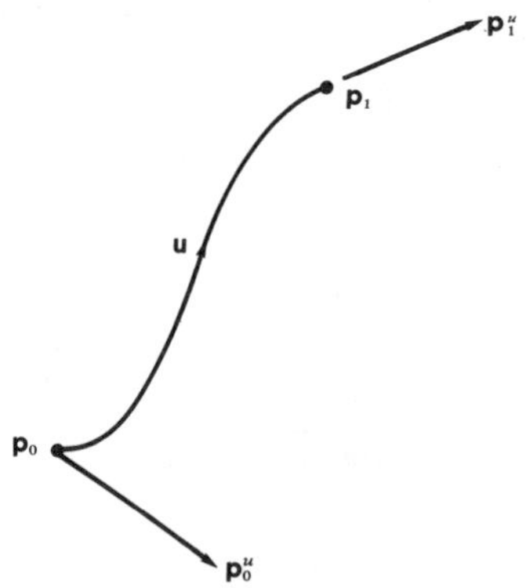

Fig. 13.10. Defining a space curve with end points and tangent vectors.

Box 13.1. Reparametrization

You can change the parametric interval in such a way that neither the shape nor the position of the curve is changed. A function $v = f(u)$ describes the precise way to change this interval. For example, sometimes it is useful to reverse the direction of parametrization of a curve. This is the simplest form of reparametrization. It is quite easy to do: In this example, $v = -u$, where v is the new parametric variable.

The diagrams are of two parametric cubic curves. They are identical, but with reversed parametrization if the following relationships are true:

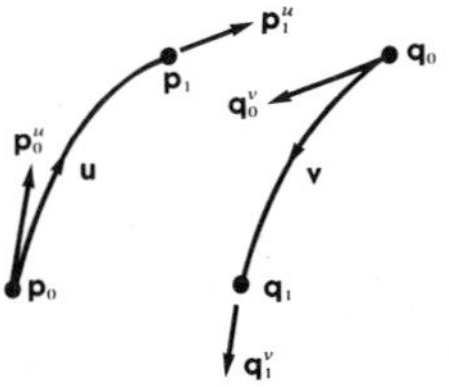

$\mathbf{q}_0 = \mathbf{p}_1, \quad \mathbf{q}_0^v = -\mathbf{p}_1^u$

$\mathbf{q}_1 = \mathbf{p}_0, \quad \mathbf{q}_1^v = -\mathbf{p}_0^u$

Here is a more general form of reparametrization for parametric cubic curves: Assume that the curve is initially parametrized from u_i to u_j. Suppose we want to change this so that the parametric variable ranges from v_i to v_j. Let the geometric coefficients initially be $\mathbf{p}_i$, $\mathbf{p}_j$, $\mathbf{q}_i^u$, and $\mathbf{q}_j^u$, and after reparametrization $\mathbf{q}_i$, $\mathbf{q}_j$, $\mathbf{q}_i^v$, and $\mathbf{q}_j^v$.

There is a simple relationship between these sets of coefficients. The end point must be related like this: $\mathbf{q}_i = \mathbf{p}_i$ and $\mathbf{q}_j = \mathbf{p}_j$, otherwise the reparametrized curve will not occupy the same position. The tangent vectors are another matter. Because they are defined by the first derivative of the parametric functions, they are sensitive to the functional relationship between u and v. A linear relationship is required to preserve the cubic form of the parametric equations and the directions of the tangent vectors. So, you must have

$$v = au + b$$

Differentiating, obtain

$$dv = adu$$

Furthermore, you know that $v_i = au_i + b$ and $v_j = au_j + b_j$, and you can readily solve for a. Then, since

$$\frac{dx}{du} = \frac{adx}{dv}$$

find that

$$\mathbf{q}^v = \frac{u_j - u_i}{v_j - v_i}\mathbf{p}^u$$

(continued)

Box 13.1. (Continued)

Now you can state the complete relationship between the two sets of geometric coefficients as:

$$\mathbf{q}_i = \mathbf{p}_i, \qquad \mathbf{q}_i^v = \frac{u_j - u_i}{v_j - v_i}\mathbf{p}_i^u$$

$$\mathbf{q}_j = \mathbf{p}_j, \qquad \mathbf{q}_j^v = \frac{u_j - u_i}{v_j - v_i}\mathbf{p}_j^u$$

This tells you that the tangent vector magnitudes must change to accommodate a change in the range of the parametric variable. The magnitudes are scaled by the ratio of the ranges of the parametric variables. The directions of the tangent vectors and the shape and position of the curve are preserved.

Again, the superscript u on x is a symbol to indicate that you have taken a derivative (it is not an exponent). If you evaluate these two equations at $u = 0$ and $u = 1$, you get

$$\begin{aligned} x_0 &= d_x \\ x_1 &= a_x + b_x + c_x + d_x \\ x_0^u &= c_x \\ x_1^u &= 3a_x + 2b_x + c_x \end{aligned} \tag{13.72}$$

Now you have four equations and four unknowns, and you will easily find a_x, b_x, c_x, and d_x (the algebraic coefficients) in terms of the boundary conditions x_0, x_1, x_0^u, and x_1^u:

$$\begin{aligned} a_x &= 2(x_0 - x_1) + x_0^u + x_1^u \\ b_x &= 3(-x_0 + x_1) - 2x_0^u - x_1^u \\ c_x &= x_0^u \\ d_x &= x_0 \end{aligned} \tag{13.73}$$

Substitute these results into Eq. (13.70) to find

$$\begin{aligned} x(u) = {} & (2x_0 - 2x_1 + x_0^u + x_1^u)u^3 \\ & + (-3x_0 + 3x_1 - 2x_0^u - x_1^u)u^2 \\ & + x_0^u u + x_0 \end{aligned} \tag{13.74}$$

Rearrange the terms and rewrite as

$$\begin{aligned} x(u) = {} & (2u^3 - 3u^2 + 1)x_0 + (-2u^3 + 3u^2)x_1 \\ & + (u^3 - 2u^2 + u)x_0^u \\ & + (u^3 - u^2)x_1^u \end{aligned} \tag{13.75}$$

Since $y(u)$ and $z(u)$ have equivalent forms, write Eq. (13.75) as a vector equation:

$$\mathbf{p}(u) = (2u^3 - 3u^2 + 1)\mathbf{p}_0 + (-2u^3 + 3u^2)\mathbf{p}_1 + (u^3 - 2u^2 + u)\mathbf{p}_0^u + (u^3 - u^2)\mathbf{p}_1^u \tag{13.76}$$

Now you can write the same equation using matrix notation. Define a matrix $\mathbf{F} = [F_1 \; F_2 \; F_3 \; F_4]$, where

$$\begin{aligned} F_1 &= 2u^3 - 3u^2 + 1 \\ F_2 &= -2u^3 + 3u^2 \\ F_3 &= u^3 - 2u^2 + u \\ F_4 &= u^3 - u^2 \end{aligned} \tag{13.77}$$

There are, of course, the polynomial coefficients of the vectors in Eq. (13.76), so that you can write

$$\mathbf{p}(u) = F_1\mathbf{p}_0 + F_2\mathbf{p}_1 + F_3\mathbf{p}_0^u + F_4\mathbf{p}_1^u \tag{13.78}$$

Now, if you define a matrix $\mathbf{B} = [\mathbf{p}_0 \; \mathbf{p}_1 \; \mathbf{p}_0^u \; \mathbf{p}_1^u]^T$, then

$$\mathbf{p}(u) = \mathbf{FB} \tag{13.79}$$

You can also write the matrix **F** as the product of two other matrices, **U** and **M**, so that

$$\mathbf{F} = \mathbf{UM} \tag{13.80}$$

where

$$\mathbf{U} = [u^3 \; u^2 \; u \; 1] \tag{13.81}$$

and

$$\mathbf{M} = \begin{bmatrix} 2 & -2 & 1 & 1 \\ -3 & 3 & -2 & -1 \\ 0 & 0 & 1 & 0 \\ 1 & 0 & 0 & 0 \end{bmatrix} \tag{13.82}$$

Now rewrite Eq. (13.79) as

$$\mathbf{p}(u) = \mathbf{UMB} \tag{13.83}$$

M is the universal transformation matrix and **B** is the boundary condition matrix (or matrix of geometric coefficients).

Since you know that

$$\mathbf{p}(u) = \mathbf{a}u^3 + \mathbf{b}u^2 + \mathbf{c}u + \mathbf{d} \tag{13.84}$$

or, in matrix form,

$$\mathbf{p}(u) = \mathbf{UA} \tag{13.85}$$

the relationship between **A** and **B** is

$$\mathbf{A} = \mathbf{MB} \tag{13.86}$$

Think for a moment about the four vectors that make up the boundary condition matrix. There is nothing extraordinary about the vectors defining the end points, but what about the two tangent vectors? A tangent vector certainly defines the slope at one end of the curve, but a vector has characteristics of both direction (slope) and magnitude. All you need to specify the slope is a unit tangent vector, say $\mathbf{t}_0$ and $\mathbf{t}_1$. But $\mathbf{p}_0$, $\mathbf{p}_1$, $\mathbf{t}_0$, and $\mathbf{t}_1$ supply only 10 (3 + 3 + 2 + 2) of the 12 conditions (sometimes called "degrees of freedom") needed to determine the algebraic coefficients **a**, **b**, **c**, and **d**. So the magnitude of a tangent vector is necessary and contributes to the shape of the curve. In fact, you can write $\mathbf{p}_0^u$ and $\mathbf{p}_1^u$ as

$$\mathbf{p}_0^u = m_0\mathbf{t}_0 \tag{13.87}$$

and

$$\mathbf{p}_1^u = m_1\mathbf{t}_1 \tag{13.88}$$

Clearly, m_0 and m_1 are the magnitudes of $\mathbf{p}_0^u$ and $\mathbf{p}_1^u$.

Use these relationships to modify Eq. (13.76):

$$\begin{aligned}\mathbf{p}(u) = {} & (2u^3 - 3u^2 + 1)\mathbf{p}_0 + (-2u^3 + 3u^2)\mathbf{p}_1 \\ & + (u^3 - 2u^2 + u)m_0\mathbf{t}_0 + (u^3 - u^2)m_1\mathbf{t}_1\end{aligned} \tag{13.89}$$

Now you will experiment with a curve; hold $\mathbf{p}_0$, $\mathbf{p}_1$, $\mathbf{t}_0$, and $\mathbf{t}_1$ constant and see what happens to the shape as $\mathbf{m}_0$ and $\mathbf{m}_1$ vary. For simplicity, study a plane curve in the x, y plane. This means that z_0, z_1, z_0^u, and $z_1^u = 0$. See Fig. 13.11. The **B** matrix for the curve drawn with a solid line ($m_0 = m_1 = 1$) is

$$\mathbf{B} = \begin{bmatrix} \mathbf{p}_0 \\ \mathbf{p}_1 \\ m_0\mathbf{t}_0 \\ m_1\mathbf{t}_1 \end{bmatrix} = \begin{bmatrix} 0 & 0 & 0 \\ 1 & 0 & 0 \\ 0.707 & 0.707 & 0 \\ 0.707 & -0.707 & 0 \end{bmatrix} \tag{13.90}$$

Think about this matrix, this array of 12 numbers. These 12 numbers uniquely define this curve. Now, by changing either m_0 or m_1 or both, you change the shape of the curve. But it is a rather special kind of change, because not only do the end points remain fixed, but the end slopes are also unchanged!

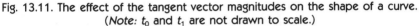

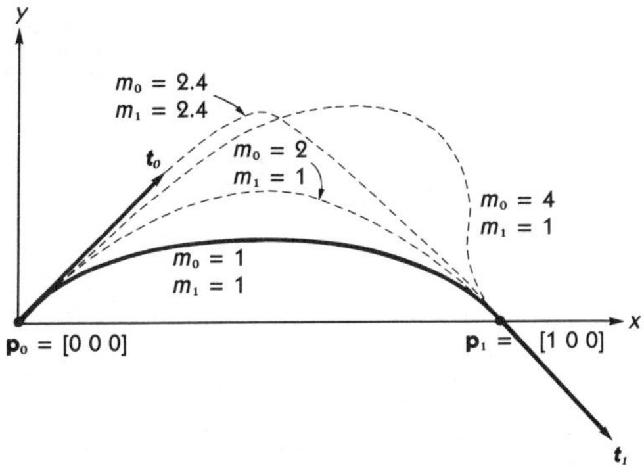

Fig. 13.11. The effect of the tangent vector magnitudes on the shape of a curve. (*Note:* t_0 and t_1 are not drawn to scale.)

The three curves drawn with dashed lines in Fig. 13.11 show the effects of varying m_0 and m_1. This is a very powerful modeling tool for designing curves, making it possible to join up end to end many curves in a smooth way and still control and change the interior shape of each individual curve. You will study this in Section 13.6. Box 13.2 shows how to adjust the tangent vectors to describe some familiar curves.

EXERCISES

1. Compute dy/dx for the following functions:

a. $y = 4x^2$
b. $y = x + 3$
c. $y = x^3 - 3x + 1$
d. $y = x^2 + 2x + 1$
e. $y = 2x^4 + x^3 + 3$

2. Find the slopes of the following curves at $x = 2$:

a. $y = x^2 + 1$
b. $y = 4x^{-3} + 2x$
c. $y = x^4 - 6x$
d. $y = -4x^{-2} + x^2$
e. $y = x^3 + 3x^2 + 3x + 1$

3. Find the coordinates of the point of zero slope for each of the curves defined in Exercise 1.

4. Compute dy/dx at $u = 0$ and $u = 1$ for each of the following parametrically defined curves:

a. $x(u) = 3 - 2u + u^3$, $y(u) = 3u^2$
b. $x(u) = 4a$, $y(u) = 3 - u^3$

Box 13.2. Approximating Canonical Curves

You will find it easy to substitute a parametric cubic curve for many of the other curves with which you may be familiar. Let us try the conic curves: hyperbola, parabola, ellipse, and circle. Study the figure. Given three points, $\mathbf{p}_0$, $\mathbf{p}_1$, and $\mathbf{p}_2$, make the following interpretation. There is a conic curve whose tangents at $\mathbf{p}_0$ and $\mathbf{p}_1$ lie along $(\mathbf{p}_2 - \mathbf{p}_0)$ and $(\mathbf{p}_1 - \mathbf{p}_2)$, respectively. The conic is also tangent to a line parallel to $(\mathbf{p}_1 - \mathbf{p}_0)$ and offset a distance ρH, where $\rho\epsilon[0, 1]$. Observe that the value of ρ determines the type of conic curve:

Hyperbola: $0.5 < \rho \leq 1.0$
Parabola: $\rho = 0.5$
Ellipse: $0 \leq \rho < 0.5$

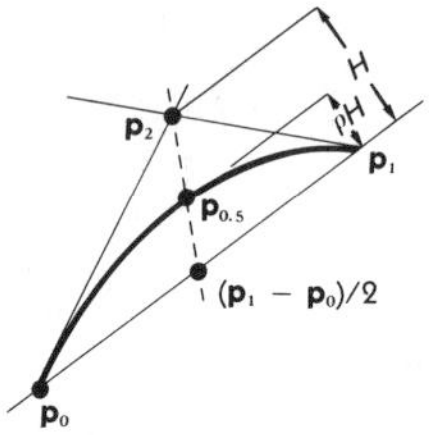

You can use these three points, $\mathbf{p}_1$, $\mathbf{p}_2$, $\mathbf{p}_3$, and ρ to define a parametric cubic curve that is also tangent to the lines discussed above. Its equation is

$$\mathbf{p} = \mathbf{F}[\mathbf{p}_0\ \mathbf{p}_1\ 4\rho(\mathbf{p}_2 - \mathbf{p}_0)\ 4\rho(\mathbf{p}_1 - \mathbf{p}_2)]^T$$

It turns out that this equation exactly fits a parabola and produces good approximations to the hyperbola and ellipse. It is interesting to note that the line connecting the points $\mathbf{p}_2$ and $(\mathbf{p}_1 - \mathbf{p}_0)/2$ intersects the curve at $\mathbf{p}_{0.5}$ and that the tangent vector $\mathbf{p}^u_{0.5}$ is parallel to $(\mathbf{p}_1 - \mathbf{p}_0)$.

You will find a complete derivation of these approximations in *Geometric Modeling*, M. E. Mortenson, John Wiley & Sons, Inc., 1985. They are rather easy to derive, and you should give it a try on your own first.

c. $x(u) = 2u^2 + u^3$, $y(u) = 7$
d. $x(u) = 3 + u + u^2 + 2u^3$, $y(u) = 5 + 3u - u^3$
e. $x(u) = 0$, $y(u) = 1 - u^2$

5. Compute m_0 and $\mathbf{t}_0$ for the following tangent vectors:

a. $\mathbf{p}^u_0 = [3\ \ -1\ \ 6]$
b. $\mathbf{p}^u_0 = [0\ \ 2\ \ 0]$
c. $\mathbf{p}^u_0 = [1\ \ 5\ \ -1]$
d. $\mathbf{p}^u_0 = [7\ \ 2\ \ 0]$
e. $\mathbf{p}^u_0 = [4\ \ 4\ \ -3]$

6. Find the **B** matrix for each of the curves in Fig. 13.11:

a. $m_0 = 2$, $m_1 = 1$
b. $m_0 = 4$, $m_1 = 1$
c. $m_0 = 2.4$, $m_1 = 2.4$

7. Find d^2y/dx^2 for the functions given in Exercise 1.

13.4. Blending Functions

The elements of the matrix **F** in Eqs. (13.77) are called **blending functions.** These functions apply to all parametric cubic curves defined by end points and tangent vectors. You also saw other blending functions that apply to parametric cubic curves defined by four points. These are the elements of the matrix **G** given in Eqs. (13.36). As you might imagine, there are many other useful blending functions (and some not so useful). In fact, you can design just about any blending functions you might want, although they may not have many desirable properties.

What blending functions do is "blend" the effects of given geometric constraints, or boundary conditions. Thus, **F** blends the contributions of $\mathbf{p}_0$, $\mathbf{p}_1$, $\mathbf{p}_0^u$, and $\mathbf{p}_1^u$ to the creation of points on a curve. **G** blends the contributions of $\mathbf{p}_1$, $\mathbf{p}_2$, $\mathbf{p}_3$, and $\mathbf{p}_4$. Figure 13.12 shows a plot of F_1, F_2, F_3, and F_4 over the interval $u \in [0,1]$, and Fig. 13.13 shows a plot of G_1, G_2, G_3, and G_4 over the same interval. Note that $F_2 = 1 - F_1$.

Study the plots of F_1, F_2, F_3, and F_4. Do you see the symmetry between F_1 and F_2? They are symmetrical about $u = 0.5$. F_4 is the mirror image of F_3. You should expect this, because there is nothing intrinsically unique about F_1 with respect to F_2, or about F_3 with respect to F_4. At $u = 0$, $F_1 = 1$ and $F_2, F_3, F_4 = 0$; while at $u = 1$, $F_2 = 1$ and $F_1, F_3, F_4 = 0$. This, too, is what you should expect. Do you see why? F_1, and therefore $\mathbf{p}_0$, dominates the shape of the curve for low values of u, while F_2, and thus $\mathbf{p}_2$, has the greatest influence for values of u near 1.

Next, study the plots of G_1, G_2, G_3, and G_4 in Fig. 13.3. Clearly, G_1 and G_4 are symmetrical parts, as are G_2 and G_3. Note that at $u = 0$, $G_1 = 1$ and $G_2, G_3, G_4 = 0$; at $u = \frac{1}{3}$, $G_2 = 1$ and $G_1, G_3, G_4 = 0$; at $u = \frac{2}{3}$, $G_3 = 1$ and $G_1, G_2, G_4 = 0$; and at $u = 1$, $G_1, G_2, G_3 = 0$.

In each case (**F** and **G**) the blending functions must have certain prop-

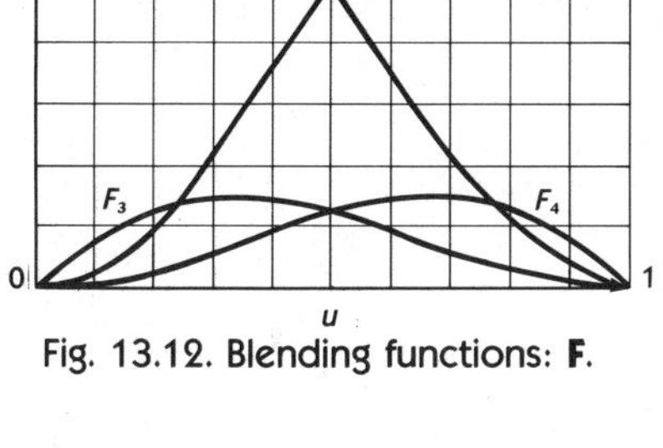

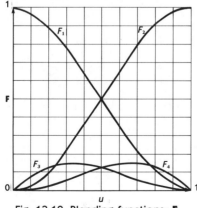

Fig. 13.12. Blending functions: **F**.

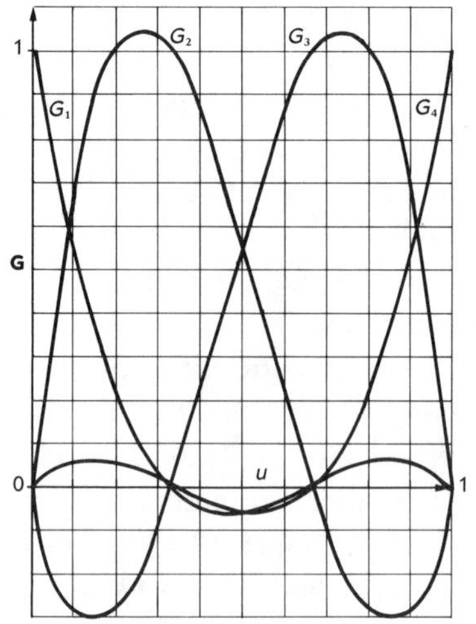

Fig. 13.13. Blending functions: **G**.

erties. These properties are determined primarily by the type of boundary conditions you use to define a curve (as we have stated) and by how you want to subsequently alter and control the shape of the curve.

13.5. Bezier Curves

Let us look briefly at another way to define a curve, with totally different blending functions. These functions were invented by Bezier, a Frenchman, and the curves bear his name: **Bezier curves**. Bezier created functions that have the following properties:

Given a set of $n + 1$ points, $\mathbf{p}_0, \mathbf{p}_1, \ldots, \mathbf{p}_n,$

1. The blending functions must interpolate the first and last points. (This means that the curve must start on $\mathbf{p}_0$ and end on $\mathbf{p}_n$.)

2. The unit tangent vector at $\mathbf{p}_0$ must be given by $(\mathbf{p}_1 - \mathbf{p}_0)/|\mathbf{p}_1 - \mathbf{p}_0|$, and the unit tangent vector at $\mathbf{p}_n$ must be given by $(\mathbf{p}_n - \mathbf{p}_{n-1})/|\mathbf{p}_n - \mathbf{p}_{n-1}|$.

3. The second derivative at $\mathbf{p}_0$ must be determined by $\mathbf{p}_0$, $\mathbf{p}_1$, and $\mathbf{p}_2$. In general, the rth derivative at an end point must be determined by its r neighboring vertices.

4. The blending functions must be symmetrical with respect to u and $1 - u$. This means that reversing the sequence of the curve-defining points does not change the shape of the curve.

The general equation for Bezier curves is

$$\mathbf{p}(u) = \sum_{i=0}^{n} \mathbf{p}_i B_{i,n}(u), \qquad u \in [0,1] \tag{13.91}$$

where the $\mathbf{p}_i$ are a set of control points defining a specific curve (there are $n + 1$ of them). The $B_{i,n}(u)$ are a set of Bezier blending functions, defined as follows:

$$B_{i,n}(u) = C(n,i)u^i(1 - u)^{n-i} \tag{13.92}$$

where $C_{n,i}$ is what mathematicians call the **binomial coefficient**.

$$C(n,i) = \frac{n!}{i!(n - i)!} \tag{13.93}$$

Observe the following conventions when computing $B_{i,n}(u)$: When i and $u = 0$, $u^i = 1$; also $0! = 1$.

Well, Bezier's blending functions are certainly different in form from those you studied earlier. Although they at first may look more complex, they are not at all once you have worked with them a short while. You will quickly discover two things about these functions: First, for $n + 1$ control points (that is, the $\mathbf{p}_i$) the $B_{i,n}(u)$ produces an nth degree polynomial, and second, the Bezier curve in general passes through only the first, $\mathbf{p}_0$, and last, $\mathbf{p}_n$, control points.

Let us look at an example of Bezier blending functions in action. Use four control points: $\mathbf{p}_0$, $\mathbf{p}_1$, $\mathbf{p}_2$, $\mathbf{p}_3$. Thus, $n + 1 = 4$, or $n = 3$. First, expand Eq. (13.91) to

$$\mathbf{p}(u) = \sum_{i=0}^{3} \mathbf{p}_i B_{i,3}(u) = \mathbf{p}_0 B_{0,3} + \mathbf{p}_1 B_{1,3} + \mathbf{p}_2 B_{2,3} + \mathbf{p}_3 B_{3,3} \tag{13.94}$$

Note that, for brevity, the functional notation, (u), is dropped.

There are four blending functions to compute:

$$\begin{aligned}
B_{0,3} &= \frac{3!}{0!(3)!} u^0(1 - u)^3 = (1 - u)^3 \\
B_{1,3} &= \frac{3!}{1!(2)!} u^1(1 - u)^2 = 3u(1 - u)^2 \\
B_{2,3} &= \frac{3!}{2!(1)!} u^2(1 - u) = 3u^2(1 - u) \\
B_{3,3} &= \frac{3!}{3!(0)!} u^3(1 - u)^0 = u^3
\end{aligned} \tag{13.95}$$

The blending functions look much less formidable once you have done the simple arithmetic called for. Substitute these functions into Eq. (13.94) to obtain

$$\mathbf{p}(u) = (1 - u)^3\mathbf{p}_0 + 3u(1 - u)^2\mathbf{p}_1 + 3u^2(1 - u)\mathbf{p}_2 + u^3\mathbf{p}_3 \quad (13.96)$$

In Fig. 13.14 you see a Bezier curve that has control points with the following coordinates:

$$\begin{aligned} \mathbf{p}_0 &= [2 \;\; 3 \;\; 0] \\ \mathbf{p}_1 &= [3 \;\; 6 \;\; 0] \\ \mathbf{p}_2 &= [7 \;\; 7 \;\; 0] \\ \mathbf{p}_3 &= [9 \;\; 4 \;\; 0] \end{aligned} \quad (13.97)$$

Note that the curve does not pass through $\mathbf{p}_1$ and $\mathbf{p}_2$ and that the curve is tangent to $\mathbf{p}_1 - \mathbf{p}_0$ at $\mathbf{p}_0$ and to $\mathbf{p}_3 - \mathbf{p}_2$ at $\mathbf{p}_2$.

The dashed line forms the **convex hull.** Recall that this is the polygonal shape that would be formed if you stretch a rubber band around the control points. It is always convex. And, for Bezier curves, it turns out that the curve always lies within the convex hull formed by the control points.

What happens if you "move" one of the points? Move $\mathbf{p}_3$ to [9 10 0]. Figure 13.15 shows the results. The new curve (shown as a solid line) is tangent to $\mathbf{p}_1 - \mathbf{p}_0$ and $\mathbf{p}_3 - \mathbf{p}_2$, as expected. Also note that the curve is within the convex hull, considerably changed with the move of $\mathbf{p}_3$.

EXERCISES

1. Compute the blending functions for a Bezier curve defined by three control points.

2. Compute the blending functions for a Bezier curve defined by five control points.

3. Compute the blending functions for a Bezier curve defined by six control points.

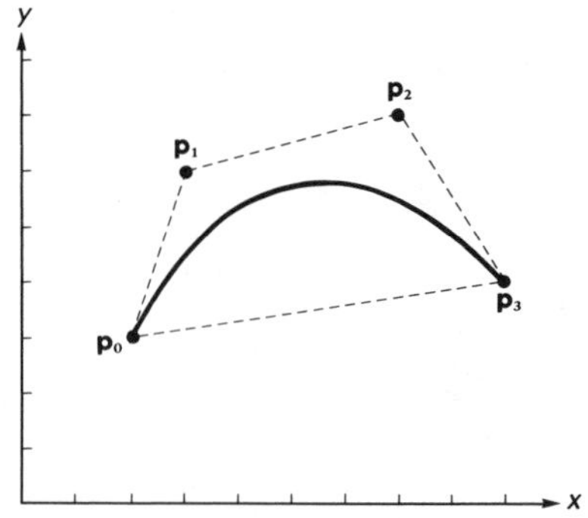

Fig. 13.14. A Bezier curve defined by four points.

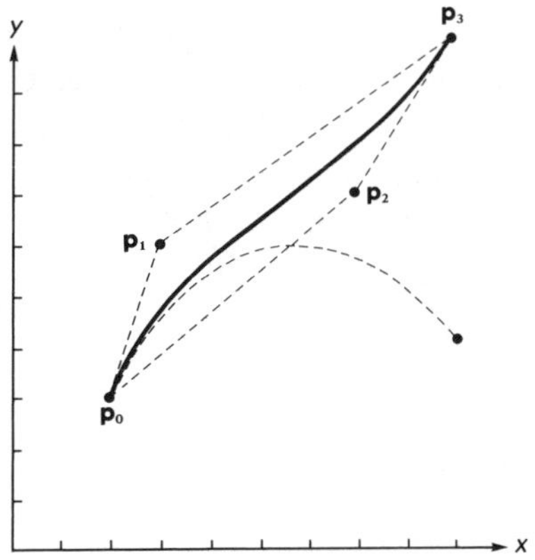

Fig. 13.15. Modifying a Bezier curve.

4. Design your own blending functions; for example, try quintic polynomials, exponentials, or trigonometric functions. Decide whether you want to define a curve using these functions with control points only or mix in some tangent vector or other geometric data (curvature, and so on).

13.6. Continuity and Composite Curves

Usually a single curve is not versatile enough to model a complex shape. For complex shapes, you must join several curves together end to end. In most cases, but certainly not all, a smooth transition from one curve to the next is desirable. Do this by making the tangent vectors of adjoining curves collinear. However, it is not necessary that their magnitudes are equal, just their direction.

Figure 13.16 shows two curves, $\mathbf{p}(u)$ and $\mathbf{q}(u)$, with tangent conti-

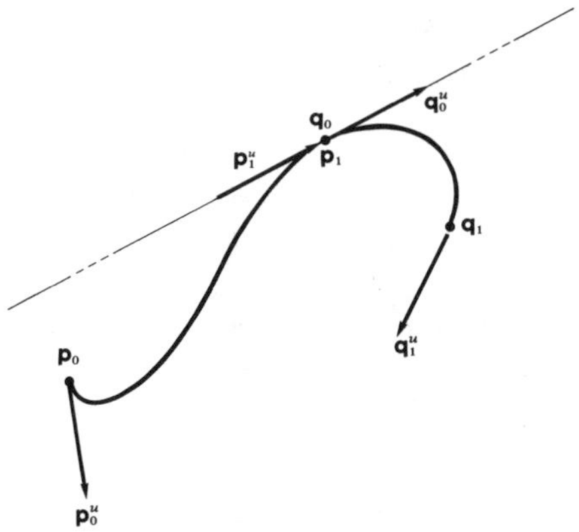

Fig. 13.16. Two curves joined with tangent continuity.

nuity. Naturally this continuity imposes certain mathematical constraints on the geometric coefficients of the respective tangents. First, since $\mathbf{p}_1$ and $\mathbf{q}_0$ must coincide, $\mathbf{p}_1 = \mathbf{q}_0$. Second, $\mathbf{p}_1^u$ and $\mathbf{q}_0^u$ must be in the same direction, although their magnitudes may differ. This means that $\mathbf{q}_0^u = k\mathbf{p}_1^u$. Now you can write the geometric coefficients of $\mathbf{q}(u)$ in terms of these constraints:

$$\mathbf{B}_q = [\mathbf{p}_1 \ \ \mathbf{q}_1 \ \ k\mathbf{p}_1^u \ \ \mathbf{q}_1^u]^T \tag{13.98}$$

A composite curve of this type has a total of 19 degrees of freedom. Compare this with the 24 degrees of freedom of two disjoint curves. See Box 13.3.

There are various kinds of continuity, denoted symbolically by a capital "C" with a numerical superscript. The simplest kind of continuity exists between two curves joined without regard for tangent continuity. Thus, at the joint there may be a kink, or abrupt and discontinuous slope. This kind of continuity is called C^0 continuity (pronounced "cee zero"). When curves are joined with tangent continuity, then they are said to have C^1

Box 13.3. Continuity

The notation used in Fig. 13.6 and Eq. (13.98) is inadequate if more than two or three curves must be used to define a complex curve. A more practical system is suggested here. If n piecewise parametric cubic curves are joined to form a composite curve of C^1 continuity, proceed as follows:

1. Label the points consecutively, $\mathbf{p}_1, \mathbf{p}_2, \ldots, \mathbf{p}_i, \ldots, \mathbf{p}_{n-1}, \mathbf{p}_n$.
2. Define unit tangent vectors, $\mathbf{t}_1, \mathbf{t}_2, \ldots, \mathbf{t}_i, \ldots, \mathbf{t}_{n-1}, \mathbf{t}_n$.
3. Define tangent vector magnitudes, $m_{1,0}, m_{1,1}, \ldots, m_{i,0}, m_{i,1}, \ldots, m_{n,0}, m_{n,1}$.

Using this notation, the geometric coefficients for curve i are $[\mathbf{p}_i \ \ \mathbf{p}_{i-1} \ \ m_{i,0}\mathbf{t}_i \ \ m_{i,1}\mathbf{t}_{i+1}]$.

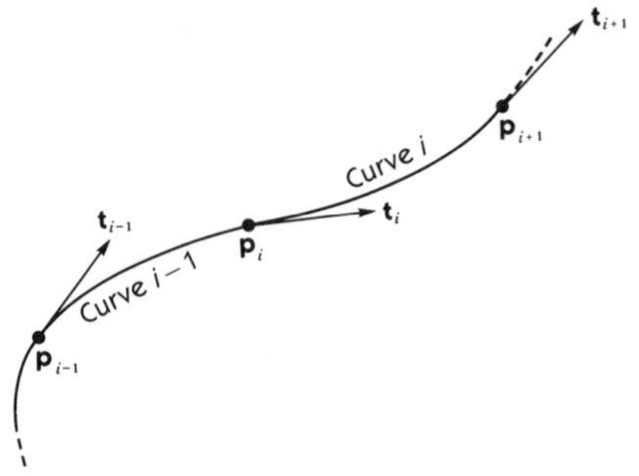

continuity ("cee one"). C^1 continuity presupposes C^0 continuity. The next level of continuity is C^2, which means that the second parametric derivation is continuous at the joint. Of course this can continue on to even higher degrees of continuity, but C^1 continuity is the most useful, with C^2 continuity used only occasionally. This technique of continuity control allows you to create very complex curves, indeed, and closed curves are easy and interesting to model in this way.

EXERCISES

1. Given two disjoint (unconnected) curves, $\mathbf{p}(u)$ and $\mathbf{q}(u)$, join $\mathbf{p}_1$ to $\mathbf{q}_0$ with a curve $\mathbf{r}(u)$ such that there is C^1 continuity across the two joints. Write the geometric coefficients, $\mathbf{B}_r$, in terms of the coefficients of $\mathbf{p}(u)$ and $\mathbf{q}(u)$.

2. How many degrees of freedom (unique coefficients) are required to define the system of three curves created in Exercise 1?

3. Use the results of Exercise 1 to construct a closed composite curve with C^1 continuity by joining $\mathbf{q}_1$ to $\mathbf{p}_0$ with a curve $\mathbf{s}(u)$. Write the geometric coefficients, $\mathbf{B}_s$, in terms of the coefficients of $\mathbf{p}(u)$ and $\mathbf{q}(u)$.

4. How many degrees of freedom does the closed composite curve of Exercise 3 have?

13.7. Displaying a Curve

When you decide to display a curve, you are faced with a rather interesting sequence of problems. First, you must project the curve onto the picture plane; next, you must clip the projected curve, as necessary, within the window; finally, you must compute points along the curve from which to construct a computer graphics image. Let us explore each of these problems in turn.

You will simplify matters considerably if you choose as the picture plane one of the principal planes, say the x,y plane. Look at the curve in Fig. 13.17. Here a pc curve is defined by the four points $\mathbf{p}_1$, $\mathbf{p}_2$, $\mathbf{p}_3$, and $\mathbf{p}_4$. They project onto the x,y plane as $\mathbf{p}_1^*$, $\mathbf{p}_2^*$, $\mathbf{p}_3^*$, and $\mathbf{p}_4^*$, and now define a two-dimensional curve. For an orthographic projection, merely set equal to zero the z component of each of the four original points. Thus,

$$\begin{aligned} \mathbf{p}_1^* &= [x_1 \ y_1 \ 0] \\ \mathbf{p}_2^* &= [x_2 \ y_2 \ 0] \\ \mathbf{p}_3^* &= [x_3 \ y_3 \ 0] \\ \mathbf{p}_4^* &= [x_4 \ y_4 \ 0] \end{aligned} \tag{13.99}$$

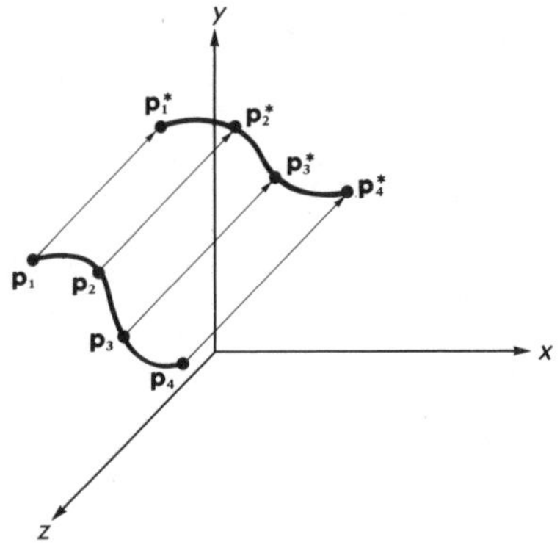

Fig. 13.17. Projecting a curve.

If the original curve is defined by its end points and tangent vectors, then for an orthographic projection onto the x,y plane it is easy to show that

$$\begin{aligned} \mathbf{p}_0^* &= [x_0 \; y_0 \; 0] \\ \mathbf{p}_0^{u*} &= [x_0^u \; y_0^u \; 0] \\ \mathbf{p}_1^* &= [x_1 \; y_1 \; 0] \\ \mathbf{p}_1^{u*} &= [x_1^u \; y_1^u \; 0] \end{aligned} \tag{13.100}$$

Once you have projected the curve and can write the equations of its projected image, then test it to see if it is contained within the window. This means to search for valid intersections. Consider the curve and window shown in Fig. 13.18. Assume that the curve is a parametric curve, then compute its intersection with each of four lines: $x = Wx_L$, $x = Wx_R$, $y = Wy_B$, and $y = Wy_T$. These yield the following four cubic equations:

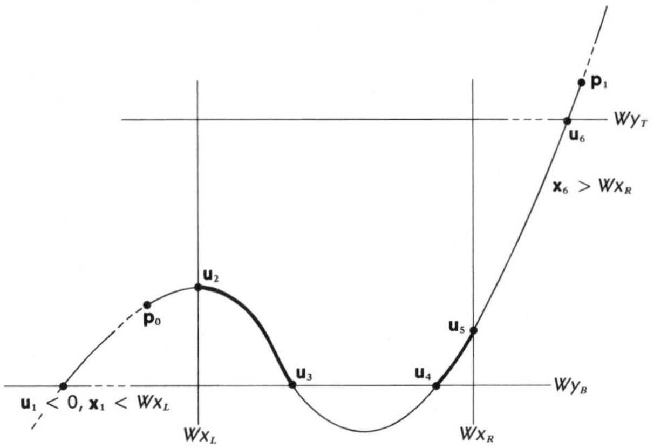

Fig. 13.18. Clipping a curve.

$$
\begin{aligned}
a_x u^3 + b_x u^2 + c_x u + d_x &= Wx_L \\
a_x u^3 + b_x u^2 + c_x u + d_x &= Wx_R \\
a_y u^3 + b_y u^2 + c_y u + d_y &= Wy_B \\
a_y u^3 + b_y u^2 + c_y u + d_y &= W_{yT}
\end{aligned}
\tag{13.101}
$$

The solutions to these equations yield six possible intersections for the example in Fig. 13.18. Not all of them are valid. All valid intersections must be in the unit interval of the curve, $u \in [0, 1]$, and within the appropriate window intervals.

The simplest way to display a curve is as a series of connected line segments. (This has certain disadvantages that will become apparent as we proceed and that can be overcome.) To do this, compute a sequence of points along the curve. Connect these points, in turn, with line segments, forming an approximation of the curve that is displayed (Fig. 13.19). The more points, the closer together they are, and the better the approximation. There is a limit to this subdivision where you can no longer discern any improvement in the displayed image. This is a function of screen size and resolution and the degree of curvature of the curve. (These are subjects for more advanced studies.)

If you divide the curve into equal increments, then where the curve is relatively flat you will usually have too many points, or where it is more curved you will have too few points. One way to avoid this is by selecting points so that there is an equal change in slope between all pairs of points. The angle θ in Fig. 13.20 characterizes the change in slope between points on the curve. The smaller the value we choose for θ, the more points are generated and the better the approximation to the true shape of the curve. (Here, again, the techniques for doing this are beyond the scope of this elementary text. However, if you wish to give it a try, here is a hint: Create an auxiliary parametric curve that is a function of slope and the original parametric variable; then at selected equal increments of slope compute the corresponding values of the parametric variable, u. These values of u

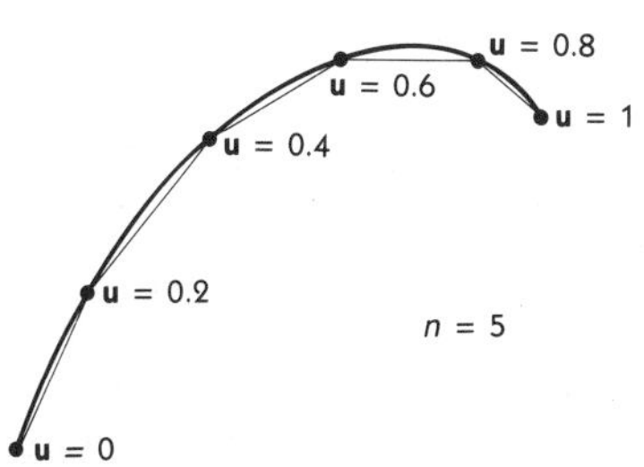

Fig. 13.19. Points on a curve: Equal parametric interval.

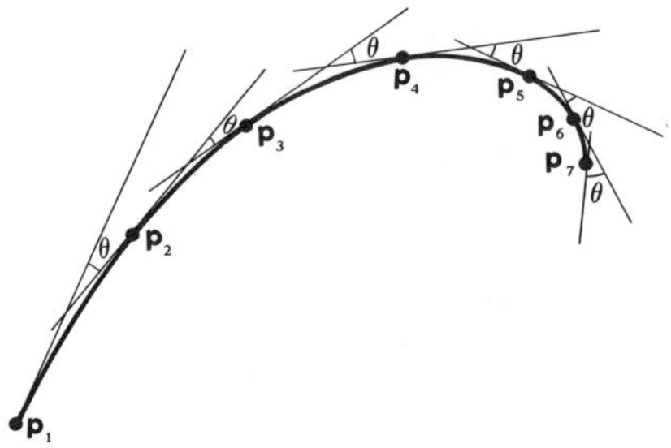

Fig. 13.20. Points on a curve: Via equal slope change criteria.

correspond directly to those on the original curve. You can take it from there.)

By one technique or another, you must eventually end up with a set of u values, for each of which you must compute corresponding x,y coordinates. The problem of computing a point on a curve (or surface, for that matter) is reduced to calculating a polynomial.

One simple, straightforward way to calculate polynomials is Horner's rule. Let us apply this to the cubic polynomial $x = a_x u^3 + b_x u^2 + c_x u + d_x$. Rewrite this equation so that only three multiplications and three additions are required to compute the solution for a given value of u:

$$x = [(a_x u + b_x)u + c]u + d \tag{13.102}$$

Also consider the general polynomial of degree n:

$$x = a_n u^n + a_{n-1}u^{n-1} + a_{n-2}u^{n-2} + \ldots + a_1 u + a_0 \tag{13.103}$$

An efficient procedure to compute x for various values of u is as follows: Define $a_0, a_1, \ldots, a_n$ as the input coefficients, along with a value for the independent variable u. The output variable is, of course, x. Generalize Horner's rule so that

	$x(u) =$
For $n = 1$	$a_1 u + a_0$
For $n = 2$	$(a_2 u + a_1)u + a_0$
For $n = 3$	$[(a_3 u + a_2)u + a_1]u + a_0$
For $n = 4$	$\{[(a_4 u + a_3)u + a_2]u + a_1\}u + a_0$

and so on.

For any n, develop a straight-line program of $2n$ steps to evaluate a general nth-degree polynomial. Clearly, n multiplications and n additions are necessary. Combining Horner's rule with a straight-line program yields, for $n = 1$, $n = 2$, and $n = 3$,

For $n = 1$

$$t \leftarrow a_1 u$$
$$x \leftarrow t + a_0$$

For $n = 2$

$$t \leftarrow a_2 u$$
$$t \leftarrow t + a_1$$
$$t \leftarrow tu$$
$$x \leftarrow t + a_0$$

For $n = 3$

$$t \leftarrow a_3 u$$
$$t \leftarrow t + a_2$$
$$t \leftarrow tu$$
$$t \leftarrow t + a_1$$
$$t \leftarrow tu$$
$$x \leftarrow t + a_0$$

14. Surfaces

JUST AS WITH curves, you probably have an intuitive sense of what a surface is. A surface is perhaps a little less abstract a concept than a curve, because you can actually touch the "surfaces" of the ordinary objects that fill our environment. It is light reflected off an object's surfaces that makes it visible. If you want to create a convincing computer graphics display of an object, then you must thoroughly understand the mathematics of surfaces.

Again, use parametric functions to describe a surface mathematically. These functions are somewhat different from those defining curves. Two parametric variables are required for surfaces, so the equations' general form looks like

$$x = x(u,w), \qquad y = y(u,w), \qquad z = z(u,w) \tag{14.1}$$

Both parametric variables are usually limited to the unit interval $u,w \in [0,1]$. This defines the simplest element of a surface, called a **patch**. Model very complex surfaces by joining together several patches.

You may want to review Section 12.5 before proceeding.

14.1. Planes

The simplest parametric surface patch is a plane. The following parametric equations define a plane patch in the x,y plane:

$$\begin{aligned} x &= (c - a)u + a \\ y &= (d - b)w + b \qquad u,w \in [0,1] \\ z &= 0 \end{aligned} \tag{14.2}$$

where u and w are the parametric variables and a, b, c, and d are constant coefficients. Figure 14.1 illustrates this plane. Also, review Eq. (12.55).

The plane patch in the figure has some rather easy-to-identify characteristics. Its four corner points correspond to vectors whose components are defined by

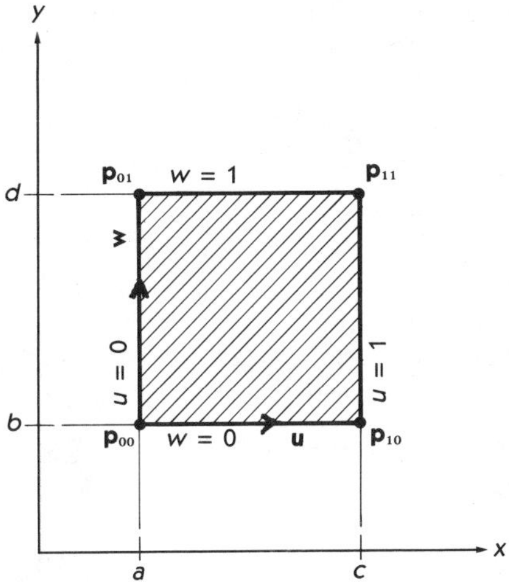

Fig. 14.1. A bounded plane.

$$\begin{aligned} u = 0, w = 0, &\quad \mathbf{p}_{00} = [a \ \ b \ \ 0] \\ u = 0, w = 1, &\quad \mathbf{p}_{01} = [a \ \ d \ \ 0] \\ u = 1, w = 0, &\quad \mathbf{p}_{10} = [c \ \ b \ \ 0] \\ u = 1, w = 1, &\quad \mathbf{p}_{11} = [c \ \ d \ \ 0] \end{aligned} \tag{14.3}$$

The boundaries are, of course, straight lines derived when the following conditions are imposed on Eqs. (14.2):

$$\begin{aligned} u = 0, &\quad x = a, \quad y = (d - b)w + b, \quad z = 0 \\ u = 1, &\quad x = c, \quad y = (d - b)w + b, \quad z = 0 \\ w = 0, &\quad x = (c - a)u + a, \quad y = b, \quad z = 0 \\ w = 1, &\quad x = (c - a)u + a, \quad y = d, \quad z = 0 \end{aligned} \tag{14.4}$$

The expressions in Eqs. (14.2) produce a very limited variety of plane patches. The most obvious limitation is that they model only planes parallel to one of the three principal planes. The boundaries are always straight lines parallel to the coordinate axes, and the boundary lines always form rectangles. You will learn how to overcome these limitations in Section 14.3, where you will find more general parametric equations for surfaces. For now, develop a facility with Eqs. (14.2) to prepare yourself for what follows. Practice thinking in terms of two parametric variables and finding points and lines on these plane patches. The following exercises will help.

EXERCISES

1. Find the parametric equations for a plane patch whose four corner points are $\mathbf{p}_{00} = [4 \ \ 1 \ \ 3]$, $\mathbf{p}_{01} = [4 \ \ 1 \ \ 7]$, $\mathbf{p}_{10} = [4 \ \ 5 \ \ 3]$, $\mathbf{p}_{11} = [4 \ \ 5 \ \ 7]$.

2. Find the four corner points of the plane patch given by $x = u - 2$, $y = 5$, $z = 3w - 4$.

3. Find the parametric equations of the four boundary lines of the plane patch given in Exercise 2.

14.2. Cylinders

A cylindrical surface is a surface generated by a straight line as it moves parallel to itself along a curve. Such a surface is easy to define with parametric functions and vector equations. Refer to Fig. 14.2. The following equation produces points on a cylindrical surface:

$$\mathbf{p}(u,w) = \mathbf{p}(u) + w\mathbf{r}, \qquad u,w \in [0,1] \tag{14.5}$$

Just how does this equation generate a cylindrical surface? First, $\mathbf{p}(u)$ generates a curve. This can be any type of curve—a plane curve or a space curve. The function could be a parametric cubic or Bezier, . . . or, you name it. Next, adding the term $w\mathbf{r}$ gives points along $\mathbf{r}$ from $w = 0$ through $w = 1$ as $\mathbf{r}$ sweeps along $\mathbf{p}(u)$ for values of u from $u = 0$ through $u = 1$.

The four boundary points of this surface are:

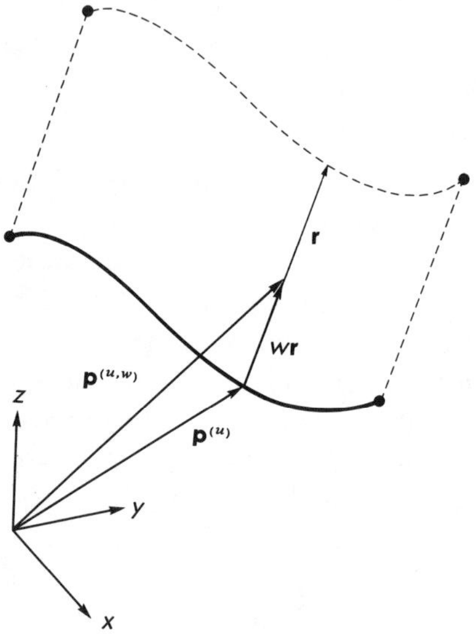

Fig. 14.2. A cylindrical surface.

$$\begin{aligned} &u = 0, \quad w = 0, \qquad \mathbf{p}_{00} = \mathbf{p}(0) \\ &u = 0, \quad w = 1, \qquad \mathbf{p}_{01} = \mathbf{p}(0) + \mathbf{r} \\ &u = 1, \quad w = 0, \qquad \mathbf{p}_{10} = \mathbf{p}(1) \\ &u = 1, \quad w = 1, \qquad \mathbf{p}_{11} = \mathbf{p}(1) + \mathbf{r} \end{aligned} \tag{14.6}$$

The four boundary curves are

$$\begin{aligned} &u = 0, \qquad \mathbf{p}(0) + w\mathbf{r} \\ &u = 1, \qquad \mathbf{p}(1) + w\mathbf{r} \\ &w = 0, \qquad \mathbf{p}(u) \\ &w = 1, \qquad \mathbf{p}(u) + r \end{aligned} \tag{14.7}$$

14.3. General Bicubic Surface

A more general kind of surface, general in the sense that it may be doubly curved with peaks and valleys, is the **bicubic surface.** It is given by the equation

$$\mathbf{p}(u,w) = \sum_{i=0}^{3} \sum_{j=0}^{3} \mathbf{a}_{ij} u^i w^j, \qquad u,w \in [0,1] \tag{14.8}$$

The $\mathbf{a}_{ij}$ vectors are the algebraic coefficients. Since both parametric variables, u and w, appear as cubic terms, the source of the name bicubic is obvious. There are sixteen $\mathbf{a}_{ij}$ vectors, each with three components. This means that you must specify 48 degrees of freedom, or coefficients, to define a unique surface. Use double subscripts because there are two parametric variables. Since the surface is bounded, it is sometimes called a surface patch, or just a patch.

Expand Eq. (14.8) to see just what you have to work with. Arrange the terms in descending order this time.

$$\begin{aligned} \mathbf{p}(u,w) = {} & \mathbf{a}_{33}u^3w^3 + \mathbf{a}_{32}u^3w^2 + \mathbf{a}_{31}u^3w + \mathbf{a}_{30}u^3 \\ & + \mathbf{a}_{23}u^2w^3 + \mathbf{a}_{22}u^2w^2 + \mathbf{a}_{21}u^2w + \mathbf{a}_{20}u^2 \\ & + \mathbf{a}_{13}uw^3 + \mathbf{a}_{12}uw^2 + \mathbf{a}_{11}uw + \mathbf{a}_{10}w \\ & + \mathbf{a}_{03}w^3 + \mathbf{a}_{02}w^2 + \mathbf{a}_{01}w + \mathbf{a}_{00} \end{aligned} \tag{14.9}$$

This 16-term polynomial in u and w defines the set of all points lying on the surface. It is the algebraic form of the bicubic patch. Using matrix notation, Eq. (14.9) becomes

$$\mathbf{p}(u,w) = \mathbf{UAW}^T \tag{14.10}$$

where $\mathbf{U} = [u^3\ u^2\ u\ 1]$, $\mathbf{W} = [w^3\ w^2\ w\ 1]$, and

$$\mathbf{A} = \begin{bmatrix} \mathbf{a}_{33} & \mathbf{a}_{32} & \mathbf{a}_{31} & \mathbf{a}_{30} \\ \mathbf{a}_{23} & \mathbf{a}_{22} & \mathbf{a}_{21} & \mathbf{a}_{20} \\ \mathbf{a}_{13} & \mathbf{a}_{12} & \mathbf{a}_{11} & \mathbf{a}_{10} \\ \mathbf{a}_{03} & \mathbf{a}_{02} & \mathbf{a}_{01} & \mathbf{a}_{00} \end{bmatrix} \tag{14.11}$$

Note that the subscripts of the vector elements in the **A** matrix correspond to those in Eq. (14.9). They have no direct relationship to the normal indexing convention for matrices. Since the **a** elements are three-component vectors, the **A** matrix is a $4 \times 4 \times 3$ array.

As with curves, the algebraic coefficients of a patch determine its shape and position in space. However, patches of the same size and shape have a different set of coefficients if they occupy different positions in space. Change any one of the 48 coefficients, and a completely different patch results.

You generate a point on the patch each time you insert a specific pair of u,w values into Eq. (14.10). And, although the u,w values are restricted by $u,w \in [0,1]$, the range of the dependent variables x, y, and z is unrestricted because the range of the algebraic coefficients is unrestricted.

Observe that a bicubic patch is bounded by four curves (see Fig. 14.3); each is a parametric cubic curve. It is a simple exercise to demonstrate this fact. For example, substitute $w = 0$ into Eq. (14.9); all terms containing w vanish, and the equation becomes:

$$\mathbf{p}(u) = \mathbf{a}_{30}u^3 + \mathbf{a}_{20}u^2 + \mathbf{a}_{10}u + \mathbf{a}_{00} \tag{14.12}$$

This is an expression for a parametric cubic curve. Of course, you can do the same for the boundary curves on $u = 0$, $u = 1$, and $w = 1$. In fact, by setting either u or w equal to some constant, you produce a curve on the surface.

As for curves, algebraic coefficients are not the most convenient way to define and control the shape of a patch, and they do not contribute much to your understanding of surface behavior. Therefore, we develop a geometric form, defining a patch in terms of certain boundary conditions that, in turn, are related to the algebraic coefficients. You need just as many geometric coefficients as algebraic coefficients, so you need 16 vectors describing boundary conditions. It is a good idea to determine them at the patch corner points. Four vectors at each corner give you the 16 you need.

Most of the geometric boundary condition vectors are obvious; refer

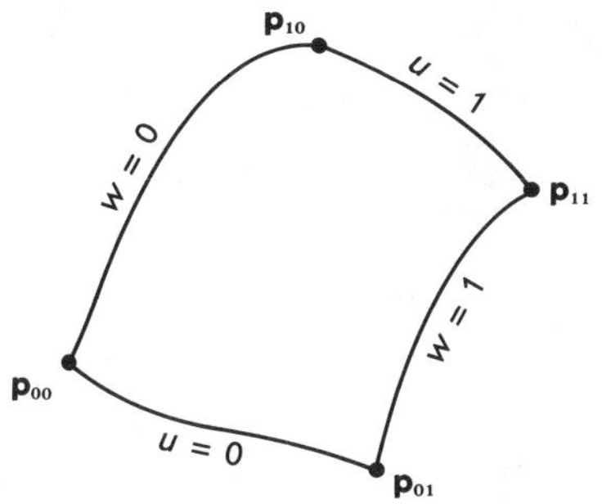

Fig. 14.3. A bicubic patch.

to Fig. 14.4. The four corner points and the eight tangent vectors to the four boundary curves provide 12 of the required 16 vectors. You need four more. You will use what are called the **twist vectors** (one at each corner, not shown in the figure). The twist vectors tell you how the tangent vectors across a patch boundary change along that boundary. For example, the twist vectors at $\mathbf{p}_{00}$ and $\mathbf{p}_{01}$ control the way $\mathbf{p}^u_{0w}$ changes along the boundary curve $u = 0$ from $\mathbf{p}^u_{00}$ to $\mathbf{p}^u_{01}$. Steven Coons was the first to explore and develop this approach.

Denote the twist vectors symbolically as $\mathbf{p}^{uw}_{00}$, $\mathbf{p}^{uw}_{01}$, $\mathbf{p}^{uw}_{10}$, and $\mathbf{p}^{uw}_{11}$. Compute them mathematically as

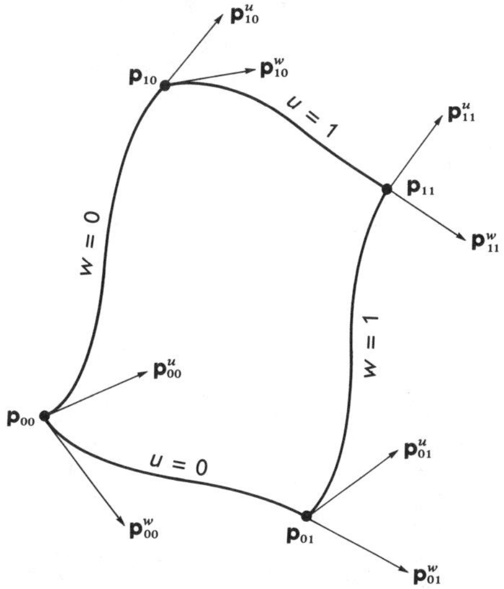

Fig. 14.4. Boundary conditions defining a bicubic patch.

$$\begin{aligned}
\mathbf{p}_{00}^{uw} &= \frac{\partial^2 \mathbf{p}(u,w)}{\partial u\,\partial w} && \text{at } u = 0, \quad w = 0 \\
\mathbf{p}_{01}^{uw} &= \frac{\partial^2 \mathbf{p}(u,w)}{\partial u\,\partial w} && \text{at } u = 0, \quad w = 1 \\
\mathbf{p}_{10}^{uw} &= \frac{\partial^2 \mathbf{p}(u,w)}{\partial u\,\partial w} && \text{at } u = 1, \quad w = 0 \\
\mathbf{p}_{11}^{uw} &= \frac{\partial^2 \mathbf{p}(u,w)}{\partial u\,\partial w} && \text{at } u = 1, \quad w = 1
\end{aligned} \tag{14.13}$$

Here is a new operation, called **partial differentiation**. It is not very different from the ordinary differentiation you already studied, except take the derivative of a function with two independent variables, $\mathbf{p}(u,w)$, and use the symbol ∂ instead of d to indicate that it is partial differentiation. The rule is simply to treat one of the independent variables as a constant while differentiating with respect to the other. Let us see how this works by computing $\mathbf{p}_{01}^{uw}$.

First, compute $\partial\mathbf{p}(u,w)/\partial w$. [Remember: Treat u in Eq. (14.9) as a constant.]

$$\begin{aligned}
\frac{\partial \mathbf{p}(u,w)}{\partial w} = {} & 3\mathbf{a}_{33}u^3w^2 + 2\mathbf{a}_{32}u^3w + \mathbf{a}_{31}u^3 \\
& + 3\mathbf{a}_{23}u^2w^2 + 2\mathbf{a}_{22}u^2w + \mathbf{a}_{21}u^2 \\
& + 3\mathbf{a}_{13}uw^2 + 2\mathbf{a}_{12}uw + \mathbf{a}_{11}u \\
& + 3\mathbf{a}_{03}w^2 + 2\mathbf{a}_{02}w + \mathbf{a}_{01}
\end{aligned} \tag{14.14a}$$

Next compute $\partial(\partial\mathbf{p}(u,w)/\partial w)/\partial u$, holding w constant in Eq. (14.4b):

$$\begin{aligned}
\left(\frac{\partial}{\partial u}\right)\left(\frac{\partial \mathbf{p}(u,w)}{\partial w}\right) &= \frac{\partial^2 \mathbf{p}(u,w)}{\partial u\,\partial w} \\
&= 9\mathbf{a}_{33}u^2w^2 + 6\mathbf{a}_{32}u^2w + 3\mathbf{a}_{31}u^2 \\
&\quad + 6\mathbf{a}_{23}uw^2 + 4\mathbf{a}_{22}uw + 2\mathbf{a}_{21}u \\
&\quad + 3\mathbf{a}_{13}w^2 + 2\mathbf{a}_{12}w + \mathbf{a}_{11}
\end{aligned} \tag{14.14b}$$

Finally, to compute $\mathbf{p}_{01}^{uw}$, the twist vector at the point where $u = 0$ and $w = 1$, substitute these values of u and w into Eq. (14.14b) to obtain

$$\mathbf{p}_{01}^{uw} = 3\mathbf{a}_{13} + 2\mathbf{a}_{12} + \mathbf{a}_{11} \tag{14.15}$$

Use the same process to compute the other twist vectors.

Now assemble all 16 vectors into a matrix. The usual order is

$$\mathbf{B} = \begin{bmatrix} \mathbf{p}_{00} & \mathbf{p}_{01} & \mathbf{p}_{00}^{w} & \mathbf{p}_{01}^{w} \\ \mathbf{p}_{10} & \mathbf{p}_{11} & \mathbf{p}_{10}^{w} & \mathbf{p}_{11}^{w} \\ \mathbf{p}_{00}^{u} & \mathbf{p}_{01}^{u} & \mathbf{p}_{00}^{uw} & \mathbf{p}_{01}^{w} \\ \mathbf{p}_{10}^{u} & \mathbf{p}_{11}^{u} & \mathbf{p}_{10}^{uw} & \mathbf{p}_{11}^{uw} \end{bmatrix} \tag{14.16}$$

There are many things worth noting in this element order. The four corner points are in the upper left quadrant of the matrix. The four twist vectors are in the lower right quadrant, while the u and w tangent vectors are in the lower left and the upper right quadrants, respectively.

There is even more information in this order. The elements in the first row are the geometric coefficients of the boundary curve along $u = 0$. The elements in the second row are the geometric coefficients of the boundary curve along $u = 1$. The first and second columns contain, in order, the geometric coefficients for the boundary curves along $w = 0$ and $w = 1$, respectively. Rows 3 and 4 and columns 3 and 4 define auxilliary curves, which describe how the cross-boundary tangent vectors vary along the boundaries.

The matrix equation for a bicubic patch in terms of the geometric coefficients is

$$\mathbf{p}(u,w) = \mathbf{UMBM}^T\mathbf{W}^T, \qquad u,w \in [0,1] \tag{14.17}$$

where $\mathbf{M}$ is the same as that given in Eq. (13.91).

The relationship between the algebraic and geometric coefficients is

$$\mathbf{A} = \mathbf{MBM}^T \tag{14.18}$$

and

$$\mathbf{B} = \mathbf{M}^{-1}\mathbf{AM}^{T-1} \tag{14.19}$$

As you should have guessed by now, there are many other ways to define a general surface. For example, you could use 16 points to define a bicubic surface, or you could use Bezier functions and control points. You should now be able to derive some of these ways of defining a surface on your own. Others require special techniques you will learn in more advanced computer graphics and geometric modeling courses. Also, see Box 14.1.

EXERCISES

1. Find the corner points $\mathbf{p}_{00}$, $\mathbf{p}_{01}$, $\mathbf{p}_{10}$, and $\mathbf{p}_{11}$ in terms of the algebraic coefficients.

2. Find each of the eight patch tangent vectors in terms of the algebraic coefficients.

Box 14.1. Surface Normal

At any point on a bicubic patch you can compute a vector normal (perpendicular) to the patch. To do this, simply compute the vector product of the tangent vectors $\mathbf{p}^u$ and $\mathbf{p}^w$ at the point:

$$\mathbf{n} = \mathbf{p}^u \times \mathbf{p}^w$$

The order in which you take the vector product determines the direction of $\mathbf{n}$. A consistent direction is required. For example, if you want the normal to point outward from the surface of a solid model:

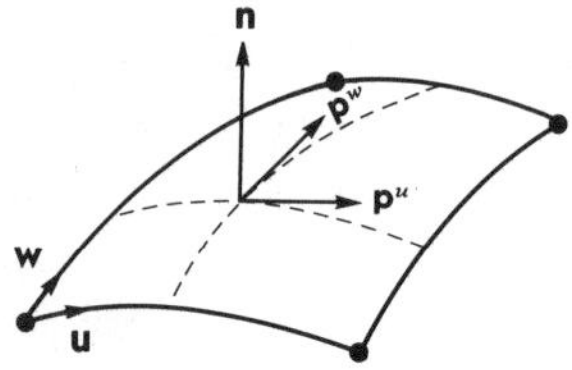

Surface normals are important in such areas of computer graphics and geometric modeling as computing silhouette curves, hidden surfaces, light reflectance, and shading effects.

14.4. Bezier Surface

A Bezier surface is defined by a grid of control points, like the Bezier curve. The control points define a **characteristic polyhedron,** analogous to the characteristic polygon of the Bezier curve. Points on a Bezier surface are given by a simple extension of the general equation for points on a Bezier curve, Eq. (13.100):

$$\mathbf{p}(u,w) = \sum_{i=0}^{m} \sum_{j=0}^{n} \mathbf{p}_{ij} B_{i,m}(u) B_{j,n}(w), \qquad u,w \in [0,1] \tag{14.20}$$

where the $\mathbf{p}_{ij}$ are vertices of the characteristic polyhedron that form an $(m + 1) \times (n + 1)$ rectangular array of points, and $B_{i,m}(u)$ and $B_{j,n}(w)$ are defined the same way as for curves [Eqs. (13.101) and (13.102)]. Note that m and n define the degrees of the blending functions, and they need not be equal. The advantage of this is that you can simplify the formulation somewhat if the surface behavior itself is simpler to describe in one of the parametric directions than in the other.

Now expand Eq. (13.20) for a 4×4 array of points. This will produce a bicubic surface patch. The matrix equation is

$$\mathbf{p}(u,w) = [(1-u)^3 \quad 3u(1-u)^2 \quad 3u^2(1-u) \quad u^3] \times \mathbf{P} \begin{bmatrix} (1-w)^3 \\ 3w(1-w)^2 \\ 3w^2(1-w) \\ w^3 \end{bmatrix} \tag{14.21}$$

where

$$\mathbf{P} = \begin{bmatrix} \mathbf{p}_{11} & \mathbf{p}_{12} & \mathbf{p}_{13} & \mathbf{p}_{14} \\ \mathbf{p}_{21} & \mathbf{p}_{22} & \mathbf{p}_{23} & \mathbf{p}_{24} \\ \mathbf{p}_{31} & \mathbf{p}_{32} & \mathbf{p}_{33} & \mathbf{p}_{34} \\ \mathbf{p}_{41} & \mathbf{p}_{42} & \mathbf{p}_{43} & \mathbf{p}_{44} \end{bmatrix} \tag{14.22}$$

The matrix **P** contains the position vectors for points that define the characteristic polyhedron. See Fig. 14.5.

Only the four corner points, $\mathbf{p}_{11}$, $\mathbf{p}_{41}$, $\mathbf{p}_{14}$, and $\mathbf{p}_{44}$, actually lie on the patch. The points $\mathbf{p}_{21}$, $\mathbf{p}_{31}$, $\mathbf{p}_{12}$, $\mathbf{p}_{13}$, $\mathbf{p}_{42}$, $\mathbf{p}_{43}$, $\mathbf{p}_{24}$, and $\mathbf{p}_{34}$ control the boundary curves. The remaining four points, $\mathbf{p}_{22}$, $\mathbf{p}_{32}$, $\mathbf{p}_{23}$, $\mathbf{p}_{33}$, control the patch interior.

14.5. Displaying a Surface

Many of the problems of displaying a surface are the same as or similar to those for a curve. If you want a "transparent" wireframe image of a surface, then merely project, clip, and plot a set of representative curves lying on the surface. At the very minimum, this might be the four bounding curves at $u = 0$, $u = 1$, $w = 0$, and $w = 1$. As you can see in Fig. 14.6a, this is barely adequate. If you include several intermediate curves, as in Fig. 14.6b, you get a more meaningful image of interior surface behavior.

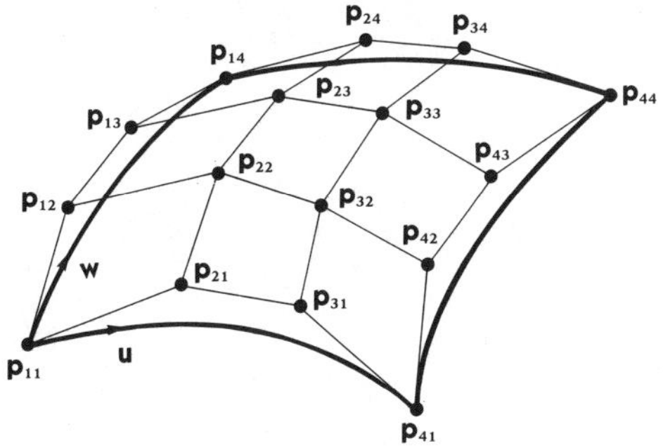

Fig. 14.5. Bicubic Bezier surface.

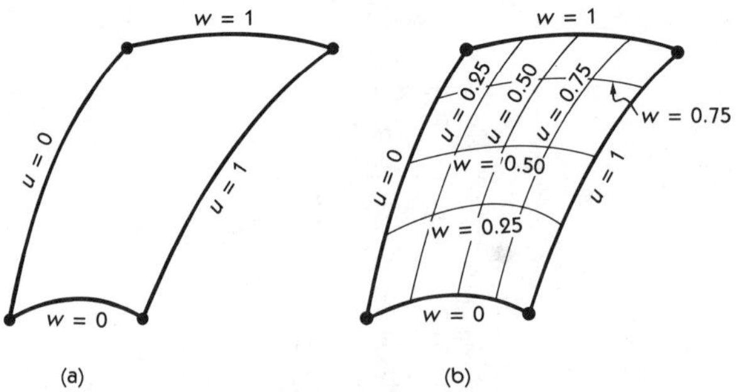

Fig. 14.6. Displaying a surface.

You will produce the most realistic display of a surface when you introduce color and shading. To do this, you need the surface normal at each point on a surface corresponding to the center of its display pixel. The relationship of the surface normal to the line of sight and the assumed incident light determines the quality and quantity of light to be emitted by the pixel. These techniques are thoroughly discussed in more advanced textbooks.

15. General Transformations

TRANSFORMING A GEOMETRIC object, whether it is a point, a curve, or a surface, means changing it in position, orientation, or shape. The simplest changes are the so-called rigid-body transformations, such as translation and rotation, that do not cause shape changes.

You will see how, by using simple vector geometry and matrix algebra, you can transform any object simply by transforming the sets of points (or vectors) that define them. In particular, you will study translation, rotation, scaling, symmetry, and reflection transformations. Finally, you will see how to combine all of these transformations by using some tricks with matrix algebra and a slightly modified coordinate bookkeeping system using what are called homogeneous coordinates.

Some of the subjects of this chapter appeared earlier. However, their restatement here, in the context of vectors, curves, and surfaces, offers new insight into their meaning.

15.1. Translation

The rigid-body translation of a curve (or other geometric object) means that every point on the curve is moved equally a given distance in a given direction, specified by a vector. Figure 15.1 shows a curve translated by **t**. Points on the translated curve are given by

$$\mathbf{p}^* = \mathbf{p} + \mathbf{t} \tag{15.1}$$

where an asterisk still indicates a transformed vector or matrix.

Equation (15.1) represents the direct pointwise translation of each and every point, **p**, on the curve. Usually this is too cumbersome, and it is preferable to transform the curve or surface matrix of geometric coefficients. For example, transform the **B** matrix for a parametric cubic curve subjected to a translation, **t**, as follows:

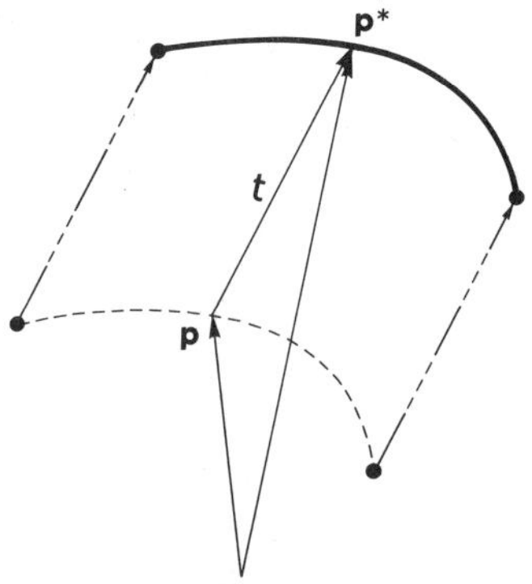

Fig. 15.1. Translation of a curve.

$$\mathbf{B}^* = \mathbf{B} + \mathbf{T} \tag{15.2}$$

where

$$\mathbf{T} = [\mathbf{t} \ \ \mathbf{t} \ \ 0 \ \ 0]^T \tag{15.3}$$

This produces

$$\mathbf{B}^* = \begin{bmatrix} \mathbf{p}_0 + \mathbf{t} \\ \mathbf{p}_1 + \mathbf{t} \\ \mathbf{p}_0^u \\ \mathbf{p}_1^u \end{bmatrix} \tag{15.4}$$

Note that only the end-point vectors are transformed. The tangent vectors are "free vectors" representing relative characteristics. They do not change under this transformation.

EXERCISES

1. Find **T** and **B*** for a bicubic patch, so that **B*** = **B** + **T**. (You will have noted, of course, that **B** symbolizes the matrix of geometric coefficients for both curves and surfaces. The distinction is usually clear from the context.)

2. Find the translation matrix that will move every point on a parametric cubic curve three units in the positive *y* direction.

3. Describe how you would translate a Bezier curve and a Bezier surface.

15.2. Rotation

There are many ways to rotate a geometric element. You will study here rotations about axes through the origin (that is, the principal axes).

The rigid-body rotation, R, of a geometric element must meet the following conditions:

1. Relative distances and angles between points and tangents on an element do not change.

2. A right-hand convention applies to signs of rotation angles.

3. The embedding coordinate system is a right-hand system.

4. A rotation about the origin has three possible components: γ, β, and θ, where γ is the angle of rotation around the x axis, β is the angle around the y axis, and θ is the angle around the z axis. In keeping with the right-hand convention, θ is positive in a counterclockwise sense when viewed from a point on the $+z$ axis looking toward the origin; β is positive in a counterclockwise sense when viewed from a point on the $+y$ axis looking toward the origin; and γ is positive in a counterclockwise sense when viewed from a point on the $+x$ axis looking toward the origin.

5. When the rotation of a geometric object is given by all three angles, the order is important. In the absence of other constraints, use the following convention:
   a. First, rotate around the z axis if $\theta \neq 0$.
   b. Next, rotate around the y axis if $\beta \neq 0$.
   c. Finally, rotate around the x axis if $\gamma \neq 0$.

Figure 15.2 shows a curve rotated through the angle θ in the positive direction around the z axis. Every point on the curve undergoes a rotation θ around the z axis, and its path lies in a plane perpendicular to the z axis and parallel to the x,y plane. For a parametric curve, the rotation θ changes

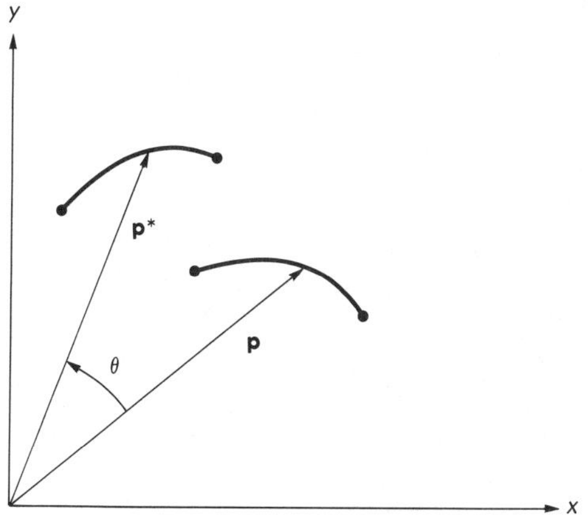

Fig. 15.2. Rotation of a curve.

(transforms) the functions $x(u)$ and $y(u)$, but not $z(u)$. Points on the rotated curve are given by

$$\mathbf{p}^* = \mathbf{pR} \tag{15.5}$$

where $\mathbf{p}$ is the original point, $\mathbf{p}^*$ is the transformed point, and $\mathbf{R}$ is a 3×3 rotation matrix.

Now derive the elements of $\mathbf{R}$. Figure 15.3 shows the geometry of a point $\mathbf{p}$ rotated through an angle θ about the z axis, so that, given $\mathbf{p}$ and θ, you can compute $\mathbf{p}^*$, the transformed point whose components are

$$x^* = |\mathbf{p}|\cos(\alpha + \theta), \qquad y^* = |\mathbf{p}|\sin(\alpha + \theta) \tag{15.6}$$

where $|\mathbf{p}| = |\mathbf{p}^*|$, since, obviously, the rotation does not affect $|\mathbf{p}|$.

From elementary trigonometry,

$$\begin{aligned} \cos(\alpha + \theta) &= \cos\alpha\cos\theta - \sin\alpha\sin\theta \\ \sin(\alpha + \theta) &= \sin\alpha\cos\theta + \cos\alpha\sin\theta \end{aligned} \tag{15.7}$$

Also, see in Fig. 15.3 that

$$\cos\alpha = \frac{x}{|\mathbf{p}|} \quad \text{and} \quad \sin\alpha = \frac{y}{|\mathbf{p}|} \tag{15.8}$$

Substitute appropriately into Eq. (15.6) to obtain

$$\begin{aligned} x^* &= x\cos\theta - y\sin\theta \\ y^* &= x\sin\theta + y\cos\theta \end{aligned} \tag{15.9}$$

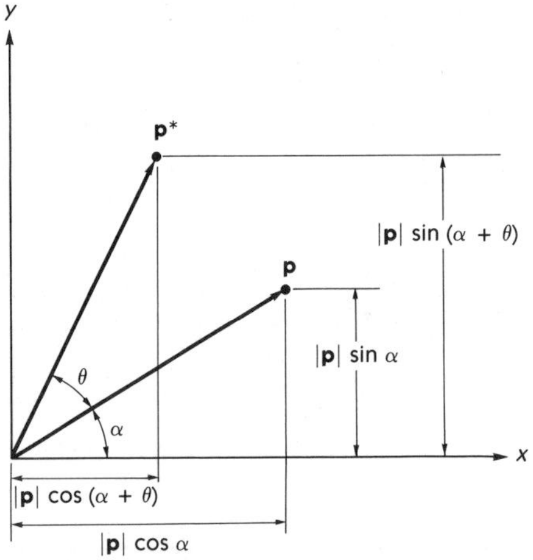

Fig. 15.3. Geometry of a rotation transformation.

Since this rotation is about the z axis, $z^* = z$. Now you have all the information you need to construct the elements of the rotation matrix $\mathbf{R}$:

$$\mathbf{R}_\theta = \begin{bmatrix} \cos\theta & \sin\theta & 0 \\ -\sin\theta & \cos\theta & 0 \\ 0 & 0 & 1 \end{bmatrix} \tag{15.10}$$

so that

$$\mathbf{p}^* = \mathbf{p}\mathbf{R}_\theta \tag{15.11}$$

for rotations about the z axis. Note that a subscript θ on $\mathbf{R}$ denotes this particular rotation. This element order in $\mathbf{R}$ assumes that $\mathbf{p}$ and $\mathbf{p}^*$ are 1×3 matrices.

Generalize this procedure to obtain the rotation transformation matrices for rotations about the y and x axes, $\mathbf{R}_\beta$ and $\mathbf{R}_\gamma$:

$$\mathbf{R}_\beta = \begin{bmatrix} \cos\beta & 0 & -\sin\beta \\ 0 & 1 & 0 \\ \sin\beta & 0 & \cos\beta \end{bmatrix} \tag{15.12}$$

and

$$\mathbf{R}_\gamma = \begin{bmatrix} 1 & 0 & 0 \\ 0 & \cos\gamma & \sin\gamma \\ 0 & -\sin\gamma & \cos\gamma \end{bmatrix} \tag{15.13}$$

It is easy to show that the rotation matrix applies equally well to the algebraic and geometric coefficient matrices of curves and surfaces; thus,

$$\mathbf{A}^* = \mathbf{A}\mathbf{R} \quad \text{and} \quad \mathbf{B}^* = \mathbf{B}\mathbf{R} \tag{15.14}$$

EXERCISES

1. If a geometric object is to be translated and rotated, show that the order in which these transformations are performed is important.

2. Compute the total rotation transformation matrix $\mathbf{R}$ when $\theta, \beta, \gamma, \neq 0$.

3. Verify and discuss the validity of Eq. (15.14).

4. Show that $\mathbf{R}_\theta \times \mathbf{R}_{-\theta} = \mathbf{I}$.

5. Derive the transformation equation(s) for rotating a point about an arbitrary point in two-dimensional space.

6. Derive the transformation equation(s) for rotating a point about an arbitrary line in three-dimensional space.

15.3. Scaling

To change the size of a curve or surface, multiply its geometric coefficients by a **scale factor.** If you apply the same scale factor to each component, then the element will change in size but not in shape. If you apply different scale factors to each of the components, then both size and shape will change.

To scale (change the size of) a parametric cubic curve, use the following transformation:

$$\mathbf{B}^* = s\mathbf{B} = \begin{bmatrix} s\mathbf{p}_0 \\ s\mathbf{p}_1 \\ s\mathbf{p}_0^u \\ s\mathbf{p}_1^u \end{bmatrix} \tag{15.15}$$

where s is the scale factor. Note that s is always positive. (If you use a negative value, you create a reflection; this concept appears in the next section.)

Figure 15.4 shows the effect of this scaling transformation. The shapes of the curves $\mathbf{p}(u)$ and $\mathbf{p}^*(u)$ are identical, but curve $\mathbf{p}^*(u)$ is in this case larger by a factor of $s = 2$. It is two times longer, and it occupies a different position in space, since the components of each point $\mathbf{p}^*$ are two times larger than the corresponding components of $\mathbf{p}$. The tangent vectors $\mathbf{p}^{*u}_0$ and $\mathbf{p}^{*u}_1$ are twice the magnitude of $\mathbf{p}_0^u$ and $\mathbf{p}_1^u$, respectively, but the direction cosines at any point are unchanged.

Note that this transformation causes scaling (expansion or contraction) with respect to the origin of the coordinate system. It is possible to per-

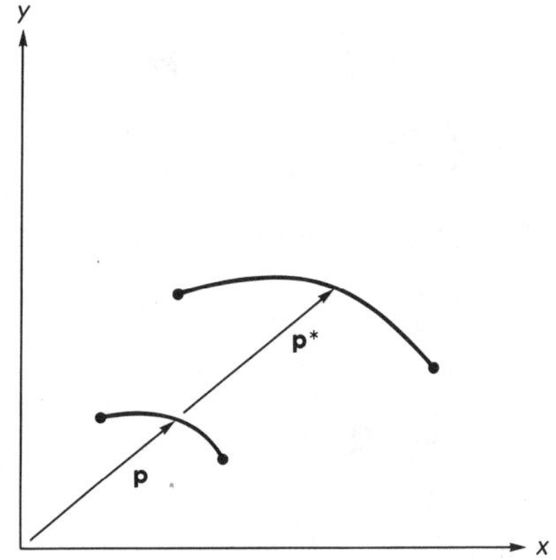

Fig. 15.4. Scale transformation of a curve.

form a scaling transformation with respect to any point, **q**. Figure 15.5 illustrates the vector geometry involved in this transformation. Note that

$$\mathbf{p}^* = \mathbf{q} + s(\mathbf{p} - \mathbf{q}) \tag{15.16}$$

Rewrite this as

$$\mathbf{p}^* = s\mathbf{p} - (s - 1)\mathbf{q} \tag{15.17}$$

The direction of the tangent vectors is unaffected, although their magnitude is scaled by s. From these results, you obtain the transformation equation for scaling a parametric cubic curve about any point in space:

$$\mathbf{B}^* = s\mathbf{B} + \mathbf{T}_s \tag{15.18}$$

where

$$\mathbf{T}_s = \begin{bmatrix} -\mathbf{q}(s-1) \\ -\mathbf{q}(s-1) \\ 0 \\ 0 \end{bmatrix} \tag{15.19}$$

So far you have applied the same scale factor to each coordinate component, but there is no reason why you must do this. There are often situations in geometric modeling where you must stretch or shrink each component by a different factor. Denote these scale factors by s_x, s_y, and s_z. The transformation operation applying them is called **differential scaling.** The general differential scaling transformation matrix for a parametric cubic curve about any point **q** is

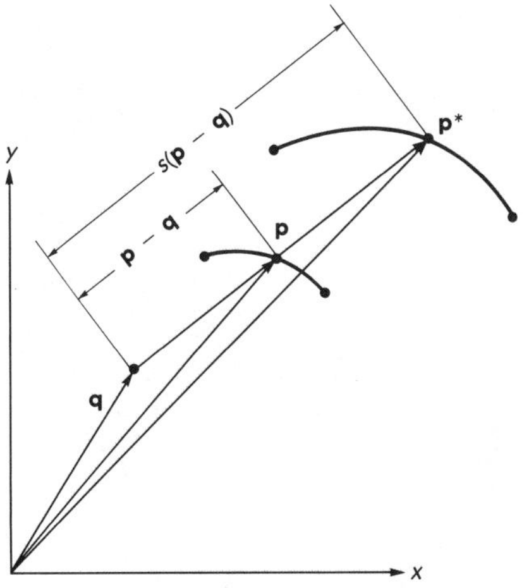

Fig. 15.5. Scaling about an arbitrary point.

$$\mathbf{B}^* = \begin{bmatrix} s_x x_0 - q_x(s_x - 1) & s_y y_0 - q_y(s_y - 1) & s_z z_0 - q_z(s_z - 1) \\ s_x x_1 - q_x(s_x - 1) & s_y y_1 - q_y(s_y - 1) & s_z z_1 - q_z(s_z - 1) \\ s_x x_0^u & s_y y_0^u & s_z z_0^u \\ s_x x_1^u & s_y y_1^u & s_z z_1^u \end{bmatrix} \tag{15.20}$$

15.4. Reflection

A curve or surface is reflected through a plane, line, or point in space to create its mirror image. The transformations necessary to do this are direct and easy to understand. Figure 15.6 shows some of the ways to reflect a curve. Here is a plane curve in the positive x,y quadrant and its three different reflected images—one in each of the other quadrants.

It is a simple procedure to construct a reflected image of a curve or surface. For example, to reflect a curve through the $y = 0$ plane, transform each point $\mathbf{p}$ on it to its reflected image $\mathbf{p}^*$ located an equal distance from the plane but on the other side of it. The distance between point $\mathbf{a}$ and point $\mathbf{p}$ is equal to the distance between $\mathbf{a}$ and $\mathbf{p}^*$. Point $\mathbf{a}$ lies on the straight line joining $\mathbf{p}$ and $\mathbf{p}^*$ at its intersection with the $y = 0$ plane. Furthermore, the vector $\mathbf{p}^* - \mathbf{p}$ is normal to this plane.

This transformation merely changes the algebraic sign of the y components of the curve coefficients. In fact, when the plane of reflection is

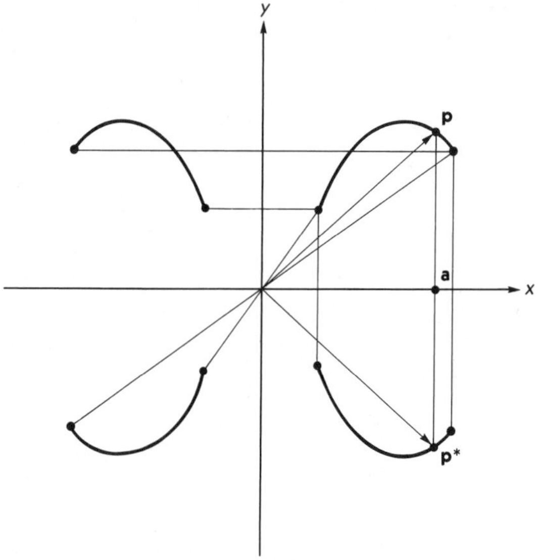

Fig. 15.6. Reflections of a curve.

one of the principal planes, transform the curve by changing the sign of the coefficients of the components corresponding to the plane. Although the example shown in the figure is a plane curve, apply the same procedures to a curve that twists through space.

Reflection may also take place across any of the principal axes or through the origin. A procedure analogous to that for reflection through a plane of symmetry applies to reflection across a principal axis or through the origin. The following relationship exists between the geometric coefficients of an initial parametric cubic curve and a reflected one:

$$\mathbf{B}^* = \mathbf{B}\mathbf{R}_f \tag{15.21}$$

where

$$\mathbf{R}_f = \begin{bmatrix} \pm 1 & 0 & 0 \\ 0 & \pm 1 & 0 \\ 0 & 0 & \pm 1 \end{bmatrix} \tag{15.22}$$

For a bicubic surface, the mathematics is only slightly more complicated:

$$\mathbf{B}^* = [\mathbf{b}_{ij}\mathbf{R}_f] \tag{15.23}$$

Interpret this to mean that each vector element $\mathbf{b}_{ij}$ of the $\mathbf{B}$ matrix is transformed by $\mathbf{R}_f$ to construct and fill a new $\mathbf{B}^*$ matrix.

EXERCISES

1. Find $\mathbf{R}_f$ for each of the following cases:

   a. Reflection through the $x = 0$ plane.
   b. Reflection through the $y = 0$ plane.
   c. Reflection through the $z = 0$ plane.
   d. Reflection through the x axis.
   e. Reflection through the y axis.
   f. Reflection through the z axis.
   g. Reflection through the origin.

2. Find the transformation equation that reflects a parametric cubic curve through the $y = a$ plane.

15.5. Homogeneous Coordinates and Transformations

Homogeneous coordinates were invented by mathematicians working in projective geometry. They are the coordinates of points in projective space (not a subject we will pursue here). You can use them to make your transformation operations easier. They allow you to combine several transformations into one matrix, and a long sequence of transformations reduces to a series of matrix multiplications. No matrix addition is required.

Using homogeneous coordinates, a three-dimensional point or vector is given by four components as

$$\mathbf{p}_h = [hx \ \ hy \ \ hz \ \ h] \tag{15.24}$$

where h is some scalar value. The subscript h on $\mathbf{p}_h$ signifies that $\mathbf{p}$ is given by homogeneous coordinates.

Homogeneous coordinates easily convert to ordinary coordinates by dividing by h:

$$x = \frac{hx}{h}, \qquad y = \frac{hy}{h}, \qquad z = \frac{hz}{h} \tag{15.25}$$

As you may note, there is no unique homogeneous coordinate representation of a point in three-dimensional space. For example, the homogeneous coordinates $[12 \ \ 8 \ \ 4 \ \ 4]$, $[6 \ \ 4 \ \ 2 \ \ 2]$, and $[3 \ \ 2 \ \ 1 \ \ 1]$ all represent the point $[3 \ \ 2 \ \ 1]$ in ordinary three-dimensional space. The computations are easier if you choose $h = 1$, so that $[x \ \ y \ \ z \ \ 1]$ in homogeneous coordinates represents the point $[x \ \ y \ \ z]$.

Make all transformations of homogeneous points by means of a 4×4 transformation matrix. To use this technique, represent curves or surfaces in their point format. Add the fourth or homogeneous coordinate h to each point. Make the required transformations, and then convert the resulting homogeneous coordinates into three-dimensional coordinates by means of Eq. (15.25).

Now let us investigate some of the possible transformations. Express these transformations as

$$\mathbf{p}_h^* = \mathbf{p}_h \mathbf{T}_h \tag{15.26}$$

Translate points using the following matrix product:

$$[x^* \ \ y^* \ \ z^* \ \ 1] = [x \ \ y \ \ z \ \ 1] \begin{bmatrix} 1 & 0 & 0 & 0 \\ 0 & 1 & 0 & 0 \\ 0 & 0 & 1 & 0 \\ t_x & t_y & t_z & 1 \end{bmatrix} \tag{15.27}$$

where t_x, t_y, and t_z are components of the vector $\mathbf{t}$ that describes the translation. Calculate the matrix product to obtain

$$[x^* \ \ y^* \ \ z^* \ \ 1] = [x + t_x \ \ \ y + t_y \ \ \ z + t_z \ \ \ 1] \tag{15.28}$$

from which you can readily compute the ordinary transformed coordinates

$$x^* = x + t_x, \qquad y^* = y + t_y, \qquad z^* = z + t_z \tag{15.29}$$

Rotate points around a principal axis with one of the three following matrix products.

For rotation around the z axis:

$$[x^* \; y^* \; z^* \; 1] = [x \; y \; z \; 1] \begin{bmatrix} \cos\theta & \sin\theta & 0 & 0 \\ -\sin\theta & \cos\theta & 0 & 0 \\ 0 & 0 & 1 & 0 \\ 0 & 0 & 0 & 1 \end{bmatrix} \tag{15.30}$$

For rotation around the y axis:

$$[x^* \; y^* \; z^* \; 1] = [x \; y \; z \; 1] \begin{bmatrix} \cos\beta & 0 & -\sin\beta & 0 \\ 0 & 1 & 0 & 0 \\ \sin\beta & 0 & \cos\beta & 0 \\ 0 & 0 & 0 & 1 \end{bmatrix} \tag{15.31}$$

For rotation around the x axis:

$$[x^* \; y^* \; z^* \; 1] = [x \; y \; z \; 1] \begin{bmatrix} 1 & 0 & 0 & 0 \\ 0 & \cos\gamma & \sin\gamma & 0 \\ 0 & -\sin\gamma & \cos\gamma & 0 \\ 0 & 0 & 0 & 1 \end{bmatrix} \tag{15.32}$$

EXERCISES

1. Deduce $\mathbf{T}_h$ for differential scaling.

16. Display and Scene Transformations

GENERATE THE COMPUTER graphics display of a geometric model by applying a sequence of transformations to the point set defining the model. The sequence usually consists of a set of matrices establishing the view orientation, followed by the projection transformation matrix. Control view changes with algorithms that create or alter these matrices.

Distinguish between **scene transformations** and **display transformations**. Scene transformations are characteristically three dimensional and operate on model data to alter the viewing orientation. Display transformations operate on the two-dimensional display data to change scale (zoom, for example) or to rotate the display around the line of sight (in the plane of the display). Note that display changes do not affect the projected view—only the viewer's relationship to the plane of the display. See Fig. 16.1 for an example of this distinction.

The kinematic relationship between the observer and the scene is also something to consider. Should the objects in the scene move, or should your eye move? Should the transformations be relative to a fixed global axis, or relative to the current display axis? Once you transform and display an object, the next view of that object is produced by assuming that either the object itself moves or your eye moves. The difference is expressed by the algebraic sign of each of the elements of the transformation matrix. These issues deserve attention when designing the user interface of interactive geometric modeling systems, such as CAD/CAM, and to do this you must understand the mathematics.

In this chapter you will examine in greater detail the orthographic and perspective transformations and explore several scene transformations: orbit, pan, and aim. First, here is a brief review of the elements of the 4×4 transformation matrix, $\mathbf{T}_h$, introduced in Chapter 15. Express $\mathbf{T}_h$ as

$$\mathbf{T}_h = \begin{bmatrix} a & b & c & p \\ d & e & f & q \\ g & i & j & r \\ l & m & n & h \end{bmatrix} \tag{16.1}$$

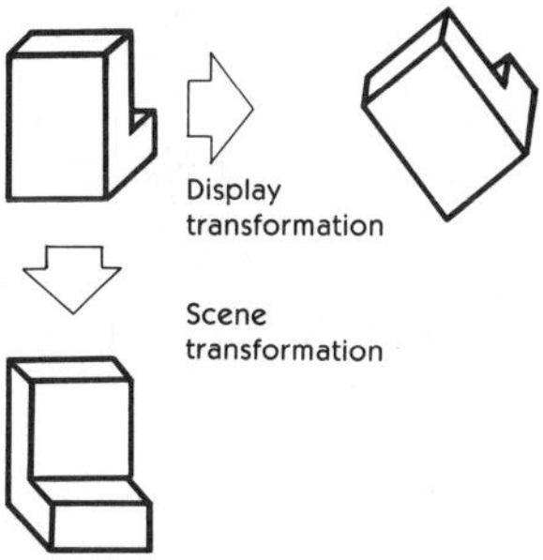

Fig. 16.1. Display and scene transformations.

Recall the transformations produced by various elements in each of the four partitions of this matrix:

Rotation:

$$\begin{bmatrix} a & b & c & 0 \\ d & e & f & 0 \\ g & i & j & 0 \\ 0 & 0 & 0 & 1 \end{bmatrix}$$

Scaling:

$$\begin{bmatrix} s_x & 0 & 0 & 0 \\ 0 & s_y & 0 & 0 \\ 0 & 0 & s_z & 0 \\ 0 & 0 & 0 & 1 \end{bmatrix}$$

Translation:

$$\begin{bmatrix} 1 & 0 & 0 & 0 \\ 0 & 1 & 0 & 0 \\ 0 & 0 & 1 & 0 \\ t_x & t_y & t_z & 1 \end{bmatrix}$$

Projection:

$$\begin{bmatrix} 1 & 0 & 0 & p \\ 0 & 1 & 0 & q \\ 0 & 0 & 1 & r \\ 0 & 0 & 0 & 1 \end{bmatrix}$$

The projection transformation elements may be unfamiliar to you. They are introduced in Section 16.2.

16.1. General Orthographic Projection

Projections are transformations that produce two-dimensional representations of three-dimensional objects. They are perhaps the most important of all transformations; without them, we could not construct a display image.

Consider the orthographic projection of any point, **p**, in space onto an arbitrary plane (Fig. 16.2). Find the projected image, $\mathbf{p}^*$, by constructing a line through **p** perpendicular to the plane. This line intersects the plane at $\mathbf{p}^*$. Clearly, $\mathbf{p}^*$ must satisfy $(\mathbf{p}^* - \mathbf{p}) \times \mathbf{n} = 0$, where **n** is the unit normal vector to the plane.

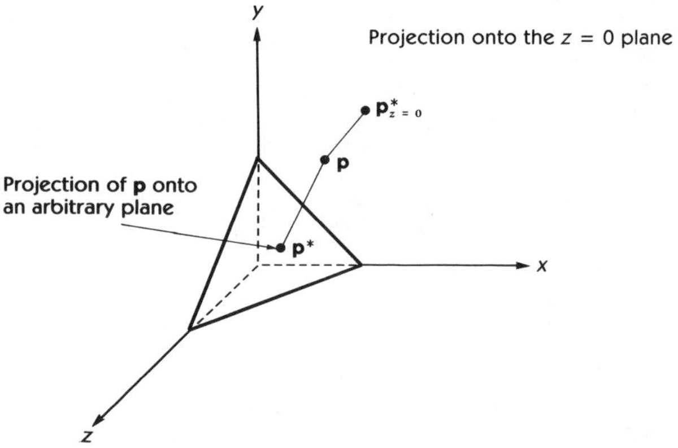

Fig. 16.2. Orthographic projection of a point.

If the plane is given by $Ax + By + Cz + D = 0$, then the following simple transformation applies:

$$\mathbf{p}_1^* = \mathbf{p}_1 - d_1\mathbf{n} \tag{16.2}$$

where

$$n_x = \frac{A}{A^2 + B^2 + C^2}$$
$$n_y = \frac{B}{A^2 + B^2 + C^2} \tag{16.3}$$
$$n_z = \frac{C}{A^2 + B^2 + C^2}$$

and

$$d_1 = \frac{Ax_1 + By_1 + Cz_1 + D}{A^2 + B^2 + C^2} \tag{16.4}$$

Note that d_1 is a directed distance. The algebraic sign associated with it indicates that it is in the same direction (+) as **n** or in the opposite direction (−).

If you can project points this way, you can also project curves. Merely project the points that define the curve; these then define the new (projected) curve.

Here is another way to project points: Study Fig. 16.3 as you follow this development. First, rotate both the plane and the point(s) (in this case,

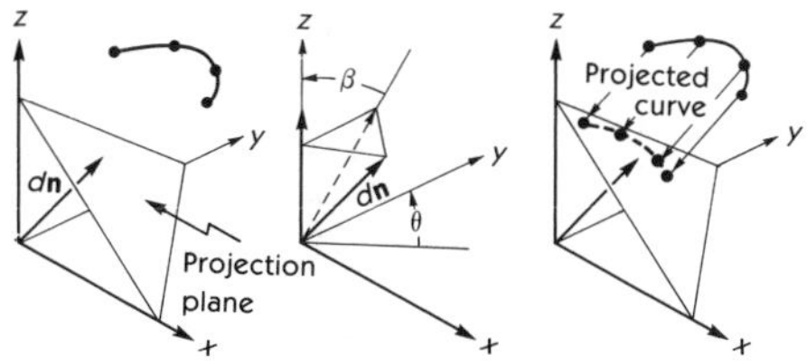

Fig. 16.3. Rotating then projecting.

points defining a curve) so that the plane is parallel to a selected principal plane. This requires finding the rotation transformation that will rotate the normal to the plane, **n**, into coincidence with the x, y, or z axis. In this example, rotate **n** through the angle θ about the z axis [where $\theta = \tan^{-1}(n_x/n_z)$]. This puts **p** into the x, z plane. Then rotate **n** through the angle β about the x axis (where $\beta = \sin^{-1} n_y$). This puts **n** into coincidence with the z axis; so the plane is now perpendicular to the z axis and intersects it at $z = d$. Apply these same two rotation transformations to the point(s). Next, project the transformed point(s) onto the plane in this new orientation, which simply results in setting their z coordinates equal to d. Finally, reverse the rotation transformations, putting the plane back in its original position, and put on it the projected points transformed likewise.

Let the first two rotation transformations yield for the points

$$\mathbf{p}' = \mathbf{p}\mathbf{T}_\theta\mathbf{T}_\beta \tag{16.5}$$

Now project $\mathbf{p}'$ onto the $z = d$ plane to yield

$$\mathbf{p}'' = [x' \;\; y' \;\; d] \tag{16.6}$$

Finally, reverse the rotations:

$$\mathbf{p}^* = \mathbf{p}'' T_{-\beta}\, \mathbf{T}_{-\theta} \tag{16.7}$$

Now you are ready for a more general approach to computing orthographic projections. The basic ingredients are: the point **p** to be projected, the projection plane, defined by $\mathbf{p}_0 + x^*\,\mathbf{u}_1 + y^*\,\mathbf{u}_2$, and the direction of projection, $\mathbf{u}_3$ (Fig. 16.4). The vector $\mathbf{p}_0$ defines the origin of a coordinate system on the projection plane (the picture plane coordinate system), with the unit vectors $\mathbf{u}_1$ and $\mathbf{u}_2$ defining the plane itself. If $\mathbf{p}^*$ is the projection of **p** onto the plane, then

$$\mathbf{p}^* = \mathbf{p} - z^*\mathbf{u}_3 \tag{16.8}$$

where z^* is to be determined. This is similar to Eq. (16.2).

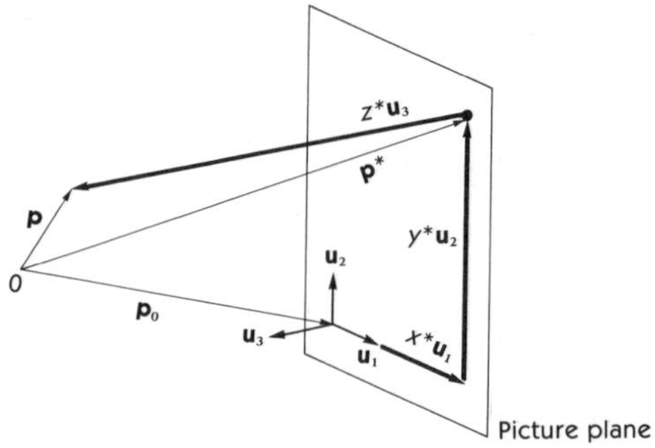

Fig. 16.4. Vector geometry of a general orthographic projection.

Now, the projected point $\mathbf{p}^*$ is also expressible in terms of vectors defining the picture plane. Thus,

$$\mathbf{p}^* = \mathbf{p}_0 + x^*\mathbf{u}_1 + y^*\mathbf{u}_2 \tag{16.9}$$

Combine Eqs. (16.8) and (16.9) to obtain

$$\mathbf{p} - z^*\mathbf{u}_3 = \mathbf{p}_0 + x^*\mathbf{u}_1 + y^*\mathbf{u}_2 \tag{16.10}$$

or

$$x^*\mathbf{u}_1 + y^*\mathbf{u}_2 + z^*\mathbf{u}_3 = \mathbf{p} - \mathbf{p}_0 \tag{16.11}$$

Solve for x^*, y^*, and z^*. For example, to find x^*, take the scalar product of all terms on both sides of the equation with $(\mathbf{u}_2 \times \mathbf{u}_3)$:

$$\begin{aligned} x^*\mathbf{u}_1 \cdot (\mathbf{u}_2 \times \mathbf{u}_3) + y^*\mathbf{u}_2 \cdot (\mathbf{u}_2 \times \mathbf{u}_3) + z^*\mathbf{u}_3 \cdot (\mathbf{u}_2 \times \mathbf{u}_3) \\ = (\mathbf{p} - \mathbf{p}_0) \cdot (\mathbf{u}_2 \times \mathbf{u}_3) \end{aligned} \tag{16.12}$$

Since $\mathbf{u}_2 \cdot (\mathbf{u}_2 \times \mathbf{u}_3) = \mathbf{u}_3 \cdot (\mathbf{u}_2 \times \mathbf{u}_3) = 0$,

$$x^* = \frac{(\mathbf{p} - \mathbf{p}_0) \cdot (\mathbf{u}_2 \times \mathbf{u}_3)}{\mathbf{u}_1 \cdot (\mathbf{u}_2 \times \mathbf{u}_3)} \tag{16.13}$$

Apply similar treatment to obtain y^* and z^*:

$$\begin{aligned} y^* &= \frac{(\mathbf{p} - \mathbf{p}_0) \cdot (\mathbf{u}_3 \times \mathbf{u}_1)}{\mathbf{u}_2 \cdot (\mathbf{u}_3 \times \mathbf{u}_1)} \\ z^* &= \frac{(\mathbf{p} - \mathbf{p}_0) \cdot (\mathbf{u}_1 \times \mathbf{u}_2)}{\mathbf{u}_3 \cdot (\mathbf{u}_1 \times \mathbf{u}_2)} \end{aligned} \tag{16.14}$$

Note that you have not yet specified a relationship between $\mathbf{u}_3$ and the plane defined by $\mathbf{u}_1$ and $\mathbf{u}_2$, nor have you specified any particular relationship between $\mathbf{u}_1$ and $\mathbf{u}_2$. Equations (16.13) and (16.14) are independent of the direction of these unit vectors. However, orthographic projection requires $\mathbf{u}_3$ to be perpendicular to the picture plane. Furthermore, it is obviously convenient to choose $\mathbf{u}_1$ and $\mathbf{u}_2$ so that they, too, are mutually perpendicular. This means that you can simplify these equations dramatically, since, for example, $\mathbf{u}_1 \cdot (\mathbf{u}_2 \times \mathbf{u}_3) = 1$ and $\mathbf{u}_2 \times \mathbf{u}_3 = \mathbf{u}_1$. So, now write

$$\begin{aligned} x^* &= (\mathbf{p} - \mathbf{p}_0) \cdot \mathbf{u}_1 \\ y^* &= (\mathbf{p} - \mathbf{p}_0) \cdot \mathbf{u}_2 \\ z^* &= (\mathbf{p} - \mathbf{p}_0) \cdot \mathbf{u}_3 \end{aligned} \tag{16.15}$$

Ordinarily, z^* helps to provide information on the visibility of $\mathbf{p}$ relative to other objects and the chosen picture plane. If you save z^* as a data item, you can later use it to reconstruct the initial point, $\mathbf{p}$, if necessary. But, in orthographic projection you do not use z^* directly in constructing the image on the picture plane.

Finally, note that $\mathbf{u}_1$, $\mathbf{u}_2$, $\mathbf{u}_3$ form a right-hand coordinate system as defined above. Frequently, the picture-plane coordinate system is a left-hand system so that on a display screen the normal relationship between the x and y axes is preserved: the positive x axis points to the right, and the positive y axis points upward. This means that the positive z axis points generally along the line of sight toward the object being viewed. The farther a point is from the viewer, the higher the value of its z coordinate.

The world coordinate system is usually a right-hand one, so the transformation of object points to the picture-plane coordinate system must also transform a right-hand to a left-hand system. Do this with a matrix that simply inverts the sign of the z coordinate:

$$\mathbf{T}_{RL} = \begin{bmatrix} 1 & 0 & 0 & 0 \\ 0 & 1 & 0 & 0 \\ 0 & 0 & -1 & 0 \\ 0 & 0 & 0 & 1 \end{bmatrix} \tag{16.16}$$

16.2. Perspective Projection

Perspective projection closely approximates the way an observer forms a visual image of an object. Objects in a scene are projected onto a picture plane from a central point, usually assumed to be the eye of the observer. The center of the picture plane is at the point of intersection between the plane and the normal to it from the observer (at *O* in Fig. 16.5). This is

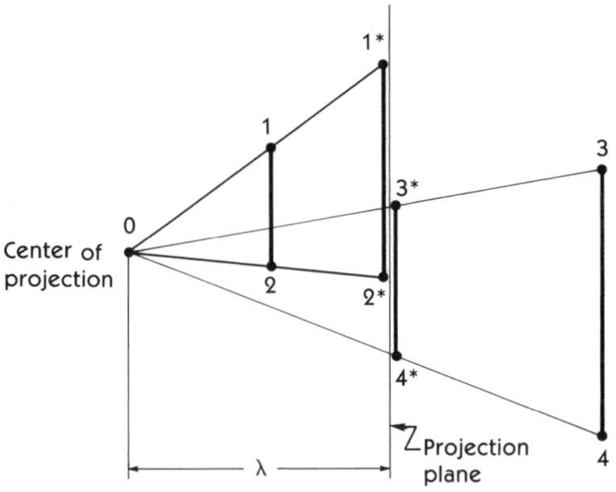

Fig. 16.5. Elements of perspective projection.

called the **center of projection.** In the figure, two line segments (that is, their end points) are projected onto the picture plane.

Now consider some of the basic vector geometry. Let λ denote the normal distance from the viewer to the picture plane (Fig. 16.6). Using some simple vector geometry, we see that $\mathbf{p}_E + k(\mathbf{p} - \mathbf{p}_E) = \mathbf{p}^*$, which you easily solve for $k = \lambda/(z + \lambda)$ and then for $\mathbf{p}^*$:

$$
\begin{aligned}
x^* &= \frac{\lambda x}{(z + \lambda)} \\
y^* &= \frac{\lambda y}{(z + \lambda)} \qquad (16.17) \\
z^* &= 0
\end{aligned}
$$

Here, homogeneous coordinates prove to be very useful. Consider the following transformation:

$$
\mathbf{p}_h^* = \mathbf{p}_h \begin{bmatrix} 1 & 0 & 0 & 0 \\ 0 & 1 & 0 & 0 \\ 0 & 0 & 0 & r \\ 0 & 0 & 0 & 1 \end{bmatrix} \qquad (16.18)
$$

where the subscript h denotes homogeneous coordinates. If $\mathbf{p}_h = [x \; y \; z \; 1]$, then for $\mathbf{p}_h^*$,

$$
\mathbf{p}_h^* = [x \; y \; 0 \; (rz + 1)] \qquad (16.19)
$$

The ordinary coordinates are

$$
\mathbf{p}^* = \left[\frac{x}{rz + 1} \quad \frac{y}{rz + 1} \quad 0 \right] \qquad (16.20)
$$

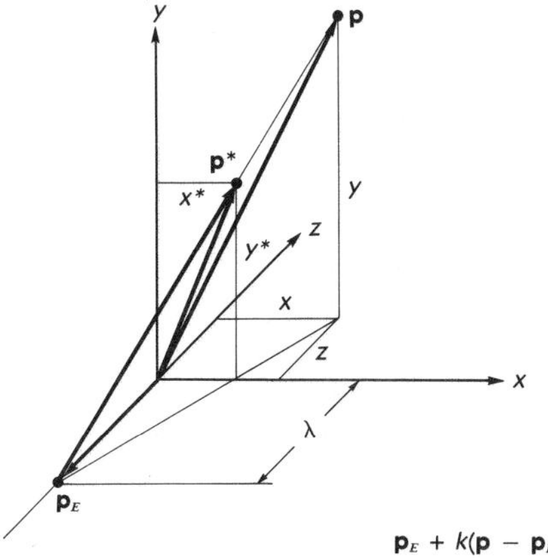

Fig. 16.6. Vector geometry of perspective projection.

If you let $r = 1/\lambda$, then

$$\mathbf{p}^* = \begin{bmatrix} \frac{\lambda x}{z + \lambda} & \frac{\lambda y}{z + \lambda} & 0 \end{bmatrix} \tag{16.21}$$

These are the same values for x^*, y^*, and z^* that you derived in Eq. (16.17). The center of projection is located at $[0 \;\; 0 \;\; -\lambda]$, and the picture plane is, of course, the $z = 0$ plane.

Now you are ready to explore the vector geometry of a more general perspective projection. You will find the basic element illustrated in Fig. 16.7. Here, $\mathbf{p}$ is the point to be projected, $\mathbf{p}_0 + x^*\mathbf{u}_1 + y^*\mathbf{u}_2$ defines the projection plane (picture plane), $\mathbf{p}^*$ is the projected point, and $\mathbf{p}_E$ is the eyepoint, or center of projection. Once again, let the vector $\mathbf{p}_0$ define the origin of the picture-plane coordinate system, with $\mathbf{u}_1$ and $\mathbf{u}_2$ mutually perpendicular unit vectors defining the picture plane. The unit vector $\mathbf{u}_3$ is normal to the picture plane, so that $\mathbf{u}_1 \times \mathbf{u}_2 = \mathbf{u}_3$. You will immediately see that

$$\mathbf{p}^* = \mathbf{p}_0 + x^*\mathbf{u}_1 + y^*\mathbf{u}_2 \tag{16.22}$$

since $\mathbf{p}^*$ is at the intersection of the projection plane and a line joining $\mathbf{p}_E$ and $\mathbf{p}$,

$$\mathbf{p}^* = z^*\mathbf{p} + (1 - z^*)\,\mathbf{p}_E \tag{16.23}$$

Combine these two equations to obtain

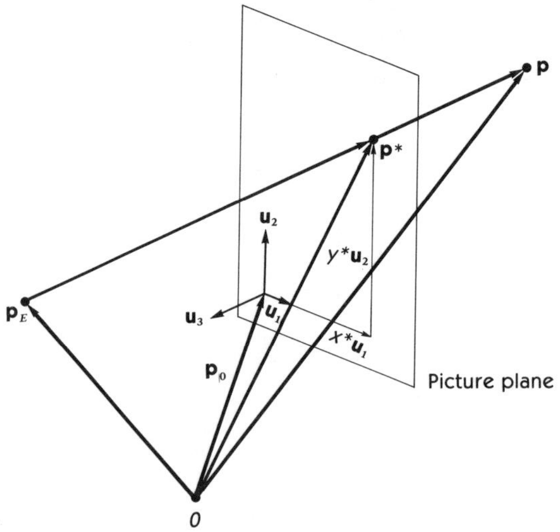

Fig. 16.7. General perspective projection.

$$\mathbf{p}_0 + x^*\mathbf{u}_1 + y^*\mathbf{u}_2 = z^*\mathbf{p} + (1 - z^*)\,\mathbf{p}_E \tag{16.24}$$

or

$$\mathbf{p}_0 + x^*\mathbf{u}_1 + y^*\mathbf{u}_2 = z^*(\mathbf{p} - \mathbf{p}_E) + \mathbf{p}_E \tag{16.25}$$

Solve this for x^*, y^*, and z^* by taking the appropriate scalar products of the equation. To solve for x^*, take the scalar product with $\mathbf{u}_2 \times (\mathbf{p} - \mathbf{p}_E)$; for y^*, use $u_1 \times (\mathbf{p} - \mathbf{p}_E)$; and for z^*, use $\mathbf{u}_1 \times \mathbf{u}_2$. So, for x^*,

$$x^* = \frac{(\mathbf{p}_E \cdot \mathbf{u}_2) \times (\mathbf{p} - \mathbf{p}_E) - (\mathbf{p}_0 \cdot \mathbf{u}_2) \times (\mathbf{p} - \mathbf{p}_E)}{(\mathbf{u}_1 \cdot \mathbf{u}_2) \times (\mathbf{p} - \mathbf{p}_E)} \tag{16.26}$$

Rewrite the expression using the property of triple vectors: $\mathbf{a} \cdot \mathbf{b} \times \mathbf{c} = \mathbf{a} \times \mathbf{b} \cdot \mathbf{c}$. Also, use the relationship $\mathbf{a} \times \mathbf{b} = -\mathbf{b} \times \mathbf{a}$ and, of course, the distributive properties of scalar and vector products (the reason will soon be apparent if you work all this out). Thus,

$$x^* = \frac{(\mathbf{p}_E \times \mathbf{u}_2) \cdot (\mathbf{p} - \mathbf{p}_E) - (\mathbf{p}_0 \times \mathbf{u}_2) \cdot (\mathbf{p} - \mathbf{p}_E)}{(\mathbf{u}_1 \times \mathbf{u}_2) \cdot (\mathbf{p} - \mathbf{p}_E)} \tag{16.27}$$

Rearrange terms and simplify to obtain

$$x^* = \frac{(\mathbf{p} - \mathbf{p}_E) \cdot [\mathbf{u}_2 \times (\mathbf{p}_0 - \mathbf{p}_E)]}{(\mathbf{p} - \mathbf{p}_E) \cdot (\mathbf{u}_1 \times \mathbf{u}_2)} \tag{16.28}$$

This procedure also produces y^*:

$$y^* = \frac{(\mathbf{p} - \mathbf{p}_E)\cdot[\mathbf{u}_1 \times (\mathbf{p}_0 - \mathbf{p}_E)]}{(\mathbf{p} - \mathbf{p}_E)\cdot(\mathbf{u}_2 \times \mathbf{u}_1)} \tag{16.29}$$

The computation of z^* is somewhat more direct and produces

$$z^* = \frac{(\mathbf{p}_0 - \mathbf{p}_E)\cdot(\mathbf{u}_1 \times \mathbf{u}_2)}{(\mathbf{p} - \mathbf{p}_E)\cdot(\mathbf{u}_1 \times \mathbf{u}_2)} \tag{16.30}$$

Simplify these equations by locating the origin of the picture-plane coordinate system so that it lies on the normal from the center of projection, at a distance d. See Fig. 16.8, where

$$\mathbf{p}_E = \mathbf{p}_0 + d\mathbf{u}_3 \tag{16.31}$$

Construct the unit vectors, such that

$$\begin{aligned} \mathbf{u}_1 &= \mathbf{u}_2 \times \mathbf{u}_3 \\ \mathbf{u}_2 &= \mathbf{u}_3 \times \mathbf{u}_1 \\ \mathbf{u}_3 &= \mathbf{u}_1 \times \mathbf{u}_2 \end{aligned} \tag{16.32}$$

Use the relationships in Eqs. (16.31) and (16.32) to rewrite Eqs. (16.28)–(16.30):

$$\begin{aligned} x^* &= \frac{-d(\mathbf{p} - \mathbf{p}_0)\cdot\mathbf{u}_1}{[(\mathbf{p} - \mathbf{p}_0)\cdot\mathbf{u}_3] - d} \\ y^* &= \frac{-d(\mathbf{p} - \mathbf{p}_0)\cdot\mathbf{u}_2}{[(\mathbf{p} - \mathbf{p}_0)\cdot\mathbf{u}_3] - d} \\ z^* &= \frac{-d}{[(\mathbf{p} - \mathbf{p}_0)\cdot\mathbf{u}_3] - d} \end{aligned} \tag{16.33}$$

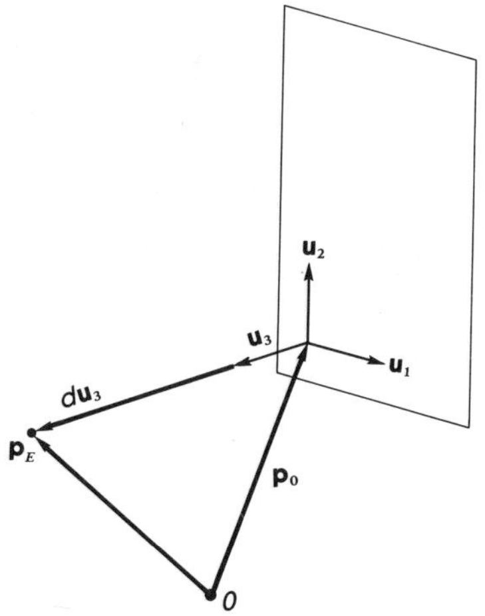

Fig. 16.8. Locating the origin of the picture plane coordinate system.

16.3. Orbit

Suppose you view an object from some arbitrary point in space, where the object remains in a fixed position and your viewing position moves from point to point. First, define the eyepoint, $\mathbf{p}_E$. Next, define the point toward which you are looking, $\mathbf{p}_V$; call this the viewpoint. These two points define the line-of-sight vector, $\mathbf{p}_V - \mathbf{p}_E$, and the collinear z direction, denoted by the unit vector, $\mathbf{u}_3$, of the picture-plane coordinate system. See the vector geometry of this arrangement in Fig. 16.9.

The picture plane is normal to the line of sight at $\mathbf{p}_0$, and the unit vectors $\mathbf{u}_1$ and $\mathbf{u}_2$ lying in it form a left-hand orthogonal triad with $\mathbf{u}_3$. The viewing distance is d. Note that you do not have to specify $\mathbf{p}_0$, since you can calculate it from the other known vectors as

$$\mathbf{p}_0 = \mathbf{p}_E + d\mathbf{u}_3 \tag{16.34}$$

Here the distance d is positive, although the coordinates of $\mathbf{p}_E$ in the picture-plane system are $(0, 0, -d)$. So, first specify $\mathbf{p}_E$, $\mathbf{p}_V$, and d.

Transformations to produce the initial view might be arranged as follows: Construct $\mathbf{u}_1$, $\mathbf{u}_2$, $\mathbf{u}_3$ at the origin of the world coordinate system, aligned with the positive x, y, and z axes. Then "translate" them to $\mathbf{p}_V$ using $\mathbf{T}_V$:

$$\mathbf{T}_V = \begin{bmatrix} 1 & 0 & 0 & 0 \\ 0 & 1 & 0 & 0 \\ 0 & 0 & 1 & 0 \\ -x_V & -y_V & -z_V & 1 \end{bmatrix} \tag{16.35}$$

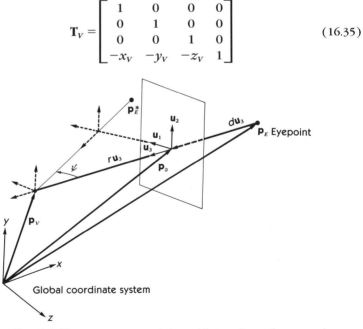

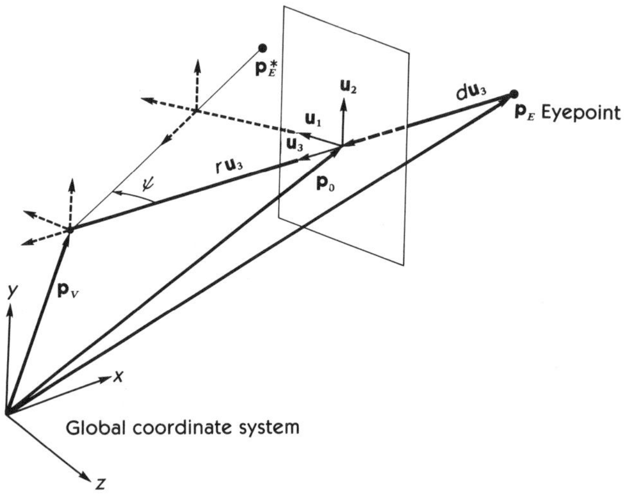

Fig. 16.9. Vector geometry of the orbit transformation.

Multiply x_V, y_V, and z_V by -1, because here you are transforming, or "moving," the coordinate system rather than points in it. Next, convert to a left-hand system using $\mathbf{T}_{RL}$ [Eq. (16.16)]. Then compute the angles of rotation that will align $\mathbf{u}_3$ with $\mathbf{p}_V - \mathbf{p}_E$, and apply the required rotation transformations, $\mathbf{T}_\theta$, $\mathbf{T}_\phi$. Usually, only two rotations are necessary. "Translate" the system to $\mathbf{p}_0$ using

$$\mathbf{T}_0 = \begin{bmatrix} 1 & 0 & 0 & 0 \\ 0 & 1 & 0 & 0 \\ 0 & 0 & 1 & 0 \\ 0 & 0 & \mathbf{r} & 1 \end{bmatrix} \tag{16.36}$$

where $\mathbf{r} = \mathbf{p}_V - \mathbf{p}_0$. The perspective projection transformation becomes:

$$\mathbf{T}_P = \begin{bmatrix} 1 & 0 & 0 & 0 \\ 0 & 1 & 0 & 0 \\ 0 & 0 & 1 & 1/d \\ 0 & 0 & 0 & 1 \end{bmatrix} \tag{16.37}$$

Finally, concatenate all of these transformations into a single expression giving the transformation of points in the world system into the picture plane:

$$\mathbf{p}^* = \mathbf{p}\mathbf{T}_V\mathbf{T}_{RL}\mathbf{T}_\theta\mathbf{T}_\phi\mathbf{T}_0\mathbf{T}_P \tag{16.38}$$

Generate subsequent views by **orbiting** around point $\mathbf{p}_V$, creating **orbit scene transformations.** The line of sight is always toward $\mathbf{p}_V$, although you may vary both d and r. For example, if you orbit "to the right" relative to the picture-plane coordinate system, then the eyepoint, $\mathbf{p}_E$, rotates about $\mathbf{p}_V$, say, through an angle ψ, in the plane defined by $\mathbf{u}_1$ and $\mathbf{u}_3$. This orbital motion can be described several ways, each leading to another set of transformation matrices appropriate for the new view.

Consider first rotating $\mathbf{p}_E$ around an axis in the direction of $\mathbf{u}_2$ and through $\mathbf{p}_V$ to produce $\mathbf{p}_E^*$, a new eyepoint. Repeat all the steps outlined above using $\mathbf{p}_E^*$ to create the new view. The orbiting type of eyepoint movement can, of course, include orbiting "up" or "down" by rotating around an axis through $\mathbf{p}_V$ and normal to the plane of $\mathbf{u}_2$ and $\mathbf{u}_3$ as well as variations in r and d. You can also rotate the view around $\mathbf{u}_3$, which does not change the projection. If you track the latest $\mathbf{p}_E^*$ relative to the global coordinate system and retain the initial eyepoint, then you can compute a "home" transformation that will restore the initial view. Note that you can orbit to the far side of an object and obtain a rear view.

16.4. Pan

Pan-scene transformations result when you apply equal vector translations of both the eyepoint, $\mathbf{p}_E$, and viewpoint, $\mathbf{p}_V$. You can pan right, left, up, or down. Figure 16.10 shows a pan to the right a distance c relative to $[\mathbf{u}_1\ \mathbf{u}_2\ \mathbf{u}_3]$. Calculate $\mathbf{p}_E^*$ and $\mathbf{p}_V^*$ from

$$\begin{aligned}\mathbf{p}_E^* &= \mathbf{p}_E + c\mathbf{u}_1 \\ \mathbf{p}_V^* &= \mathbf{p}_V + c\mathbf{u}_1\end{aligned} \tag{16.39}$$

Compute the other scene transformation components just as easily, and thereby complete the definition for a subsequent projection transformation. Note that the system $[\mathbf{u}_1\ \mathbf{u}_2\ \mathbf{u}_3]$ is translated parallel to its initial orientation, which also means that the projection plane is similarly translated to the new viewing position.

Figure 16.11 shows the effect of the pan transformations on the pro-

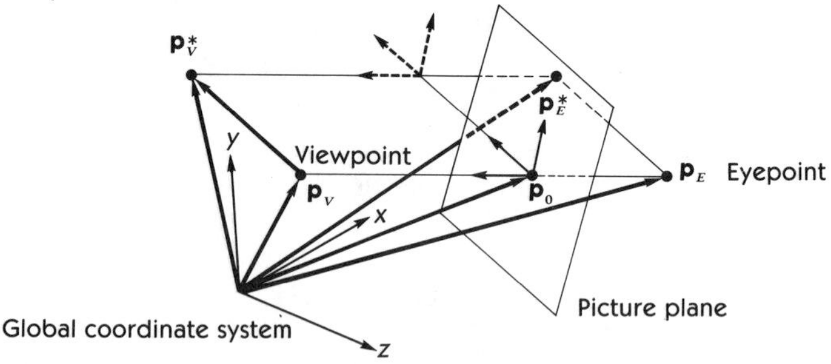

Fig. 16.10. Pan transformation.

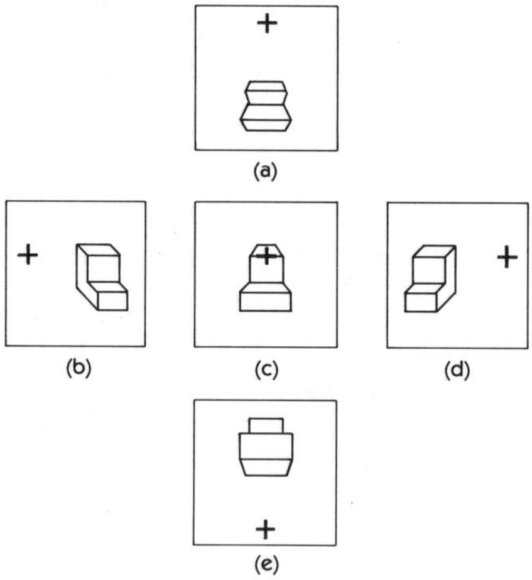

Fig. 16.11. The effects of pan transformations.

jection of a simple object. A cross marks the location of the viewpoint relative to the object in each scene. The eyepoint is located some arbitrary distance away from the picture plane (the page, in this case) and on the normal through the viewpoint. Note that the pan transformation can never generate the view of the opposite side of the object: A large enough pan motion will move the object out of the display in the opposite direction.

16.5. Aim

Aim-scene transformations come about by moving the viewpoint while maintaining the eyepoint in a fixed position. This is analogous to a person standing in one spot and looking to the right or left, up or down, forward or backward, or any rotation in between, to view the surroundings.

Relocate the viewpoint by a sequence of rotations of the line of sight, $\mathbf{p}_V - \mathbf{p}_E$, around $\mathbf{p}_E$ (Fig. 16.12). After constructing the initial display, define an aim movement by specifying an axis of rotation and an angle. The example in the figure shows a rotation, ψ, around the $\mathbf{u}_2$ axis. Thus, we determine new scene transformation components by first translating $[\mathbf{u}_1 \;\; \mathbf{u}_2 \;\; \mathbf{u}_3]$ into $\mathbf{p}_E$ and then, in the case of this example, rotating these unit vectors and $(\mathbf{p}_V - \mathbf{p}_E)$ around $\mathbf{u}_2$ through ψ. Following this rotation, reverse the translation of $[\mathbf{u}_1 \;\; \mathbf{u}_2 \;\; \mathbf{u}_3]$, and all the vector elements are now in place for a new projection.

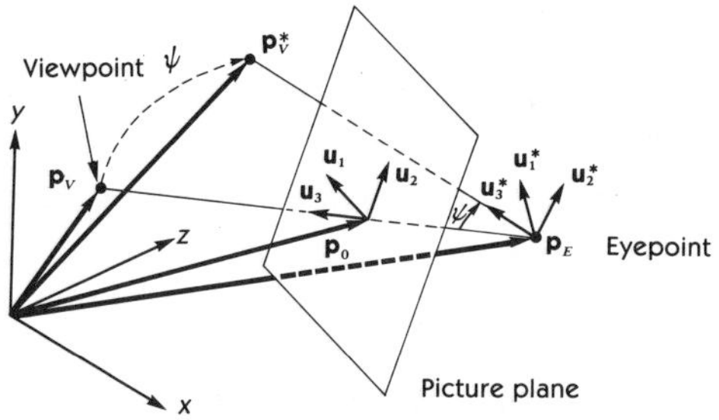

Fig. 16.12 Aim transformation.

17. Half-Spaces

THIS CHAPTER AND Chap. 18 introduce more advanced topics that are finding increasing application in geometric modeling and computer graphics. The mathematics of half-spaces, for example, formalizes many of the window and clipping operations and resolves containment problems. Topology is a step more abstract, although there are many direct applications to constructing and analyzing geometric models.

An unbounded straight line or plane curve divides the two-dimensional space into two semiinfinite regions, called **half-spaces.** Similarly, an unbounded plane or surface divides the three-dimensional space into two semiinfinite regions. These are also called half-spaces. Closed curves and surfaces, such as circles and spheres, also divide their spaces into regions, one finite and one infinite. These, too, are called half-spaces.

You can combine half-spaces using the union, limit, and difference operators to create geometric models of two- and three-dimensional shapes, including objects, clipping volumes, and shading and visibility volumes. This chapter introduces the techniques for doing this. One general principle for these techniques is: Preserve dimensional homogeneity. You should not mix two- and three-dimensional half-spaces.

17.1. Two-Dimensional Half-Spaces

Recall that in two-dimensional Cartesian space the general equation of a straight line is $ax + by + c = 0$. A straight line divides the two-dimensional space into two semiinfinite regions—half-spaces. This line also serves as the boundary of these half-spaces. So, for a half-space bounded by a straight line, let

$$h(x,y) = ax + by + c \tag{17.1}$$

where h denotes a half-space. Thus, $h(x,y)$ says that points in the half-space are a function of (depend on) the values of x and y. Any combination of values of x and y that satisfies the equation so that $h(x,y) = 0$ are on the line, the boundary of the half-space. Other values of x and y produce an inequality, either $h(x,y) > 0$ or $h(x,y) < 0$. Use the following conventions to classify a point with respect to a given half-space.

1. If the coordinates of a point produce $h(x,y) = 0$, then the point is on the boundary of the half-space.

2. If the coordinates of a point produce $h(x,y) > 0$, then the point is inside the half-space.

3. If the coordinates of a point produce $h(x,y) < 0$, then the point is outside the half-space.

A shorter form of notation is $h = h(x,y)$. Now look at an example.

In Fig. 17.1a, the line $x - 2y - 6 = 0$ divides the x,y plane into two half-spaces. If $h(x,y) = x - 2y - 6$ and you use the classification convention defined above, then the point $x = 0$, $y = 0$ lies outside the half-space. Since $h(x,y) = x - 2y - 6$, you obtain $h(0,0) = -6$, or $h(0,0) < 0$. On the other hand, at the point $x = 8$, $y = 0$, you obtain $h(8,0) = 2$ or $h(8,0) > 0$, and the point is inside the half-space.

Change the sign of $h(x,y)$ and you reverse the inside/outside classification. Thus, if $h(x,y) = -x + 2y + 6$, as in Fig. 17.1b, then the point at $x = 0$, $y = 0$, for example, is inside the half-space. The **complement** of $h(x,y)$ is $-h(x,y)$.

You are not restricted to using straight lines to define half-spaces. For example, in Fig. 17.2a a parabola forms the boundary of the half-space $h(x,y)$

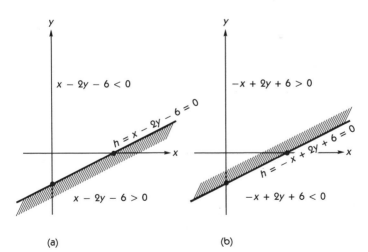

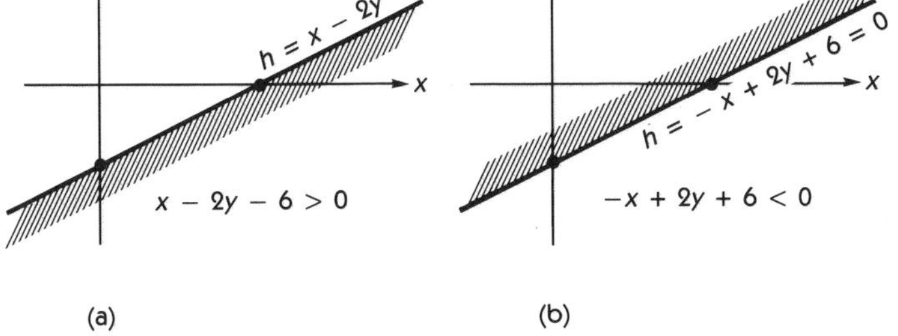

Fig. 17.1. Two-dimensional half-space defined by a straight line.

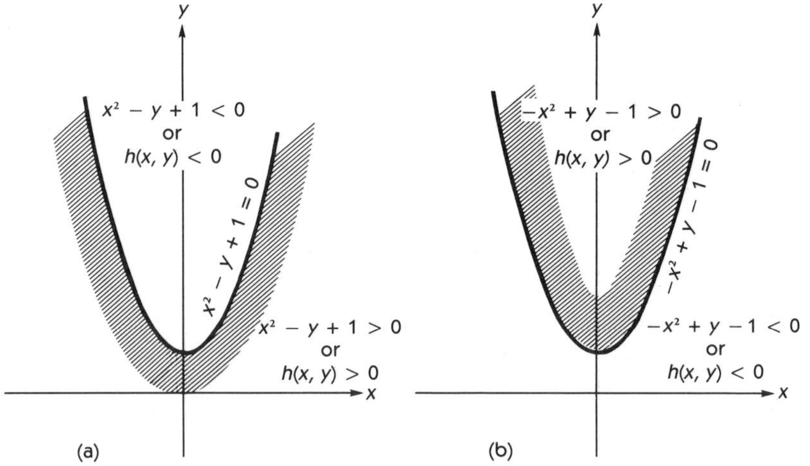

Fig. 17.2. Two-dimensional half-space with a parabolic curve boundary.

$= x^2 - y + 1$. Here $h(0,0) > 0$, and the reverse is true of its complement.

A final example is the circle defining the half-space $h(x,y) = (x - 2)^2 + (y - 2)^2 - 1$ (Fig. 17.3a). The complement of this, in Fig. 17.3b, defines a circular "solid" area. Again, points on the boundary yield $h = 0$, those inside $h > 0$, and those outside $h < 0$.

Note that any unbounded plane curve can define a half-space.

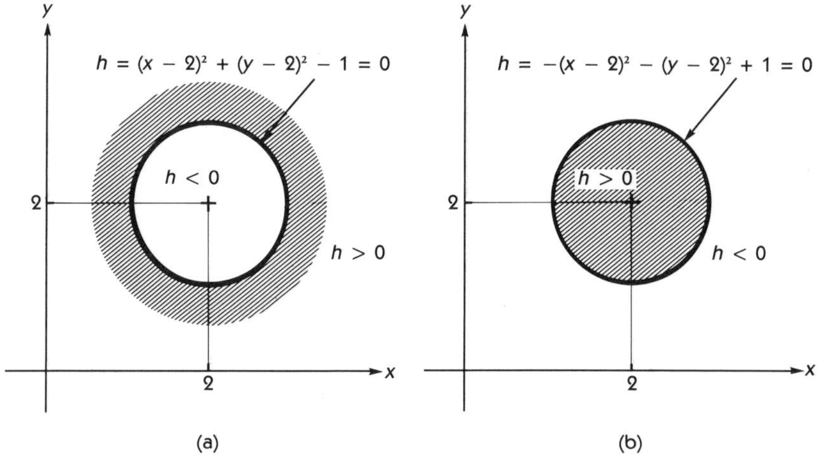

Fig. 17.3. Two-dimensional half-space bounded by a circle.

EXERCISES

1. Classify the following points with respect to $h_1 = -y + 3$.

a. $\mathbf{p}_1 = [0\ 0]$
b. $\mathbf{p}_2 = [0\ 5]$
c. $\mathbf{p}_3 = [-4\ 3]$
d. $\mathbf{p}_4 = [-3\ -1]$
e. $\mathbf{p}_5 = [5\ 0]$
f. $\mathbf{p}_6 = [1\ -4]$
g. $\mathbf{p}_7 = [6\ -3]$
h. $\mathbf{p}_8 = [3\ -2]$
i. $\mathbf{p}_9 = [3\ 4]$
j. $\mathbf{p}_{10} = [6\ 9]$

2. Classify the points given in Exercise 1 with respect to $h_2 = -x - 2$.

3. Classify the points given in Exercise 1 with respect to $h_3 = -2x + 3y - 6$.

4. Classify the points given in Exercise 1 with respect to the complement of h_3.

5. Which of the following points are inside both $h_4 = -x^2 - y^2 + 9$ and $h_5 = (x - 1)^2 + y^2 - 1$?

a. $\mathbf{p}_1 = [-1\ 4]$
b. $\mathbf{p}_2 = [0\ 3]$
c. $\mathbf{p}_3 = [-1\ 2]$
d. $\mathbf{p}_4 = [1\ 2]$
e. $\mathbf{p}_5 = [6\ 1]$
f. $\mathbf{p}_6 = [1\ 0.5]$
g. $\mathbf{p}_7 = [-3\ 0]$
h. $\mathbf{p}_8 = [0\ 0]$
i. $\mathbf{p}_9 = [1.5\ 0]$
j. $\mathbf{p}_{10} = [-1\ -1]$
k. $\mathbf{p}_{11} = [1\ -1]$
l. $\mathbf{p}_{12} = [2\ -1]$
m. $\mathbf{p}_{13} = [-3\ -2]$
n. $\mathbf{p}_{14} = [-2\ -4]$
o. $\mathbf{p}_{15} = [5\ -3]$

6. Which of the points defined in Exercise 5 are on the boundary of either h_4 or h_5?

7. Which of the points defined in Exercise 5 are outside either h_4 or h_5, or both?

8. If $h_1 = x - y^2 + 2$ and $h_2 = -x + y + 4$, accurately sketch the boundaries of the region containing points inside both these half-spaces.

17.2. Three-Dimensional Half-Spaces

A plane given by $Ax + By + Cz + D = 0$ divides three-dimensional space into two semiinfinite regions—half-spaces. Just as a straight line or curve serves as the boundary of a two-dimensional half-space, so too does a plane serve as the boundary of a three-dimensional half-space. Thus, a half-space bounded by a plane is given by

$$h(x,y,z) = Ax + By + Cz + D \tag{17.2}$$

Here $h(x,y,z)$ is a function of x, y, and z.

Use the same convention to classify points with respect to three-dimensional half-spaces as for two-dimensional half-spaces. Thus, if the coordinates of a point yield $h(x,y,z) = 0$, then the point is on the boundary. The point is outside the half-space if $h(x,y,z) < 0$, and inside if $h(x,y,z) > 0$.

Study the example in Fig. 17.4. Here the half-space is defined by $h = y - 4$. Any point whose y coordinate is 4 is on the boundary of the half-space. If $y > 4$, then $h > 0$, and the point is inside the half-space. Conversely, if $y < 4$, then the point is outside.

Next, study the half-space in Fig. 17.5. Here $h = -x - 5y + 20$. Is the origin inside or outside this half-space? It is inside, since $h = -(0) - 5(0) + 20 = 20$. What about the point whose coordinates are (5,7)? It is outside the half-space, since $h = -(5) - 5(7) + 20 = -20$.

In Fig. 17.6, the plane $3x + 3y + 4z - 24 = 0$ is the boundary of the half-space $h = 3x + 3y + 4z - 24$ or its complement $h^c = 3x - 3y - 4z + 24$. Note that the superscript lowercase letter c can denote the complement of a half-space. The origin is outside h and inside h^c.

A spherical half-space (shown in Fig. 17.7) is given by

$$h = (x - x_c)^2 + (y - y_c)^2 + (z - z_c)^2 - r^2 \qquad (17.3)$$

where x_c, y_c, z_c are the coordinates of the center point and r is the radius. For example, if the sphere has a radius of 2 and its center is (4,4,8), then

$$h = (x - 4)^2 + (y - 4)^2 + (z - 8)^2 - 4 \qquad (17.4)$$

This defines a three-dimensional unbounded space with a spherical "hole" embedded in it, since any point inside the sphere yields $h < 0$ and is

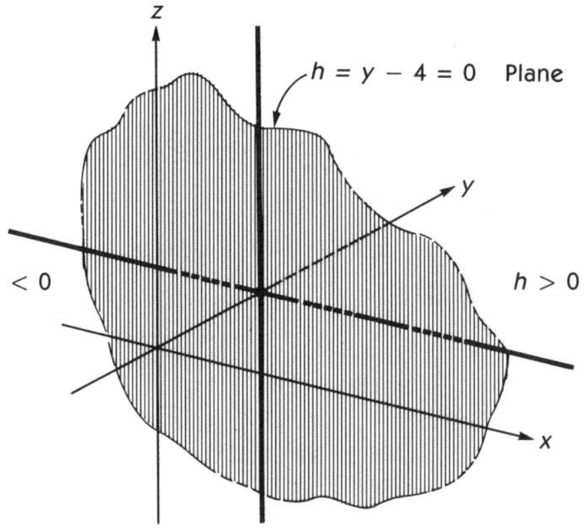

Fig. 17.4. Three-dimensional half-space bounded by the plane $y = 4$.

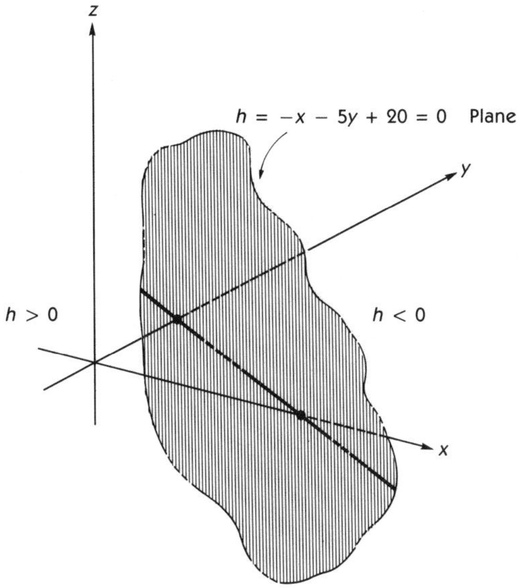

Fig. 17.5. Three-dimensional half-space bounded by the plane $-x - 5y + 20 = 0$.

outside the half-space. On the other hand, the complement of h is

$$h^c = -(x - 4)^2 - (y - 4)^2 - (z - 8)^2 + 4 \qquad (17.5)$$

This is a bounded, closed spherical half-space, and points inside the sphere are inside the half-space.

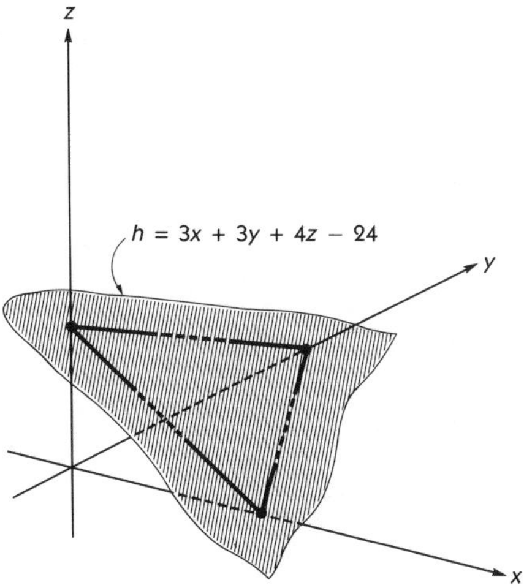

Fig. 17.6. Three-dimensional half-space bounded by an arbitrary plane.

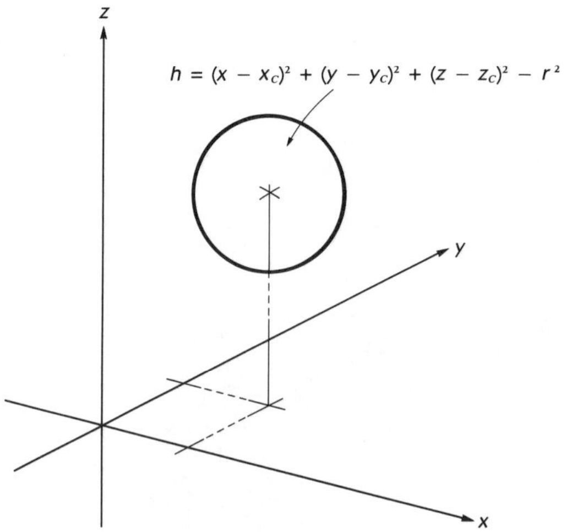

Fig. 17.7. Three-dimensional half-space bounded by a sphere.

The half-space in Fig. 17.8 is a cylinder given by

$$h = -x^2 - z^2 + 9 \tag{17.6}$$

Show that the origin is inside this cylindrical half-space.

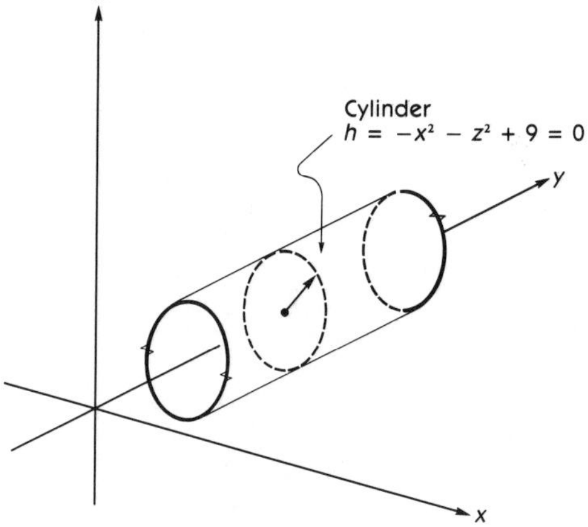

Fig. 17.8. Three-dimensional half-space bounded by a cylinder.

EXERCISES

1. Classify the following points with respect to the half-space $h_1 = -z + 4$.

a. $\mathbf{p}_1 = [0\ 0\ 0]$
b. $\mathbf{p}_2 = [2\ -5\ 6]$
c. $\mathbf{p}_3 = [3\ 1\ -4]$
d. $\mathbf{p}_4 = [-7\ 5\ 4]$
e. $\mathbf{p}_5 = [8\ 1\ 7]$
f. $\mathbf{p}_6 = [11\ -3\ 5]$
g. $\mathbf{p}_7 = [0\ 0\ 4]$
h. $\mathbf{p}_8 = [4\ 8\ 0]$
i. $\mathbf{p}_9 = [12\ 9\ 4]$
j. $\mathbf{p}_{10} = [-9\ 3\ 3]$

2. Classify the following points with respect to the half-space $h_2 = 16 - x^2 - y^2 - z^2$.

a. $\mathbf{p}_1 = [0\ 0\ 0]$
b. $\mathbf{p}_2 = [2\ 1\ 0]$
c. $\mathbf{p}_3 = [-5\ 2\ 4]$
d. $\mathbf{p}_4 = [-3\ 5\ 6]$
e. $\mathbf{p}_5 = [1\ 0\ 1]$
f. $\mathbf{p}_6 = [0\ -4\ 0]$
g. $\mathbf{p}_7 = [2\ 7\ -3]$
h. $\mathbf{p}_8 = [0\ 0\ 4]$
i. $\mathbf{p}_9 = [2\ 1\ 1]$
j. $\mathbf{p}_{10} = [3\ -6\ 4]$

17.3. Intersections of Half-Spaces

Half-spaces can combine to form complex shapes that are closed and bounded. To do this, use Boolean operators, principally the intersect operator. Again, you must preserve dimensional homogeneity. Two-dimensional half-spaces combine only with other two-dimensional half-spaces, and three-dimensional half-spaces combine only with other three-dimensional half-spaces. Let us first investigate intersections of two-dimensional half spaces.

If $h_1 = x + y - 8$ and $h_2 = x - y - 3$, then express the intersection of these two half-spaces as

$$g = h_1 \cap h_2 \tag{17.7}$$

where g denotes a combination of two or more half-spaces. Note that g is not necessarily a closed finite region; see Fig. 17.9. Table 17.1 presents the possible point classifications with respect to the intersection of these two half-spaces.

There are several things worth noting in this table. First, any point outside either h_1 or h_2 is outside $h_1 \cap h_2$. Second, every point on the boundary of $h_1 \cap h_2$ is on the boundary of either h_1 or h_2 and inside the other. The exception to this is that any point on the boundary of both h_1 and h_2 is on the boundary of $h_1 \cap h_2$. Finally, every point inside $h_1 \cap h_2$ must be inside both h_1 and h_2.

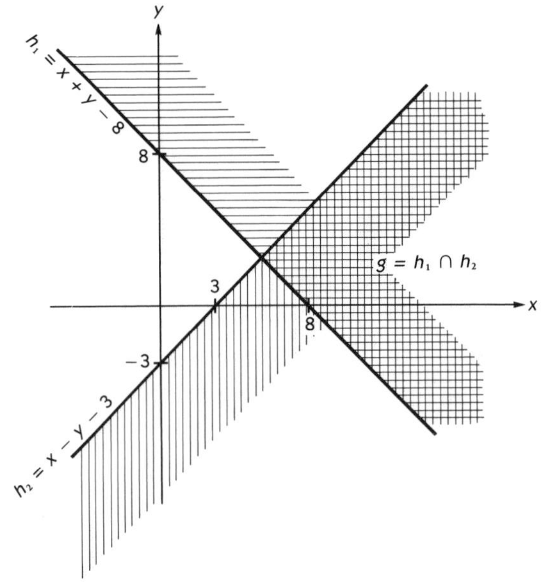

Fig. 17.9. Intersection of two two-dimensional half-spaces.

The classification conditions in this table apply to the intersection of any two half-spaces. These conditions are independent of both the shape and dimensionality of the half-spaces.

Figure 17.10 shows the intersection of four half-spaces that defines a rectangular region. In this case the result is finite and closed. Express this as

$$g = h_1 \cap h_2 \cap h_3 \cap h_4 \tag{17.8}$$

Table 17.1. $h_1 \cap h_2$: Point Classification

	If						Then		
Condition	ih_1	bh_1	oh_1	ih_2	bh_2	oh_2	$i(h_1 \cap h_2)$	$b(h_1 \cap h_2)$	$o(h_1 \cap h_2)$
1	X			X			X		
2	X				X			X	
3	X					X			X
4		X		X				X	
5		X			X			X	
6		X				X			X
7			X	X					X
8			X		X				X
9			X			X			X

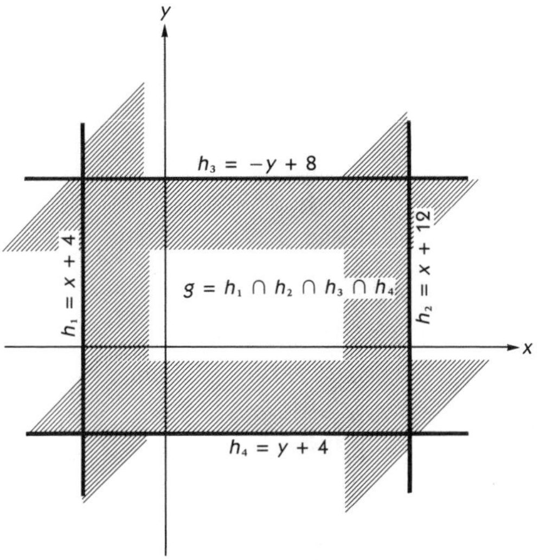

Fig. 17.10. Intersection of two-dimensional half-spaces to form a bounded rectangular shape.

or more concisely as

$$g = \bigcap_{i=1}^{4} h_i \tag{17.9}$$

using the summation notation discussed in Box 17.1. Experiment with simple combinations to see if you can create order-dependent shapes using a fixed set of half-spaces.

Listing all of the point classification conditions is cumbersome with more than two half-spaces, so instead follow these three classification rules:

1. If and only if a point is inside all h_i, then it is inside g.

2. If and only if a point is outside at least one h_i, then it is outside g.

3. If and only if a point is on the boundary of at least one h_i and inside the remaining h_i, then it is on the boundary of g.

Verify that these rules apply to the results of half-space intersections shown in Figs. 17.11 and 17.12. Note that in Fig. 17.12, h_4 creates a hole, but the rules still apply.

The g is the same dimension as the h_i that form it. In Fig. 17.13, six three-dimensional half-spaces defined by planes intersect to form a cube. In Fig. 17.14, two three-dimensional half-spaces defined by planes and one defined by a cylindrical surface intersect to form a cylindrical solid.

Box 17.1 Boolean Summation

Express sequences of combining operations on geometric elements using Boolean operators **union** and **intersect** in compact notation as follows

$$b = \bigcup_{i=1}^{n} g_i$$

When expanded, this looks like

$$b = g_1 \cup g_2 \cup g_3 \cup g_4 \cup \cdots \cup g_n$$

This means that to construct a body or shape take the sequential accumulated union of a series of n other bodies or shapes. Do the same thing with the intersect operator; thus,

$$b = \bigcap_{i=1}^{n} g_i$$

or

$$b = g_1 \cap g_2 \cap g_3 \cap \cdots \cap g_n$$

You can also combine the union and intersect notation to yield

$$b = \bigcup_{i=1}^{m} \bigcap_{j=1}^{n} g_{ij}$$

This means to compute the union of m sets of shapes, each defined by a series of no more than n intersections of simpler shapes. When expanded, this becomes

$$\begin{aligned} b = & (g_{11} \cap g_{12} \cap g_{13} \cap \cdots \cap g_{1n}) \\ & \cup (g_{21} \cap g_{22} \cap g_{23} \cap \cdots \cap g_{2n}) \cup \cdots \\ & \cup (g_{m1} \cap g_{m2} \cap g_{m3} \cap \cdots \cap g_{mn}) \end{aligned}$$

The general formulation for intersections of this type, whether two or three dimensional, is

$$g = \bigcap_{i=1}^{n} h_i \tag{17.10}$$

where n is the number of half-spaces. Note that this process by itself does not guarantee a finite g. In fact, g can be null if one of the h_i does not, indeed, intersect the net intersection of the other h_i. More advanced techniques solve the problem of verifying the finiteness and nonnullity of g.

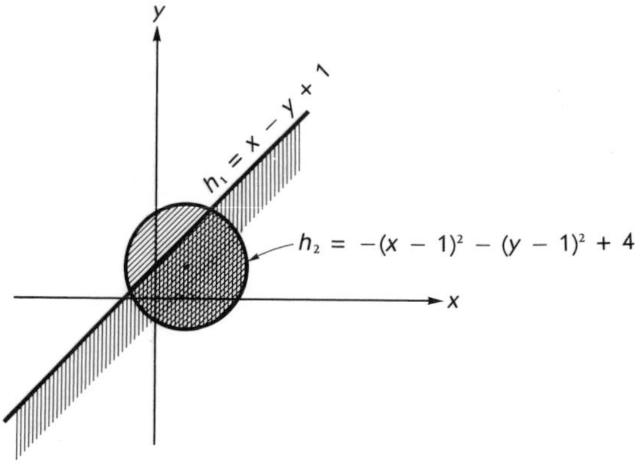

Fig. 17.11. Intersection of two-dimensional half-spaces to form a bounded truncated circular shape.

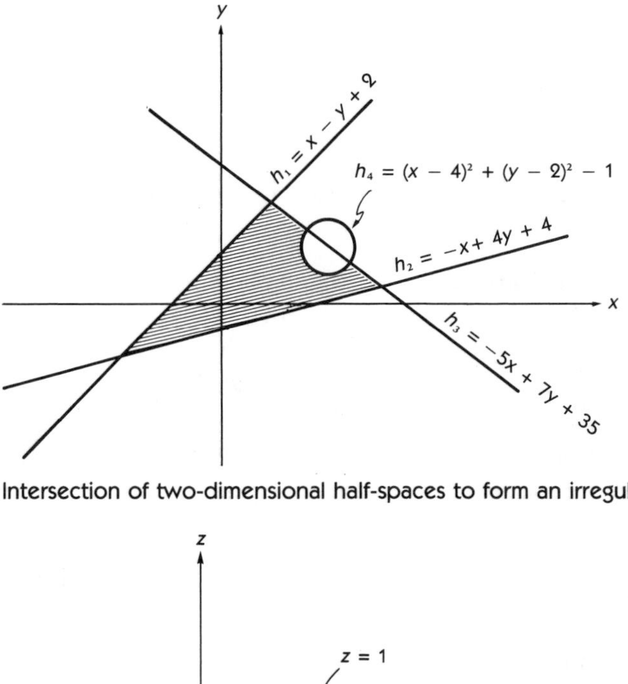

Fig. 17.12. Intersection of two-dimensional half-spaces to form an irregular shape.

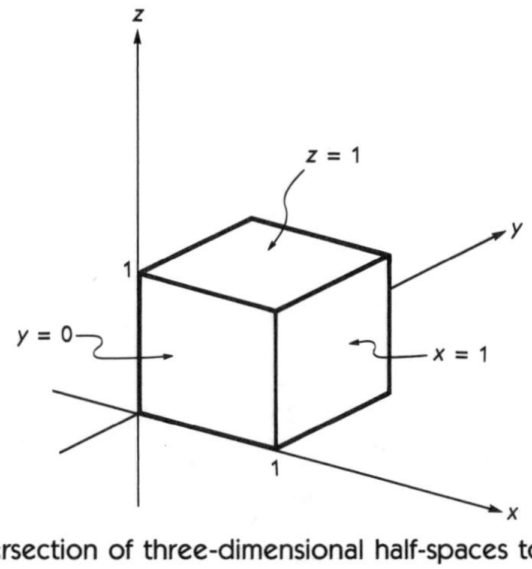

Fig. 17.13. Intersection of three-dimensional half-spaces to form a cube.

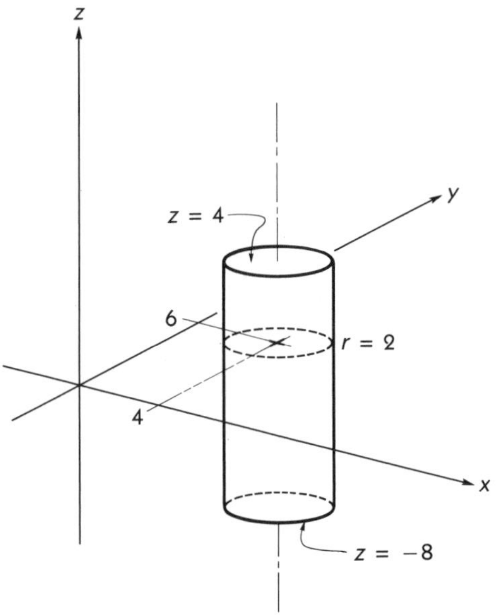

Fig. 17.14. Intersection of three-dimensional half-spaces to form a cylindrical solid.

Also combine half-spaces using both the intersect operator and the union operator. Perform sets of intersections first, then combine the results with the union operator. The solid in Fig. 17.15 is produced in this way. Here you create three separate blocks by intersecting appropriate half-spaces and combine the results with the union operator. To do this, use the following half-spaces. Note that each is identified with a double subscript. The reason for this will become clear as you progress. Thus,

$$\begin{array}{lll} h_{1,1} = x, & h_{2,1} = x, & h_{3,1} = x \\ h_{1,2} = -x + 4, & h_{2,2} = -x + 3, & h_{3,2} = -x + 3 \\ h_{1,3} = y, & h_{2,3} = y, & h_{4,2} = y - 4 \\ h_{1,4} = -y + 6, & h_{2,4} = -y + 2, & h_{5,2} = -y + 6 \\ h_{1,5} = z, & h_{2,5} = z - 2, & h_{6,2} = z - 2 \\ h_{1,6} = -z + 2, & h_{2,6} = -z + 8, & h_{7,2} = -z + 8 \end{array} \tag{17.11}$$

One way to define the shape shown in Fig. 17.15 and constructed of these half-spaces is

$$\begin{aligned} g = {} & (h_{1,1} \cap h_{1,2} \cap h_{1,3} \cap h_{1,4} \cap h_{1,5} \cap h_{1,6}) \\ & \cup (h_{2,1} \cap h_{2,2} \cap h_{2,3} \cap h_{2,4} \cap h_{2,5} \cap h_{2,6}) \\ & \cup (h_{3,1} \cap h_{3,2} \cap h_{3,3} \cap h_{3,4} \cap h_{3,5} \cap h_{3,6}) \end{aligned} \tag{17.12}$$

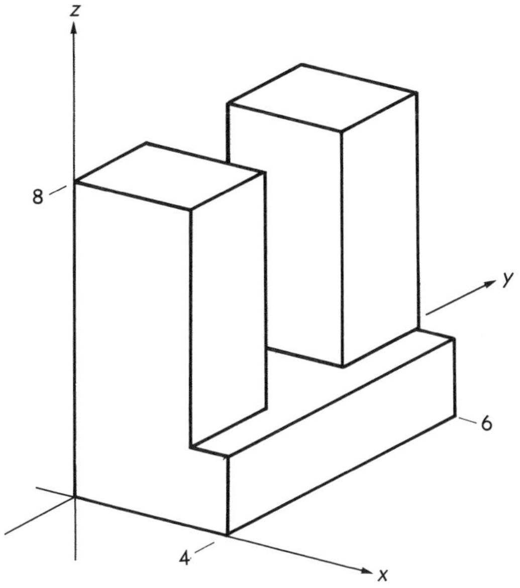

Fig. 17.15. A series of three-dimensional half-space intersections and their subsequent union to form a complex solid.

Or, use a much more concise summation notation to yield

$$g = \bigcup_{i=1}^{3} \bigcap_{j=1}^{6} h_{ij} \tag{17.13}$$

This statement says, in effect: First perform all the intersections. There are three sets, one each for $i = 1$, $i = 2$, and $i = 3$. Then take the union of these sets. So, first set $i = 1$ and exhaust the j's. Next, set $i = 2$ and exhaust the j's. Finally, set $i = 3$ and once more exhaust the j's.

Use the difference operator to create the shape in Fig. 17.16. To do this, define a slightly different set of half-spaces:

$$\begin{aligned}
&h_{1,1} = x, && h_{2,1} = x - 3, && h_{3,1} = x \\
&h_{1,2} = -x + 4, && h_{2,2} = -x + 4, && h_{3,2} = -x + 4 \\
&h_{1,3} = y, && h_{2,3} = y, && h_{3,3} = y - 2 \\
&h_{1,4} = -y + 6, && h_{2,4} = -y + 6, && h_{3,4} = -y + 4 \\
&h_{1,5} = z, && h_{2,5} = z - 2, && h_{3,5} = z - 2 \\
&h_{1,6} = -z + 8, && h_{2,6} = -z + 8, && h_{3,6} = -z + 8
\end{aligned} \tag{17.14}$$

Next create three intermediate shapes defined by

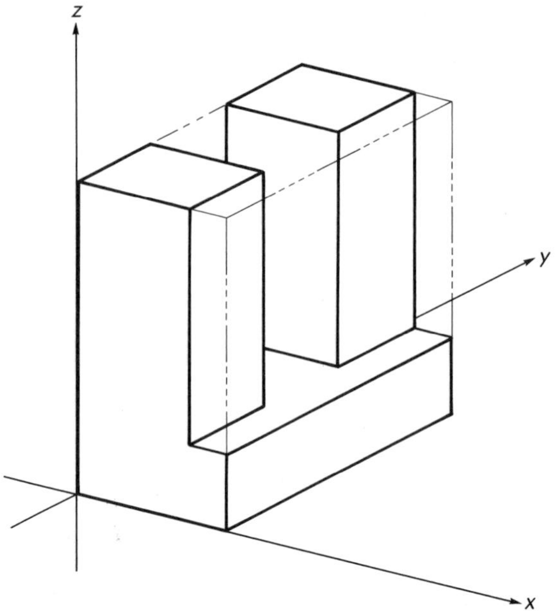

Fig. 17.16. A series of three-dimensional half-space intersections and their subsequent difference to form a complex solid.

$$g_i = \bigcap_{j=1}^{6} h_{ij}, \qquad i = 1,2,3 \tag{17.15}$$

Finally, combine these g_i's using the difference operator to obtain

$$g = g_1 - g_2 - g_3 \tag{17.16}$$

EXERCISES

1. Classify the following points with respect to the solid defined in Fig. 17.13.

   a. $\mathbf{p}_1 = [-1\ 0\ 2]$
   b. $\mathbf{p}_2 = [0\ 1\ 1]$
   c. $\mathbf{p}_3 = [0.5\ 0.5\ 0]$
   d. $\mathbf{p}_4 = [1\ 2\ 1]$
   e. $\mathbf{p}_5 = [0.25\ 0.5\ 0.5]$

2. Classify the following points with respect to the solid defined in Fig. 17.14.

   a. $\mathbf{p}_1 = [5\ 5\ 3]$
   b. $\mathbf{p}_2 = [4\ 4\ -7]$
   c. $\mathbf{p}_3 = [6\ 4\ 5]$
   d. $\mathbf{p}_4 = [4\ 8\ 0]$
   e. $\mathbf{p}_5 = [7\ 4\ 2]$

3. Given $h_1 = x - y + 2$, $h_2 = y + 1$, $h_3 = -x + 4$, and $h_4 = x - 6$,

a. Find $g = h_1 \cap h_2 \cap h_3 \cap h_4$; sketch the individual half-spaces.
b. Find $g = h_3 \cap h_4 \cup h_1 \cap h_2$; sketch the results.
c. What happens if, instead of h_4, you use h_4^c? Sketch the result.

18. Topology

WHEN YOU STUDY **topology,** you study properties of geometric shapes that do not change when these shapes are deformed. Imagine that you have rubber models of the shapes; you can bend, stretch, and twist them in any way whatsoever, but you are not allowed to cut or tear them. You will discover properties of these shapes that remain constant. Many of these properties will be intuitively obvious; others are more subtle, but nonetheless easy to understand.

The ideas in this chapter are very basic and only hint at the richness of this branch of geometry. You will probably find you will want to learn much more about the subject.

18.1. Topological Equivalence

Two geometric shapes may look quite different but turn out to be **topologically equivalent.** Two shapes are topologically equal to each other if one can be deformed into the other. The four shapes in Fig. 18.1 are topologically equal. You can easily imagine distorting any of the nonspherical shapes into a sphere. Now look at Fig. 18.2. All of these shapes are topologically equal, since all can be distorted into the shape of a torus or donut.

Can the toruslike shapes be distorted into a spherical shape? No. So the shapes in Fig. 18.2 are not topologically equal to those in Fig. 18.1. The surfaces of these two sets of shapes reflect their topological differences. For example, all simple non-self-intersecting closed curves that you can construct on the surface of a sphere are equivalent. Imagine moving several of these closed curves around on the sphere's surfaces, stretching, shrinking, and deforming them until they become congruent and superimposed (Fig. 18.3a). There are three families of closed curves on a torus (Fig. 18.3b), none of which can be brought into correspondence with a member of a different family. Study curves 1, 2, and 3. Each of these curves

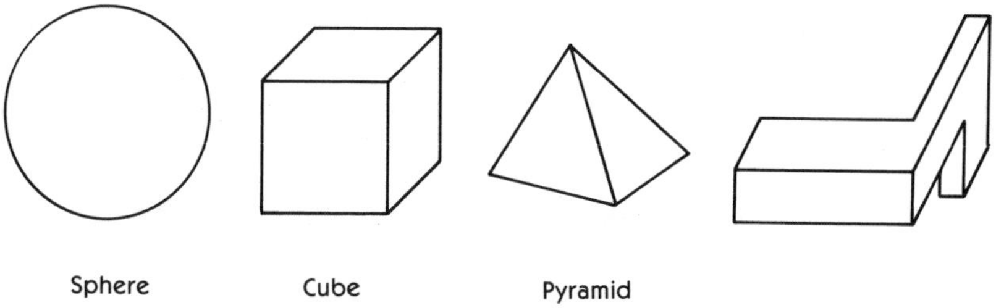

Fig. 18.1. Topologically equivalent shapes.

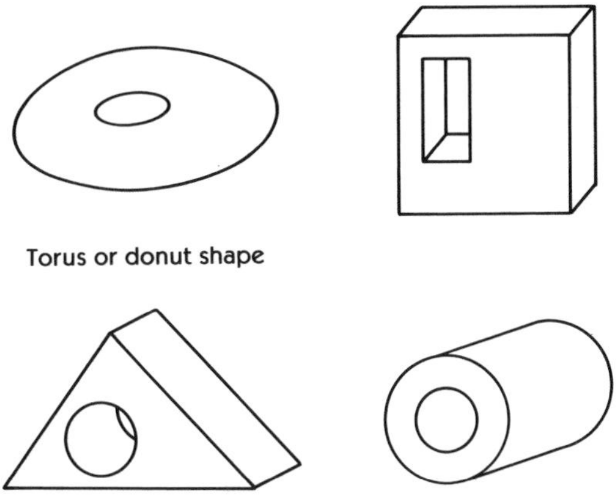

Fig. 18.2. More topologically equivalent shapes.

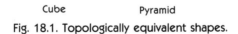

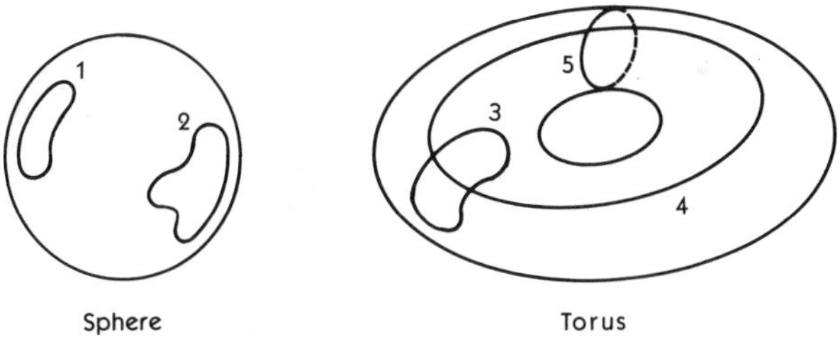

Fig. 18.3. Curves on surfaces.

can be shrunk to a point. This cannot be done to curves 4 and 5 without cutting the surface of the torus. In fact, closed curves, like 1, 2, and 3, form or define **topological disks** on the surface on which they lie, because they can be shrunk to a point. Closed curves 4 and 5 do not define topological disks.

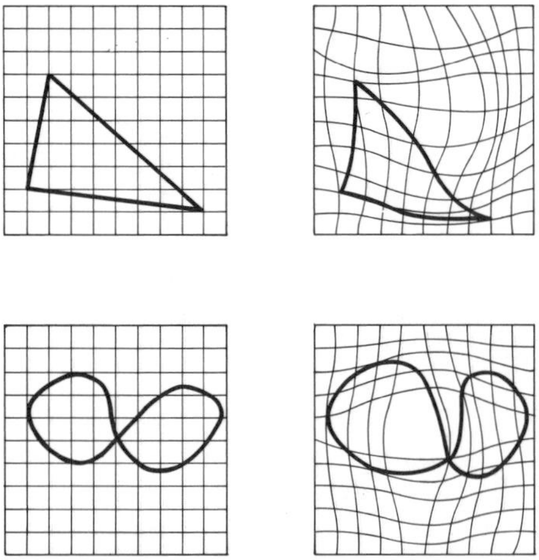

Fig. 18.4. Deformation of curves on a surface.

You could readily find other properties of curves on surfaces that undergo rubber-sheet deformations. Look at the examples in Fig. 18.4. Here the property of self-intersection is preserved. What about metric properties—length, angle, area, and so forth? Are these preserved? No, they are not, because, again, you can imagine stretching or compressing a surface, causing an increase or decrease in any or all of these metric properties. That is why they are not topological properties.

18.2. Intersection Properties

Consider the intersections of the closed curves and straight lines in Fig. 18.5. The following properties are true if these elements all lie in the same surface:

1. An infinitely long straight line or curve always intersects a closed curve an even number of times, if it intersects at all.

2. Two closed curves intersect an even number of times, if they intersect at all.

Refining these properties can help you to decide if a point is inside or outside a closed curve or closed surface. Study Fig. 18.6. You will see that:

1. A point is outside a closed curve or surface if a semiinfinite line drawn from it intersects the closed curve or surface an even number of times.

2. A point is inside a closed curve or surface if a semiinfinite line drawn from it intersects the closed curve or surface an odd number of times.

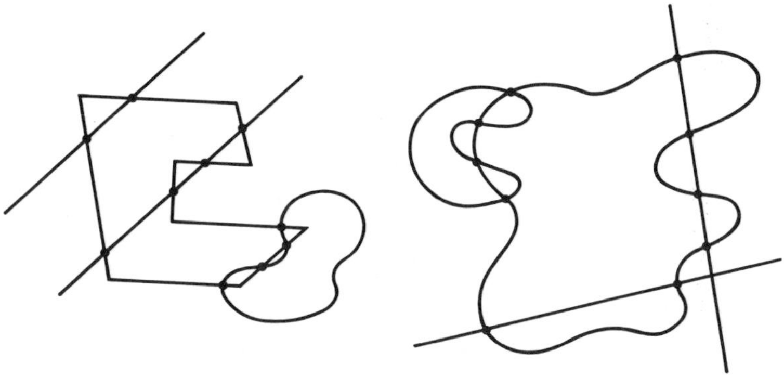

Fig. 18.5. Intersection properties of lines and closed curves.

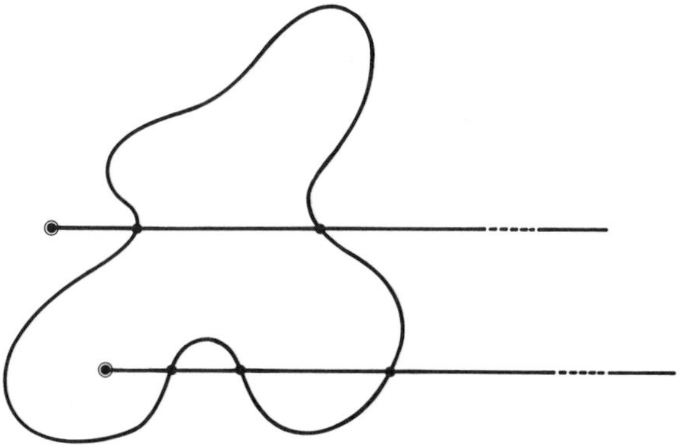

Fig. 18.6. Inside/outside.

Note that you need one additional rule when counting intersections: Do not count tangent points.

Here is another property to consider: If an unbounded plane intersects a closed surface, then the intersection is one or more closed curves. (A closed curve can have straight or "curved" sides. Thus, a square is a closed curve.)

18.3. Orientation

If you have never made a surface called a Möbius strip, now is a good time to do it. Take a strip of paper about 12 in. long and 1 in. wide. Glue or tape the two ends together to form a loop, but before you do, give one end a twist of 180°, so that the complete loop will have this twist built

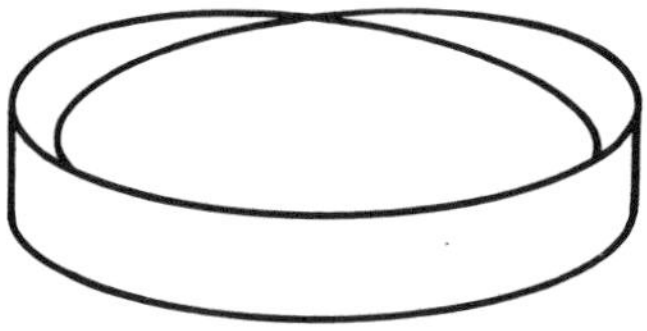

Fig. 18.7. A Möbius strip.

into it. See Fig. 18.7; this is a Möbius strip, and it has many interesting properties that an ordinary, untwisted loop does not have.

An inhabitant of a Möbius strip observes a curious fact. If it starts out at some point and takes a trip all the way around the strip, when it gets back to its initial position it finds that left and right are reversed. This happens because left and right are not intrinsically defined. Externally, whether a turn appears left or right depends on the side of the surface you are looking from. It is an extrinsic property of the surface and depends on setting up an external reference. So, you must specify that the observation is from the top side or from the bottom side.

Right and left are characteristics of the two-dimensional Möbius strip inhabitant's motions, not characteristics of the surface. If you visualize yourself as an inhabitant of the Möbius strip, you can define right and left on the surface, but the definition works only locally. You cannot look at some point on the surface and then decide in advance that one direction is either right or left. You must first move around on the surface. There is nothing to guarantee that, as you move around the surface, the commands left and right will generate the same orientation each time you return to a given point. This potential reversal and confusion is exactly what happens on the Möbius strip.

A surface on which left and right are never reversed is called **orientable,** and you can establish a consistent left and right definition on the surface. If you find a path that confuses left and right, the surface is called **nonorientable.**

You can demonstrate this same property of orientability by using rotation, establishing initial clockwise and counterclockwise rotations. Then see if there exists a closed path that results in a rotation reversal.

18.4. Euler's Formula and Connectivity

On any closed surface you can construct a network (called a **net**) of edges and vertices analogous to those defining polyhedra. The edges, obviously do not have to be straight lines. The net must have the following properties:

1. Each edge is terminated by two vertices.
2. Each edge subtends two faces. (Faces can be curved, of course.)
3. Each vertex subtends three or more edges.
4. Each face, each loop of edges, must be a topological disk.
5. The net must divide the entire surface into topological disks.

Now, define a connectivity number, n, and modify Euler's formula so that

$$V - E + F = 2 - n \tag{18.1}$$

For a sphere and all topologically equivalent shapes, $n = 0$. For all toruslike shapes, $n = 2$, and $n = 4$ for all shapes like a solid figure-eight. This means that you can use Eq. (18.1) to determine n and thus determine the type of surface. Look at the three examples in Fig. 18.8. In Fig. 18.8a, the net on the sphere has the following characteristics: $V = 8$, $E = 16$, $F = 10$, and $n = 0$. These values do indeed satisfy Eq. (18.1). In Fig. 18.8b, find the following characteristics of the net on the toruslike shape: $V = 16$, E

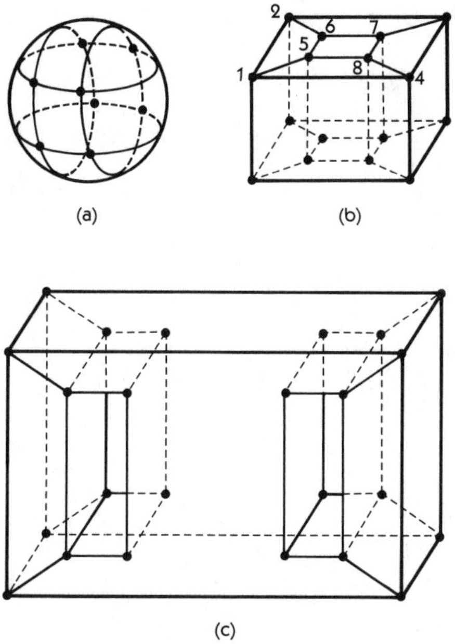

Fig. 18.8. The connectivity number n.

= 32, F = 16, n = 2. Again, Eq. (18.1) is satisfied. And, finally, for the solid figure-eight shape in Fig. 18.8c, find that: V = 24, E = 44, F = 18, n = 4, satisfying the equation.

Take another look at Fig. 18.8b. Do you see why it is necessary to have edges like 1–5, 2–6, 3–7, and 4–8? *Hint:* If these edges were missing, would the face contained between the loop of edges 1–2–3–4–1 and 5–6–7–8–5 be a topological disk?

Answers to Selected Exercises

Chapter 1

SECTION 1.1

1. a. Inside
   b. Inside
   c. Outside
   d. Inside
   e. Outside
   f. Inside
   g. Outside
   h. Outside
   i. Inside
   j. Inside

3. a. Interval x_A contains *d*, *e*, *f*, *h*, and *j*.
   b. Interval x_B contains *a*, *b*, *c*, *f*, *i*, and *j*.
   c. Interval x_C contains *a*, *b*, *d*, *e*, *f*, *h*, and *j*.
   d. Interval x_D contains *a*, *b*, and *f*.

SECTION 1.2

1. a. $\mathbf{p}_1^* = (6, -4)$
   b. $\mathbf{p}_2^* = (1, -2)$
   c. $\mathbf{p}_3^* = (6, -3)$
   d. $\mathbf{p}_4^* = (4, -3)$
   e. $\mathbf{p}_5^* = (4, 0)$
   f. $\mathbf{p}_6^* = (7, 2)$
   g. $\mathbf{p}_7^* = (2, 2)$
   h. $\mathbf{p}_8^* = (-2, -1)$
   i. $\mathbf{p}_9^* = (1, -7)$
   j. $\mathbf{p}_{10}^* = (0, 0)$

SECTION 1.3

1. a. $\mathbf{p}_1^* = (-6, -4, +2)$
   b. $\mathbf{p}_2^* = (0, -3, 3)$
   c. $\mathbf{p}_3^* = (-10, -2, -1)$
   d. $\mathbf{p}_4^* = (0, 0, 0)$
   e. $\mathbf{p}_5^* = (-9, -13, 2)$
   f. $\mathbf{p}_6^* = (-1, -11, 1)$
   g. $\mathbf{p}_7^* = (-15, -5, -1)$
   h. $\mathbf{p}_8^* = (-4, -7, 0)$
   i. $\mathbf{p}_9^* = (2, 1, 10)$
   j. $\mathbf{p}_{10}^* = (-5, -4, 2)$

2. $r = \sqrt{x^2 + y^2 + z^2}$
   $\theta = \tan^{-1}(y/x)$
   $\phi = \cos^{-1}(z/\sqrt{x^2 + y^2 + z^2})$

3. a. $r = 0$, $\theta = 0$, $\phi = 0$
b. $r = 6.164$, $\theta = 9.462°$, $\phi = 80.664°$
c. $r = 5.385$, $\theta = 153.435°$, $\phi = 123.856°$
d. $r = 7.483$, $\theta = 33.690°$, $\phi = 105.503°$
e. $r = 9.487$, $\theta = -108.435°$, $\phi = 90°$
f. $r = 8.660$, $\theta = -54.462°$, $\phi = 96.631°$
g. $r = 9.539$, $\theta = -173.660°$, $\phi = 108.351°$
h. $r = 4.123$, $\theta = -56.310°$, $\phi = 119.018°$
i. $r = 12.369$, $\theta = 32.005°$, $\phi = 49.701°$
j. $r = 1$, $\theta = 0°$, $\phi = 90°$

SECTION 1.5

1. $x_s = \left(\dfrac{x - Wx_L}{Wx_R - Wx_L}\right)Vx_R$, $y_s = \left(\dfrac{y - Wy_B}{Wy_T - Wy_B}\right)Vy_T$ since $Vx_L = 0$ and $Vy_B = 0$.

Chapter 2

SECTION 2.1

1. Define a polar coordinate system as the set of all points in a plane defined by the real numbers (r, θ), where $r \in [0, \infty]$ and $\theta \in [-\pi, \pi]$. The origin is the point with $r = 0$ and $\theta = 0$. The x axis is the set of points $\mathbf{p} = (r, 0)$, where $r \in [0, \infty]$. The positive y axis is the set of points $\mathbf{p} = (r, \pi/2)$, and the negative y axis is the set of points $\mathbf{p} = (r, -\pi/2)$.

4. a. 14.526
b. 13.491
c. 5.987
d. 13.491
e. 0
f. 10.000
g. 6.557
h. 14.522
i. 9.959
j. 8.124

9. a. (2.5, 6.5, 5.5)
b. (2, 1.5, 2.5)
c. (3.9, 7.65, −1)
d. (−0.5, 4, 0.5)
e. (0, 0, 1)
f. (2, 0, 0)
g. (2.5, 3.5, −1.5)
h. (1.2, 0.4, 1.35)
i. (3.5, −0.65, 0.85)
j. (6.5, 8.5, 1)

SECTION 2.2

1. Given $\mathbf{p}_0 = (x_0, y_0)$, then
$\mathbf{p}_1 = (x_0 + \Delta, y_0 + \Delta)$
$\mathbf{p}_2 = (x_0 + 2\Delta, y_0 + 2\Delta)$
$\mathbf{p}_3 = (x_0 + 3\Delta, y_0 + 3\Delta)$
$\mathbf{p}_4 = (x_0 + 4\Delta, y_0 + 4\Delta)$

3. $\Delta_1 = (0, 4)$
$\Delta_2 = (4, 0)$
$\Delta_3 = (0, -4)$
$\Delta_4 = (-4, 0)$

SECTION 2.3

1. $\mathbf{p}_1, \mathbf{p}_8, \mathbf{p}_9$

SECTION 2.4

1. $x^* = (x + x_T)\cos\theta - (y + y_T)\sin\theta$
$y^* = (x + x_T)\sin\theta + (y + y_T)\cos\theta$

3. Translating and then rotating a point does not, in general, produce the same result as rotating and then translating the point. Thus, the order in which you perform a set of two or more sequential transformations (combining rotations and translations) is important.

4. $\phi = -\theta$

Chapter 3

SECTION 3.1

1. $\sigma_x^2 + \sigma_y^2 + \sigma_z^2 = \dfrac{(x_1 - x_0)^2 + (y_1 - y_0)^2 + (z_1 - z_0)^2}{L^2}$

But, $(x_1 - x_0)^2 + (y_1 - y_0)^2 + (z_1 - z_0)^2 = L^2$;
Thus, $\sigma_x^2 + \sigma_y^2 + \sigma_z^2 = 1$

3. a. $L = 12.267$, $\sigma_x = -0.228$, $\sigma_y = -0.954$, $\sigma_z = 0.196$
b. $L = 8.824$, $\sigma_x = 0.136$, $\sigma_y = 0.805$, $\sigma_z = -0.578$
c. $L = 9.271$, $\sigma_x = 0.464$, $\sigma_y = 0.658$, $\sigma_z = 0.593$
d. $L = 13.137$, $\sigma_x = -0.403$, $\sigma_y = 0.913$, $\sigma_z = 0.053$

7. Length is unchanged. Signs of direction cosines are reversed.

9. a. $x = 4$, $y = 3$, $z = -4u + 10$
b. $x = -6u + 5$, $y = 4u - 4$, $z = 7u$
c. $x = -u + 1$, $y = 0$, $z = 0$
d. $x = 0$, $y = -u + 1$, $z = 0$
e. $x = 0$, $y = 0$, $z = -u + 1$

SECTION 3.2

1. a. (1, 0, 0), (2, 0, 0), (3, 0, 0), (4, 0, 0), (5, 0, 0), (6, 0, 0), (7, 0, 0), (8, 0, 0), (9, 0, 0)

b. (−0.5, 0.5, 0)
c. (7, 3, 6), (7, 3, 3)
d. (−2.5, 7.25, −1.75), (−1, 8.5, −3.5), (0.5, 9.75, −5.25)
e. (1.5, 0.25, 3.25), (3, 0.5, 0.5), (4.5, 0.75, −2.25)

SECTION 3.3

1. Given $\mathbf{p}_0 = (6, 4, 8)$ and $\mathbf{p}_1 = (8, 8, 12)$, then

$$x = 2u + 6, y = 4u + 4, z = 4u + 8$$

$$\text{and } u_x = (x - 6)/2, u_y = (y - 4)/4, u_z = (z - 8)/4$$

a. $u_x = 0$, $u_y = 0$, $u_z = 1$. $\mathbf{q}_1$ is off the line.
b. $u_x = 1$, $u_y = 1$, $u_z = 2$. $\mathbf{q}_2$ is off the line.
c. $u_x = -1$, $u_y = -1$, $u_z = -1$. $\mathbf{q}_3$ is on back extension of line.
d. $u_x = 3$, $u_y = -3$, $u_z = 3$. $\mathbf{q}_4$ is off the line.
e. $u_x = 0.5$, $u_y = 0.5$, $u_z = 0.5$. $\mathbf{q}_5$ is on the line.
f. $u_x = 2$, $u_y = 0$, $u_z = 1$. $\mathbf{q}_6$ is off the line.
g. $u_x = 2$, $u_y = 2$, $u_z = 2$. $\mathbf{q}_7$ is on forward extension of line.
h. $u_x = 0.25$, $u_y = 0.25$, $u_z = 2.5$. $\mathbf{q}_8$ is on the line.
i. $u_x = 0.25$, $u_y = 0.5$, $u_z = 0$. $\mathbf{q}_9$ is off the line.
j. $u_x = 0$, $u_y = 1$, $u_z = 0$. $\mathbf{q}_{10}$ is off the line.

SECTION 3.4

1. a. $x_a = 2u_a + 2$, $y_a = 2u_a + 4$, $z_a = -10u_a + 6$
$x_b = 6u_b$, $y_b = 8u_b$, $z_b = -7u_b + 1$
No intersection.
b. $x_a = 2u_a + 2$, $y_a = 2u_a + 4$, $z_a = -10u_a + 6$
$x_b = -1.5u_b + 4$, $y_b = 1.5u_b + 3$, $z_b = -1.5u_b + 5$
No intersection.
c. $x_a = 2u_a + 2$, $y_a = 2u_a + 4$, $z_a = -10u_a + 6$
$x_b = -3u_b + 3$, $y_b = -3u_b + 5$, $z_b = 15u_b + 1$
The lines overlap.
d. $x_a = -11u_a + 10$, $y_a = -9u_a + 8$, $z_a = 0$
$x_b = -9u_b + 13$, $y_b = 5u_b + 2$, $z_b = 0$
The lines intersect at $u_a = 0.287$, $u_b = 0.683$.
Thus, $\mathbf{p}_i = (6.843, 5.417, 0)$
e. $x_a = -3u_a + 5$, $y_a = 0$, $z_a = 0$
$x_b = 2u_b + 8$, $y_b = 0$, $z_b = 0$
Both line segments lie on the x axis. They do not overlap.

SECTION 3.5

1. a. Outside window
b. Inside window

c. Inside window
d. Intersects Wy_T and Wx_L. Clipped segment:
   $\mathbf{p}_0 = (4, 10)$, $\mathbf{p}_1 = (2, 6)$
e. Inside window
f. Intersects Wy_B
g. Partially coincident with Wx_L
h. Intersects Wy_B and Wy_T
i. Intersects Wx_R
j. Outside window

SECTION 3.6

1. a. Line 1 = (1, 3), (4, 5)
   Line 2 = (4, 5), (4, 8)
   Line 3 = (4, 8), (9, 5)
   Line 4 = (9, 5), (5, 1)
   Line 5 = (5, 1), (7, −3)

b.
$$\begin{aligned}&\text{Line 1}\ \begin{cases}(1, 3)\\ (4, 5)\end{cases}\\ &\text{Line 2}\ \begin{cases}(4, 5)\\ (4, 8)\end{cases}\\ &\text{Line 3}\ \begin{cases}(4, 8)\\ (9, 5)\end{cases}\\ &\text{Line 4}\ \begin{cases}(9, 5)\\ (5, 1)\end{cases}\\ &\text{Line 5}\ \begin{cases}(5, 1)\\ (7, -3)\end{cases}\end{aligned}$$

c. $\mathbf{p}_0$ (1, 8)
$$\Delta\text{'s}\ \begin{cases}(3, 2)\\ (0, 3)\\ (5, -3)\\ (-4, -4)\\ (2, -4)\end{cases}$$

Chapter 4

SECTION 4.1

1. Solve the four simultaneous equations for A, B, C, and D:

$$\begin{aligned}Ax + By + Cz + D &= 0\\ Aa + D &= 0\\ Bb + D &= 0\\ Cc + D &= 0\end{aligned}$$

SECTION 4.2

1. a. Same side as $\mathbf{p}_R$
b. On
c. Same side as $\mathbf{p}_R$
d. Opposite side
e. Opposite side

3. a. Same side
b. On
c. On
d. Opposite side
e. Opposite side

SECTION 4.3

1. a. $u_i = -0.333$
b. $u_i = 1.000$
c. $u_i = 1.5$
d. The line lies in the plane.
e. $u_i = 0.5$

Chapter 5

SECTION 5.1

3. a. $\mathbf{p}_1^* = (1, 9, -10)$
b. $\mathbf{p}_2^* = (1, 8, 8)$
c. $\mathbf{p}_3^*$ not visible (behind observer)
d. $\mathbf{p}_4^*$ not visible (behind observer)
e. $\mathbf{p}_5^*$ not visible (behind observer)

5. The midpoint of an arbitrary line defined by $\mathbf{p}_0$ and $\mathbf{p}_1$ is $x_{0.5} = 0.5(x_1 - x_0) + x_0$, $y_{0.5} = 0.5(y_1 - y_0) + y_0$, and $z_{0.5} = 0.5(z_1 - z_0) + z_0$. Project this point onto the $z = 0$ plane, for example, to yield: $x_{0.5}^* = 0.5(x_1 - x_0) + x_0$, $y_{0.5}^* = 0.5(y_1 - y_0) + y_0$ and $z_{0.5}^* = 0$. Alternatively, project the line defined by $\mathbf{p}_0$ and $\mathbf{p}_1$ onto the $z = 0$ plane to yield $\mathbf{p}_0^* = (x_0, y_0, 0)$ and $\mathbf{p}_1^* = (x_1, y_1, 0)$. The midpoint of this projected line is: $x_{0.5}^* = 0.5(x_1 - x_0) + x_0$, $y_{0.5}^* = 0.5(y_1 - y_0) + y_0$ and $z_{0.5}^* = 0$. This is the same as the projection of the midpoint, above. QED.

SECTION 5.2

2. a. $\mathbf{p}_1^* = (-5.455, 3.636, 0)$
b. $\mathbf{p}_2^* = (3, 10, 0)$
c. $\mathbf{p}_3^* = (10, 7.143, 0)$

d. $\mathbf{p}_4^* = (20, -45, 0)$
e. $\mathbf{p}_5^* = (-2.5, 0, 0)$

Chapter 6

SECTION 6.1

1. a. Stellar
   b. Concave
   c. Convex
   d. Concave
   e. Convex

7. a. $L = 20.040$, $\mathbf{p}_{CG} = (0.2, 7)$
   b. $L = 15.078$, $\mathbf{p}_{CG} = (5.667, 6.333)$
   c. $L = 17.211$, $\mathbf{p}_{CG} = (11.5, 6.5)$
   d. $L = 22.141$, $\mathbf{p}_{CG} = (0.75, 0.5)$
   e. $L = 18.000$, $\mathbf{p}_{CG} = (10.25, -1.75)$

Chapter 7

SECTION 7.2

1. a. Tetrahedron: $4 - 6 + 4 = 2$
   b. Cube: $8 - 12 + 6 = 2$
   c. Octahedron: $6 - 12 + 8 = 2$
   d. Dodecahedron: $20 - 30 + 12 = 2$
   e. Icosahedron: $12 - 30 + 20 = 2$

SECTION 7.3

1. a. Tetrahedron: 180°
   b. Cube: 270°
   c. Octahedron: 240°
   d. Dodecahedron: 324°
   e. Icosahedron: 300°

2. a. 450°
   b. 450°
   c. 540°
   d. 270°
   e. 270°

9.

$$F = \begin{bmatrix} 1 & 2 & 3 & 4 & 0 & 0 \\ 2 & 5 & 8 & 3 & 0 & 0 \\ 5 & 6 & 7 & 8 & 0 & 0 \\ 6 & 13 & 14 & 7 & 0 & 0 \\ 7 & 14 & 15 & 8 & 0 & 0 \\ 4 & 12 & 8 & 11 & 0 & 0 \\ 8 & 9 & 10 & 11 & 0 & 0 \\ 8 & 15 & 16 & 9 & 0 & 0 \\ 9 & 16 & 17 & 10 & 0 & 0 \\ 1 & 12 & 13 & 6 & 5 & 2 \\ 1 & 4 & 11 & 10 & 17 & 12 \\ 12 & 17 & 16 & 15 & 14 & 13 \end{bmatrix}$$

Chapter 8

SECTION 8.1

1. b. The length of the side of the square is a negative quantity.
   e. Values for only two arguments are given.
   f. Values for more than three arguments are given.

3. a. $\mathbf{p}_0 = (-2, -2)$, $\mathbf{p}_1 = (2, -2)$, $\mathbf{p}_2 = (2, 2)$, $\mathbf{p}_3 = (-2, 2)$
   b. $\mathbf{p}_0 = (4, -1)$, $\mathbf{p}_1 = (9, -1)$, $\mathbf{p}_2 = (9, 4)$, $\mathbf{p}_3 = (4, 4)$
   c. $\mathbf{p}_0 = (5, 4)$, $\mathbf{p}_1 = (7, 4)$, $\mathbf{p}_2 = (7, 6)$, $\mathbf{p}_3 = (5, 6)$
   d. $\mathbf{p}_0 = (-6, -6)$, $\mathbf{p}_1 = (0, -6)$, $\mathbf{p}_2 = (0, 0)$, $\mathbf{p}_3 = (-6, 0)$
   e. $\mathbf{p}_0 = (-4, 1)$, $\mathbf{p}_1 = (-1, 1)$, $\mathbf{p}_2 = (-1, 4)$, $\mathbf{p}_3 = (-4, 4)$

5. a. $\mathbf{p}_{max} = (-2, 7)$, $\mathbf{p}_{CG} = (-2.5, 6.5)$
   b. $\mathbf{p}_{max} = (2, 6)$, $\mathbf{p}_{CG} = (0, 4)$
   c. $\mathbf{p}_{max} = (7, 6)$, $\mathbf{p}_{CG} = (5.5, 4.5)$
   d. $\mathbf{p}_{max} = (9, 8)$, $\mathbf{p}_{CG} = (6.5, 5.5)$
   e. $\mathbf{p}_{max} = (11, 10)$, $\mathbf{p}_{CG} = (7.5, 6.5)$
   f. $\mathbf{p}_{max} = (-5, 2)$, $\mathbf{p}_{CG} = (-6, 1)$
   g. $\mathbf{p}_{max} = (-2, 0)$, $\mathbf{p}_{CG} = (-5, -3)$
   h. $\mathbf{p}_{max} = (-4, -2)$, $\mathbf{p}_{CG} = (-5, -3)$
   i. $\mathbf{p}_{max} = (5, 0)$, $\mathbf{p}_{CG} = (2.5, -2.5)$
   j. $\mathbf{p}_{max} = (5, 0)$, $\mathbf{p}_{CG} = (4, -1)$

9. Write $\mathbf{p}_{CG} = (\mathbf{p}_{min} + \mathbf{p}_{max})/2$ in terms of x and y; thus, $x_{CG} = (x_{min} + x_{max})/2$. Since $s = x_{max} - x_{min}$, and $x_{min} = x_0$, then $s = x_{max} - x_0$ and $x_{max} = x_0 + s$. Therefore, $x_{CG} = x_0 + s/2$, which is in agreement with Eq. (8.3). A similar approach applies to y_{CG}.

SECTION 8.2

1. c. s_y is negative.
   e. s_y is zero.
   g. s_x and s_y are negative.
   h. Five arguments are given.

3. a. $\mathbf{RN}_1(-2, -2, 4, 4)$
   b. $\mathbf{RN}_2(4, -1, 5, 5)$
   c. $\mathbf{RN}_3(5, 4, 2, 2)$

5. a. $\mathbf{RN}_1(-8, 5, 7, 4)$
   b. $\mathbf{RN}_2(-4, 1, 2, 6)$
   c. $\mathbf{RN}_3(-3, 0, 5, 2)$
   d. $\mathbf{RN}_4(2, 8, 4, 4)$
   e. $\mathbf{RN}_5(2, 8, 10, 5)$
   f. $\mathbf{RN}_6(7, 1, 4, 5)$
   g. $\mathbf{RN}_7(-5, -5, 4, 4)$
   h. $\mathbf{RN}_8(0, -4, 9, 4)$
   i. $\mathbf{RN}_9(4, -2, 4, 1)$
   j. $\mathbf{RN}_{10}(5, -10, 3, 7)$

SECTION 8.3

1. a. $r = 0$, which produces a point.
   b. r is negative.
   e. Four arguments are specified.
   h. Only two arguments are specified.

3. a. $\mathbf{CR}_1(4, 8, 4)$
   b. $\mathbf{CR}_2(-5, 5, 2.5)$
   c. $\mathbf{CR}_3(0, 0, 4)$
   d. $\mathbf{CR}_4(7, -1, 2)$
   e. $\mathbf{CR}_5(-10, -5, 3)$

SECTION 8.4

4. a. $(\mathbf{CR}_1 \cup \mathbf{RN}_1 \cup \mathbf{RN}_2) - \mathbf{CR}_2$, where
   $\mathbf{CR}_1 = \mathbf{CR}_1(5, 5, 2.5)$
   $\mathbf{CR}_2 = \mathbf{CR}_2(5, 5, 1)$
   $\mathbf{RN}_1 = \mathbf{RN}_1(1, 4, 8, 2)$
   $\mathbf{RN}_2 = \mathbf{RN}_2(4, 1, 2, 8)$
   b. $(\mathbf{RN}_1 - \mathbf{CR}_1 - \mathbf{RN}_2) \cup \mathbf{CR}_2$, where
   $\mathbf{CR}_1 = \mathbf{CR}_1(1, 1, 1.5)$
   $\mathbf{CR}_2 = \mathbf{CR}_2(5.5, 5.5, 1.5)$
   $\mathbf{RN}_1 = \mathbf{RN}_1(1, 1, 6, 6)$
   $\mathbf{RN}_2 = \mathbf{RN}_2(5.5, 5.5, 1.5, 1.5)$

c. $(\mathbf{RN}_1 - \mathbf{CR}_2 - \mathbf{CR}_4 - \mathbf{CR}_5 - \mathbf{CR}_6) \cap \mathbf{CR}_1$, where
$\mathbf{CR}_1 = \mathbf{CR}_1(4, 4, 4)$
$\mathbf{CR}_2 = \mathbf{CR}_2(2, 2, 1.25)$
$\mathbf{CR}_3 = \mathbf{CR}_3(6, 2, 1.25)$
$\mathbf{CR}_4 = \mathbf{CR}_4(6, 6, 1.25)$
$\mathbf{CR}_5 = \mathbf{CR}_5(2, 6, 1.25)$
$\mathbf{RN}_1 = \mathbf{RN}_1(0, 0, 8, 8)$

d. $(\mathbf{CR}_1 \cup \mathbf{CR}_2 \cup \mathbf{CR}_3 \cup \mathbf{CR}_4) \cap \mathbf{RN}_1$, where
$\mathbf{CR}_1 = \mathbf{CR}_1(0, 0, 3)$
$\mathbf{CR}_2 = \mathbf{CR}_2(6, 0, 3)$
$\mathbf{CR}_3 = \mathbf{CR}_3(6, 6, 3)$
$\mathbf{CR}_4 = \mathbf{CR}_4(0, 6, 3)$
$\mathbf{RN}_1 = \mathbf{RN}_1(0, 0, 6, 6)$

e. $(\mathbf{CR}_1 - \mathbf{CR}_2 - \mathbf{RN}_2) \cup [(\mathbf{CR}_3 \cup \mathbf{RN}_1) \cap \mathbf{CR}_1]$, where
$\mathbf{CR}_1 = \mathbf{CR}_1(6, 6, 4)$
$\mathbf{CR}_2 = \mathbf{CR}_2(6, 6, 2.5)$
$\mathbf{CR}_3 = \mathbf{CR}_3(6, 6, 1)$
$\mathbf{RN}_1 = \mathbf{RN}_1(0, 5.5, 11, 1)$
$\mathbf{RN}_2 = \mathbf{RN}_2(1, 5, 10, 2)$

Chapter 9

SECTION 9.1

1. b. s is assigned a negative number.
c. Five arguments are given.
e. Only three arguments are given.
f. $s = 0$, resulting in a point.
h. s is assigned a negative number.

3. a. $\mathbf{p}_{CG,1} = (0.5, 0.5, 0.5)$
b. $\mathbf{p}_{CG,2} = (-1, 4, 1)$
c. $\mathbf{p}_{CG,3} = (6.35, 2.95, 3.75)$
d. $\mathbf{p}_{CG,4} = (-5, -5, -5)$
e. $\mathbf{p}_{CG,5} = (25.1, 20.9, 3.6)$

5. a. $\mathbf{p}_1 \in b\mathbf{CB}_1$
b. $\mathbf{p}_2 \in i\mathbf{CB}_1$
c. $\mathbf{p}_3 \in o\mathbf{CB}_1$
d. $\mathbf{p}_4 \in b\mathbf{CB}_1$
e. $\mathbf{p}_5 \in o\mathbf{CB}_1$

SECTION 9.2

1. a. s_y is negative.
   d. Only five arguments are given.
   e. Too many (seven) arguments are given.
   i. s_y is zero.

3. a. $\mathbf{p}_{CG,1} = (1.5, 4, 0.5)$
   b. $\mathbf{p}_{CG,2} = (0, 0, 0)$
   c. $\mathbf{p}_{CG,3} = (5.5, 2, 5)$
   d. $\mathbf{p}_{CG,4} = (9.5, -3.5, 2.5)$
   e. $\mathbf{p}_{CG,5} = (0.65, 3.00, 6.10)$

5. a. $\mathbf{p}_1 \in o\mathbf{BK}_1$
   b. $\mathbf{p}_2 \in b\mathbf{BK}_1$
   c. $\mathbf{p}_3 \in b\mathbf{BK}_1$
   d. $\mathbf{p}_4 \in o\mathbf{BK}_1$
   e. $\mathbf{p}_5 \in i\mathbf{BK}_1$

SECTION 9.3

1. b. $a = 4$, undefined
   d. Too many arguments
   e. $a = 1.2$, not an integer (1, 2, or 3)
   h. $l = -2.0$, a negative value for the length
   j. Only five arguments

3. a. $\mathbf{p}_{CG,1} = (0, 0, -4)$
   b. $\mathbf{p}_{CG,2} = (4, 1, 0.5)$
   c. $\mathbf{p}_{CG,3} = (0, 6, 0)$
   d. $\mathbf{p}_{CG,4} = (6, -2, 1)$
   e. $\mathbf{p}_{CG,4} = (8, 4.5, -6)$

5. a. $\mathbf{p}_1 \in o\mathbf{CL}_1$
   b. $\mathbf{p}_2 \in b\mathbf{CL}_1$
   c. $\mathbf{p}_3 \in i\mathbf{CL}_1$
   d. $\mathbf{p}_4 \in b\mathbf{CL}_1$
   e. $\mathbf{p}_5 \in i\mathbf{CL}_1$

SECTION 9.4

1. b. $r = 0$
   d. $r = -2$

3. a. $C = 6.283$ $A = 12.566$ $V = 4.189$ $\mathbf{p}_{CG} = (0, 0, 0)$
   b. $C = 6.283$ $A = 12.566$ $V = 4.189$ $\mathbf{p}_{CG} = (3, 3, 0)$
   c. $C = 12.566$ $A = 50.265$ $V = 33.510$ $\mathbf{p}_{CG} = (-2, 4, 6)$

d. $C = 15.708$ $A = 78.540$ $V = 65.450$ $\mathbf{p}_{CG} = (7.5, 5, 2)$
e. $C = 31.416$ $A = 314.159$ $V = 523.599$ $\mathbf{p}_{CG} = (0, 0, 10)$

5. a. $\mathbf{SP}_1\langle\text{intersect}\rangle\mathbf{SP}_2$
b. $\mathbf{SP}_3\langle\text{inside, tangent}\rangle\mathbf{SP}_1$
c. $\mathbf{SP}_1\langle\text{outside}\rangle\mathbf{SP}_4$
d. $\mathbf{SP}_1\langle\text{outside, tangent}\rangle\mathbf{SP}_5$
e. $\mathbf{SP}_1\langle\text{inside, tangent}\rangle\mathbf{SP}_6$

7. a. $\mathbf{SP}_1\langle\text{intersect}\rangle\mathbf{CL}_1$
b. $\mathbf{SP}_1\langle\text{outside}\rangle\mathbf{CL}_2$
c. $\mathbf{SP}_1\langle\text{inside, tangent}\rangle\mathbf{CL}_3$
d. $\mathbf{CL}_4\langle\text{inside}\rangle\mathbf{SP}_1$
e. $\mathbf{SP}_1\langle\text{outside, tangent}\rangle\mathbf{CL}_5$

SECTION 9.5

5. a. $\mathbf{CB}_1 \cap \mathbf{SP}_1$, where $\mathbf{CB}_1 = \mathbf{CB}_1(-4, 0, -4, 4)$ and $\mathbf{SP}_1 = \mathbf{SP}_1(0, 0, 0, 4)$
b. $\mathbf{SP}_1 \cap \mathbf{BK}_1$, where $\mathbf{SP}_1 = \mathbf{SP}_1(0, 0, 0, 4)$ and $\mathbf{BK}_1 = \mathbf{BK}_1(-2, -4, -4, 4, 8, 8)$

Chapter 10

SECTION 10.1

1. a. $\mathbf{T} = (3, -4)$
b. $\mathbf{T} = (9, 0)$
c. $\mathbf{T} = (5, 2)$
d. $\mathbf{T} = (-8, -6)$
e. $\mathbf{T} = (1, 7, -1)$
f. $\mathbf{T} = (0, 0, 10)$
g. $\mathbf{T} = (6, 6, 6)$
h. $\mathbf{T} = (-2, -4, 0)$
i. $\mathbf{T} = (0, 11, 8)$
j. $\mathbf{T} = (3, 0, 3)$

3. $\mathbf{T} = (2, 0, 0)$, $\mathbf{SP}(2, 0, 0, 1)$
$\mathbf{T} = (2, 5, 0)$, $\mathbf{SP}(2, 5, 0, 1)$
$\mathbf{T} = (0, 5, 0)$, $\mathbf{SP}(0, 5, 0, 1)$
$\mathbf{T} = (0, 0, 5)$, $\mathbf{SP}(0, 0, 5, 1)$
$\mathbf{T} = (2, 0, 5)$, $\mathbf{SP}(2, 0, 5, 1)$
$\mathbf{T} = (2, 5, 5)$, $\mathbf{SP}(2, 5, 5, 1)$
$\mathbf{T} = (0, 5, 5)$, $\mathbf{SP}(0, 5, 5, 1)$

SECTION 10.3

1. a. **CR**(−2, 5, 3)
   b. **CR**(0, 0, 2)
   c. **SP**(6.2, 1.7, 0, 1)
   d. **BK**(7.25, 0, 0, 0.6, 0.6, 14.2)
   e. **CL**(0, 0, −2.5, 3, 1, 2)
   f. **CL**(8.1, 9.7, 0.25, 2, 0.5, 5)
   g. **RN**(−2.5, −2.5, 5, 12)
   h. **SP**(1.5, 0.75, 0, 6.5)
   i. **BK**(8.25, 3.15, 6.5, 14.5, 9, 12.5)
   j. **CR**(3.1, 2.7, 1.5)

3. **S** = (0.5), **T** = (0.5, 0.5, 0.5)

Chapter 11

SECTION 11.1

1. a. $a_{23} = 3$
   b. $a_{12} = 4$
   c. $a_{31} = 0$
   d. $b_{11} = 6$
   e. $b_{32} = 9$
   f. 3×3
   g. 3×2
   h. **A**
   i. $a_{11} = 7, a_{22} = 1, a_{33} = 5$
   j. $a_{12} = 9, a_{13} = 0, a_{23} = 2$

3. No.

5. $\begin{bmatrix} 0 & 0 \\ 0 & 0 \end{bmatrix}$

7. a. $a_{12} = -2, a_{13} = -6, a_{23} = -7$
   b. $a_{11} = 0, a_{22} = 0, a_{33} = 0$

SECTION 11.2

1. $-\mathbf{A} = [-7 \;\; -3 \;\; -1]$

3. a. $\begin{bmatrix} 2 & 0 \\ 5 & 13 \end{bmatrix}$
   b. $\begin{bmatrix} 5 & -4 \\ 5 & 6 \\ -5 & 3 \end{bmatrix}$

c. $\begin{bmatrix} 1 & 11 & -8 \\ -9 & 8 & 2 \\ -7 & -10 & 2 \end{bmatrix}$

d. [9 0 6 8]

e. $\begin{bmatrix} 2 & 0 & 0 \\ 0 & 2 & 0 \\ 0 & 0 & 2 \end{bmatrix}$

5. a. $x = 4, y = -2$
b. $x = 3, y = 3, z = 10$
c. $a = -2, b = -4, c = -1, d = -5, e = -7, f = 0$

7. a. $(\mathbf{A}^T)^T = \mathbf{A}$
b. $(\mathbf{A} + \mathbf{B})^T = \begin{bmatrix} 5 & 6 & 8 \\ -1 & 2 & 11 \end{bmatrix}$
c. $\mathbf{A}^T + \mathbf{B}^T = \begin{bmatrix} 4 & 1 & 6 \\ -2 & 0 & 7 \end{bmatrix} + \begin{bmatrix} 1 & 5 & 2 \\ 1 & 2 & 4 \end{bmatrix} = \begin{bmatrix} 5 & 6 & 8 \\ -1 & 2 & 11 \end{bmatrix}$
d. $\mathbf{B}^T + \mathbf{A}^T = \mathbf{A}^T + \mathbf{B}^T$

11. **p** is of order 1×4.

SECTION 11.3

1. a. -4
b. -13
c. 0
d. 0
e. 17

3. $|\mathbf{A}| = 8$

5. $|\mathbf{A}^T| = |\mathbf{A}| = 8$

SECTION 11.4

1. $\begin{bmatrix} 1 & 0 & 0 \\ 0 & 1 & 0 \\ 0 & 0 & 1 \end{bmatrix}$ **2.** $\frac{1}{30}\begin{bmatrix} 5 & 5 & -5 \\ -5 & 13 & -1 \\ 5 & -1 & 7 \end{bmatrix}$ **3.** $\begin{bmatrix} 1 & 0 & 0 \\ 1 & -2 & 3 \\ -1 & 1 & -1 \end{bmatrix}$

5. Inverse does not exist, since the determinant = 0.

7. $x = 2, y = 1, z = -3$

9. $x = 2, y = 0, z = 1$

Chapter 12

SECTION 12.1

1. $\mathbf{a} = [5 \ \ 6]$
   $\mathbf{b} = [5 \ \ -5]$
   $\mathbf{c} = [0 \ \ 7]$
   $\mathbf{d} = [-7 \ \ 0]$
   $\mathbf{e} = [-5 \ \ 3]$

3. $\mathbf{a}_u = [0.640 \ \ 0.768]$
   $\mathbf{b}_u = [0.707 \ \ -0.707]$
   $\mathbf{c}_u = [0 \ \ 1]$
   $\mathbf{d}_u = [-1 \ \ 0]$
   $\mathbf{e}_u = [0.857 \ \ 0.514]$

5. a. $\begin{bmatrix} a_1 \\ a_2 \\ a_3 \end{bmatrix} x + \begin{bmatrix} b_1 \\ b_2 \\ b_3 \end{bmatrix} y = \begin{bmatrix} c_1 \\ c_2 \\ c_3 \end{bmatrix}$

   b. $a_1x + b_1y = c_1$
   $a_2x + b_2y = c_2$
   $a_3x + b_3y = c_3$

7. a. $[5 \ \ -1 \ \ 7 \ \ 4]\begin{bmatrix} x_1 \\ x_2 \\ x_3 \\ x_4 \end{bmatrix} = 8$

   b. $5x_1 - x_2 + 7x_3 + 4x_4 = 8$

9. a. $\mathbf{a}_u = [-0.275 \ \ 0 \ \ 0.962]$
   b. $\mathbf{b}_u = [0.784 \ \ 0.196 \ \ 0.588]$
   c. $\mathbf{c} = [-10 \ \ -2 \ \ 1]$
   d. $\mathbf{c} = [-6 \ \ 0 \ \ 21]$
   e. $\mathbf{c} = [2 \ \ 1 \ \ 10]$

11. $\mathbf{a}_u = \mathbf{b}_u$

SECTION 12.2

1. a. $\mathbf{i} \cdot \mathbf{i} = 1$
   b. $\mathbf{i} \cdot \mathbf{j} = 0$
   c. $\mathbf{i} \cdot \mathbf{k} = 0$
   d. $\mathbf{j} \cdot \mathbf{j} = 1$
   e. $\mathbf{j} \cdot \mathbf{k} = 0$
   f. $\mathbf{k} \cdot \mathbf{k} = 1$

2. a. 29
b. 3
c. −8
d. 11
e. −16
f. 56
g. 3
h. −16
i. 1
j. 0.168

SECTION 12.3

1. a. $\mathbf{i} \times \mathbf{i} = 0$
b. $\mathbf{j} \times \mathbf{j} = 0$
c. $\mathbf{k} \times \mathbf{k} = 0$
d. $\mathbf{i} \times \mathbf{j} = \mathbf{k}$
e. $\mathbf{j} \times \mathbf{k} = \mathbf{i}$
f. $\mathbf{k} \times \mathbf{i} = \mathbf{j}$
g. $\mathbf{j} \times \mathbf{i} = -\mathbf{k}$
h. $\mathbf{k} \times \mathbf{j} = -\mathbf{i}$
i. $\mathbf{i} \times \mathbf{k} = -j$

3. a. $\mathbf{a} \times \mathbf{a} = 0$
b. $\mathbf{a} \times \mathbf{b} = [2\ \ -10\ \ -2]$
c. $\mathbf{b} \times \mathbf{a} = [-2\ \ 10\ \ 2]$
d. $\mathbf{b} \times \mathbf{c} = [-22\ \ -10\ \ 19]$
e. $\mathbf{c} \times \mathbf{a} = [-12\ \ 0\ \ -6]$

SECTION 12.4

1. a. $\mathbf{p} = \mathbf{a} + u\mathbf{b}$
b. $\mathbf{p} = \mathbf{b} + u\mathbf{c}$
c. $\mathbf{p} = \mathbf{c} + u\mathbf{a}$
d. $\mathbf{p} = \mathbf{a} + u\mathbf{a} = \mathbf{a}(u + 1)$
e. $\mathbf{p} = \mathbf{b} + u\mathbf{c}$, where $\mathbf{c} = [0\ \ 0\ \ 1]$

3. a. $x = u, y = u, z = u$
b. $x = -3 + 5u, y = 1 - u, z = 6 + u$
c. $x = 1 + 4u, y = 1 - 4u, z = -4 + 13u$
d. $x = 6 - 16u, y = 8 - 8u, z = 8 - 11u$
e. $x = 0, y = 0, z = 1 - 2u$

5. Identical segments, with opposite directions of parametrization.

7. $\mathbf{p} = 0.5(\mathbf{p}_1 - \mathbf{p}_0)u + 0.5(\mathbf{p}_0 + \mathbf{p}_1)$

SECTION 12.5

1. $\mathbf{p} = \mathbf{a} + u\mathbf{b} + v\mathbf{c}$

2. $\mathbf{p} = u\mathbf{i} + v\mathbf{k}$

Chapter 13

SECTION 13.1

1. a. $\mathbf{a} = [2\ \ -10\ \ 16]$, $\mathbf{b} = [1\ \ 4\ \ -12]$, $\mathbf{c} = [0\ \ 2\ \ 2]$
   b. $\mathbf{a} = [-1\ \ -4\ \ 4]$, $\mathbf{b} = [3\ \ 2\ \ -10]$, $\mathbf{c} = [-1\ \ 0\ \ 4]$
   c. $\mathbf{a} = [-14\ \ 10\ \ -14]$, $\mathbf{b} = [23\ \ -17\ \ 13]$, $\mathbf{c} = [-3\ \ 7\ \ 1]$
   d. $\mathbf{a} = [10\ \ 6\ \ 6]$, $\mathbf{b} = [-15\ \ -17\ \ -13]$, $\mathbf{c} = [7\ \ 7\ \ 8]$
   e. $\mathbf{a} = [4\ \ 20\ \ -20]$, $\mathbf{b} = [-4\ \ -14\ \ 20]$, $\mathbf{c} = [0\ \ -1\ \ 2]$

3. Since $\mathbf{UMB} = \mathbf{UA}$, and $\mathbf{U} = [1 \times 3]$, $\mathbf{M} = [3 \times 3]$, $\mathbf{B} = [3 \times 3]$, and $\mathbf{A} = [3 \times 3]$, then $[1 \times 3][3 \times 3][3 \times 3] = [1 \times 3][3 \times 3]$.

5. $$\mathbf{M}^{-1} = \begin{bmatrix} 0 & 0 & 1 \\ \frac{1}{4} & \frac{1}{2} & 1 \\ 1 & 1 & 1 \end{bmatrix}$$

9. $$\mathbf{B} = \begin{bmatrix} x_0 & y_0 & 0 \\ x_{0.5} & y_{0.5} & 0 \\ x_1 & y_1 & 0 \end{bmatrix}$$

SECTION 13.2

1. At $u = 0$: $G_1 = 1$, $G_2 = 0$, $G_3 = 0$, $G_4 = 0$.

3. At $u = \frac{1}{3}$: $G_1 = 0$, $G_2 = 1$, $G_3 = 0$, $G_4 = 0$.

5. $x_1 = x_2 = x_3 = x_4 = 0$.

SECTION 13.3

1. a. $8x$
   b. 1
   c. $3x^2 - 3$
   d. $2x + 2$
   e. $8x^3 + 3x^2$

3. At zero slope: $dy/dx = 0$
   a. $8x = 0$; $x = 0$, $y = 0$
   b. $1 \neq 0$; the function has a constant slope of 1 (it is a straight line)

c. $3x^2 - 1 = 0$; $x = \pm 1$, $y = -1, 3$
d. $2x + 2 = 0$; $x = -1$, $y = 0$
e. $8x^3 + 3x^2 = 0$; $x = 0, 0, -3$, $y = 3, 3, 138$

5. a. $m_0 = 6.782$, $\mathbf{t}_0 = [0.442 \ \ -0.147 \ \ 0.885]$
b. $m_0 = 2$, $\mathbf{t}_0 = [0 \ \ 1 \ \ 0]$
c. $m_0 = 5.196$, $\mathbf{t}_0 = [0.192 \ \ 0.962 \ \ -0.192]$
d. $m_0 = 7.280$, $\mathbf{t}_0 = [0.962 \ \ 0.275 \ \ 0]$
e. $m_0 = 6.403$, $\mathbf{t}_0 = [0.625 \ \ 0.625 \ \ -0.469]$

7. a. 8
b. 0
c. $6x$
d. 2
e. $24x^2 + 6x$

SECTION 13.5

1. $B_{0,2} = (1 - u)^2$
$B_{1,2} = 2u(1 - u)$
$B_{2,2} = u^2$

3. $B_{0,5} = (1 - u)^5$
$B_{1,5} = 5u(1 - u)^4$
$B_{2,5} = 10u^2(1 - u)^3$
$B_{3,5} = 10u^3(1 - u)^2$
$B_{4,5} = 5u^4(1 - u)$
$B_{5,5} = u^5$

SECTION 13.6

1. $\mathbf{B}_r = [\mathbf{p}_1 \ \ \mathbf{q}_0 \ \ k_0\mathbf{p}_1^u \ \ k_1\mathbf{q}_0^u]^T$

3. $\mathbf{B}_s = [\mathbf{q}_1 \ \ \mathbf{p}_0 \ \ l_0\mathbf{q}_1^u \ \ l_1\mathbf{p}_0^u]^T$

Chapter 14

SECTION 14.1

1. $x = 4$, $y = 4u + 1$, $z = 4w + 3$

3. $u = 0 \rightarrow x = -2$, $y = 5$, $z = 3w - 4$
$u = 1 \rightarrow x = -1$, $y = 5$, $z = 3w - 4$
$w = 0 \rightarrow x = u - 2$, $y = 5$, $z = -4$
$w = 1 \rightarrow x = u - 2$, $y = 5$, $z = -1$

SECTION 14.2

1. $\mathbf{p}_{00} = \mathbf{a}_{00}$

$\mathbf{p}_{01} = \mathbf{a}_{03} + \mathbf{a}_{02} + \mathbf{a}_{01} + \mathbf{a}_{00}$

$\mathbf{p}_{10} = \mathbf{a}_{30} + \mathbf{a}_{20} + \mathbf{a}_{10} + \mathbf{a}_{00}$

$$\mathbf{p}_{11} = \mathbf{a}_{33} + \mathbf{a}_{32} + \mathbf{a}_{31} + \mathbf{a}_{30} + \mathbf{a}_{23} + \mathbf{a}_{22} + \mathbf{a}_{21} + \mathbf{a}_{20} + \mathbf{a}_{13} + \mathbf{a}_{12} + \mathbf{a}_{11} + \mathbf{a}_{10} + \mathbf{a}_{03} + \mathbf{a}_{02} + \mathbf{a}_{01} + \mathbf{a}_{00}$$

Chapter 15

SECTION 15.1

1. $\mathbf{T} = \begin{bmatrix} \mathbf{t} & \mathbf{t} & 0 & 0 \\ \mathbf{t} & \mathbf{t} & 0 & 0 \\ 0 & 0 & 0 & 0 \\ 0 & 0 & 0 & 0 \end{bmatrix}$

SECTION 15.2

1. $\mathbf{B}^* = \mathbf{BR} + \mathbf{T}$ or $\mathbf{B}^* = [\mathbf{B} + \mathbf{T}]\mathbf{R}$
   In general, $\mathbf{BR} + \mathbf{T} \neq [\mathbf{B} + \mathbf{T}]\mathbf{R}$, since $\mathbf{BR} + \mathbf{T} \neq \mathbf{BR} + \mathbf{TR}$.

3. For curves: $\mathbf{B}, \mathbf{A} = 4 \times 3$ matrices. $\mathbf{BR}, \mathbf{AR} = [4 \times 3][3 \times 3] = [4 \times 3]$, and each component or element of **B** or **A** is appropriately transformed. Doing the matrix algebra for each readily verifies this. Note that the elements of **A** are vector components and treated the same as **B** elements.

For surfaces: $\mathbf{B}, \mathbf{A} = 4 \times 4 \times 3$ matrices. Using subscripts to identify the elements, we have B_{ijk} and A_{ijk}, where $i,j = 1,2,3,4$ and $k = 1,2,3$. Suppress i or j elements so that four new matrices are formed: $\mathbf{B}_1 = B_{1jk}$, $\mathbf{B}_2 = B_{2jk}$, $\mathbf{B}_3 = B_{3jk}$, and $\mathbf{B}_4 = B_{4jk}$ (similarly for **A**). Then $\mathbf{B}_1, \mathbf{B}_2, \mathbf{B}_3, \mathbf{B}_4 = 4 \times 3$ matrices, and we can now compute $\mathbf{B}_1^* = \mathbf{B}_1\mathbf{R}$, and so on. Finally, $\mathbf{B}_1^*, \mathbf{B}_2^*, \mathbf{B}_3^*$, and $\mathbf{B}_4^*$ are assembled into $\mathbf{B}^*$.

SECTION 15.4

1. a. $\mathbf{R}_f = \begin{bmatrix} -1 & 0 & 0 \\ 0 & 1 & 0 \\ 0 & 0 & 1 \end{bmatrix}$

   b. $\mathbf{R}_f = \begin{bmatrix} 1 & 0 & 0 \\ 0 & -1 & 0 \\ 0 & 0 & 1 \end{bmatrix}$

   c. $\mathbf{R}_f = \begin{bmatrix} 1 & 0 & 0 \\ 0 & 1 & 0 \\ 0 & 0 & -1 \end{bmatrix}$

d. $\mathbf{R}_f = \begin{bmatrix} 1 & 0 & 0 \\ 0 & -1 & 0 \\ 0 & 0 & -1 \end{bmatrix}$

e. $\mathbf{R}_f = \begin{bmatrix} -1 & 0 & 0 \\ 0 & 1 & 0 \\ 0 & 0 & -1 \end{bmatrix}$

f. $\mathbf{R}_f = \begin{bmatrix} -1 & 0 & 0 \\ 0 & -1 & 0 \\ 0 & 0 & 1 \end{bmatrix}$

g. $\mathbf{R}_f = \begin{bmatrix} -1 & 0 & 0 \\ 0 & -1 & 0 \\ 0 & 0 & -1 \end{bmatrix}$

SECTION 15.5

1. $\mathbf{T}_h = \begin{bmatrix} s_x & 0 & 0 & 0 \\ 0 & s_y & 0 & 0 \\ 0 & 0 & s_z & 0 \\ 0 & 0 & 0 & 1 \end{bmatrix}$

Chapter 17

SECTION 17.1

1. a. Inside
b. Inside
c. Inside
d. Inside
e. Outside
f. Inside
g. Outside
h. Boundary
i. Boundary
j. Outside

SECTION 17.2

1. a. Inside
b. Outside
c. Inside
d. Boundary
e. Outside
f. Outside

g. Boundary
h. Inside
i. Boundary
j. Inside

SECTION 17.3

1. a. Outside
   b. Boundary
   c. Boundary
   d. Outside
   e. Inside

Index